INTERMEDIATE SPOKEN
CHINESE

A PRACTICAL APPROACH TO FLUENCY IN SPOKEN MANDARIN

进阶中文：听与说
進階中文：聽與説

CORNELIUS C. KUBLER

TUTTLE Publishing

Tokyo | Rutland, Vermont | Singapore

The Tuttle Story: "Books to Span the East and West"

Many people are surprised to learn that the world's largest publisher of books on Asia had its beginnings in the tiny American state of Vermont. The company's founder, Charles E. Tuttle, belonged to a New England family steeped in publishing. And his first love was naturally books—especially old and rare editions.

Immediately after WW II, serving in Tokyo under General Douglas MacArthur, Tuttle was tasked with reviving the Japanese publishing industry, and founded the Charles E. Tuttle Publishing Company, which thrives today as one of the world's leading independent publishers.

Though a westerner, Charles was hugely instrumental in bringing knowledge of Japan and Asia to a world hungry for information about the East. By the time of his death in 1993, Tuttle had published over 6,000 books on Asian culture, history and art—a legacy honored by the Japanese emperor with the "Order of the Sacred Treasure," the highest tribute Japan can bestow upon a non-Japanese.

With a backlist of 1,500 titles, Tuttle Publishing is more active today than at any time in its past—inspired by Charles Tuttle's core mission to publish fine books to span the East and West and provide a greater understanding of each.

Published by Tuttle Publishing, an imprint of Periplus Editions (HK) Ltd.

www.tuttlepublishing.com

Copyright © 2013 Cornelius C. Kubler
All photos © Cornelius C. Kubler except for:

Front cover/title page, top righthand image: © iStockphoto. com/Peng Wu. Page 359: © Roza; Unit 24 Part 1, © 1000words; Unit 24 Part 2, © Sam D\'ouz; Unit 24 Part 3, Mohamad Ridzuan Abdul Rashid (George Town), © Rindradjaja (food stall); Unit 24 Part 4, © Rafal Cichawa, all Dreamstime.com.

ISBN 978-0-8048-4018-7
Interior design: Anne Bell Carter

Assistance received from the following in the videotaping of the basic conversations for this course is gratefully acknowledged: Unit 11, Part 2: 7-Eleven Corporation of Taiwan; Part 4: China Petroleum station, corner of Xinyi Road and Tonghua Street, Taipei; Unit 12, Part 2: Suzhou Jie Department Store, Beijing; Unit 13, Part 2: Heping Supermarket, Taipei; Part 3: Fengcai Shoe and Handbag Store, Taipei; Part 4: Tiantian Children's Fashions, Taipei; Unit 14, Parts 1 and 2: Dong Ji Restaurant, Beijing; Parts 3 and 4: Jufulou Manchurian Restaurant, Beijing; Unit 15, Parts 1, 2, and 3: Quanjude Roast Duck Restaurant, Beijing; Unit 16, Part 1: Xiangyanglou Restaurant, Taipei; Unit 20, Parts 1 and 2: Chinese Classic Art Development Center, New York City; Unit 22, Part 2: Foreign Affairs Police, Taipei; Part 3: National Taiwan Normal University, Taipei; Unit 23, Part 3: Yale-China Chinese Language Centre, Chinese University of Hong Kong; Unit 24, Part 3: Penang Chinese Girls' Private High School; Part 4: SBS House of Notebooks, Gurney Plaza, Penang.

Library of Congress Cataloging-in-Publication Data for this title is on record.

Distributed by:

North America, Latin America & Europe
Tuttle Publishing
364 Innovation Drive
North Clarendon, VT 05759-9436 U.S.A.
Tel: 1 (802) 773-8930
Fax: 1 (802) 773-6993
info@tuttlepublishing.com
www.tuttlepublishing.com

Japan
Tuttle Publishing
Yaekari Building, 3rd Floor
5-4-12 Osaki Shinagawa-ku
Tokyo 141 0032
Tel: (81) 3 5437-0171
Fax: (81) 3 5437-0755
sales@tuttle.co.jp
www.tuttle.co.jp

Asia Pacific
Berkeley Books Pte. Ltd.
61 Tai Seng Avenue #02-12
Singapore 534167
Tel: (65) 6280-1330
Fax: (65) 6280-6290
inquiries@periplus.com.sg
www.periplus.com

First edition
15 14 13   8 7 6 5 4 3 2 1   1306EP

Printed in Hong Kong

TUTTLE PUBLISHING® is a registered trademark of Tuttle Publishing, a division of Periplus Editions (HK) Ltd.

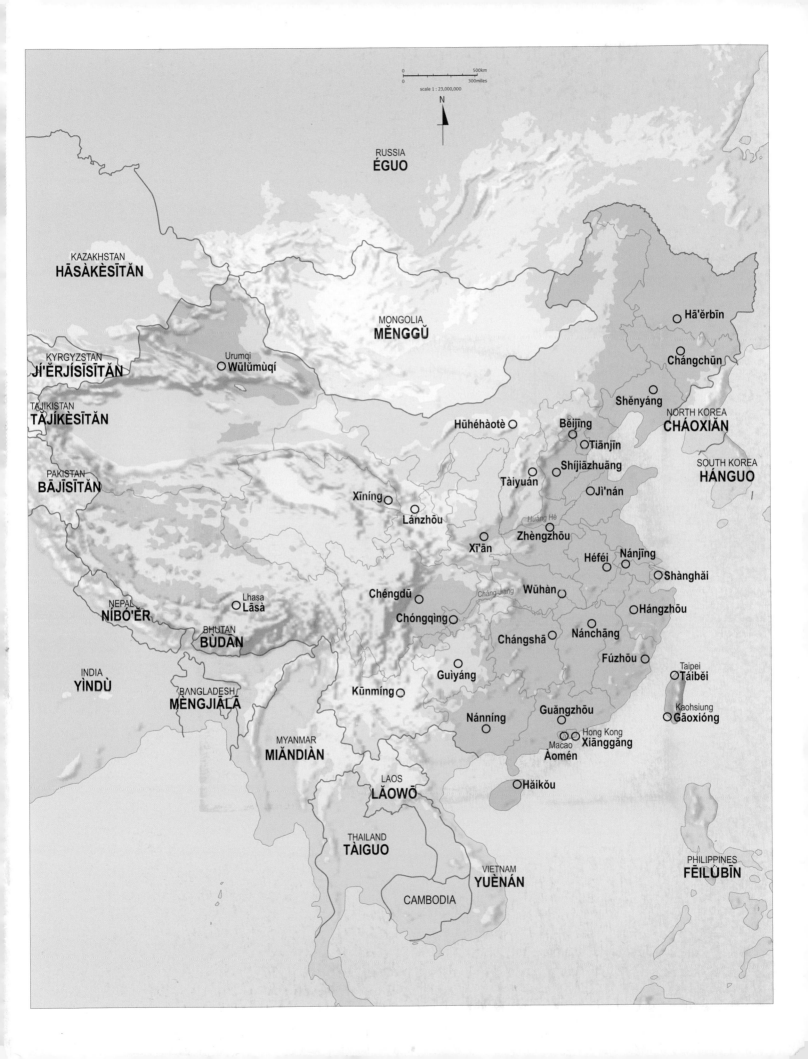

A Note to the Learner

Welcome to the second volume of an unusual, and highly effective, two-volume course in spoken Chinese.

As a native English speaker, your working hard to learn Chinese isn't enough; you have to work smart in order to learn this very different language efficiently. No matter why you've chosen to learn Chinese—for business, travel, cultural studies, or another goal—the *Basic Chinese* approach of two separate but integrated tracks will help you learn it most efficiently and successfully.

There are no Chinese characters to be found here because you don't need characters to learn to speak Chinese. In fact, learning the characters for everything you learn to say is an inefficient way to learn Chinese, one that significantly slows down your progress.

To help you learn to speak and understand Chinese as efficiently as possible, *Intermediate Spoken Chinese* gives you the Chinese language portions of this course not via characters, but instead through **video** and **audio** featuring native speakers (on the accompanying discs). And in the pages of this book, the Chinese is represented in Hanyu Pinyin, the official Chinese romanization system.

- *Intermediate Spoken Chinese* should be used in conjunction with the accompanying **Intermediate Spoken Chinese Practice Essentials**.

- If you wish to learn Chinese reading and writing, which is certainly to be recommended for most learners, you should—together with or after the spoken course—use the companion course **Intermediate Written Chinese**. It corresponds with *Intermediate Spoken Chinese* and systematically introduces the highest-frequency characters (simplified and traditional) and words in context in sentences and reading passages as well as in realia such as street signs, menus, and advertisements.

- For instructors and those learners with prior knowledge of Chinese characters, an *Intermediate Spoken Chinese* **Character Transcription** is also available. It contains transcriptions into simplified and traditional characters of *Intermediate Spoken Chinese* and can be downloaded free from the *Intermediate Spoken Chinese* page at www.tuttlepublishing.com. Please note that the character transcription isn't intended, and shouldn't be used, as the primary vehicle for beginning Chinese language students to learn reading and writing.

- The *Basic Chinese* **Instructor's Guide**, also available free from the publisher, contains detailed suggestions for using these materials as well as a large number of communicative exercises for use by instructors in class or by tutors during practice sessions.

请注意

《进阶中文：听与说》为专门练习口语的教材，内附有两张光盘，因此全书内只列有汉语拼音和英文注释，不使用汉字。学习者宜与配套的《进阶中文：听与说》练习册一起使用。

此套中文教材另编有《进阶中文：读与写》及《进阶中文：读与写》练习册，专供读写课使用。《进阶中文：听与说》另配有汉字版，将《进阶中文：听与说》中所有对话和补充生词的拼音版转为汉字，并分简繁体，供教师和已有汉字基础的学习者参考、使用。此套教材亦配有教师手册，指导教师如何使用此教材，且提供大量课堂练习，极为实用。

請注意

《進階中文：聽與說》為專門練習口語的教材，內附有兩張光盤，因此全書內只列有漢語拼音和英文注釋，不使用漢字。學習者宜與配套的《進階中文：聽與說》練習冊一起使用。

此套中文教材另編有《進階中文：讀與寫》及《進階中文：讀與寫》練習冊，專供讀寫課使用。《進階中文：聽與說》另配有漢字版，將《進階中文：聽與說》中所有對話和補充生詞的拼音版轉為漢字，並分簡繁體，供教師和已有漢字基礎的學習者參考、使用。此套教材亦配有教師手冊，指導教師如何使用此教材，且提供大量課堂練習，極為實用。

Contents

Acknowledgments

I am indebted to a great many people in Beijing, Taipei, Hong Kong, Macao, Singapore, Malaysia, and the United States for their assistance in the preparation of this course. It's not possible to mention everyone who participated, but special thanks are due the following for their contributions:

For assistance with the preparation of the basic conversations that serve as the core of this course: Jerling G. Kubler, Lu Zhi, Amory Yi-mou Shih, Wu Zong, and Yang Wang.

For recording situational dialogs used as source material for some of the basic conversations: Cao Jianying, Chang Ling-lan, Li Yueying, Li Zhenwen, Liu Shu-yen, Eileen H. Seng, Amory Yi-mou Shih, Tony Chungyan Yang, and Yang-Hou Kun.

For assistance in preparing the accompanying drills and exercises: Huang Ya-Yun, Jerling G. Kubler, Yang Wang; and my student research assistants Jenny Chen, Hoyoon Nam, Alexander T. Ratté, and Tron Wang.

For assistance in preparing the accompanying audio recordings: Jerling G. Kubler, Jun Yang, Weibing Ye and over one hundred other native speakers in Beijing, Taipei, Hong Kong, Macao, Singapore, and Malaysia. Of these, Dr. Jun Yang, Senior Lecturer in Chinese at the University of Chicago, deserves special recognition for the many hours he spent recording the majority of the Build Ups for the basic conversations.

For serving as actors in the accompanying video recordings or for assistance with arrangements for the videotaping: Flora Banker, Lindsay Benedict, Chen Limin, Chiu Ming-hua, Chou Shu-yen, Cynthia Cramsie, Darryl Crane, M. O. Danun, Chris Folino, Foo Si Min, Susan Harmon, Ho Tsu-chi, Brad Hou, Hou Lanfen, Mr. and Mrs. Hsueh Fu-hua, Ingrid Hsue, Hu Weiguo, Angie Huse, Jonathan Isaacs, Yun Yong Khang, Teng Jian Khoo, Jerling G. Kubler, Kuo Chih-hsiung, James Lambert, Gavin LaRowe, Siu-lun Lee, Roger Levy, Debbie Lee, Heidi Lee, Li Chen, Li Mei, Li Yingyou, Li Zhenqiang, Li Zhenwen, Liang Chunshen, Liao Hao-hsiang, Liu Jifeng, Liu Xiaodong, Kevin Lo, Michelle Lopez, Sweeheong Low, Ziqing Low, Lü Lin, Ma Yulan, Rachel Mac-Cleery, Mao Hui-ling, Maja Mave, Max Mayrhofer, Nicholas Minekime, Emily Murray, Chin Kwee Nyet, Gwendolyn Pascoe, David Rieth, Todd Roma, Thomas Rowley, Michael Saso, Mr. and Mrs. Amory Shih, Matthew Stein, Peter Stein, Su Weiming, Beth Sutter, Tang Chu-shih, Tang Wei-ying, Alex Tsebelis, Natasha Tyson, Wang Lixin, Michael Warres, Tim White, Wong Ho Put, Wu Hsian-jong, Yang Chunxue, Yang Ping, Yap Mae, Charles Yonts, Yun Yong Khang, Zhou Lei, and others.

For performing and granting permission to record and use their classical Chinese music in the audio and video recordings: Bai Miao, Chang Jing, and Tian Weining. In the recordings, Part 1 of each unit features the **gǔzhēng**, a 21-stringed plucked instrument similar to the zither; Part 2 features the **èrhú**, a two-stringed bowed instrument; Part 3 features the **yángqín** or dulcimer; and Part 4 features the **sānxián**, a three-stringed plucked instrument.

For assistance with the editing and dubbing of the accompanying audio and video recordings: An Zi; Bruce Wheat and Philip Remillard of the Office of Instructional Technology at Williams College; and my student research assistants Hoyoon Nam and Freeman Ningchuan Zhu.

For assistance with computer-related work: Adam Jianjun Wang, Senior Instructional Technology specialist at Williams College; student research assistants Daniel Gerlanc, Hoyoon Nam, Daniel Nelson, and Freeman Zhu; and Carl E. Kubler. Of these, Daniel Nelson and Daniel Gerlanc deserve special recognition for their continued support of the project over a period of several years.

For clerical assistance with various tasks related to the preparation of the manuscript: Donna L. Chenail of the Faculty Secretarial Office at Williams College; and my student research assistants Jenny Chen, Steven P. S. Cheng, Angie Chien, Niki Fang, Hoyoon Nam, Amy Sprengelmeyer, Tron Wang, and Freeman Zhu.

For assistance in checking the Chinese contained in this volume and/or providing helpful comments and suggestions: Cecilia Chang, Jingqi Fu, Han Bing, Hsu Yu-yin, Jerling G. Kubler, Liao Hao-hsiang, Nicholas Minekime, Eric Pelzl, Cathy Silber, Tseng Hsin-I, Chen Wang, Yang Wang, Tony Chung-yan Yang, and Li Yu. Of these, Yang Wang, my coauthor for the accompanying *Intermediate Spoken Chinese Practice Essentials*, deserves special recognition for her detailed review of the entire manuscript. I also wish to thank the students in my Chinese 101-102 courses at Williams College from 1992 through 2012 for numerous suggestions and corrections, as well as for their inspiration and encouragement. Students at St. Mary's College of Maryland, where the course was field-tested with the assistance of Professor Jingqi Fu, and at Wisconsin Lutheran College, where the course was field-tested with the assistance of Professor Eric Pelzl, similarly provided helpful comments. Professor Pelzl deserves special thanks for his many insightful comments and excellent suggestions.

For meticulous editing and many other helpful suggestions during the production of this course: Sandra Korinchak, Senior Editor at Tuttle Publishing. I wish, once again, to express my appreciation for their enthusiastic support of the project and its development to Tuttle's Publisher Eric Oey and Vice President Christina Ong; and to Nancy Goh, Tan Cheng Har, and the Tuttle Sales and Marketing Team for their expertise and assistance throughout.

It will be obvious to those familiar with the field of Teaching of Chinese as a Foreign Language how this course builds upon the work of others. I would like to single out the following, whose work has been especially helpful and inspiring to me: Y. R. Chao, Chien Wang-Chen, John DeFrancis, Beverly Hong, Thomas E. Madden, Victor Mair, Shou-hsin Teng, Galal Walker, and A. Ronald Walton. I should express here my appreciation to my own teachers of Chinese language and linguistics: Nicholas C. Bodman, Paul Jen-kuei Li, John McCoy, Mei Kuang, Tsu-lin Mei, Pei Shin Ni, Ting Pang-hsin, Harold Shadick, and Pilwun Wang. I wish also to acknowledge my debt to my teacher of Japanese, the late Eleanor H. Jorden, whose innovative contributions to the field of Teaching of Japanese as a Foreign Language served both as inspiration and example during the development of this course. Finally, I wish to express thanks to my wife, Jerling G. Kubler; my son, Carl E. Kubler; and my mother, Gisela H. Kubler, for their advice, support, and patience over a period of many years.

Logistical and/or financial support from the following is gratefully acknowledged: Hong Gang Jin at the Associated Colleges in China Program in Beijing; Hsin Shih-Chang, Shouhsin Teng, and Tseng Chin-Chin at the Graduate Institute of Teaching Chinese as a Second Language at National Taiwan Normal University in Taipei; the Mellon Foundation and the Center for Educational Technology at Middlebury College; Michael Saso at the Institute of Asian Studies in Beijing; Jenny F. So and staff at the Institute of Chinese Studies at the Chinese University of Hong Kong; Tuttle Publishing; Wu Jingjyi at the Foundation for Scholarly Exchange in Taipei; Weiping Wu at the Yale-China Chinese Language Center of the Chinese University of Hong Kong; and, last but not least, Williams College, especially the Center for Technology in the Arts and Humanities, the Oakley Center for the Humanities and Social Sciences, and the Office of the Dean of the Faculty.

I should state here that the ultimate rationale behind the preparation of this course is to improve communication between Americans and the citizens of the various Chinese-speaking societies and thereby contribute, in however small a way, toward promoting understanding and peace between our peoples.

Cornelius C. Kubler
Department of Asian Studies
Williams College
Williamstown, Massachusetts, USA

Orientation

About This Course

The *Basic Chinese* series constitutes an introductory course in modern Chinese (Mandarin), the language with the largest number of native speakers in the world, the official language of mainland China and Taiwan, and one of the official languages of Singapore. The focus of this course, which is designed for adult English-speaking learners, is on communicating in Chinese in practical, everyday situations. It successfully meets the needs of a wide range of users, from college and university students to business people and government personnel. With some adjustments in the rate of progress, high school students may also be able to use these materials to their advantage. By availing themselves of the detailed usage notes and making good use of the workbook, the video, and the audio, it's even possible for motivated self-learners to work through these materials on their own, though it would be desirable for them to meet with a teacher or native speaker for an hour or two per week, if possible.[1] Although users with specialized needs will, in the later stages of their study, require supplementary materials, we believe this course provides a solid general foundation or "base" (hence the title of the course) that all learners of Chinese need, on which they may build for future mastery.

The course is divided into spoken and written tracks, each with various types of ancillary materials. The following diagram will clarify the organization of the whole course:

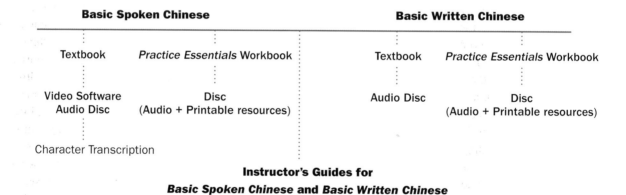

Several modes of study are possible for these materials: (1) the spoken series only; (2) a lesson in the spoken series followed a few days, weeks, or months later by the corresponding lesson in the written series; and (3) a lesson in the spoken and written series studied simultaneously. What isn't possible is to study the

---

1. For specific suggestions on how to use this course for self study, self-learners should see "A Note for Independent Learners" on pp. 19–20 of the first volume of this course, *Basic Spoken Chinese*.

written series first or only, since the written series assumes knowledge of the pronunciation system and relevant grammatical and cultural information, which are introduced in the spoken series.

Students embarking upon the study of Chinese should be aware that, along with Japanese, Korean, and Arabic, Chinese is one of the most difficult languages for native English speakers. This course makes no pretensions of being an "easy" introduction to the language. However, students can be assured that if they make the effort to master thoroughly the material presented here, they will acquire a solid foundation in Chinese.

The proficiency goals in speaking and reading by completion of *Intermediate Spoken Chinese* and *Intermediate Written Chinese* are Intermediate-High on the American Council on the Teaching of Foreign Languages (ACTFL) Chinese Proficiency Guidelines, which correlates with S-1+/R-1+ on the U.S. government Interagency Language Roundtable (ILR) Language Skill Level Descriptions. The last few lessons of *Intermediate Spoken Chinese* are on the cusp of the ACTFL Advanced or ILR S-2 level. By the time they complete this volume, learners will be able to conduct simple, practical conversations with Chinese speakers on a variety of everyday topics (cf. Table of Contents). They will not yet be able to conduct formal conversations on professional topics, a skill that in the case of Chinese takes a considerably longer time to develop.

Some of the special features of the *Basic Chinese* series include:

Separate but integrated tracks in spoken and written Chinese. Most textbooks for teaching basic Chinese teach oral and written skills from the same materials, which are covered at a single rate of progress. Students typically study a dialog, learn how to use in their speech the words and grammar contained in the dialog, and also learn how to read and write every character used to write the dialog. But the fact is that, due to the inherent difficulty of Chinese characters, native English speakers can learn spoken Chinese words much faster than they can learn the characters used to write those words. As East Asian language pedagogues Eleanor H. Jorden and A. Ronald Walton have argued,[2] why must the rate of progress in spoken Chinese be slowed down to the maximum possible rate of progress in written Chinese? Moreover, in Chinese, more than in most languages, there are substantial differences between standard spoken style and standard written style, with many words and grammar patterns that are common in speech being rare in writing or vice versa. For all these reasons, this course uses separate but related materials for training in spoken and written Chinese. However, reflecting the fact that written Chinese is based on spoken Chinese, and so as to mutually reinforce the four skills (listening, speaking, reading, and writing), the written track is closely integrated with the spoken track. A day's spoken lesson is based on a Basic Conversation typically introducing one to three new grammar patterns and 20 to 25 new spoken words, while the corresponding written lesson introduces six new high-frequency characters and a number of words that are written using them, chosen from among (but not including all of) the characters used to write the Basic Conversation of the corresponding lesson. Experience shows that the learning of written skills in Chinese proceeds more efficiently if learners study for reading and writing the characters for words they have previously learned for speaking and comprehension. Under this approach, when learners take up a new lesson in written Chinese, they already know the pronunciations, meanings, and usages of the new words, needing only to learn their written representations—which considerably lightens the learning load. Such an approach also allows students and instructors maximum flexibility concerning at which point, how, and even whether, to introduce reading and writing.

Graduated approach. There is so much to learn to become proficient in Chinese that Chinese language learning can easily become overwhelming. By dividing large tasks into a series of many smaller ones, the learning of Chinese becomes more manageable. Therefore, each spoken lesson consists of only one fairly short (five- to twelve-line) Basic Conversation, while each written lesson introduces only six new characters. An added bonus to this approach is the sense of accomplishment learners feel through frequent completion of small goals, rather than getting bogged down in long lessons that seem never-ending.

Naturalness of the language. A special effort has been made to present natural, idiomatic, up-to-date Chinese as opposed to stilted "textbook style." This will be evident, for example, in the use of interjections, pause

2. Cf. Eleanor H. Jorden and A. Ronald Walton, "Truly Foreign Languages: Instructional Challenges" in *The Annals of the American Academy of Political and Social Science,* March 1987.

fillers, and final particles, which occur more frequently in this text than in most other Chinese language textbooks. Occasionally, for comprehension practice, we have included recordings of slightly accented Mandarin speech, so as to familiarize learners with some of the more common variations in pronunciation they are likely to encounter.

Authenticity of the language. Chinese, like English, is a language spoken in a number of different societies, with multiple standards and varying usages. Although the emphasis of this course is on the core that is common to Mandarin Chinese wherever it's spoken, linguistic differences among the major Chinese speech communities as well as recent innovations are taken up where appropriate. Of the 96 basic conversations in *Basic Spoken Chinese* and *Intermediate Spoken Chinese*, the audio and video for 56 of them were recorded in Beijing, with another 31 recorded in Taipei, 3 in Hong Kong, one in Macao, 2 in Singapore, 2 in Malaysia, and one in the U.S. The relatively small number of terms that are restricted in use to a particular speech area are so indicated.

Emphasis on the practical and immediately useful. We have tried to present material that is high in frequency and has the most immediate "pay-off value" possible. An effort has been made to include the most useful words, grammar patterns, situations, and functions, based on several published frequency studies as well as research by the author. The units of this course have been arranged in order of general usefulness and practical importance. Although the course is designed to be studied from beginning to end, learners with time for only, say, the first five or ten units will at least be exposed to many of the most useful vocabulary items and structural patterns.

Eclecticism of method. We believe that language is so complex and the personalities of learners so different, that no single method or approach can possibly meet the needs of all learners at all times. For this reason, the pedagogical approach we have chosen is purposefully eclectic. This course is proficiency-oriented and situational in approach with a carefully ordered underlying grammatical foundation. We have borrowed freely from the audio-lingual, communicative, functional-notional, and grammar-translation approaches.

Maximum flexibility of use. Student and teacher needs and personalities vary widely, as do the types of programs in which Chinese is taught. We have tried to leave options open whenever possible. This is true, for example, in the question of how to teach pronunciation; whether to teach the spoken skills only or also the written skills; when to introduce reading and writing; whether to teach simplified or traditional characters or both; and which of the exercises to do and in which order to do them. There is detailed discussion of all these and other questions in the *Instructor's Guide*.

Attention to sociolinguistic and cultural features. Knowing how to say something with correct grammar and pronunciation isn't sufficient for effective communication. Learners must know what to say and what not to say, when to say it, and how to adjust what they say for the occasion. How do the gender, age, and social position of the speaker and listener affect language? Finally, language doesn't exist apart from the culture of its speakers. What are the cultural assumptions of Chinese speakers? These are some of the matters to which we have tried to pay attention.

Extensive built-in review. In order to promote long-term retention of the material learned, a great effort has been made to recycle vocabulary and grammar periodically in later units in the textbook and *Practice Essentials* after they have been introduced. In addition, there is a review and study guide at the end of every unit.

Attention to the needs of learners with prior knowledge of Chinese. While the course is designed for beginners and assumes no prior knowledge of Chinese, it tries to take into account the special situation and needs of learners who possess some prior knowledge of the language acquired from home or residence overseas. Consequently, there are special notes on features of standard Mandarin pronunciation and usage that differ from the Cantonese or Taiwanese-influenced Mandarin to which some learners may have been exposed.

Organization and Use

Intermediate Spoken Chinese is a continuation of *Basic Spoken Chinese*, also published by Tuttle Publishing. Learners should have thorough control of the material in the ten units of that volume before beginning this one. This volume is titled "Intermediate" because the expectation is that conscientious learners will be able to attain the ACTFL Intermediate-High proficiency level in spoken Chinese by the time they complete it. *Intermediate Spoken Chinese* is designed for the second and third semesters of fast-paced college and university Chinese language programs that schedule one or more hours a day of class in small groups with an additional 2-3 hours daily of student preparation and self-study. At college or university programs that progress at a more moderate pace, where students have fewer than 5 hours per week of classroom instruction and don't have so much time available for outside preparation, this volume would be suitable for second-year Chinese courses. In high schools, this volume would be suitable for third and fourth year Chinese courses.

Intermediate Spoken Chinese introduces most of the remaining high-frequency grammatical patterns of spoken Chinese that weren't introduced in *Basic Spoken Chinese*, a vocabulary of 1,387 items,[3] and the sociolinguistic and cultural information needed for learners to use these linguistic components appropriately. In addition, another 426 Additional Vocabulary items are presented for optional learning. The textbook for *Intermediate Spoken Chinese* contains 14 units divided into 56 parts or lessons that involve common daily life situations in which Americans typically find themselves interacting with Chinese speakers in the various Chinese-speaking societies. On the first page of each unit are listed the topic and communicative objectives for the unit. The communicative objectives reflect important language functions and give the learning a purpose. Learners should be sure to read through the objectives, since they will be more receptive to learning if they understand the purpose of the learning and have an idea of what to expect.

Every unit is divided into four parts, each of which includes the following sections:

Context. On the first page of each part you'll see the title of the lesson, an image of the situation drawn from the on-location video, and a description of the situation. We always explain the sociolinguistic and cultural context, for example, where the conversation is taking place, who the speakers are, their positions in society, how well they know each other, their age, their gender, etc. It's important that you study the image and read the description, so you have a clear idea of the context for the Basic Conversation you'll be studying.

Basic Conversation. The basic conversations, which constitute the core of each lesson, normally consist of a conversation between one American and one (or occasionally more than one) Chinese speaker. The purpose of the basic conversations is to introduce high-frequency structural patterns, vocabulary, and cultural information that is relevant to learners' likely future needs in a situation-oriented format. To help make each conversation "come to life" and to show details of the sociolinguistic and cultural background, audio and video recordings of the basic conversations have been prepared, which should be used in conjunction with the textbook. The basic conversations are next presented in "Build Up" format, with each sentence of the Basic Conversation broken down into manageable chunks with pauses provided for repetition, so as to help learners gain fluency. In the textbook, the "Build Up" is presented in two columns: romanization, on the left; and English translation and word class, on the right. By working with the audio recordings and textbook, the student should thoroughly memorize the Basic Conversation so he or she can perform it (in class with the instructor and other students the next day, or, for independent learners, by using the software's conversation options) prior to beginning the drills and exercises. To a significant extent, the student has mastered the lesson to the degree that he or she has internalized the Basic Conversation. Of course, memorization of the Basic Conversation is only the first step in attaining communicative competence.

Supplementary Vocabulary. This section presents important supplementary vocabulary that, in many cases, is related in some way to the material introduced in the Basic Conversation. The Supplementary Vocabulary, which is included on the audio recordings after the Basic Conversation, is required for learning and may reoccur later in the course without further explanation.

---

3. Since *Basic Spoken Chinese* introduces 931 words, this makes a total of 2,318 words introduced in the two volumes of the spoken course.

Additional Vocabulary. This section, which exists only for some lessons, presents other useful words related to the content of the lesson for the learner's reference. The Additional Vocabulary, which is designed for students with extra time who desire to be challenged, isn't required to be learned and will not reoccur in later lessons.

Grammatical and Cultural Notes. The major new grammatical structures in the Basic Conversation are here explained and exemplified from the point of view of the native English-speaking learner. There are also miscellaneous comments on the Basic Conversation, Supplementary Vocabulary, and Additional Vocabulary. A special effort has been made to incorporate important sociolinguistic and cultural information as well as practical advice for the learner of Chinese. Unlike the first volume, in this volume we occasionally introduce in the example sentences some words learners have not formally learned in the lessons, but since the examples are always in Pinyin romanization and are accompanied by complete English translations, this shouldn't present a problem and should actually be a good way for learners to further expand their Chinese vocabulary.

Review and Study Guide. At the end of every unit, there is a review and study guide consisting of: (1) the new vocabulary introduced in the Basic Conversation and Supplementary Vocabulary of the four parts of the unit, arranged according to word class; and (2) a list of the major new grammar patterns introduced in the unit, with an indication of where they first occurred.

Abbreviations

Word Classes*

[A]	Adverb
[AT]	Attributive
[AV]	Auxiliary Verb
[BF]	Bound Form
[CJ]	Conjunction
[CV]	Coverb
[EV]	Equative Verb
[EX]	Expression
[I]	Interjection
[IE]	Idiomatic Expression
[L]	Localizer
[M]	Measure
[MA]	Moveable Adverb
[N]	Noun
[NU]	Number
[P]	Particle
[PH]	Phrase
[PR]	Pronoun
[PT]	Pattern

[PV]	Postverb
[PW]	Place Word
[QW]	Question Word
[RC]	Resultative Compound
[RE]	Resultative Ending
[SN]	Surname
[SP]	Specifier
[SV]	Stative Verb
[TW]	Time Word
[V]	Verb
[VO]	Verb-Object Compound

Other Abbreviations and Symbols

(B)	Beijing
(T)	Taipei
lit.	literally
SV	Supplementary Vocabulary
AV	Additional Vocabulary
*	(indicates that what follows is incorrect)

* For explanations of the above word classes, see the section on "Word Classes of Spoken Chinese" on the disc.

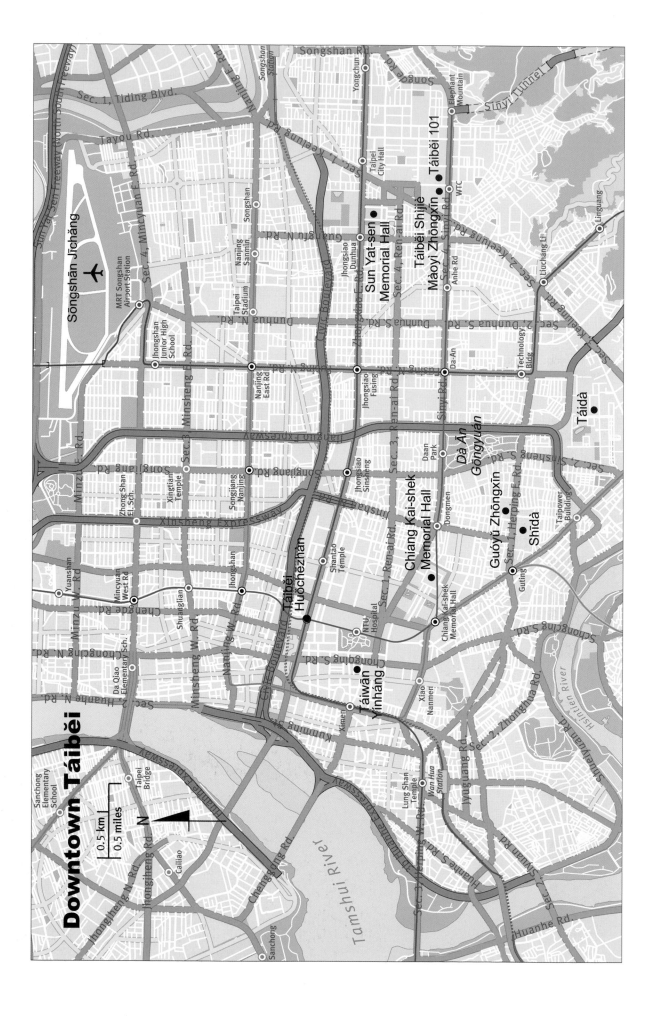

Getting Around Taipei

COMMUNICATIVE OBJECTIVES

Once you've mastered this unit, you'll be able to use Chinese to:

1. Hail a taxi in Taipei and tell the driver your destination.

2. Complain that the driver is driving too fast and tell her or him to slow down.

3. Pay the driver and tell her or him to keep the change.

4. Inquire about taking a bus or the MRT in Taipei: which number or line to take, how often they come, buying the ticket, etc.

5. Ask directions from a pay phone when you can't find someone's home.

6. Give instructions to a gasoline station attendant when you stop for gas.

By Taxi to the Bank of Taiwan

Sandra Russell, an American graduate student in Taipei, hails a taxi for herself and a friend. She tells the driver the destination and they chat for a while. On arrival, she asks what the fare is and pays the driver.

 ## Basic Conversation 11-1

1. **RUSSELL** **Máfan dào Chóngqìng Nán Lùde Táiwān Yínháng, xièxie.**
   Please go to the Bank of Taiwan on Chongqing South Road, thanks.

2. **DRIVER** **Nǐde Guóyǔ shuōde bú cuò ó! Zài náli xuéde?**
   You speak Mandarin really well! Where did you learn it?

3. **RUSSELL** **Wǒ zài Měiguo, dàlù gēn Táiwān dōu xuéguo.**
   I studied it in America, mainland China, and Taiwan.

4. **DRIVER** **Nǐ lái Táiwān duō jiǔ le?**
   How long have you been in Taiwan?

5. **RUSSELL** **Láile sān'ge duō yuè le.**
   I've been here for more than three months.

   (after a while) **Āiyò! Nǐ kāide tài kuàile, xiàsǐ rén le! Kě bu kéyi kāi màn yìdiǎn?**
   Whew! You're driving too fast, that was terrifying! Could you slow down a bit?

6. **DRIVER** **Méi wèntí, fàngxīn la.**
   No problem, relax.

   (after a while) **Qiánmiàn jiù dàole.**
   It's up ahead.

7. **RUSSELL** *(when the cab comes to a stop)* **Duōshǎo qián?**
   How much is it?

8. **DRIVER** **Jiǔshiwǔkuài.**
   95 NT.

9. **RUSSELL** **Yìbǎikuài, bú yòng zhǎole.**
   Here's 100 NT, keep the change.

10. **DRIVER** **Xièxie.**
    Thanks.

Build Up

1. **Russell**

Chóngqìng	Chongqing (city in Sichuan) **[PW]***
Chóngqìng Nán Lù	Chongqing South Road **[PW]**
yínháng	bank **[PW]** (M: **jiā**)
Táiwān Yínháng	Bank of Taiwan **[PW]**
Máfan dào Chóngqìng Nán Lùde	Please go to the Bank of Taiwan
Táiwān Yínháng, xièxie.	on Chongqing South Road, thanks.

2. **Driver**

Guóyǔ (T)	Mandarin (language) **[N]**
ó	(indicates interest or excitement) **[P]**
shuōde bú cuò ó	is spoken well
Nǐde Guóyǔ shuōde bú cuò ó!	You speak Mandarin really well!
Zài náli xuéde?	Where did you learn it?

3. **Russell**

dàlù	mainland **[PW]**
Wǒ zài Měiguo, dàlù gēn	I studied it in America, mainland China, and
Táiwān dōu xuéguo.	Taiwan.

4. **Driver**

le	(indicates action continuing up to the present) **[P]**
duō jiǔ le	how long has it been
Nǐ lái Táiwān duō jiǔ le?	How long have you been in Taiwan?

5. **Russell**

Láile sān'ge duō yuè le.	I've been here for more than three months.
xià	frighten **[V]**
-sǐ	to the point of death **[RE]**
xiàsǐ	frighten to death **[RC]**
xiàsǐ rén le	it frightens people to death
màn	be slow **[SV]**
kāi màn yìdiǎn	drive a little more slowly
Āiyò! Nǐ kāide tài kuàile, xiàsǐ rén le!	Whew! You're driving too fast, that was
Kě bu kéyi kāi màn yìdiǎn?	terrifying! Could you slow down a bit?

6. **Driver**

wèntí	problem **[N]**
méi wèntí	there is no problem, "no problem" **[IE]**
fàngxīn	be at ease, relax **[VO]**
la	(combined form of **le** and **a**) **[P]**
fàngxīn la	relax
Méi wèntí, fàngxīn la.	No problem, relax.
Qiánmiàn jiù dàole.	It's up ahead.

7. **Russell**

Duōshǎo qián?	How much is it?

* Throughout this book, as was the practice in *Basic Spoken Chinese*, if an item in the Basic Conversation or Supplementary Vocabulary section shows a word class abbreviation [in brackets] after the English translation, this indicates that the item occurs at that point for the *first time* in the course. It should be given special attention for learning, since knowledge of it will be assumed in the rest of the course.

8. Driver

Jiǔshiwǔkuài.   95 NT.

9. Russell

bú yòng zhǎo   you don't need to give change

Yìbǎikuài, bú yòng zhǎole.   Here's 100 NT, keep the change.

10. Driver

Xièxie.   Thanks.

 ## Supplementary Vocabulary

1. **yàojǐn**   be important [SV]
    bú yàojǐn   be unimportant; "never mind" [IE]
    Nǐ wàngle dài qián bú yàojǐn,   That you forgot to bring money doesn't matter;
    wǒ yǒu.   I've got some.

2. **zuò**   sit in/on; take; by (car, train, boat, airplane) [CV]
    jìchéngchē (T)   taxi [N] (M: **liàng**)
    zuò jìchéngchē   by taxi
    Wǒmen zuò jìchéngchē qù ba.   Let's go by taxi.

3. **jiějué**   solve [V]
    jiějué wèntí   solve problems
    Nèiyang bù néng jiějué wèntí.   You can't solve problems that way.

4. **wèntí**   question [N]
    Lǎoshī, wǒ yǒu yíge wèntí.   Teacher, I have a question.

Grammatical and Cultural Notes

1.   When telling a taxi driver where to go, it's also common simply to state your destination, for example, **Chóngqìng Nánlù Táiwān Yínháng** "the Bank of Taiwan on Chongqing South Road." Adding **Máfan dào...** "Could I trouble you to go to..." at the beginning and **xièxie** "thank you" at the end makes this request polite.

2A. Although the term **Guóyǔ** "Mandarin" is now used primarily in Taiwan, it's occasionally still heard in Hong Kong and mainland China.

2B. **ACCENTED MANDARIN.** The driver in this basic conversation doesn't speak standard Mandarin; his Mandarin is influenced by his native language, Taiwanese. For example, in line 2, instead of **shuō** he says **suō**; and in line 8, instead of **jiǔshiwǔkuài** he says **jiǔsiwǔkuài**. The type of pronunciation you're learning for your active use in this course is that of standard Mandarin, which is based on the dialect of Beijing and is considered the Chinese national language. While the majority of Chinese speakers throughout all of China can understand standard Mandarin without any problem, speakers from areas other than Beijing and environs frequently use non-standard, dialect-influenced pronunciations in their Mandarin. In the speech of non-standard Mandarin speakers there are fewer unstressed syllables and there is less use of the (r) suffix. Other common features of non-standard Mandarin include:

(a) Initials **zh-**, **ch-**, and **sh-** may lose the **h** to become **z-**, **c-**, and **s-** so that, for example, **zhū** "pig" sounds like **zū** "rent," **chǎo** "noisy" sounds like **cǎo** "grass," and **shān** "mountain" sounds like **sān** "three."

(b) Initial **f-** may change to **hu-** so that, for example, **fàn** "cooked rice" sounds like **huàn** "change."

(c) The distinction between initials **l-** and **n-** may be lost so that, for example, **lán** "blue" and **nán** "difficult" sound the same.

(d)   The distinction between finals **-in** and **-ing** and between finals **-en** and **-eng** may be lost so that, for example, **xìn** "letter" and **xìng** "be surnamed" sound the same, or so that **děng** "wait" sounds like **děn**.

Bank of Taiwan headquarters on Chongqing South Road in Taipei

(e)   Tones may differ from standard Mandarin. For example, in the Mandarin dialect of Tianjin, only 75 miles from Beijing, syllables which would be Tone One in standard Mandarin are pronounced like standard Mandarin Tone Three, and syllables which would be Tone Two in standard Mandarin are pronounced as Tone One. Also, Mandarin as spoken by many speakers from Taiwan and southern mainland China has fewer neutral tones than when spoken by northern speakers. However, this doesn't mean that you don't need to learn standard Mandarin tones; when native Chinese speakers use tones in a non-standard manner, there is still a *system* to their speech (e.g., their Tone Three may correspond regularly to standard Mandarin Tone One), so standard speakers will subconsciously make the proper adjustments and still understand them. If you, as a non-native Chinese speaker, pronounce tones "any old way," there will be no system, and you're likely to be misunderstood.

You may be wondering how Chinese can communicate if all these distinctions in pronunciation are lost; and, in particular, how you'll ever get all this straight. The short answer to the first question is that context usually makes the meaning clear. As regards the second question, for the time being just be aware that non-standard pronunciations exist, so that if you try out your Chinese in the local Chinese restaurant and hear someone say **Wǒ sì Céndū rén** rather than standard Mandarin **Wǒ shi Chéngdū rén** "I'm from Chengdu," you won't be overly surprised and will have a general idea of what is going on. The important thing for you to focus on now is learning how to speak and understand Mandarin with standard pronunciation. In time, as your Chinese language experience increases, you'll gradually get used to common accented Mandarin pronunciations.

2C.   The sentence final particle **ó**, which indicates interest or excitement, is especially common in Taiwan. It's sometimes also used to indicate lively, friendly warnings. Examples:

> **Màn diǎnr ó!**   "Hey, buddy, slow down!"
>
> **Bù zǎole ó!**   "Hey, it's getting late, you know!"

2D.   **COMPLIMENTS.** Chinese people are quick to compliment foreigners who can speak some Mandarin. In fact, no matter how long a foreigner has lived in China or how good their Chinese is, Chinese people will often express amazement that they can speak any Chinese at all; this rapidly gets tiring, especially for long-time foreign residents, but the best attitude probably is to grin and bear it. Chinese people traditionally don't accept most compliments that are made to them, so if you're complimented for your Chinese, it would be better if you didn't just say **Xièxie** "thank you." Instead, you should politely decline such compliments with **Nǎli, nǎli** "Not at all" or **Mámahūhū** "It's only so-so" (lit. "horse-horse tiger-tiger") or **Hái chàde hěn yuǎn ne** "I still have a long ways to go" or **Shuǐpíng yǒuxiàn** "My level is limited." As for offering compliments to others, note that in Chinese society, you usually offer compliments only to someone equal or inferior in status. It would be presumptuous, for example, for a student to compliment a teacher on a class or lecture, for how (from the Chinese perspective) is the student able to judge? In English, students might compliment a teacher by saying "Hey, Professor, that was a great class!" but in Chinese you'd be more likely to say something like **Wǒ jīntiān gēn lǎoshī xuédàole hěn duō dōngxi** "Today I learned many things from the teacher."

2E.   **Zài nǎli xuéde?** "Where did you learn it?" is short for **Nǐ shi zài nǎli xuéde?** In rapid conversation, the **shi** of the **shi...de** construction is frequently omitted.

3.   Unless clarified otherwise, **dàlù** "mainland" usually refers to the Chinese mainland.

4A.   **LE TO INDICATE TIME CONTINUING UP THROUGH THE PRESENT.** Examine the question **Nǐ lái Táiwān duō jiǔ le?** Literally, this means something like "You come to Taiwan how long has it been?" In smoother English, we can translate this question as "How long have you been in Taiwan?" Now look at the answer to this question in line 5: **Láile sān'ge duō yuè le** "I've been here for more than three months." In sentences indicating duration of time, a sentence-final particle **le** at the end of the sentence indicates that the action of the verb has been continuing for a period of time up to and including the present. This is like the English construction "have been VERB-ing (for a certain period of time)." The pattern is:

SENTENCE INDICATING DURATION OF TIME	LE
Wǒ xué Rìyǔ xuéle liùge yuè	**le.**
"I've been studying Japanese for six months."	

More examples of **le** to indicate time continuing up through the present:

Lǎo Liú chīfàn chīle sān'ge zhōngtóu le!

"Old Liu has been eating for three hours!"

Xiǎo Wáng jiéhūn yǐjīng liǎngnián duō le.

"Little Wang has been married for more than two years."

Gù Lǎoshī zài wǒmen xuéxiào jiāole èrshiniánde Zhōngwén le.

"Professor Gu has been teaching Chinese at our school for 20 years."

Be careful to distinguish sentences that have only a verb **-le** from those that have both a verb **-le** and a sentence-final particle **le** at the end of the sentence. Verb **-le** alone indicates completed action; verb **-le** and sentence **le** occurring together in a sentence indicate duration of time continuing up through the present. Contrast the following pairs:

Tā zài nèijiā màoyì gōngsī gōngzuòle wǔnián.

"She worked at that trading company for five years." (she's not working there now)

Tā zài nèijiā màoyì gōngsī gōngzuòle wǔnián le.

"She's been working at that trading company for five years." (she's still working there now)

Tā xué Zhōngwén xuéle liǎngnián.

"She studied Chinese for two years." (e.g., when she was a student in college twenty years ago)

Tā xué Zhōngwén xuéle liǎngnián le.

"She's been studying Chinese for two years." (and she's still studying it now)

There is one exception to the rule about **le** at the end of a sentence to indicate time continuing up through the present. If there is an adverb like **zhǐ** "only" or **cái** "only" modifying the verb, then there is no **le** at the end of the sentence, even if the sense is that the action of the verb continues up through the present. The reason is that with **zhǐ** or **cái**, the focus is on relative shortness of time, not on continuity of time through the present. For example, consider the exchange below:

Speaker A: **Nǐ xué Zhōngwén xuéle duō jiǔ le?**

"How long have you been studying Chinese?"

Speaker B: **Wǒde tóngxué dōu xuéle yìnián le, kěshi wǒ zhǐ xuéle bànnián.**

"My classmates have all been studying for one year, but I've only been studying for half a year."

4B.   The question **Nǐ lái Táiwān duō jiǔ le?** "How long have you been in Taiwan?" is actually an abbreviated form of **Nǐ lái Táiwān láile duō jiǔ le?** with exactly the same meaning. Either construction is correct.

5A. **IMPERATIVES CONSISTING OF VERB + STATIVE VERB + YÌDIĂN(R).** In utterance 5, look at **kāi màn yidian** "drive more slowly." This is a common pattern for telling someone how to do something. A pronoun such as **nǐ** may optionally be added at the beginning. The **yìdiăn(r)** at the end is often in the neutral tone. To sum up, the pattern is:

VERB	STATIVE VERB	YÌDIĂN(R)
kāi	màn	yidian

"drive more slowly"

More examples of this pattern:

Kāi kuài yidianr.	"Drive a little faster."
Zǒu màn yidianr.	"Walk more slowly."
Nǐ shuō qīngchu yidian.	"Speak more clearly."
Xiě hǎokàn yidian.	"Write it nicer." (lit. "Write it more good-looking by a little.")

5B. Learn the resultative verb ending **-sǐ** "to the point of death" or "extremely," as in **xiàsǐ** "frighten to death." Other common resultative verbs ending in **-sǐ** include **mángsǐ** "so busy one is going to die—extremely busy," **lèisǐ** "so tired one is going to die—extremely tired," and **gāoxìngsǐ** "so happy one is going to die—incredibly happy." Be aware the ending **-sǐ** is used mostly in statements, not in questions. So you could say **Wǒ lèisǐle** "I'm exhausted" but you couldn't ask someone *Nǐ lèisǐle ma? "Are you exhausted?"

5C. Like its English equivalent, the question **Kě bu kéyi kāi màn yidian?** "Could you drive a little more slowly?" functions not as a question to be pondered and answered but rather as a polite request to do something. Other ways to convey the same meaning would be **Qǐng nǐ kāi màn yidian** and **Kāi màn yidian, hǎo bu hǎo?**

5D. Taiwan taxi drivers are renowned for their dare-devil driving. Don't be hesitant to ask your driver to slow down if you think he or she is driving dangerously.

9A. **Bú yòng zhǎole** is a common way to say "keep the change" (lit. "don't need to make change").

9B. Although tips aren't usually given to taxi drivers in Taiwan, it's customary to round off fares and let drivers keep small change. In Beijing, taxi drivers aren't allowed to take tips.

SV2A. As you may have guessed, the coverb **zuò** "by (car, bus, train, boat, airplane)" derives from the verb **zuò** "sit," so the example sentence **Wǒmen zuò jìchéngchē qù ba** "Let's go by taxi" could be translated literally as "Let's sit in a taxi and go."

SV2B. The formal written word for "taxi" in Taiwan is **chūzū qìchē**, the same as in mainland China. But in conversation, most people in Taiwan refer to taxis as **jìchéngchē** (lit. "calculate journey vehicle").

SV3–4. The noun **wèntí** can mean "question" as well as "problem." The context usually makes the meaning clear.

"Which Bus Do I Take to Muzha?"

Elizabeth Brill, an American who is teaching English for a year at an English language institute in Taiwan, wants to find out which bus she should take to get to Muzha, a suburb of Taipei. After trying but failing to make sense of the signs at a bus stop, she decides to ask a passerby, who suggests she ask at a 7-Eleven store across the street.

 Basic Conversation 11-2

1. BRILL **Qǐng wèn, dào Mùzhà qù yào zuò jǐhào?**
Excuse me, what number bus do you take to get to Muzha?

2. PASSERBY **Āiyà, wǒ hǎo jiǔ méi zuò gōngchē le, bù xiǎode. Nǐ dào duìmiànde Tǒngyī qù wènwen kàn. Yàoburán, nǐ yě kéyǐ zuò jiéyùn qù Mùzhà.**
Gosh, I haven't taken a bus for a long time, I don't know. Go to the 7-Eleven across the street and ask. Or you could also take the MRT to Muzha.

3. BRILL *(asks the clerk at a 7-Eleven)* **Qǐng wèn, dào Mùzhà qù yào zuò jǐhào?**
Excuse me, what number bus do you take to get to Muzha?

4. CLERK **Èr-sān-liù huòshi èr-sān-qī dōu kéyǐ dào.**
You can get there on 236 or 237.

5. BRILL **Dàgài duō jiǔ yìbān?**
About how often is there a bus?

6. CLERK **Èr-sān-qī bǐjiào jiǔ. Èr-sān-liù hǎoxiàng wǔfēn zhōng yìbān, hěn kuàide la.**
237 takes longer. For 236, I think there's a bus every five minutes, it won't be long.

7. BRILL **Xièxie. Wǒ shùnbiàn mǎi yìzhāng sānbǎikuàide chúzhípiào.**
Thanks. While I'm at it, I'll buy a stored-value ticket for 300 NT.

8. CLERK **Ò, bù hǎo yìsi. Sānbǎikuàide màiwánle. Zhǐ shèngxia liùbǎikuàide éryǐ.**
Oh, I'm sorry. The 300 NT ones are sold out. Only the 600 NT ones are left.

9. BRILL **Nà wǒ mǎi yìzhāng liùbǎikuàide ba.**
Then I guess I'll buy a 600 NT one.

10. CLERK **Hǎo. Yígòng liùbǎikuài. Xièxie.**
All right. That's 600 NT in all. Thanks.

Build Up

---

1.   Brill

Mùzhà   Muzha (suburb of Taipei) [PW]

Qǐng wèn, dào Mùzhà qù yào zuò jǐhào?   Excuse me, what number bus do you take to get to Muzha?

---

2.   Passerby

hǎo   very [A]

hǎo jiǔ   for a very long time

gōngchē   public bus [N] (M: **liàng**)

hǎo jiǔ méi zuò gōngchē le   hasn't taken a bus for a long time

xiǎode   know [V]

duìmiàn   across [PW]

Tǒngyī   7-Eleven® (name of store) [PW]

duìmiànde Tǒngyī   the 7-Eleven across the street

qù wènwen kàn   try and ask

yàoburán   otherwise, or [MA]

jiéyùn   mass rapid transit, MRT [N]

zuò jiéyùn qù Mùzhà   go to Muzha by MRT

Āiyà, wǒ hǎo jiǔ méi zuò gōngchē le,   Gosh, I haven't taken a bus for a long time,
bù xiǎode. Nǐ dào duìmiànde Tǒngyī qù   I don't know. Go to the 7-Eleven across the
wènwen kàn. Yàoburán, nǐ yě kéyǐ zuò   street and ask. Or you could also take
jiéyùn qù Mùzhà.   the MRT to Muzha.

---

3.   Brill

Qǐng wèn, dào Mùzhà qù yào zuò jǐhào?   Excuse me, what number bus do you take to get to Muzha?

---

4.   Clerk

huòshi   or [CJ]

Èr-sān-liù huòshi èr-sān-qī dōu kéyǐ dào.   You can get there on 236 or 237.

---

5.   Brill

Dàgài duō jiǔ yìbān?   About how often is there a bus?

---

6.   Clerk

wǔfēn zhōng yìbān   one run every five minutes

Èr-sān-qī bǐjiào jiǔ. Èr-sān-liù hǎoxiàng   237 takes longer. For 236, I think there's
wǔfēn zhōng yìbān, hěn kuàide la.   a bus every five minutes, it won't be long.

---

7.   Brill

shùnbiàn   conveniently, in passing [A]

chúzhípiào (T)   stored-value ticket [N] (M: **zhāng**)

Xièxie. Wǒ shùnbiàn mǎi yìzhāng   Thanks. While I'm at it, I'll buy a
sānbǎikuàide chúzhípiào.   stored-value ticket for 300 NT.

---

8.   Clerk

bù hǎo yìsi   be embarrassing, be embarrassed [PH]

wán   finish [V]

-wán   finish [RE]

màiwán   finish selling, be sold out [RC]

sānbǎikuàide màiwánle   the 300 NT ones have sold out

shèngxia   be left over [RC]

| Ò, bù hǎo yìsi. Sānbǎikuàide màiwánle. | Oh, I'm sorry. The 300 NT ones are sold out. |
| Zhǐ shèngxia liùbǎikuàide éryǐ. | Only the 600 NT ones are left. |

---

9. Brill

| Nà wǒ mǎi yìzhāng liùbǎikuàide ba. | Then I guess I'll buy a 600 NT one. |

---

10. Clerk

| Hǎo. Yígòng liùbǎikuài. Xièxie. | All right. That's 600 NT in all. Thanks. |

 ## Supplementary Vocabulary

1. **huò**   or [CJ]
    dìtiě   subway [N]
    Zuò gōngchē huò dìtiě dōu kéyi dào.   You can get there by bus or subway.

2. **jiàn**   see [V]
    Míngtiān jiàn!   See you tomorrow!

3. **qíguài**   be strange [SV]
    mèng   dream [N]
    zuòmèng   have a dream [VO]
    Wǒ zuòle yíge hěn qíguàide mèng.   I had a strange dream.

Additional Vocabulary*

1. **dǎchà**   interrupt [VO]
    Duìbuqǐ, wǒ dǎ ge chà.   Excuse me for interrupting.

2. **Tángrénjiē**   Chinatown [PW]
    Jiùjīnshānde Tángrénjiē hǎo dà.   San Francisco Chinatown is big.

3. **lǎowài**   foreigner [N]
    Nèige lǎowài Hànyǔ jiǎngde bú cuò ó!   That foreigner speaks Chinese pretty well!

Grammatical and Cultural Notes

1A. Muzha (often written as "Mucha," which is Wade-Giles romanization) is a suburb to the southeast of Taipei. National Chengchi University, the Taipei Zoo, and the famous **Zhǐnán** Temple are all located there.

1B. For "what number (bus)," some speakers say **jǐhào** while others say **jǐlù**. This is true in both Taiwan and mainland China.

1C. Taipei has an extensive municipal bus network with over a dozen bus companies in a unified system. The fare is based on the number of sections crossed. Depending on how far the bus has traveled on its route, you either insert your ticket or put cash into the machine when you get on (a light will indicate **SHÀNG**) or when you get off (in which case the light will indicate **XIÀ**).

2A. **NEGATIVE TIME SPENT.** Look at the sentence **Wǒ hǎo jiǔ méi zuò gōngchē le** "I haven't taken a bus for a long time." As we learned in 4-1: 4A, time spent expressions (i.e., for how long something did in fact happen) come AFTER the verb; but now note that, quite to the contrary, negative time spent expressions (i.e., for how long something didn't happen) come BEFORE the verb. Contrast the following:

---

* As in *Basic Spoken Chinese*, the Additional Vocabulary is for learners with extra time who desire to be challenged, and isn't required to be learned.

Wǒ xuéle sānnián le.

"I've been studying it for three years." (time spent, time expression comes after verb)

Wǒ sānnián méi xuéle.

"I haven't studied it for three years." (negative time spent, time expression comes before verb)

Study these additional examples (and see also note 2D below on the use of **le**):

Tā láile yíge xīngqīle.	"He has been (come) here for a week."
Tā yíge xīngqī méi láile.	"He hasn't been (come) here for a week."
Tā gōngzuòle sān'ge yuè.	"She worked for three months."
Tā sān'ge yuè méi gōngzuò.	"She didn't work for three months."

2B. Notice **hǎo jiǔ** "for a very long time." The same word **hǎo** that functions as a stative verb meaning "be good" can also function as an adverb meaning "very," similar in meaning to but less formal than **hěn**. (Compare English "a good long while," where "good" similarly functions as an adverb and means "very.") Actually, you've previously seen **hǎo** in the sense of "very" in the phrase **hǎo jiǔ bú jiànle** "haven't seen you for a very long time," where **hǎo jiǔ** means the same as **hěn jiǔ** (1-2: 2A). Some more examples of **hǎo** meaning "very":

Hǎo guì ya!	"They're very expensive!"
Wǒ hǎo lèi ya!	"I'm very tired!"
Hǎo duō rén qùle.	"A lot of people went."

Speakers from Taiwan, Hong Kong, and Guangdong province sometimes use this **hǎo** that means "very" in conjunction with the **hǎo** that means "good to...," saying things like **hǎo hǎochī** "to be very good to eat" and **hǎo hǎowán** "to be lots of fun," but such usage isn't fully accepted in Beijing.

2C. **Gōngchē** is an abbreviation of **gōnggòng qìchē** "public bus."

2D. The **le** in **Wǒ hǎo jiǔ méi zuò gōngchē le** "I haven't taken a bus for a long time" indicates that the situation of not having taken a bus for a long time is continuing up through the present. The sentence could also have been said without the final le as **Wǒ hǎo jiǔ méi zuò gōngchē** "I didn't take a bus for a long time," but then it would not have been clear that this situation is continuing up through the present.

2E. The frequently used verb **xiǎode** means "know" and is a synonym of **zhīdao**. **Xiǎode** is especially common in southern China and Taiwan. Some speakers pronounce the negative as **bù xiǎodé**.

2F. **Tǒngyī** "7-Eleven" (lit. "united"). Since educated people in Taiwan have all studied English, this chain is often referred to in English as "7-Eleven."

2G. **Qù wènwen kàn** "Go and ask" (lit. "go and try and ask"). The reduplicated verb **wènwen** here is a mild imperative; the reduplication shows tentativeness and non-insistence, hence is politer and less abrupt than **wèn** alone would be. You certainly could say **Qù wèn** "Go ask," but this would normally be said only among intimates (e.g., close friends, spouses, parent to child) and would not be said to strangers.

2H. The moveable adverb **yàoburán** "otherwise" is well worth learning. It's sometimes abbreviated to **yào bù**. Both **yàoburán** and **yào bù** are frequently followed by a **jiù** "then" later in the same clause. Another example:

Rúguǒ tiānqi hǎode huà, wǒmen jiù chūqu, yàoburán wǒmen jiù bù chūqu.

"If the weather is good, then we'll go out; otherwise we won't go out."

5–6. **NUMBER OF TIMES WITHIN A PERIOD OF TIME.** In line 5 examine the question **Duō jiǔ yìbān?** "How often is there a bus?" and in line 6 examine the response **Wǔfēn zhōng yìbān** "One every five minutes." To express the number of times something happens during a certain period of time, mention first the period of time you're talking about and then the number of times during that period. If there is a verb, it occurs in the middle. Note that in English, the order is often the reverse of the Chinese. The pattern is:

PERIOD OF TIME	(VERB)	NUMBER OF TIMES
yìnián	(qù)	sāncì

"(go) three times a year"

More examples of this pattern:

shífēn zhōng yìbān	"one bus every ten minutes"
yìtiān liǎngcì	"twice a day"
yíge yuè lái liǎngcì	"come twice a month"

7A. **Shùnbiàn** is an adverb meaning "take advantage of the fact that you're already doing one thing to do another thing." The literal meaning is "follow convenience." In good English, we can translate as "while you're at it" or "in passing."

7B. **Chúzhípiào**, "stored-value ticket," refers to a ticket with a magnetic stripe on which is stored the remaining monetary value of the card. These cards are available in several different denominations. The syllable **chú-** is a bound form meaning "to store," as in the word **chúcún** "store." In mainland China, this syllable is pronounced **chǔ-**.

8A. **Bù hǎo yìsi** is most commonly used alone as an expression meaning "That's embarrassing," but it can also be used within sentences, where it functions as the equivalent of a stative verb meaning "be embarrassed." This phrase is very useful as a general-purpose apology, for example, if you need to reach over someone, or if you should accidentally bump against someone in a crowd, or if you need to make your way through a crowd. Sometimes it can also indicate unwillingness to do something out of politeness. Examples:

Tā hěn bù hǎo yìsi.	"She was very embarrassed."
Wǒ juéde bú tài hǎo yìsi.	"I feel somewhat embarrassed."
Nǐ hěn máng, wǒ bù hǎo yìsi zài dǎrǎole.	"You're very busy, I'm embarrassed to bother you any more."

Hǎo yìsi is used most commonly with a preceding **bù**, but it can sometimes be used alone in the sense of "not be embarrassed," as in:

Nǐ zuòle nèiyàngde shìr, hái hǎo yìsi shuō!

"You did something like that, and you actually have the nerve to talk about it!"

8B. The common resultative ending **-wán** indicates completion or depletion; thus **màiwánle** means "sold with the result that everything was depleted" or, in better English, "sold out." In English, we often say we've finished something without specifying what it is exactly that we've finished, so we can speak of "finishing lunch" or "finishing a book." In Chinese, the action which has been finished is usually mentioned, so you'd have to say **chīwánle wǔfàn** or **kànwánle shū**. You could NEVER say *Wǒ wánle wǔfàn** to mean "I finished lunch." (Actually, if you just say **Wǒ wánle**, it means "I'm done for" or "I'm going to die"!) Here are some more examples with the resultative ending **-wán**:

Wǒ shuōwánle.	"I've finished speaking."
Tā yǐjīng chīwánle.	"She has already finished eating."
Wǒmen dōu zuòwánle.	"We've finished doing all of it."

8C. Do you remember the pattern **zhǐ...éryǐ** "only" that you learned in 10-1: 6A? This is typical Taiwanese Mandarin usage, though it's sometimes used in mainland China as well. Another example:

Wǒ zhǐ búguò gēn nǐ kāi ge wánxiào éryǐ, bié shēngqì!

"I was only kidding you, don't get angry!"

SV1. The conjunction **huò** "or" is a more formal equivalent of **huòshi**, introduced in line 4 of this conversation, and of **huòzhě**, which you learned in 8-1.

SV2. The verb **jiàn** means "see." You've encountered it before in the expressions **zàijiàn** "goodbye" (lit. "again see") and **hǎo jiǔ bú jiànle** "haven't seen you for a very long time."

SV3. The stative verb **qíguài** "be strange" can also be used at the beginnings of sentences as a one-word comment or exclamation. For example (when talking about something one is looking for):

Qíguài, dào nǎr qùle? Wǒ zěmme zhǎobudào ne?

"Strange, where did it go? Why can't I find it?"

AV1. The verb-object compound **dǎchà** "make an interruption, interrupt" can be very useful as an opening gambit in a conversational exchange. It's quite common to say, as in the sample sentence: **Duìbuqǐ, wǒ dǎ ge chà** "Excuse me for interrupting..." (lit. "Sorry, I make an interruption").

AV2. **Tángrénjiē** refers to Chinatowns overseas. This word literally means "streets of the people of Tang." Since the Tang Dynasty was one of the most prosperous in Chinese history, the Cantonese (who made up the majority of early Chinese immigrants to the U.S.) sometimes referred to themselves as **Táng rén** "people of Tang," from whence came the term **Tángrénjiē**.

AV3. **Lǎowài** is an informal equivalent of **wàiguo rén** which is often used by Chinese when speaking about foreigners. It has no negative connotation; indeed, **lǎo** often indicates respect (cf. **lǎoshī** "teacher"). Formerly, foreigners were sometimes called **yáng guǐzi** "foreign devils," but this term is now considered very rude and is no longer used.

People waiting at a bus stop on Heping East Road in Taipei

Asking Directions to a Friend's House

Mark Donnelly has been invited to the Taipei home of his friend Zhou Zengmo. Donnelly has been driving back and forth on his motorcycle searching for his friend's house for some time but, even though Zhou gave him directions, he can't find the right street. He calls Zhou from a public telephone to ask for more precise directions.

 Basic Conversation 11-3

1. ZHOU

Wéi?
Hello?

2. DONNELLY

Lǎo Zhōu a, wǒ shi Xiǎo Dǒng. Wǒ gēn nǐ shuō a, wǒ zhuànlái zhuànqù zěmme zhǎo yě zhǎobudào nǐ shuōde nèitiáo xiàngzi.
Old Zhou, it's me, Mark. Listen, I've been driving back and forth and no matter how hard I try, I just can't find that lane you mentioned.

3. ZHOU

Nǐ xiànzài zài náli a?
Where are you now?

4. DONNELLY

Wǒ zài nǐ shuōde nèige xiǎo miào ménkǒu dǎ gōngyòng diànhuà gěi nǐ.
I'm calling you from a public phone at the entrance to that little temple you mentioned.

5. ZHOU

Hǎo, wǒ gàosu nǐ, nǐ jìxù wàng yóujú nèibian zǒu, chàbuduō liǎngbǎigōngchǐ jiù huì kàndào yìjiā jiājù diàn. Diàn bú tài dà, nǐ shāowēi zhùyì yixia, búyào cuòguo. Cóng nèitiáo xiàngzi zhuǎnjìnlái zuǒshǒubiān dì'èrdòng sānlóu jiù shi wǒmen jiā.
O.K., I'll tell you, you continue going over toward the post office; after about 200 meters you'll see a furniture store. The store isn't very large, pay some attention, don't miss it. Turning in from that lane, the second building on the left-hand side, third floor, is our home.

6. DONNELLY

Hǎo, zhīdaole. Yìhuǐr jiàn.
O.K., I know now. See you in a little while.

 Build Up

1. Zhou
Wéi?   Hello?

2. **Donnelly**

Zhōu	Zhou [SN]
a	(pause filler) [P]
Lǎo Zhōu a	Old Zhou
gēn...shuō	tell (someone something) [PT]
wǒ gēn nǐ shuō	I tell you
zhuàn	turn, go around [V]
zhuànlái	come turning around [RC]
...-lái...-qù	...all over the place [PT]
zhuànlái zhuànqù	turn around all over the place
zěmme zhǎo yě zhǎobudào	no matter how search can't find
xiàngzi	lane [N]
nǐ shuōde nèitiáo xiàngzi	that lane you were talking about

Lǎo Zhōu a, wǒ shi Xiǎo Dǒng. Wǒ gēn nǐ shuō a, wǒ zhuànlái zhuànqù zěmme zhǎo yě zhǎobudào nǐ shuōde nèitiáo xiàngzi.

Old Zhou, it's me, Mark. Listen, I've been driving back and forth and no matter how hard I try, I just can't find that lane you mentioned.

3. **Zhōu**

Nǐ xiànzài zài náli a?   Where are you now?

4. **Donnelly**

miào	temple, shrine [N]
nǐ shuōde nèige xiǎo miào	that little temple you mentioned
gōngyòng	public [AT]
gōngyòng diànhuà	public telephone [PH]
dǎ gōngyòng diànhuà gěi nǐ	call you from a public telephone

Wǒ zài nǐ shuōde nèige xiǎo miào ménkǒu dǎ gōngyòng diànhuà gěi nǐ.

I'm calling you from a public phone at the entrance to that little temple you mentioned.

5. **Zhou**

gàosu	tell [V]
wǒ gàosu nǐ	I tell you
yóujú	post office [PW]
wàng yóujú nèibian zǒu	go toward the post office over there
gōngchǐ	meter [M]
chàbuduō liǎngbǎigōngchǐ	about two hundred meters
kàndào	see [RC]
jiājù	furniture [N] (M: **jiàn**)
diàn	shop, store [N] (M: **jiā**)
jiājù diàn	furniture store [PH]
huì kàndào yìjiā jiājù diàn	will see a furniture store
shāowēi (B)	somewhat, slightly [A]
zhùyì	pay attention to [V/VO]
shāowēi zhùyì yixia	pay a little attention
-guò	(indicates motion past or by) [RE]
cuòguo	miss [RC]
búyào cuòguo	don't miss (it)
zhuǎnjìnlái	turn in [RC]
cóng nèitiáo xiàngzi zhuǎnjìnlái	from that lane turn in
shǒu	hand [N] (M: **zhī**)
zuǒshǒu	left hand [PW]
zuǒshǒubiān	left-hand side [PW]
dòng	(for buildings) [M]
zuǒshǒubiān dì'èrdòng	the second building on the left

Hǎo, wǒ gàosu nǐ, nǐ jìxù wàng yóujú nèibian zǒu, chàbuduō liǎngbǎigōngchǐ jiù

O.K., I'll tell you, you continue going over toward the post office; after about 200 meters

huì kàndào yìjiā jiājù diàn. Diàn bú tài dà, ní shāowēi zhùyì yixia, búyào cuòguo. Cóng nèitiáo xiàngzi zhuǎnjinlái zuǒshǒubiān dì'èrdòng sānlóu jiù shi wǒmen jiā.	you'll see a furniture store. The store isn't very large, pay some attention, don't miss it. Turning in from that lane, the second building on the left-hand side, third floor, is our home.

6. Donnelly
    yìhuǐr jiàn   "see you in a little while" [IE]
Hǎo, zhīdaole. Yìhuǐr jiàn.   O.K., I know now. See you in a little while.

🔘 Supplementary Vocabulary

1. **fángzi**   house [N] (M: **dòng**)
Nèisāndòng fángzi dōu shi tāde.   **Those three houses are all hers.**

2. **yòushǒu**   right hand [PW]
    yòushǒubiān   right-hand side [PW]
Nǐ zhǎode fángzi bú zài   The house you're looking for isn't
zuǒshǒubiān, zài yòushǒubiān.   on the left, it's on the right.

3. **gōngyòng cèsuǒ**   public toilet [PH]
Gōngyòng cèsuǒ dōu hěn zāng.   Public toilets are all dirty.

4. **gēn...jiǎng**   tell (someone something) [PT]
    gēn tā jiǎng   tell him
Nǐ bié gēn tā jiǎng wǒ huì qù.   Don't tell him that I'll go.

Grammatical and Cultural Notes

1. The speakers in the video for this lesson both have a strong Taiwan accent. The most notable feature of this accent is that the **h** in the standard retroflex initials **zh- ch- sh-** is dropped. Such an accent is actually quite common not only in Taiwan but also in the Mandarin spoken in most of southern and western China as well. Below is a transcription of the Basic Conversation for this lesson with all the non-standard pronunciations that were recorded on the video <u>underlined</u> (note that the Build Up of the basic conversation was recorded by a speaker of standard Mandarin, so it doesn't contain non-standard pronunciations):

    A: **Lǎo <u>Z</u>ōu a, wǒ <u>s</u>i Xiǎo Dǒng. Wǒ gēn nǐ <u>s</u>uō a, wǒ <u>z</u>uànlái <u>z</u>uànqù zěmme <u>z</u>ǎo yě <u>z</u>ǎobudào nǐ <u>s</u>uōde nèitiáo xiàngzi.**

    B: **Nǐ xiànzài zài náli a?**

    A: **Wǒ zài nǐ <u>s</u>uōde nèige xiǎo miào ménkǒu dǎ gōngyòng diànhuà gěi nǐ.**

    B: **Hǎo, wǒ gàosu nǐ, nǐ jìxù wàng yóujú nèibian zǒu, <u>c</u>àbuduō liǎngbǎigōng<u>c</u>ǐ jiù huì kàndào yìjiā jiājùdiàn. Diàn bú tài dà, nǐ <u>s</u>āowēi <u>z</u>ùyì yixia, búyào cuòguo. Cóng nèitiáo xiàngzi <u>z</u>uǎnjinlái zuǒ<u>s</u>ǒubiān dì'èrdòng sānlóu jiù <u>s</u>i wǒmen jiā.**

    A: **Hǎo, <u>z</u>īdaole. Yìhuǐr jiàn.**

2A. The **a** in **Lǎo Zhōu** a is a pause filler. Like the pause filler **ne** (7-1: 10B), it gives the speaker more time to plan the rest of his utterance and makes his speech seem smoother, less abrupt, and more conversational.

2B. **GĒN...SHUŌ.** The pattern **gēn...shuō** means "tell (somebody) (something)." This is one common way to say "tell" (another way is introduced in note 5A below). The pattern is:

PERSON₁	GĒN	PERSON₂	SHUŌ
Wǒ	**gēn**	**tā**	**shuōle.**
"I told her."			

More examples:

> **Qǐng nǐ gēn tā shuō wǒ xiànzài hěn máng.**
> "Please tell him that I'm busy right now."

> **Wǒ yǐjīng gēn nǐ shuōguo bù zhīdào duōshǎo cì le!**
> "I've already told you I don't know how many times!"

2C. The **a** in **Wǒ gēn nǐ shuō a** is again a pause filler (cf. 2A above). Some speakers have a habit of using such pause fillers very frequently, there often being a whole series of phrases, each of which ends in **a**.

2D. In 7-1: 1B we learned about common phonetic changes that can take place in the sentence-final particle **a** so that, depending on the sound that precedes it, it changes to **ya**, **wa**, **ra**, **na**, or **nga**. In this sentence, we encounter two variants of **a**: the **a** in **Lǎo Zhōu a**, which is actually pronounced like **wa**, so the whole phrase sounds like **Lǎo Zhōu wa**; and the **a** in **Wǒ gēn nǐ shuō a**, which is actually pronounced like **ya**, so the whole phrase sounds like **Wǒ gēn nǐ shuō ya**. Always pay attention to how **a** changes depending on the preceding sound.

2E. **VERB-LÁI VERB-QÙ.** The very common and useful pattern VERB-**lái** VERB-**qù** expresses the sense of "do something back and forth," "do something here and there," "do something all over the place," or "do something again and again." The basic pattern is:

VERB	-LÁI	VERB	-QÙ
zhǎo	lái	zhǎo	qù

"look all over"

Examples of the pattern VERB-**lái** VERB-**qù**:

zǒulái zǒuqù	"walk back and forth"
zhuànlái zhuànqù	"go around all over"
kànlái kànqù	"look at over and over again"
xiǎnglái xiǎngqù	"think over and over again," "rack one's brains"
bānlái bānqù	"move all over the place"
mánglái mángqù	"be busy all over the place," "be very busy"
fēilái fēiqù	"fly back and forth"
tǎolùnlái tǎolùnqù	"discuss again and again"
yánjiūlái yánjiūqù	"research again and again"

Sentences containing the pattern VERB-**lái** VERB-**qù**:

> **Wǒ zhǎolái zhǎoqù, zěmme zhǎo yě zhǎobuzháo.**
> "I looked all over the place, but no matter how hard I tried, I just couldn't find it."

> **Shuōlái shuōqù, háishi xué diànnǎo bǐjiào róngyi zhǎo gōngzuò.**
> "You can say what you want, the fact remains it's easier finding a job if you've studied computer science."

> **Nǐmen Měiguo rén wèishemme lǎo shi qīnlái qīnqù?**
> "Why are you Americans always kissing people all over the place?" (**qīn** is a verb meaning "kiss")

2F. Some speakers, including the one in the video and the conversation for listening, pronounce **zhuàn** "turn, go around" with a third tone as **zhuǎn**. Thus, the more standard **zhuànlái zhuànqù** "go around all over" is then pronounced **zhuǎnlái zhuǎnqù**. While both pronunciations occur, **zhuàn** is considered better usage (**zhuǎn** is a closely related word written with same character that means "turn" that you learned in 9-1 and that occurs in line 5 of this Basic Conversation in **zhuǎnjìnlái** "turn in."

2G.   **ZĚMME (VERB) YĚ NEGATIVE VERB.** The pattern **zěmme** (VERB) **yě** + NEGATIVE VERB means "no matter (how hard one tries, no matter what one does), one doesn't/didn't/can't/couldn't (do something)." The first occurrence of the verb is optional, but the second occurrence of the verb (i.e., the negative verb form) is mandatory. The pattern is:

SUBJECT	ZĚMME	(VERB)	YĚ	NEGATIVE VERB
Wǒ	zěmme	(zhǎo)	yě	zhǎobudào.

"No matter how hard I searched, I couldn't find it."

Examples:

Wǒ zěmme yě mǎibudào.	"No matter what I did, I wasn't able to buy one."
Wǒ zěmme yě shuìbuzháo.	"No matter how hard I tried, I just couldn't fall asleep."
Tā zěmme xué yě xuébuhuì.	"No matter how hard she tried, she just couldn't learn it."
Tā zěmme xiě yě xiěbuhǎo.	"No matter how he wrote it, he just couldn't write it well."

2H.   As we've seen before, many speakers pronounce **nèi-** "that" as **nà-**. Thus, in line 2 of the video for this lesson, and also in the conversation for listening, **nèitiáo xiàngzi** "that lane" is pronounced as **nàtiáo xiàngzi**; in line 4, **nèige** "that" is pronounced as **nàge**; and in line 5, **nèibian** "over there" is pronounced as **nàbian**, and **nèitiáo** is again pronounced as **nàtiáo**. Both **nèi-** and **nà-** are correct.

4.   You were introduced to the expression **dǎ diànhuà** "make a telephone call" in 8-3. There are two ways to indicate to whom a telephone call is made; you say either **gěi...dǎ diànhuà** "call (somebody) on the telephone" or, as in this line, **dǎ diànhuà gěi...**, with exactly the same meaning. Examples:

Qǐng nǐ gěi Wáng Xiānsheng dǎ diànhuà.	"Please call Mr. Wang."
Qǐng nǐ dǎ diànhuà gěi Wáng Xiānsheng.	(same meaning as above)

5A.   **Gàosu** "tell (somebody) (something)" is a very common and useful verb. It must always have an indirect object, with a direct object being optional. For example:

Qǐng nǐ gàosu wǒ. (indirect object only)	"Please tell me."
Qǐng nǐ gàosu wǒ wèishemme. (both direct and indirect objects)	"Please tell me why."

The verb **gàosu** has an alternate form **gàosong** which is used by some speakers in northern China.

5B.   In mainland China and Taiwan, **yóujú** "post offices" offer more services than in the U.S. You can send letters, make long distance telephone calls, send telegrams, deposit or withdraw money, and subscribe to newspapers and magazines.

5C.   **METRIC SYSTEM.** The official system of measurement in both mainland China and Taiwan is the metric system. The key terms are:

gōngfēn "centimeter"	**gōngkè** "gram"
gōngchǐ "meter"	**gōngjīn** "kilogram, kilo"
gōnglǐ "kilometer"	**gōngshēng** "liter"

5D.   The Chinese word for "slightly, somewhat" is pronounced by some speakers as **shāowēi** and by other speakers as **shāowéi**. You can say either.

5E.   **Cuòguo** means "miss," e.g., miss seeing something that you had planned to see or miss an opportunity. A common collocation is **cuòguo jīhui** "miss an opportunity." Examples:

> **Tā méi zhùyì, cuòguo jīhui le.**   "He didn't pay attention and missed his chance."
>
> **Nǐ bié cuòguo zhèige hǎo jīhui!**   "Don't miss this good opportunity!"

5F.   **Nǐ shāowēi zhùyì yixia**, literally "You slightly pay attention a little," is a politer, softer, and less direct way of saying **Nǐ zhùyì** "You pay attention." When speaking politely to non-intimates, Chinese people often add words such as **shāowēi** and **yixia** so as to tone down the force of the command.

5G.   **Zhuǎnjìnlái** means "turn in (coming closer to the speaker)." If the speaker had meant "turn in (going further away from the speaker)," he would have said **zhuǎnjìnqù**.

6.   The changed status **le** on **zhīdao** indicates that while the speaker didn't know the directions before, he does now.

SV1.   Distinguish **fángzi** "house" from **jiā** "family, home," which you learned in 4 3. **Fángzi** is the bricks and mortar that constitute a physical house, while **jiā** refers to the family that lives in that house. Sometimes in English we say things like "at my house we speak French and English" when we really mean "in my family." In this case, in Chinese you'd normally say **wǒmen jiāli** and not **wǒmen fángzili**. Though **Wǒ zài wǒde fángzili shuō Fǎguo huà** isn't incorrect, it would rarely be said and literally means that the second you step out the door of your house, you no longer speak French.

SV3.   Instead of **gōngyòng cèsuǒ** "public toilet," some Chinese speakers say **gōnggòng cèsuǒ**, with exactly the same meaning.

SV4A.   **GĒN...JIǍNG. Gēn...jiǎng** "tell (somebody) (something)" is a synonym of **gēn...shuō** in 2B above. The pattern is:

PERSON₁	GĒN	PERSON₂	JIǍNG
Wǒ	gēn	tā	jiǎngle.
"I told her."			

Examples:

> **Qǐng nǐ gēn tā jiǎng wǒmen yǐjīng dàole.**
> "Please tell her that we've already arrived."

> **Wǒ gēn nǐ jiǎng, yídìng yào zǎo yìdiǎnr jiějué zhèige wèntí.**
> "I tell you, this problem definitely needs to be solved as soon as possible."

To sum up, in this lesson, you've been introduced to three ways to say "tell (someone) (something)," namely, **gēn...shuō**, **gēn...jiǎng**, and **gàosu** (cf. note 5A in this lesson). Compare the following three sentences, all of which mean "Don't tell her/him that I didn't go":

> **Bié gēn tā shuō wǒ méi qù.**
> **Bié gēn tā jiǎng wǒ méi qù.**
> **Bié gàosu tā wǒ méi qù.**

SV4B.   **RAPID SPEECH.** The type of standard Mandarin pronunciation we've been learning so far applies to Mandarin when spoken slowly and carefully. In rapid speech, especially as spoken by native Mandarin speakers from northern China, various kinds of sound changes typically occur. (This is also true of English; consider the pronunciation of "incomplete" as "ingcomplete" and of "What do you want to do?" as "Wudja wanna do?")

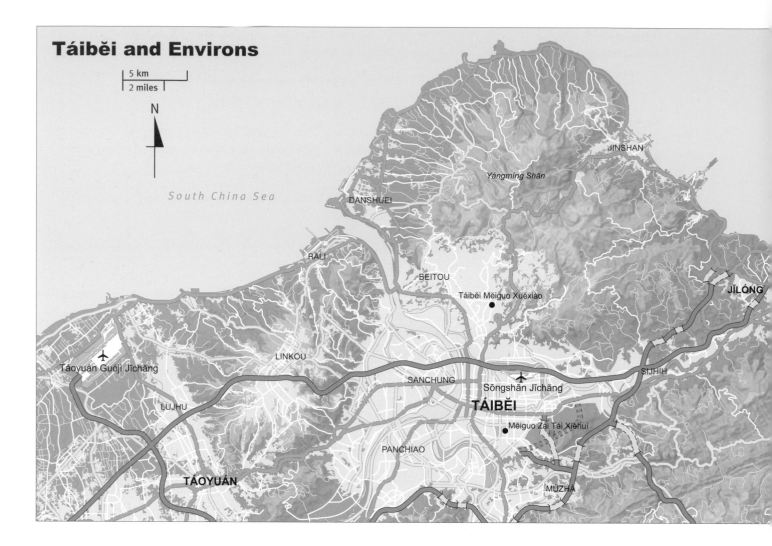

Táiběi and Environs

Now look at the last example in the previous note: **Bié gàosu tā wǒ méi qù** "Don't tell her/him that I didn't go." When Chinese people say this rapidly, it may sound somewhat like **Bié gào ta wǒ méi qù**. Below we'll describe some of the sound changes that are common in Chinese rapid speech. (This section is for your future reference; you don't have to learn this material now, nor should you try to speak this way yourself, at least not until your Mandarin is at a much more advanced level. Your goal should be always to make good use of the context and try to the extent possible to *understand* Mandarin when spoken this way.)

1. Certain sounds may influence certain other sounds occurring after them. For example, **n** before **b** or before **m** often changes into **m**. Examples: **qiānbǐ** "pencil" becomes **qiāmbǐ**, and **sānmáo qián** "30 cents" becomes **sāmmáo qián**.

2. In the speech of many people, the consonant **n** at the end of a syllable may be nasalized when the next syllable starts with a **y**, an **h**, or a vowel sound. Examples: **piányi** "cheap," **zhēn hǎo** "truly good," and **hěn è** "very hungry."

3. In two-syllable words where the second syllable begins with an **m-**, is unstressed, and doesn't occur before a pause, the two syllables are often combined into a single syllable ending in **m**. Examples: **wǒmen** "we" becomes **wǒm**, **shénme** "what" becomes **shém**, and **zěnme** "how" becomes **zěm**.

4. Some other common two-syllable words may be combined into a single syllable. Examples: **zhèiyang** may become **jiàng**, or **nèiyang** may become **niàng**.

5.   If the previous syllable is Tone Four, vowels occurring after the voiceless initials **c-**, **f-**, **q-**, **s-**, and **sh-** in unstressed syllables themselves become voiceless and sound as though they were whispered. Examples: **bù hǎo yìsi** "be embarrassed" sounds like **bù hǎo yìs**, **bú kèqi** "you're welcome" sounds like **bú kèq**, and **dòufu** "bean curd" sounds like **dòuf**.

6.   Especially in the speech of people from Beijing, and especially with the commonest words in the spoken language, there is a tendency to slur syllables together. For example, **wǒ gàosu nǐ** "I tell you" may sound like **wǒ gào ni**. Moreover, the initials **ch-**, **sh-**, and **zh-** when occurring in unstressed syllables are often pronounced very lightly, losing much of their consonantal quality and retaining only the **r**-sound. For example, **wǒ bù zhīdào** "I don't know" may become **wǒ bērdào** or **Wáng Xiānshēng** "Mr. Wang" may sound somewhat like **Wáng xianr**.

7.   In three-syllable words and expressions where the first syllable is Tone One or Tone Two and the second syllable is Tone Two or unstressed, the second syllable often changes to Tone One. Examples: **Jiā'nádà** "Canada" becomes **Jiā'nādà**, and **zǒu yuānwang lù** "go a long way for nothing" changes to **zǒu yuānwāng lù**.

Filling Up at a Gas Station

An American business-
man in Taipei stops at
a gasoline station for a
fill-up.

 Basic Conversation 11-4

1. GAS STATION ATTENDANT	**Huānyíng guānglín! Qǐng wèn, nǐ jiā shémme yóu?** Welcome! Excuse me, what kind of gas do you want?	
2. AMERICAN BUSINESSMAN	**Jiǔ wǔ. Èrshigōngshēng. M, wǒ kàn hái shi jiāmǎn hǎole.** 95. Twenty liters. Uh, I think you might as well just fill it up.	
3. GAS STATION ATTENDANT	**Hǎode. Qǐng kàn, xiànzài cóng líng kāishǐ.** All right. Look, it's now starting from zero.	

(after filling the car with gasoline)

Hǎole, yígòng sìbǎi qīshiwǔyuán.
O.K., that makes 475 NT in all.

4. AMERICAN BUSINESSMAN	**Zhè shi wǔbǎikuài.** This is 500 NT.	
5. GAS STATION ATTENDANT	**Qǐng wèn, nǐde tǒngyī biānhào shi...** Excuse me, your unified serial number is...	
6. AMERICAN BUSINESSMAN	**Búbìle.** It's not necessary.	
7. GAS STATION ATTENDANT	**Búbìle?** It's not necessary?	

(returns with the change)

Hǎo, zhǎo nǐ èrshiwǔyuán. Xièxie!
O.K., here's 25 NT in change. Thank you!

8. AMERICAN BUSINESSMAN	**Hǎoxiàng yóujià yòu yào zhǎngle?** It looks likes the price of gas is going up again?	

9. GAS STATION ATTENDANT

Èi, duì a. Cóng míngtiān qǐ yóujià yòu yào tiáozhěngle, suóyi jīntiān jiāyóude chē tèbié duō. Nǐ kàn, dà-pái-cháng-lóng ó!

Yeah, that's right. Starting tomorrow, the price of gas is going to be adjusted again, so today there're especially many cars filling up. Just look at how they've formed a long line!

 **Build Up**

1. **Gas station attendant**

huānyíng guānglín	"we welcome your honorable presence" [IE]
yóu	oil [N]
jiāyóu	add gasoline, buy gas [VO]
nǐ jiā shémme yóu	you'll add which kind of gas
Huānyíng guānglín! Qǐng wèn, nǐ jiā shémme yóu?	Welcome! Excuse me, what kind of gas do you want?

2. **American businessman**

gōngshēng	liter [M]
èrshigōngshēng	twenty liters
kàn	think, consider [V]
wǒ kàn	the way I see things
mǎn	be full [SV]
-mǎn	full [RE]
jiāmǎn	fill up [RC]
hái shi jiāmǎn hǎole	it would be better to fill up
Jiǔ wǔ. Èrshigōngshēng. M, wǒ kàn hái shi jiāmǎn hǎole.	95. Twenty liters. Uh, I think you might as well just fill it up.

3. **Gas station attendant**

cóng líng kāishǐ	start from zero
Hǎode. Qǐng kàn, xiànzài cóng líng kāishǐ.	All right. Look, it's now starting from zero.
hǎole	"all right," "O.K." [IE]
yuán	dollar (monetary unit) [M]
sìbǎi qīshiwǔyuán	four hundred and seventy-five yuan
Hǎole, yígòng sìbǎi qīshiwǔyuán.	O.K., that makes 475 NT in all.

4. **American businessman**

Zhè shi wǔbǎikuài.	This is 500 NT.

5. **Gas station attendant**

tǒngyī	unite, unify [V]
biānhào	serial number [N]
tǒngyī biānhào	unified serial number
Qǐng wèn, nǐde tǒngyī biānhào shi...	Excuse me, your unified serial number is...

6. **American businessman**

Búbìle.	It's not necessary.

7. **Gas station attendant**

Búbìle?	It's not necessary?
Hǎo, zhǎo nǐ èrshiwǔyuán. Xièxie!	O.K., here's 25 NT in change. Thank you!

8. American businessman

yóujià	price of gasoline [N]
zhǎng	rise, go up [V]
yòu yào zhǎngle	is going to rise again
Hǎoxiàng yóujià yòu yào zhǎngle?	It looks likes the price of gas is going up again?

9. Gas station attendant

èi	"yeah" [I]
cóng...qǐ	starting from... [PT]
cóng míngtiān qǐ	starting from tomorrow
tiáozhěng	adjust [V]
yóujià yòu yào tiáozhěngle	price of gas will again be adjusted
tèbié	especially [A]
dà-pái-cháng-lóng	form a long line [EX]
Èi, duì a. Cóng míngtiān qǐ yóujià yòu yào tiáozhěngle, suóyi jīntiān jiāyóude chē tèbié duō. Nǐ kàn, dà-pái-cháng-lóng ó!	Yeah, that's right. Starting tomorrow, the price of gas is going to be adjusted again, so today there're especially many cars filling up. Just look at how they've formed a long line!

Supplementary Vocabulary

1. qí ride, straddle (bicycle, motorcycle, horse) [V]
  mótuōchē motorcycle [N]
  Tā xǐhuan qí mótuōchē. She likes to ride motorcycles.

2. tíngchē park a car, park [VO]
  tíngchēchǎng parking lot [PW]
  Rúguǒ zhǎobuzháo tíngchēchǎng, If I can't find a parking lot,
  zěmme bàn? what should I do?

3. jiāyóuzhàn gasoline station [PW]
  Wǒ děi dào jiāyóuzhàn qù jiāyóu. I have to go to the gas station for a fill-up.

4. qìyóu gasoline [N]
  jiàqián price [N]
  tè (B) especially [A]
  Zuìjìn qìyóude jiàqián tè guì. Recently the price of gas has been especially high.

Grammatical and Cultural Notes

1A. The idiomatic expression **huānyíng guānglín** "we welcome your honorable presence" is very formal and very polite. It can be used by a host to welcome guests or, as here, by employees of a commercial establishment to welcome customers.

1B. The verb-object compound **jiāyóu** (lit. "add oil") means "add gasoline, buy gas, refuel." Be aware that besides this meaning, the expression can also mean "step on the gas," i.e., step on the gas pedal of a car to increase the flow of gasoline to the motor. Furthermore, this expression can also be used to cheer players on in a competition, e.g., **Jiāyóu, jiāyóu!** "Step on it!" or "Go team!"

2A. **Jiǔ wǔ** "95" refers to the octane rating of the gasoline. There are some speakers who, instead of reading this off as a series of two numbers, "nine" and "five," pronounce it as one number and say **jiǔshiwǔ** "ninety-five."

2B. **Gōngshēng** "liter" is one in the series of measure words that begins with **gōng-** that refers to units of the metric system (11-3: 5C).

2C.   **Wǒ kàn hái shi jiāmǎn hǎole** "I think you might as well just fill it up." The verb **kàn**, which you learned as meaning "look, see" in 3-2 and as "read" in 9-4 has an additional meaning of "think" or "consider." In this sense, it occurs only after **wǒ** in an affirmative sentence, or after **nǐ** in an interrogative sentence. Examples:

> **Wǒ kàn wǒmen jiù bié máfan tā le ba!**
> "It seems to me that it would be best if we didn't bother him."

> **Wǒ kàn tā bú huì láile, wǒmen zǒu ba.**
> "I don't think she's going to come; let's go."

> **Nǐ kàn wǒmen xiànzài yīnggāi zěmme bàn ne?**
> "What do you think we ought to do now?"

3.   Because some dishonest gas station owners have at times pumped less gasoline than they claimed they did, service station attendants in Taiwan now often direct customers' attention to the fact that the pump gauge is at zero at the beginning of the transaction.

5A.   **Tǒngyī** "unite, unify" is the verb that would be used, for example, when discussing whether or how mainland China and Taiwan should "unite." Example:

> **Tāmen xīwàng Zhōngguo dàlù hé Táiwān néng hépíng tǒngyī.**
> "They hope that mainland China and Taiwan can unite peacefully."

5B.   **Tǒngyī biānhào** "united serial number" is a number that is entered on the gasoline receipts for those customers for whom gasoline is a deductible business expense.

7.   The question **Búbìle?** "It's not necessary?" is an intonation question pronounced with rising intonation (cf. 2-3: 1C).

8.   **Hǎoxiàng yóujià yòu yào zhǎngle?** "It looks likes the price of gas is going up again?" Just like the previous line, this whole line is also an intonation question pronounced with rising intonation.

8–9.   **YÒU YÀO...LE.** The pattern **yòu yào...le** means "will...again" (lit. "again will..."). A verb always fills the slot after **yào** and before the **le**. The pattern is:

> | SUBJECT | YÒU YÀO | VERB | LE |
> |---------|---------|------|-----|
> | Tāmen | yòu yào | lái le. | |
>
> "They're coming again."

We see **Yóujià yòu yào zhǎngle** "The price of gas is going to rise again" in line 8, and **Yóujià yòu yào tiáozhěngle** "The price of gas is going to be adjusted again" in line 9. **Yòu** "again," which normally means "again" for past situations, is here used in spite of this being a future situation because the sense is that "the price of gas has gone up time and time again in the past and now here we go again." The **le** at the end of this pattern indicates anticipated change in a future situation (3-2: 6D). Some more examples with the pattern **yòu yào...le**:

Nǐ yòu yào jiāyóu le?	"You're going to stop for gas again?"
Tīngshuō míngtiān yòu yào xiàyǔ le.	"I heard tomorrow it's going to rain again."
Nǐ zěmme yòu yào qù Zhōngguo le?	"How come you're going to go to China again?"

> **Wǒ zuótiān gāng cóng Shànghǎi huílai, míngtiān yòu yào qù Guǎngzhōu le.**
> "I just got back from Shanghai yesterday; tomorrow I'm leaving again for Guangzhou."

Gas station on Xinsheng South Road in Taipei

9A.   **CÓNG...QǏ. Cóng** means "from" and **qǐ** literally means "rise" or "arise." The pattern **cóng...qǐ** means "beginning from/with/on/in," "starting from...," or "from...on." A time word, place word, or question word fills the slot between the **cóng** and the **qǐ**. The pattern is:

CÓNG	TW/ PW/QW	QǏ
cóng	míngtiān	qǐ

"starting tomorrow"

In this pattern, the **qǐ** can occur independently, as above and in the first two examples below, or the **qǐ** can be suffixed to a one-syllable verb, as in the last two examples below. If **qǐ** is suffixed to a verb, the meaning is "begin (verb)." Some more examples of the pattern **cóng...qǐ**:

Cóng xiàge yuè qǐ, wǒmen měitiān yào xué shíge zì.

"Beginning next month, we're going to learn ten characters a day."

Cóng xué Zhōngwénde dìyītiān qǐ, wǒmen shàngkède shíhour bù shuō Yīngwén.

"From the first day of learning Chinese, when we have class we don't speak English."

Wǒ zhēn bù zhīdào gāi cóng nǎr shuōqǐ.

"I really don't know where I should start (talking) from."

Yào jiějué wèntí, yīnggāi cóng nǎr zuòqǐ?

"If you want to solve problems, from where should you begin?"

The pattern **cóng...qǐ** is often the same or nearly the same in meaning as the pattern **cóng...kāishǐ** "starting from..." (10-1: 4A).

9B. Note the verb **tiáozhěng** "adjust." **Tiáozhěng yóujià** "adjust the price of gasoline" and **tiáozhěng jiàqián** "adjust price(s)" are common collocations. Another noun that is often used as the object of **tiáozhěng** is **shíjiān** "time." Example:

> **Qǐngwèn, shíjiān néng bu néng tiáozhěng yixia?**
> "Excuse me, could the time (for an appointment) be adjusted?"

9C. To say "there are especially many cars filling up," you'd say **jiāyóude chē tèbié duō**, literally "the cars filling up with gas are especially many." **Yǒu** "there is/there are" would not normally be used here.

9D. The common adverb **tèbié** "especially" can be used everywhere Chinese is spoken. In mainland China (but not in Taiwan), **tè** alone is sometimes used in place of **tèbié** when modifying stative verbs, as in **tè hǎo** "especially good" or **tè guì** "especially expensive."

9E. The four-character expression **dàpái chánglóng** "form a long line" literally means "greatly line up long dragons" and is used to refer to long lines of cars, people, etc.

9F. Note that through assimilation with the final **-ng** of the preceding **lóng**, the **ó** at the end of **dà-pái-cháng-lóng ó** sounds as though it were written **ngó**, so that the whole phrase is pronounced **dà-pái-cháng-lóng ngó**.

Unit 11: Review and Study Guide

New Vocabulary

ADVERBS

hǎo	very
shāowēi	somewhat, slightly
shùnbiàn	conveniently, in passing
tè	especially
tèbié	especially

ATTRIBUTIVES

gōngyòng	public

CONJUNCTIONS

huò	or
huòshi	or

COVERBS

zuò	sit in/on; take; by (car, boat, train, airplane)

EXPRESSIONS

dà-pái-cháng-lóng	form a long line

IDIOMATIC EXPRESSIONS

bú yàojǐn	be unimportant; "never mind"
hǎole	"all right," "O.K."
huānyíng guānglín	"welcome honorable presence"
méi wèntí	"no problem"

yìhuǐr jiàn	"see you in a little while"

INTERJECTIONS

èi	"yeah"

MEASURES

dòng	(for buildings)
gōngchǐ	meter
gōngshēng	liter
yuán	dollar (monetary unit)

MOVEABLE ADVERBS

yàoburán	otherwise, or

NOUNS

biānhào	serial number
chúzhípiào	stored-value ticket
dìtiě	subway
diàn	shop, store
fángzi	house
gōngchē	public bus
Guóyǔ	Mandarin (language)
jìchéngchē	taxi
jiājù	furniture
jiàqián	price
jiéyùn	mass rapid transit, MRT
mèng	dream

miào	temple, shrine
mótuōchē	motorcycle
qìyóu	gasoline
shǒu	hand
wèntí	question; problem
xiàngzi	lane
yóu	oil
yóujià	price of gasoline

PARTICLES

a	(pause filler)
la	(combined form of **le** and **a**)
le	(indicates action continuing up to the present)
ó	(indicates interest or excitement)

PATTERNS

cóng...qǐ	starting from..., beginning from...
gēn...jiǎng	tell (someone something)
gēn...shuō	tell (someone something)
VERB-lái...VERB-qù	VERB all over the place

PHRASES

bù hǎo yìsi	be embarrassing, be embarrassed
gōngyòng cèsuǒ	public toilet
gōngyòng diànhuà	public telephone
jiājù diàn	furniture store

PLACE WORDS

Chóngqìng	Chongqing (city in Sichuan)
Chóngqìng Nán Lù	Chongqing South Road
dàlù	mainland
duìmiàn	across
jiāyóuzhàn	gasoline station
Mùzhà	Muzha (suburb of Taipei)
Táiwān Yínháng	Bank of Taiwan
tíngchēchǎng	parking lot
Tǒngyī	Seven-Eleven® (name of store)
yínháng	bank
yóujú	post office
yòushǒu	right hand
yòushǒubiān	right-hand side
zuǒshǒu	left hand
zuǒshǒubiān	left-hand side

RESULTATIVE COMPOUNDS

cuòguo	miss
jiāmǎn	fill up
kàndào	see
màiwán	finish selling, be sold out
shèngxia	be left over
xiàsǐ	frighten to death
zhuǎnjìnlái	turn in

RESULTATIVE ENDINGS

-guò	(indicates motion past or by)
-lái	(indicates motion toward speaker)
-mǎn	full
-sǐ	to the point of death
-wán	finish

STATIVE VERBS

mǎn	be full
màn	be slow
qíguài	be strange
yàojǐn	be important

SURNAMES

Zhōu	Zhou

VERBS

gàosu	tell
jiàn	see
jiějué	solve
kàn	think, consider
qí	ride, straddle (bicycle, motorcycle, horse)
tiáozhěng	adjust
tǒngyī	unite, unify
wán	finish
xià	frighten
xiǎode	know
zhǎng	rise, go up
zhuàn	turn, go around
zhùyì	pay attention **to**

VERB-OBJECT COMPOUNDS

fàngxīn	be at ease, relax
jiāyóu	add gasoline, buy gas
tíngchē	park a car, park
zuòmèng	have a dream

Major New Grammar Patterns

-LE...LE TO INDICATE TIME CONTINUING UP THROUGH PRESENT WITH TIME EXPRESSION AFTER VERB: Tā gōngzuòle sān'ge yuè le. "She's been working for three months." (11-1)

IMPERATIVES CONSISTING OF VERB + STATIVE VERB + YÌDIǍN(R): kāi màn yidian "drive more slowly" (11-1)

NEGATIVE TIME SPENT WITH TIME EXPRESSION BEFORE VERB: Tā sān'ge yuè méi gōngzuòle. "She hasn't been working for three months." (11-2)

NUMBER OF TIMES WITHIN A PERIOD OF TIME: Duō jiǔ yìbān? "One (bus) every how often?", **Sānfēn zhōng yìbān.** "One (bus) every three minutes." (11-2)

GĒN...SHUŌ and GĒN...JIǍNG: Qǐng nǐ gēn tā shuō. "Please tell him.", **Qǐng nǐ gēn tā jiǎng wǒmen yǐjīng dàole.** "Please tell her that we've already arrived." (11-3)

VERB-LÁI VERB-QÙ: zǒulái zǒuqù "walk back and forth" (11-3)

ZĚMME (VERB) YĚ NEGATIVE VERB: Tā zěmme (zhǎo) yě zhǎobudào. "No matter how hard she searched she couldn't find it." (11-3)

YÒU YÀO...LE: Yóujià yòu yào zhǎngle. "The price of gas is going to rise again." (11-4)

CÓNG...QǏ: cóng míngtiān qǐ "starting from tomorrow" (11-4)

Shopping (I)

COMMUNICATIVE OBJECTIVES

Once you've mastered this unit, you'll be able to use Chinese to:

1. Buy ice pops at a street vendor's stand.
2. Purchase pens at a small department store.
3. Go shopping for vegetables at a vegetable stand.
4. Go shopping for fruit at a fruit stand.
5. Ask where to go to purchase various items.
6. Complain if something is too expensive and inquire if there are cheaper ones.
7. Discuss alternatives: this one or that one? Red ones or blue ones? etc.
8. Talk about different kinds of vegetables and fruit.
9. Talk about different kinds of writing instruments and office supplies.
10. Ask someone what they're majoring in at their college or university, and answer the same question when you are asked.
11. Discuss the names of common academic fields and majors.

P A R T 1

Buying Ice Pops

Sam White, an American graduate student doing research in Beijing for his dissertation, is returning to his dormitory from lunch. Just outside the entrance to his university, he sees an ice pop seller. It being a hot summer day, he decides to buy two ice pops.

 Basic Conversation 12-1

1. ICE POP SELLER	**Bīnggùnr, bīnggùnr! Wǔmáo qián yìgēnr.**
	Ice pops, ice pops! Fifty cents apiece.
2. WHITE	**Mǎi liǎnggēnr.**
	I'll take two.
3. ICE POP SELLER	**Nǎiyóude háishi xiǎodòude?**
	Cream or red bean?
4. WHITE	**Yíyàng yìgēnr ba.**
	Why don't we make it one of each.
5. ICE POP SELLER	**Yígòng yíkuài.**
	In all that will be one yuan.
6. WHITE	**Gěi nín wǔkuài.**
	This is five yuan.
7. ICE POP SELLER	**Zhǎo nín sìkuài. Nín náhǎo!**
	Here's four yuan in change. Hold them carefully!

 Build Up

1. Ice pop seller

bīng	ice [N]
bīnggùn(r) (B)	ice pop [N]
gēn(r)	(for long, thin things) [M]
yìgēnr	one (long, thin thing)
wǔmáo qián yìgēnr	fifty cents for one
Bīnggùnr, bīnggùnr! Wǔmáo qián yìgēnr.	Ice pops, ice pops! Fifty cents apiece.

2.   White
Mǎi liǎnggēnr.   I'll take two.

3.   Ice pop seller
nǎiyóu   cream [N]
nǎiyóude   cream one
háishi   or [CJ]
xiǎodòu   red bean [N]
xiǎodòude   red bean one
Nǎiyóude háishi xiǎodòude?   Cream or red bean?

4.   White
yàng(r)   kind, variety [M]
yíyàng   one kind
yíyàng yìgēnr   one of each kind
Yíyàng yìgēnr ba.   Why don't we make it one of each.

5.   Ice pop seller
Yígòng yíkuài.   In all that will be one yuan.

6.   White
Gěi nín wǔkuài.   This is five yuan.

7.   Ice pop seller
ná   hold, take [V]
-hǎo   so that something is good [RE]
náhǎo   hold well, hold firmly [RC]
Zhǎo nín sìkuài. Nín náhǎo!   Here's four yuan in change. Hold them carefully!

 ## Supplementary Vocabulary

1. **dú**   read aloud; study [V]
   dúshū   study [VO]
   hěn huì dúshū   know very well how to study
   Zhōngguo xuésheng chàbuduō   Chinese students are almost all very
   dōu hěn huì dúshū.   good at studying.

2. **niànshu**   study [VO]
   Tā jiù xǐhuan wánr,   He only likes to have fun,
   bù xǐhuan niànshū.   he doesn't like to study.

3. **zhuānyè (B)**   major, specialization [N]
   Wǒ hái méi juédìng wǒde zhuānyè.   I haven't yet decided on my major.

4. **zhǔxiū (T)**   major in; major [V/N]
   Nǐ yào zhǔxiū shémme?   What do you want to major in?

5. **xì**   department [N]
   Zhōngwén xì   department of Chinese
   yánjiūsuǒ   graduate program
   Zhōngwén yánjiūsuǒ   graduate program in Chinese
   Tā niàn Zhōngwén xì,   He's studying in the Chinese department; his
   tāde tàitai niàn Zhōngwén yánjiūsuǒ.   wife is studying in the graduate program in Chinese.

Additional Vocabulary: Common Academic Fields and Majors

1.	kuàijì	accounting [N]	32. dìlǐ	geography [N]
2.	guǎnggào shèjì	advertising design [PH]	33. dìzhìxué (B)	geology [N]
3.	Fēizhōu yánjiū	African studies [PH]	34. lìshǐ	history [N]
4.	nóngyè	agriculture [N]	35. zīliào guǎnlǐ	information management [PH]
5.	Měiguo yánjiū	American studies [PH]	36. guójì màoyì	international business [PH]
6.	rénlèixué	anthropology [N]	37. guójì guānxi	international relations [PH]
7.	kǎogǔxué	archeology [N]	38. xīnwénxué	journalism [N]
8.	jiànzhù	architecture [N]	39. fǎlǜ	law [N]
9.	yìshù	art [N]	40. túshūguǎnxué	library science [N]
10.	yìshùshǐ	art history [N]	41. yǔyánxué	linguistics [N]
11.	Yàzhōu yánjiū (B)	Asian studies [PH]	42. wénxué	literature [N]
12.	tiānwén	astronomy [N]	43. cáiliào kēxué	material science [PH]
13.	shēngwù huàxué	biochemistry [N]	44. shùxué	mathematics [N]
14.	shēngwù	biology [N]	45. jīxiè gōngchéng	mechanical engineering [PH]
15.	zhíwùxué	botany [N]	46. yīxué	medicine [N]
16.	shāngyè	business, commerce [N]	47. yīnyuè	music [N]
17.	shāngyè guǎnlǐ	business administration [PH]	48. Jìndōng yánjiū	Near Eastern studies [PH]
18.	huàxué	chemistry [N]	49. hùlǐ	nursing [N]
19.	tǔmù gōngchéng	civil engineering [PH]	50. yíngyǎngxué	nutrition [N]
20.	dàzhòng chuánbō	communications [PH]	51. zhéxué	philosophy [N]
21.	bǐjiào wénxué	comparative literature [PH]	52. tǐyù	physical education [N]
22.	jìsuànjī	computer science [N]	53. wùlǐ	physics [N]
23.	wǔdǎo	dance [N]	54. zhèngzhìxué	political science [N]
24.	xìjù	drama [N]	55. gōnggòng xíngzhèng	public administration [PH]
25.	jīngjì	economics [N]	56. xīnlǐxué	psychology [N]
26.	jiàoyù	education [N]	57. zōngjiào	religion [N]
27.	diànjī gōngchéng	electrical engineering [PH]	58. shèhuìxué	sociology [N]
28.	gōngchéng	engineering [N]	59. tǒngjìxué	statistics [N]
29.	Yīngwén	English [N]	60. xìjù	theater [N]
30.	Ōuzhōu yánjiū	European studies [PH]	61. dòngwùxué	zoology [N]
31.	sēnlínxué	forestry [N]		

Grammatical and Cultural Notes

1A. As we begin with this lesson the first of two units on the subject of shopping, it's worth mentioning that merchants and shopkeepers are a valuable resource for you to practice your Chinese. Unlike Chinese students, who often prefer practicing their English with foreigners, Chinese merchants and shopkeepers are usually quite willing to follow your lead, since they're obviously eager to be in your good graces and perhaps earn your business. Even if you purchase nothing, they sometimes feel they gain "face" by interacting with foreigners. If the shopkeepers or salespeople aren't too busy with other customers, you should feel free to engage them in conversation about a variety of topics. Department stores are especially well suited for this purpose, since they typically have large numbers of sales staff who are often happy to engage in conversation with Chinese-speaking foreign visitors.

1B. While the practice is decreasing with modernization, small vendors in China traditionally call out their wares.

1C. In Taiwan, ice pops are called **bīngbàng**.

1D. **AMOUNT OF MONEY PER ITEM.** In this line, consider the expression **wǔmáo qián yìgēnr**. Note the pattern for indicating the amount of money that one item of a certain category of items costs:

MONEY AMOUNT	YĪ	MEASURE
wǔmáo qián	yì	gēnr

"fifty cents apiece" (talking about ice pops)

Some more examples:

bákuài qián yíge	"eight dollars each" (talking about watermelons)
shíkuài qián yìbǎ	"ten dollars each" (talking about umbrellas)
yìqiānkuài yìtái	"a thousand dollars each" (talking about computers)

Instead of the order MONEY AMOUNT + **YĪ** + MEASURE, the order **YĪ** + MEASURE + MONEY AMOUNT is also possible, so instead of **wǔmáo qián yìgēnr** you could also say **yìgēnr wǔmáo qián**, with exactly the same meaning.

2. **Mǎi liǎnggēnr** "buy two." As is quite common in colloquial Chinese, the subject (**wǒ** "I") has here been omitted, since it's understood from the context.

3A. **Nǎiyóude** "cream one(s)" is short for **nǎiyóu bīnggùnr** "cream ice pop(s)," just as **xiǎodòude** "red bean one(s)" is short for **xiǎodòu bīnggùnr** "red bean ice pop(s)."

3B. **A HÁISHI B.** One very common way to ask about alternatives in choice-type questions is with the pattern **A háishi B** "A or B," where **háishi** is a conjunction meaning "or." The pattern is:

A	**HÁISHI**	**B**
Zhèige	háishi	nèige?

"This one or that one?"

Examples:

Jīntiān háishi míngtiān?	"Today or tomorrow?"
Nǐ yào dàde háishi yào xiǎode?	"Do you want big ones or do you want small ones?"
Nǐ yào qù Běijīng háishi yào qù Táiběi?	"Do you want to go to Beijing or do you want to go to Taipei?"

The last two sentences would often be abbreviated to:

Nǐ yào dàde háishi xiǎode?	"Do you want big ones or small ones?"
Nǐ yào qù Běijīng háishi Táiběi?	"Do you want to go to Beijing or Taipei?"

IMPORTANT: Note carefully that **háishi** alone is sufficient to create choice-type questions. Question particle **ma** is not added to choice-type questions containing **háishi**.

3C. **HÁISHI VS. HUÒ/HUÒSHI/HUÒZHĚ.** It's important to compare and contrast **háishi** "or" that you learn in this lesson with several other words that also translate as "or." In lesson 8-1 you were introduced to **huòzhě** "or" and in lesson 11-2 you were introduced to two other closely related words for "or," namely, **huòshi** and **huò**. **Huòzhě**, **huòshi**, and **huò** are used differently from **háishi** "or" and aren't interchangeable with it. The key difference is that **háishi** is used to express "or" in choice-type questions where the speaker is giving the listener alternatives and asking the listener to choose one of those alternatives. On the other hand, **huòshi**, **huòzhě**, and **huò** are used to express "or" in statements (or occasionally in questions that ask about something else, not which of several alternatives). The contrast between the following two sentences will clarify the difference:

Nǐ yào qù Běijīng háishi Táiběi?	"Do you want to go to Beijing or to Taipei?"
Tā yào qù Běijīng huòshi Tiānjīn.	"He wants to go to Beijing or Tianjin."

Study the following additional examples of the difference between **háishi** and **huòshi**:

Tā yào qù Zhōngguo dàlù háishi Táiwān?	"Does she want to go to mainland China or Taiwan?"

Tīngshuō tā yào qù Zhōngguo dàlù huòshi Táiwān.

"I heard she wants to go to mainland China or Taiwan."

Wǒ bù zhīdào tā yào qù Zhōngguo dàlù háishi Táiwān.

"I don't know whether she wants to go to mainland China or Taiwan."

Wǒ bù zhīdào tā yào qù Zhōngguo dàlù huòshi Táiwān.

"I didn't know she wants to go to mainland China or Taiwan."

4. **Yíyàng yìgēnr** literally means "one kind (of flavor), one stick (of ice pop)," that is, "of each kind of flavor, I want one ice pop" or, in better English, "one of each."

6–7. For the sake of clarity, it's common when you're giving change or paying out money to someone to say **Gěi nín...** or **Zhǎo nín...** followed by the words for the sum of money. In both line 6 and line 7, the subject **wǒ** "I" has been omitted and is understood.

7A. Distinguish the verb **ná** "take (with the hand), hold" from **dài** "take along, bring along" (cf. lesson 2-4). **Ná** means "hold" or "take" physically with one's hands. Here are some more examples with **ná**:

Qǐng nǐ názǒu.	"Please take it away."
Tā shǒuli názhe shémme?	"What is she holding in her hand?"

7B. **Nín náhǎo** "Hold them (i.e., the ice pops) carefully" indicates concern by the vendor for the customer. The resultative ending **-hǎo** indicates a desirable outcome of the action of the verb, so **náhǎo** could be translated as "hold it good." The resultative ending **-hǎo** can also have a meaning very similar to **-wán** "finish," with which it's often interchangeable, the only difference being that **-hǎo** sometimes has an added flavor of "finish something to the point where it's good" or "finish something to the point where it's ready for the next step." Examples:

Wǒ xiěhǎole.	"I've finished writing it."
Nǐ chīhǎole ma?	"Are you finished eating?"
Mén guānhǎole méiyou?	"Have you closed the door?"
Yīfu wǒ yǐjīng xǐhǎole.	"I've finished washing the clothes."

SV3–5, AV1–61. **ACADEMIC FIELDS AND MAJORS.** Common questions with the noun **zhuānyè** "major" are: **Nǐ niàn shémme zhuānyè?** "What's your major?" (lit. "You study what major?") and **Nǐde zhuānyè shi shémme?** "What is your major?" In Taiwan you say **Nǐ zhǔxiū shémme?** "What are you majoring in?" The various academic fields and majors listed in numbers 1–61 of the Additional Vocabulary are arranged in alphabetical order of the English equivalents. To say "I want to study (a certain field)," say **Wǒ yào niàn...**; to say "department of...," say **...xì**; and to say "graduate school of...," say **...yánjiūsuǒ**.

AV11. An alternate pronunciation of **Yàzhōu yánjiū** "Asian studies" that you'll hear in Taiwan and occasionally elsewhere is **Yǎzhōu yánjiū**.

AV17. Another term for **shāngyè guǎnlǐ** "business administration" or "business management" is **qǐyè guǎnlǐ**.

AV33. An alternate pronunciation of **dìzhìxué** "geology" that you'll hear in Taiwan and occasionally elsewhere is **dìzhíxué**.

AV39. The term for "law school" is **fǎxuéyuàn**.

AV46. The term for "medical school" is **yīxuéyuàn**.

Purchasing Pens

Jonathon Little, an American who is working as an intern in a law office in Beijing, goes to a department store to purchase some ball-point pens.

Basic Conversation 12-2

1. LITTLE   **Wǒ xiǎng shìshi zhèizhǒng yuánzhūbǐ, xíng ma?**
             Could I try out this kind of ball-point pen?

2. CLERK   **Xíng. Nín yào hóngde, lánde, háishi hēide?**
             Sure. Do you want a red one, a blue one, or a black one?

3. LITTLE   **Lánde ba. Duōshǎo qián yìzhī?**
             A blue one, I guess. How much are they each?

4. CLERK   **Liǎngkuài qián yìzhī.**
             They're two yuan each.

5. LITTLE   *(tries out a blue pen)* **Yǒu piányi diǎnde ma?**
             Do you have cheaper ones?

6. CLERK   **Yǒu. Zhèiyangrde yíkuài wǔ yìzhī.**
             We do. This kind is one dollar fifty apiece.

7. LITTLE   *(tries out the cheaper pen)* **Nǐ gěi wǒ liǎngzhī. Wǒ hái xiǎng mǎi yìběn Hàn-Yīng zìdiǎn, yìzhāng Běijīng shì dìtú hé yífèn bàozhǐ.**
             Give me two of them. I also want to buy a Chinese-English dictionary, a map of Beijing and a newspaper.

8. CLERK   **Duìbuqǐ, wǒmen zhèr bú mài zhèixiē dōngxi. Zìdiǎn hé dìtú, nín kéyi dào gébìde shūdiàn qù mǎi. Mǎi bàozhǐ, nín děi qù yóujú huò bàotíng.**
             Sorry, we don't sell these things here. The dictionary and the map you can go to the bookstore next door to buy. To buy a newspaper you'll have to go to a post office or a newspaper kiosk.

9. LITTLE   *(after paying for the pens and receiving change from the clerk)* **Xièxie.**
             Thank you.

10. CLERK **Bú kèqi, xīwàng nǐ xiàcì zài lái. Nǐ hái yào diǎnr shémme ma?**
You're welcome, hope you come again next time. Would you like anything else?

11. LITTLE **Bú yàole, xièxie.**
No, thank you.

12. CLERK **Bú yàole, à.**
So you don't want anything else.

(notices that Little has forgotten to take the pens)

Bié wàngle zhèige!
Don't forget this!

Build Up

1. Little

shì	try [V]
shìshi	try out
wǒ xiǎng shìshi	I'd like to try out
zhǒng	kind [M]
zhèizhǒng	this kind
bǐ	writing instrument [N] (M: **zhī**)
yuánzhūbǐ (B)	ball-point pen [N] (M: **zhī**)
zhèizhǒng yuánzhūbǐ	this kind of ball-point pen
Wǒ xiǎng shìshi zhèizhǒng yuánzhūbǐ, xíng ma?	Could I try out this kind of ball-point pen?

2. Clerk

lánde	blue one(s)
hēide	black one(s)
Xíng. Nín yào hóngde, lánde, háishi hēide?	Sure. Do you want a red one, a blue one, or a black one?

3. Little

zhī	(for pens, pencils) [M]
Lánde ba. Duōshǎo qián yìzhī?	A blue one, I guess. How much are they each?

4. Clerk

Liǎngkuài qián yìzhī.	They're two yuan each.

5. Little

piányi diǎn(r)	a little cheaper
piányi diǎnde	ones that are a little cheaper
Yǒu piányi diǎnde ma?	Do you have cheaper ones?

6. Clerk

zhèiyangrde	ones like these
Yǒu. Zhèiyangrde yíkuài wǔ yìzhī.	We do. This kind is one dollar fifty apiece.

7. Little

běn(r)	(for books, dictionaries) [M]
Hàn-Yīng	Chinese-English [AT]
zìdiǎn	dictionary [N] (M: **běn**)
yìběn Hàn-Yīng zìdiǎn	a Chinese-English dictionary
shì	city, municipality [N]

Běijīng shì	the city of Beijing
dìtú	map [N] (M: **zhāng**)
yìzhāng Běijīng shì dìtú	a map of Beijing city
fèn(r)	(for newspapers, magazines) [M]
bàozhǐ	newspaper [N] (M: **fèn**)
yífèn bàozhǐ	a newspaper
Nǐ gěi wǒ liǎngzhī. Wǒ hái xiǎng mǎi yìběn Hàn-Yīng zìdiǎn, yìzhāng Běijīng shì dìtú hé yífèn bàozhǐ.	Give me two of them. I also want to buy a Chinese-English dictionary, a map of Beijing and a newspaper.

8. Clerk

xiē	some [M]
zhèixiē	these [SP+M]
zhèixiē dōngxi	these things
gébì	next door [PW]
shū	book [N] (M: **běn**)
shūdiàn	book store [PW]
gébìde shūdiàn	the book store next door
bàotíng	newspaper kiosk [PW]
yóujú huò bàotíng	a post office or a newspaper kiosk
Duìbuqǐ, wǒmen zhèr bú mài zhèixiē dōngxi. Zìdiǎn hé dìtú, nín kéyǐ dào gébìde shūdiàn qù mǎi. Mǎi bàozhǐ, nín děi qù yóujú huò bàotíng.	Sorry, we don't sell these things here. The dictionary and the map you can go to the bookstore next door to buy. To buy a newspaper you'll have to go to a post office or a newspaper kiosk.

9. Little

Xièxie.	Thank you.

10. Clerk

Bú kèqi, xīwàng nǐ xiàcì zài lái. Nǐ hái yào diǎnr shémme ma?	You're welcome, hope you come again next time. Would you like anything else?

11. Little

Bú yàole, xièxie.	No, thank you.

12. Clerk

Bú yàole, à.	So you don't want anything else.
Bié wàngle zhèlge!	Don't forget this!

Supplementary Vocabulary

1. qiānbǐ	pencil [N] (M: **zhī**)
2. zhǐ	paper [N] (M: **zhāng**)
3. běnzi	notebook [N]
4. zázhì	magazine [N] (M: **fèn**, **běn**)

Additional Vocabulary: More Writing Instruments

1. fěnbǐ	chalk [N] (M: **zhī**)
2. gāngbǐ	fountain pen [N] (M: **zhī**)
3. máobǐ	Chinese brush [N] (M: **zhī**)

Grammatical and Cultural Notes

1A. The verb **shì** "try" often occurs reduplicated with a following **kàn** as **shìshi kàn** "try and see" (3-2: 2B). For example, **Wǒ dǎbukāi, nǐ shìshi kàn** "I can't open it, you try and see (if you can)."

1B. An alternate word for **yuánzhūbǐ** "ball-point pen" that you'll hear in Taiwan and occasionally elsewhere is **yuánzǐbǐ**. **Yuánzǐ** means "atom," so this word literally means "atomic pen."

2A. In the video and the various audio recordings of this basic conversation, there is some variation in the use of **nǐ** as opposed to **nín**. While speakers from Beijing tend to distinguish these two pronouns carefully, speakers from other parts of mainland China and Taiwan tend not to use **nín** so often. But as a non-native speaker, you'd do well always to use **nín** toward those older or higher in social status than you.

2B. When referring to pens, **hóngde** "red one," **lánde** "blue one," and **hēide** "black one" would most likely mean pens that write in the color mentioned; in other contexts, **hóngde**, **lánde**, and **hēide** could indicate objects that themselves are colored the color mentioned.

3. **MEASURES.** In English, numbers like "one" or "two" and demonstratives like "this" or "that" can occur directly before most nouns, so we can say "two tables," "this person," "that book" and so on. However, there are a few English nouns (called "mass nouns") that can only be counted by means of a measure word; for example, we can't say "two cattles" or "a sand" but must instead say "two head of cattle" or "a grain of sand." In Chinese, all nouns act like English mass nouns; that is to say, every Chinese noun must be preceded by a measure if it's counted or specified. There are two basic patterns involving measures, the first involving a number and the second involving a specifier:

NUMBER	MEASURE	NOUN
liǎng	ge	rén

"two people"

SPECIFIER	MEASURE	NOUN
zhèi	zhāng	zhuōzi

"this table"

Other specifiers you've had beside **zhèi-** include **nèi-** "that," **něi-** "which?", **měi-** "each," **dì-** (forms ordinal numbers), **shàng-** "last," and **xià-** "next."

In Chinese, there are many specific measures, each limited to certain nouns or categories of nouns.[1] Some measures have fairly clear meanings, e.g., **zhāng**, which is used for flat things, or **tiáo**, which is used for long, narrow things. You can sometimes predict which measure a given noun is likely to use, and sometimes you can use two or more measures with the same noun, depending on the meaning you wish to convey (e.g., **yìzhī xié** "a shoe" vs. **yìshuāng xié** "a pair of shoes"). However, many measure words are arbitrary and are best learned together with the noun they modify.[2]

The general measure **ge** can be used with many nouns, including human beings, abstract entities, containers of all kinds, rings, and other solid three-dimensional objects. As a general strategy, use **ge** when you don't know what the appropriate measure for a noun is. Though use of the specific measure is preferred, **ge** will be understood and will be less jarring than an incorrect measure or no measure at all.

---

1. For a complete list of all the measures introduced in *Basic Spoken Chinese* and *Intermediate Spoken Chinese*, see the Table of Measures on the disc.

2. If there is a specific measure for a new noun, it will be indicated in parentheses after the English translation in the Build Up. If no specific measure is listed, you can assume that the noun uses the general measure **ge**.

Below are examples containing the new measures introduced in this lesson:

zhèizhī qiānbǐ	"this pencil"
nèiběn shū	"that book"
něizhāng dìtú	"which map?"
wǔfèn bàozhǐ	"five newspapers"
měizhāng zhǐ	"each piece of paper"

The above are simple measure constructions. More complex measure constructions, where more and different kinds of words come between the measure and the noun, are also possible. Examples:

yìzhǒng xīnde yuánzhūbǐ	"a new kind of ball-point pen"
nèiběn hěn xiǎode Yīng-Hàn zìdiǎn	"that very small English-Chinese dictionary"

There are a few common Chinese measures that typically occur alone without a following noun and which translate into English nouns. Examples: **tiān** "day," **nián** "year," **suì** "year of age." For "one day" be careful to say **yìtiān** (and NOT *yíge tiān), for "two years" say **liǎngnián** (and NOT *liǎngge nián), and for "ten years of age" say **shísuì** (and NOT *shíge suì).

There is one other important point about measures. If the noun you're talking about is clear from the context, then you can—and Chinese speakers often do—omit the noun entirely and use only the specifier and/or number plus measure. For example, consider the following conversation at a bookstore:

A: **Něiběn?**	"Which one?"
B: **Zhèiběn.**	"This one."
A: **Yígòng yào jǐběn?**	"How many do you want in all?"
B: **Zhǐ yào yìběn.**	"I only want one."

The noun being referred to (**shū** "book") is never mentioned since it's clear from the context.

5.　Note the pattern STATIVE VERB + **(yì)diǎn** in the question **Yǒu piányi diǎnde ma?** "Are there cheaper ones?" (5-3: 4E).

7A.　**Nǐ gěi wǒ liǎngzhī** "Give me two of them." The native Chinese speakers who helped develop this Basic Conversation suggested this line, since customers generally don't need to speak as politely as salespeople. However, it would be politer for you, as a non-native, to say **Nín gěi wǒ liǎngzhī ba** "Why don't you give me two of them."

7B.　**Zìdiǎn** (lit. "character dictionary") refers to a dictionary focusing on the meanings of individual characters. This kind of dictionary has traditionally been the most common for Chinese. A dictionary where the basic unit of entry is the word (which in Chinese typically has two syllables, like **péngyou** "friend") is called a **cídiǎn** (lit. "word dictionary").

Kiosk on campus of Beijing Language and Culture University

7C.　**Hàn-Yīng zìdiǎn** "Chinese-English dictionary." **Hàn-Yīng** "Chinese-English" is a so-called attributive, which means it precedes and modifies a noun but couldn't be used as a stative verb in the predicate. The elements **Hàn** "Chinese" and **Yīng** "English" are here equal in importance. This is one of the few kinds of grammatical constructions in Chinese where the element that comes first (**Hàn**) doesn't describe what follows (**Yīng**). Other combinations based on this pattern include:

Yīng-Hàn "English-Chinese"	**Dé-Hàn** "German-Chinese"
Fǎ-Hàn "French-Chinese"	**Rì-Hàn** "Japanese-Chinese"
Hàn-Fǎ "Chinese-French"	**Hàn-Rì** "Chinese-Japanese"
Hàn-Dé "Chinese-German"	

The syllable **Hàn** in all the above terms (as well as in **Hànyǔ** and **Hànzì**) means "Chinese." It comes from the word for the Han Dynasty (206 BCE to 220 CE), which was one of the most prosperous and successful periods in Chinese history.

7D.   **Shì** is a more formal word for "city" than **chéng**, which you learned in lesson 5-3. **Shì** usually occurs immediately after the name of a city, e.g., **Běijīng shì** "the city of Beijing." It's fine to say the name of a city without adding **shì**, but adding **shì** sounds more complete and more formal. If you want to simply say "city," without giving the name of a particular city, then don't use **shì** at all but instead use **chéng**, for example:

> **Qǐng wèn, zuì jìnde chéng lí zhèr yǒu duō yuǎn?**
>
> "How far from here is the nearest city?"

8A.   **XIĒ AS MEASURE IN ZHÈIXIĒ, NÈIXIĒ, AND NĚIXIĒ.** In line 8, note **zhèixiē dōngxi** "these things." The measure **xiē** indicates plural and has the basic meaning "some." There are three common combinations of SPECIFIER + **xiē** which you should learn at this time:

SPECIFIER	XIĒ	ENGLISH
zhèi	**xiē**	these
nèi	**xiē**	those
něi	**xiē**	which?

Zhèixiē, **nèixiē**, and **něixiē** can all be used to modify a following noun (e.g., **Zhèixiē dōngxi shi wǒde** "These things are mine"), or they can be used alone as pronouns with the noun omitted (e.g., **Zhèixiē shi wǒde** "These are mine"). **Zhèixiē** has an alternate form **zhèxiē**, **nèixiē** has an alternate form **nàxiē**, and **něixiē** has an alternate form **nǎxiē**. Note that when **zhè** and **nà** are used as pronouns to indicate plural, the **xiē** is optional, not required; so to say "What are these?" you could say either **Zhè shi shémme dōngxi?** or **Zhèixiē shi shémme dōngxi?** The **xiē** is used only when there is a need to make plurality explicit. Also, **xiē** is never used if a specific number is mentioned, so to say "these three books" you must say **zhèisānběn shū** and you CANNOT say **zhèixiē sānběn shū**. Now some more examples with **zhèixiē**, **nèixiē**, and **něixiē**:

> **Zhèixiē dōngxi hǎokàn, nèixiē bú tài hǎokàn.**
>
> "These things look nice; those don't look very nice."

> **Nèixiē zì, yǒude xuéguole, yǒude hái méiyou xuéguo.**
>
> "Those characters, some of them we've learned, others we haven't yet learned."

> **Nǐ kéyi gàosu ta nǐ yào qù něixiē dìfang.**
>
> "You can tell her which places you want to go to."

8B.   In the second sentence of this line, **zìdiǎn** "dictionary" and **dìtú** "map," which are really the objects of the verb **mǎi** "buy," are preposed—placed at the beginning of the sentence—and become the topics of the sentence.

8C.   In this line you learn the words **shū** "book" and **shūdiàn** "book store." Review the following expressions containing the syllable **shū** "book" that you've encountered previously: **túshūguǎn** "library" (1-1), **shūfáng**

"book-room, study" (5-4), **shūjià** "bookshelf" (5-4), **jiāoshū** "teach books, teach" (6-3), **dúshū** "to study" (12-1), and **niànshū** "to study" (12-1).

8D. To say "In the book it says…" say **Shūshang shuō…** (lit. "On the book it says"). But to say "In the book it doesn't say…" you must in Chinese say **Shūshang méi(you) shuō…** (lit. "On the book it didn't say"). In Chinese you CANNOT say *Shūshang bù shuō....

8E. Remember that, as we noted in 12-1: 3C, the difference between **háishi** "or" and **huò** "or" (and its synonyms **huòshi** and **huòzhě**) is that **háishi** is used in questions that ask that a choice be made from among two or more alternatives, while **huò**, **huòshi**, and **huòzhě** are usually used in statements. Two good contrasting examples are contained in this Basic Conversation. In line 2, we have **háishi** in a choice-type question:

> **Nǐ yào hóngde, lánde, háishi hēide?**
>
> "Do you want a red one, a blue one, or a black one?"

Then, in line 8, we see **huò** in a statement:

> **Mǎi bàozhǐ, nín děi qù yóujú huò bàotíng.**
>
> "To buy a newspaper you'll have to go to a post office or a newspaper kiosk."

10. **MORE ON QUESTION WORDS USED AS INDEFINITES.** In utterance 10, look at the question **Nǐ hái yào diǎnr shémme ma?** At first glance, this may look to you as though it meant "What else do you want?" But surely you remember the rule that if there is a question word in a sentence that is meant as a question, then there is no **ma** at the end of the sentence, right? But here there is a **ma**, so what is going on? Well, it just so happens that if a question word like **shémme** "what" or **shéi** "who" occurs in a sentence that is already a question because of a **ma** at the end or because of an affirmative-negative verb construction like **yào bu yào**, then the question word no longer asks a question but rather carries an indefinite sense. In this case, instead of meaning "what?", **shémme** means "something" or "anything"; and instead of meaning "who?", **shéi** means "someone" or "anyone." Examples:

Nín hái yào diǎnr shémme ma?	"Would you like something else?"
Nǐ yào bu yào chī yidianr shémme?	"Would you like to eat a little something?"
Yǒu méiyou shéi bù xǐhuan xiǎodòurde?	"Is there anyone who doesn't like red bean ones?"

Be careful to distinguish true question word questions such as **Nín hái yào shémme?** "What else do you want?" from **ma** questions that contain an indefinite **shémme** such as **Nín hái yào diǎnr shémme ma?** "Do you want anything else?"

12. The particle **à** in this sentence indicates comprehension on the part of the speaker.

Shopping for Vegetables

Rosy Huang, a Chinese-American woman living for a year in Taipei, goes shopping for tomatoes.

 Basic Conversation 12-3

1. HUANG		**Lǎobǎn, fānqié zěmme mài?** Sir, how much are tomatoes?
2. VEGETABLE SELLER		**Bànjīn èrshiwǔkuài.** 25 NT for half a catty.
3. HUANG		**Zěmme zhèmme guì a?** How come they're so expensive?
4. VEGETABLE SELLER		**Tàitai, zhè shi jīntiān cái dàode. Bǎozhèng xīnxiān.** Ma'am, these just arrived today. I guarantee they're fresh.
5. HUANG		**Gěi wǒ bànjīn hǎole.** Then give me half a catty.
6. VEGETABLE SELLER		**Hǎo, bànjīn. Yào bu yào mǎi diǎn shālācài huòshi qíncài? Zhèixiē dōu shi cóng Měiguo jìnkǒude, bǐ Lí Shānde hǎo. Yòu piàoliang yòu cuì.** O.K., half a catty. Would you like to buy some lettuce or celery? These are both imported from the U.S., and they're better than those from Li Shan. They both look nice and they're crisp.
7. HUANG		**Jīntiān bú yàole. Jiù mǎi fānqié ba.** Not today. I'll just buy the tomatoes.
8. VEGETABLE SELLER		**Hǎo.** Fine.
9. HUANG		*(gives him the money)* **Èrshiwǔkuài.** 25 NT.
10. VEGETABLE SELLER		**Hǎo, duō xiè. Zài lái a!** O.K., thanks. Come again!

Build Up

1. **Huang**

fānqié	tomato [N]
Lǎobǎn, fānqié zěmme mài?	Sir, how much are tomatoes?

2. **Vegetable seller**

jīn	catty (unit of weight) [M]
bànjīn	half a catty
Bànjīn èrshiwǔkuài.	25 NT for half a catty.

3. **Huang**

zěmme zhèmme...	how come so... [PT]
zěmme zhèmme guì	how come so expensive
Zěmme zhèmme guì a?	How come they're so expensive?

4. **Vegetable seller**

cái	not until, just [A]
jīntiān cái dàode	didn't arrive until today
bǎozhèng	guarantee [V]
xīnxiān	be fresh [SV]
bǎozhèng xīnxiān	(I) guarantee (they're) fresh
Tàitai, zhè shi jīntiān cái dàode.	Ma'am, these just arrived today.
Bǎozhèng xīnxiān.	I guarantee they're fresh.

5. **Huang**

Gěi wǒ bànjīn hǎole.	Then give me half a catty.

6. **Vegetable seller**

shālā	salad [N]
cài	vegetable [N]
shālācài (T)	lettuce [N]
qíncài	Chinese celery [N]
shālācài huòshi qíncài	lettuce or celery
jìnkǒu	import [V/N]
cóng Měiguo jìnkǒu	import from America
lí(r)	pear [N]
Lí Shān	"Pear Mountain," Li Shan [PW]
bǐ Lí Shānde hǎo	better than those from Li Shan
piàoliang	be pretty, look nice [SV]
cuì	be crisp [SV]
yòu piàoliang yòu cuì	both nice-looking and crisp
Hǎo, bànjīn. Yào bu yào mǎi diǎn shālācài huòshi qíncài? Zhèixiē dōu shi cóng Měiguo jìnkǒude, bǐ Lí Shānde hǎo. Yòu piàoliang yòu cuì.	O.K., half a catty. Would you like to buy some lettuce or celery? These are both imported from the U.S., and they're better than those from Li Shan. They both look nice and they're crisp.

7. **Huang**

Jīntiān bú yàole. Jiù mǎi fānqié ba.	Not today. I'll just buy the tomatoes.

8. **Vegetable seller**

Hǎo.	Fine.

9. Huang
    Èrshíwǔkuài.   25 NT.

10. Vegetable seller
    duō xiè   "many thanks" [IE]
    Hǎo, duō xiè. Zài lái a!   O.K., thanks. Come again!

Supplementary Vocabulary

1. shūcài	vegetable [N]
2. qīngcài	green vegetable [N]
3. báicài	cabbage [N]
4. càichǎng	market [N]
5. chūkǒu	export [V/N]

Additional Vocabulary: More Vegetables

1. kǔguā	bitter melon [N]	11. qīngdòu	pea [N]
2. húluóbo	carrot [N]	12. dòumiáo	pea sprouts [N]
3. càihuā	cauliflower [N]	13. tǔdòu (B)	potato [N]
4. luóbo	Chinese radish [N]	14. mǎlíngshǔ (T)	potato [N]
5. yùmǐ	corn/sweetcorn [N]	15. xiānggū	shiitake mushroom [N]
6. huánggua	cucumber [N]	16. Hélándòu	snow pea [N]
7. qiézi	eggplant/aubergine [N]	17. bōcài	spinach [N]
8. dòujiǎo	green beans [N]	18. xīhóngshì	tomato [N]
9. qīngjiāo	green pepper/capsicum [N]	19. xīlánhuā	Western broccoli [N]
10. shēngcài (B)	lettuce [N]	20. dōngguā	winter melon [N]

Grammatical and Cultural Notes

1A. The term **fānqié** "tomato" literally means "foreign eggplant" (**qiézi** is the word for "eggplant"). In northern China, the colloquial term for "tomato" is **xīhóngshì**, literally "Western red persimmon." As is obvious from these terms, the tomato isn't indigenous to China. Also, it's interesting to note that, in the West, tomatoes are considered vegetables, but in China, they're often considered to be fruit, which is actually more accurate from a botanical standpoint. So don't be surprised if you should be given a fruit plate for dessert that includes tomatoes in it.

Vegetable stand in Tai Po, Hong Kong

1B. Note in this line the pattern for asking how much something costs: **Fānqié zěmme mài?** "How much are tomatoes?" (lit. "How do tomatoes sell?"). Of course, any of the following questions would also be acceptable for asking how much tomatoes cost:

Fānqié duōshǎo qián?	"How much are tomatoes?"
Fānqié yìjīn duōshǎo qián?	"How much are tomatoes per catty?"
Fānqié yìjīn mài duōshǎo qián?	"How much does a catty of tomatoes sell for?"

2. A **jīn**, usually translated as a "catty," is a Chinese unit of weight that is traditionally about 1⅓ pounds in weight. In Taiwan, one **jīn** (there also called **Táijīn**) equals 600 grams. In mainland China, the **jīn** has been rounded off to 500 grams or half a kilo. Contrast the pronunciation of **yìjīn** "one catty" with that of **yǐjīng** "already."

3. **ZĚMME ZHÈMME....** As we learned in 8-3, one meaning of **zěmme** is "how come, why"; and as we learned

in 2-2, **zhèmme** (which has an alternate pronunciation **zèmme**) means "so." The whole expression **zĕmme zhèmme...** means "how come (something/somebody is or does something) so...." **Zĕmme zhèmme...** is most commonly followed by a stative verb but can also be followed by an auxiliary verb or regular verb. There is frequently a final particle **a** (or variant of **a** such as **ya, wa, ra, na, nga**) at the end of the sentence. Instead of **zhèmme** you can also use **nèmme** (with the same meaning of "so" but referring to something further away). The basic pattern is:

SUBJECT	ZĔMME ZHÈMME	SV/AV/V	A?
Fānqié	zĕmme zhèmme	guì	a?

"How come tomatoes are so expensive?"

More examples:

Zhèijiān wūzi zĕmme zhèmme lĕng a?	"How come this room is so cold?"
Zhōngguo zì zĕmme zhèmme nán a?	"How come Chinese characters are so difficult?"
Tā zĕmme nèmme xĭhuan chī táng a?	"How come he likes to eat candy so much?"
Nĭ zĕmme zhèmme pà tā?	"How come you're so scared of him?"

4. **CÁI VS. JIÙ.** Cái and jiù are both adverbs that sometimes translate as "then," but they're used in very different ways. Depending on the context, **cái** can be translated as "then and only then," "not until then," or "only." **Jiù**, on the other hand, can be translated as "then," "then already," and "as early as." The essential difference between the two is that **cái** means later or more than expected, while **jiù** means earlier or fewer than expected. Like all regular adverbs, **cái** and **jiù** occur after the subject and before the verb. Compare these two sentences, the first one with **jiù** and the second one with **cái**:

Xiǎo Wáng yīnggāi qīdiǎn dào, kěshi tā liùdiǎn bàn jiù láile.

"Little Wang was supposed to arrive at 7:00, but he came at 6:30 (that early)."

Xiǎo Lǐ yě yīnggāi qīdiǎn dào, kěshi tā qīdiǎn bàn cái lái.

"Little Li was also supposed to arrive at 7:00, but he didn't come until 7:30."

Some more examples with **cái**:

Zhè shi jīntiān cái dàode.	"This arrived only today (and not before)."
Zhōu Tàitai míngtiān cái lái.	"Mrs. Zhou won't come until tomorrow."
Bái Xiānsheng jīnnián cái dào Měiguo.	"It wasn't until this year that Mr. Bai came to the U.S."
Wǒ gàosu ta sāncì, tā cái dǒng.	"He didn't understand until I had told him three times."

Wǒ èrshisuì jiù bìyèle; tā sānshisuì cái bìyè.

"I graduated at the age of 20; she didn't graduate until she was 30."

Wǒ yě bù zhīdào zĕmme bàn cái héshì.

"And I don't know what would be appropriate for me to do."

Wǒmen qù zhǎo shéi cái néng jiějué zhèige wèntí?

"Who should we go look for who can solve this problem?"

Wǒmen shàngcì rén bù duō, liùge cài jiù gòule; zhèicì rén bǐjiào duō, wǒ kàn shíge cài cái gòu.

"Last time there weren't many people, so six dishes were enough; this time there are more people, so I think only ten dishes would be enough."

Notice that, as is clear from the examples above, after **cái** a verb doesn't have a **-le** suffixed to it. Also, be aware that in English, the translation of a phrase with **cái** often calls for a negative verb plus "until," but in the Chinese, there is no negative.

6A.   **Yào bu yào mǎi diǎn shālācài huòshi qíncài?** "Do you want to buy some lettuce or celery?" Because of the **huòshi**, we know this isn't a question asking about "lettuce vs. celery," but rather a question about "wanting to buy or not wanting to buy." As we noted in 12-1: 3C, you should distinguish carefully between the different words in Chinese for "or": **huòshi** (and its variants **huòzhě** and **huò**) vs. **háishi**. To review, **háishi** is used in questions that ask the listener to choose between alternatives. On the other hand, **huòshi** and its variants are usually used in statements, or (as here) in questions that ask about something else, not which of two alternatives. Contrast:

> **Nǐ yào mǎi shēngcài háishi qíncài?**
>
> "Do you want to buy lettuce or celery?" (i.e., "Which of these two vegetables do you want to buy?")

> **Nǐ yào bu yào mǎi diǎn shēngcài huòshi qíncài?**
>
> "Do you want to buy a little lettuce or celery?" (i.e., "Do you want to buy a vegetable, like lettuce or celery? Or don't you want to buy anything today?")

6B.   In this line, **zhèixiē** is used as a pronoun meaning "these," with the noun to which it refers (most likely **qīngcài** "green vegetables") deleted. **Zhèixiē** is sometimes pronounced **zhèxiē**, as in the video recording for this lesson. See note 12-2: 8A for more information on **xiē**.

6C.   Learn the pattern **cóng...jìnkǒu** "import from...." Example:

> **Zhèixiē dōngxi dōu shi cóng wàiguo jìnkǒude.**
>
> "These things were all imported from foreign countries."

6D.   **Lí Shān** "Pear Mountain" is located in Taichung County in central Taiwan and is famous for its many pear orchards. **Lí** is the word for "pear."

6E.   **Zhèixiē...bǐ Lí Shānde hǎo** "These...are better than the ones from Li Shan." Do you remember the use of the coverb **bǐ** to express unequal comparison? If not, review 10-4: 8B.

6F.   **Yòu piàoliang yòu cuì** "They're both pretty and crispy." Do you remember the pattern **yòu...yòu...** "both... and..."? If not, review 10-2: 2C.

SV2, AV3.   The **qīng** in the words **qīngcài** "green vegetable" and **qīngjiāo** "green pepper" is the traditional Chinese color word meaning "green-blue," the color of nature. Professor William Baxter of the University of Michigan has translated this color into English as "grue"!

AV1–20.   **VEGETABLES.** The names of these vegetables are listed in alphabetical order of the English translations. Note that the shapes of some vegetables are different in Asia from America. For example, carrots are thicker but cucumbers and eggplants are thinner. Traditionally, Chinese people don't often eat raw vegetables.

At a Fruit Stand

Ellen Anderson, an American student who is studying Chinese in Beijing, shops for pears at a local fruit stand.

Basic Conversation 12-4

1. ANDERSON		**Qǐng gěi wǒ yāo èrjīn Yālír. Gěi tiāo xīnxiān yidianrde.** Please weigh me out two catties of Ya pears. Pick out fresher ones.
2. FRUIT VENDOR		**Yào yíkuài yìjīnde háishi yào yíkuài wǔ yìjīnde?** Do you want the one yuan per catty ones or the 1.50 per catty ones?
3. ANDERSON		**Wǒ yào yíkuài wǔde.** I want the 1.50 ones.
4. FRUIT VENDOR		**Yíkuài wǔde bǐ yíkuàide dàde duō.** The 1.50 ones are much bigger than the one yuan ones. *(after he has weighed out the pears)* **Hái yào biéde ma? Mǎi diǎnr xiāngjiāo zěmmeyàng?** Do you want anything else? How about buying some bananas?
5. ANDERSON		**Xiāngjiāo duōshǎo qián yìjīn?** How much are bananas per catty?
6. FRUIT VENDOR		**Liǎngkuài èr yìjīn.** They're 2.20 per catty.
7. ANDERSON		**Nín gěi wǒ lái liǎngjīn ba.** Why don't you give me two catties. *(after the fruit vendor has put all the fruit in a bag)* **Yígòng duōshǎo qián?** How much in all?
8. FRUIT VENDOR		**Zǒnggòng shi qīkuài sì.** In all it's 7.40.

9. ANDERSON	**Gěi nín shíkuài.**
	This is ten yuan.
10. FRUIT VENDOR	**Zhǎo nín liǎngkuài liù. Qǐng nín diǎn yíxiàr.**
	Here's 2.60 in change. Please count your change.
11. ANDERSON	**Xièxie. Zàijiàn!**
	Thank you. Goodbye!
12. FRUIT VENDOR	**Zàijiàn!**
	Goodbye!

🔘 Build Up

1. Anderson

yāo (B)	weigh out [V]
qǐng gěi wǒ yāo	please weigh out for me
Yālí(r)	Ya pear [N]
èrjīn Yālír	two catties of Ya pears
tiāo	pick out, select [V]
gěi tiāo	pick out for (me)
xīnxiān yidianrde	fresher ones
Qǐng gěi wǒ yāo èrjīn Yālír. Gěi tiāo xīnxiān yidianrde.	Please weigh me out two catties of Ya pears. Pick out fresher ones.

2. Fruit vendor

yíkuài yìjīnde	the one yuan per catty ones
yíkuài wǔ yìjīnde	the 1.50 per catty ones
Yào yíkuài yìjīnde háishi yào yíkuài wǔ yìjīnde?	Do you want the one yuan per catty ones or the 1.50 per catty ones?

3. Anderson

Wǒ yào yíkuài wǔde.	I want the 1.50 ones.

4. Fruit vendor

dàde duō	be much bigger
Yíkuài wǔde bǐ yíkuàide dàde duō.	The 1.50 ones are much bigger than the one yuan ones.
biéde	other things, others
hái yào biéde ma	do you want anything else
xiāngjiāo	banana [N] (M: **gēn**)
mǎi diǎnr xiāngjiāo	buy some bananas
Hái yào biéde ma? Mǎi diǎnr xiāngjiāo zěmmeyàng?	Do you want anything else? How about buying some bananas?

5. Anderson

Xiāngjiāo duōshǎo qián yìjīn?	How much are bananas per catty?

6. Fruit vendor

Liǎngkuài èr yìjīn.	They're 2.20 per catty.

7. Anderson

lái	bring, give [V]
lái liǎngjīn	bring two catties
gěi wǒ lái liǎngjīn	bring two catties for me

Nín gěi wǒ lái liǎngjīn ba. | Why don't you give me two catties.
Yígòng duōshǎo qián? | How much in all?

---

8. **Fruit vendor**
   zǒnggòng | in all [A]
Zǒnggòng shi qīkuài sì. | In all it's 7.40.

---

9. **Anderson**
Gěi nín shíkuài. | This is ten yuan.

---

10. **Fruit vendor**
   diǎn | count, check [V]
   qǐng nín diǎn yíxiàr | please count
Zhǎo nín liǎngkuài liù. Qǐng nín diǎn yíxiàr. | Here's 2.60 in change. Please count your change.

---

11. **Anderson**
Xièxie. Zàijiàn! | Thank you. Goodbye!

---

12. **Fruit vendor**
Zàijiàn! | Goodbye!

 # Supplementary Vocabulary

A. Fruits

1. **shuǐguǒ** | fruit [N]
2. **píngguǒ** | apple [N]
3. **júzi** | orange [N]
4. **táozi** | peach [N]
5. **pútao** | grape [N]

B. General

6. **bāo** | wrap [V]
   -qǐlái | (general resultative ending) [RE]
   bāoqilai | wrap up [RC]
Qǐng nín gěi wǒ bāoqilai. | Please wrap it up for me.

7. **qióng** | be poor [SV]
   yǒuqián | be rich [SV]
   yǒuqián rén | rich people
Wǒmen bù qióng, kěshi yě bú shi yǒuqián rén. | We're not poor, but neither are we rich people.

8. **tīngdào** | hear [RC]
Wǒ yào nǐ chūqu! Nǐ tīngdàole ma? | I want you to go out! Did you hear?

9. **-jiàn** | see, perceive [RE]
   kànjian | see [RC]
   kànbujiàn | can't see
Tài yuǎnle, wǒ kànbujiàn. | It's too far, I can't see it.

10. **tīngjian** | hear [RC]
Nǐ tīngjian dǎléi le ma? | Did you hear it thunder?

Additional Vocabulary: More Fruits

1.	**yángtáo**	carambola, star fruit [N]		8.	**mángguǒ**	mango [N]
2.	**pútáoyòu**	grapefruit [N]		9.	**mùguā**	papaya [N]
3.	**bālè**	guava [N]		10.	**wéndàn**	pomelo [N]
4.	**Hāmìguā**	Hami melon [N]		11.	**cǎoméi**	strawberry [N]
5.	**níngméng**	lemon [N]		12.	**xīguā**	watermelon [N]
6.	**lìzhī**	litchi [N]				
7.	**liánwù**	Malaysian wax apple [N]				

Grammatical and Cultural Notes

1A.   The verb **yāo** "weigh out" is common in Beijing. Another verb for "weigh out" that can be used wherever Chinese is spoken is **chēng** "weigh out" (cf. 13-1). Yet another option is to use **lái** in the sense of "bring," as in line 7 of this conversation.

1B.   Either **liǎng** or **èr** can be used with the measure **jīn** "catty." So both **liǎngjīn Yālír** and **èrjīn Yālír** would be correct in the sense of "two catties of Ya pears."

1C.   **Yālí(r)** is a kind of pear grown in north China, especially Hebei Province. In English they're often called "Asian pear."

1D.   **Gěi tiāo** is here short for **nǐ gěi wǒ tiāo** "you choose for me."

1E.   Never split a pear with someone else, especially someone you care for, as the expression **fēn lí** "divide a pear" sounds exactly the same as **fēnlí** "separate (of people)."

2.   In the video, the speaker says **Yào yíkuài qián yìjīnde háishi yào yíkuài wǔ yìjīnde?** "Do you want the one yuan per catty ones or the 1.50 per catty ones?" In the audio recording, the speaker leaves out the word **qián**. Either way of saying this is correct.

4A.   **BǏ FOLLOWED BY STATIVE VERB + -DE DUŌ.** You already learned in 10-4: 8B that the coverb **bǐ** is used to express unequal comparison, as in:

> **Zhèige bǐ nèige dà.**   This one is bigger than that one."

Now we'll learn how to form sentences such as "This one is much bigger than that one." This is said by beginning with a basic **bǐ** sentence and then adding **-de duō** after the stative verb at the end of the sentence. The pattern is:

TOPIC	BǏ	OBJECT	STATIVE VERB	-DE DUŌ
Zhèige	bǐ	nèige	hǎo	de duō.

"This one is much better than that one."

More examples of **bǐ** followed by STATIVE VERB + **-de duō**:

> **Zhèizhǒng běnzi bǐ nèizhǒng běnzi piányide duō.**
> "This kind of notebook is much cheaper than that kind of notebook."

> **Zhèizhǒng píngguǒ bǐ nèizhǒng píngguǒ hǎochīde duō.**
> "This kind of apple tastes much better than that kind of apple."

If the stative verb of the sentence is itself **duō**, then it's quite possible to have the combination **duōde duō**. For example:

Zhèige dàxuéde xuésheng bǐ nèige dàxuéde xuésheng duōde duō.

"There are many more students at this college than at that college."

We encourage you to use the pattern with **-de duō**, but you should be able to understand two related patterns that are used by some speakers. One uses the pattern STATIVE VERB + **duōle**, while the other uses the pattern STATIVE VERB + **hěn duō** or STATIVE VERB + **hǎo duō**. Compare the following four sentences, all of which mean "This kind is much more expensive than that kind":

With **-de duō**:   **Zhèizhǒng bǐ nèizhǒng guìde duō.**
With **duōle**:   **Zhèizhǒng bǐ nèizhǒng guì duōle.**
With **hěn duō**:   **Zhèizhǒng bǐ nèizhǒng guì hěn duō.**
With **hǎo duō**:   **Zhèizhǒng bǐ nèizhǒng guì hǎo duō.**

Fruit market on Yong'an Road in Beijing

7.   Notice in this utterance how **lái** (lit. "come") is used as a kind of "dummy verb" that substitutes for a more specific verb. Here **lái** means "have something come" or "bring." The sentence **Nín gěi wǒ lái liǎngjīn ba** literally means something like "Why don't you have two catties come for me?" or, in better English, "Bring me two catties" or "Give me two catties." **Lái** can substitute for many different verbs; depending on the context, it can be translated as "bring," "give," "have," "do," etc. **Lái** can be used this way when purchasing items in stores, ordering dishes or beverages in restaurants, making musical selections, etc. Some more examples of this use of **lái**:

Xiān lái yidianr chá.   "Bring some tea first."
Xiàmian lái ge "tango," zěmmeyàng?   "Next let's have a tango, how about it?"
Wǒ bú huì, nǐ lái ba!   "I can't, you do it!"

10.   It's customary to check one's change carefully immediately upon receiving it.

SV2.   Contrast the pronunciations of **píngguǒ** "apple" and **bīnggùn(r)** "ice pop"!

SV3.   **Júzi** technically means "tangerine," but in everyday conversation it's the equivalent of English "orange." Watch the pronunciation of this word and distinguish it carefully from **zhúzi** "bamboo"!

SV8–10.   In lesson 11-3, you had already learned **kàndào** "see." So now you have learned these four very common resultative compounds:

tīngdào   "hear"
kàndào   "see"
tīngjian   "hear"
kànjian   "see"

The meanings of the verbs ending in the resultative ending **-dào** are the same as those ending in the resultative ending **-jiàn**, but the ones with **-dào** are slightly more common in Taiwan and southern mainland China while the ones with **-jiàn** are slightly more common in northern China.

Also, note the difference between **kàn** and **kànjian/kàndào**, on the one hand; and between **tīng** and **tīngjian/tīngdào**, on the other. **Kàn** "look" and **tīng** "listen" refer only to the simple actions of "looking" and "listening"; but when **-jiàn** or **-dào** are added as resultative complements, they indicate that something has been "seen" or "heard." So you could say, for example:

Wǒ kànle, kěshi méi kànjian.   "I looked, but I didn't see it."

AV1–12.   **FRUITS.** The names of these fruits are arranged in alphabetical order of the English equivalents.

Unit 12: Review and Study Guide

New Vocabulary

ADVERBS

cái	not until, just
zŏnggòng	in all

ATTRIBUTIVES

Hàn-Yīng	Chinese-English

CONJUNCTIONS

háishi	or

IDIOMATIC EXPRESSIONS

duō xiè	"many thanks"

MEASURES

bĕn(r)	(for books, dictionaries)
fèn(r)	(for newspapers, magazines)
gēn(r)	(for long, thin things)
jīn	catty (500 grams)
xiē	some
yàng(r)	kind, variety
zhī	(for pens, pencils)
zhŏng	kind

NOUNS

báicài	cabbage
bàotíng	newspaper kiosk
bàozhĭ	newspaper
bĕnzi	notebook
bĭ	writing instrument
bīng	ice
bīnggùn(r)	ice pop
cài	vegetable
càichăng	market
chūkŏu	export
dìtú	map
fānqié	tomato
jìnkŏu	import
júzi	orange

lí(r)	pear
năiyóu	cream
píngguŏ	apple
pútao	grape
qiānbĭ	pencil
qíncài	celery
qīngcài	green vegetable
shālā	salad
shālācài	lettuce
shì	city, municipality
shū	book
shūcài	vegetable
shuĭguŏ	fruit
táozi	peach
xì	department
xiāngjiāo	banana
xiăodòu	red bean
Yālí(r)	Ya pear
yuánzhūbĭ	ball-point pen
zázhì	magazine
zhĭ	paper
zhuānyè	major, specialization
zhŭxiū	major
zìdiăn	dictionary

PATTERNS

zĕmme zhèmme...	how come so...

PLACE WORDS

gébì	next door
Lí Shān	"Pear Mountain," Li Shan
shūdiàn	book store

RESULTATIVE COMPOUNDS

bāoqilai	wrap up

kànjian	see
náhăo	hold well, hold firmly
tīngdào	hear
tīngjian	hear

RESULTATIVE ENDINGS

-hăo	so that something is good
-jiàn	see, perceive
-qĭlái	(general resultative ending)

SPECIFIER + MEASURE

zhèxiē	these

STATIVE VERBS

cuì	be crisp
piàoliang	be pretty, look nice
qióng	be poor
xīnxiān	be fresh
yŏuqián	be rich

VERBS

bāo	wrap
băozhèng	guarantee
chūkŏu	export
diăn	count, check
dú	read aloud; study
jìnkŏu	import
lái	bring, give
ná	hold, take
shì	try
tiāo	pick out, select
yāo	weigh out
zhŭxiū	major in

VERB-OBJECT COMPOUNDS

dúshū	study
niànshū	study

Major New Grammar Patterns

A HÁISHI B IN QUESTIONS: Nĭ yào qù Bĕijīng háishi Táibĕi? "Do you want to go to Beijing or to Taipei?" **(12-1)**

A HUÒSHI B IN STATEMENTS: Wŏ yào qù Bĕijīng huòshi Tiānjīn. "I want to go to Beijing or Tianjin." **(12-1)**

AMOUNT OF MONEY PER ITEM: wŭmáo qián yìgēnr "fifty cents apiece (for ice pops)." **(12-1)**

MEASURES: yìzhŏng yuánzhūbĭ "a kind of ball-point pen," **zhèizhī qiānbĭ** "this pencil," **nèibĕn shū** "that book," **wŭfèn bàozhĭ** "five newspapers," **nĕizhāng dìtú** "which map?", etc. **(12-2)**

CÁI: Zhè shi jīntiān cái dàode. "This arrived only today (and not before then)." **(12-3)**

ZĔMME ZHÈMME...: Fānqié zĕmme zhèmme guì a? "How come tomatoes are so expensive?" **(12-3)**

BĬ FOLLOWED BY STATIVE VERB + -DE DUŌ: Zhèizhŏng bĕnzi bĭ nèizhŏng bĕnzi piányide duō. "This kind of notebook is much cheaper than that kind of notebook." **(12-4)**

Shopping (II)

COMMUNICATIVE OBJECTIVES

Once you've mastered this unit, you'll be able to use Chinese to:

1. Buy meat at a traditional market.
2. Go shopping in a supermarket.
3. Purchase shoes in a shoe store.
4. Buy pants in a clothing store.
5. Discuss clothing and shoe sizes: one size bigger, etc.
6. Inquire whether you can exchange something if it doesn't fit.
7. Request a better price and discuss discounts.
8. Ask if you may use a credit card to pay for your purchases or if you must pay cash.
9. Express similarity and dissimilarity: "Are shoe sizes in Taiwan the same or different from those in the U.S.?"
10. Emphasize your main point while conceding minor points: "It's pretty, all right, it's just too expensive!"
11. Talk about different kinds of stores and establishments.
12. Discuss different varieties of meat, seafood, and other food products.
13. Talk about various articles of apparel, footwear, and accessories.

Buying Meat at a Traditional Market

Cindy Han, an American student in Beijing, has agreed to cook an American-style meal for her Chinese friends. She goes shopping for meat at a traditional Beijing market.

Basic Conversation 13-1

1. HAN	**Qǐng nín gěi wǒ chēng shíkuài qiánde zhūròu.** Please weigh out ¥10 worth of pork for me.
2. MEAT SELLER	**M.** Uh-huh.
3. HAN	*(points to a piece of pork)* **Nèibianrde shòu yidianr, nín gěi wǒ qiē nèibianrde ba.** That over there is leaner, why don't you cut that over there for me.
4. MEAT SELLER	**Qíshí dōu chàbuduō.** Actually, it's all about the same.
	(after she has cut the pork) **Hái yào biéde ma?** Do you want anything else?
5. HAN	**Bú yàole, jiù zhèixiē ba. Gěi nín qián.** No, just this, I suppose. Here's the money.
	(after she has paid) **Ò, láojià, nǎr mài miànbāo?** Oh, excuse me, where do they sell bread?
6. MEAT SELLER	**Miànbāo diàn, shípǐn diàn dōu mài.** Bakeries and grocery stores both sell it.
7. HAN	**Yuǎn bu yuǎn?** Are they far away?
8. MEAT SELLER	**Jìnjíle, yìdiǎnr yě bù yuǎn. Jiù zài pángbiānrde hútòngrli.** They're very close, not far at all. They're right in the next alley.
9. HAN	**Xièxie.** Thanks.

Build Up

1. Han

chēng	weigh, weigh out [V]
qǐng nín gěi wǒ chēng	please you weigh out for me
zhū	pig [N] (M: **zhī**)
ròu	meat [N]
zhūròu	pork [N]
shíkuài qiánde zhūròu	ten dollars' worth of pork
Qǐng nín gěi wǒ chēng shíkuài qiánde zhūròu.	Please weigh out ¥10 worth of pork for me.

2. Meat seller

M.	Uh-huh.

3. Han

qiē	cut, slice [V]
nín gěi wǒ qiē	you cut for me
Nèibianrde shòu yidianr,	That over there is leaner,
nín gěi wǒ qiē nèibianrde ba.	why don't you cut that over there for me.

4. Meat seller

chàbuduō	be about the same [PH]
Qíshí dōu chàbuduō.	Actually, it's all about the same.
Hái yào biéde ma?	Do you want anything else?

5. Han

Bú yàole, jiù zhèixiē ba. Gěi nín qián.	No, just this, I suppose. Here's the money.
miànbāo	bread [N] (M: **tiáo** "loaf")
nǎr mài miànbāo	where is bread sold
Ò, láojià, nǎr mài miànbāo?	Oh, excuse me, where do they sell bread?

6. Meat seller

miànbāo diàn	bakery [PH]
shípǐn	food product; groceries [N]
shípǐn diàn	grocery store [PH]
Miànbāo diàn, shípǐn diàn dōu mài.	Bakeries and grocery stores both sell it.

7. Han

Yuǎn bu yuǎn?	Are they far away?

8. Meat seller

-jíle	extremely [PT]
jìnjíle	extremely close
yìdiǎn(r) yě bù...	not at all, not the least bit [PT]
yìdiǎnr yě bù yuǎn	not at all far
hútòng(r) (B)	small street, lane, alley [N]
pángbiānrde hútòngrli	in the next alley
Jìnjíle, yìdiǎnr yě bù yuǎn.	They're very close, not far at all.
Jiù zài pángbiānrde hútòngrli.	They're right in the next alley.

9. Han

Xièxie.	Thanks.

Supplementary Vocabulary

1. jī	chicken [N] (M: **zhī**)
jīròu	chicken meat [N]
niú	cow, ox [N] (M: **tóu**)
niúròu	beef [N]
Nǐ xiǎng chī niúròu háishi jīròu?	Would you like to eat beef or chicken?
2. yáng	sheep [N] (M: **zhī**)
yángròu	mutton [N]
Běifāng rén ài chī yángròu.	Northerners like to eat mutton.
3. yāzi	duck [N] (M: **zhī**)
Tā yǎngle jǐbǎizhī yāzi.	He raised several hundred ducks.
4. yāròu	duck meat [N]
féi	be fatty (of food) [SV]
Yāròu hǎochī, kěshi tài féile.	Duck meat tastes good, but it's too fatty.
5. xiā	shrimp [N] (M: **zhī**)
Tā bù néng chī yú, xiā.	She can't eat fish and shrimp.
6. chīsù	eat vegetarian food [VO]
Wǒ bù chī ròu, wǒ chīsù.	I don't eat meat; I'm a vegetarian.
7. fùjìn	in the vicinity, nearby [PW]
Fùjìn yǒu shípǐn diàn ma?	Is there a grocery store nearby?

Grammatical and Cultural Notes

1. **Shíkuài qiánde zhūròu** literally means "ten dollars of pork." In good English, we would have to add the words "worth of," i.e., "ten dollars' worth of pork." Another example of a quantity expression followed by **-de** which modifies a noun is **Tā xuéle sānniánde Zhōngwén** "She studied three years of Chinese."

4. The adverb **qíshí** "actually" can be useful for making smooth revisions or corrections of what another speaker—or even the speaker herself or himself—has said previously.

5. Note the use of **nǎr** in the question **Nǎr mài miànbāo?** "Where (do they) sell bread?" or "Where is bread sold?"

8A. **-JÍLE AS A VERB SUFFIX TO EXPRESS "EXTREMELY."** Especially in Northern Mandarin, the suffix **-jíle** is often attached to stative verbs to indicate "extremely." This suffix is most commonly attached to one-syllable stative verbs like **hǎo** "be good" and **màn** "be slow," but it may also be attached to two-syllable stative verbs like **hǎochī** "be good to eat" and **hǎokàn** "be attractive." The basic pattern is:

SUBJECT	STATIVE VERB	-JÍLE
Miànbāo diàn	**jìn**	**-jíle.**

"The bakery is extremely close."

More examples:

Hǎojíle!	"Great!"
Nèige rén huàijíle!	"That person is very bad!"
Wǒ zuìjìn mángjíle.	"Recently, I've been extremely busy."
Kǎoshì nánjíle.	"The test was extremely difficult."

Hǎochījíle!	"It's delicious!"
Hǎokànjíle!	"It's beautiful!"
Tā gāoxìngjíle.	"She was extremely happy."

The suffix **-jíle** is sometimes also used with regular verbs, for example, with **xǐhuan** as in **Wǒ xǐhuanjíle** "I like it extremely much," but you can't make up these constructions at will; say only what you've heard a native speaker use. And if you use **-jíle**, don't use **hěn** or **fēicháng**. Also, **-jíle** is usually not negated with **bù** (so you could NOT say **bù hǎokànjíle). In Taiwan and southern mainland China, the forms with **-jíle** are understood but aren't as common as in North China.

8B.   YÌDIǍN(R) YĚ BÙ... AND YÌDIǍN(R) YĚ MÉI.... The very common structure **yìdiǎn(r) yě bù** literally means "a little bit also not," i.e., "not even by a little" or in good English "not the least bit" or "not at all." It may be followed by stative verbs, auxiliary verbs, and other kinds of verbs. The basic pattern is:

YÌDIǍN(R)	YĚ	BÙ	SV/AV/V
Yìdiǎnr	yě	bù	yuǎn.

"It's not far at all."

Some more examples:

Wǒ yìdiǎn(r) yě bú lèi.	"I'm not at all tired."
Wǒ yìdiǎn(r) yě bú huì xiǎng tā.	"I don't miss him in the least."
Wǒ yìdiǎn(r) yě bù xǐhuan tā.	"I don't like her at all."

In this pattern, the adverb **dōu** can always be substituted for the **yě**. Examples with **yìdiǎn(r) dōu bù**:

Wǒ juéde Zhōngwén yìdiǎnr dōu bù nán.	"I feel that Chinese isn't at all difficult."
Zhèrde dōngxi yìdiǎn dōu bú guì.	"The things here aren't at all expensive."

If the verb is **méiyou** "not have, there is/aren't," then **méiyou** is used instead of **bù**. A preposed object may be added between the **yìdiǎn(r)** and the **yě** or **dōu**. Examples:

Wǒ yìdiǎn qián yě méiyou.	"I don't have any money at all."
Wǒ yìdiǎn yě méiyou.	"I don't have any at all."

Similarly, in the case of negative completed action, **méi(you)** is used instead of **bù**. Examples:

Wǒ gěi tā zuòde fàn, tā yìdiǎnr dōu méi chī.	"She didn't eat any of the food I made for her."
Tā yìdiǎn yě méiyou biàn.	"He hasn't changed at all."

Remember that this pattern can be used only in the negative, as in **Rìwén, wǒ yìdiǎnr yě bú huì** "I don't know any Japanese at all." You could NEVER say a sentence like **Rìwén, wǒ yìdiǎnr yě huì. If you intend to say "I know a little Japanese," you should say **Wǒ huì yìdiǎnr Rìwén**.

8C.   THE HÚTÒNG OF BEIJING. The noun **hútòng(r)** refers to the characteristic small and narrow streets, lanes, or alleys that used to be very common in traditional Beijing. In other parts of mainland China and Taiwan, the word **xiàngzi** "lane" that you learned in 11-3 would usually be used instead of **hútòng(r)**. In old Beijing, series of traditional courtyard residences with tiled roofs, called **sìhéyuànr**, were typically joined one to the next, thus creating the **hútòng**. **Hútòng** have existed in Beijing since the Yuan Dynasty (1271–1368). At their high point, they numbered over 6,000. Since the People's Republic of China was founded in 1949, large numbers of **hútòng** have been demolished to make way for roads and more modern structures. In recent years, attempts have been made to preserve some of the **hútòng** for posterity. Tours of Beijing's **hútòng** are available and quite popular with foreign students and tourists.

SV1–5.   In China, if the word **ròu** is used alone, it usually refers to pork, the favorite meat of the Han Chinese people. If there is a need to specify the kind of meat, this can be added before the word **ròu**, e.g., **niúròu** "beef," **yángròu** "mutton," and **zhūròu** "pork." What do you think would be the meaning of **gǒuròu**?

SV1A.   As with English "chicken," the Chinese noun **jī** can refer either to the animal or to its flesh, so to say "I want to eat chicken" it's possible to say either **Wǒ yào chī jī** or **Wǒ yào chī jīròu**. On the other hand, **niú** "cow" refers only to the animal, so to say "I want to eat beef" you must say **Wǒ yào chī niúròu**.

SV1B.   Be sure to pronounce the **niú** of **niúròu** "beef" accurately, being careful to distinguish the syllable **niú** from the very different syllable **nǚ** as in **nǚde** "woman, female."

SV4.   The stative verb **féi** means "be fatty" when referring to food. To say that a person or an animal is "fat," use the stative verb **pàng** that you learned in 5-3. On the other hand, the stative verb **shòu** "be thin, lean" that you also learned in 5-3 can refer to people, animals, or foods.

SV5.   Be careful to distinguish the pronunciation of **xiā** "shrimp" from that of **sha** "sand, gravel" (10-2).

Stand selling fish at Hong Kong outdoor market

In a Supermarket

Holly Young, an American college student, is studying Chinese and teaching English in Taipei. She shares an apartment with a young Taiwanese woman by the name of Su Ning. One morning, Su asks Young if she would like to go shopping with her at the neighborhood supermarket. Young agrees, and the two young women go shopping together.

Basic Conversation 13-2

1. SU   **Holly, wǒ yào qù chāoshì mǎi diǎn dōngxi. Nǐ yào bu yào hàn wǒ yìqǐ qù?**
   Holly, I'm going to the supermarket to buy some stuff. Do you want to go together with me?

2. YOUNG   **Hǎo a. Wǒ yě zhèng xiǎng mǎi diǎn kāfēi, tǔsī shemmede.**
   Sure. I was just thinking of buying some coffee, white bread, and so forth.

   (after they arrive at the supermarket)

3. SU   **Zhèiyang hǎole. Wèile jiéshěng shíjiān, nǐ mǎi nǐde, wǒ mǎi wǒde. Wǒmen wǔfēn zhōng yǐhòu zài chūkǒude guìtái jiàn, zěmmeyàng?**
   How about this? To save time, you buy your things and I'll buy mine. In five minutes we'll meet at the counter by the exit. How about it?

4. YOUNG   **Hǎo zhǔyì!**
   Good idea!

   (after they've finished shopping)

5. SU   **Nǐ juéde Táiwān gēn Měiguode chāoshì bíqilai zěmmeyàng?**
   How do you feel supermarkets in Taiwan compare with those in America?

6. YOUNG   **Dōu chàbuduō. Dàgài bǐ Měiguode xiǎo yìdiǎn, yě bú xiàng zài Měiguo nèmme pǔbiàn.**
   About the same. Probably a bit smaller than in America, and not so widespread as in America.

7. SU   **Kěnéng yào mànmān lái ba. Wǒ xiǎng yǐhòu huì yìnián bǐ yìnián pǔbiànde.**
   All in its own good time. I think in the future they'll become more widespread each year.

Build Up

1. **Su**
   chāoshì   supermarket [N] (M: **jiā**)

wǒ yào qù chāoshì	I want to go to the supermarket
hàn (T)	with [CV]
hàn wǒ yìqǐ qù	go together with me
Holly, wǒ yào qù chāoshì mǎi diǎn dōngxi.	Holly, I'm going to the supermarket to buy some
Nǐ yào bu yào hàn wǒ yìqǐ qù?	stuff. Do you want to go together with me?

2. Young

kāfēi	coffee [N]
tǔsī	white bread [N] (M: **tiáo** "loaf")
...shemmede	...and so on [PT]
kāfēi, tǔsī shemmede	coffee, white bread, and so on
Hǎo a. Wǒ yě zhèng xiǎng mǎi diǎn	Sure. I was just thinking of buying some
kāfēi, tǔsī shemmede.	coffee, white bread, and so forth.

3. Su

zhèiyang hǎole	this way it will be good
wèile...	in order to..., for... [PT]
jiéshěng	save [V]
wèile jiéshěng shíjiān	in order to save time
nǐ mǎi nǐde	you buy yours
wǒ mǎi wǒde	I buy mine
chūkǒu(r)	exit [PW]
guìtái	counter [N]
zài chūkǒude guìtái	at the counter by the exit
zài chūkǒude guìtái jiàn	see each other at the counter by the exit
Zhèiyang hǎole. Wèile jiéshěng shíjiān, nǐ mǎi	How about this? To save time, you buy your
nǐde, wǒ mǎi wǒde. Wǒmen wǔfēn zhōng yǐhòu	things and I'll buy mine. In five minutes we'll
zài chūkǒude guìtái jiàn, zěmmeyàng?	meet at the counter by the exit. How about it?

4. Young

zhǔyì	idea, plan [N]
Hǎo zhǔyì!	Good idea!

5. Su

bíqilai	compare [RC]
A gēn B bǐqǐlái	comparing A and B [PT]
Táiwān gēn Měiguode chāoshì bíqilai	Taiwan compared with America's supermarkets
Nǐ juéde Táiwān gēn Měiguode	How do you feel supermarkets in Taiwan
chāoshì bíqilai zěmmeyàng?	compare with those in America?

6. Young

xiàng	resemble, be like [V]
bú xiàng zài Měiguo	not like America
pǔbiàn	be widespread, common [SV]
nèmme pǔbiàn	so common
bú xiàng zài Měiguo nèmme pǔbiàn	not so common as in America
Dōu chàbuduō. Dàgài bǐ Měiguode xiǎo yìdiǎn,	About the same. Probably a bit smaller than in
yě bú xiàng zài Měiguo nèmme pǔbiàn.	America, and not so widespread as in America.

7. Su

mànmān	slowly
mànmān lái	"take one's time" [IE]
kěnéng yào mànmān lái	it's possible it needs to take its time
yìnián bǐ yìnián	one year compared with the next
huì...-de	be likely to, would, will [PT]
huì yìnián bǐ yìnián pǔbiànde	be likely to become more common each year

Kěnéng yào mànmàn lái ba. Wǒ xiǎng yǐhòu huì yìnián bǐ yìnián pǔbiànde.

All in its own good time. I think in the future they'll become more widespread each year.

Supplementary Vocabulary

1. **rùkǒu(r)**
Zhèr shi chūkǒu, bú shi rùkǒu!

entrance [PW]
This here is the exit, not the entrance!

2. **jiéshěng**
Tāmen jiā tèbié jiéshěng.

be frugal [SV]
Their family is particularly frugal.

Additional Vocabulary

1. **Yìfēn qián, yìfēn huò.**

"You get what you pay for." [EX]

Grammatical and Cultural Notes

1A. The noun **chāoshì** "supermarket" is an abbreviated form of **chāojí shìchǎng**, which quite literally means "super market." You can say either the short or the long form.

1B. The coverb **hé** "with," to which you were introduced in 7-1, is pronounced by many Taiwan speakers as **hàn**. Interestingly, the pronunciation **hàn** is originally from the Beijing area and was made official in several early twentieth century dictionaries. It was brought to Taiwan in 1945 by the Nationalist Chinese government after they recovered Taiwan from the Japanese and has been taught there ever since. Later, the more common pronunciation **hé** was made official on the mainland. We recommend you say **hé**, which will be understood in Taiwan also, but you should be prepared to understand **hàn** when you hear it.

1C. The pattern **hàn...yìqǐ** "together with..." is a useful pattern for expressing togetherness. **Hàn...yìqǐ** is a synonym of **hé...yìqǐ** and **gēn...yìqǐ**, which were introduced in 7-3: 4C. Example:

Wǒ hàn nǐ yìqǐ qù.   "I'll go together with you."

2A. **FOREIGN BORROWINGS IN CHINESE.** In this utterance, the nouns **kāfēi** "coffee" and **tǔsī** "white bread" are borrowings from English. **Tǔsī** was borrowed from the English word "toast," but in Chinese it refers to the kind of white bread that can be used for making toast, regardless of whether it has or hasn't been toasted, which demonstrates that sometimes the meaning of a loanword in the borrowing language can be different from in the source language. Now, all languages are subject to the influence of other languages with which their speakers come into contact. English, for example, has borrowed huge numbers of expressions from French, Latin, and many other languages, including Chinese. Did you know that the English words "gung ho," "ketchup," and "tea," among others, are all borrowings from Chinese? In the

> Did you know that the English words "gung ho," "ketchup," and "tea," among others, are all borrowings from Chinese?

past, Chinese borrowed many terms from Sanskrit, Mongolian, Manchu, and several Central Asian languages. Then in the nineteenth century, Chinese borrowed large numbers of words from Japanese (which had created them out of Chinese characters to translate various Western terms), for example, words like **kēxué** "science," **jīngjì** "economics," and **shèhuì** "society." Since the beginning of large-scale contact with the West in the nineteenth century, Chinese—which for many centuries flooded the vocabularies of Japanese, Korean, and Vietnamese—has been directly influenced by European languages, especially English. Most foreign borrowings in Chinese are nouns, of which many are cultural borrowings; with the foreign concept or item came the name. Two common types of borrowings are loanwords and loan translations. Loanwords are words borrowed directly into another language, with the foreign phonetic material adapted to the borrowing language's sound system. **Kāfēi**, **shālā**, and **tǔsī** are all examples of loanwords. On the other hand, loan translations are words consisting of translations of the meaning of foreign words. **Diànhuà** "telephone" (lit. "electric speech"), **diànnǎo** "computer" (lit. "electric brain"), and **huǒchē** "train" (lit. "fire vehicle") are all examples of loan translations. There are even borrowings that are half loanword and half loan translation, for example, **mótuōchē** "motorcycle." Traditionally, Chinese has adopted many more loan translations than loanwords. While there continue to be new borrowings from English entering standard Chinese, since the 1990s there have also been many new terms borrowed from the Chinese used in Hong Kong and Taiwan.

2B.   **...SHEMMEDE.** The very common pattern **...shemmede** "and so on," "and so forth" is attached to the end of a series of two or more nouns (or occasionally other word classes) when you wish to indicate that there exist more members of the same series but don't want to list them all. The pattern is:

SERIES OF NOUNS	SHEMMEDE
kāfēi, tǔsī	**shemmede**
"coffee, white bread, and so on"	

More examples:

> **Tā mǎile zìdiǎn, bàozhǐ, dìtú shemmede.**
>
> "She bought dictionaries, newspapers, maps, and so on."

> **Wǒ xūyào báicài, qíncài, fānqié shemmede.**
>
> "I need cabbage, celery, tomatoes, and so forth."

> **Wǒmen jīntiān yào chīfàn, mǎi dōngxi, kàn wǒ biǎojiě shemmede.**
>
> "Today we're going for a meal, going shopping, visiting an aunt of mine and so forth."

3A.   **Zhèiyang hǎole** "This way it will be good" or "(If it's) like this (then it will be) all right" is an example of the pattern **...hǎole**, which was introduced in 2-2: 6D. The sentence **Zhèiyang hǎole** is often used as a discourse marker and conversation management device to make a proposal to others. It indicates that the speaker has just come up with an idea for how to do something or how to solve a certain problem.

3B.   **WÈILE TO EXPRESS PURPOSE.** One way to express purpose is with the coverb expression **wèile** "in order to, so as to, to, for." The pattern is:

WÈILE	PURPOSE CLAUSE	MAIN CLAUSE
Wèile	**jiéshěng shíjiān,**	**nǐ mǎi nǐde, wǒ mǎi wǒde.**
"In order to save time, you buy your things, and I'll buy my things."		

Some more examples with **wèile** to express purpose:

> **Wèile jiéshěng qián, tāmen juédìng bù chī zǎofàn le.**
>
> "So as to save money, they decided not to eat breakfast."

> **Wèile zhǎo tā zuì xǐhuan hēde kāfēi, tā wènle hǎojǐjiā kāfēi diàn.**
>
> "In order to find the coffee he liked to drink most, he asked at quite a few coffee shops."

> **Wèile néng mǎidào piào, tā yídàzǎo jiù qù páiduì le.**
>
> "To be able to buy a ticket, she went to stand in line very early in the morning."

> **Wèile zǎo yidianr dào Shànghǎi, tā juédìng gǎizuò fēijī qu, bú zuò huǒchē le.**
> "To get to Shanghai earlier, he decided to change to a plane and not take the train."

> **Wèile xué zuì biāozhǔnde Zhōngwén, tā bāndao Běijīng qule.**
> "To learn the most standard Chinese, she moved to Beijing."

If the subject or topic of the purpose clause is the same as that of the main clause, then the subject or topic can precede the **wèile**. For example, the last example above could be said with exactly the same meaning as:

> **Tā wèile xué zuì biāozhǔnde Zhōngwén, bāndao Běijīng qule.**

It's also possible for the main clause to come first and for the purpose clause with **wèile** to come at the end of the sentence, but in that case it's necessary to add a **shi** before **wèile**. Example:

> **Tā bāndao Běijīng qu shi wèile xué zuì biāozhǔnde Zhōngwén.**

3. In 12-3 you learned **chūkǒu** in the sense of "export." Now in this line you learn another meaning of this word, namely, "exit."

4. **Hǎo zhǔyì** is a common comment about someone else's suggestion or plan. The meaning is "That's a good idea" or "That's a good plan." In local Beijing dialect, **zhǔyì** is often pronounced **zhúyi**. Here are some more examples with **zhǔyì**:

> **Tā yòu gǎile zhǔyì le.**   "She changed her mind again."
> **Nǐ chū ge zhǔyì ba.**   "Why don't you come up with a plan."

5. **A GĒN B BǏQǏLÁI.** In this line, look at the question **Táiwān gēn Měiguode chāoshì bíqilai zěmmeyàng?** "How do supermarkets in Taiwan compare with those in America?" (lit. "Taiwan compared with America's supermarkets how is it?") This question is actually an abbreviation of a fuller form **Táiwānde chāoshì gēn Měiguode chāoshì bíqilai zěmmeyàng?** "Taiwan's supermarkets compared with America's supermarkets how are they?" The pattern **A gēn B bǐqǐlái** "comparing A and B" is used to compare two items with each other. Some sort of a comment or, as here, question then follows. **Bǐqǐlái** is the pronunciation with full tones on each syllable, but in normal conversation the word is usually pronounced **bíqilai**. The basic pattern is:

A	GĒN	B	BǏQǏLÁI	COMMENT

> **Zhèrde gēn nàrde bíqilai zěmmeyàng?**
> "How do the ones here compare with the ones there?"

Another example of this pattern:

> **Nǐ juéde Běijīngde tiānqi gēn Huáshèngdùnde tiānqi bíqilai zěmmeyàng?**
> "What do you think of Beijing's weather compared to Washington's weather?"

There is a related pattern, **A gēn B bǐjiàoqǐlái**, that has the same meaning and is used in the same way as **A gēn B bǐqǐlái**.

6A. **XIÀNG.** The verb **xiàng** means "resemble, be like." The sentence **Táiwānde chāoshì bú xiàng zài Měiguo nèmme pǔbiàn** literally means "Taiwan's supermarkets aren't like in America that common," or in better English, "In Taiwan supermarkets aren't as common as in America." Here are some more examples of **xiàng**:

> **Wǒ juéde nǐ hěn xiàng nǐ bàba.**
> "I feel you greatly resemble your father."

Tā shi Zhōngguo rén, kěshi tā bǐ Měiguo rén gèng xiàng Měiguo rén.

"He's Chinese, but he's even more like Americans than Americans."

Xiàng zuótiān nèiyàngrde shì, suīrán kěxī, dànshi yě hěn nán bìmiǎn.

"Like that kind of matter yesterday, though it's a pity, it's also very hard to avoid."

Tā zhǐ huì shuō jǐjù jiǎndānde Zhōngguo huà, xiàng "nǐ hǎo," "xièxie," "zàijiàn."

"He can say only a few simple things in Chinese, like 'how are you,' 'thank you,' and 'goodbye.'"

In 10-4: 8D we learned the pattern **A méiyou B nèmme C** "A is not as C as B" as the negative of the **bǐ** construction, for example:

QUESTION:	**Zhèige bǐ nèige hǎo ma?**	"Is this one better than that one?"
NEGATIVE REPLY:	**Zhèige méiyou nèige nèmme hǎo.**	"This one isn't as good as that one."

Now that you have learned **xiàng** "resemble, be like," you should be aware that the pattern **A bú xiàng B nèmme C** is a synonym of **A méiyou B nèmme C** as the negative of the **bǐ** construction. So for the negative reply above, the speaker could just as well have replied:

NEGATIVE REPLY: **Zhèige bú xiàng nèige nèmme hǎo.**

"This one isn't as good as that one."

6B.   In the video, both speakers pronounce **pǔbiàn** in lines 6 and 7 as **pǔpiàn**, which is a common alternate pronunciation.

7A.   In the sentence **Kěnéng yào mànmān lái ba**, the auxiliary verb **yào** means "need to, should," so the whole sentence means "It's possible it needs to come slowly" or "It's possible it needs to take its time." Depending on the context, **yào** can have a wide range of meanings including "want," "want to," "cost," "take," "be going to," "will," "request," "need to," and "should."

7B.   Note the form **mànmān** "slowly." This derives from the stative verb **màn** "to be slow," which has here been reduplicated to become an adverb; note the change to Tone One in the second syllable. Beijing speakers may add an **(r)** suffix and say **mànmānr**, while other speakers may say both syllables with Tone Four as **mànmàn**. All these forms are correct. For now, just learn the idiomatic expression **mànmān lái** "take one's time." There is more information on reduplicated stative verbs as adverbs in 19-2: 2B.

7C.   **HUÌ...-DE.** The pattern **huì...-de**, which is usually translated as "be likely to, would, will," expresses a speaker's conviction that something will most likely be a certain way. The **huì** and the **-de** surround the predicate of the sentence. The basic pattern is:

SUBJECT	HUÌ	PREDICATE	-DE
Táiwānde chāoshì	**huì**	**yìnián bǐ yìnián pǔbiàn**	**de.**

"Taiwan's supermarkets will become more widespread each year."

The **huì...-de** pattern is especially common in Southern Mandarin, including the Mandarin of Taiwan. Of course, **huì** can also be used alone with basically the same meaning, but the addition of a final **-de** lends additional assurance or assertion to the statement. Some more examples:

Xiǎo Liú huì láide.	"Little Liu will come."
Xiǎo Zhào bú huì láide.	"Little Zhao isn't likely to come."
Dōngxi yídìng huì zhǎodàode.	"I'm sure the stuff will be found."
Tā yídìng huì shēngqìde.	"He'll definitely get angry."

Tā huì hěn bù gāoxìngde.	"She'll be very upset."
Wǒ bú huì gàosu tāde.	"I won't tell her."
Kuài zǒu ba, bùrán nǐ huì chídàode.	"Leave quickly, otherwise you're likely to arrive late."

Wǒ xiǎng zhèrde dōngxi yǐhòu huì yuè lái yuè guìde.

"I think things here will in the future become more and more expensive."

7D.   **YĪ + MEASURE + BǏ + YĪ + MEASURE.** In this line, look at the sentence **Wǒ xiǎng yǐhòu huì yìnián bǐ yìnián pǔbiànde** "I think in the future they're likely to become more widespread each year." The meaning of the pattern **yī** + MEASURE + **bǐ** + **yī** + MEASURE is "(measure) by (measure)" or "one (measure) at a time." The pattern is:

YĪ	MEASURE	BǏ	YĪ	MEASURE
yì	nián	bǐ	yì	nián

"year by year"

More examples of the pattern **yī** + MEASURE + **bǐ** + **yī** + MEASURE:

Měiguode shū yìnián bǐ yìnián guì.

"Books in America are getting more expensive year by year."

Nǐde Zhōngwén yìtiān bǐ yìtiān hǎo!

"Your Chinese is getting better day by day!"

Zhèixiē dìtú, yìzhāng bǐ yìzhāng piàoliang.

"These maps, one is more attractive than the next."

SV1.   **STRESS.** Examine the sentence **Zhèr shì CHŪkǒu, bú shì rùkǒu!** "This here is the exit, not the entrance!" To emphasize that this is the exit rather than the entrance, the syllable **chū** of **chūkǒu** "exit" is stressed. You should be aware that in speaking Chinese, not only initials, finals, and tones are important but also other factors such as stress and intonation. The discussion of stress below is for your future reference; you don't have to learn this information now.

Elderly couple shopping for meat in Beijing supermarket

In Mandarin, stress involves an increase in the loudness, an increase in the length, and a widening of the pitch range of a sound. Widening of the pitch range means that a stressed Tone One syllable will be pronounced at a higher level; a stressed Tone Two syllable will rise higher; a stressed Tone Three syllable will be lower; and a stressed Tone Four syllable will fall from a higher than normal position to a lower than normal position. There are in Mandarin two kinds of stress: syllable stress and word stress. Syllable stress has to do with which syllable in a word is stressed. Word stress has to do with which word in a sentence is stressed. There are four degrees of stress in Mandarin: primary, secondary, tertiary, and unstressed (which is actually the same as so-called neutral tone).

If there is only one syllable in a word, it receives primary stress (primary stress will, in this paragraph only, be indicated by CAPITAL LETTERS). Examples: **SHŪ** "book," **WǑ** "me," **TĀ** "her." In the case of most two-syllable words, primary stress falls on the second syllable, with the first syllable receiving secondary stress. Examples: **xiànZÀI** "now," **jùJUÉ** "refuse," **yīSHĒNG** "doctor." However, if the second syllable is unstressed (so-called "neutral tone"), then the first syllable receives primary stress (e.g., **ZHĪdao** "know"). In words of three or more syllables, the last syllable has primary stress, the first syllable has secondary stress, and the medial syllable or syllables have tertiary stress. Examples: **huāshēngTÁNG** "peanut candy," **zìláiSHUǏ** "running water," **dàfànDIÀN** "hotel." Personal and place names are fully stressed on each syllable, no matter how many syllables there are (e.g., **ZHŌU ĒNLÁI, BĚIJĪNG, ZHĀNGJIĀKǑU**).

There may be one element in a sentence which a speaker wishes to emphasize or contrast with other elements. In this case, the speaker has the option of pronouncing this element with stress. The position of the stress may vary depending on the meaning. For example, consider several possible responses to the intonation question **Ò, yuánlái nǐ yě zhùzai Zhōngshān Běi Lù?** "Oh, so you also live on Zhongshan North Road?" (in the examples below, the word that is stressed will be indicated in CAPITAL LETTERS):

1. **Bú shi Zhōngshān Běi Lù, shi DŌNGshan Běi Lù.** "It's not Zhongshan North Road, it's DONGshan North Road."

2. **Bú shi Zhōngshān Běi Lù, shi ZhōngHUÁ Běi Lù.** "It's not Zhongshan North Road, it's ZhongHUA North Road."

3. **Bú shi Zhōngshān Běi Lù, shi Zhōngshān NÁN Lù.** "It's not Zhongshan North Road, it's Zhongshan SOUTH Road."

4. **Bú shi Zhōngshān Běi Lù, shi Zhōngshān Běi JIĒ.** "It's not Zhongshan North Road, it's Zhongshan North STREET."

AV1.   POPULAR SAYINGS. In this lesson we take up the first of a number of popular sayings you'll learn in this course. **Yìfēn qián, yìfēn huò** means "You get what you pay for," literally, "One penny of money, one penny of product." This is an example of a so-called **súyǔ** "popular saying" or "folk adage," of which there are thousands in Chinese. Unlike the **chéngyǔ** to which you were introduced in 10-4: 8G, which almost always consist of four characters and are typically composed in Classical Chinese, **súyǔ** are often more than four characters in length and are composed in colloquial Chinese.

Purchasing New Shoes

Rosy Huang, a Chinese-American woman living with her family in Taipei for a year, wants to purchase a pair of black high-heeled shoes.

🎧 Basic Conversation 13-3

1. HUANG	**Wǒ xūyào yìshuāng hēisède gāogēnxié.**
	I need a pair of black high-heeled shoes.

| 2. SHOE SALESMAN | **Nǐ chuān jǐhàode?** |
| | What size do you wear? |

| 3. HUANG | **Wǒ zài Měiguo chuān qíhàode. Bù zhīdào nǐmende hàomǎ gēn Měiguode hàomǎ yíyàng bu yíyàng?** |
| | In America I wear size seven. I wonder if your sizes are the same as or different from American sizes? |

| 4. SHOE SALESMAN | **Hàomǎ bù yíyàng la, búguò wǒ kéyi bāng nǐ shìshi kàn.** |
| | The sizes are different, but I can help you try some on and see. |

(takes out a pair of shoes for her to try on)

Zhèishuāng dàxiǎo zěmmeyàng?
How is the size of this pair?

| 5. HUANG | **Hǎoxiàng tài xiǎole. Yǒu méiyou dà yíhàode?** |
| | They seem too small. Do you have any that are one size larger? |

| 6. SHOE SALESMAN | **Zhèishuāng dà yíhào, nǐ shìshi kàn.** |
| | This pair is one size bigger, try it on. |

| 7. HUANG | **Zhèishuāng gāng hǎo. Zhèishuāng mài duōshǎo qián?** |
| | This pair is just right. How much does this pair sell for? |

| 8. SHOE SALESMAN | **Yìqiān bā.** |
| | 1,800 NT. |

| 9. HUANG | **M, piàoliang shi piàoliang, dànshi yìqiān bā tài guìle. Shǎo suàn yidian, hǎo bu hǎo?** |
| | Hm, they do look nice, but 1,800 NT is too expensive. Could you reduce the price a little? |

10. SHOE SALESMAN	Gāng shàngshìde, méiyou bànfa.
	They just came on the market, nothing I can do.
11. HUANG	Nà wǒ zài kànkan.
	Then I'll look around some more.
12. SHOE SALESMAN	Hǎode. Yǒu xūyào huānyíng zài lái.
	O.K. If you need anything, you're welcome to come again.

Build Up

1. Huang

shuāng	pair [M]
yìshuāng	a pair
gāogēn(r)xié	high-heeled shoes [N]
yìshuāng hēisède gāogēnxié	a pair of black high-heeled shoes
Wǒ xūyào yìshuāng hēisède gāogēnxié.	I need a pair of black high-heeled shoes.

2. Shoe salesman

chuān	put on, wear (shoes, clothes) [V]
Nǐ chuān jǐhàode?	What size do you wear?

3. Huang

bù zhīdào	(I) wonder [A+V]
hàomǎ(r)	number [N]
yíyàng	one kind; the same [NU+M]
A gēn B yíyàng	A is the same as B [PT]
yíyàng bu yíyàng	the same or different
nǐmende hàomǎ gēn Měiguode hàomǎ	are your numbers the same as or
yíyàng bu yíyàng	different from American numbers
Wǒ zài Měiguo chuān qíhàode. Bù zhīdào	In America I wear size seven. I wonder if
nǐmende hàomǎ gēn Měiguode hàomǎ yíyàng	your sizes are the same as or different from
bu yíyàng?	American sizes?

4. Shoe salesman

hàomǎ bù yíyàng	the numbers are different
bāng	help [V]
shìshi kàn	try and see
bāng nǐ shìshi kàn	help you to try some on and see
Hàomǎ bù yíyàng la, búguò wǒ kéyi	The sizes are different, but I can help
bāng nǐ shìshi kàn.	you try some on and see.
dàxiǎo	size [N]
Zhèishuāng dàxiǎo zěmmeyàng?	How is the size of this pair?

5. Huang

dà yíhào	bigger by one size
dà yíhàode	ones that are a size bigger
Hǎoxiàng tài xiǎole. Yǒu	They seem too small. Do you have
méiyou dà yíhàode?	any that are one size larger?

6. Shoe salesman

Zhèishuāng dà yíhào, nǐ shìshi kàn.	This pair is one size bigger, try it on.

7. **Huang**	
gāng hǎo	just right
Zhèishuāng gāng hǎo.	This pair is just right. How much
Zhèishuāng mài duōshǎo qián?	does this pair sell for?

8. **Shoe salesman**	
Yìqiān bā.	1,800 NT.

9. **Huang**	
piàoliang shi piàoliang	as for being pretty they're pretty all right
suàn	figure, calculate [V]
shǎo suàn yidian	figure by a little less, make cheaper
M, piàoliang shi piàoliang, dànshi yìqiān bā	Hm, they do look nice, but 1,800 NT is too ex-
tài guìle. Shǎo suàn yidian, hǎo bu hǎo?	pensive. Could you reduce the price a little?

10. **Shoe salesman**	
shàngshì	come on the market [VO]
gāng shàngshìde	they just came on the market
Gāng shàngshìde, méiyou bànfa.	They just came on the market, nothing I can do.

11. **Huang**	
Nà wǒ zài kànkan.	Then I'll look around some more.

12. **Shoe salesman**	
xūyào	need [N]
yǒu xūyào	if there is a need
huānyíng zài lái	(we) welcome you to come again
Hǎode. Yǒu xūyào huānyíng zài lái.	O.K. If you need anything, you're welcome to come again.

Supplementary Vocabulary

1. **wánquán**	completely [A]
Zhèizhǒng zhǐ gēn nèizhǒng zhǐ	This kind of paper is completely
wánquán bù yíyàng.	different from that kind of paper.

2. **wàzi**	sock [N] (M: **shuāng** "pair")
Zhèishuāng wàzi shi gānjìngde	Is this pair of socks clean or dirty?
háishi zāngde?	

Additional Vocabulary: Buying Footwear

1. **xuēzi**	boots [N] (M: **shuāng** "pair")
2. **yǔxié**	galoshes [N] (M: **shuāng** "pair")
3. **liángxié**	sandals [N] (M: **shuāng** "pair")
4. **biànxié**	slippers [N] (M: **shuāng** "pair")
5. **tuōxié**	slippers [N] (M: **shuāng** "pair")
6. **qiúxié**	sneakers, athletic shoes (M: **shuāng** "pair")
7. **yùndòngxié**	sneakers, athletic shoes (M: **shuāng** "pair")
8. **xiédiàn**	shoe store [N] (M: **jiā**)
9. **Huò bǐ sānjiā bù chīkuī.**	"It pays to shop around." [EX]

Grammatical and Cultural Notes

1A. Note the measure **shuāng** "pair" as in **yìshuāng hēisède gāogēnxié** "a pair of black high-heeled shoes." The English word "pair" sometimes means "one of something" (as in "a pair of pants") and sometimes means "two of something" (as in "a pair of shoes"). Chinese **shuāng** is always used for two separate and identical items. Thus, **shuāng** is used for pairs of socks, shoes, sandals, and chopsticks; but **shuāng** CANNOT be used for pairs of pants, trousers, shorts, or glasses.

1B. If you're just looking around in a store and a clerk asks what you want, you can say **Wǒ zhǐ shi kànkan éryǐ** "I'm just looking" or **Wǒ zhǐ shi suíbiàn kànkan** "I'm just looking randomly."

2. The verb **chuān** "put on, wear" literally means "pierce" or "pass through." **Chuān** is used for "wearing" things that have an opening in them, e.g., shirts, pants, shoes, and socks, since a part of the body must "pass through" an opening when you wear them. **Chuān** isn't used for "wearing" watches, belts, ties, hats, or jewelry, for which you use a different verb (cf. 13-4: SV7 for a fuller discussion of Chinese equivalents of English "wear").

3A. The speaker in the Build Up says **qíhàode** "number seven ones," with a rising Tone Two on **qī** because of the following falling Tone Four. The tone change on **qī** is optional here, and other speakers would say **qīhàode**. Either pronunciation is fine for you to use.

3B. The literal meaning of **bù zhīdào** is, of course, "(I) don't know." **Bù zhīdào** "I wonder if..." or "I wonder whether..." when used at the beginning of a sentence alerts the listener to the fact that a question is coming and renders the question more gentle and less abrupt. Another example:

> **Bù zhīdào nǐ xīngqīliù wǎnshang yǒu méiyou kòng?**
>
> "I wonder if you'd be free Saturday evening?"

Be aware that **yàoshi** or **rúguǒ** couldn't be used to express this kind of "if" that really means "whether." You could NEVER say *Bù zhīdào yàoshi nǐ xīngqīliù wǎnshang yǒu méiyou kòng? Simply put, if in the English you could substitute "whether" for the "if," then you can't use **yàoshi** or **rúguǒ**, but instead should use an affirmative-negative verb construction like **yǒu méiyou**.

3C. The noun **hàomǎ(r)** "number" may co-occur with **diànhuà** "telephone" to form **diànhuà hàomǎ(r)** "telephone number."

3D. **A GĒN B YÍYÀNG TO EXPRESS SIMILARITY.** The pattern **A gēn B yíyàng** "A is the same as B" (lit. "A is the same kind as B") is a common and useful pattern for expressing similarity and, in the negative, dissimilarity. The basic pattern is:

A	GĒN	B	YÍYÀNG

Zhèige gēn nèige yíyàng.
"This one is the same as that one."

Yíyàng means "one kind," so the sentence **Zhèige gēn nèige yíyàng** literally means "This one and that one are of one kind." Some more examples:

Wǒ gēn nǐ yíyàng.	"I'm the same as you."
Nǐmen Měiguo rén dōu yíyàng!	"You Americans are all the same!"
Zuò gōngchē gēn zuò diànchē yíyàng.	"Taking the bus would be the same as taking the trolley."
Zài zhèr chīfàn gēn zài nàr chīfàn dōu yíyàng.	"Eating here would be the same as eating there."

To indicate in what particular respect the two things compared are similar, stative verbs or other verbal expressions can be added after the **yíyàng**, which then functions adverbially. For example:

Wǒ gēn nǐ yíyàng gāo. "I'm as tall as you."

Wǒ gēn nǐ yíyàng xǐhuan chī Zhōngguo cài. "I like eating Chinese food as much as you do."

Sùshè lí túshūguǎn gēn sùshè lí shítáng yíyàng yuǎn.
"The dorm is as far from the library as the dorm is far from the dining hall."

The pattern **A gēn B yíyàng** is most often used as a predicate, but it can also be used as an attributive. For example:

Wǒ yào mǎi yìtái gēn nǐ nèitái yíyàngde diànnǎo.
"I want to buy a computer like that one of yours."

To express dissimilarity, in other words, that two things aren't the same or similar, put a **bù** before the **yíyàng** and say **A gēn B bù yíyàng**. The pattern is:

A	GĒN	B	BÙ	YÍYÀNG

Zhèige   gēn   nèige   bù   yíyàng.
"This one isn't the same as that one."

Zhōng gēn biǎo bù yíyàng. "Clocks and watches are different."

But in refuting a statement expressing similarity, the **bù** is usually prefixed to the entire expression:

Zhōng bù gēn biǎo yíyàng.
"Clocks aren't the same as watches." (someone just said they were, and you disagree)

Diànchē bù gēn huǒchē yíyàng kuài.
"Trolleys aren't as fast as trains." (someone just said they were, and you disagree)

To make questions with the **A gēn B yíyàng** pattern, either add **ma** or use an affirmative-negative verb construction. Examples:

Zhèige gēn nèige yíyàng ma? "Is this one the same as that one?"
Zhèizhǒng gēn nèizhǒng yíyàng bu yíyàng? "Is this kind the same as that kind?"

Additional notes:

a. Some speakers will abbreviate **yíyàng bu yíyàng to yí bù yíyàng**, so the last example above could be said as **Zhèige gēn nèige yí bù yíyàng?**

b. Instead of **A gēn B yíyàng**, there is an alternate pattern **A hé B yíyàng** (in Taiwan this is pronounced as **A hàn B yíyàng**), with the same meaning.

c. The **gēn** or **hé/hán** of this pattern is sometimes omitted, for example: **Zhōngguo, Měiguo dōu yíyàng yǒu yìsi** "China and America are equally interesting."

d. Another way to approach similarity and dissimilarity is with the verb **yǒu**, for example: **Tāde Zhōngwén yǒu nǐde zhèmme hǎo ma?** "Is her Chinese as good as yours?"

e. Yet another way to approach similarity is with **xiàng** (13-2: 6A): **Tāde Zhōngwén xiàng nǐde zhèmme hǎo ma?** "Is her Chinese as good as yours?"

4A.   Look at the sentence **Wǒ kéyi bāng nǐ shìshi kàn** "I can help you try and see." The verb **bāng** "help" is a so-called "pivot verb." In this sentence, the **nǐ** serves simultaneously as the the object of **bāng** (**bāng nǐ** "help you") and as the subject of the following clause (**nǐ shìshi kàn** "you try and see").

4B.   Look at the noun **dàxiǎo** "size" in **Zhèishuāng dàxiǎo zěmmeyàng?** "How is the size of this pair?" Obviously, **dàxiǎo** consists of the stative verb **dà** "to be big" combined with its antonym **xiǎo** "to be small." **Dàxiǎo** could be translated literally as "the bigness and smallness of something." A number of abstract nouns are created by this process of combining antonym pairs. Additional examples include:

chángduǎn	"long short — length"
duōshǎo	"much little — amount; how much"
gāo'ǎi	"tall short — height"
kuàimàn	"fast slow — speed"
kuānzhǎi	"wide narrow — width"
qīngzhòng	"light heavy — weight"
yuǎnjìn	"far near — distance"

5.   **STATIVE VERBS FOLLOWED BY QUANTITY EXPRESSIONS.** A stative verb may be followed by a quantity expression that limits or otherwise clarifies its meaning. The pattern is:

STATIVE VERB	QUANTITY EXPRESSION
dà	yíhào

"be bigger by one number," "be one size bigger"

Two more examples:

Zhèige guì wǔkuài.	"This one is five dollars more expensive."
Nèibān huǒchē màn liǎngge zhōngtóu.	"That train is two hours slower."

7.   Note the two related but different senses of **gāng** in lines 7 and 10. **Zhèishuāng gāng hǎo** means "This pair is just right" but **Gāng shàngshide** means "They just came on the market." The first **gāng** means "just, exactly" while the second means "just, a moment ago, very recently."

9A.   **CONCESSIVE CLAUSES WITH X SHI X.** Concessive clauses involve clauses where speakers concede certain aspects of an argument before making their main point. Concessive clauses are commonly used in Chinese when analyzing the weak and strong points of people, things, situations, etc. The X in the concessive clause can be a stative verb, some other kind of verb, or even a phrase. The second clause, where the main point is made, is usually introduced by **dànshi** "but," **kěshi** "but," **búguò** "however," or **jiù shi** "it's just that." The basic pattern is:

X	SHI	X,	DÀNSHI / KĚSHI / BÚGUÒ / JIÙ SHI + COMMENT
Piàoliang	shi	piàoliang,	dànshi yìqiān bā tài guìle.

"As for being pretty, they (i.e., the shoes) are pretty, but 1,800 is too expensive."

In English, the concessive clause can sometimes be translated with "all right" or "to be sure," or sometimes just by contrastive stress. Some more examples of concessive clauses with **X shi X**...:

Nèige dìfang yuǎn shi yuǎn, dànshi wǒ hái shi xiǎng qù.

"That place is far away, to be sure, but I still want to go."

Shoe store on Heping East Road in Taipei

Tā cōngming shi cōngming, dànshi duì rén bù hǎo.

"She's smart, all right, but she's not kind to others."

Gōngzuò máng shi máng, kěshi dàjiā dōu hěn gāoxìng.

"Work is busy, all right, but everyone is happy."

Wǒ lái shi lái, búguò děi bādiǎn yǐhòu.

"I'll come, to be sure, but it'll have to be after eight o'clock."

Nèige xuésheng shuōhuà màn shi màn, kěshi fāyīn hěn biāozhǔn.

"That student sure is slow when he speaks, but his pronunciation is very standard."

The second iteration of the verb in the concessive clause can take an aspectual suffix, for example:

Wǒ qù shi qùguo, kěshi méi kànjian tā.

"As far as going there is concerned, I did go, but I didn't see her."

Tā lái shi láile, dànshi wǒ méi zài jiā.

"He did come, but I wasn't home."

There can optionally be an adverb before the second X, but never only before the first X. In other words, you could say either **Nàrde dōngxi guì shi guì...** or **Nàrde dōngxi guì shi hěn guì...** "The things there are very expensive, all right...," but you could NEVER say *Nàrde dōngxi hěn guì shi guì....

9B.   **Shǎo suàn yidian, hǎo bu hǎo?** "Could you reduce the price a little?" This is obviously a very useful question. Other ways to say this include **Néng bu néng shǎo suàn yidian?** and **Néng bu néng piányi yidian?**

11.   In the given context, the sentence **Nà wǒ zài kànkan** could mean either "Then I'll look around some more" or "Then I'll think it over some more." Remember that besides meaning "look," **kàn** can also mean "consider, think" (cf. 11-4). Regardless of the interpretation, the function of this sentence is to serve as a polite way of informing the salesperson that the customer isn't going to buy the shoes at the present time.

12.   The phrase **Yǒu xūyào** "There is a need" here contains an implied "if," so that it really means "If there is a need" or, in better English, "If you need anything." A fuller version of this phrase would be **Rúguǒ nǐ yǒu shémme xūyàode huà** "If you have any need."

AV1–7.   **FOOTWEAR.** The names of these different types of footwear are arranged in alphabetical order of the English translation.

AV2.   The literal meaning of **yǔxié** "galoshes" is "rain shoes."

AV9.   The literal meaning of **Huò bǐ sānjiā bù chīkuī** "It pays to shop around" is "(When buying) goods, (if you) compare three establishments, (you) won't suffer a loss." This is another example of a **súyǔ** or "popular saying" (cf. 13-2: AV1).

Buying Pants

Rosy Huang, a Chinese-American woman living with her family in Taipei for a year, goes shopping for pants for her six-year-old son at a children's clothing store in Taipei.

Basic Conversation 13-4

1. HUANG   **Xiáojie, nǐmen yǒu méiyou xiǎo nánshēng chuānde chángkù?**
Miss, do you have long pants that little boys wear?

2. CLERK   **Yǒu, qǐng guòlai kànkan. Xiǎoháir jǐsuì le?**
Yes, please come over and take a look. How old is the child?

3. HUANG   **Liùsuì duō, kuài qīsuì le.**
He's six, almost seven.

4. CLERK   **Chuān jiǔhào yīnggāi méiyou wèntí. Kànkan zhèitiáo.**
Size nine should be no problem. Take a look at this pair.

5. HUANG   **Yánsè hái bú cuò, dànshi bù zhīdào huì bu huì tài dà huò tài xiǎo?**
The color is fine, but I wonder if it's going to be too big or too small?

6. CLERK   **Méi guānxi. Jiǎrú bù héshìde huà, qītiān yǐnèi kéyi nálai huàn.**
That's O.K. If it doesn't fit, you can bring it here within seven days for exchange.

7. HUANG   **Duōshǎo qián?**
How much is it?

8. CLERK   **Zhèizhǒng kùzi běnlái shi wǔbǎi sì yìtiáo, zhèige lǐbài gānghǎo dǎ duìzhé, zhǐ yào liǎngbǎi qī.**
These pants originally were 540 NT per pair, this week they just happen to be 50% off, only 270 NT.

9. HUANG   **Hǎo, wǒ mǎi yìtiáo. Kéyi shuākǎ ma?**
All right, I'll buy a pair. Can I use a credit card?

10. CLERK   **Duìbuqǐ, wǒmen bù shōu xìnyòngkǎ.**
I'm sorry, we don't accept credit cards.

11. HUANG   **Hǎo ba, nà wǒ gěi nǐ xiànjīn. Zhè shi sānbǎikuài.**
O.K., then I'll give you cash. This is 300 NT.

(clerk leaves briefly, then returns)

12. CLERK   **Zhǎo nín sānshí. Fāpiào zài lǐmiàn. Xièxie! Huānyíng zài lái.**
Here's 30 NT in change. The receipt is inside. Thank you! Please come again.

 **Build Up**

1. Huang
xiǎo nánshēng — young male student, little boy [PH]
chángkù — long pants [N] (M: **tiáo**)
xiǎo nánshēng chuānde chángkù — long pants worn by little boys
Xiáojie, nǐmen yǒu méiyou xiǎo nánshēng chuānde chángkù? — Miss, do you have long pants that little boys wear?

2. Clerk
guòlai — come over [RC]
guòlai kànkan — come over and take a look
Yǒu, qǐng guòlai kànkan. — Yes, please come over and take a
Xiǎoháir jǐsuì le? — look. How old is the child?

3. Huang
Liùsuì duō, kuài qīsuì le. — He's six, almost seven.

4. Clerk
chuān jiǔhào — wear size nine
yīnggāi méiyou wèntí — there should be no problem
Chuān jiǔhào yīnggāi méiyou wèntí. — Size nine should be no problem.
Kànkan zhèitiáo. — Take a look at this pair.

5. Huang
hái bú cuò — not too bad
huì bu huì — is or isn't likely to be
tài dà huò tài xiǎo — too big or too small
Yánsè hái bú cuò, dànshi bù zhīdào huì bu huì tài dà huò tài xiǎo? — The color is fine, but I wonder if it's going to be too big or too small?

6. Clerk
jiǎrú — if [MA]
jiǎrú...-de huà — if... [PT]
héshì — be the right size, fit [SV]
jiǎrú bù héshìde huà — if it doesn't fit
...yǐnèi — within... [PT]
qītiān yǐnèi — within seven days
nálai — bring here [RC]
kéyi nálai huàn — may bring it here and exchange it
Méi guānxi. Jiǎrú bù héshìde huà, qītiān yǐnèi kéyi nálai huàn. — That's O.K. If it doesn't fit, you can bring it here within seven days for exchange.

7. Huang
Duōshǎo qián? — How much is it?

8. Clerk
kùzi — pants [N] (M: **tiáo**)

zhèizhǒng kùzi	this kind of pants
běnlái	originally [MA]
wǔbǎi sì yìtiáo	540 NT per pair
gānghǎo	just, as it happens [MA]
dǎzhé	give a discount [VO]
duìzhé	50% discount [N]
dǎ duìzhé	give a 50% discount [PH]
gānghǎo dǎ duìzhé	just happen to be 50% off
zhǐ yào liǎngbǎi qī	they cost only 270 NT

Zhèizhǒng kùzi běnlái shi wǔbǎi sì yìtiáo, zhèige lǐbài gānghǎo dǎ duìzhé, zhǐ yào liǎngbǎi qī.

These pants originally were 540 NT per pair, this week they just happen to be 50% off, only 270 NT.

---

9. Huang

shuākǎ	imprint a credit card [VO]

Hǎo, wǒ mǎi yìtiáo. Kéyi shuākǎ ma?

All right, I'll buy a pair. Can I use a credit card?

---

10. Clerk

shōu	accept [V]
xìnyòngkǎ	credit card [N] (M: **zhāng**)

Duìbuqǐ, wǒmen bù shōu xìnyòngkǎ.

I'm sorry, we don't accept credit cards.

---

11. Huang

xiànjīn	cash [N]

Hǎo ba, nà wǒ gěi nǐ xiànjīn. Zhè shi sānbǎikuài.

O.K., then I'll give you cash. This is 300 NT.

---

12. Clerk

qǐng shāo hòu	"please wait briefly" [IE]

Hǎode, qǐng shāo hòu.

O.K., just a minute, please.

fāpiào	itemized bill; receipt [N] (M: **zhāng**)

Zhǎo nín sānshí. Fāpiào zài lǐmiàn. Xièxie! Huānyíng zài lái.

Here's 30 NT in change. The receipt is inside. Thank you! Please come again.

Supplementary Vocabulary

1.	duǎn	be short (not long) [SV]
2.	duǎnkù	short pants [N] (M: **tiáo**)
3.	yīfu	clothes [N] (M: **jiàn**)
4.	chènshān	shirt [N] (M: **jiàn**)
5.	qúnzi	skirt [N] (M: **tiáo**)
6.	xiǎo nǚshēng	little girl [PH]
7.	dài	put on, wear (watch, hat, jewelry) [V]
	biǎo	watch (for telling time) [N] (M: **zhī**)
	shǒubiǎo	wristwatch [N] (M: **zhī**)

Nǐ dàile shǒubiǎo le ma?

Did you wear your wristwatch?

8.	guòqu	go over, pass by [RC]
9.	náqu	take away [RC]
10.	-guòlai	(indicates movement from there to here) [RE]
	bānguolai	move over [RC]

Tā yě bānguolaile.

She moved over here, too.

11. -guòqu   (indicates movement from here to there) [RE]
   náguoqu   take over [RC]
   Tā náguoqule.   He took it over there.

12. ...zhīnèi   within... [PT]
   Sāntiān zhīnèi kéyi huàn.   It can be exchanged within 3 days.

 ## Additional Vocabulary: Clothing and Accessories

1.	huàzhuāng	apply makeup [VO]	19.	tàng	iron [V]
2.	pídài	belt [N] (M: **tiáo**)	20.	jiákè	jacket [N] (M: **jiàn**)
3.	màozi	cap, hat [N] (M: **dǐng**)	21.	niúzǎikù	jeans [N] (M: **tiáo**)
4.	Zhōngshānzhuāng	Chinese-style loose-fitting jacket [N] (M: **tào**)	22.	shǒushì	jewelry [N] (M: **jiàn**)
			23.	shuǐxǐ	launder with water [V]
5.	mián'ǎo	Chinese-style padded jacket [N] (M: **jiàn**)	24.	xǐyīdiàn	laundry (the store) [PW] (M: **jiā**)
6.	qípáo	Chinese-style woman's dress [N] (M: **jiàn**)	25.	zuò yīfu	make clothes [PH]
			26.	liàozi	material, fabric [N] (M: **kuài**)
7.	yīshang (B)	clothes [N] (M: **jiàn**)	27.	bǔ	mend [V]
8.	fúzhuāng diàn	clothing store [PH] (M: **jiā**)	28.	xiàngliàn	necklace [N] (M: **tiáo**)
9.	dàyī	coat [N] (M: **jiàn**)	29.	shuìyī	pajama [N] (M: **jiàn**)
10.	shūzi	comb [N] (M: **bǎ**)	30.	yǔyī	raincoat [N] (M: **jiàn**)
11.	huàzhuāngpǐn	cosmetics [N]	31.	jièzhi	ring [N] (M: **méi**)
12.	bǎihuò gōngsī	department store [PH] (M: **jiā**)	32.	yùndòngzhuāng	sportswear [N] (M: **tào**)
13.	yángzhuāng	dress (Western-style) [N] (M: **jiàn**)	33.	xīzhuāng	suit (Western-style) [N] (M: **tào**)
			34.	tàiyáng yǎnjìng	sunglasses [PH] (M: **fù**)
14.	gānxǐ	dry clean [V]	35.	máoyī	sweater [N] (M: **jiàn**)
15.	ěrhuán	earring [N] (M: **fù** "pair")	36.	yǔsǎn	umbrella [N] (M: **bǎ**)
16.	shǒupà	handkerchief [N] (M: **tiáo**)	37.	nèikù	underpants [N] (M: **tiáo**)
17.	yǎnjìng	(eye) glasses [N] (M: **fù**)	38.	nèiyī	underwear [N] (M: **jiàn**)
18.	shǒutào(r)	glove [N] (M: **shuāng** "pair")	39.	bèixīn	vest [N] (M: **jiàn**)
			40.	dǎ lǐngdài	wear a tie [PH]

Grammatical and Cultural Notes

2. **Guòlai** "come over (here)" is a resultative compound verb composed of **guò** "pass over" and the resultative ending **-lai** "come." You can also say **guòqu** "go over (there)." Compare:

> **Qǐng nǐ guòlai.**   "Please come over here."
> **Nǐ zěmme bú guòqu gēn tāmen jiǎnghuà ne?**   "How come you don't go over and talk with them?"

3. **Kuài qīsuì le** is an example of **le** to indicate anticipated change in a situation, i.e., "he will soon be seven years old" (cf. 3-2: 6D).

4. **Chuān jiǔhào yīnggāi méiyou wèntí** literally means "(If he) wears size nine, there should be no problem." Instead of **Chuān jiǔhào**, some speakers would say **Chuān jiǔhàode** "(If he) wears size nine ones" (i.e., pants). Also, the **yīnggāi** here indicates not the "should" of obligation but the "should" of probability, i.e., the speaker thinks that probably there should be no problem, though she isn't indicating absolute certainty.

6A. **JIǍRÚ...-DE HUÀ.** The pattern **jiǎrú...-de huà** "if" works the same way and has the same meaning as the patterns **yàoshi...-de huà** and **rúguǒ...-de huà**. These patterns all indicate that if a certain condition is met, a certain result will occur. **Yàoshi** is very colloquial and is used mostly in northern China, while **jiǎrú** and **rúguǒ** can be used everywhere Chinese is spoken. The clause with **jiǎrú** (or **yàoshi** or **rúguǒ**) precedes the condition while **-de huà**, which literally means "the words that," follows it. (In English, the "if" clause can precede or follow the condition.) The **-de huà** is common but can be omitted. The pattern is:

JIĂRÚ	CONDITION	(-DE HUÀ),	RESULT
Jiărú	míngtiān tiānqi hăo	de huà,	wŏ yídìng qù.

"If the weather tomorrow is good, I'll definitely go."

More examples:

Jiărú tā bù láide huà, nĭ dăsuan zĕmme bàn?

"What do you plan to do if she doesn't come?"

Jiărú míngtiān bù héshìde huà, hòutiān yĕ kéyi.

"If tomorrow isn't convenient, the day after tomorrow is O.K., too."

6B. In 10-2 you learned the stative verb **héshì** in the sense of "be appropriate," as in **qiūtiān zuì héshì** "fall is the most appropriate" (season for visiting a place). Now you learn **héshì** in its more basic meaning of "be the right size, fit." Examples:

Zhèidĭng màozi hĕn héshì.   "This hat fits just right."

6C. **TIME EXPRESSION + YĬNÈI.** The pattern TIME EXPRESSION + **yĭnèi** means "within a certain period of time." Note that, unlike English, in Chinese the time expression always comes first. The pattern is:

TIME EXPRESSION	YĬNÈI
yìnián	yĭnèi

"within one year"

More examples:

sāntiān yĭnèi	"within three days"
yíge yuè yĭnèi	"within a month"
wŭnián yĭnèi	"within five years"

Zhīnèi, introduced in the Supplementary Vocabulary of this lesson, has the same meaning and is used in the same way as **yĭnèi**. Example:

shítiān zhīnèi   "within ten days"

6D. **Nálai** is another example of a resultative compound. It's composed of **ná** "take" and the resultative ending **-lái** "come." The verb **nálai** as a whole means "bring here." Compare **náqu** "take there."

8A. The moveable adverb **bĕnlái** "originally" is a near synonym of **yuánlái** "originally" that you learned in 7-1. Some more examples:

Bĕnlái wŏ xiăng qù, kĕshi yŭ tài dàle, suóyi méi qù.

"Originally I wanted to go, but it was raining too hard, so I didn't go."

Bĕnlái wŏ bù măi, kĕshi jiàqián piányi, dōngxi yòu hăo, suóyi jiù măile.

"Originally I wasn't going to buy it, but the price was cheap and the item was good, so I bought it."

8B. **DĂZHÉ TO EXPRESS "GIVE A DISCOUNT."** To indicate that a discount is being given off an original price, the verb-object compound **dăzhé** is used. A number indicating for how many tenths of the original price the item will be sold is inserted between the **dă** and the **zhé**. The pattern is:

DĂ	NUMBER OF TENTHS	ZHÉ
dă	jiŭ	zhé

"sell at 9/10 of the original price" (i.e., give a 10% discount)

Some more examples with **dǎzhé**:

dǎ bāzhé	"sell at ⁸⁄₁₀ of the original price" (=20% discount)
dǎ qīzhé	"sell at ⁷⁄₁₀ of the original price" (=30% discount)
dǎ liùzhé	"sell at ⁶⁄₁₀ of the original price" (=40% discount)
dǎ bāwǔzhé	"sell at 85% of the original price" (=15% discount)

Be careful not to confuse the number of tenths of the original price (the Chinese point of view) with the percentage amount of the discount (the American point of view). For example, **dǎ liùzhé** means "sell at a 40% discount" NOT "sell at a 60% discount." Instead of **dǎ wǔzhé** "sell at a 50% discount," you can also say **dǎ duìzhé** "sell at half price." Finally, **dǎzhé** can also be used alone, as in the following example:

Néng bu néng dǎzhé?   "Could you discount it?

9–10.   Distinguish carefully between the verb-object compound **shuākǎ** "to swipe or imprint a credit card" and the noun **xìnyòngkǎ** "credit card." Even though credit cards are now more widely used in mainland China and Taiwan than before, these economies are still largely cash economies, so you'll need to bring cash to buy things most of the time. Exceptions are shopping malls, major hotels and restaurants, large foreign stores, and establishments that cater to foreigners. But be aware that those places that accept credit cards generally tend to have higher prices than those that don't.

10.   The verb **shōu** "accept" would also be used for saying that an applicant was or wasn't accepted by a university to which he or she had applied. Example:

Zhèige dàxué shōu wǒ le, búguò nèige dàxué méi shōu wǒ.

"This university accepted me, however that university didn't accept me."

12.   Department stores in Taiwan always provide receipts, but smaller stores sometimes are reluctant to do so, as they frequently don't report full revenues to the government so as to lower their value-added tax (VAT) and income tax obligations. To serve as incentive for customers to request a **fāpiào** "itemized bill, receipt," each **fāpiào** has a number printed on it and is automatically entered in a bimonthly lottery with substantial cash prizes.

SV1.   **Duǎn** means "be short" in the sense of "not long," e.g., of clothes or arms. To indicate "be short" in the sense of "not be tall," you'd use **ǎi**, which was introduced in 1-3.

SV7.   **CHINESE EQUIVALENTS OF ENGLISH "WEAR."** There are two Chinese verbs that translate as "put on" or "wear": **dài**, in this lesson, and **chuān**, which was introduced in 13-3. The distinction between the two is that **chuān** (which literally means "pierce" or "pass through") is used for "wearing" things that have an opening in them, e.g., shirts, pants, shoes, and socks (since a part of the body must "pass through" an opening when you wear them). On the other hand, **dài** is used for "wearing" things that don't have an opening in them, which aren't part of one's basic apparel, e.g., hats, gloves, watches, jewelry, earrings, glasses, and false teeth. Grammatically, both **dài** and **chuān** are action verbs more like English "put on" than like "wear." Therefore, to say "I'm wearing..." say **Wǒ dàile...** or **Wǒ chuānle...** with a completed action **-le**; to say "I'm not wearing..." say **Wǒ méi dài...** or **Wǒ méi chuān...** with **méi** to indicate past negative of an action verb. So to say "She's not wearing gloves" you have to say **Tā méi dài shǒutào**; and to say "He's not wearing socks" you have to say **Tā méi chuān wàzi**. If instead you said **Tā bú dài shǒutào**, that would actually mean "She doesn't (usually) wear gloves;" and if you said **Tā bù chuān wàzi**, that would mean "He doesn't (usually) wear socks."

AV1–40.   **CLOTHING AND ACCESSORIES.** The names of these types of clothing, accessories, and related terms are arranged in alphabetical order of the English equivalents.

AV4.   **Zhōngshānzhuāng** is a Chinese-style loose-fitting jacket named after Sun Yat-sen (**Sūn Zhōngshān**), the father of modern China, who frequently wore them and made them popular.

AV6. A **qípáo** is a close-fitting woman's dress with high collar and slit on the side. Even though now considered Chinese, it originated with the Manchus during the Qing Dynasty.

AV36. Don't give a **yǔsǎn** "umbrella" as a gift, because **yǔsǎn** (which can also be abbreviated to **sǎn**) sounds somewhat like **sàn** "to part, disperse," which is obviously a bad thing for friends to do.

Unit 13: Review and Study Guide

New Vocabulary

ADVERBS

wánquán	completely

COVERBS

hàn	with

IDIOMATIC EXPRESSIONS

mànmān lái	"take one's time"
qǐng shāo hòu	"please wait briefly"

MEASURES

shuāng	pair

MOVEABLE ADVERBS

běnlái	originally
gānghǎo	just, as it happens
jiǎrú	if

NOUNS

biǎo	watch (for telling time)
chángkù	long pants
chāoshì	supermarket
chènshān	shirt
dàxiǎo	size
duǎnkù	short pants
duìzhé	50% discount
fāpiào	itemized bill; receipt
gāogēn(r)xié	high-heeled shoes
guìtái	counter
hàomǎ(r)	number
hútòng(r)	alley
jī	chicken
jīròu	chicken meat
kāfēi	coffee
kùzi	pants
miànbāo	bread
niú	cow, ox
niúròu	beef
qúnzi	skirt
ròu	meat
shípǐn	food product; groceries
shǒubiǎo	wristwatch
tǔsī	white bread

wàzi	sock
xiā	shrimp
xiànjīn	cash
xìnyòngkǎ	credit card
xūyào	need
yáng	sheep
yángròu	mutton
yāròu	duck meat
yāzi	duck
yīfu	clothes
zhū	pig
zhūròu	pork
zhǔyì	idea, plan

NUMBER + MEASURE

yíyàng	one kind; the same

PATTERNS

A gēn B bǐqǐlái	comparing A and B
A gēn B yíyàng	A is the same as B
huì...-de	be likely to, would, will
jiǎrú...-de huà	if...
...shemmede	...and so on
...yǐnèi	within...
...zhīnèi	within...
-jíle	extremely
wèile...	in order to..., for...
yìdiǎn(r) yě bù...	not at all, not the least bit

PHRASES

chàbuduō	be about the same
dǎ duìzhé	give a 50% discount
miànbāo diàn	bakery
shípǐn diàn	grocery store
xiǎo nánshēng	little boy
xiǎo nǚshēng	little girl

PLACE WORDS

chūkǒu(r)	exit
fùjìn	in the vicinity, nearby

rùkǒu(r)	entrance

RESULTATIVE COMPOUNDS

bānguolai	move over
bǐqilai	compare
guòlai	come over
guòqu	go over, pass by
náguoqu	take over
nálai	bring here
náqu	take away

RESULTATIVE ENDINGS

-guòlai	(indicates movement from there to here)
-guòqu	(indicates movement from here to there)

STATIVE VERBS

duǎn	be short (not long)
féi	be fatty (of food)
héshì	be the right size, fit
jiéshěng	be frugal
pǔbiàn	be widespread, common

VERBS

bāng	help
chēng	weigh, weigh out
chuān	put on, wear (shoes, clothes)
dài	wear (watch, hat, jewelry)
jiéshěng	save
qiē	cut, slice
shōu	accept
suàn	figure, calculate
xiàng	resemble, be like

VERB-OBJECT COMPOUNDS

chīsù	eat vegetarian food
dǎzhé	give a discount
shàngshì	come on the market
shuākǎ	imprint a credit card

Major New Grammar Patterns

-JÍLE: Miànbāo diàn jìnjíle. "The bakery is extremely close." **(13-1)**

YÌDIĂN(R) YĚ BÙ...: Wǒ yìdiǎn(r) yě bú lèi. "I'm not at all tired." **(13-1)**

...SHEMMEDE: kāfēi, tǔsī shemmede "coffee, white bread, and so on" **(13-2)**

WÈILE TO EXPRESS PURPOSE: Wèile jiéshěng shíjiān, nǐ mǎi nǐde, wǒ mǎi wǒde. "In order to save time, you buy your things, and I'll buy my things." **(13-2)**

A GĒN B BÍQILAI: Táiwānde chāoshì gēn Měiguode bíqilai zěmmeyàng? "How are Taiwan's supermarkets compared to America's?" **(13-2)**

HUÌ...-DE: Táiwānde chāoshì huì yìnián bǐ yìnián pǔbiànde. "Taiwan's supermarkets will become more widespread each year." **(13-2)**

YĪ + MEASURE + BǏ + YĪ + MEASURE: yìnián bǐ yìnián guì "more expensive year by year" **(13-2)**

A GĒN B YÍYÀNG TO INDICATE SIMILARITY: Zhèige gēn nèige yíyàng. "This one is the same as that one." **(13-3)**

STATIVE VERBS FOLLOWED BY EXPRESSIONS OF QUANTITY: dà yíhào "be bigger by one number," "be one size bigger" **(13-3)**

CONCESSIVE CLAUSES WITH X SHI X...: Piàoliang shi piàoliang, dànshi yìqiān bā tài guìle. "As for being pretty, they're pretty all right, but 1,800 is too expensive." **(13-3)**

JIĂRÚ...-DE HUÀ: Jiǎrú tā bù láide huà, nǐ dǎsuan zěmme bàn? "What do you plan to do if she doesn't come?" **(13-4)**

TIME EXPRESSION + YǏNÈI: sāntiān yǐnèi "within three days" **(13-4)**

DǍZHÉ TO EXPRESS "GIVE A DISCOUNT": dǎ jiǔzhé "sell at 9/10 of the original price" (=10% discount), **dǎ duìzhé** "sell at half price" **(13-4)**

Eating and Drinking (I)

COMMUNICATIVE OBJECTIVES

Once you've mastered this unit, you'll be able to use Chinese to:

1. Discuss with a friend where to go for a meal.
2. Ask for the menu and order a meal in a restaurant.
3. Talk about some common Chinese dishes, staple foods, soups, and beverages.
4. Reserve a formal banquet in a restaurant.
5. Arrange a menu for a banquet: cold appetizers, main courses, soups, desserts, etc.
6. Discuss the names of some common flavors, seasonings, and condiments, and give instructions for how much or how little of each you want.
7. Talk about some of the different cuisines of China.
8. Discuss the names of common eating utensils.

PART 1

Ordering a Meal in a Restaurant

Dave Warres, an American studying at Capital Normal University in Beijing, and his Chinese roommate, Li Xiaodong, have decided to go out for lunch. They're walking along a street near the university, trying to decide where to eat.

 Basic Conversation 14-1

1. LI   **Nǐ kàn zámmen zài něige fànguǎnr chī?**
Which restaurant do you think we should eat at?

2. WARRES   **Suíbiàn, něige dōu xíng.**
As you like, any one is fine.

3. LI   **Nèijiā rén shǎo, zámmen jiù zài nàr ba.**
That one doesn't have many people, why don't we eat there.

(they enter and sit down)

Nǐ xiān kànkan càidānr, kànkan nǐ xiǎng chī shémme.
You look at the menu first; see what you'd like to eat.

4. WARRES   **Shémme dōu kéyi. Nǐ diǎn ba.**
Anything's fine. Why don't you order.

5. WAITRESS   **Liǎngwèi yào diǎnr shémme?**
What would the two of you like?

6. LI   **Yíge Yúxiāng Ròusī, yíge Mǎyǐ Shàngshù, yíge Mápó Dòufu. Chàbuduōle. Zài lái liǎngwǎn jīdàn tāng.**
One Fish Fragrant Meat Shreds, one Ants Climbing a Tree, and one Pockmarked Old Woman's Tofu. That's about it. And bring two bowls of egg soup.

 **Build Up**

1. Li

zámmen (B)	we (you and I) **[PR]**
fànguǎn(r)	restaurant **[PW]** (M: **jiā**)
Nǐ kàn zámmen zài něige fànguǎnr chī?	Which restaurant do you think we should eat at?

2. Warres

suíbiàn   "as you wish" [IE]
něige dōu xíng   any one is fine
Suíbiàn, něige dōu xíng.   As you like, any one is fine.

3. Li

Nèijiā rén shǎo, zámmen jiù zài nàr ba.   That one doesn't have many people, why don't we eat
                                               there.
cài   dish of food [N]
càidān(r)   menu [N] (M: **zhāng**)
Nǐ xiān kànkan càidānr, kànkan nǐ xiǎng   You look at the menu first; see what you'd like
chī shémme.   to eat.

4. Warres

shémme dōu kéyi   anything is fine
diǎn   order, choose [V]
Shémme dōu kéyi. Nǐ diǎn ba.   Anything's fine. Why don't you order.

5. Waitress

Liǎngwèi yào diǎnr shémme?   What would the two of you like?

6. Li

ròusī(r)   meat shred [N]
Yúxiāng Ròusī   Fish Fragrant Meat Shreds [PH]
mǎyǐ   ant [N] (M: **zhī**)
shù   tree [N] (M: **kē**)
Mǎyǐ Shàngshù   Ants Climbing a Tree [PH]
dòufu   tofu [N]
Mápó Dòufu   Pockmarked Old Woman's Tofu [PH]
wǎn   bowl [M]
dàn   egg [N]
jīdàn   chicken egg [N]
tāng   soup [N] (M: **wǎn**)
jīdàn tāng   egg soup [PH]
liǎngwǎn jīdàn tāng   two bowls of egg soup
Yíge Yúxiāng Ròusī, yíge Mǎyǐ Shàngshù,   One Fish Fragrant Meat Shreds, one Ants Climbing a
yíge Mápó Dòufu. Chàbuduōle.   Tree, and one Pockmarked Old Woman's Tofu.
Zài lái liǎngwǎn jīdàn tāng.   That's about it. And bring two bowls of egg soup.

Supplementary Vocabulary

1. dāozi   knife [N] (M: **bǎ**)
2. chāzi   fork [N]
3. sháozi   spoon [N]
4. fànwǎn   rice bowl [N]

5. yòng   use [V]
   xǐ   wash [V]
   xǐ shǒu   wash one's hands
   xǐshǒujiān   bathroom [PW] (M: **jiān**)
Wǒ xiǎng yòng yixia xǐshǒujiān.   I'd like to use the bathroom.

6. yòng   using, with [CV]
   kuàizi   chopsticks [N] (M: **shuāng** "pair")
Wǒ huì yòng kuàizi chīfàn, kěshi   I can eat with chopsticks, but I don't use them
wǒ yòngde bú tài hǎo.   very well.

7. diǎncài
Nǐmen xiǎng diǎn shémme cài?

order dishes of food [VO]
What dishes would you like to order?

8. gòu
Yìwǎn fàn gòu bu gou?

be enough [SV/A]
Is one bowl of rice enough?

Additional Vocabulary: Fast Food Restaurants

1. Kěndéjī
2. Màidāngláo

Kentucky Fried Chicken® [PW]
McDonald's® [PW]

Grammatical and Cultural Notes

1A. **ZÁMMEN AS INCLUSIVE "WE."** In this line we encounter the last of the personal pronouns, **zámmen**. This pronoun, which in rapid speech is often contracted to **zám** or even **zém**, is used primarily in Beijing and environs to indicate "inclusive we/our/us," referring to both the speaker and the person(s) spoken to. For those Chinese speakers who use **zámmen, wǒmen** has a separate meaning of "exclusive we/our/us," i.e., not including the person(s) spoken to. As examples of these two different words for "we," study the following sentences:

> **Míngtiān wǒmen dàside tóngxué dōu yào qù Xiāng Shān wánr; nǐ rúguǒ méi shìrde huà, zámmen yíkuàir qù, hǎo ma?**
>
> "Tomorrow we college seniors (of which you aren't one) are all going to Fragrant Hills to have some fun; if you're not busy, why don't we (you and I) go together?"

> **Nǐmen shi Měiguo rén, wǒmen shi Zhōngguo rén, kěshi zámmen dōu shi tóngxué!**
>
> "You all are Americans, and we (not including you) are Chinese, but we (including you) are all class-mates!"

Since the majority of Chinese speakers use **wǒmen** for both the inclusive and exclusive senses of "we," it would be quite acceptable for you to use **wǒmen** for both kinds of "we." However, if you live in Beijing for any length of time, you'll want to learn how to use **zámmen**. In any case, you should be able to comprehend **zámmen** and understand the subtle distinction when you hear it.

1B. There are in Chinese several different words for "restaurant." The most basic, which you encounter in this line, is **fànguǎn(r)**. Be sure to distinguish **fànguǎn(r)** from **fàndiàn**, which you learned in 5-3. Nowadays **fàndiàn** is ordinarily used to refer to relatively large hotels with modern facilities, including a restaurant or restaurants.

2. **MORE ON QUESTION WORDS USED AS INDEFINITES.** In this line, consider the phrase **Něige dōu xíng** "Any one (i.e., restaurant) will do." As you've seen before (cf. 7-2: 7B and 12-2: 10), Chinese question words may in certain environments function as indefinites. There is in Chinese a pattern consisting of QUESTION WORD + **dōu** + VERB; in this pattern, the question word takes on an indefinite meaning of "any" or "every." The question word may serve as the topic or subject of the sentence, or it may serve as the preposed object or even in some other grammatical role. The pattern is:

QUESTION WORD	DŌU	VERB
Něige	dōu	xíng.

"Any one will do."

Here are additional examples of the pattern QUESTION WORD + **dōu** + VERB:

Zài xuéxiàoli shéi dōu rènshi ta.	"At school everyone knows her."
Zài Shànghǎi nǎr dōu shi rén!	"In Shanghai there are people everywhere!"
Jǐsuì dōu kéyi.	"Any age is fine."
Duōjiǔ dōu méi guānxi.	"It doesn't matter how long."
Tā shéi dōu xǐhuan.	"She likes everyone."
Tā shémme dōu chī.	"He'll eat anything."
Wǒ nǎr dōu zhǎoguo.	"I've looked everywhere."
Shémme yàngrde dōu hǎo.	"Any kind will be fine."
Něijiā fànguǎnr dōu xíng.	"Any restaurant will do."

The pattern QUESTION WORD + **dōu** + VERB can be used when the verb is negative, but there is an alternative pattern QUESTION WORD + **yě** + VERB which is especially common with negative verbs. (This is the **yě** which by itself means "also.") In negative sentences, when question words are followed by **yě** or **dōu**, the question words also function as indefinites but they indicate exclusiveness, i.e., "nobody," "no one," "nowhere," "nothing," etc. Examples:

Shéi yě bù zhīdào.	"Nobody knows."
Tā shéi yě bù xǐhuan.	"She likes no one."

Wǒ zài Běijīngde shíhou mángzhe shàngkè, nǎr yě méi qù.
"While I was in Beijing, I was busy taking classes and didn't go anywhere."

Wǒ zuótiān shémme shì dōu méi zuò. "Yesterday I didn't do anything."

Zhè shi wǒ xīn mǎide xiàngjī, shéi yě bú jiè.
"This is my new camera that I just bought; I'm not lending it to anybody."

Duōshǎo qián dōu bú gòu tā yòng.   "No amount of money is enough for her."

3A. In lines 1 and 2, the general measure **ge** is used when referring to **fànguǎnr** "restaurant." In this line, **jiā**, the specific measure for the noun **fànguǎnr**, is used. While either **ge** or **jiā** is correct, **jiā** carries a more specific meaning, making clear that you're talking about an establishment like a restaurant, bank, or hospital.

3B. **Nèijiā rén shǎo** is a good example of a topic-comment sentence. A literal translation might be "As regards that one (i.e., restaurant), the people are few."

3C. In the audio of the Basic Conversation, the **nàr** in **Zámmen jiù zài nàr ba** "Let's eat there" is pronounced so it sounds almost like **nèr**. Some speakers regularly pronounce **nàr** as **nèr**.

3D. **Zámmen jiù zài nàr ba** is, of course, a shortened form of **Zámmen jiù zài nàr chī ba**.

3E. In addition to **càidānr** or **càidān** for "menu," there are also people who say **càidānzi**. Large and medium-sized restaurants usually have printed menus, while in small restaurants the choices available may be written on a chalk blackboard or on slips of paper pasted on the walls. Just as in English, **càidān** can also refer to the "menu" of a computer software program.

4A. The noun **cài**, which you learned in 12-3 as meaning "vegetable," can also mean "a cooked dish of food." In this sense, it can refer to both vegetable and meat dishes. A related expression is **zuòcài** "to cook." For example:

Lǎo Lǐ hěn huì zuò Zhōngguo cài.	"Old Li is very good at cooking Chinese food."

4B. **Shémme dōu kéyi** "Anything will do" is another example of a question word used as an indefinite followed by **dōu**. But note that **shémme dōu** can never be used alone at the end of a sentence or before a noun; it must always be followed by a verb. So to answer the question **Nǐ yào shémme?** "What do you want?", you could say **Shémme dōu kéyi** "Anything would be fine," since **kéyi** is a verb; but you could NEVER say ***Shémme dōu** alone to mean "Anything." To say "They don't have anything," you should say **Tāmen shémme dōu méiyou**; you could NEVER say ***Shémme dōu tāmen méiyou**.

5. Notice **liǎngwèi** "the two of you." This might be said by a waiter when asking what two people wish to order, or by a host when inviting a couple to enter her or his home.

6A. **Yúxiāng Ròusī**, which we translate as "Fish Fragrant Meat Shreds," is also sometimes translated as "Sichuan-style Shredded Pork." Despite the word **yú** "fish" in the name, no fish is actually used. **Yúxiāng** refers to a style of cooking from Sichuan that includes a sauce made with hot bean paste, scallions, garlic, ginger, soy sauce, and vinegar.

6B. **Mǎyǐ Shàngshù** "Ants Climbing a Tree" is another classic dish in Sichuan cuisine. It consists of bits of ground pork poured over Chinese vermicelli. The bits of ground pork on top of the vermicelli resemble ants on the twigs of a tree, hence the name of the dish.

6C. **Mápó Dòufu** "Pockmarked Old Woman's Tofu" is a hot and spicy dish from Sichuan. It consists of bean curd, finely minced pork, and hot bean paste. The name stems from the tradition that a pockmarked old woman invented the dish.

Yúxiāng Ròusī or "Fish Fragrant Meat Shreds"

6D. The Chinese word for "egg" is **dàn**. In English, unless otherwise specified, "eggs" are chicken eggs, but in Chinese you have to say **jīdàn** for "chicken eggs," since **yādàn** "duck eggs" and yet other types of eggs are also commonly eaten. The measure to express "dozen" is **dá**, so to say "a dozen chicken eggs" you'd say **yìdá jīdàn**. In English "dozen" can be used to count inanimate or animate nouns (e.g., "a dozen people," "a dozen eggs"), but in Chinese **dá** can only be used with inanimate nouns. Also, note that in English we sometimes say "dozens of...," but since Chinese uses the decimal system, in Chinese this would be **jǐshíge....**

6E. Chinese people drink soup much more than people in the West. In fact, at many meals there may be soup but no beverage. Chinese speakers always say **hē tāng** "drink soup." In English, depending on the speaker and the kind of soup, either "drink soup" or "eat soup" are possible.

SV3. For "spoon," instead of **sháozi**, some Chinese speakers say **sháor**; and there are yet others who say **chízi**, **tāngchí**, or **tiáogēng**.

Mápó Dòufu or "Pockmarked Old Woman's Tofu"

Mǎyǐ Shàngshù or "Ants Climbing a Tree"

Jīdàn Tāng or "Egg Soup"

SV5.　**Xǐshǒujiān** "bathroom" (lit. "room for washing hands") is a euphemism for **cèsuǒ** "toilet," which was introduced in 5-3. Of course, the English word "bathroom" is itself a euphemism.

SV6A.　**ALL ABOUT CHOPSTICKS.** Learn the word **kuàizi** "chopsticks." For a pair of chopsticks, use the measure **shuāng** and say **yìshuāng kuàizi**; for just one chopstick (which you won't have occasion to say very often), use the measure **gēn** and say **yìgēn kuàizi**. To say "eat with chopsticks," use the coverb **yòng** "use" and say **yòng kuàizi chīfàn**, literally "use chopsticks to eat." If you're not ethnically Chinese, you'll often get asked if you can use chopsticks; a polite response would be as in SV6: **Wǒ huì yòng kuàizi chīfàn, kěshi wǒ yòngde bú tài hǎo** "I know how to use chopsticks, but I don't use them very well." As regards chopsticks etiquette, don't cross them over and don't use them with the back of your hand up, which is considered impolite. If the food is hard to handle, it's perfectly acceptable to use a Chinese soup spoon (called **tāngchí**) in conjunction with chopsticks. Choose a piece of

> Once a piece of food has been handled with chopsticks, it must be taken, as it's considered poor manners to pick through a dish in search of the most appetizing morsel.

food near you, never reaching farther to choose a better piece. Once a piece of food has been handled with chopsticks, it must be taken, as it's considered poor manners to pick through a dish in search of the most appetizing morsel. So study a plate first, eye your goal, and seize it quickly. Don't use chopsticks to tear apart large pieces of food; instead, use chopsticks to pick up the larger pieces and bite off a little at a time. When not using your chopsticks, there will sometimes be chopstick holders for your use; otherwise, place your chopsticks next to the plate or across your plate pointing north and south. However, in no case should you stick the chopsticks upright into a bowl of rice or any other food, since this resembles sticking incense sticks into an incense bowl when making offerings to the dead, which would be considered most inauspicious at a meal! More modern or hygiene-conscious Chinese now often use **gōngsháo** "public serving spoons" or **gōngkuài** "public chopsticks," i.e., a pair of chopsticks for each dish that is used exclusively to dish up food to individual plates. If you're concerned about hygiene and are in a situation where people are eating from communal dishes with their personal chopsticks, you could politely ask: **Wǒmen kéyi yòng gōngkuài ma?** "Could we use public chopsticks?" If you're concerned the chopsticks you've been given may not be clean, you could request disposable chopsticks: **Yǒu méiyou fāngbiànkuài?** "Are there disposable chopsticks?" (lit. "convenient chopsticks"). Other words for disposable chopsticks are **wèishēngkuài** (lit. "hygienic chopsticks") and **yícìxìng kuàizi** (lit. "one-time chopsticks").

SV6B.　Note the coverb **yòng** "using, with" as in **yòng kuàizi chīfàn** "eat with chopsticks." **Yòng** is also used when you want to say "speak or write in a certain language." Example:

　　　Qǐng nǐ yòng Zhōngwén xiě.　"Please write in Chinese."

SV8.　Be careful how you use the word **gòu** "enough." **Gòu** can be used as a stative verb, for example:

　　　Wǒde qián bú gòu.　　　"I don't have enough money." (lit. "My money isn't enough.")

Gòu can also be used as an adverb before another stative verb:

　　　Nǐde shēngyīn bú gòu dà!　"Your voice isn't loud enough!"

However, there is a restriction on **gòu** so that unlike most stative verbs (and unlike English "enough"), **gòu** can't be used as an adjective before a noun. In other words, you could NEVER say *Nǐ yǒu méiyou gòu qián? "Do you have enough money?" Instead you'd have to say **Nǐde qián gòu bu gòu?** (lit. "Your money is enough not enough?")

PART 2

Ordering a Meal in a Restaurant (cont.)

Li and Warres finish ordering their meal (continued from the previous lesson).

 Basic Conversation 14-2

1. LI   **Mápó Dòufu shǎo fàng diǎnr làjiāo, wǒ pà zhèiwèi Měiguo péngyou shòubuliǎo.**
For the Pockmarked Old Woman's Tofu don't put in too many hot peppers, I'm afraid my American friend wouldn't be able to stand it.

2. WARRES   **Duō fàng diǎnr yě méi guānxi, wǒ néng chī làde.**
It's O.K. if you put in a lot, I can eat hot spicy foods.

3. WAITRESS   **Hǎo lei. Zhǔshí yào shémme? Mǐfàn háishi mántou?**
All right. What do you want for your main food? Rice or steamed buns?

4. LI   **Sìliǎng mǐfàn, liǎngge mántou.**
Four ounces of rice and two steamed buns.

5. WAITRESS   **Hē diǎnr shémme?**
What would you like to drink?

6. LI   **Yǒu píjiǔ ma, nín zhèr?**
Do you have beer here?

7. WAITRESS   **Yǒu.**
Yes.

8. LI   **Nà jiù xiān lái yìpíng ba. Jiù zhèixiē le ba. Wǒmen yǒu jíshì, máfan nín kuài dianr shàngcài.**
Then why don't you first bring us one bottle. That's all, I guess. We're in a great hurry, so please bring the food as fast as you can.

9. WAITRESS   **Xíng.**
O.K.

Build Up

1. Li	
fàng	put, place [V]
làjiāo	hot pepper [N]
shǎo fàng diǎnr làjiāo	put in fewer hot peppers
pà	fear, be afraid of [V]
shòu	endure, suffer [V]
-liǎo	be able to [RE]
shòubuliǎo	not to be able to endure [RC]
Mápó Dòufu shǎo fàng diǎnr làjiāo,	For the Pockmarked Old Woman's Tofu don't
wǒ pà zhèiwèi Měiguo péngyou shòubuliǎo.	put in too many hot peppers, I'm afraid my
	American friend wouldn't be able to stand it.

2. Warres	
duō fàng diǎnr	put in more
yě méi guānxi	is also O.K.
là	be peppery hot [SV]
wǒ néng chī làde	I can eat hot spicy ones
Duō fàng diǎnr yě méi guānxi,	It's O.K. if you put in a lot, I can eat hot
wǒ néng chī làde.	spicy foods.

3. Waitress	
lei (B)	(sentence final particle) [P]
hǎo lei	"all right," "O.K." [IE]
zhǔshi (B)	staple food, main food [N]
zhǔshí yào shémme	as staple food what do you want
mǐ	rice (uncooked) [N]
mǐfàn	rice (cooked) [N]
mántou	steamed bun [N]
mǐfàn háishi mántou	rice or steamed buns
Hǎo lei. Zhǔshí yào shémme?	All right. What do you want for your
Mǐfàn háishi mántou?	main food? Rice or steamed buns?

4. Li	
liǎng	ounce (50 grams) [M]
sìliǎng	four ounces
sìliǎng mǐfàn	four ounces of cooked rice
Sìliǎng mǐfàn, liǎngge mántou.	Four ounces of rice and two steamed buns.

5. Waitress	
hē	drink [V]
Hē diǎnr shémme?	What would you like to drink?

6. Li	
jiǔ	liquor [N]
píjiǔ	beer [N]
Yǒu píjiǔ ma, nín zhèr?	Do you have beer here?

7. Waitress	
Yǒu.	Yes.

8. Li	
píng	bottle [M]

yìpíng	one bottle
xiān lái yìpíng	first bring one bottle
jiù zhèixiē le ba	only these I suppose
jíshì	urgent matter [N] (M: **jiàn**)
wǒmen yǒu jíshì	we have an urgent matter
shàngcài	bring food to a table [VO]
kuài dianr shàngcài	bring food to the table faster
Nà jiù xiān lái yìpíng ba. Jiù zhèixiē le ba. Wǒmen yǒu jíshì, máfan nín kuài dianr shàngcài.	Then why don't you first bring us one bottle. That's all, I guess. We're in a great hurry, so please bring the food as fast as you can.

9. **Waitress**

Xíng.	O.K.

Supplementary Vocabulary

1.	suān	be sour [SV]
2.	tián	be sweet [SV]
3.	kǔ	be bitter [SV]
4.	xián	be salty [SV]
5.	píngzi	bottle [N]
6.	mǎn	reach a certain age or time limit [V]
	nián mǎn èrshiyīsuì	years to reach 21 years of age
	hē jiǔ	drink alcoholic beverages
	Zài Měiguo, nián mǎn èrshiyīsuì cái kéyi hē jiǔ.	In the U.S., only when you've reached the age of 21 can you drink alcohol.

Grammatical and Cultural Notes

1A. The verb **fàng** "put, place" is very common and useful. It's often used with the postverb **-zài** to create **fàngzai** "put in, put at, put on." The **-zài** makes clear where the "putting" is supposed to end up. In rapid speech, the postverb **-zài** is sometimes omitted, but we recommend that for now you always use it. Examples:

Zhèige fàngzai zhèr, nèige fàngzai nàr.	"Put this here and put that there."
Qǐng nǐ bǎ shūbāo fàngzai yǐzi dǐxia.	"Please put your book bags under your chairs."
Nèixiē dōngxi nǐ fàngzai nǎr le?	"Where did you put those things?"

1B. **DUŌ AND SHǍO BEFORE VERBS TO INDICATE "MORE" AND "LESS."** Consider, in this line, the phrase **shǎo fàng diǎnr làjiāo** "put in fewer hot peppers" or "don't put in too many hot peppers;" and, in line 2, the phrase **duō fàng diǎnr yě méi guānxi** "if you put in more it's also O.K." or "it's O.K. even if you put in a lot." The stative verbs **duō** and **shǎo** can be used as adverbs directly before some verbs to indicate "more" and "less." You actually encountered this pattern previously in the phrase **qǐng duō zhǐjiào** "please instruct me more" in 2-4. In this pattern, **yìdiǎn(r)** or some other quantity expression is often, though not always, added after the verb. If both **yìdiǎn(r)** and an object are present, then the object is placed after the **yìdiǎn(r)**. The basic patterns are:

DUŌ	VERB	YÌDIǍNR	OBJECT
duō	kàn	yìdiǎnr	shū

"study more"

SHǍO	VERB	YÌDIǍNR	OBJECT
shǎo	fàng	yìdiǎnr	làjiāo

"put in fewer hot peppers"

Here are some more examples:

Shǎo chī diǎnr.	"Eat a little less." or "Don't eat so much."
Duō chuān diǎnr yīfu!	"Wear some more clothes!"
Duō xiě jǐge zì.	"Write a few more characters."
Duō zhù jǐtiān.	"Stay a few more days."
Duō zuòshì, shǎo shuōhuà.	"Do more, talk less."

Especially in the case of actions that have already been completed, **duō** can sometimes imply "too much" and **shǎo** can sometimes imply "too little." For example:

Nèige zì, nǐ duō xiěle yìbǐ.	"You wrote one stroke too many for that character."
Hǎoxiàng nǐ shǎo gěile shíkuài qián.	"It seems you paid ten dollars too little."

Attention: In certain non-Mandarin dialects such as Cantonese, the sentence order with **duō** and **shǎo** is the opposite of Mandarin. In those dialects, the equivalents of **duō** and **shǎo** regularly come after the verb, rather than before the verb as in Mandarin. So you may sometimes hear Cantonese speakers utter sentences like ***Chī duō yìdiǎn** when they speak Mandarin. But this isn't good Mandarin. Standard Mandarin requires that the **duō** come before the verb, so you should say **Duō chī yìdiǎn** "Eat a little more."

1C. Distinguish **pà** "to fear" from **kǒngpà** "I'm afraid that" or "probably" (cf. 3-4). **Pà** means "fear" or "be afraid of" while **kǒngpà** indicates one's overall estimation of a situation, a little like **dàgài**. Unlike **pà**, which is a verb, **kǒngpà** is a moveable adverb, so you must say **Wǒ pà gǒu** "I fear dogs" and you could NOT say ***Wǒ kǒngpà gǒu**.

1D. Look at the resultative compound verb **shòubuliǎo** "be unable to endure." The resultative ending **-liǎo** means "be able to" or "have the physical ability to." It can be used only in conjunction with the potential infixes **-de-** "be able to" or **-bu-** "not be able to" and never with a verb alone (so you could never say just ***shòuliǎo**). Some examples of other resultative compounds with **-liǎo**:

POSITIVE	NEGATIVE
zuòdeliǎo	**zuòbuliǎo**
"be able to do"	"be unable to do"
chīdeliǎo	**chībuliǎo**
"be able to eat"	"be unable to eat"
hēdeliǎo	**hēbuliǎo**
"be able to drink"	"be unable to drink"

Some example sentences with the resultative ending **-liǎo**:

Nǐ kāideliǎo chē ma?	"Are you able to drive?" (e.g., when asked of people who may have had too much alcohol)
Jīntiān wǒ zǒubuliǎo nèmme yuǎnde lù.	"Today I can't walk that far."
Nèiwèi lǎo tàitai hǎobuliǎole.	"That old lady isn't going to get better."

Wǒ Zhōngwén bù hǎo, xiěbuliǎo nèmme chángde bàogào.
"My Chinese isn't good, I can't write that long a report."

2A. **Wǒ néng chī làde** means **Wǒ néng chī làde cài** "I can eat hot spicy dishes." The other flavors introduced in the Supplementary Vocabulary of this lesson can similarly be used with a **-de** at the end to indicate foods characterized by that flavor, for example:

Nǐ zěmme zhèmme ài chī suānde?	"How come you like eating sour foods so much?"
Guǎngdōng rén xǐhuan chī tiánde.	"The Cantonese people like to eat sweet things."
Wǒ néng chī kǔde.	"I can eat bitter foods."
Wǒ bù néng chī xiánde.	"I can't eat salty foods."

2B. There is a famous saying containing the stative verb **là** "be peppery hot" that goes like this: **Sìchuān rén bú pà là, Jiāngxī rén là bú pà, Hú'nán rén pà bú là!** "People from Sichuan aren't afraid of peppery hot flavor; people from Jiangxi, peppery hot flavor, they're not afraid of that either; but people from Hunan are afraid that their food is not peppery hot!"

3A. The expression **hǎo lei**, which is a variant of **hǎole** "all right" or "O.K.," has become quite common in Beijing in recent years.

3B. Note the concept of **zhǔshí** "staple food" or "main food." **Zhǔshí** would be food like rice, steamed buns, noodles, or dumplings which are what really "make you full" and which are eaten along with vegetables and meat (which are sometimes called **fùshí** "non-staple foods"). These terms are often used in mainland China but are seldom used in Taiwan.

3C. Be sure to pronounce the tones in **zhǔshí** "staple food" correctly, and distinguish this word from the unrelated word **zhūshǐ** "pig manure"!

3D. Note the important difference between **mǐ** "uncooked rice" and **mǐfàn** "cooked rice" (**fàn** alone can also mean "cooked rice"). There is also a color, **mǐsè**, "the color of uncooked rice," which is tan or light brown but definitely not white. Also, if you've finished all the rice in your rice bowl but are still hungry and want more rice, be careful not to say **Wǒ hái yào fàn**, because **yào fàn** has a secondary meaning of "to beg," which some Chinese find very inauspicious. Instead, you should say **Zài lái yìwǎn fàn** "Another bowl of rice" or, even more politely, **Wǒ hái xiǎng zài tiān yìwǎn fàn**, which means "I'd like to add one more bowl of rice."

4A. **Liǎng** is a measure meaning "Chinese ounce." To avoid pronouncing **liǎng** twice, which would be considered as not pleasant sounding, Chinese speakers usually say **èrliǎng** for "two ounces" instead of the expected **liǎngliǎng**.

4B. In dining halls in mainland China, rice and other staple foods such as **jiǎozi** "dumplings" are usually sold by weight. In Taiwan, rice is sold by the bowl while dumplings are sold by the piece or per ten.

6A. **Jiǔ** refers to any kind of alcoholic beverage from light beer to hard liquor. English "drink alcoholic beverages" is **hē jiǔ** in Chinese. A recent Chinese government-sponsored campaign to promote safe driving had as its slogan: **Hē jiǔ bù kāichē, kāichē bù hē jiǔ** "If/when you drink don't drive, and if/when you drive don't drink" (note the implied "if" or "when").

6B. The **pí-** of **píjiǔ** "beer" is a phonetic borrowing from Western languages (cf. English "beer," French "bière," German "Bier"). Like other languages, Chinese has loanwords (cf. 13-2: 2A). Normally, Chinese speakers prefer loan translations like **huǒchē** "train" (lit. "fire vehicle"), where the meaning of the foreign original, rather than the sound, is transferred. The number of purely phonetic borrowings, such as **léidá** "radar," has in the past not been very great. There are also partial phonetic borrowings such as **píjiǔ**, where one syllable renders the sound of a foreign word and another syllable (**jiǔ**) indicates the general meaning.

6C. **AFTERTHOUGHTS.** Examine the question **Yǒu píjiǔ ma, nín zhèr?** "(Do you) have beer, you here?" In this line, the phrase **nín zhèr** "you here" would normally come first in the sentence, as in **Nín zhèr yǒu píjiǔ ma?** "Do you here have beer?" However, the first words that came to the speaker's mind when he was about to say this sentence were the verb and object (**yǒu píjiǔ**), and only later—as an afterthought—did he add the subject (**nín zhèr**). Some more examples of afterthoughts:

Màn zǒu, nín.	"Take your time, you." OR "You take your time."
Zěmme la, nǐ?	"What happened to you?"
Zhēn guì a, zhèrde dōngxi.	"The things here are really expensive."
Duō piàoliang a, nèibianrde shān!	"How beautiful the hills over there are!"

The use of afterthoughts occurs wherever Chinese is spoken, but is especially common in Beijing. There is no need for you, as a nonnative speaker of Chinese, to make a special effort to use afterthoughts in your speech, but if it occasionally happens "naturally," that would be just fine.

Three **mántou** or "steamed buns"

8A. The **le** in **jiù zhèixiē le ba** "only these I suppose" is optional. When used, as here, it implies that originally the speaker had considered ordering additional items but then changed his mind and decided to order only these items; in other words, a changed situation has occurred in the speaker's mind.

8B. Why does the same speaker use **wǒmen** in this line but **zámmen** in line 1 of 14-1 (the first half of this conversation)? In line 1 of 14-1, the Chinese student is speaking directly to his American friend, while here in line 8 of 14-2, he's speaking to the waitress about himself and his American friend. He uses exclusive **wǒmen** because he wishes to make clear that he's excluding the waitress, i.e., the ones who are in a hurry are **wǒmen** "we" ("my American friend and I") and not **zámmen** "we" ("you and I").

SV1–4. The so-called "five flavors of Chinese cooking" are **suān** "be sour," **tián** "be sweet," **kǔ** "be bitter," **là** "be peppery hot" (which appeared in line 2 of the Basic Conversation), and **xián** "be salty." A basic categorization of flavors in China is into **tiánde** and **xiánde**. Often **xiánde** just means "those foods that aren't sweet."

SV3. The stative verb **kǔ** "to be bitter" can be used figuratively as well as literally. The verb-object compound **chīkǔ** means "eat bitterness," i.e., "have a difficult time." There is also a famous saying in Classical Chinese: **Chī dé kǔ zhōng kǔ, fāng wéi rén shàng rén** "Only when one has eaten the bitterest of the bitter will one be a human being above all others."

Arranging a Banquet

Professor Michael Vitale, who is directing a study abroad program in Beijing while on sabbatical, goes to the Ju Fu Lou Manchurian restaurant to arrange a welcoming banquet for his new students.

 Basic Conversation 14-3

1. VITALE		**Láojià, wǒ xiǎng dìng zhuō jiǔxí.**
		Excuse me, I'd like to make a reservation for a banquet.
2. RESTAURANT MANAGER		**Shémme shíhou? Duōshǎo rén?**
		When? For how many people?
3. VITALE		**Shí'èrhào, xīngqīliù, wǎnshang liùdiǎn. Wǒ gūjì chàbuduō yǒu èrshíge rén cānjiā.**
		The twelfth, Saturday, at 6:00 P.M. I reckon there will be about twenty people attending.
4. RESTAURANT MANAGER		**Wǒ kàn fēnchéng liǎngzhuō hǎo, nín juéde zěmmeyàng?**
		I think dividing into two tables would be best, what do you think?
5. VITALE		**Xíng a.**
		Fine.
6. RESTAURANT MANAGER		**Nín dǎsuan dìng shémme biāozhǔnde? Yǒu měi rén shíyuánde, èrshíyuánde. Gāojí yìdiǎnrde huà, yě yǒu měi rén sìshíyuánde, wǔshíyuánde.**
		What price level do you plan to book? There are 10 and 20 yuan per person ones. A little higher class, there are also 40 and 50 yuan per person ones.
7. VITALE		**Ò, měi rén sìshiyuánde ba.**
		Oh, I guess one at 40 yuan for each person.

 Build Up

1. **Vitale**

dìng	reserve, book [V]
zhuō	(for banquets) [M]

jiǔxí	banquet [N] (M: **zhuō**)
dìng zhuō jiǔxí	reserve a banquet
Láojià, wǒ xiǎng dìng zhuō jiǔxí.	Excuse me, I'd like to make a reservation for a banquet.

2.   Restaurant manager

Shémme shíhou? Duōshǎo rén?	When? For how many people?

3. Vitale

gūjì	reckon, estimate [V]
cānjiā	take part in [V]
yǒu èrshige rén cānjiā	there are 20 people attending
Shí'èrhào, xīngqīliù, wǎnshang liùdiǎn.	The twelfth, Saturday, at 6:00 P.M. I reckon
Wǒ gūjì chàbuduō yǒu èrshíge rén cānjiā.	there will be about twenty people attending.

4. Restaurant manager

fēn	divide, separate [V]
fēnchéng	divide into [V+PV]
fēnchéng liǎngzhuō	separate into two tables
nín juéde zěmmeyàng	how do you feel
Wǒ kàn fēnchéng liǎngzhuō hǎo,	I think dividing into two tables would be best,
nín juéde zěmmeyàng?	what do you think?

5. Vitale

Xíng a.	Fine.

6. Restaurant manager

dǎsuan	plan [AV/V]
biāozhǔn	level, standard [N]
dìng shémme biāozhǔn	reserve what (price) level
dìng shémme biāozhǔnde	reserve one at what (price) level
měi rén shíyuánde	one where each person is 10 yuan
gāojí	be high-class [SV]
gāojí yìdiǎnrde huà	if it's a little higher class
Nín dǎsuan dìng shémme biāozhǔnde? Yǒu měi rén shíyuánde, èrshíyuánde. Gāojí yìdiǎnrde huà, yě yǒu měi rén sìshíyuánde, wǔshíyuánde.	What price level do you plan to book? There are 10 and 20 yuan per person ones. A little higher class, there are also 40 and 50 yuan per person ones.

7. Vitale

Ò, měi rén sìshíyuánde ba.	Oh, I guess one at 40 yuan for each person.

Supplementary Vocabulary

1. zhǔxí	chairman [N]
Máo Zhǔxí	Chairman Mao
2. Xīcān	Western-style food [N]
3. Zhōngcān	Chinese-style food [N]
4. zuòfàn	cook [VO]

Additional Vocabulary: Foods and Eating

1. diǎnxin	pastry, light refreshments [N]
2. dàn'gāo	cake [N]

3. wèijīng
Qǐng búyào fàng wèijīng.

monosodium glutamate, MSG [N]
Please don't put in any MSG.

4. Fàn hòu bǎibù zǒu, huódào jiǔshíjiǔ.

"(If) after meals (you) walk one hundred paces, (you'll) live to be ninety-nine." [EX]

Grammatical and Cultural Notes

1A.   Note the expression **dìng zhuō jiǔxí** "reserve a banquet." Here are some more things that you can reserve with the verb **dìng**: **dìng zhuōzi** "reserve a table," **dìng fángjiān** "reserve a room," **dìng piào** "reserve a ticket," and **dìng yíge shíjiān** "reserve a time."

1B.   **Zhuō** is here short for **yìzhuō**. The number **yī** is often omitted before measures in rapid, colloquial conversation.

3.   Use of **gūjì** "estimate, reckon" in the sense of "think" is a relatively new usage in mainland Chinese Mandarin. In more traditional usage, as in Taiwan, **gūjì** is rather low in frequency and means "estimate, reckon" in its original sense. For this sentence, speakers from Taiwan would use **xiǎng** "think" or **rènwéi** "believe."

4.   Note **fēnchéng** "divide into." The postverb **-chéng** means "into"; like all postverbs, it's attached to a regular verb (cf. 10-1: 2C). Here are more examples of postverb constructions with the postverb **-chéng**: **huànchéng** "exchange for," **gǎichéng** "change into," **kànchéng** "see as," **qiēchéng** "slice into," **shuōchéng** "say as," **xiěchéng** "write into," and **zuòchéng** "make into."

6A.   **Dìng shémme biāozhǔnde** means **dìng shémme biāozhǔnde jiǔxí**, that is, "reserve a banquet at what level" or "book a banquet at what price category." Dinners for larger groups are often arranged on a set price per person or per table basis. There are typically inexpensive, moderate, and expensive menus from which to choose, which may vary widely from restaurant to restaurant and from region to region. In general, a good rule of thumb for foreign diners is that the more you pay for a meal, the less you'll probably like it, since the more expensive menus tend to include rarer and more exotic dishes such as shark's fin soup, sea slug, and fish maw.

6B.   As a noun, **biāozhǔn** can also be used to mean "standard," as in **Wǒmen xuéxiàode biāozhǔn hěn gāo** "Our school's standards are high." **Biāozhǔn** can also be used as a stative verb to mean "be standard," for example: **Nǐde Pǔtōnghuà hěn biāozhǔn** "Your Mandarin is very standard."

6C.   In the sentence **Yǒu měi rén shíyuánde, èrshíyuánde** "There are 10 and 20 yuan per person ones," the speaker says **měi rén** rather than the expected **měige rén**. Normally, the specifier **měi-** "each" is followed by a measure before a following noun, so to say **měige rén** would certainly not be incorrect. However, in the case of a few nouns including **rén** "person," **xīngqī** "week," and **yuè** "month," the measure **ge** is optional after **měi-**.

6D.   In the expression, **gāojí yìdiǎnrde huà**, the **-de huà** alone implies the conditional "if." However, it's also possible to use an explicit word for "if" followed by **-de huà**. Familiarize yourself with these three patterns that all mean "if":

> **Jiǎrú ...-de huà, ...**
>
> **Rúguǒ...-de huà, ...**
>
> **Yàoshi...-de huà, ...**

6E.   Some other nouns that may be described as **gāojí** "high-class" include **qìchē** "car," **bīnguǎn** "guest house," **fàndiàn** "hotel," and **dìfang** "place."

AV3.   **Wèijīng** "monosodium glutamate" or "MSG" is a flavor enhancer that is extracted from seaweed which is used extensively in Chinese cooking. It's especially common in soups. Some people suffer unpleasant side effects from ingesting it, such as headaches or flushes. If you're sensitive to MSG and don't want any in your food, just say: **Qǐng búyào fàng wèijīng** "Please don't put in any MSG."

Arranging a Banquet (cont.)

Professor Vitale
and the restaurant
manager continue
discussing the menu
for the banquet
(continued from the
previous lesson).

 Basic Conversation 14-4

1. RESTAURANT MANAGER	**Cài shi nín zìjǐ diǎn ne, háishi yóu wǒmen pèi ne?**
	Will you order the dishes yourself, or should they be arranged by us?
2. VITALE	**Wǒ duì nǐmen Dōngběi fēngwèirde cài bú tài shúxi, hái shi nín gěi wǒmen pèi ba.**
	I'm not very familiar with your Manchurian cuisine; it might be better if you arranged it for us.
3. RESTAURANT MANAGER	**Hǎo ba. Sìge lěngpán, bādào cài, yíge tāng, hái yǒu yídào tiánshí. Xíng ma?**
	All right. Four cold dishes, eight hot dishes, a soup, and a dessert. Will that do?
4. VITALE	**Kéyi, kéyi.**
	Fine.
5. RESTAURANT MANAGER	**Qǐng liúxià nínde xìngmíng, dìzhǐ, diànhuà, yǐbiàn wǒmen tóng nín liánxì.**
	Please leave your name, address, and phone number, so that we can contact you.
6. VITALE	**Hǎo, zhè shi wǒde míngpiàn. Máfan nín!**
	All right, this is my name card. Much obliged!

 Build Up

1. **Restaurant manager**

zìjǐ	oneself [PR]
nín zìjǐ	you yourself
yóu	by [CV]
pèi	coordinate, arrange [V]
yóu wǒmen pèi	arrange by us

| Cài shi nín zìjǐ diǎn ne, háishi yóu wǒmen pèi ne? | Will you order the dishes yourself, or should they be arranged by us? |

2. Vitale

duì	to, toward [CV]
Dōngběi	the Northeast, Manchuria [PW]
fēngwèi(r)	special local flavor [N]
Dōngběi fēngwèirde cài	Manchurian cuisine
shúxi	be familiar [SV]
duì...shúxi	be familiar with... [PT]
wǒ duì nǐmen Dōngběi fēngwèirde cài	I'm not very familiar with
bú tài shúxi	your Manchurian cuisine
hái shi nín gěi wǒmen pèi ba	it would be better if you arranged it for us

Wǒ duì nǐmen Dōngběi fēngwèirde cài bú tài shúxi, hái shi nín gěi wǒmen pèi ba.
I'm not very familiar with your Manchurian cuisine; it might be better if you arranged it for us.

3. Restaurant manager

lěngpán(r)	cold dish [N]
dào	(for courses of food) [M]
bādào cài	eight courses of hot dishes
tiánshí	dessert [N]

Hǎo ba. Sìge lěngpán, bādào cài, yíge tāng, hái yǒu yídào tiánshí. Xíng ma?
All right. Four cold dishes, eight hot dishes, a soup, and a dessert. Will that do?

4. Vitale

Kéyi, kéyi.
Fine.

5. Restaurant manager

-xià	down [RE]
liúxià	leave behind [RC]
liúxià nínde xìngmíng	leave your name
yǐbiàn...	so that..., in order to... [PT]
tóng	with [CV]
liánxì	contact [V]
tóng...liánxì	contact (someone) [PT]
tóng nín liánxì	contact you

Qǐng liúxià nínde xìngmíng, dìzhǐ, diànhuà, yǐbiàn wǒmen tóng nín liánxì.
Please leave your name, address, and phone number, so that we can contact you.

6. Vitale

Hǎo, zhè shi wǒde míngpiàn. Máfan nín!
All right, this is my name card. Much obliged!

Supplementary Vocabulary

1. pánzi	dish, plate [N]
2. chǎofàn	fried rice [N]
3. chǎomiàn	fried noodles [N]

Additional Vocabulary: Common Chinese Cuisines

1. Běijīng cài	Beijing food [PH]
2. Dōngběi cài	Manchurian food [PH]
3. Shànghǎi cài	Shanghai food [PH]
4. Guǎngdōng cài	Cantonese food [PH]
5. Táiwān cài	Taiwanese food [PH]

| 6. Chuāncài | Sichuan food [N] |
| 7. Xiāngcài | Hunan food [N] |

Grammatical and Cultural Notes

1A. Note the question **Cài shi nín zìjǐ diǎn ne, háishi yóu wǒmen pèi ne?** "Will you order the dishes yourself, or should they be arranged by us?" The word **cài** "dishes" is, of course, a preposed object here, and **shi** in the first phrase means something like "is it the case that" or "is it a situation of." Therefore, we could translate this question literally as "As regards the dishes, is it the case that you yourself order, or by us arrange?"

1B. The pronoun **zìjǐ** "oneself" often occurs immediately after a noun or pronoun to indicate emphasis. Examples:

wǒ zìjǐ	"I myself"
nǐ zìjǐ	"you yourself"
tāmen zìjǐ	"they themselves"
Wáng tàitai zìjǐ	"Mrs. Wang herself"

Zìjǐ can also occur alone. For example:

Zìjǐ zuòfàn, zìjǐ chī méi shémme yìsi.   "To have to cook by yourself and eat by yourself is a drag."

1C. Note the two **ne** in the question **Cài shi nín zìjǐ diǎn ne, háishi yóu wǒmen pèi ne?** "Will you order the dishes yourself, or should they be arranged by us?" It's not uncommon to add a **ne** at the end of each of the alternatives in choice-type questions with **háishi**.

1D. **THE COVERB YÓU "BY, FROM."** Examine the coverb **yóu** in the question **Cài shi nín zìjǐ diǎn ne, háishi yóu wǒmen pèi ne?** "Will you order the dishes yourself, or should they be arranged by us?" **Yóu** means "by" or "from" and indicates the person who performs the action of the verb or who is responsible for something. Some more examples of **yóu**:

Zhèijiàn shì yóu nǐ lái guǎn.

"Why don't you handle this matter." (lit. "This matter by you be handled.")

Zhèijiàn shìr yóu wǒ lái zuò ba.

"Let me do this." (lit. "This matter by me be done.")

1E. **Pèi** means "coordinate, match, arrange." When arranging a formal Chinese menu, it's very important that the proper kinds of foods be coordinated or matched with each other.

1F. In the video for this lesson, the large glass jar on the left side of the restaurant counter contains a deer penis (**lùbiān**, lit. "deer whip") immersed in wine. Some Chinese people will pay a premium to drink such concoctions in the belief that the reproductive organs of animals can cure sexual dysfunction and improve virility.

2A. **DUÌ...SHÚXI.** Look at the sentence **Wǒ duì nǐmen Dōngběi fēngwèirde cài bú tài shúxi** "I'm not very familiar with your Manchurian cuisine." The pattern **duì...shúxi** means "be familiar with." The basic pattern is:

DUÌ	OBJECT	SHÚXI
toward	(object)	be familiar
"be familiar with"		

Notice that the pattern for saying "to be familiar with" is **duì...shúxi** and NOT *gēn...shúxi, as you might expect from the vantage point of English. Also, the stative verb **shúxi** "be familiar" has an alternate pronunciation **shóuxi**, which is quite common and which is in fact used by the speaker in the conversation for listening.

2B.   The coverb **duì** "to" or "toward" is quite common. Here is another example:

> **Tā duì nǐ hěn hǎo.**   "He is very good to you."

3A.   The **lěngpán(r)** is usually a large plate with several kinds of cold appetizers that starts off a formal dinner.

3B.   While **tiánshí** "dessert" is served on formal occasions as at banquets, at home Chinese people usually eat only fruit for dessert.

5A.   YĪBIÀN. **Yǐbiàn** "so as to facilitate...," "so that...," or "in order that..." is a somewhat formal way to indicate purpose. **Yǐbiàn** is similar in meaning to **wèile** but is more formal, includes the ideal of "facilitate" and, unlike **wèile**, can never occur at the beginning of a sentence. Another difference between **yǐbiàn** and **wèile** is that **yǐbiàn** can be followed by nouns or pronouns as well as verbs, but **wèile** (in the sense of "in order to") must be followed by a verb. Another example with **yǐbiàn**:

> **Yǐnyòngde cáiliào yīng zhùmíng chūchù, yǐbiàn cházhèng.**
>
> "For materials cited one should indicate the source, so as to facilitate verification."

5B.   TÓNG...LIÁNXÌ. The pattern **tóng...liánxì** means "contact (someone)." The basic pattern is:

TÓNG	OBJECT	LIÁNXÌ
with	(someone)	contact

"to contact (someone)"

Examples with the pattern **tóng...liánxì**:

> **Qǐng nín zǎo yìdiǎn tóng tā liánxì.**
>
> "Please contact her as soon as possible."

> **Qǐng liúxià nínde xìngmíng, dìzhǐ, diànhuà, yǐbiàn wǒmen tóng nín liánxì.**
>
> "Please leave your name, address, and phone number, so that we can contact you."

Instead of the coverb **tóng**, the coverbs **gēn** and **hé/hàn** can also be used in this pattern. In English, the verb "contact" is transitive and takes a direct object ("contact him"). The Chinese verb **liánxì**, on the other hand, is intransitive and cannot take an object; it must be used with a coverb like **tóng** or **gēn**. This is the reason why many Chinese people, when speaking English, produce ungrammatical sentences like "I will contact with you tomorrow." Of course, when Americans speak Chinese, they often make far worse mistakes!

AV1–7.   **CUISINES OF CHINA.** China has many different cuisines. Except for Beijing food and Shanghai food, which are named for cities, most Chinese cuisines are named for the province or area from where they originate. Basically, northerners eat many different wheat products while southerners prefer rice. Northern food tends to be salty, food in the southeast is often sweet, and southwestern food is typically very spicy. As a result of improved transportation as well as large-scale migrations to different provinces in the last century due to wars and political movements, most Chinese cuisines are now available in most parts of China.

AV1.   **Běijīng cài** "Beijing food," which is often slightly oily and more salty than that of other regions, is noted for its lamb and duck. Garlic, scallions, leeks, chives, and vinegar are used generously. Since wheat is the basic grain in north China, Beijing cuisine includes many flour products such as noodles, dumplings, and buns. Many so-called Beijing dishes, including **kǎoyā** "roast duck," actually originate from Shandong.

AV2.   **Dōngběi cài** "Manchurian food" makes frequent use of pine nuts. Candied apples and pears are other specialties. Formerly, bear paw was a famous Manchurian specialty.

AV3.   Since Shanghai is a seaport and there are many lakes and rivers in the region, **Shànghǎi cài** "Shanghai food" includes many kinds of seafood as well as freshwater fish and shellfish. Shanghai cuisine tends to be rather rich and oily, with much sugar and soy sauce used in cooking.

AV4. **Guǎngdōng cài** "Cantonese food" is the style of Chinese cooking with which Americans are most familiar. Cantonese food is mildly seasoned and colorful, including many steamed or sweet-sour dishes and all kinds of sauces.

AV5. **Táiwān cài** "Taiwanese food" is rather mild in seasoning, using little salt, with numerous soups and noodle dishes. Since Taiwan is an island and most cities are located near the coast, **Táiwān cài** includes much seafood.

AV6. **Chuāncài** "Sichuan food" is hot and spicy, with lots of red chilis, peppers, scallions, and garlic. This type of cuisine includes many **suānlà** "hot and sour" dishes. **Chuān** is an abbreviation for Sichuan province.

AV7. **Xiāngcài** "Hunan food" is also hot and spicy and, in general, quite similar to Sichuan cuisine, though it may be richer and oilier and include more steamed foods. **Xiāng** is an abbreviation for Hunan province.

Unit 14: Review and Study Guide

New Vocabulary

AUXILIARY VERBS
dǎsuan — plan

COVERBS
duì — to, toward
tóng — with
yòng — using, with
yóu — by

IDIOMATIC EXPRESSIONS
hǎo lei — "all right," "O.K."
suíbiàn — "as you wish"

MEASURES
dào — (for courses of food)
liǎng — ounce (50 grams)
píng — bottle
wǎn — bowl
zhuō — (for banquets)

NOUNS
biāozhǔn — level
cài — dish of food
càidān(r) — menu
chǎofàn — fried rice
chǎomiàn — fried noodles
chāzi — fork
dàn — egg
dāozi — knife
dòufu — tofu
fànwǎn — rice bowl
fēngwèi(r) — special local flavor

jīdàn — chicken egg
jíshì — urgent matter
jiǔ — liquor
jiǔxí — banquet
kuàizi — chopsticks
làjiāo — hot pepper
lěngpán(r) — cold dish
mántou — steamed bun
mǎyǐ — ant
mǐ — rice (uncooked)
mǐfàn — rice (cooked)
pánzi — dish, plate
píjiǔ — beer
píngzi — bottle
ròusī(r) — meat shred
sháozi — spoon
shù — tree
tāng — soup
tiánshí — dessert
Xīcān — Western-style food
xǐshǒujiān — bathroom
Zhōngcān — Chinese-style food
zhǔshí — staple/main food
zhǔxí — chairman

PARTICLES
lei — (sentence final particle)

PATTERNS
duì...shúxi — be familiar with...

tóng...liánxì — contact (someone)
yǐbiàn... — so that...

PHRASES
jīdàn tāng — egg soup
Mápó Dòufu — Pockmarked Old Woman's Tofu
Mǎyǐ Shàngshù — Ants Climbing a Tree
Yúxiāng Ròusī — Fish Fragrant Meat Shreds

PLACE WORDS
Dōngběi — the Northeast, Manchuria
fànguǎn(r) — restaurant

PRONOUNS
zámmen — we (you and I)
zìjǐ — oneself

RESULTATIVE COMPOUNDS
liúxià — leave behind
shòubuliǎo — not to be able to endure

RESULTATIVE ENDINGS
-liǎo — be able to
-xià — down

STATIVE VERBS
gāojí — be high-class
gòu — be enough
kǔ — be bitter
là — be peppery hot

shúxi	be familiar
suān	be sour
tián	be sweet
xián	be salty

VERBS

cānjiā	take part in
diǎn	order, choose
dìng	reserve, book
fàng	put, place
fēn	divide, separate
gūjì	reckon, estimate
hē	drink
liánxì	contact
mǎn	reach a certain age or time limit
pà	fear
pèi	coordinate, arrange
shòu	endure, suffer
xǐ	wash

yòng	use

VERB-OBJECT COMPOUNDS

diǎncài	order dishes of food
shàngcài	bring food to a table
zuòfàn	cook

Major New Grammar Patterns

QUESTION WORDS AS INDEFI-NITES: Něige dōu xíng. "Any one will do.", **Nǎr dōu yíyàng.** "It's the same everywhere.", **Wǒ shémme dōu chī.** "I eat everything.", **Tā shéi yě bù xǐhuan.** "She likes no one." (14-1)

DUŌ AND SHǍO BEFORE VERBS TO INDICATE "MORE" AND "LESS": Duō kàn yìdiǎnr shū. "Read more books.", **Shǎo fàng**

diǎnr làjiāo. "Put in fewer hot peppers." (14-2)

AFTERTHOUGHTS: Yǒu píjiǔ ma, nín zhèr? "Do you have beer here?" (14-2)

THE COVERB YÓU "FROM, BY": Cài shi nín zìjǐ diǎn ne, háishi yóu wǒmen pèi ne? "Will you order the dishes yourself, or should they be arranged by us?" (14-4)

DUÌ...SHÚXI: Wǒ duì nǐmen Dōngběi fēngwèirde cài bú tài shúxi. "I'm not very familiar with your Manchurian cuisine." (14-4)

TÓNG...LIÁNXÌ: Qǐng nín tóng wǒmen liánxì. "Please contact us." (14-4)

YǏBIÀN...: Qǐng liúxià nínde xìng-míng, dìzhǐ, diànhuà, yǐbiàn wǒmen tóng nín liánxì. "Please leave your name, address, and phone number, so that we can contact you." (14-4)

Eating and Drinking (II)

COMMUNICATIVE OBJECTIVES

Once you've mastered this unit, you'll be able to use Chinese to:

1. Host or participate as a guest in a formal banquet.
2. Make and reply to formal welcoming comments at a banquet.
3. Toast the guests or hosts at a dinner, employing appropriate toasting etiquette.
4. Explain to others when they put food on your plate that you'd prefer to help yourself.
5. Converse about the food served at a dinner.
6. Tell the hosts or other guests, when they urge you to eat more, that you've had enough.
7. Describe how to eat Peking duck: take a pancake, put scallions and sweet fermented flour sauce on it, add duck skin and meat, and roll it up.
8. Offer words of thanks at the conclusion of a banquet.
9. Invite someone to your home for dinner, or accept or decline an invitation if you are invited to dinner.
10. Talk about making and eating various kinds of dumplings.

P A R T 1

The Peking Duck Banquet

American professor Peter McCoy has recently arrived in Beijing, where he teaches American history at Beijing Normal University. Professor Jiang Zixiang has invited McCoy and his wife, as well as a number of Chinese guests, to a welcoming banquet at the Quan Ju De Roast Duck Restaurant. The banquet begins with welcoming comments and a toast by Professor Jiang to Professor and Mrs. McCoy.

Basic Conversation 15-1

1.	PROFESSOR JIANG	**Wǒ xiān lái jiǎndānde shuō jǐjù. Jīntiān a, wǒmen dàjiā zài zhèr jùcān shi huānyíng Mò Jiàoshòu hé fūren lái wǒmen xuéxiào gōngzuò. Zhù Mò Jiàoshòu zài zhèli gōngzuò shùnlì, shēnghuó yúkuài! Xiànzài wǒmen lái jìng tāmen èrwèi yìbēi!**

I'll first simply say a few words. Today all of us have gathered here for a meal to welcome Professor and Mrs. McCoy to our school to work. We wish Professor McCoy that his work here go smoothly and that his life be happy! Now let's show our respect and toast the two of them with a glass of wine!

2.	PROFESSOR MCCOY	**Xièxie dàjiā, xièxie, xièxie. Wǒmen hěn gāoxìng yǒu jīhui dào Zhōngguo lái. Tóngshí yě fēicháng gǎnxiè dàjiā jǐge xīngqī lái gěi wǒmende bāngzhù hé zhàogu. Kǒngpà yǐhòu máfan dàjiāde dìfang hái hěn duō.**

Thank you, everyone. We're very pleased to have the chance to come to China. At the same time, we also very much appreciate the help and care you've given us the past few weeks. I'm afraid in the future we'll still need to call on you frequently.

Build Up

1. Professor Jiang

lái	(indicates one is about to do something) [AV]
wǒ xiān lái shuō jǐjù	I'll first say a few words
jiǎndān	be simple [SV]
-de	(adverbial marker) [P]
jiǎndānde	simply
jù	sentence, phrase [M]
jǐjù	a few sentences
jiǎndānde shuō jǐjù	simply to say several sentences
dàjiā	everybody, everyone [PR]

wǒmen dàjiā	all of us
jùcān	get together for a meal [VO]
wǒmen dàjiā zài zhèr jùcān	all of us get together to eat here
Mò	Mo [SN]
fūren	madam, lady [N]
zhù	wish [V]
shùnlì	be smooth [SV]
gōngzuò shùnlì	(may one's) work be smooth
shēnghuó	life [N]
yúkuài	be happy [SV]
shēnghuó yúkuài	(may one's) life be happy
jìng	respectfully toast, drink to [V]
bēi	glass, cup (for beverages) [M]
yìbēi	a cup or glass
jìng tāmen èrwèi yìbēi	toast the two of them with a glass

Wǒ xiān lái jiǎndānde shuō jǐjù. Jīntiān a, wǒmen dàjiā zài zhèr jùcān shi huānyíng Mò Jiàoshòu hé fūren lái wǒmen xuéxiào gōngzuò. Zhù Mò Jiàoshòu zài zhèli gōngzuò shùnlì, shēnghuó yúkuài! Xiànzài wǒmen lái jìng tāmen èrwèi yìbēi!

I'll first simply say a few words. Today all of us have gathered here for a meal to welcome Professor and Mrs. McCoy to our school to work. We wish Professor McCoy that his work here go smoothly and that his life be happy! Now let's show our respect and toast the two of them with a glass of wine!

---

2. **Professor McCoy**

tóngshí	at the same time [MA]
fēicháng	extremely [A]
gǎnxiè	thank [V]
fēicháng gǎnxiè dàjiā	very much thank everyone
jǐge	a few, several
jǐge xīngqī lái	in the past few weeks
bāngzhù	help [N/V]
zhàogu	care [N]
bāngzhù hé zhàogu	help and care
máfan dàjiāde dìfang	the areas where we'll trouble
hái hěn duō	everyone are still very many

Xièxie dàjiā, xièxie, xièxie. Wǒmen hěn gāoxìng yǒu jīhui dào Zhōngguo lái. Tóngshí yě fēicháng gǎnxiè dàjiā jǐge xīngqī lái gěi wǒmende bāngzhù hé zhàogu. Kǒngpà yǐhòu máfan dàjiāde dìfang hái hěn duō.

Thank you, everyone. We're very pleased to have the chance to come to China. At the same time, we also very much appreciate the help and care you've given us the past few weeks. I'm afraid in the future we'll still need to call on you frequently.

Supplementary Vocabulary

1. jùzi
Zhèige jùzi shi shémme yìsi?

sentence [N]
What does this sentence mean?

2. zhàogu
    xiǎo háizi
Ta hěn huì zhàogu xiǎo háizi.

take care of [V]
small child [PH]
She really knows how to care for children.

3. kuàilè
Zhù nǐ shēngrì kuàilè!

be happy [SV]
Happy birthday to you!

Grammatical and Cultural Notes

1A. This lesson takes place in one of the famous Quan Ju De roast duck restaurants in Beijing. Founded in 1864 in the third year of the reign of the Tongzhi Emperor during the late Qing Dynasty, the original Quan Ju De was located at the corner of Hepingmen in Xuanwu District. Many state-level banquets have been held there. There are now Quan Ju De branches throughout Beijing and other Chinese cities; there are even several branches overseas.

1B. The **lái** in **wǒ xiān lái jiǎndānde shuō jǐjù** is the same **lái** that means "come," but here it merely indicates in a general way the speaker's intention, i.e., that he is about to do something. It can be omitted without any change in the meaning. This kind of **lái** sounds very colloquial and gives the speaker a bit more time to think about how he or she will finish the sentence. More examples:

Xiànzài wǒ lái wèn nǐ.	"Now I'm going to ask you."
Nǐ xiūxi ba, ràng wǒ lái nòng.	"Why don't you rest and let me do it."
Nǐ shēntǐ bù shūfu, wǒ lái zuò ba.	"You don't feel well; why don't I do it."
Zhèxiē wèntí wǒmen lái yánjiū yixia.	"Let us study these problems."

1C. **-DE AS ADVERBIAL MODIFIER TO EXPRESS MANNER.** If there is an adverbial expression of two syllables or more that precedes a verb, a **-de** is usually added after the adverbial expression and before the verb. This is especially common in the case of two-syllable stative verbs; when **-de** is added to the stative verb, it makes the stative verb into an adverb that expresses manner. For example, **jiǎndān** means "be simple," but **jiǎndānde** means "simply," as in **jiǎndānde shuō jǐjù** "to simply say a few sentences." Some more examples:

shāngxīnde kū	"sadly cry"
rènzhēnde liànxí	"diligently practice"
gāoxìngde tiàoqilai	"happily jump"
hěn kuàide guò mǎlù	"quickly cross the street"
búduànde mǎi xīn yīfu	"constantly buy new clothes"

1D. The **a** in **jīntiān a** is a pause filler (11-3: 2A).

1E. Learn the common and useful pronoun **dàjiā** "everybody, everyone." It can be used alone or after plural pronouns. Note here **wǒmen dàjiā** "all of us." The plural pronouns **wǒmen**, **nǐmen**, and **tāmen** can optionally be used before **dàjiā**. There is often a **dōu** after **dàjiā** to further stress that "everybody" is involved.

1F. **Tāmen èrwèi** "the two of them." **Èrwèi** is sometimes used instead of **liǎngwèi**. However, **liǎngwèi** would also be correct here.

1G. **Bēi** is the measure that means "glass" or "cup" of some beverage, so you'd say **yìbēi** "one glass" or **zhèibēi** "this cup" or **jǐbēi** "how many cups?" The expression for "a large glass" is **dàbēi** and "a small glass" is **xiǎobēi**. The noun for "cup" is **bēizi** and the noun for "glass" is **bōlibēi**. The word for "tea cup" is **chábēi**.

1H. **BANQUET ETIQUETTE.** Eating is one of the very best ways to meet Chinese people and make friends; in fact, for many Chinese, the epitome of happiness is a group of 12 friends or relatives seated around a table, with many expensive delicacies and even more alcohol, accompanied by loud conversation, laughter, wine drinking games, and singing. Banquets and formal dinner parties are ubiquitous in Chinese society. They represent an important forum for social, economic, and even political interchange, and allow participants to maintain and enhance their social status. As Professor Eric Shepherd has pointed out, the purposes of banquets include "to welcome a friend home or see him off on a journey, to gain or give face, to introduce two or more unfamiliar parties, to establish and strengthen relationships, to reaffirm familial ties, to request assistance, to reciprocate for help received, to celebrate important occasions such as weddings, holidays and promotions, to express gratitude, to repair strained relationships, and to get together with friends and consume rare foods and fine spirits."*

If the dinner is at a restaurant, as is the usual practice, there is no need to bring a gift; on the other hand, if the invitation is to someone's home, which is considered a special honor, you should bring a suitable gift, e.g., a large basket of special fruit, a box of small cakes, or one or two bottles of imported spirits. Getting invited to people's homes is special, since many Chinese have small apartments and can't easily invite guests; if you must decline an invitation to a Chinese person's home, explain the exact reason why, so that they don't misunderstand and think you dislike them or consider their home too primitive.

If you're hosting, you can entertain at a restaurant just like most Chinese would, or you can entertain at home, which will be a special treat for your guests. If you do entertain at home, Western food will be expected, and many Chinese will enjoy the novelty. Don't attempt to cook Chinese style unless you're truly very good. Invitations are best handled through a phone call via a third party, such as your secretary; this reduces the awkwardness if the invitation should be declined. If you entertain at home, resist the urge to be informal; Chinese people love formality. Picnics, pizza, or barbecues don't usually go over very well. On the other hand, a buffet with various kinds of hot vegetable, meat, and seafood dishes, where everyone can take whatever they like, would be appropriate. When entertaining, liquor is obligatory, even if you yourself don't drink; without it, most of your guests will be disappointed.

> If you entertain at home, resist the urge to be informal; Chinese people love formality. Picnics, pizza, or barbecues don't usually go over very well. On the other hand, a buffet with various kinds of hot vegetable, meat, and seafood dishes, where everyone can take whatever they like, would be appropriate.

It's customary at banquets for the host to start the evening with a few remarks and for the guest of honor to reply in kind; so be prepared if you're playing either of these roles. Typically, at the end of each person's remarks, a toast will be proposed. As each new dish is brought to the table, the host may propose another toast. During the meal, the host will usually toast the other guests; this may be in order of rank or simply in the order in which the guests are seated. Of course, the guests should also toast the host. At banquets with more than one table, the host and hostess, sometimes accompanied by the guest of honor, often rise with their glasses and make a round of all the tables, starting at their own, drinking a toast at each. The guests at each table then stand for the toast.

A formal Chinese banquet consists of a dozen or more courses, served one after another. A common mistake made by foreigners is to eat too much of the first few dishes, since the best dishes are often saved until the end. Dishes are shared by all those present; unlike in the West, you're not offered a separate entree for you alone. This practice is a reflection of Chinese society, which emphasizes the group rather than the individual. Food is enjoyed for its **sè**, **xiāng**, **wèi** "appearance, aroma, and taste," as well as for its texture, rarity, medicinal value, and symbolism.

Wait until the host invites you to start eating. The guest of honor is expected to partake of each new dish first, with the other guests following. The dishes will typically be on a lazy Susan, and it's considered polite to rotate the lazy Susan to the next diner after you have taken your portion. It's best not to decline any food that is being offered. It will give the host face if you take something from each dish and eat and praise it, but if you really don't want to eat it, you can always leave it on your plate or in your bowl. If you eat everything up each time, this is a signal that you're hungry for more, so someone is sure to add another helping to your dish. If you're the host, you should start the dinner by offering food to your guests. It's the responsibility of the host to see to it that guests' drinking glasses are refilled and that food is being added to the guests' plates during the meal; the host may serve guests personally, or the guests to your right and left may serve you. Even if you're only a

---

* Eric T. Shepherd, *Eat Shandong*, National East Asian Languages Resource Center, The Ohio State University, Columbus, Ohio, 2005, p. 21.

guest, you should serve beverages and food to those seated to your right and left before serving yourself—this will impress Chinese people with your thoughtfulness and good manners.

Chinese banquets usually start at 6:00 or 6:30 PM and end by 8:30 or 9:00. Chinese people generally don't sit around long after a meal is over. Once the last course has been served, the guest of honor should thank the host, toast him or her, toast all the guests together, and then slowly get up to leave. Neither the host nor any of the other guests can ordinarily get up before the guest of honor, unless they have another commitment, in which case they must formally excuse themselves (cf. line 7 in Basic Conversation 16-3). Depending on the formality of the occasion and the personality of the host, Chinese will sometimes take turns singing after the dinner, so it's best to be prepared; if you're able to offer a rousing rendition of your college song, "Old Mac-Donald," "Row, Row, Row Your Boat," or "Puff the Magic Dragon," you'll be sure to bring down the house.

1I.   HOW TO HANDLE INTERPRETING. There may be times when giving toasts or speeches that you encounter the need for English-Chinese interpreting. If you ask someone else to interpret, whether a professional interpreter or a friend, give them an English version of your remarks beforehand if at all possible, so that they may better be prepared and not caught by surprise. The most common practice is to deliver the whole speech in English first, followed by a Chinese interpretation. But if you should desire simultaneous interpretation, be sure to keep your sentences short, pausing frequently between sentences. Speak loudly and distinctly at a moderate pace, eschewing both very formal and very colloquial terms. If you should encounter the need to interpret between two parties yourself, be aware that the interpreter normally stands or sits between the two parties and slightly behind them. Always interpret in the first person, exactly as the speakers say something, rather than using indirect speech, which adds to the complications of interpretation. For example, in your interpretation you should say "This is the best offer my company can make," not "Mr. Jones said that this is the best offer his company can make." Even if your Chinese is very good, it can sometimes be advantageous to ask an interpreter to interpret for you, since doing so will save you energy and give you extra time to think about what your Chinese interlocutor has said and what you should say next.

2A.   **Note the moveable adverb **tóngshí "at the same time." You've seen the bound form **tóng-** "same" previously in the following nouns:

tóngshì	"colleague" (2-3)
tóngwū	"roommate" (2-2)
tóngxué	"classmate" (2-1)
tóngzhì	"comrade" (9-4)

Pay attention to recurring components in related words, as this will help you expand your vocabulary.

2B.   TIME EXPRESSION + (YĬ)LÁI. In this line, notice the expression **jǐge xīngqī lái** "for the past few weeks." The pattern TIME EXPRESSION + **(yǐ)lái** means "(in) the last..." or "(during) the past...." A time expression followed by **yǐlái** or **lái** indicates a period from a certain point in the past extending up to and including the present. Examples:

zhèijǐge yuè yǐlái	"the last few months"
zhèiyìnián yǐlái	"during the past year"
zhèijǐtiān lái	"these past few days"
duō nián lái	"for many years"

2C.   **Here, **bāngzhù functions as a noun. However, it can also function as a verb. Example:

Qǐng nǐ bāngzhù wǒ, hǎo ma? "Please help me, all right?"

2D.   Máfan dàjiāde dìfang hái hěn duō literally means "the places where (we'll) trouble everyone are still very many," that is, "There are still lots of areas where we'll be needing your help." Often, where in English we would say "There are many...," Chinese will use a noun followed by the stative verb **duō** "be many." Two more examples:

> **Zhèr shān hěn duō.**
>
> "There are many mountains here." (lit. "Here mountains are many.")

> **Měiguo háizi língyòngqián tài duōle.**
>
> "American children have too much pocket money." (lit. "American children pocket money is too much.")

The preferred, most natural position for an adjective in Chinese is as stative verb at the end of the sentence, while in English the preferred position is as adjective before a noun. In Chinese, the focus is on the stative verb at the end of the sentence; therefore, if you say something like ***Měiguo háizi yǒu tài duōde língyòngqián**, the focus will seem strange to a Chinese native speaker and the whole sentence will sound like a poor translation from English.

SV2.   **Xiǎo háizi** "small child." The following words containing the bound form **hái-** "child" have already been introduced:

háizi	"child" (1-2)
xiǎohái(r)	"small child" (6-2)
nánháir	"boy" (7-1)
nǚháir	"girl" (7-1)

In addition to the above, **nánháizi** "boy" and **nǚháizi** "girl" are also common.

SV3A.   In this lesson two words for "happy" are introduced—**kuàilè** and **yúkuài**—and in 2-2 you had previously encountered **gāoxing**. All three of these are stative verbs that all mean "be happy," but they aren't used in exactly the same way. In general, **kuàilè** expresses deeper and longer term "happiness," while **gāoxing** expresses a person's feelings at one particular moment in time, which could easily change from one moment to the next. The sense of **yúkuài** is somewhere between **kuàilè** and **gāoxing**.

SV3B.   BIRTHDAYS. **Zhù nǐ shēngrì kuàilè** literally means "(I) wish you (that your) birthday is happy." This sentence is sometimes sung four times as the Chinese translation of "Happy Birthday to You." Traditionally, only older people celebrated birthdays, but due to Western influence, urban families now celebrate birthdays for their children with cake and presents much as in the West. At birthday dinners for older persons, long noodles may be served, symbolizing "long" life. These "long-life noodles" shouldn't be cut or sliced, since that would be most inauspicious. Peaches are another symbol of longevity and are also given or eaten on birthdays. On birthdays and other happy occasions such as Chinese New Year, Chinese people are reluctant to talk about unpleasant topics such as death, illness, or accidents, so be careful what you talk about!

The Peking Duck Banquet (cont.)

As the host and guests continue their eating and drinking, the duck is brought to the table (continued from the previous conversation).

 Basic Conversation 15-2

1. **PROFESSOR MCCOY** **Wǒ tíyì wèile zhǔrén hé zàizuò gèwèide jiànkāng gān yìbēi!**
I propose a toast to the health of the host and everyone here.

2. **PROFESSOR JIANG** **Mò Jiàoshòu, nín chángchang zhèige cài.**
Professor McCoy, try this dish.

3. **PROFESSOR MCCOY** **Xièxie, wǒ zìjǐ lái. M, wèidao zhēn bú cuò.**
Thank you, I'll help myself. Mmm, it tastes really good.

4. **CHINESE GUEST** **Mò Jiàoshòu, Mò Fūren, wǒ lái jìng nín èrwèi yìbēi. Zhōngguo cài nǐmen hái chīdeguàn ma?**
Professor McCoy, Mrs. McCoy, let me drink a toast to the two of you. So how do you like eating Chinese food?

5. **MRS. MCCOY** **Wǒmen hěn xǐhuan chī. Lái, wǒmen yě jìng nín yìbēi!**
We like to eat it very much. Come, let's also drink a toast to you!

6. **PROFESSOR JIANG** **Zhè shi yā zhēn'gānr. Nín chīdelái ma?**
This is duck gizzard and liver. Do you like it?

7. **PROFESSOR MCCOY** **Bú cuò. Yuè chī yuè hǎochī!**
It's good. The more I eat, the better it tastes!

8. **PROFESSOR JIANG** **Èi, kǎoyā láile! Mò Jiàoshòu, nín yǐqián chīguo kǎoyā méiyou?**
Hey, the duck is here! Professor McCoy, have you ever eaten roast duck before?

9. **PROFESSOR MCCOY** **Zǎo jiù tīngshuōguo, dàn yìzhí méi chīguo.**
I heard of it long ago, but have never eaten it before.

Build Up

---

1. **Professor McCoy**

tíyì	propose [V]
zhǔrén	host [N]
zàizuò	be present (at a banquet or meeting) [V]
gè-	each, every [SP]
gèwèi	everyone (polite)
jiànkāng	health [N]
zhǔrén hé zàizuò gèwèide jiànkāng	the health of the host and everyone here
gānbēi	drink a toast [VO]
gān yìbēi	drink a toast
Wǒ tíyì wèile zhǔrén hé zàizuò gèwèide jiànkāng gān yìbēi!	I propose a toast to the health of the host and everyone here.

---

2. **Professor Jiang**

cháng	taste [V]
chángchang zhèige cài	taste this dish
Mò Jiàoshòu, nín chángchang zhèige cài.	Professor McCoy, try this dish.

---

3. **Professor McCoy**

lái	(verb substitute) [V]
wǒ zìjǐ lái	I'll help myself
wèidao	taste [N]
wèidao zhēn bú cuò	the taste is really not bad
Xièxie, wǒ zìjǐ lái. M, wèidao zhēn bú cuò.	Thank you, I'll help myself. Mmm, it tastes really good.

---

4. **Chinese guest**

-guàn	be used to [RE]
chīguàn	be used to eating something [RC]
chīdeguàn	can get used to eating something
Mò Jiàoshòu, Mò Fūren, wǒ lái jìng nín èrwèi yìbēi. Zhōngguo cài nǐmen hái chīdeguàn ma?	Professor McCoy, Mrs. McCoy, let me drink a toast to the two of you. So how do you like eating Chinese food?

---

5. **Mrs. McCoy**

Wǒmen hěn xǐhuan chī.	We like to eat it very much. Come,
Lái, wǒmen yě jìng nín yìbēi!	let's also drink a toast to you!

---

6. **Professor Jiang**

yā zhēn'gān(r)	duck gizzard and liver [PH]
chīdelái	can or like to eat something [RC]
nín chīdelái ma	do you like to eat it
Zhè shi yā zhēn'gānr. Nín chīdelái ma?	This is duck gizzard and liver. Do you like it?

---

7. **Professor McCoy**

yuè...yuè...	the more...the more... [PT]
yuè chī yuè hǎochī	the more I eat the more delicious it is
Bú cuò. Yuè chī yuè hǎochī!	It's good. The more I eat, the better it tastes!

---

8. **Professor Jiang**

kǎo	bake, roast [V]
kǎoyā	roast duck [N]

chīguo kǎoyā méiyou	have or haven't eaten roast duck
Èi, kǎoyā láile! Mò Jiàoshòu,	Hey, the duck is here! Professor McCoy,
nín yǐqián chīguo kǎoyā méiyou?	have you ever eaten roast duck before?

....

9. Professor McCoy

zǎo jiù	long ago, long since [PH]
zǎo jiù tīngshuōguo	heard of it long ago
dàn	but [CJ]
yìzhí	always, all along [A]
dàn yìzhí méi chīguo	but always never had eaten
Zǎo jiù tīngshuōguo, dàn	I heard of it long ago, but have never
yìzhí méi chīguo.	eaten it before.

 ## Supplementary Vocabulary

1. **kèrén**	guest [N]
zuì	become drunk [V]
-zuì	drunk [RE]
hēzuì	get drunk [RC]
Zhǔrén, kèrén dōu hēzuìle.	The host and guests are all drunk.
2. **gānbēi**	"Cheers!," "Bottoms up" [IE]
Lǎo Lǐ, gānbēi!	Old Li, cheers!

Additional Vocabulary: Guests

1. **zhǔkè**	main guest [N]
2. **péikè**	accompanying guest [N]
3. **guǐ**	devil, ghost [N]
jiǔguǐ	wino, lush [N]
Nǐ lí tā yuǎn yidianr, tīngshuō tā shi ge jiǔguǐ.	Stay away from him, I hear he's a wino.

Grammatical and Cultural Notes

1. Examine the sentence **Wǒ tíyì wèile zhǔrén hé zàizuò gèwèide jiànkāng gān yìbēi!** The **wèile** in this sentence means "for" or "on behalf of" and is followed by nouns. So the literal meaning of this sentence would be "I propose for the host and everyone here's health to drink dry a cup!" The **wèile** that you learned in 13-2 means "in order to" and is followed by verbs, e.g., **wèile jiéshěng shíjiān** "in order to save time."

2. It's customary for the host to invite the guest of honor to try each new dish as it's brought to the table. The host will frequently serve those guests sitting nearby. As each new dish arrives at the table, a toast will often be proposed.

3A. As we saw in 12-4: 7, the verb **lái**, lit. "come," can substitute for other verbs with more specific meanings. In the sentence **Wǒ zìjǐ lái**, **lái** stands for **ná** "take (food)." If someone is about to serve you, it's very common to say **Wǒ zìjǐ lái**, which is then equivalent to English "I'll help myself." Another common suggestion from hosts to guests at dinner parties is **Zài lái yìdiǎnr ba!** "Have some more!"

3B. Look at **Wèidao zhēn bú cuò** "The taste is really good." The adverb **zhēn** "really" is a bit tricky. It can only be used in the pattern **zhēn** + STATIVE VERB and can never be used within a subordinate clause with **-de**. So to say "That's a really good book" you could NEVER say *_**Nà shi yìběn zhēn hǎode shū**. Instead, you must say **Nèiběn shū zhēn hǎo** "That book is really good."

4. **Nín èrwèi** "the two of you" is equivalent to **nǐmen èrwèi** but is even more polite. Except in a few set phrases like these, you'd always use **liǎng-** before the measure **wèi** and say **liǎngwèi**.

5. If you're the guest of honor, you need to keep track of who has toasted you. At some point during the dinner, you should return the toast of everyone who has toasted you.

6. The resultative compound **chīdelái** means "can eat something" or "like to eat something." You can also say **chībulái** "not be able to eat something" or "not like to eat something"; however, *chīlái doesn't exist. More examples with **chīdelái** and **chībulái** and also with the similar **zuòdelái** and **zuòbulái**:

> **Hǎishēn nǐ chīdelái ma?**
>
> "Are you able to eat sea cucumber?"

> **Hěn duō Zhōngguo rén dōu chībulái Měiguode "cheese."**
>
> "Many Chinese can't eat American cheese."

> **Xīcān wǒ zuòdelái, Zhōngguo cài wǒ kě zuòbulái.**
>
> "I can make Western food, but I really can't make Chinese food."

Remember **chīdeguàn** in line 4 above? **Chīdelái** and **chīdeguàn** are related in meaning and can both often be translated as "like to eat." However, there is a subtle difference, in that **chīdeguàn** literally means "can get used to eating," there being an implication that eating has occurred a number of times in the past; whereas **chīdelái** simply means "be able to eat something," with no implication that someone has eaten something previously in the past.

7. **YUÈ...YUÈ....** In 10-1: 4B we discussed the pattern **yuè lái yuè...** "more and more..., " as in **yuè lái yuè rè** "hotter and hotter." Now, in this lesson, you learn the related, very important pattern **yuè...yuè...** "the more...the more....," as in **Yuè chī yuè hǎochī** "The more I eat, the better it tastes." The slots after the two **yuè** are filled by some kind of verb—regular verb, stative verb, or auxiliary verb. The basic pattern is:

> | YUÈ | VERB₁ | YUÈ | VERB₂ |
> |---|---|---|---|
> | Yuè | chī | yuè | hǎochī. |
>
> "The more I eat, the better it tastes." (lit. "More eat more good-tasting.")

Note that in English, nouns or pronouns can occur after the word "more" (as in the example above); but in Chinese, **yuè** is an adverb, so as with all Chinese adverbs, **yuè** must precede the verb and can NEVER precede a noun or pronoun (so you could not say *yuè wǒ chī to mean "the more I eat"). Some more examples of the pattern **yuè...yuè...**:

> **Yǔ yuè xià yuè dà.**
>
> "The more it rained, the heavier the rain became." (lit. "Rain more descended more big.")

> **Tā yuè lǎo yuè qíguài!**
>
> "The older he gets, the stranger he gets!" (lit. "He more old more strange!")

> **Zhèige háizi yuè dà yuè cōngming.**
>
> "The older this child gets, the smarter she is." (lit. "This child more big more smart.")

Northern-style Chinese restaurant on Chengfu Road in Beijing

Jiàoshòu yuè jiāo yuè shòu!

"Professors, the more they teach the thinner they get!" (lit. "Professors more teach more thin"; this is an example of Chinese humor, since **jiāo** "teach" and **shòu** "be thin" when said together sound almost like **jiàoshòu** "professor"!)

In the examples above, the subject of the two **yuè** is the same. However, it's also possible to have sentences where the subject of each **yuè** is different. For example:

Tāde Zhōngwén yuè xué yuè hǎo.

"As for her Chinese, the more she learns the better it gets."

Nèipiān bàogào wǒ yuè xiě yuè cháng!

"That report, the more I write it, the longer it gets!"

Mǎi dōngxi, yuè piányi yuè hǎo.

"When you're buying things, the cheaper the better." (lit. "the more cheap the more better")

Wǒ juéde Zhōngwén yuè xué yuè yǒu yìsi.

"I feel that the more you study Chinese, the more interesting it gets."

In addition to **yuè...yuè...**, you can also use the negative patterns **yuè...yuè bù...** or **yuè bù...yuè bù....** For example:

Nèiběn shū wǒ yuè kàn yuè bù xǐhuan.

"That book, the more I read in it, the less I liked it."

Nǐ yuè bú yùndòng, shēntǐ yuè bú jiànkāng.

"The more you don't exercise, the more unhealthy your body will be."

Those of you interested in grammar might note that **yuè lái yuè...** is really a variant of **yuè...yuè...**, in which the dummy verb **lái** (cf. 12-4: 7 and note 3A above) fills the slot after the first **yuè**.

8A. **Kǎoyā** "roast duck" is here short for **Běijīng Kǎoyā** "Beijing Roast Duck." This is crisp, glazed duck which is sliced and served on thin pancakes with scallions and **tiánmiànjiàng** "sweet flour sauce."

8B. **AFFIRMATIVE-NEGATIVE QUESTIONS WITH -GUO AND MÉIYOU.** Note the **méiyou** at the end of **Nín yǐqián chīguo kǎoyā méiyou?** "Have you ever eaten roast duck before?" This question form, with **méiyou** at the end of the sentence, is the preferred affirmative-negative question form for verbs with **-guo** in Northern China. Some more examples:

Nǐ qùguo Nánjīng méiyou?	"Have you ever been to Nanjing?"
Tā xuéguo Zhōngwén méiyou?	"Has she ever studied Chinese?"

We don't recommend you say the following, but be aware that some native speakers will use affirmative-negative question forms and ask **Nín chīguo méi chīguo kǎoyā?** "Have you ever eaten roast duck before?", which can even be abbreviated to **Nín chī méi chīguo kǎoyā?**

In Southern China and Taiwan, in place of the above question patterns, it's very common to use **yǒu méiyou** before the verb with **-guo**. This is common even in North China in the case of long, complex questions where the listener might otherwise not know that what is being said is a question until the very end of the question. Examples:

Nín yǒu méiyou chīguo kǎoyā?	"Have you ever eaten roast duck?"
Nǐ yǒu méiyou qùguo Nánjīng?	"Have you ever been to Nanjing?"
Tā yǒu méiyou xuéguo Zhōngwén?	"Has she ever studied Chinese?"

The answers to such questions are as follows:

QUESTION: **Nǐ yǒu méiyou qùguo Nánjīng?** "Have you ever been to Nanjing before?"

NEGATIVE LONG ANSWER: **Wǒ méi qùguo Nánjīng.** "I've never been to Nanjing before."

NEGATIVE SHORT ANSWER: **Méiyou.** "I haven't."

POSITIVE LONG ANSWER: **Wǒ qùguo Nánjīng.** "I've been to Nanjing."

POSITIVE SHORT ANSWER: **Qùguo.** "I have."

Even though many speakers from Southern China and Taiwan will say the following, be aware that it isn't considered good Chinese to say ***Yǒu** or ***Wǒ yǒu qùguo Nánjīng** as the positive answers. Instead, you should use the verb + **-guo**

9A.   **Zǎo jiù** indicates that something happened long ago, has been going on for a long time, or took place earlier than expected. Examples:

Wǒ zǎo jiù zhīdaole.   "I've known for a long time."

Tāmen liǎngge zǎo jiù rènshile.

"The two of them have known each other for a long time." OR "The two of them met long ago."

Wǒ zǎo jiù xiǎng qǐng nǐ dào jiāli lái chī dùn fàn le.

"I've been wanting to have you over to my home for a meal for a long time now."

9B.   **Yìzhí**, which you've learned as meaning "straight" in terms of physical distance (cf. 8-1), can also be used in an abstract sense with time. In other words, **yìzhí méi chīguo** means "straight in time, from a long time ago until the present, I haven't ever eaten it" or, in better English, "I've never eaten it before."

SV1.   **Hēzuì** "get drunk" literally means "drink (to the point where one gets) drunk."

SV2.   **Gānbēi** "Cheers!" or "Bottoms up!" literally means "dry glass."

AV3.   **Jiǔguǐ** "wino, lush" literally means "alcohol devil."

The Peking Duck Banquet (cont.)

Professor Jiang explains to Professor McCoy how one eats Peking Duck, after which one of the Chinese guests puts more food on Mrs. McCoy's plate (continued from the previous conversation).

 ### Basic Conversation 15-3

1. PROFESSOR JIANG

   Nín děi xiān ná zhāng báobǐng, bǎ tiánmiànjiàng túzai bǐngshang, zài fàng-shang cōng, ránhòu bǎ yāròu fàngzai zhōngjiān. Bǎ bǐng juánqilai jiù kéyi chīle.

   You have to first take a pancake and spread the sweet flour sauce onto the pancake, then put on scallions, and after that put the duck meat in the middle. Roll up the pancake and you can eat it.

2. PROFESSOR MCCOY

   Hǎo, wǒ shìshi kàn. M, hǎochī]íle!

   All right, let me try. Mmm, it's delicious!

3. ANOTHER CHINESE GUEST *(as she puts more food on Mrs. McCoy's plate)* **Mò Fūren, nín chīde tài shǎole. Zài lái yidianr zhèige cài ba!**

   Mrs. McCoy, you're not eating enough. Have a little more of this dish!

4. MRS. MCCOY

   Wǒ yǐjīng chīle hěn duōle. Bié jǐn gěi wǒ jiācài, nín zìjǐ yě chī a!

   I've already had a lot. Don't only serve me food; you yourself eat, too!

5. PROFESSOR JIANG

   Mò Jiàoshòu, nín zěmme bù chīle? Duō chī diǎnr ba!

   Professor McCoy, how come you're not eating anymore? Have some more!

6. PROFESSOR MCCOY

   Wǒ chīde tài duōle, shízài chībuxiàle.

   I've eaten too much, I really can't eat any more.

   (when all have finished)

   Jīntiānde cài tài fēngfùle! Fēicháng gǎnxiè zhǔrén yǐjí zàizuòde gèwèi.

   There was so much food today! Very special thanks to our hosts and to everyone here.

Build Up

1. **Professor Jiang**

báo	be thin (in dimensions) [SV]
bǐng	pancake, biscuit [N] (M: **zhāng**)
báobǐng	pancake [N] (M: **zhāng**)
xiān...zài...	first...then... [PT]
nín děi xiān ná zhāng báobǐng	you must first take a pancake
bǎ	(moves object before verb) [CV]
miàn	flour; pasta, noodles [N]
jiàng	thick sauce [N]
tiánmiànjiàng	sweet flour sauce [N]
tú	smear, daub [V]
túzai	smear onto [V+PV]
bǎ tiánmiànjiàng túzai bǐngshang	take the sweet flour sauce and smear it onto the pancake
fàngshang	put on [RC]
cōng	scallion [N]
zài fàngshang cōng	then put on scallions
zhōngjiān	in the middle [PW]
fàngzai	put in, put on [V+PV]
bǎ yāròu fàngzai zhōngjiān	put the duck meat in the middle
juǎn	roll up [V]
juǎnqilai	roll up [RC]
bǎ bǐng juǎnqilai	roll up the pancake

Nín děi xiān ná zhāng báobǐng, bǎ tiánmiànjiàng túzai bǐngshang, zài fàngshang cōng, ránhòu bǎ yāròu fàngzai zhōngjiān. Bǎ bǐng juǎnqilai jiù kéyi chīle.

You have to first take a pancake and spread the sweet flour sauce onto the pancake, then put on scallions, and after that put the duck meat in the middle. Roll up the pancake and you can eat it.

2. **Professor McCoy**

Hǎo, wǒ shìshi kàn. M, hǎochījíle!   All right, let me try. Mmm, it's delicious!

3. **Another Chinese guest**

Mò Fūren, nín chīde tài shǎole.   Mrs. McCoy, you're not eating enough.
Zài lái yidianr zhèige cài ba!   Have a little more of this dish!

4. **Mrs. McCoy**

jǐn	only [A]
jiā	pick up (with chopsticks) [V]
jiācài	pick up food (with chopsticks) [VO]

Wǒ yǐjīng chīle hěn duōle. Bié jǐn gěi wǒ jiācài, nín zìjǐ yě chī a!

I've already had a lot. Don't only serve me food; you yourself eat, too!

5. **Professor Jiang**

duō chī diǎnr	eat a little more

Mò Jiàoshòu, nín zěmme bù chīle?   Professor McCoy, how come you're
Duō chī diǎnr ba!   not eating anymore? Have some more!

6. **Professor McCoy**

chībuxià	can't eat [RC]

Wǒ chīde tài duōle, shízài chībuxiàle.   I've eaten too much, I really can't eat any more.

fēngfù	be abundant [SV]

yìjí
Jīntiānde cài tài fēngfùle! Fēicháng
gǎnxiè zhǔrén yìjí zàizuòde gèwèi.

and [CJ]
There was so much food today! Very special
thanks to our hosts and to everyone here.

 ## Supplementary Vocabulary

1. hòu
Zhèijiàn yīfu tài báole,
nèijiàn bǐjiào hòu.

be thick [SV]
This piece of clothing is too thin,
that one is thicker.

Grammatical and Cultural Notes

1A.   **Zhāng** here means **yìzhāng**. As we've seen before, in colloquial, rapid speech, the number **yī** "one" is some-times omitted before measures when it means "a." (It's not omitted when it means "one." So to say "I have a friend" you could say **Wǒ yǒu ge péngyou**, but to say "I have one friend" you must say **Wǒ yǒu yíge péngyou**.)

1B.   **Báo** means "thin" in dimensions, such as the "thin pancake" (**báobǐng**) that is talked about here. To indicate "thin" in the sense of "not fat," you must use the word **shòu**, which you learned in 5-3.

1C.   **BǍ CONSTRUCTION TO MOVE OBJECT BEFORE VERB.** Do you remember two of the classroom ex-pressions that you learned at the very beginning of this course? They are:

(a)   **Qǐng nǐmen bǎ gōngkè gěi wǒ.** "Please you all give me your homework."

(b)   **Qǐng nǐmen bǎ kǎojuàn gěi wǒ.** "Please you all give me your test papers."

Now, in this first utterance of this Basic Conversation, examine these three phrases that all contain the coverb **bǎ**:

(a)   **bǎ tiánmiànjiàng túzai bǐngshang** "take the sweet flour sauce and smear it onto the pancake"

(b)   **bǎ yāròu fàngzai zhōngjiān** "take the duck meat and put it in the middle"

(c)   **bǎ bǐng juánqilai** "take the pancake and roll it up"

The so-called **bǎ** construction is extremely common. **Bǎ** was originally a verb meaning "grasp, hold, take," though it's now seldom used with those meanings. Its most common use by far is as a coverb, serving to move the object of the verb to a position before the verb and to indicate that the object is being disposed of or handled in a certain way. For example, consider these two sentences:

(a)   **Tā guānshang mén le.** "She closed the door."

(b)   **Tā bǎ mén guānshangle.** "She closed the door." (lit. "She took the door and closed it.")

In the second sentence, **bǎ** has transformed the regular SUBJECT + VERB + OBJECT order to SUBJECT + **bǎ** + OBJECT + VERB, so that the object of the verb is moved to a position in front of the verb. Although both of the above sentences as well as a third version with a preposed object (**Mén tā guānshangle**) are equally good and mean about the same thing, the version with **bǎ** is especially common and is typical of spoken Chinese. If we had to distinguish between the meaning of (a) and (b), we could say that in (b) there is special focus on what is being done to the door. To sum up, the basic pattern with **bǎ** is:

SUBJECT	BǍ	OBJECT	VERB
Tā	bǎ	mén	guānshangle.

"She closed the door." (lit. "She took the door and closed it.")

There are several things to keep in mind when using **bǎ**:

(1)   The verb must be transitive, in other words, it must be capable of having an object; and it must have a sense of disposal or control. Therefore, intransitive verbs like **lái** "come," **yǒu** "have," or **zài** "be located at" aren't compatible with the **bǎ** construction.

(2)   The object after **bǎ** is always definite or specific in meaning. **Tā bǎ sānzhāng zhuōzi bānzǒule** can mean only "He moved those three tables" or "He moved the three tables." To say "He moved three tables," you'd have to say **Tā bānzǒule sānzhāng zhuōzi**.

(3)   The verb at the end of the sentence cannot be in its simple form, i.e., it must have some kind of verb ending attached (e.g., **-le**, **-shang**, **-lai**) or be reduplicated. Less commonly, a monosyllabic verb at the end of the sentence may be preceded by a number expression that specifies the quantity of the verb such as **Tā bǎ mén yì guān** "She closed the door."

(4)   As with other coverbs, negative **bù** and **méi** are placed before **bǎ** or a preceding auxiliary, not before the main verb of the sentence, so you'd say **Tā hái méi bǎ mén guānshang** "She hasn't yet closed the door."

Two ladies at High Tea at the Peninsula Hotel in Hong Kong

(5)   The potential form of a resultative compound (i.e., the form with infixed **-de-** that means "can..." or with **-bu-** that means "can't...") cannot be used as the main verb in a **bǎ** sentence. In other words, you could NEVER say ****Wǒ bǎ mén dǎbukāi** for "I can't open the door." Instead, you'd say **Wǒ dǎbukāi mén** or **Mén wǒ dǎbukāi**. If you wish to express ability in a sentence where there is a **bǎ**, use **néng** or **kéyi** before the **bǎ**. For example, **Nǐ jīntiān néng bu néng bǎ gōngzuò zuòwán?** "Are you able to finish the work today?"

(6)   If there is an object in the sentence, and the verb is a postverb, then either **bǎ** is required or else the object is preposed. For example, **Qǐng nǐ bǎ shū fàngzai zhèr** OR **Shū qǐng nǐ fàngzai zhèr** "Please put the books here."

(7)   **Bǎ** can't be used with complements ending in **-jiàn** "perceive" as in **kànjian** "see" or **tīngjian** "hear," so you could NOT say ****Wǒ bǎ nèige rén kànjianle** "I saw that man." Similarly, **bǎ** can't be used with certain verbs indicating emotions, so you could NOT say ****Wǒ bǎ tā xǐhuanle** "I liked him."

If the above rules seem complicated, then just memorize a couple of useful sentences with **bǎ** and use them as often as you can; and as always, observe closely how Chinese speakers and writers use **bǎ**. Gradually, you'll gain a "feel" for **bǎ**. As a general strategy, you're encouraged to use **bǎ** whenever you can, but when in doubt, you can always use a preposed object (as in **Shū tā fàngzai nàr le** "She put the books there"). Here are some more example sentences with the **bǎ** construction:

Qǐng bǎ chēzi tíngzai tíngchēchǎng.

"Please park the car in the garage." (lit. "Please take the car and park it in the garage.")

Qǐng nǐ bǎ zhuōzi fàngzai zhèr, bǎ yǐzi fàngzai nàr.

"Please put the tables here and put the chairs over there."

Wǒ xiànzài méiyou dàyī, yīnwei wǒ qiánjǐtian bǎ dàyī jiègei péngyou le.

"I don't have a coat now, because a couple of days ago, I lent my coat to a friend."

Nǐ zěmme yòu bǎ wǒde shēngrì gěi wàngle ne?

"How come you forgot my birthday again?"

Wǒ bǎ wèntí dōu wènwánle.

"I've asked all my questions."

Nǐ yīnggāi bǎ nǐ gāngcái jiǎngde huà xiěxiàlái!

"You should write down what you just said!"

Nǐ yīngāi bǎ nǐ mèimei jièshao gěi tā!

"You should introduce your sister to him!"

Bié bǎ zhèijiàn shìr gàosu biérén!

"Don't tell anybody else about this!"

1D.   Both **túzai** "smear onto" and **fàngzai** "put in" are postverbs. The **-zài** indicates the direction of the action, i.e., where the result of the activity is supposed to end up. This contrasts with ordinary coverb constructions with **zài**, which describe where the action takes place. Contrast the following:

Qǐng nǐ xiězai zhèr.   "Please write it (e.g., a dedication in a book) here."

Qǐng nǐ zài zhèr xiě.   "Please write it here." (i.e., in this room now, not at home later)

1E.   **XIĀN...ZÀI....** Look at the first part of this utterance: **Nín děi xiān ná zhāng báobǐng...zài fàngshang cōng** "You have to first take a pancake...then put on scallions." When used alone, **xiān** means "first" and **zài** means "again." However, these two adverbs are also commonly used together in the paired adverb pattern **xiān...zài...** "first..., then...," which shows the sequence of the actions when there are two actions happening one after another. Any kind of verb or verb phrase may fill the slots after **xiān** and **zài**. The clause with **xiān** and the clause with **zài** may have the same subject or they may have two different subjects, as in the last example below. The basic pattern is:

XIĀN	VERB PHRASE$_1$	ZÀI	VERB PHRASE$_2$

Xiān   ná zhāng báobǐng,   **zài**   fàngshang cōng.

"First take a pancake, then put on scallions."

Some more examples of the pattern **xiān...zài...**:

Xiān xué shuō Zhōngguo huà, zài xué xiě Zhōngguo zì.

"First learn how to speak Chinese, then learn how to write Chinese characters."

Wǒmen xiān xiūxi yìhuǐr zài qù, hǎo bu hǎo?

"Let's rest a while before going, O.K.?" (lit. "We first rest a while and then go, O.K.?")

Wǒmen xiān kànkan yǒu duōshǎo rén lái chīfàn, zài juédìng mǎi duōshǎo cài.

"We'll first see how many people are coming to eat, and then decide how much food to buy."

Měiguo rén xiān hē tāng zài chīfàn, Zhōngguo rén xiān chīfàn zài hē tāng.

"Americans drink their soup first, and then eat; Chinese people eat first, and then drink their soup."

Nǐmen xiān lái fànguǎnr, wǒ zài diǎncài.

"You all first come to the restaurant and then I'll order food."

1F.   Some speakers in Beijing pronounce **zhōngjiān** "in the middle" as **zhōngjiànr** (with both an **-r** at the end and a different tone).

1G.   The resultative compound verb **juánqilai** means "roll up," so the phrase **bǎ bǐng juánqilai** means "take the pancake and roll it up" or "roll up the pancake." The ending **-qilai** in **juánqilai** has a different meaning from that in **kànqilai** "in the looking at" that you learned in 6-2.

3A.   The **lái** here, as we've seen before in 12-4: 7, is serving as a "dummy verb" filling in for a more specific verb like **ná** "take" or **jiā** "pick up with your chopsticks."

3B.   In the recording of the basic conversation for listening, the speaker actually says **zhège cài** "this dish" rather than **zhèige cài**. Be aware that to say "this," you can say either **zhèige** or **zhège**, and to say "that" you can say either **nèige** or **nàge**.

4A.   **Wǒ yǐjīng chīle hěn duōle** "I've already eaten a lot (and I'm still eating)." The final **le** here indicates that the action of eating has been going on for a period of time extending up through the present and is still continuing (11-1: 4A).

4B.   **Bié jǐn gěi wǒ jiācài** "Don't only serve me food." It's considered polite to serve those seated next to one.

5.   It's customary for hosts to urge guests to have additional helpings of food. If you eat everything on your plate, you'll most likely be served more. This is because eating everything on your plate indicates you're still hungry, and a good host never allows his or her guests to remain hungry. Thus, even though it's wasteful, if you've truly had enough, you should leave a little food on your plate. This is true of banquets only and would not apply to family members eating at home.

6A.   **Wǒ chīde tài duōle, shízài chībuxiàle** "I've eaten too much, I really can't eat any more." This sentence is useful as an explanation for why you don't wish to eat more. The negative potential resultative compound **chībuxià** literally means "eat but can't get down" or "unable to get down." Here, the implication is that you can't eat more because you're full; but in a different context, it could also be because you're sick, e.g., **Wǒ bìngle, suóyi shémme yě chībuxiàle** "I'm sick, so I can't get anything down."

6B.   When describing the various dishes served at dinners or banquets, some speakers prefer the word **fēngshèng** "be rich, sumptuous" to **fēngfù** "be abundant."

6C.   At the end of the meal, the guest of honor should make polite comments and offer thanks prior to getting up to depart.

Making Dumplings

Jenny Tai, a Chinese-American woman studying in Beijing, learns how to make boiled dumplings at a Chinese friend's home.

 Basic Conversation 15-4

1. CHINESE   **Zhēnní, nǐ yuànyi zhèige zhōumò qù wǒ nàr chī jiǎozi ma?**
              Jenny, would you like to go to my place this weekend to eat dumplings?

2. TAI   **Dāngrán yuànyi la!**
              Of course I'd like to!

              (at her friend's home that weekend)

              Zhè jiù shi nǐ shuōde jiǎozi ma? Hǎo piàoliang! Zhè shi shémme ya?
              These are the dumplings you talked about? They're beautiful! What's this?

3. CHINESE   **Zhè shi jiǎozi xiànr.**
              This is the dumpling filling.

4. TAI   **Dōu yǒu shémme?**
              What all is in it?

5. CHINESE   **Zhǔyào shi ròu hé báicài. Chúle zhèixiē zhīwài, hái yǒu xiē tiáoliào: cōng, jiāng, jiàngyóu, yán hé xiāngyóu.**
              It's mainly meat and cabbage. Besides these, there are also some condiments: scallions, ginger, soy sauce, salt and sesame oil.

6. TAI   **Zhēn xiāng a! Wénde wǒ dōu èle. Néng bu néng xiān zhǔ jǐge ràng wǒ chángchang?**
              Smells real good! Smells so good, I'm hungry. Could you boil a few first and let me taste them?

7. CHINESE   **Dāngrán kéyi la. Xiànzài wǒ jiù qù zhǔ.**
              Of course I can. I'll go boil them right now.

              (returns from the kitchen with a plate of dumplings) **Qǐng chī ba, bié kèqi.**
              Please eat some, don't be polite.

8. TAI   **Wà, hǎochījíle!**
                 Wow, they're incredibly delicious!

9. CHINESE   **Hǎochī jiù duō chī yidianr!**
                 If they're good, have some more!

 **Build Up**

---

1. Chinese
   Zhēnní   (Chinese for "Jenny")
   yuànyi   be willing to, like to [AV]
   zhōumò   weekend [N]
   zhèige zhōumò   this weekend
   qù wǒ nàr   go over there where I am
   jiǎozi   dumpling [N]
   Zhēnní, nǐ yuànyi zhèige zhōumò   Jenny, would you like to go to my place
   qù wǒ nàr chī jiǎozi ma?   this weekend to eat dumplings?

---

2. Tai
   Dāngrán yuànyi la!   Of course I'd like to!
   Zhè jiù shi nǐ shuōde jiǎozi ma?   These are the dumplings you talked
   Hǎo piàoliang! Zhè shi shémme ya?   about? They're beautiful! What's this?

---

3. Chinese
   xiàn(r)   filling [N]
   jiǎozi xiànr   dumpling filling
   Zhè shi jiǎozi xiànr.   This is the dumpling filling.

---

4. Tai
   Dōu yǒu shémme?   What all is in it?

---

5. Chinese
   zhǔyào   mainly [A]
   zhǔyào shi ròu hé báicài   it's mainly meat and cabbage
   chúle...zhīwài   besides...; except for... [PT]
   chúle zhèixiē zhīwài   besides these
   tiáoliào   condiment, seasoning [N]
   hái yǒu xiē tiáoliào   there are also some condiments
   jiāng   ginger [N]
   jiàngyóu   soy sauce [N]
   yán   salt [N]
   xiāngyóu   sesame oil [N]
   Zhǔyào shi ròu hé báicài. Chúle zhèixiē zhīwài,   It's mainly meat and cabbage. Besides these,
   hái yǒu xiē tiáoliào: cōng, jiāng, jiàngyóu,   there are also some condiments: scallions,
   yán hé xiāngyóu.   ginger, soy sauce, salt and sesame oil.

---

6. Tai
   wén   smell something [V]
   è   be hungry [SV]
   wénde wǒ dōu èle   I've smelled it to the extent that I've even become
                                             hungry
   zhǔ   boil [V]
   xiān zhǔ jǐge   boil several first
   ràng wǒ chángchang   let me taste
   Zhēn xiāng a! Wénde wǒ dōu èle. Néng Smells real good! Smells so good, I'm hungry.
   bu néng xiān zhǔ jǐge ràng wǒ chángchang?   Could you boil a few first and let me taste them?

7. Chinese
Dāngrán kéyi la. Xiànzài wǒ jiù qù zhǔ.   Of course I can. I'll go boil them right now.

    kèqi   be polite [SV]
    bié kèqi   "don't be polite" [IE]
Qǐng chī ba, bié kèqi.   Please eat some, don't be polite.

8.   Tai
    wà   "wow" [I]
Wà, hǎochījíle!   Wow, they're incredibly delicious!

9.   Chinese
Hǎochī jiù duō chī yidianr!   If they're good, have some more!

Supplementary Vocabulary

    1. kě   be thirsty [SV]
      hēde   things to drink
Wǒ hǎo kě. Yǒu méiyou shémme hēde?   I'm very thirsty. Is there anything to drink?

    2. chúle...yǐwài   besides...; except for... [PT]
      chúle nǐ yǐwài   besides you
Chúle nǐ yǐwài, hái yǒu shéi qù?   Besides you, who else is going?

Additional Vocabulary: Eating Dumplings

    1. shuǐjiǎo   boiled dumpling [N]
    2. zhēngjiǎo   steamed dumpling [N]
    3. sùjiǎo   vegetarian dumpling [N]
    4. guōtiē   potsticker [N]
    5. cù   vinegar [N]
    6. làjiāojiàng   hot pepper sauce [N]

Grammatical and Cultural Notes

1A.   The pronunciation of **yuànyi** "like to, be willing to" deserves special comment, as the final **-n** of the first syllable isn't pronounced as **-n**. If a syllable ending in **-n** is followed immediately by a syllable beginning with **y-**, **w-**, **h-**, or a vowel, then the **-n** of the first syllable is often not fully pronounced. In this case, the tongue doesn't quite reach the roof of the mouth, and the vowel in the first syllable is nasalized, so **yuànyi** is pronounced almost as if it were **yuàyi**, except that the **a** is nasalized. Examples of this phenomenon we've had earlier include **piányi** "cheap" (3-3) and **zhēn hǎochī** "really delicious" (6-1). Another example, using the word **è** "be hungry" that you learn in this lesson, is **hěn è** "very hungry."

1B.   The word **zhōumò** "weekend" is a fairly recent creation in Chinese, having been modeled after the Western concept and word "weekend." **Zhōu** is a bound form meaning "week" while **mò** is a bound form meaning "end." It's fine for you to use this word, though you'll notice that Chinese people tend to use it less than Americans do.

1C.   **Qù wǒ nàr** "go to me there" or "go over to my place." When a person (pronoun, noun, or personal name) is the object of a verb of movement such as **dào** "arrive/to," **lái** "come," or **qù** "go," the person must be followed by the place words **zhèr/zhèli** "here" or **nàr/nàli** "there" and cannot stand alone. Whereas in English it's possible to have a verb like "come" or "go" followed directly by "to" and a pronoun (e.g., "come to me," "go to her"), in Chinese the place words **zhèr/zhèli** (for action in the direction of the speaker) or **nàr/nàli** (for action away from the speaker) must appear after the pronoun. More examples:

Nǐ dào wǒ zhèr lái.	"Come to me." (lit. "Come to me here.")
Qǐng nǐ dào tā nàr qù.	"Please go to him." (lit. "Please go to him over there.")
Qǐng nǐ qù Lǎo Bái nàli.	"Please go to Old Bai." (lit. "Please go to Old Bai over there.")

You could NEVER say *__Nǐ dào wǒ__ or *__Qǐng nǐ dào tā qù__ or *__Qǐng nǐ qù Lǎo Bái__.

1D. **Nǐ yuànyi zhèige zhōumò qù wǒ nàr chī jiǎozi ma?** "Would you like to go to my place this weekend to eat dumplings?" Instead of **qù wǒ nàr** "go over to my place," in English we would probably say "come over to my place." However, Chinese speakers are in general more conscious of their actual position when speaking than are English speakers. Since at the time she is speaking the speaker of this line isn't at her home, she uses **qù** rather than **lái**. Were she at her home when speaking, e.g., on the telephone, she would no doubt say **lái wǒ zhèr**.

1E. **Jiǎozi** are dumplings which are of a crescent shape. The outside is made of white dough while the inside is stuffed with a mixture of meat and/or vegetables. **Jiǎozi** can be boiled (in which case they're also called **shuǐjiǎo**, AV1), steamed (**zhēngjiǎo**, AV2), or fried (**guōtiē**, AV4). To say "make dumplings," you say **bāo jiǎozi** (lit. "wrap dumplings," cf. **bāo** "wrap" in 12-4).

4. The **dōu** in **Dōu yǒu shémme?** "What all is in it?" is the "forward-looking" kind of **dōu** that was discussed in 7-1: 3. It anticipates the answer in line 5 (**ròu hé báicài** "meat and cabbage"). But note that in the answer, there is no **dōu**.

5A. Here are some more examples with the common adverb **zhǔyào** "mainly":

> **Tā cháng shēngbìng, zhǔyào shi yīnwei chōuyān chōude tài duōle.**
>
> "The main reason why he often gets sick is because he smokes too much."

> **Tā zuìjìn shēntǐ bú tài hǎo, zhǔyào shì yīnwei gōngzuò tài mángle.**
>
> "Recently she hasn't been in very good health; it's mainly because she's too busy with her work."

> **Tāmen xiànzài bù xiǎng yào háizi, zhǔyào shi yīnwei tāmen dōu hái zài niànshū.**
>
> "They don't want children now; it's mostly because they're both still in school."

> **Dìyícì shàngkè, lǎoshī zhǔyào jièshaole yixia zhè xuéqī wǒmen yào xué xiē shémme.**
>
> "At the first class session, the teacher mostly introduced what we're going to learn this semester."

5B. **CHÚLE...ZHĪWÀI AND CHÚLE...YǏWÀI.** The patterns **chúle...zhīwài** and **chúle...yǐwài** literally mean "removing...apart"; a common English translation is "besides" or "in addition to." What comes between the two parts of the pattern can be a noun, pronoun, or verb phrase. The main clause that follows often contains the adverbs **hái**, **yě**, or **yòu**. To sum up, the basic pattern is:

CHÚLE	NOUN / PRONOUN / VERB	ZHĪWÀI / YǏWÀI	MAIN CLAUSE
Chúle	zhèixiē	zhīwài,	hái yǒu xiē tiáoliào.

"Besides these, there are also some seasonings."

Some more examples of **chúle...zhīwài** and **chúle...yǐwài**:

> **Chúle Xībānyáyǔ zhīwài, tā hái huì Fǎyǔ hé Déyǔ.**
>
> "Besides Spanish, she also knows French and German."

> **Chúle tā yǐwài, wǒ hái yǒu biéde péngyou.**
>
> "Besides her, I also have other friends."

> **Tāmen bānshang chúle Měiguo rén yǐwài, yě yǒu Rìběn rén.**
>
> "In their class besides Americans, there are also Japanese."

> **Nèibǎ yǐzi chúle yǒu diǎn jiù yǐwài, yánsè yě bú tài hǎokàn.**
>
> "Besides being a little old, that chair is also an ugly color."

> **Tā chúle bù xǐhuan chī ròu yǐwài, yě bù xǐhuan chī yú.**
>
> "Besides not liking to eat meat, he also doesn't like to eat fish."

If a sense of exclusion is indicated by the main clause of the sentence through the use of a negative verb and words like "all," "every," "any" or "other," then **chúle...zhīwài** and **chúle...yǐwài** are often best translated into English as "except (for)." Examples:

> **Chúle nǐ yǐwài, wǒ méiyou biéde péngyou.**
>
> "I don't have any other friends except you."

> **Chúle Běijīng yǐwài, shémme dìfang wǒ dōu méi qùguo.**
>
> "Except for Beijing, I haven't been anywhere."

> **Chúle tā zhīwài, wǒmen dōu qùguo Chángchéng le.**
>
> "Except for her, we've all been to the Great Wall."

> **Chúle Lǎo Lǐ yǐwài, biéde rén wǒ dōu bú rènshi.**
>
> "Except for Old Li, I don't know any of the other people."

> **Tā chúle chīfàn hē jiǔ zhīwài, shémme yě méi zuò.**
>
> "He didn't do anything except eat and drink wine."

Plate of **shuǐjiǎo** or "boiled dumplings"

> **Shàngge yuè wǒmen zhèr chúle shísānhào, shísìhào zhèiliǎngtiān méi xiàyǔ yǐwài, měitiān dōu xiàyǔle.**
>
> "Last month we had rain here every day, except for the thirteenth and the fourteenth, when it didn't rain."

Some speakers sometimes drop the **zhīwài** or **yǐwài** and use only **chúle**. However, we urge you to use the full forms of these patterns. Also, note that in English the dependent clause with "besides," "in addition to" or "except" can come before or after the main clause; in other words, you can say "Besides him, I have many other friends" or "I have many other friends besides him." In Chinese, however, the clause with **chúle...zhīwài** or **chúle...yǐwài** must come first.

5D. **Xiāngyóu** "sesame oil" is also called **máyóu**.

6A. **-DE TO INDICATE EXTENT.** Another function of the particle **-de** when it appears after a verb and before a result expression is to indicate the extent of the action of the verb. The example in this line is **Wénde wǒ dōu èle** "(I) have smelled them to the extent that I've even become hungry." The pattern is:

SUBJECT	VERB	-DE	EXTENT / RESULT
Wǒ	mángde		méi shíjiān shuìjiào.

"I'm so busy that I don't even have time to sleep."

Some more examples:

> **Tā qìde shuōbuchū huà lái.**　"She was so angry that she couldn't speak."
>
> **Tā gāoxìngde dōu tiàoqilaile.**　"He was so happy that he jumped up."
>
> **Lǎo Wáng shuō xiàohua shuōde měige rén dōu xiàochū shēng laile.**
> "Old Wang told jokes to the point where everyone burst into laughter."

In the pattern with **-de** to indicate extent, adverbs like **hěn** "very" or **nèmme** cannot be used before the verb, so you could NEVER say ***Wǒ hěn mángde méi shíjiān chīfàn**.

6B.　The **dōu** in **Wénde wǒ dōu èle** means "already." Another example of this **dōu**: **Tā dōu bāsuì le** "She's already 8 years old."

6C.　Look at **Néng bu néng xiān zhǔ jǐge ràng wǒ chángchang?** "Could you boil a few first and let me taste them?" As in English, the **néng bu néng** "can (you) or can't you" here doesn't involve a question about physical ability but rather creates a polite request that the other person boil some dumplings and let the speaker try them. Compare the English question "Can you turn off the light?" If someone asks you this, the normal response isn't "Yes, I can" or "No, I can't," but rather the performance of the request to turn off the light.

7A.　The **jiù** in **Xiànzài wǒ jiù qù zhǔ** "I'll go boil them right now" means "right away" and the **qù** expresses purpose. A literal translation of this sentence would be "Now I'll right away go in order to boil (them)."

7B.　**Bié kèqi** "don't be polite" is a common polite expression. The implication is that the guest should go ahead and eat the dumplings rather than hesitating to do so out of politeness. **Búyào kèqi** is a synonym of **bié kèqi**.

Unit 15: Review and Study Guide

New Vocabulary

ADVERBS
fēicháng　extremely
jǐn　only
yìzhí　always, all along
zhǔyào　mainly

AUXILIARY VERBS
lái　(indicates one is about to do something)
yuànyi　be willing to, like to

CONJUNCTIONS
dàn　but
yǐjí　and

COVERBS
bǎ　(moves object before verb)

IDIOMATIC EXPRESSIONS
bié kèqi　"don't be polite"
gānbēi　"Cheers!", "Bottoms up"

INTERJECTIONS
wà　"wow"

MEASURES
bēi　(for beverages)

jù　sentence, phrase

MOVEABLE ADVERBS
tóngshí　at the same time

NOUNS
bāngzhù　help
báobǐng　pancake
bǐng　pancake, biscuit
cōng　scallion
fūren　madam, lady
jiāng　ginger
jiàng　thick sauce
jiàngyóu　soy sauce
jiànkāng　health
jiǎozi　dumpling
jùzi　sentence
kǎoyā　roast duck
kèrén　guest
miàn　flour; pasta, noodles
shēnghuó　life
tiánmiànjiàng　sweet flour sauce
tiáoliào　seasoning
wèidao　taste
xiàn(r)　filling

xiāngyóu　sesame oil
yán　salt
zhàogu　care
zhōumò　weekend
zhǔrén　host

PARTICLES
-de　(adverbial marker)

PATTERNS
chúle...yǐwài　besides...; except for...
chúle...zhīwài　besides...; except for...
xiān...zài...　first...then...
yuè...yuè...　the more...the more...

PHRASES
xiǎo háizi　small child
yā zhēn'gān(r)　duck gizzard and liver
zǎo jiù　long ago, long since

PLACE WORDS
zhōngjiān　in the middle

PRONOUNS
dàjiā　everybody, everyone

RESULTATIVE COMPOUNDS

chībuxià	can't eat
chīdelái	can or like to eat something
chīguàn	be used to eating something
fàngshang	put on
hēzuì	get drunk
juánqilai	roll up

RESULTATIVE ENDINGS

-guàn	**be used to**
-zuì	**drunk**

SPECIFIERS

gè-	each, every

STATIVE VERBS

báo	be thin (in dimensions)
è	be hungry

fēngfù	be abundant
hòu	be thick
jiǎndān	be simple
kě	be thirsty
kèqi	be polite
kuàilè	be happy
shùnlì	be smooth
yúkuài	be happy

SURNAMES

Mò	Mo

VERBS

cháng	taste
gǎnxiè	thank
jiā	pick up (with chopsticks)
jìng	toast, drink to
juǎn	roll up

kǎo	bake, roast
lái	(verb substitute)
tíyì	propose
tú	smear, daub
wén	smell something
zàizuò	be present
zhàogu	take care of
zhǔ	boil
zhù	wish
zuì	become drunk

VERB-OBJECT COMPOUNDS

gānbēi	drink a toast
jiācài	pick up food (with chopsticks)
jùcān	get together for a meal

Major New Grammar Patterns

-DE AS ADVERBIAL MODIFIER TO EXPRESS MANNER: jiǎndānde shuō jǐjù "say a few phrases simply" (15-1)

TIME EXPRESSION + (YǏ)LÁI: zhèijǐge yuè yǐlái "the last few months" (15-1)

YUÈ…YUÈ…: Yuè piányi yuè hǎo. "The cheaper the better." (15-2)

AFFIRMATIVE-NEGATIVE QUESTIONS WITH -GUO AND MÉIYOU: Nǐ chīguo kǎoyā méiyou? "Have you ever eaten roast duck?" (15-2)

BǍ CONSTRUCTION: Qǐng nǐ bǎ shū fàngzai zhèr. "Please put the books here." (15-3)

XIĀN…ZÀI…: Xiān xué Zhōngwén, zài qù Zhōngguo. "First learn Chinese, then go to China." (15-3)

CHÚLE…ZHĪWÀI AND CHÚLE… YǏWÀI: Chúle tā zhīwài, wǒ hái yǒu biéde péngyou. "Besides her, I also have other friends.", **Chúle nǐ yǐwài, wǒ méiyou biéde péngyou.** "I don't have any friends except you." (15-4)

-DE TO INDICATE EXTENT: Wǒ mángde méi shíjiān chīfàn. "I'm so busy that I don't have time to eat." (15-4)

Eating and Drinking (III)

COMMUNICATIVE OBJECTIVES

Once you've mastered this unit, you'll be able to use Chinese to:

1. Ask whether someone has eaten yet and propose that you go to a restaurant to eat together.
2. Discuss how the food is.
3. Ask for the check.
4. Offer to pay for the meal and respond appropriately when the other person insists on treating you.
5. Host or participate as a guest in a dinner party held in a private home.
6. Engage in polite conversation and rituals associated with eating and drinking that are common at Chinese dinner parties.
7. Explain to your hosts when they urge you to drink alcoholic beverages that you don't drink, or that you've had enough, and propose drinking some other beverage in lieu of alcohol.
8. Explain and apologize to the hosts and guests if you must leave a dinner party early.
9. Make appropriate comments to the hosts and guests at the end of a dinner.
10. Talk about different kinds of meals as well as various foods, snacks, and beverages.

Eating with a Colleague in a Restaurant

It's shortly after 1:00 P.M. at an English language "cram school" in downtown Taipei. Zeng Xianfen, a Taiwanese employee of the school, notices Donna Neal, an American teacher, at her desk in the main office and suggests they go out together for lunch. They go to a restaurant and have lunch, after which Zeng asks for the bill and insists on treating Neal.

Basic Conversation 16-1

1. ZENG **Hài, Donna!**
Hi, Donna!

(after she returns some materials to a cabinet) **Chīguo fàn méiyou?**
Have you eaten yet?

2. NEAL **Hái méi. Gāngcái bǔle yìtáng kè. Nǐ ne?**
Not yet. I just made up a class. And you?

3. ZENG **Wǒ yě hái méi chī. Zěmmeyàng? Yào bu yào yíkuàir qù chī?**
I haven't eaten yet either. How about it? Do you want to go eat together?

4. NEAL **Hǎo a!**
Sure!

(a bit later, at a restaurant)

5. RESTAURANT HOSTESS **Huānyíng guānglín. Jǐwèi?**
Welcome! How many?

6. ZENG **Liǎngge.**
Two.

(after they've started eating)

Yú zěmmeyàng? Hǎo bu hǎochī?
How's the fish? Is it good?

7. NEAL **Mán nènde, jiù shi cì duōle yidian.**
Very tender, it's just there are a few too many fish bones.

8. ZENG *(to the waitress, when they're finished)* **Mǎidān.**
The check, please.

| 9. NEAL | **Duōshǎo qián? Wǒ lái fù ba.** |
| | How much is it? I'll pay. |

| 10. ZENG | **Bù, jīntiān wǒ qǐngkè.** |
| | No, today I'm treating. |

| 11. NEAL | **Hái shi wǒ lái ba!** |
| | Come on, let me pay. |

| 12. ZENG | **Ài, bié kèqi. Yídùn biànfàn éryǐ.** |
| | Oh, don't be polite. It's only a simple meal. |

| 13. NEAL | **Bù hǎo yìsi, ràng nǐ pòfèile. Gǎitiān wǒ zuòdōng ba.** |
| | How embarrassing to let you go to such expense. Next time I'll be the host. |

Build Up

---

1. Zeng

| **hài** | "hi" [I] |
| **Hài, Donna!** | Hi, Donna! |

| **-guo** | (expresses completed action) [P] |
| **Chīguo fàn méiyou?** | Have you eaten yet? |

---

2. Neal

gāngcái	just now, just [TW]
bǔkè	make up a class [VO]
táng	(for classes) [M]
yìtáng kè	a class
gāngcái bǔle yìtáng kè	(I) just made up a class
Hái méi. Gāngcái bǔle yìtáng kè. Nǐ ne?	Not yet. I just made up a class. And you?

---

3. Zeng

yíkuài(r)	together [A/PW]
yíkuàir qù chī	go eat together
Wǒ yě hái méi chī. Zěmmeyàng?	I haven't eaten yet either. How about it?
Yào bu yào yíkuàir qù chī?	Do you want to go eat together?

---

4. Neal

| **Hǎo a!** | Sure! |

---

5. Restaurant hostess

| **Huānyíng guānglín. Jǐwèi?** | Welcome! How many? |

---

6. Zeng

| **Liǎngge.** | Two. |
| **Yú zěmmeyàng? Hǎo bu hǎochī?** | How's the fish? Is it good? |

---

7. Neal

mán...de	quite [PT]
nèn	be tender [SV]
mán nènde	quite tender
cì	fish bone [N]
duōle yidian	there is a little too much
cì duōle yidian	there're a few too many fish bones
Mán nènde, jiù shi cì duōle yidian.	Very tender, it's just there are a few too many fish bones.

8. Zeng

măidān	pay the check, figure up the bill [IE]
Măidān.	The check, please.

9. Neal

fù	pay [V]
wǒ lái fù	I'll pay
Duōshǎo qián? Wǒ lái fù ba.	How much is it? I'll pay.

10. Zeng

qǐngkè	treat (someone to something) [VO]
Bù, jīntiān wǒ qǐngkè.	No, today I'm treating.

11. Neal

Hái shi wǒ lái ba!	Come on, let me pay.

12. Zeng

ài	(indicates strong sentiment) [I]
dùn	(for meals) [M]
biànfàn	simple meal [N]
yídùn biànfàn	a simple meal
Ài, bié kèqi. Yídùn biànfàn éryǐ.	Oh, don't be polite. It's only a simple meal.

13. Neal

pòfèi	go to great expense [V]
gǎi	change [V]
gǎitiān	on some other day [TW]
zuòdōng	serve as host [VO]
Bù hǎo yìsi, ràng nǐ pòfèile.	How embarrassing to let you go to such
Gǎitiān wǒ zuòdōng ba.	expense. Next time I'll be the host.

 ## Supplementary Vocabulary

1. **bǔxíbān**	cram school [N]
2. **fúwùyuán**	attendant, waiter, waitress [N]
3. **lǎo**	be tough (of food) [SV]
Jīntiānde niúròu hěn lǎo.	The beef today is very tough.
4. **fùqián**	pay money [VO]
Shì bu shi yào xiān fùqián?	Are you supposed to pay first?

Additional Vocabulary: Meals and Snacks

1. **zǎocān**	breakfast [N]
2. **zǎodiǎn**	breakfast [N]
3. **wǔcān**	lunch [N]
4. **xiàwǔ chá**	afternoon tea [N]
5. **wǎncān**	supper [N]
6. **xiāoyè**	late night snack [N]

Grammatical and Cultural Notes

1A.   The interjection **hài** was borrowed from the English greeting "hi" and is now commonly used by students in the larger cities in both mainland China and Taiwan.

1B.   **-GUO TO EXPRESS COMPLETED ACTION.** As we've already seen in earlier lessons, the verb suffix **-guo** can express experience, as in **Nǐ qùguo Běijīng ma?** "Have you ever been to Beijing?" A different use of **-guo** is to express completed action, much like verb suffix **-le**. The pattern is:

VERB	-GUO
chī	-guo

"has eaten" or "have eaten"

One common and useful example of **-guo** to express completed action is:

> **Nǐ chīguo fàn le ma?**
> "Have you eaten?"

The answers to the above question would be either **Wǒ chīguo fàn le** "I've eaten" or **Wǒ hái méi chīguo fàn** "I haven't eaten yet." Context will usually make clear which of the two types of **-guo** is involved. When a non-Chinese person is asked **Nǐ chīguo Zhōngguo fàn ma?**, this would ordinarily be interpreted as "Have you ever eaten Chinese food?" On the other hand, **Nǐ chīguo fàn le ma?** would be understood as "Have you eaten (yet)?," since it wouldn't make sense to ask someone if they had ever eaten.

1C.   **Chīguo fàn méiyou?** "Have you eaten yet?" is here a genuine question. In other contexts, especially around meal times, it's merely a greeting that shows concern for the other person. Frequently, as here, the subject **nǐ** "you" is omitted. Also notice that, in the Basic Conversation for listening, **chīguo** is pronounced as *cīguo, a non-standard pronunciation used by many speakers in Taiwan and southern China.

Cram schools on Nanyang Street in downtown Taipei

2A.   You've often seen **hái méi** "not yet" before a verb (e.g., **Tā hái méi qù** "She hasn't gone yet"). Here in utterance 2 we see that **Hái méi** can occur alone to mean "not yet." To emphasize that something is still in progress and hasn't yet been completed, Beijing speakers would often add a final **ne** and say **Hái méi ne** "Not yet" or even just **Méi ne**, with the same meaning. Another example:

> Speaker A: **Lǎo Zhāng láile ma?** "Has Old Zhang come yet?"
> Speaker B: **Hái méi ne.** "Not yet."

2B.   Here are some more examples of the time word **gāngcái** "just now" or "just":

Tā gāngcái láiguo.	"He was here just a moment ago."
Nǐ gāngcái dào nǎr qùle?	"Where did you just go?"
Gāngcái shì bu shi yǒu rén chōuguo yān?	"Did someone just smoke?"

In 9-3 you learned the adverbs **gāng** and **gānggāng**, which both mean "just." Even though **gāngcái**, **gāng**, and **gānggāng** can all translate into English as "just" and are sometimes interchangeable, there are some differences in usage and also some situations where they aren't interchangeable. The distinctions are as follows:

(1) **Gāngcái** always means not long before speaking, i.e., in the recent past, so we could translate it as "just now." **Gāng** and **gānggāng** can indicate the recent past but can also be used for events that happened long ago, e.g., **Nǐ gāng kāishǐ xué Zhōngwénde shíhou juéde hěn nán ma?** "When you had just started learning Chinese, did you feel it was hard?" **Gāngcái** couldn't be used in the preceding sentence.

(2) As a time word, **gāngcái** can occur either before the subject or before the verb, but **gāng** and **gānggāng** are adverbs and can only occur before the verb. So you can say either **Gāngcái Lǎo Zhāng gěi wǒ dǎ diànhuà le** or **Lǎo Zhāng gāngcái gěi wǒ dǎ diànhuà le** "Old Zhang just called me;" but you can say only **Lǎo Zhāng gāng gěi wǒ dǎ diànhuà le** and NOT *Gāng Lǎo Zhāng gěi wǒ dǎ diànhuà le.

(3) As a time word, **gāngcái** can also function like a noun, which **gāng** and **gānggāng** can't do. Examples:

> **Gāngcáide yǎnjiǎng hěn jīngcǎi.**
> "The lecture a moment ago was brilliant."

> **Xiànzài bǐ gāngcái nuǎnhuo yìdiǎnr, gāngcái tài lěng.**
> "Now it's a bit warmer than a moment ago; a moment ago it was too cold." (e.g., someone has just turned on the heat)

(4) **Gāngcái** can be used with negative as well as positive verbs, e.g., **Nǐ wèishemme gāngcái bù mǎi? Xiànzài yǐjīng màiwánle!** "Why didn't you buy it just now? Now they're sold out!" On the other hand, **gāng** is usually used only with positive verbs.

2C.   **Bǔkè** "make up a class" can be said by both instructors and students.

2D.   **Gāngcái bǔle yìtáng kè** "(I) just made up a class." Since the context is clear, the pronoun **wǒ** "I" has been omitted. As we've seen before, this is very common in colloquial Chinese.

3A.   **Zěmmeyàng?** literally means "How?" The implication is "How would it be?" In better English, we might also say "How about it?" or "What do you think?" The question **Zěmmeyàng?** here occurs before the proposal (**Yào bu yao yíkuàir qù chī?** "Do you want to go eat together?") in order to introduce the proposal and render it less blunt.

3B.   Learn the common Mandarin adverb **yíkuài(r)** "together," e.g., **Wǒmen yíkuàir chīfàn ba** "Let's eat together." **Yíkuài(r)** can also serve as a place word, e.g., **Jīntiān zámmen dōu zài yíkuàir** "Today all of us are together" or **Tā gēn tā nánpéngyou zǒuzai yíkuàir** "She's walking together with her boyfriend." **Yíkuài(r)** is a synonym of **yìqǐ**, which you learned in 7-3. The main difference between the two is that **yíkuài(r)** is more colloquial and is used mostly in North China (even though the speaker who says it here happens to be from Taiwan), while **yìqǐ** can be used either in speaking or writing and is common throughout China.

6A.   Instead of **liǎngge** some speakers would say **liǎngwèi**, even when referring to themselves, because of influence from the **wèi** in the preceding question **Jǐwèi?** Other speakers feel that **wèi** shouldn't be used when speaking of themselves.

6B.   **SPECIAL MEANINGS IN NUMBERS.** When guests enter Taiwanese restaurants and announce how many persons there are in their party, it has become the custom when referring to parties of four people not to say **sìge rén** or **sìwèi** but instead to say **sān jiā yī** "three plus one." The reason is to avoid the word **sì** "four," which is considered by some Chinese to be inauspicious since it sounds somewhat like the word **sǐ** "die." For the same reason, some hospitals and apartment buildings in Taiwan and Hong Kong lack a 4th floor and 14th floor; and red envelopes with gifts of money (called **hóngbāo**) never contain the sum of 400 or 4,000 **kuài**. To give some examples of auspicious numbers, the number **liù** "six" is considered lucky because it sounds somewhat like the word **liú** "to flow" and the word **liūliū** "smooth"—which are considered lucky words for business. The number **bā** "eight" is considered a lucky number because it rhymes with the verb **fā** "get rich," and the number **jiǔ** "nine" is thought to be auspicious because it's a homonym with the **jiǔ** in **yǒngjiǔ** "forever."* In the various Chinese-speaking societies, special meanings are often found in numbers, as demonstrated by the thousands of dollars sometimes bid on specially numbered license plates or telephone numbers, or the many hours a bride and groom will queue at the marriage registry for an auspicious wedding date, or the many computer passwords that contain the numbers 6, 8, and 9!

7A.   **MÁN...-DE.** While the adverb **mán** "quite," which is similar in meaning to **tǐng**, can occur alone, it's very often used in the pattern **mán...-de**, which surrounds stative verbs or other types of verb phrases. The pattern is:

> | MÁN | VERB | -DE |
> | --- | --- | --- |
>
> mán   hǎochī   de
> "quite tasty"

Some more examples of **mán...-de**:

mán lèide	"quite tired"
mán bú cuòde	"quite good"
mán yǒu yìside	"quite interesting"

Instead of **mán...-de**, some speakers give the syllable **mán** a Tone Three and say **mǎn...-de**.

7B.   Depending on the context, **cì** can mean "(fish) bone," "thorn," "splinter," or "sliver." If you need to be more specific, you can say **yúcì** "fish bone."

7C.   **STATIVE VERB + LE + (YI)DIAN(R) TO EXPRESS EXCESS.** Examine the phrase in this line **jiù shi cì duōle yidian** "it's only that the fish bones are a little too many" or "it's just that there are a few too many fish bones." A stative verb like **duō** followed by **le** plus **yidian(r)** can indicate "too many" or "too much." The basic pattern is:

> | STATIVE VERB | LE | (YI)DIAN(R) |
> | --- | --- | --- |
>
> duō   le   yidianr
> "a little too much" or "a little too many"

Some more examples:

Zhèige cài hǎochī shi hǎochī, jiù shi làle yidianr.
"This dish is good all right, it's just a little too spicy hot."

Nèijiā diànde dōngxi hǎo shi hǎo, jiù shi guìle yidian.
"The things in that store are good enough, they're just a bit too expensive."

Zhèitiáo kùzi chuānqilai yòu shūfu, jiàqián yòu piányi, jiù shi duǎnle yìdiǎndiǎn.
"This pair of pants is both comfortable and inexpensive, it's just that it's a tiny bit too short."

8.   **PAYING THE CHECK IN A RESTAURANT.** The expression **mǎidān** "pay the check" is a borrowing from Hong Kong Cantonese but has become very common in Taiwan and mainland China. More traditional equivalents would be **Zhàngdān!** "The bill!", **Jiézhàng!** "I'd like to pay the bill" (lit. "Clear the bill"), and **Qǐng suàn**

---

* For this reason, 9/9/1999 was considered an extremely auspicious wedding date in China. On this same day, 165 couples married in Singapore.

yixia zhàng "Please add up the bill." In this Basic Conversation, Zeng asks for the bill because she is the one who originally proposed going out to lunch, and also because she is Taiwanese and, after all, the other person is a foreigner. Chinese tradition knows no such thing as Dutch treat. Nothing looks worse to Chinese people than for several Americans to go out to eat, figure out how much each of them owes, and then throw some money in the middle of the table. Even in cases where Americans have lived in mainland China or Taiwan a long time, Chinese people who go out to eat with them will oftentimes still consider themselves the "host" and the American the "guest" and will try to pay, even when it was the American who proposed going out to eat in the first place. Nevertheless, you should insist on inviting your Chinese friends about as often as they invite you. Once you've gotten to know a Chinese person well, they may start allowing you to invite occasionally. This is often a sign that they have begun to consider you a real friend and not just a "foreign guest." When the time comes to pay the bill, it's considered a real honor to be the one who ends up paying. One useful strategy for achieving this goal is, toward the end of the meal, to say you're going to the bathroom but actually to go to the counter and secretly pay the bill. If you offered to pay but the other person insisted on covering the tab, you should say something like the first sentence in utterance 13 below: **Bù hǎo yìsi, ràng nǐ pòfèile** "Very embarrassing, I let you go to great expense." It's important to keep track of who owes whom. It would not be appropriate to accept an invitation more than two times in a row without reciprocating in some manner—whether by inviting the person to a meal, giving them a gift, or providing help of some kind. The preceding information applies to working adults who have an income. In the case of Chinese students who are eating together at a restaurant, they will often split the bill evenly.

> **Once you've gotten to know a Chinese person well, they may start allowing you to invite occasionally. This is often a sign that they have begun to consider you a real friend and not just a "foreign guest."**

9. **Wǒ lái fù ba** "I'll pay" (lit. "Why don't I come and pay?"). This **lái** indicates the speaker's intention to do something, a little like English "allow me to" or "let me." Some more examples:

Wǒ lái kànkan.	"Let me take a look."
Wǒ lái mǎi ba.	"Let me buy them." (e.g., tickets)
Wǒ lái jiē.	"I'll answer." (e.g., the telephone)

10. The verb-object compound **qǐngkè** can have two different meanings. In this sentence it means "invite someone as a guest" or "treat" them, that is, pay for them. However, **qǐngkè** can also mean "invite guests," in other words, have a dinner party. Some examples of both usages:

Wǒmen qù kàn diànyǐng ba, wǒ qǐngkè.
"Let's go see a movie, my treat."

Wǒ xīngqīliù yào qǐngkè. Nǐ néng lái ma?
"On Saturday I'm hosting a dinner party. Can you come?"

Wáng Xiānsheng, Wáng Tàitai hěn xǐhuan qǐngkè.
"Mr. and Mrs. Wang like having guests over."

There are also situations where the meaning is ambiguous, as in:

Tā méiyou qǐng nǐ ma?   "He didn't treat you?" or "He didn't invite you?"

11. The **lái** in this sentence is a verb substitute that substitutes for a more specific verb, the meaning of which depends on the context (15-2). In this case, the **lái** substitutes for **fù** "pay."

13A. **Gǎi tiān** "change the day" or "on some other day." This is a very useful phrase if you want to propose an alternative to a speaker's suggestion. For example, if someone suggests you and they do something together but you have no time or interest, you could say:

> **Wǒ jīntiān yǒu yidianr shì, gǎi tiān zài shuō ba.**
>
> "I have something I have to do today; let's try again some other day."

It would be rude and cause the other person to lose face if you were to turn them down flat.

13B. The verb **gǎi** means "change." As regards the difference between **gǎi** and the verb **biàn** which you learned in 10-1 and which also means "change," **biàn** mostly refers to a spontaneous change on the part of a person or thing, e.g., **Tiānqi biànle** "The weather has changed" or **Shínián méi jiànle, nǐ yìdiǎnr yě méi biàn!** "I haven't seen you for ten years, and you haven't changed a bit!" On the other hand, **gǎi** and the related verb **gǎibiàn**, which often take an object, mean "cause someone or something to turn into someone or something else." Here are two more examples with **gǎi**:

> **Zhèige zì xiěcuòle, qǐng nǐ gǎi yixia.**
>
> "This character was written wrong; please correct it."

> **Běijīng zhèige chéngshì gǎiguo jǐcì míngzi; 1928 nián Guómíndǎng zhèngfǔ bǎ "Běijīng" gáichéng "Běipíng," 1949 nián "Běipíng" yòu gǎihuí "Běijīng" le.**
>
> "The city of 'Beijing' has changed its name several times; in 1928 the Guomindang government changed 'Beijing' to 'Beiping'; in 1949 'Beiping' was again changed back to 'Beijing.'"

13C. While it isn't necessary to tip in restaurants in Taiwan, it's customary to round off the amount of the bill. For example, given a bill of NT 387, you might say:

> **Gěi nǐ sìbǎikuài, bú yòng zhǎole.**   "Here's NT 400, no need for change."

Also, while no service charge is added in smaller restaurants such as the one in this conversation, in higher-class establishments a service charge of 10% is automatically added to the bill. The Chinese word for "tip" is **xiǎofèi** and for "service charge" it's **fúwùfèi**.

SV1. A **bǔxíbān** or "cram school" is a privately run supplementary school or class designed to help students score well on examinations. **Bǔxíbān** range from small, home-based operations, sometimes run by the students' regular teachers as a way to supplement their income, to huge institutions with hundreds of instructors and thousands of students. They are common in all the Chinese-speaking societies, and in Japan and Korea as well.

SV2. A common way to call a waiter or waitress to your table in mainland China is by calling out **fúwùyuán**. In Taiwan, you'd usually just call out **xiānsheng** or **xiáojie**.

SV3. **Jīntiānde niúròu hěn lǎo** "The beef today is very tough." In English, stress often gives a syllable a high or falling pitch pattern (e.g., "The beef today is VERY tough"). But in Chinese, while the tone of a syllable may be exaggerated or the syllable it's part of may be lengthened due to stress, the tone doesn't change: Tone One is still level, Tone Two still rises, Tone Three is still low, and Tone Four still falls. Be very careful to guard against the tendency that native speakers of English have to pronounce stressed Chinese syllables with English stress. For example, the Chinese equivalent of "The beef today is VERY tough" must never be pronounced with a high or falling pitch on **hěn**! The **hěn** is still Tone Three (which here changes to Tone Two because of the following Tone Three syllable **lǎo**.) In class when practicing with your teacher and when working on your own with the audio and video recordings, note carefully where the stresses fall and try to imitate them in your own speech.

AV4. In recent years, afternoon tea has become quite popular among well-to-do people in larger cities such as Taipei, Hong Kong, and Shanghai.

P
A
R
T

2

A Dinner Party at Home

Larry Wells, an American who used to teach English in Taiwan, returns to Taipei for a short visit. His good friends, Mr. and Mrs. Yang, invite him to a dinner at their home to welcome him back. They've also invited Mr. and Mrs. Zhang and Mr. Shi, all of whom are old friends of Wells. After Mr. Yang welcomes Wells and Wells thanks him, Mr. Shi proposes a toast to Wells.

Basic Conversation 16-2

| 1. MR. YANG | **Jīntiān wǒmen tì Lǎo Wèi jiēfēng. Huānyíng nǐ huídào Táiwān lái! Zàizuòde yě dōu shi lǎo péngyou. Lái, wǒmen jìng Lǎo Wèi!** |
| | Today we're having a welcome dinner for Larry. Welcome back to Taiwan! Those present are all old friends. Come, let's toast Larry! |

| 2. WELLS | **Xièxie, xièxie, shízài bù gǎn dāng.** |
| | Thank you, I really don't dare accept this honor. |

| 3. MR. SHI | **Lǎo Wèi, lái, wǒ jìng nǐ! Gānbēi zěmmeyàng?** |
| | Larry, come, here's to you! Bottoms up, O.K.? |

| 4. WELLS | **Liàng qiǎn, liàng qiǎn. Nǐ gān, wǒ suíyì ba.** |
| | I'm not much of a drinker. You drink bottoms up, I'll just have a little. |

| 5. MR. SHI | **Éi, nǐ shi hǎiliàng. Lái, gānbēi, gānbēi!** |
| | Hey, your capacity is limitless. Come on, bottoms up! |

| 6. WELLS | **Gōngjìng bù rú cóng mìng. Nà wǒ xiān-gān-wéi-jìngle!** |
| | It's better to obey than to show respect. So I'll drink bottoms up first to show my respect! |

Build Up

1. Mr. Yang

tì	for [CV]
Wèi	Wei [SN]
jiēfēng	give a welcome dinner [VO]
tì Lǎo Wèi jiēfēng	give a welcome dinner for Old Wei
huílai	come back [RC]

huídào	come back to [V+PV]
huídào Táiwān lái	return to Taiwan
Jīntiān wǒmen tì Lǎo Wèi jiēfēng. Huānyíng nǐ huídào Táiwān lái! Zàizuòde yě dōu shi lǎo péngyou. Lái, wǒmen jìng Lǎo Wèi!	Today we're having a welcome dinner for Larry. Welcome back to Taiwan! Those present are all old friends. Come, let's toast Larry!

2. Wells

gǎn	dare to [AV]
bù gǎn dāng	"don't dare accept" [IE]
Xièxie, xièxie, shízài bù gǎn dāng.	Thank you, I really don't dare accept this honor.

3. Mr. Shi

Lǎo Wèi, lái, wǒ jìng nǐ! Gānbēi zěmmeyàng?	Larry, come, here's to you! Bottoms up, O.K.?

4. Wells

qiǎn	be shallow [SV]
liàng qiǎn	"capacity is shallow" [IE]
suíyì	"as you like" [IE]
Liàng qiǎn, liàng qiǎn. Nǐ gān, wǒ suíyì ba.	I'm not much of a drinker. You drink bottoms up, I'll just have a little.

5. Mr. Shi

hǎi	ocean, sea [N]
hǎiliàng	"ocean capacity" [IE]
Éi, nǐ shi hǎiliàng. Lái, gānbēi, gānbēi!	Hey, your capacity is limitless. Come on, bottoms up!

6. Wells

bù rú...	not be as good as... [PT]
gōngjìng bù rú cóng mìng	"to show respect is not as good as following orders" [EX]
xiān-gān-wéi-jìng	drink bottoms up before someone else to show respect [EX]
Gōngjìng bù rú cóng mìng. Nà wǒ xiān-gān-wéi-jìngle!	It's better to obey than to show respect. So I'll drink bottoms up first to show my respect!

Supplementary Vocabulary

1. hé	river [N] (M: **tiáo**)
2. hú	lake [N]
3. shēn	be deep [SV]
4. Shí	Shi [SN]
5. shítou	stone [N] (M: **kuài**)
6. yǔliàng	rainfall [N]
7. huíqu	go back [RC]

Additional Vocabulary

1. Bǎi wén bù rú yí jiàn.	"Seeing is believing." [EX]

Grammatical and Cultural Notes

1A. **Wǒmen tì Lǎo Wèi jiēfēng** "We're having a welcome dinner for Old Wei." The meaning of **tì** is "for," "substitute for," "on behalf of," or "in place of." Some more examples:

> **Wǒ tì nǐ qù.**
>
> "I'll go on your behalf." or "I'll go for you."

Wǒ tài mángle, nǐ tì wǒ qù, hǎo ma?

"I'm too busy; you go in my place, O.K.?"

Tā bú huì Yīngwén, nǐ kéyi tì tā dǎ diànhuà ma?

"Since she doesn't know English, could you call for her?"

Instead of **tì...jiēfēng** "give a welcome dinner for...," there are some speakers who prefer **gěi...jiēfēng**.

1B. **Huídào Táiwān lái** "come back to Taiwan" would be said if the speaker of this sentence were in Taiwan. If the speaker weren't in Taiwan, then you'd say **huídào Táiwān qù** "go back to Taiwan." The **lái** and **qù** at the end are common but optional. More examples:

huídào Měiguo lái	"come back to America" (you could NEVER say *dào Měiguo huílai)
fēihuí Zhōngguo qù	"fly back to China" (you could NEVER say *fēidào Zhōngguo huíqu)
zǒuhuí wūzili qù	"walk back into the room"

As regards the resultative compound verb **huílai** "come back," in Chinese this can mean only "return to a particular place." Unlike English "come back," **huílai** doesn't have the additional meaning "come another time." So for English "Mr. Smith isn't in right now, please come back tomorrow," you could not use **huílai**; instead, you'd have to say **Qǐng nǐ míngtiān zài lái** "Please come again tomorrow."

2. **Bù gǎn dāng** is an humble phrase that literally means "(I) don't dare accept (an honor)." In more colloquial English, we might say "I don't deserve it" or "I feel flattered."

3–5. **DRINKING ETIQUETTE.** As with eating at banquets (15-1: 1H), the main goal of drinking at Chinese banquets is to repay social obligations, give others face, and build up **guānxi** "connections" for the future, at the same time that you try to have a good time yourself. Unlike Americans and their beloved cocktails, Chinese people don't drink alcohol before the meal begins; moreover, when the meal comes to a close or the food runs out, they stop drinking alcohol. The first toast is frequently a general one, made by the host and hostess to all of the guests, usually as soon as the first dish is presented. Then the host and hostess will toast the guest of honor and other guests, with couples usually drinking as a unit, though they are free to drink as individuals if they wish. Everyone then can, and usually does, toast everyone else, with couples usually drinking as a unit. Let the host and other guests toast you first, but then be sure to reciprocate, keeping your rank in mind. If there are other Westerners (say, your boss) present who are clearly senior to you, you should defer to them and let them do most of the toasting and talking. In that case, you'll have more opportunity to enjoy the food!

If someone proposes a toast to you, it would be rude not to accept at all. While it would give the person proposing the toast the most face if you drank as commanded (**Gānbēi!** "Bottoms up!"), there are ways of getting around this. You could offer excuses like **Liàng qiǎn** "My capacity for drinking liquor is low" (cf. line 4), but the other person might claim that you're being modest and that actually you're **hǎiliàng** "ocean capacity," referring to great capacity for drinking liquor (cf. line 5). Another alternative would be for you to say **Wǒ bú huì hē jiǔ** "I don't drink alcohol" (lit. "I don't know how to drink alcohol") or **Wǒ duì jiǔjīng guòmǐn** "I'm allergic to alcohol" or **Wǒ shēntǐ bù hǎo, bù néng hē jiǔ** "I'm in poor health and can't drink alcohol." Yet another strategy would be to accept the proposal to toast but substitute a non-alcoholic beverage for the alcoholic one (cf. line 2 in 16-4). Or, as in line 4 of this Basic Conversation, you could propose that the people involved not **gānbēi** but rather **suíyì**, i.e., have as much or as little alcohol as they feel like. If you **suíyì**, it's acceptable merely to take a sip from your glass or even just to moisten your lips. With the exception of beer, guests drink alcohol only when toasting or toasted, never alone, so if you're thirsty, it's time to propose a toast to someone. You don't even necessarily have to say anything; just catch someone's eye, raise your glass (preferably with both hands), look the other person in the eyes, and drink.

Relatives gather for dinner in a middle class home in Taipei

Yellow rice wine called **shàoxīngjiǔ** (15% alcohol content) is often served at Chinese dinners. Even stronger alcoholic drinks that are sometimes offered include **máotái** (55% alcohol content), **gāoliang** (60% alcohol content), and **báigānr** (up to 70% alcohol content). These are all manufactured from various grains and are completely clear and therefore look like water, but don't be fooled! To quench thirst, beer, soft drinks, juice and/or mineral water are usually also provided.

At dinner parties the "finger-guessing game" **huáquán** is sometimes played. Two players first fill their cups to the brim. The object of the game is to guess the total number of fingers held up by both players. On the count of three, both players loudly call out any number from 0 to 10. At the same time, each player holds up one hand showing the number of fingers they want to show. Whoever guesses the correct number of fingers on both hands wins. The loser must then drink bottoms up without spilling a drop; if he or she spills, there may be penalties of various kinds, including drinking extra wine. If both players guess correctly, then it's considered a tie and repeated; if none guess correctly, the procedure is repeated until one player wins.

6A. **A BÙ RÚ B. Gōngjìng bù rú cóng mìng** "to show respect is not as good as following orders" is a set expression, but you should learn the common and useful grammatical pattern **A bù rú B** "A isn't as good as B" that is contained in it. The literal meaning of **bù rú** is "not be as good as," "not be equal to," or "be inferior to." The basic pattern is:

A	BÙ RÚ	B
Nǐ	bù rú	tā

"You're not as good as she is." or "You're not her equal."

Bù rú is a bit formal in style. Here are additional examples of the pattern **A bù rú B**:

> **Zhèr bù rú nàr.**
>
> "It's not as good here as it is there."

> **Wǒ zuòcài bù rú wǒ bàba.**
>
> "I can't cook as well as my father."

> **Tīngshuō Měiguode yīliáo bǎoxiǎn zhìdu bù rú Jiā'nádà.**
>
> "I've heard the U.S. medical insurance system is inferior to Canada."

> **Lǐ Jiàoshòude Yīngyǔ kěnéng bù rú Zhāng Jiàoshòu, kěshi xuéwèn zuòde bǐ Zhāng Jiàoshòu hǎo duō le.**
>
> "It's possible that Professor Li's English isn't as good as Professor Zhang's, but his scholarship is much better than Professor Zhang's."

> **Tā Zhōngwén shuōde bù rú tā tàitai hǎo.**
>
> "He doesn't speak Chinese as well as his wife."

> **Zhù xiàonèi bù rú zhù xiàowài shěngqián.**
>
> "Living on campus isn't as economical as living off campus."

Sometimes **bù rú**, when used at the beginning of a sentence or phrase, is used to make a polite suggestion and can imply "it would be better to...." Example:

> **Xiàyǔ le, bù rú míngtiān zài qù.**   "It's raining; it would be better to go tomorrow."

6B.   The two expressions making up utterance 6 would seem logically to be contradictory. However, keep in mind these are merely stock phrases, to which relatively little thought is being given.

SV3.   **Shēn** "deep" and, in line 4, **qiǎn** "shallow," can be used not only to describe water but also to describe colors (to review color words, cf. 9-1: SV3–8). Examples:

shēn hóng	"dark red"
qiǎn lánsè	"light blue"
shēn yánsède yīfu	"dark-colored clothes"

AV1.   **Bǎi wén bù rú yí jiàn** is another example of a **súyǔ** "popular saying" (13-2: AV1). The literal meaning is "100 hear not equal one see," that is, "hearing something a hundred times isn't as good as seeing it once." Notice the use of **bù rú**, explained in note 6A above. A good English equivalent might be "a picture is worth a hundred words" or "seeing is believing."

A Dinner Party at Home (cont.)

The eating and drinking continues. Mrs. Yang puts some more food on Wells' plate, after which Mr. and Mrs. Zhang announce they have to leave the dinner party early (continued from the previous conversation).

Basic Conversation 16-3

1. MR. ZHANG

Lái, Lǎo Wèi, wǒ yě jìng nǐ. Gānbēi!
Come, Larry, let me toast you, too. Bottoms up!

2. WELLS

Bànbēi ba.
How about half a glass.

(after a while, to Mrs. Yang) **Dàsǎo, nǐ jīntiān yùbeile zhèmme duō cài a!**
Older sister, you prepared so many dishes today!

3. MRS. YANG

Méi shémme cài, shízài jiǎndānde hěn. Búyào kèqi! Lái, zhè shi Tángcù Lǐjī, wǒ jìde nǐ zuì ài chīde.
The food is nothing special, really very simple. Don't be polite! Here, this is Sweet and Sour Pork, I remember this was your favorite.

4. WELLS

M, wèir wénzhe zhēn xiāng a! Zhēn shi liǎngsānnián méi chīdàole.
Mmm, the aroma smells really great! I really haven't had it for a couple of years now.

5. MRS. YANG

Wǒ yě jìde nǐ ài chī làde. Wǒ tèdì wèi nǐ zuòle Málà Zábànr. Nǐ gòubuzháo ba? Wǒ gěi nǐ jiā yidianr.
I remember too that you love to eat hot spicy food. I specially made Sesame Hot Spicy Medley for you. I guess you can't reach it? Let me serve you some.

6. WELLS

Gòudezháo, gòudezháo, wǒ zìjǐ lái.
I can reach it, I'll help myself.

7. MR. ZHANG

(looks at his watch) **Duìbuqǐ, wǒmen yǒu yidianr shì, děi xiān zǒu yíbù. Wǒ gēn nèirén jìng gèwèi!**
Excuse us, we have something we have to do, we must leave early. My wife and I would like to toast everyone!

(Mr. and Mrs. Zhang toast the others, then rise)

Gèwèi màn yòng, shīpéile.
Enjoy your meal, sorry we have to leave.

Build Up

---

1. **Mr. Zhang**
Lái, Lǎo Wèi, wǒ yě jìng nǐ. Gānbēi! | Come, Larry, let me toast you, too. Bottoms up!

---

2. **Wells**
Bànbēi ba. | How about half a glass.

dàsǎo	wife of oldest brother [N]
yùbei	prepare [V]
zhèmme duō cài	so many dishes of food
yùbeile zhèmme duō cài	prepared so many dishes of food
Dàsǎo, nǐ jīntiān yùbeile zhèmme duō cài a!	Older sister, you prepared so many dishes today!

---

3. **Mrs. Yang**

méi shémme cài	there isn't any food
jiǎndānde hěn	it's very simple
shízài jiǎndānde hěn	really very simple
búyào kèqi	"don't be polite" [IE]
Tángcù Lǐjī	Sweet and Sour Pork [PH]
wǒ jìde nǐ zuì ài chīde	I remember what you like to eat most
Méi shémme cài, shízài jiǎndānde hěn.	The food is nothing special, really very simple.
Búyào kèqi! Lái, zhè shi Tángcù Lǐjī,	Don't be polite! Here, this is Sweet and Sour
wǒ jìde nǐ zuì ài chīde.	Pork, I remember this was your favorite.

---

4. **Wells**

wèir	smell, aroma [N]
wénzhe	in the smelling of it
wèir wénzhe zhēn xiāng	the aroma smells really fragrant
liǎngsānnián	two or three years
chīdào	succeed in eating [RC]
liǎngsānnián méi chīdào	didn't eat for two or three years
M, wèir wénzhe zhēn xiāng a!	Mmm, the aroma smells really great! I
Zhēn shi liǎngsānnián méi chīdàole.	really haven't had it for a couple of years now.

---

5. **Mrs. Yang**

tèdì	especially [A]
wèi	for [CV]
wǒ tèdì wèi nǐ zuòle	I especially made for you
Málà Zábànr	Sesame Hot Spicy Medley [PH]
gòu	reach (by stretching) [V]
gòubuzháo	be unable to reach [RC]
nǐ gòubuzháo ba	I suppose you can't reach
wǒ gěi nǐ jiā yidianr	I'll pick some up for you
Wǒ yě jìde nǐ ài chī làde. Wǒ	I remember too that you love to eat hot spicy
tèdì wèi nǐ zuòle Málà Zábànr. Nǐ	food. I specially made Sesame Hot Spicy Medley
gòubuzháo ba? Wǒ gěi nǐ jiā yidianr.	for you. I guess you can't reach it? Let me serve
	you some.

---

6. **Wells**

gòudezháo	be able to reach [RC]
Gòudezháo, gòudezháo, wǒ zìjǐ lái.	I can reach it, I'll help myself.

---

7. **Mr. Zhang**

bù	step, pace [M]

yíbù	one step
zǒu yíbù	walk one step, take a step
xiān zǒu yíbù	"take one step first" [IE]
nèirén	one's wife (polite) [N]

Duìbuqǐ, wǒmen yǒu yidianr shì, děi xiān zǒu yíbù. Wǒ gēn nèirén jìng gèwèi!

Excuse us, we have something we have to do, we must leave early. My wife and I would like to toast everyone!

màn yòng	"take your time eating" [IE]
shīpéi	"sorry to have to leave" [IE]

Gèwèi màn yòng, shīpéile.

Enjoy your meal, sorry we have to leave.

Supplementary Vocabulary

1. xiǎochī	snack [N]
2. biàndāng (T)	box lunch [N]

Additional Vocabulary: More Foods and Cooking Methods

1. miàntiáo(r)	noodles [N]	6. zhēng	steam [V]
2. húntun	won-ton, ravioli soup [N]	7. chǎo	stir-fry [V]
3. làobǐng	meat-filled pancake [N]	8. zhá	deep fry [V]
4. sānmíngzhì	sandwich [N]	9. dùn	stew [V]
5. Yóutài miànbāo	bagel [N]		

Grammatical and Cultural Notes

2.   **Dàsǎo**, literally "wife of oldest brother" or "sister-in-law," can also, as here, be used as a term of respect for the wife of anyone whom you might call **dàgē** "older brother," that is, a close friend who is senior in age or position or for whom you wish to show respect even if he isn't one's senior. To use **xiānsheng** and **tàitai** would be considered too formal, as though you were purposely creating distance. Kinship terms aren't restricted in use to blood relatives. For example, the children of friends and neighbors are often called **xiǎodì** "little brother" or **xiǎomèi** "little sister," and your parents' friends are often called **bófù** "uncle" and **bómǔ** "aunt."

3A.   **Méi shémme cài** literally means "there isn't any food," but this is merely **kèqi huà** "polite talk" and is the functional equivalent of English "it's nothing special." As you can imagine, some hungry foreigners who thought they had been invited to a dinner party have been very much confused upon hearing this statement!

3B.   **STATIVE VERB + -DE + HĚN.** The meaning of the pattern STATIVE VERB + **-de** + **hěn** is "very (STATIVE VERB)." **Jiǎndānde hěn** literally means "simple to the extent of being very," that is, "very simple." You could, of course, also just say **hěn jiǎndān** "very simple," but the use of the STATIVE VERB + **-de** + **hěn** pattern adds emphasis as well as variety. This pattern is closely related to the pattern with **-de** that indicates extent (15-4: 6A). The pattern is:

SUBJECT	STATIVE VERB	-DE	HĚN
Cài	jiǎndān	de	hěn.

"The food is very simple."

Some more examples of STATIVE VERB + **-de** + **hěn**:

Tā hǎode hěn.	"He's fine."
Zhèrde dōngxi guìde hěn.	"The things here are very expensive."
Wǒ zuìjìn mángde hěn.	"I've been very busy lately."
Tāde Zhōngwén hǎode hěn.	"Her Chinese is very good."

3C.   **(SHI)...-DE TO EMPHASIZE A SITUATION.** Examine the last **-de** in **Wǒ jìde nǐ zuì ài chīde** "I remember that you loved to eat it most." This is an example of so-called "situational **-de**," which describes how things are, that is, that a certain feature is part of a certain situation. Situational **-de** gives a statement an air of solidity and makes a situation seem permanent. A **shi** can optionally be placed after the subject, so you could just as well say **Wǒ jìde nǐ shi zuì ài chīde**. Both the **shi** and the **-de** are optional. Some more examples:

> **Nǐ nèiyàng shuō shi bú duìde.**
>
> "It's not right of you to speak that way."

> **Wáng Jiàoshòu duì yǔyánxué hěn yǒu yánjiūde.**
>
> "Professor Wang is very knowledgeable about linguistics."

> **Wǒ yuèmǔ chīle wǔshiniánde Zhōngguo cài, xīcān tā shi chībuláide.**
>
> "My mother-in-law has eaten Chinese food for fifty years; she just wouldn't be able to get used to eating Western food."

4A.   **-ZHE AS CONTINUOUS ASPECT SUFFIX MEANING "IN THE VERBING."** In this line, look at the sentence **Wèir wénzhe zhēn xiāng** "The aroma smells really great!" (lit. "The aroma, in my smelling it, is really fragrant"). This use of the aspect suffix **-zhe** is actually quite like the use of VERB + **-qilai** to indicate "in the VERBing" that we introduced in 6-2: 5A (e.g., **Nǐ kànqilai hěn niánqīng** "You look very young"). Indeed, instead of the sentence in the Basic Conversation here, we could also say **Wèir wénqilai zhēn xiāng**, with the same meaning. In 9-4: 2A, we introduced **-zhe** as a suffix that can indicate continuous aspect, that is, that some action is prolonged and continuing for a duration of time. When **-zhe** is suffixed onto an action verb, it often

Xiǎocài or "appetizer" choices in a Taipei restaurant

corresponds to English "-ing." The adverb **zhèng** "just now" sometimes occurs before the **-zhe** and sentence final particle **ne** often co-occurs after the **-zhe**, so this pattern is often manifested as **zhèng** + VERB + **-zhe ne**. We should also compare continuous aspect suffix **-zhe** with the use of **zài** as an auxiliary verb to indicate progressive aspect (10-3: 2A). In general, we can say that with the auxiliary **zài**, the emphasis is on the progression of an activity, while with continuous aspect suffix **-zhe**, the emphasis is on the continuation of the results of an action. To make this clearer, compare these two examples:

(a) **Tā zài chuān yīfu ne.**

"She's putting on her clothes." (the emphasis is on the progression of the action of "putting on")

(b) **Tā chuānzhe yíjiàn hóngsède máoyī.**

"She's wearing a red sweater." (the emphasis is on the results of the "putting on," that is, the "wearing")

Such clear distinctions as for (a) and (b) above don't apply for all verbs; for some verbs, the meaning with the auxiliary **zài** and with the continuous aspect suffix **-zhe** is essentially the same. To sum up, the pattern with **-zhe** as continuous aspect suffix is:

VERB	-ZHE
chuān	zhe
"wearing"	

Here, now, are some more examples of **-zhe** as progressive aspect suffix:

Mén hái kāizhe ne.	"The door is still open."
Nǐ shóuli názhe shémme ne?	"What are you holding in your hand?"
Zhèijiàn yīfu chuānzhe tǐng shūfude.	"This dress is very comfortable."
Zhànzhe bǐ zuòzhe hǎo.	"Standing is better than sitting."
Mén wàibianr zhànzhede nèige rén shi shéi?	"Who is that standing outside the doorway?"
Dàshǐ zhèng kāizhe huì ne.	"The ambassador is just having a meeting."
Wàitou zhèng xiàzhe yǔ ne.	"It's raining outside right now."
Tā zhèng shuōzhe huà ne.	"She is just now speaking."

The negative form of a verb with the continuous aspect suffix **-zhe** is **méi(you)** + VERB + **-zhe**. However, this is not very common. Example:

Mén kāizhe, chuānghu méi kāizhe.   "The door is open; the windows aren't open."

4B.   **APPROXIMATE NUMBERS.** Consider in this line the approximate number expression **liǎngsānnián** "two or three years." Approximations involving single digits can be indicated in Chinese by juxtaposing two consecutive numbers followed by a measure, without any overt expression for "or" or "and." The numbers involved can be simple numbers, money amounts, times, numbers of people, etc. Examples:

yìliǎngge	"one or two"
liǎngsān'ge	"two or three"
liǎngsānfēn zhōng	"two or three minutes"
sānsìtiān	"three or four days"
wǔliùge rén	"five or six people"
liǎngsānkuài qián	"two or three bucks"
qībādiǎn zhōng	"7:00 or 8:00"

Approximate numbers are very common in Chinese, as there is a certain hesitation about committing oneself too exactly to a certain number and running the risk of later being proven wrong. Approximate numbers leave "wriggle room." The combination **liǎngsān-** is especially common. One doesn't normally juxtapose **jiǔ** and **shí** for "nine or ten," since that could also be taken to mean "ninety" (though **jiǔshídiǎn zhōng** "9:00 or 10:00" is sometimes said).

4C.   **Zhēn shi liǎngsānnián méi chīdàole** "I really haven't had it for two or three years now." The time expression **liǎngsānnián** "for two or three years" here appears before rather than after the verb because this is a case of negative time spent (11-2: 2A). Were it positive time spent (e.g., **Tā xuéle liǎngsānnián le** "She's been studying it for two or three years"), the time expression would go after the verb.

4D.   Contrast the pronunciation of **chīdào** "eat so something arrives in one's mouth, succeed in eating something, eat" and **chídào** "arrive late, be late." Some more examples of **chīdào**:

> **Zài Táiwān chīdedào Rìběn cài ma?**
>
> "Is one able to eat Japanese food in Taiwan?"

> **Zài Měiguo chībudào dìdàode Zhōngguo cài!**
>
> "In America, you can't eat (or "can't get") authentic Chinese food!"

5.   **Wǒ tèdì wèi nǐ zuòle Málà Zábànr** "I specially made Sesame Hot Spicy Medley for you." The coverb **wèi** means "for." Here are some more examples with the coverb **wèi**:

Tā xǐhuan wèi dàjiā bànshì.	"She likes to do things for everyone."
Māma wèi wǒ zuòle hěn duō hǎochīde dōngxi.	"Mom made lots of delicious things for me."
Wèi wǒmende yǒuyì gānbēi!	"Let's drink to our friendship!"
Wǒ wèi nǐ gāoxìng.	"I'm happy for you."
Nǐ bié wèi zhèige bù gāoxìng.	"Don't be unhappy on account of this."

7A.   The idiomatic expression **xiān zǒu yíbù** "take one step first" usually refers to a person's departing from a dinner table before the others do. However, occasionally it can also refer to someone's dying before others; therefore, superstitious people sometimes try to avoid this expression.

7B.   **Wǒ gēn nèirén** "my wife and I" literally means "I and wife." In English we're taught by our parents and in school that it's rude to say "I" first, and that you should name the other person before "I." In Chinese there is no such rule. Therefore, it's normal to say **wǒ gēn nǐ** "I and you," **wǒ hé Lǎo Zhāng** "I and Old Zhang," etc.

7C.   The polite expression **màn yòng**, literally "slowly use," is commonly said when one person gets up before others are finished eating. It means "take your time eating," in other words, "please don't rush just because I have to leave."

7D.   **Shīpéi** is another polite expression. It literally means "lose accompaniment" and is used when one person has to leave and so is unable to continue accompanying others at a meal or other function. In smoother English, we might say "Sorry to have to leave."

7E.   Line 7 illustrates useful language when you have to leave a dinner party early. The person or persons leaving normally propose a toast to those remaining behind. You should, of course, notify the host beforehand if you anticipate having to leave early. Also, it's best to wait until the finest dish of food has been served, as this means you've received and accepted the host's **shèngyì** "great kindness" in inviting you.

SV2.   **Biàndāng**, introduced to Taiwan during the Japanese occupation, are boxed lunches that have become increasingly popular over the years. Some people make them at home and bring them to work, where they're put in a wok to be steamed shortly before the lunch hour. Other people buy commercially prepared **biàndāng** at stands and restaurants. The price range in Taiwan is from about $2.00 U.S. to the very extravagant. In mainland China, the equivalent word is **héfàn** "box lunch."

AV4.   **Sānmíngzhì** "sandwich" is a borrowing from English. **Sānmíngzhì** are available at coffee shops in Western restaurants. In Taiwan, a type of breakfast sandwich under this name has become popular in recent years.

AV5.   **Yóutài miànbāo** "bagel" literally means "Jewish bread." Some Chinese speakers use this term, but others don't.

A Dinner Party at Home (cont.)

Mr. Yang tries to get Wells to consume some more liquor, but Wells declines. After more eating and drinking, the dinner concludes with Wells thanking the hosts and other guests. Everyone then moves to the living room for fruit and tea (continued from the previous conversation).

 Basic Conversation 16-4

1. MR. YANG   *(after returning from escorting Mr. and Mrs. Zhang to the elevator)* **Lǎo Wèi, lái, zài hē jiǔ! Wǒ jìng nǐ!**
Larry, come on, have some more liquor! To you!

2. WELLS   **Wǒ yǐjīng hēde tài duōle. Shízài shi bù néng zài hēle. Wǒ yǐ guǒzhī dài jiǔ hǎo ba.**
I've already had too much to drink. I really can't drink any more. I'll substitute juice for liquor.

(after a while, to Mrs. Yang)

Dàsǎo zuòde cài zhēn shi "sè xiāng wèir jùquán." Guǎnzi yě bǐbushàng!
Older sister, the food you cook really is perfect in color, aroma, and taste. Not even a restaurant could compare!

3. MRS. YANG   **Náli, náli, yìdiǎnr jiācháng cài éryǐ. Búguò ne, cài suírán bù zěmmeyàng, nǐ hái shi yào chībǎo ó!**
Thank you. It's just a little home-style cooking. But though the food is nothing special, you do have to get enough to eat, you know!

4. WELLS   **Wǒ dōu yǐjīng chīchēngle. Shízài shi tài hǎochīle. Zhèmme fēngshèngde yídùn fàn, Dàsǎo jīntiān xīnkǔle. Wǒ jìng Dàgē, Dàsǎo!**
I've already eaten so much, I'm going to burst. It was really delicious. Such a sumptuous meal; Older Sister worked very hard today. Let me toast the two of you!

(he toasts Mr. and Mrs. Yang, then looks at the other guests)

Yòu máfan gèwèi dà lǎo yuǎnde lái. Wǒ jìng gèwèi! Jiù suàn shi ménqiánqīng ba.
And I made you all go to the trouble of coming here from far away. Here's to all of you! Let's just consider this a last "bottoms up."

5. MR. YANG   **Gèwèi qǐng dào kètīng zuò. Hē diǎn chá, chī diǎn shuǐguǒ!**
Everyone please go to the living room and have a seat. Drink some tea and eat some fruit!

Build Up

---

1.   Mr. Yang

Lǎo Wèi, lái, zài hē jiǔ! Wǒ jìng nǐ!

Larry, come on, have some more liquor! To you!

---

2.   Wells

hēde tài duōle	have drunk too much
yǐ	take [CV]
guǒzhī	juice [N]
dài	take the place of [V]
yǐ A dài B	take A to substitute for B [PT]
yǐ guǒzhī dài jiǔ	substitute juice for liquor

Wǒ yǐjīng hēde tài duōle. Shízài
shi bù néng zài hēle. Wǒ yǐ guǒzhī
dài jiǔ hǎo ba.

I've already had too much to drink. I really
can't drink any more. I'll substitute juice
for liquor.

"sè xiāng wèir jùquán"	"color, aroma, taste all complete" [EX]
guǎnzi	restaurant [PW]
bǐbushàng	not be able to compare [RC]
guǎnzi yě bǐbushàng	even a restaurant can't compare

Dàsǎo zuòde cài zhēn shi "sè xiāng
wèir jùquán." Guǎnzi yě bǐbushàng!

Older sister, the food you cook really is perfect
in color, aroma, and taste. Not even a restaurant could
compare!

---

3.   Mrs. Yang

jiācháng cài	home-style cooking [PH]
yìdiǎnr jiācháng cài éryǐ	only a little home-style cooking
suírán... (T)	although... [PT]
cài suírán bù zěmmeyàng	though the food is not special
bǎo	be full, satiated [SV]
-bǎo	full, satiated [RE]
chībǎo	eat one's fill [RC]
nǐ hái shi yào chībǎo ó	you still have to eat your fill

Náli, náli, yìdiǎnr jiācháng cài éryǐ.
Búguò ne, cài suírán bù zěmmeyàng,
nǐ hái shi yào chībǎo ó!

Thank you. It's just a little home-style cooking.
But though the food is nothing special, you do
have to get enough to eat, you know!

---

4.   Wells

-chēng	fill to the point of bursting [RE]
chīchēng	eat until one bursts [RC]
wǒ dōu yǐjīng chīchēngle	I'm already so full I'll burst
fēngshèng	be sumptuous [SV]
zhèmme fēngshèngde yídùn fàn	so sumptuous a meal
xīnkǔ	endure hardship [SV]
dàsǎo jīntiān xīnkǔle	Older Sister toiled hard today

Wǒ dōu yǐjīng chīchēngle. Shízài
shi tài hǎochīle. Zhèmme fēngshèngde
yídùn fàn, Dàsǎo jīntiān xīnkǔle.
Wǒ jìng Dàgē, Dàsǎo!

I've already eaten so much, I'm going to burst.
It was really delicious. Such a sumptuous
meal; Older Sister worked very hard today.
Let me toast the two of you!

lǎo	very [A]
lǎo yuǎn	very far
dà lǎo yuǎnde lái	come from very far away
suàn	consider as [V]
ménqiánqīng	finish drinking up alcoholic beverages before leaving [EX]

| jiù suàn shi ménqiánqīng | consider it as drinking up all the remaining alcohol before leaving |
| Yòu máfan gèwèi dà lǎo yuǎnde lái. Wǒ jìng gèwèi! Jiù suàn shi ménqiánqīng ba. | And I made you all go to the trouble of coming here from far away. Here's to all of you! Let's just consider this a last "bottoms up." |

5. Mr. Yang

kètīng	living room [PW] (M: **jiān**)
qǐng dào kètīng zuò	please go to the living room and sit
chá	tea [N]
hē diǎn chá	drink some tea
Gèwèi qǐng dào kètīng zuò. Hē diǎn chá, chī diǎn shuǐguǒ!	Everyone please go to the living room and have a seat. Drink some tea and eat some fruit!

Supplementary Vocabulary

1. shuǐ	water [N]
2. qìshuǐ(r)	soda [N]
3. kělè	cola [N]
4. cāntīng	dining room (in a house); dining hall, restaurant [PW] (M: **jiān**)
5. dàikè	teach in place of someone else [VO]
dàikè lǎoshī	substitute teacher
Tā suīrán zhǐ shi dàikè lǎoshī, kěshi jiāode bú cuò.	Although she's only a substitute teacher, she teaches rather well.

Additional Vocabulary: More Beverages and a Popular Saying

1. xìngrénlù	almond milk [N]
2. píngguǒzhī	apple juice [N]
3. kāishuǐ	boiled water [N]
4. Kěkǒu Kělè	Coca-Cola® [N]
5. yēzhī	coconut milk [N]
6. zhāpí (B)	draft beer [N]
7. bīngshuǐ	ice water [N]
8. niúnǎi	milk [N]
9. kuàngquánshuǐ	mineral water [N]
10. júzizhī	orange juice [N]
11. chéngzhī	orange juice [N]
12. Bǎishì Kělè	Pepsi-Cola® [N]
13. chúnjìngshuǐ	purified water, distilled water [N]
14. Qīxǐ	Seven-Up® [N]
15. Xuěbì	Sprite® [N]
16. Zǎofàn chīde bǎo, wǔfàn chīde hǎo, wǎnfàn chīde shǎo.	"Breakfast eat your fill, lunch eat well, supper eat little." [EX]

Grammatical and Cultural Notes

2A.   **YǏ A DÀI B.** Consider in this line the sentence **wǒ yǐ guǒzhī dài jiǔ** "I'll take juice to substitute for wine" or "I'll substitute juice for wine." The pattern **yǐ A dài B** "take A to substitute for B" is a useful pattern for you to learn. It would be considered bad manners if someone raised his or her glass to toast you and you refused entirely, since this would cause the other party to lose face. Therefore, if you really can't drink alcohol and don't wish to **suíyì**, then you can use this pattern and propose substituting some non-alcoholic beverage such as **guǒzhī** "juice," **qìshuǐ** "soda," or **chá** "tea" for the alcohol. To sum up, the basic pattern is:

yǐ   guǒzhī   dài   jiǔ
"substitute juice for wine"

More examples of the pattern **yǐ A dài B**:

> **Wǒmen yǐ chá dài jiǔ ba.**
>
> "Let's drink tea in place of wine." (lit. "Let's take tea and substitute it for wine." This is quite commonly said.)

> **Wǒ yǐ qìshuǐ dài jiǔ.**
>
> "I'm substituting soda for liquor." (lit. "I take soda and substitute it for liquor.")

2B.   Many speakers prefer **sè xiāng wèi jùquán**, without an **-r** on **wèi**.

2C.   **Guǎnzi** "restaurant" is a synonym of **fànguǎn(r)**, which you learned in 14-1. Other words for "restaurant" or "dining hall" that you have learned so far include **cāntīng** (16-4) and **shítáng** (1-1).

2D.   **TOPIC + YĚ + NEGATIVE VERB.** Toward the end of this utterance, notice **Guǎnzi yě bǐbushàng** "Not even a restaurant could compare." A topic followed by **yě** (or **dōu**) plus a negative verb often carries the connotation "not even." A fuller version of this would add a **lián**: **lián guǎnzi yě bǐbushàng**, with the same meaning. The basic pattern is:

TOPIC	YĚ / DŌU	NEGATIVE VERB
Guǎnzi	yě	bǐbushàng.

"Not even a restaurant could compare."

Some more examples of the pattern TOPIC + **yě/dōu** + NEGATIVE VERB:

Wǒ shínián yě xuébuhuì.	"Even in ten years I couldn't learn it."
Nǐ yìqiānkuài yě mǎibudào.	"You couldn't buy it even for a thousand dollars."
Nǐ sònggěi wǒ wǒ yě bú yào.	"Even if you gave it to me as a present, I wouldn't want it."

3A.   The **ne** in **búguò ne** "however" is a pause filler (7-1: 10B).

3B.   **SUĪRÁN...KĚSHI, SUĪRÁN...DÀNSHI, AND SUĪRÁN...HÁI SHI.** These three patterns all mean "although…" or "though…." The moveable adverb **suīrán** occurs in the first or dependent clause, with **kěshi** "but," **dànshi** "but," or **hái shi** "still" in the second or independent clause. The basic pattern is:

SUĪRÁN...,	KĚSHI / DÀNSHI / HÁI SHI....
Cài suīrán bù zěmmeyàng,	nǐ hái shi yào chībǎo!

"Though the food is nothing special, you've got to get enough to eat!"

There are four things you need to remember about **suīrán**:

(1)   In English we use "although" and "though" alone, without a following "but." However, in Chinese **suīrán** must be used together with a following **kěshi**, **dànshi**, or **hái shi**.

(2)   In English we can have the "although" or "though" phrase as either the first or the second clause of a sentence, but in Chinese, the phrase with **suīrán** usually comes first.

(3)   Since **suīrán** is a moveable adverb, it can occur before or after the subject. In other words, you could say either of the following two sentences:

Suīrán wǒ hěn xǐhuan nèiběn shū, dànshi tài guìle, wǒ juédìng bù mǎile.

"Although I like that book very much, it's too expensive, I decided not to buy it."

Wǒ suīrán hěn xǐhuan nèiběn shū, dànshi tài guìle, wǒ juédìng bù mǎile.

"Although I like that book very much, it's too expensive, I decided not to buy it."

(4)   An alternate pronunciation of **suīrán** "although" that you'll hear in Taiwan and occasionally elsewhere is **suírán**. This is how the word is pronounced in the recording of this Basic Conversation.

Now, some more examples of **suīrán...kěshi**, **suīrán...dànshi**, and **suīrán...hái shi**:

Nǐ suīrán bú è, kěshi yě děi chī yidian dōngxi.

"Though you're not hungry, you still have to eat something."

Tā suīrán hěn cōngming, dànshi bú tài yònggōng.

"Even though he's smart, he's not very hard-working."

Suīrán tiānqi bù hǎo, wǒ hái shi yào qù.

"I'm still going to go, though the weather isn't good."

3C.   Remember that **ó** is a sentence final particle that can indicate a friendly warning (11-1: 2C).

4A.   **Dà lǎo yuǎnde lái** "come from very far away" (lit. "come in a very far away manner," cf. 15-1: 1C). **Lǎo** here means "very," **lǎo yuǎn** means "very far," and **dà** intensifies the meaning of the whole: "come from very far away." Here is a related sentence with **lǎo yuǎn**:

Wǒmen cóng lǎo yuǎnde dìfang lái.   "We come from a far away place."

4B.   **Jiù suàn shi ménqiánqīng ba** literally means "(This) can be considered as 'clear before the door,'" i.e., "Let's consider this as drinking up the remainder of our alcoholic beverages before we get up to leave." This is said when drinking up all the remaining alcohol in one's glass at the end of a dinner.

5.   **IMPORTANCE OF TEA IN CHINESE CULTURE. Chá** "tea" is a special beverage in China. It implies conversation and relaxation. Inviting someone to drink tea is a gesture of friendship, as tea serves to facilitate communication, somewhat like cocktails in the United States. Never ask for milk, cream, sugar, or lemon with your tea unless you're in a Western-style hotel; most Chinese find it curious and regrettable to "spoil" tea in this way. If a Chinese guest comes to your home, the first thing you should do is pour them some tea. Don't even ask if they want any, or they will feel obligated to decline. Drinking tea is important for good health; besides providing warmth during cold weather, it provides fluids, which are important in the dry Northern Chinese climate, and in the case of green tea, there may even be additional health benefits. When drinking tea, there is a custom (originally from Guangdong but which has spread to Beijing and Taipei and elsewhere) of rapping your knuckles on the table to show your respect and appreciation to the person filling your tea cup; when you stop rapping, the person knows to stop pouring.

SV1.   **Shuǐ** "water." For reasons of hygiene, it's important that you not drink tap water when in China. You should drink only boiled water (**kāishuǐ**, AV3), bottled mineral water (**kuàngquánshuǐ**, AV9), or purified water (**chúnjìngshuǐ**, AV13). In Western hotels you can ask for ice water (**bīngshuǐ**, AV7), but this isn't something that Chinese people would drink or that smaller restaurants would have available.

SV2.   **Qìshuǐ(r)** "soda" refers to any carbonated soft drink, i.e., soda pop, but not club soda.

AV1–15.   **BEVERAGES.** The names of these beverages have been listed in alphabetical order of the English translations.

AV4. **Kěkǒu Kělè** "Coca-Cola" not only sounds like English "Coca-Cola" but also has an appropriate meaning; in Classical Chinese, it means "can mouth it, can be happy." **Kě** is similar to modern Chinese **kéyi**; **kǒu** "mouth" is the same **kǒu** as the measure for people and is also the **kǒu** in **rénkǒu** "population;" **lè** is the **lè** of **kuàilè** "be happy."

AV6. An alternate word for **zhāpí** "draft beer" that you'll hear in Taiwan and occasionally elsewhere is **shēng píjiǔ**, which literally means "raw beer."

AV12. **Bǎishì Kělè** "Pepsi-Cola" literally means "(in) one hundred things can be happy (when drinking Pepsi-Cola)."

AV14. **Qīxǐ** "Seven-Up" literally means "the seven happinesses." **Xǐ** is the **xǐ** of **xǐhuan** "like."

Unit 16: Review and Study Guide

New Vocabulary

ADVERBS

lǎo	very
tèdì	especially
yíkuài(r)	together

AUXILIARY VERBS

gǎn	dare to

COVERBS

tì	for
wèi	for
yǐ	take

EXPRESSIONS

gōngjìng bù rú cóng mìng	"to show respect is not as good as following orders"
ménqiánqīng	finish drinking up alcoholic beverages before leaving
"sè xiāng wèir jùquán"	"color, aroma, taste all complete"
xiān-gǎn-wéi-jìng	drink bottoms up before someone else to show respect

IDIOMATIC EXPRESSIONS

bù gǎn dāng	"don't dare accept"
búyào kèqi	"don't be polite"
hǎiliàng	"ocean capacity"
liàng qiǎn	"capacity is shallow"
mǎidān	"pay the check, "figure up the bill"
màn yòng	"take your time eating"
shīpéi	"sorry to have to leave"

suíyì	"as you like"
xiān zǒu yíbù	"take one step first"

INTERJECTIONS

ài	(indicates strong sentiment)
hài	"hi"

MEASURES

bù	step, pace
dùn	(for meals)
táng	(for classes)

NOUNS

biàndāng	box lunch
biànfàn	simple meal
bǔxíbān	cram school
chá	tea
cì	fish bone
dàsǎo	wife of oldest brother
fúwùyuán	attendant, waiter, waitress
guǒzhī	juice
hǎi	ocean, sea
hé	river
hú	lake
kělè	cola
nèirén	one's wife (polite)
qìshuǐ(r)	soda
shítou	stone
shuǐ	water
wèir	smell, aroma
xiǎochī	snack
yǔliàng	rainfall

PARTICLES

-guo	(expresses completed action)

PATTERNS

bù rú...	not be as good as...
mán...de	quite
suīrán...	although...
yǐ A dài B	take A to substitute for B

PHRASES

jiācháng cài	home-style cooking
Málà Zábànr	Sesame Hot Spicy Medley
Tángcù Lǐjī	Sweet and Sour Pork

PLACE WORDS

cāntīng	dining room (in a house); dining hall, restaurant
guǎnzi	restaurant
kètīng	living room

RESULTATIVE COMPOUNDS

bǐbushàng	not be able to compare
chībǎo	eat one's fill
chīchēng	eat until one bursts
chīdào	succeed in eating
gòubuzháo	be unable to reach
gòudezháo	be able to reach
huílai	come back
huíqu	go back

RESULTATIVE ENDINGS

-bǎo	full, satiated
-chēng	fill to the point of bursting

STATIVE VERBS

bǎo	be full, satiated
fēngshèng	be sumptuous

lǎo	be tough (of food)	gāngcái	just now	yùbei	prepare
nèn	be tender	**VERBS**		**VERB-OBJECT COMPOUNDS**	
qiǎn	be shallow	dài	take the place of	bǔkè	make up a class
shēn	be deep	fù	pay	dàikè	teach in place of someone
xīnkǔ	endure hardship	gǎi	change		
SURNAMES		gòu	reach (by stretching)	fùqián	pay money
Shí	Shi			jiēfēng	give a welcome dinner
Wèi	Wei	pòfèi	go to great expense	qǐngkè	invite, treat (someone to something)
TIME WORDS		suàn	consider as	zuòdōng	serve as host
gǎitiān	on some other day				

Major New Grammar Patterns

-GUO TO EXPRESS COMPLETED ACTION: Nǐ chīguo fàn le ma? "Have you eaten?" (16-1)

STATIVE VERB + LE + (YI) DIAN(R) TO EXPRESS EXCESS: Zhèige cài làle yidian. "This dish is a little too spicy hot." (16-1)

A BÙ RÚ B: Tā Zhōngwén shuōde bù rú tā tàitai hǎo. "He doesn't speak Chinese as well as his wife." (16-2)

STATIVE VERB + -DE + HĚN: Cài jiǎndānde hěn. "The food is very simple." (16-3)

-ZHE AS PROGRESSIVE ASPECT SUFFIX MEANING "IN THE VERB-ING": Zhèige cài wénzhe zhēn xiāng a! "This dish of food (in the smelling of it) smells really good!" (16-3)

APPROXIMATE NUMBERS: liǎngsānnián "two or three years" (16-3)

YǏ A DÀI B: Wǒ yǐ guǒzhī dài jiǔ. "I'll substitute juice for wine." (16-4)

SUĪRÁN...KĚSHI/DÀNSHI: Tā suīrán hěn cōngming, dànshi bú tài yònggōng. "Even though she's smart, she's not very hard-working." (16-4)

On the Telephone

COMMUNICATIVE OBJECTIVES

Once you've mastered this unit, you'll be able to use Chinese to:

1. Make and take telephone calls and engage in relevant telephone talk: ask to speak to a certain person, ask to be connected to a certain extension, state who you are, say goodbye, etc.

2. Ask someone to speak up if you can't hear them clearly.

3. Leave a message for someone who isn't there.

4. Discuss with someone on the telephone when and where to meet.

5. Call on the telephone to inquire about an apartment that has been advertised: how large is it? Is it furnished? Are utilities included? etc.

6. Talk about the rooms of an apartment or house: living room, dining room, study, bedrooms, bathroom, kitchen, etc.

7. Discuss different kinds of furniture: sofa, dining table, desk, bed, closet, etc.

"Want to Go to the Show?"

Jim Donovan calls his Chinese friend Wang Dapeng on the telephone to ask if Wang would like to accompany him to a musical performance at the Beijing International Club. Wang picks up the phone.

Basic Conversation 17-1

1. WANG   *(answering the telephone, which is ringing)* **Wéi? Qǐng wèn, nín zhǎo shéi?**
             Hello? Who would you like to speak with?

2. DONOVAN   **Wáng Dàpéng Xiānshēng zài ma?**
             Is Mr. Wang Dapeng in?

3. WANG   **Wǒ jiù shì a. Qǐng wèn, nǐ shi něiwèi?**
             Speaking. Excuse me, who is this?

4. DONOVAN   **Wǒ shi Xiǎo Táng. Nǐ zěmmeyàng?**
             I'm Little Tang. How are you?

5. WANG   **Hài, bié tíle! Zhèjǐtiān zhēn bǎ wǒ mánghuàile. Nǐ yǒu shémme shìr ma?**
             Oh, don't mention it! The last few days I've really been incredibly busy. Something up?

6. DONOVAN   **Xiǎo Wáng, wǒ gēn nǐ shuō, zhèige xīngqīliù wǎnshàng Guójì Jùlèbù yǒu yīnyuèhuì. Bù zhīdào nǐ yǒu méiyou kòngr?**
             Little Wang, listen. This Saturday evening the International Club is having a concert. I wonder if you'd be free?

7. WANG   **Yǒu a. Xīngqīliù jǐdiǎn zhōng?**
             Sure. What time on Saturday?

8. DONOVAN   **Yīnyuèhuì shi qīdiǎn zhōng. Zámmen tíqián yíkè zhōng zài Guójì Jùlèbù ménkǒur jiàn, xíng ma?**
             The concert is at seven o'clock. We'll meet 15 minutes beforehand at the entrance to the International Club, O.K.?

9. WANG   **Xíng, yì-yán-wéi-dìng. Ò, duìle, nǐ néng duō gǎo jǐzhāng piào ma? Xiǎo Liú, Xiǎo Zhào tāmen duì yīnyuè yě tǐng gǎn xìngqude.**
             O.K., agreed. Oh, yes, could you get a few more tickets? Little Liu and Little Zhao are also quite interested in music.

10. DONOVAN   **Zhè, wǒ gūjì wèntí bú dà.**
                I think there should be no big problem with that.

11. WANG   **Hǎo, jiù zhèiyangr ba. Dào shíhour jiàn!**
                O.K., then that's how it will be. See you when the time comes!

12. DONOVAN   **Jiù zhèiyangr dìngle. Báibái!**
                Then it's settled like this. Bye!

Build Up

1. **Wang**
Wéi? Qǐng wèn, nín zhǎo shéi?   Hello? Who would you like to speak with?

2. Donovan
   Wáng Dàpéng   Wang Dapeng (Chinese name)
   Wáng Dàpéng Xiānshēng zài ma?   Is Mr. Wang Dapeng in?

3. Wang
   wǒ jiù shì   it's me
   Wǒ jiù shì a. Qǐng wèn, nǐ shi něiwèi?   Speaking. Excuse me, who is this?

4. Donovan
   Táng   Tang [SN]
   Wǒ shi Xiǎo Táng. Nǐ zěmmeyàng?   I'm Little Tang. How are you?

5. Wang
   hài   (indicates exasperation) [I]
   tí   mention [V]
   bié tíle   don't mention it
   zhèjǐtiān   these last few days
   huài   be bad [SV]
   -huài   be bad [RE]
   mánghuài   extremely busy [RC]
   bǎ wǒ mánghuàile   made me extremely busy
   Hài, bié tíle! Zhèjǐtiān zhēn bǎ wǒ   Oh, don't mention it! The last few days I've
   mánghuàile. Nǐ yǒu shémme shìr ma?   really been incredibly busy. Something up?

6. Donovan
   wǒ gēn nǐ shuō   let me tell you
   guójì   international [AT]
   jùlèbù   club [PW]
   Guójì Jùlèbù   International Club [PW]
   huì   gathering, meeting [N]
   yīnyuè   music [N]
   yīnyuèhuì   concert [N]
   kòng(r)   free time [N]
   yǒukòng(r)   have free time [VO]
   nǐ yǒu méiyou kòngr   do you have free time
   Xiǎo Wáng, wǒ gēn nǐ shuō, zhèige xīngqīliù Little Wang, listen. This Saturday evening
   wǎnshàng Guójì Jùlèbù yǒu yīnyuèhuì.   the International Club is having a concert.
   Bù zhīdào nǐ yǒu méiyou kòngr?   I wonder if you'd be free?

7. **Wang**
Yǒu a. Xīngqīliù jǐdiǎn zhōng?   Sure. What time on Saturday?

8. Donovan

tíqián	move up (a time or date) [V]
tíqián yíkè zhōng	move up a quarter of an hour
Yīnyuèhuì shi qīdiǎn zhōng. Zámmen tíqián yíkè zhōng zài Guójì Jùlèbù ménkǒur jiàn, xíng ma?	The concert is at seven o'clock. We'll meet 15 minutes beforehand at the entrance to the International Club, O.K.?

9. Wang

yì-yán-wéi-dìng	be agreed with one word [EX]
ò, duìle	oh, that's right
gǎo jǐzhāng piào	get several tickets
Liú	Liu [SN]
gǎn	feel [V]
xìngqu	interest [N]
gǎn xìngqu	feel or have interest
duì...gǎn xìngqu	be interested in... [PT]
duì yīnyuè gǎn xìngqu	be interested in music
Xíng, yì-yán-wéi-dìng. Ò, duìle, nǐ néng duō gǎo jǐzhāng piào ma? Xiǎo Liú, Xiǎo Zhào tāmen duì yīnyuè yě tǐng gǎn xìngqude.	O.K., agreed. Oh, yes, could you get a few more tickets? Little Liu and Little Zhao are also quite interested in music.

10. Donovan

wèntí bú dà	the problem is not great
Zhè, wǒ gūjì wèntí bú dà.	I think there should be no big problem with that.

11. Wang

Hǎo, jiù zhèiyangr ba. Dào shíhour jiàn!	O.K., then that's how it will be. See you when the time comes!

12. Donovan

dìng	settle, decide [V]
báibái	"bye-bye" [IE]
Jiù zhèiyangr dìngle. Báibái!	Then it's settled like this. Bye!

Supplementary Vocabulary

1. **shìnèi diànhuà**	local telephone call [PH]

Additional Vocabulary: Using the Telephone

1. **diànhuàbù**	telephone directory [N] (M: **běn**)
2. **cháhàotái**	directory assistance [N]
3. **zǒngjī**	switchboard [N]
4. **bō**	dial (a number) [V]
5. **dǎtōng**	call and get through [RC]
6. **dǎbutōng**	call but not be able to get through [RC]
7. **méi rén jiē**	there is no one who answers [PH]
8. **jiǎnghuà zhōng**	be in the midst of talking [PH]
9. **chángtú diànhuà**	long distance telephone call [PH]

Grammatical and Cultural Notes

1. **BODY MOVEMENTS.** In the video for this lesson, note how the American walks in large strides, his body bouncing up and down, his arms swinging back and forth at his sides. In general, Americans tend to move their bodies much more than Chinese, who are sparing and restrained in their movements. As someone who

isn't native to Chinese culture, it's not realistic—and might even be counterproductive—for you to attempt to adopt a completely different Chinese persona, but perhaps you could achieve some sort of compromise between the American and Chinese ways of doing things. On a related note, watch your posture! Don't adopt too relaxed a posture, especially when in the presence of someone who is superior to you in position. When standing, stand erect, don't lean against things, and don't put your hands in your pockets; when sitting, don't slouch in your chair, don't cross your legs, and for heaven's sake don't put your feet up on the coffee table in front of you. Similarly, you shouldn't prop your chin on your elbow, which is considered uncouth and disrespectful. Realize that your body movements, posture, and comportment will have an effect on how Chinese people—your teacher, your friends, your business partners—relate to you.

2–3. **TELEPHONE TALK.** Do you remember how to say "call someone on the phone"? This should be said as **gěi...dǎ diànhuà** (8-3: 2B). Remember that **dǎ** literally means "hit," so to say "I'll call you," you must not say anything like **Wǒ huì dǎ nǐ**, since that would mean "I'll hit you"; instead, you should say **Wǒ huì gěi nǐ dǎ diànhuà**.

Since there are so many people in China with the same surname, it's usually better to give the full name of the person you wish to speak with. For example, **Wáng Dàpéng Xiānshēng zài ma?** "Is Mr. Wang Dapeng in?" Other ways to express who it is you wish to speak with are **Qǐng...tīng diànhuà** and **Qǐng...jiē diànhuà**.

If calling from a company or organization, Chinese people usually first identify themselves by giving their own name or affiliation, for example: **Wéi, wǒ shi Zhāng Dàmíng** or **Nín hǎo, Běijīng Dàxué**. If the other party asks for someone and it's you who is answering, then say **Wǒ jiù shì** "It's me" or "Speaking" (lit. "I precisely it is"). In English we often say "This is so-and-so," but in Chinese telephone conversations you'd never say *Zhè shi....

One way to ask the equivalent of "Who is this?" on the telephone is **Nǐ shi něiwèi?**, literally, "You are which one?" As in English, it would be considered rude to just ask **Nǐ shi shéi?** "Who are you?" Here are several other ways to ask "Who is this?":

Nín shi něiwèi?	(lit. "You are which person?")
Nín něiwèi?	(lit. "You are which [polite] person?")
Nín nǎr?	(lit. "You are where?")
Nín shi nǎr?	(lit. "You are where?")
Nín náli a?	(lit. "You are where?")
Nín náli zhǎo?	(lit. "Where are you looking?")

For "What is your phone number?" most people ask **Nǐde diànhuà (shi) duōshǎo (hào)?** and there are some who ask **Nǐde diànhuà jǐhào?** To say "Please call me back" say **Qǐng gěi wǒ huí diànhuà**. To say "Sorry, wrong number," say **Duìbuqǐ, wǒ dǎcuòle** (or **Duìbuqǐ, nín dǎcuòle** if it is the other party that made the mistake).

Chinese people are sometimes rather rude on the telephone until they have figured out who you are, where you fit in, and what it is you're calling about. This is beginning to change as the result of governmental campaigns to urge citizens to speak politely and say **Nín hǎo**, but it's still largely true, especially outside of urban areas. So identify yourself and your purpose in calling as quickly and clearly as possible. Chinese phone calls often take place at deafening decibel levels, with speakers yelling into handsets or cell phones. This dates back to the days of bad connections, when there was often much static and one had to speak loudly to make oneself understood. The volume can sometimes hurt your ears, so you may wish to hold your phone some distance away from your ear. Also, Chinese people will often bring phone calls to an end very abruptly, much less gradually than Americans. For example, they might suddenly just say **Hǎo, hǎo** and then hang up. It's easy for Americans to think there has been some problem or that the Chinese person on the other end has become angry, but understand this is just the custom and doesn't usually mean the other party is upset.

One final note about Chinese telephone talk: In English, we'll sometimes say on the telephone something like "I haven't spoken with you for a long time!" But you shouldn't say anything like this in Chinese, as it would imply that for a long time you and the other person weren't on speaking terms!

5A.   The interjection **hài** can indicate exasperation, sorrow, or regret.

5B.   **Bié tíle!** "Don't mention it!" After negative imperatives with **bié** or **búyào** "don't," there is often a **le** at the end of the sentence. More examples:

> **Nǐ bié qùle.**   "Don't go."
>
> **Búyào zài shuōle.**   "Don't say it again."

5C.   **EXTENDED USE OF BǍ.** Look at **Zhèjǐtiān zhēn bǎ wǒ mánghuàile** "These past few days I've been incredibly busy" (lit. "These last few days really have taken me and made me so busy that I'm going to break down"). As we see in the preceding sentence, the coverb **bǎ** can be used in an extended sense. Some more examples of the extended use of **bǎ**:

> **Nǐ zhēn bǎ wǒ qìsǐle!**
>
> "You're making me furious!" (lit. "You really have taken me and made me angry to the point where I'm going to die!")
>
> **Tāde huà bǎ wǒmen shuōde yǎnlèi dōu diàoxialaile.**
>
> "What he said made us shed tears." (lit. "His words took us and talked to such an extent that tears even fell.")

5D.   **Mánghuài** "extremely busy" literally means "be busy to the extent that you've gone bad." Some more examples of resultative compounds with the resultative ending **-huài** "be bad, go bad":

> **Nǐ bǎ diànnǎo nònghuàile!**   "You've broken the computer!"
>
> **Wǒ bǎ dùzi chīhuàile.**   "I ate something bad so that I now have stomach problems."
>
> **Nèige xiǎo háizi zài nàr xuéhuàile.**   "That child learned bad things there."

The stative verb **huài** "be bad" is very common and useful. For example:

> **Nèige rén zhēn huài, nǐ zuì hǎo fángzhe tā!**
>
> "That person is really bad, you better safeguard yourself against him!"

There are also many collocations with **huài** such as **huài rén** "a bad person," **zuò huài shì** "do bad things," etc. When pronouncing **huài** "be bad," be sure to create sufficient friction on the **h-**. **Huài** should sound quite different from **wài** as in **wàiguo** "foreign country."

5E.   Since **Nǐ yǒu shémme shìr ma?** "Something up?" is already a question due to the final **ma**, the **shémme** here has an indefinite meaning of "any" or "some" and does not mean "what." Literally, **Nǐ yǒu shémme shìr ma?** means "Do you have any matter?" or "Do you have something?"

6A.   In utterance 6, observe the very common phrase **Wǒ gēn nǐ shuō** "I say to you" or "Let me tell you." The pattern **A gēn B shuō C**, literally "A to B says C," is one common way to say "tell" (11-3: 2B). Instead of **gēn** you can also use **hé**, and instead of **shuō** you can also say **jiǎng** (11-3: SV4A).

> **Nǐ bié gēn tā shuō wǒ méi qù.**
>
> "Don't tell her I didn't go."
>
> **Tā yǐjīng gēn lǎobǎn shuōle nèijiàn shì le.**
>
> "She already told the boss about that matter."

Wǒ gēn nǐ jiǎng, wǒmen gōngsī zhèige lǐbài tèbié máng.

"Listen, our company is especially busy this week."

6B.   **Guójì Jùlèbù** "International Club" is a long established organization in Beijing that caters to the expatriate community. Some Chinese citizens also participate in its activities.

6C.   The word **guójì** "international" is a member of the word class we call Attributive [AT]. This means it can occur as an adjective before nouns but CANNOT occur as a stative verb in the predicate (so you couldn't say *Tāmen jiā hěn guójì to mean "Their family is very international"). Examples of common noun phrases with **guójì**:

guójì fàndiàn	"international hotel"
guójì jīchǎng	"international airport"
guójì màoyì	"international trade"
guójì xuésheng	"international student"

In new-style, urban Chinese as spoken by the younger generation, attributives and nouns are sometimes used as stative verbs, for example:

Zhèige fànguǎnr hěn Déguo.

"This restaurant is very German."

Nèige yǎnyuán céngjīng hěn nèidì, rújīn hěn Gǎngtái, yǐhòu kěnéng huì hěn guójì.

"That actress used to be known only on the mainland; currently she's very popular in Hong Kong and Taiwan, and in the future she may become known internationally."

It's too early to tell if such usages will take root in Chinese or are merely a temporary fad. In any case, this is currently not considered standard usage and we don't recommend that you speak this way.

6D.   Though it may at first not be obvious to you, the word **jùlèbù** is actually a phonetic rendering of the English word "club." The dialect of Chinese that "club" was first borrowed into most likely pronounced standard Mandarin **j-** as **g-**, which is closer to the English **c-** in "club" (cf. the section on foreign borrowings in Chinese, 13-2: 2A).

8.   **Yīnyuèhuì shi qīdiǎn zhōng** "The concert is at seven o'clock." The **shi** in this sentence loosely connects the topic (**yīnyuèhuì**) with the comment (**qīdiǎn zhōng**). The sense is "As for the concert, it's a situation of (beginning at) 7:00."

9A.   **Yì-yán-wéi-dìng** is a **chéngyǔ** or four-character expression (10-4: 8G). It literally means "(with only) one word (the matter) is settled." Chinese people are very fond of using **chéngyǔ**, which succinctly express meanings that would otherwise take a number of words to express. Contextually appropriate use of **chéngyǔ** tends to impress hearers as to the eloquence and educational level of the speaker. You should memorize the **chéngyǔ** introduced in this course and, if the context is appropriate, use them frequently to improve your Chinese fluency and impress your interlocutors.

9B.   **Ò, duìle** "Oh, that's right" or "Oh, yes" can be said when, in the midst of a conversation, you've suddenly thought of something new and wish to introduce it into the conversation or, somewhat more deviously, when you purposely desire to change the topic but wish to make the transition seem natural and spontaneous. Example:

Ò, duìle, wǒ yǒu yíjiàn shìqing xiǎng wèn nǐ.   "Oh, yeah, there's something I wanted to ask you."

9C. The verb **gǎo** entered Mandarin from other dialects and means "do, get, make." It can substitute for many verbs, here substituting for the verb **zhǎodào**, which could also be used. Such use of **gǎo** as an all-purpose verb replacement has become extremely common in mainland China in recent decades. In Taiwan, **gǎo** isn't nearly so common and often has a negative implication (cf. **Nǐ gǎocuòle** "You got it wrong").

9D. **Nǐ néng duō gǎo jǐzhāng piào ma?** "Can you get a few more tickets?" Notice that the function of this sentence, like the English equivalent, isn't to ask whether the listener is able to get tickets but to request that he do so.

9E. **Xiǎo Liú, Xiǎo Zhào tāmen** "Little Liu and Little Zhao, they." In Chinese, after mentioning the specific members of a class or category, it's very common to close by mentioning the larger category. Another example:

> **Zhāng Xiānsheng, Lǐ Xiānsheng, Gāo Xiānsheng tāmen sān'ge rén**
>
> "Mr. Zhang, Mr. Li, and Mr. Gao, the three of them"

9F. **DUÌ...GǍN XÌNGQU AND DUÌ...YǑU XÌNGQU.** The pattern **duì...gǎn xìngqu** "be interested in..." (lit. "toward...feel interest") is very common and useful for expressing what a certain person is interested in. An alternate pattern with the same meaning is **duì...yǒu xìngqu**, literally "toward...have interest." To sum up, the two patterns are:

DUÌ	(WHAT PERSON IS INTERESTED IN)	GǍN/YǑU XÌNGQU
duì	yīnyuè	gǎn xìngqu
"be interested in music"		

More examples:

> **Nǐ duì shémme gǎn xìngqu?** "What are you interested in?"
>
> **Wǒ duì Zhōngguo wénhuà gǎn xìngqu.** "I'm interested in Chinese culture."

The question forms would be as follows:

> **Nǐ duì Zhōngguo wénhuà gǎn xìngqu ma?**
>
> **Nǐ duì Zhōngguo wénhuà yǒu xìngqu ma?**
>
> **Nǐ duì Zhōngguo wénhuà gǎn bu gǎn xìngqu?**
>
> **Nǐ duì Zhōngguo wénhuà yǒu méiyou xìngqu?**
>
> (all of the above mean "Are you interested in Chinese culture?")

The negative forms would be:

> **Wǒ duì Zhōngguo wénhuà bù gǎn xìngqu.**
>
> **Wǒ duì Zhōngguo wénhuà méiyou xìngqu.**
>
> (all of the above mean "I'm not interested in Chinese culture.")

Be sure to contrast the patterns **A duì B gǎn xìngqu** and **A duì B yǒu xìngqu** "A is interested in B," on the one hand, with the pattern **A yǒu yìsi** "A is interesting," on the other. Observe and contrast:

> **Wǒ duì yīnyuè hěn yǒu xìngqu.** "I'm very much interested in music."
>
> **Yīnyuè hěn yǒu yìsi.** "Music is very interesting."

You could NEVER say ***Wǒ duì yīnyuè hěn yǒu yìsi** to mean "I'm very much interested in music."

10. **Wǒ gūjì wèntí bú dà** literally means "I reckon that the problem is not big," i.e., "I think it should be no big problem."

11A.   **Jiù zhèiyàngr** literally means "precisely this way." The whole phrase **Hǎo, jiù zhèiyàngr ba** "O.K., then that is how it will be" is a common and useful discourse marker that signals the end of a conversation or of a topic within a conversation. It confirms and summarizes the main points of the conversation. A common variant is **Nà jiù zhèiyàngr ba** "Well, then this is how it will be."

11B.   **Dào shíhour jiàn** "see you when the time comes" literally means "when the time comes, see (you)."

12.   In telephone conversations among high school and college students, **báibái**, which obviously derives from English "bye-bye," has become very widespread both in mainland China and Taiwan. In Taiwan, **báibái** can even be used in informal speech when you're not on the telephone. The same is true of **hài** "hi" as a greeting, and of **ōukèi** "O.K." Such usage is meant to indicate that speakers are cosmopolitan, educated, and familiar with English. In the speech of Chinese intellectuals who have studied abroad, English nouns and occasionally other types of words are also sometimes inserted into Chinese discourse, e.g., **zhèige procedure** "this procedure," **nèiyang bǐjiào róngyi handle** "that way it's a little easier to handle," **jiǎrú shi nèizhǒng case -de huà** "if it's a case like that," and **nèige rén fēichángde nàisī** ("nice").

AV1.   **Diànhuàbù** "telephone directory." In China, telephone books are used much less frequently than in the U.S. On the one hand, they're less widely available, but another reason is because they're cumbersome to use. Name cards, which Chinese people collect in special plastic albums and from which they develop personal telephone directories, serve this purpose to some extent. You're urged to collect and develop your own personal telephone directory.

AV2.   At least in part because of the difficulty of looking up Chinese characters, Chinese people call **cháhàotái** "directory assistance" more often than Americans do.

Telephone Tag

Carl Johnson, an employee at Sino-American Travel Agency in Beijing, tries to call his Chinese business associate He Zhiwen on the telephone but can't get through to him.

 ## Basic Conversation 17-2

1. JOHNSON	**Wéi? Qǐng nín zhuǎn sān qī yāo.**
	Hello? Please transfer me to 371.
2. OPERATOR	**Duìbuqǐ, sān qī yāo fēnjī zhànxiàn. Nín shi děng yìhuǐr háishi guò yìhuǐr zài dǎ?**
	I'm sorry, extension 371 is busy. Will you wait a while or call back later?
3. JOHNSON	**Wǒ děng yideng.**
	I'll wait.
4. OPERATOR	*(after a while)* **Wéi? Nín kéyi gēn sān qī yāo fēnjī jiǎnghuàle.**
	Hello? You can speak with extension 371 now.
5. PERSON ANSWERING TELEPHONE	**Wéi? Nín zhǎo shéi?**
	Hello? Who do you want?
6. JOHNSON	**Qǐng nín gěi wǒ zhǎo yixiar Hé Zhìwén.**
	Could you please find He Zhiwen for me?
7. PERSON ANSWERING TELEPHONE	**Hé Zhìwén, shi ma? Hǎo, qǐng děng yixia, wǒ qù gěi nín zhǎo. Bié guà, à!**
	He Zhiwen? All right, please wait a minute, I'll go find him for you. Don't hang up, O.K.?
	(after a while) **Wéi? Hé Zhìwén zhèng zài kāihuì ne. Nín yào gěi tā liú ge huàr ma?**
	Hello? He Zhiwen is in a meeting right now. Do you want to leave him a message?
8. JOHNSON	**Tā kāiwán huì, qǐng nín ràng tā gěi wǒ dǎ ge diànhuà. Wǒ xìng Zhēnsēn, Zhōng-Měi Lǚxíngshède. Nín yì tí, tā jiù zhīdaole.**
	When he's finished with his meeting, please have him give me a call.

My name is Johnson, from Sino-American Travel Agency. As soon as you mention it, he'll know.

9. PERSON ANSWERING TELEPHONE   **Hǎode, wǒ jìxialaile. Děng tā kāiwán huì, wǒ jiù gàosu ta.**
O.K., I've written it down. As soon as he's finished with his meeting, I'll tell him.

10. JOHNSON   **Máfan nín.**
Much obliged.

Build Up

1. Johnson
zhuǎn   transfer [V]
Wéi? Qǐng nín zhuǎn sān qī yāo.   Hello? Please transfer me to 371.

2. Operator
fēnjī   extension [N]
zhànxiàn   be busy (of a telephone) [VO]
sān qī yāo fēnjī zhànxiàn   extension 371 is busy
guò yìhuǐr   when a little while has passed
guò yìhuǐr zài dǎ   call again in a little while
Duìbuqǐ, sān qī yāo fēnjī zhànxiàn.   I'm sorry, extension 371 is busy.
Nín shì děng yìhuǐr háishi guò yìhuǐr zài dǎ? Will you wait a while or call back later?

3. Johnson
děng yideng   wait
Wǒ děng yideng.   I'll wait.

4. Operator
Wéi? Nín kéyi gēn sān qī yāo fēnjī jiǎnghuàle. Hello? You can speak with extension 371 now.

5. Person answering telephone
Wéi? Nín zhǎo shéi?   Hello? Who do you want?

6. Johnson
Hé Zhìwén   He Zhiwen (Chinese name)
Qǐng nín gěi wǒ zhǎo yixiar Hé Zhìwén.   Could you please find He Zhiwen for me?

7. Person answering telephone
guà   hang, hang up [V]
bié guà   don't hang up
Hé Zhìwén, shi ma? Hǎo, qǐng děng yixia,   He Zhiwen? All right, please wait a minute,
wǒ qù gěi nín zhǎo. Bié guà, à!   I'll go find him for you. Don't hang up, O.K.?

kāihuì   hold or attend a meeting [VO]
zhèng zài...   just be in the midst of... [PT]
zhèng zài kāihuì ne   just be attending a meeting
liúhuà(r)   leave a message [VO]
gěi tā liú ge huàr   leave a message for him
Wéi? Hé Zhìwén zhèng zài kāihuì ne.   Hello? He Zhiwen is in a meeting right now.
Nín yào gěi tā liú ge huàr ma?   Do you want to leave him a message?

8. Johnson
kāiwán   finish holding (a meeting) [RC]

tā kāiwán huì	when he's finished his meeting
qǐng nín ràng tā gěi wǒ	please you have him give me
dǎ ge diànhuà	a telephone call
Zhēnsēn	(Chinese for "Johnson")
lǚxíng	travel [V]
lǚxíngshè	travel agency [PW]
yī…jiù…	as soon as [PT]
nín yì tí tā jiù zhīdaole	as soon as you mention it he'll know
Tā kāiwán huì, qǐng nín ràng tā gěi wǒ dǎ ge diànhuà. Wǒ xìng Zhēnsēn, Zhōng-Měi Lǚxíngshède. Nín yì tí, tā jiù zhīdaole.	When he's finished with his meeting, please have him give me a call. My name is Johnson, from Sino-American Travel Agency. As soon as you mention it, he'll know.

....

9. Person answering telephone

jì	record [V]
xiàlai	come down [RC]
-xiàlai	down [RE]
jìxialai	write down, note down [RC]
děng…	as soon as…, once… [PT]
děng tā kāiwán huì	once he's done with his meeting
Hǎode, wǒ jìxialaile. Děng tā kāiwán huì, wǒ jiù gàosu ta.	O.K., I've written it down. As soon as he's finished with his meeting, I'll tell him.

....

10. Johnson

Máfan nín.	Much obliged.

 ## Supplementary Vocabulary

1. lǚxíng	trip [N]
2. chuánzhēn	facsimile, fax [N]
3. shànglái	come up [RC]
-shànglái	up [RE]
náshànglái	take up (to speaker) [RC]
Qǐng nǐ náshànglái.	Please bring it up.
4. shàngqu	go up [RC]
-shàngqu	up [RE]
náshàngqu	take up (away from speaker) [RC]
Qǐng nǐ náshàngqu.	Please take it up (away from me).
5. xiàqu	go down [RC]
-xiàqu	down [RE]
náxiaqu	take down (away from speaker) [RC]
Tā yǐjīng náxiaqule.	She's already taken it down.

Additional Vocabulary: Communications Technology

1. dálùjī	telephone answering machine [N]
2. qǐng liúyán	"please leave a message" [PH]
3. yǔyīn xìnxiāng	mailbox for voice mail [PH]
4. shǒujī	cellular phone [N]

Grammatical and Cultural Notes

2A.   In addition to meaning "extension," as here, **fēnjī** can also mean the extension telephone itself.

2B. **Zhànxiàn** "be busy (of a telephone)" literally means "occupy the wire" or "occupy the line." Instead of **zhàn-xiàn**, some people say **jiǎnghuà zhōng** "in the midst of talking" or **dǎbutōng** "can't get through."

2C. **Nín shi děng yìhuǐr háishi guò yìhuǐr zài dǎ?** "Are you going to wait a while or call back later?" The **shi** here means "be a case of" or "be a situation where." The literal meaning of the question would be "You're a case of waiting for a while, or a case of when a while has passed again calling?"

3. **REDUPLICATED MONOSYLLABIC VERBS WITH -YI-.** Consider in this line the reduplicated verb **děng yideng** "wait a bit." Many one-syllable verbs like **děng** can be reduplicated with an optional **-yi-** "one" in the middle to give a relaxed, casual sense to the verb. The second iteration of the verb is usually neutral tone. Examples:

BASIC FORM	REDUPLICATED FORM WITH -YI-	REDUPLICATED FORM WITHOUT -YI-	ENGLISH MEANING
kàn	kàn yikan	kànkan	take a look
zǒu	zǒu yizou	zóuzou	take a walk
tán	tán yitan	tántan	talk a bit

The reduplicated forms can generally be converted to VERB + **yixia**, so that **děng yideng** and **děng yixia** are interchangeable, both meaning "wait a bit" or "wait a second."

6. **Qǐng nín gěi wǒ zhǎo yixiar Hé Zhìwén** "Please find He Zhiwen for me." The coverb **gěi** here means "for." Look also at line 7: **Wǒ qù gěi nín zhǎo** "I'll go find him for you."

7A. **ZHÈNG ZÀI + VERB + NE TO EXPRESS PROGRESSIVE ASPECT.** Examine the sentence **Hé Zhìwén zhèng zài kāihuì ne** "He Zhiwen is in a meeting right now." In 10-3: 2A we discussed the use of **zài** as an auxiliary verb to indicate progressive aspect. This **zài** is commonly, as in this sentence, accompanied by a preceding adverb **zhèng** "just" and a sentence final particle **ne**, which serve to strengthen the sense that an action is in progress. Here are some more examples of the pattern **zhèng zài** + VERB + **ne** to express that an action is in progress:

Xiǎo Lǐ zhèng zài chīfàn ne.	"Little Li is just eating right now."
Nǐ zhèng zài zuò shémme ne?	"What are you doing right now?"
Wǒ zhèng zài liànxí xiě Hànzì ne.	"I'm just now practicing writing Chinese characters."

7B. The verb-object compound **kāihuì** "hold a meeting" or "attend a meeting" usually implies a formal meeting involving three or more people. If only two people are involved, you'd use a different term like **tánhuà** "talk" or **jiànmiàn** "see." To express English "I'd like to meet with you at 10:00" said to one person, you would in Chinese not use **kāihuì** but instead could say **Wǒ shídiǎn xiǎng gēn nǐ tántan** "I'd like to speak with you at 10:00."

7C. **CHINESE MEETINGS.** Practically every organization in China—whether company, government office, or university—has a special **huìkèshì** "reception room" (lit. "receive guest room") that is furnished with over-stuffed sofas with doilies, which is where guests are received and where meetings are held. It's in general best to arrive exactly on time, neither too early nor too late. Members of visiting groups enter the **huìkèshì** in order of rank. High-level participants are received at the entrance or even at their car and are escorted back at the end of the meeting. In a meeting that consists of both Chinese and foreigners, the highest-ranking member of the foreign group usually sits to the right of the highest-ranking Chinese. If there is a conference table, the highest-ranking members may sit across from each other. Meetings often begin with small talk ("How was your trip? You must be tired. Is this your first time in China? Are you married? How many children do you have? How do you like Chinese food?" etc.). The reason for all this small talk is that it's considered impolite and impersonal to begin talking business immediately. Engaging in small talk is important, as it helps the participants get to know each other better and builds up trust. The lower-ranking participants in the meeting often say very little. It's mostly the chief Chinese and chief American who will talk, unless one of them calls on one of the others.

8A.   Consider **Tā kāiwán huì, qǐng nín ràng tā gěi wǒ dǎ ge diànhuà** "When he finishes holding the meeting, please have him give me a call." As you learned in 11-2: 8B, the resultative ending **-wán** means "finish (the action of the verb)." When used with a verb-object compound like **kāihuì**, **-wán** is inserted in the middle of a construction, before the object. Some more examples of **-wán**:

Nǐ chīwánle ma?	"Are you finished eating?"
Duìbuqǐ, dōu màiwánle.	"Sorry, they're all sold out." (e.g., tickets)
Tā yǐjīng bǎ shū kànwánle.	"She has already finished reading the book."

8B.   **Wǒ xìng Zhēnsēn, Zhōng-Měi Lǚxíngshède.**

"My name is Johnson, from Sino-American Travel Agency."

This sentence derives from a deeper structure **Wǒ xìng Zhēnsēn, wǒ shi Zhōng-Měi Lǚxíngshède rén**, literally "I'm surnamed Johnson, I'm a person from Sino-American Travel Agency." It's common to identify one's affiliation with a company or institution using **-de** in this manner. Some more examples:

Tā shi Běijīng Dàxuéde.	"She's from Peking University."
Wǒ shi Měiguo Dàshǐguǎnde.	"I'm with the U.S. Embassy."
Wǒ shi Xī'nán Hángkōng Gōngsīde.	"I'm from Southwest Airlines."

8C.   **YĪ...JIÙ....** The paired adverb pattern **yī...jiù...** most commonly expresses an instanteous response to a certain situation and is often translated as "as soon as..." or "the moment..." or "the minute..." or "no sooner...." However, this pattern may also express a general habitual situation, in which case it's translated as "whenever." The subject of the **yī** clause may be the same as or different from the subject of the **jiù** clause; if the subject is the same, it's often omitted in the **jiù** clause. The pattern is:

SUBJECT	YĪ	VERB₁	SUBJECT	JIÙ	VERB₂
Tā	**yì**	**lái,**	**wǒ**	**jiù**	**zǒule.**

"The minute he came, I left."

Some more examples with **yī...jiù...**:

Wǒ yí kàn jiù zhīdaole.	"I knew the minute I looked."
Tā yì máng jiù zháojí.	"As soon as he's busy, he gets excited."
Wǒ yì chī yú jiù bù shūfu.	"Whenever I eat fish, I don't feel good."
Tā měitiān yí xiàkè jiù huíjiā.	"She goes home each day as soon as classes are over."
Wǒ yì gēn tā shuōhuà, tā jiù shēngqìle.	"The moment I spoke with him, he got angry."

Wèishemme yǒude rén yì xué jiù huì ne?

"Why is it that some people master something the minute they start learning it?"

Note the following:

(1)   As we've seen before in other environments, the syllable **yī** usually changes to **yì** before a syllable with a first, second, or third tone, and to **yí** before a syllable with a fourth tone.

(2)   Both **yī** and **jiù** are adverbs and therefore must be followed by verbs, never by nouns or pronouns; in other words, the **yī** and **jiù** always follow the subjects of their clauses. To say "As soon as you left, he came," you'd have to say **Nǐ yì zǒu, tā jiù láile**; you could NEVER say *Yì nǐ zǒu, jiù tā láile.

(3)   There is never a **-le** or **-guo** at the end of the first clause with **yī**, as this is a dependent clause which doesn't take aspect particles.

9A.   Look at the sentence **Děng tā kāiwán huì, wǒ jiù gàosu ta** "As soon as he's finished with his meeting, I'll tell him." The verb **děng**, which literally means "wait," can be placed immediately in front of a sentence consisting of several actions with the meaning "wait until (action one), then (action two)." In better English, it can often be translated as "as soon as" or "once" or simply "when." It's often followed by a **jiù** "then" or **zài** "then" in the second clause. Here's another example:

Děng wǒ zhīdaole, zài gàosu ni.   "I'll tell you once I know."

9B.   Notice the neutral tone **ta** in **wǒ jiù gàosu ta** "I'll tell him." In rapid, colloquial Chinese, pronoun objects often lose their tones.

10.   **Máfan nín** literally means "(I) trouble you (to do this)."

AV1.   **Dálùjī** literally means "answer record machine."

AV2.   **Qǐng liúyán** literally means "please leave speech." **Yán** is the Classical Chinese word for "word," "speech," or "language."

AV3.   **Xìnxiāng** is the noun meaning "mailbox," and **xìn** is the noun meaning "letter."

Calling about an Advertisement for an Apartment

Lydia Dunn, who has just enrolled as a graduate student in art history at National Taiwan University in Taipei, is looking for an apartment. From a campus telephone booth, she calls the telephone number listed in a newspaper advertisement to find out more information.

 **Basic Conversation 17-3**

1. TAIWANESE LANDLORD	**Wéi?** Hello?
2. DUNN	**Wéi? Wǒ zài bàoshang kàndào nǐmende guǎnggào—** Hello? In the newspaper I saw your advertisement—
3. TAIWANESE LANDLORD	**Duìbuqǐ, nǐde diànhuà záyīn tài dàle, tīngbuqīngchu. Qǐng nǐ shuō dà shēng yìdiǎn.** I'm sorry, there's too much static on your line, I can't hear clearly. Please speak a little louder.
4. DUNN	**Wéi? Wǒ shuō wǒ zài bàoshang kàndào nǐmende guǎnggào (M.), yǒu gōngyù yào chūzū (Shìde.). Bù zhīdào zūchuqule méiyou?** Hello? I said that I saw your advertisement in the newspaper (Yeah.), you have an apartment to rent out (Yes.). I wonder if it has been rented out or not?
5. TAIWANESE LANDLORD	**Hái méiyou, dànshi yǒu rén lái kànguo, hǎoxiàng mán yǒu xìngqude (Ò.). Rúguǒ nǐ xiǎng lái kànde huà, zuìhǎo zǎo yìdiǎn.** Not yet, but somebody came to look at it, and they seem to be quite interested (Oh.). If you want to come look at it, you'd better come soon.
6. DUNN	**Qǐng wèn, gōngyù yǒu duō dà?** Excuse me, how big is the apartment?
7. TAIWANESE LANDLORD	**Chàbuduō yǒu sānshiwǔpíng. Yǒu kètīng, cāntīng, sānjiān wòshì, yùshì gēn chúfáng.** It's about 35 ping. It has a living room, dining room, three bedrooms, bathroom and kitchen.

 **Build Up**

1. Taiwanese landlord
Wéi?   Hello?

2. Dunn
bào   newspaper [N] (M: **fèn**)
zài bàoshang   in the newspaper
guǎnggào   advertisement [N]
Wéi? Wǒ zài bàoshang kàndào   Hello? In the newspaper I saw
nǐmende guǎnggào—   your advertisement—

3. Taiwanese landlord
záyīn   noise, static [N]
záyīn tài dàle   static is too loud
-qīngchu   clear [RE]
tīngqīngchu   hear clearly [RC]
tīngbuqīngchu   not be able to hear clearly
dà shēng   in a loud voice [PH]
shuō dà shēng yìdiǎn   speak in a louder voice
Duìbuqǐ, nǐde diànhuà záyīn tài dàle,   I'm sorry, there's too much static on your line,
tīngbuqīngchu. Qǐng nǐ shuō dà shēng yìdiǎn. I can't hear clearly. Please speak a little louder.

4. Dunn
gōngyù   apartment [N]
yǒu gōngyù yào chūzū   you have an apartment to rent
shìde   "yes" [IE]
zū   rent [V]
-chūqu   out [RE]
zūchuqu   rent out [RC]
Wéi? Wǒ shuō wǒ zài bàoshang   Hello? I said that I saw your advertisement
kàndào nǐmende guǎnggào (M.), yǒu   in the newspaper (Yeah.), you have
gōngyù yào chūzū (Shìde.). Bù zhīdào   an apartment to rent out (Yes.). I wonder
zūchuqule méiyou?   if it has been rented out or not?

5. Taiwanese landlord
zuìhǎo   it would be best, had better [MA]
yǒu xìngqu   have interest, be interested
Hái méiyou, dànshi yǒu rén lái kànguo,   Not yet, but somebody came to look at it, and
hǎoxiàng mán yǒu xìngqude (Ò.). Rúguǒ   they seem to be quite interested (Oh.). If you
nǐ xiǎng lái kànde huà, zuìhǎo zǎo yìdiǎn. want to come look at it, you'd better come soon.

6. Dunn
yǒu duō dà   is how big
Qǐng wèn, gōngyù yǒu duō dà?   Excuse me, how big is the apartment?

7. Taiwanese landlord
píng (T)   (unit of area, 36 sq. ft.) [M]
jiān   (for rooms) [M]
wòshì   bedroom [PW] (M: **jiān**)
yùshì   bathroom [PW] (M: **jiān**)
chúfáng   kitchen [PW] (M: **jiān**)
Chàbuduō yǒu sānshiwǔpíng. Yǒu kètīng,   It's about 35 ping. It has a living room, dining
cāntīng, sānjiān wòshì, yùshì gēn chúfáng. room, three bedrooms, bathroom and kitchen.

Supplementary Vocabulary

1. **chuānghu**   window [N]
   Bú yòng guān chuānghu, kāizhe hǎole.   You don't need to close the windows, it will be fine to keep them open.

2. **kōngtiáo**   air conditioning [N]
3. **shēngyīn**   sound; voice [N]
4. **xiǎo shēng**   in a low voice, quietly [PH]
5. **ānjìng**   be quiet [SV]
6. **chǎo**   be noisy [SV]
7. **lìkè**   immediately [A]

Additional Vocabulary: Rooms and Buildings

1. **gélóu**   attic [PW]
2. **yángtái**   balcony [PW]
3. **dìxiàshì**   basement [PW]
4. **wòfáng**   bedroom [PW] (M: **jiān**)
5. **fàntīng**   dining room [PW] (M: **jiān**)
6. **diàntī**   elevator [PW]
7. **chēkù**   garage [PW]
8. **kèfáng**   guest room [PW] (M: **jiān**)
9. **lóutī**   staircase [PW]

Grammatical and Cultural Notes

2. In English we say "in the newspaper" but in Chinese one says **bàoshang** "on the newspaper." One could NEVER say *****bàoli**.

3A. The Taiwanese landlord has a Taiwanese accent in her Mandarin. For example, instead of standard Mandarin **tīngbuqīngchu** she says **tīngbuqīngcu**. Later, in line 7, instead of standard **chàbuduō** she says **càbuduō**.

3B. **Qǐng nǐ shuō dà shēng yidian** literally means "Please you speak in a little bigger voice," i.e., "Please speak up a little." Here is another example with **dà shēng**:

> **Bié nèmme dà shēng, hǎo bu hǎo?**   "Don't be so loud, O.K.?"

Also, compare **dà shēng** with SV4 **xiǎo shēng** "in a low voice, quietly," as in:

> **Qǐng nǐmen xiǎo shēng dianr!**   "You all please be a little quieter!"

4A. Examine the sentence **Wǒ shuō wǒ zài bàoshang kàndào nǐmende guǎnggào** "I said that I saw your advertisement in the newspaper." There is no verb suffix **-le** indicating completed action attached to the verb **shuō** here because **shuō** has as its object a whole clause (i.e., the long quotation that follows the verb **shuō**). When verbs like **shuō** or **wèn** "ask" are used to introduce direct or indirect quotations, no **-le** is used even though the action of "saying" or "asking" is completed.

4B. The parenthetical comments (**M.**) "Yeah" and (**Shìde.**) "Yes" in this line as well as (**Ò.**) "Oh" in line 5 are examples of so-called backchannel comments by the other speaker (7-4: 6C). It's important when conversing with a Chinese speaker to indicate that you're following her or his comments by using such backchannel comments; this is especially important when speaking on the telephone, since your interlocutor doesn't have visual cues available.

4C.   **Zū** alone means "rent (from someone else)," while **zūchuqu** is a resultative compound meaning "rent out (to someone else)."

5.   **ZUÌHǍO.** This common moveable adverb means "it would be best" or "had better." Since **zuìhǎo** is a moveable adverb, it can occur either before or after the subject; but it occurs most frequently after the subject and before the verb. **Zuìhǎo** is frequently used before the negative imperatives **bié** and **búyào** "don't" to express "You better not...." The most common pattern with **zuìhǎo** is:

SUBJECT	ZUÌHǍO	VERB PHRASE
Nǐ	**zuìhǎo**	**bié wèn ta.**

"You (had) better not ask him."

It's true that **zuìhǎo** sometimes can be translated as "it would be best if" (e.g., **Nǐ zuìhǎo bié qù** "It would be best if you didn't go"), but be careful never to add a **rúguǒ** or **yàoshi** in such a sentence. Some more examples of **zuìhǎo**:

Zuìhǎo duō dài yidian qián.

"You had best bring a lot of money."

Nǐ qù yǐqián, zuìhǎo xiān gàosu nǐ fùmǔ.

"It would be best if you told your parents before you go."

Nèijiàn shì zuìhǎo xiān bié gàosu biérén.

"It would be best if you didn't tell anyone else about that."

Nǐ zuìhǎo zǎo yìdiǎn dào chēzhàn qù, yàoburán kěnéng huì gǎnbushàng huǒchē.

"You better go to the station early, otherwise you might not make the train."

Nǐ zuìhǎo xiān chī diǎn dōngxi, yàoburán děng yìhuǐr yì mángqilai, jiù méi shíjiān le.

"You better eat something first, otherwise in a while when you get busy, you won't have time."

When pronouncing **zuìhǎo**, be careful to distinguish it from **zuìhòu** "in the end." Also, distinguish **zuìhǎo** "it would be best, had better" from **zhǐhǎo** "can only, have no choice but" (8-4: 5B). Finally, distinguish **zuìhǎo** from the combination of the adverb **zuì** and the stative verb **hǎo** as in **zuì hǎo**, which simply means "best." For example:

Zhèige zuì hǎo.

"This one is the best."

Zhèisān'ge rén lǐtou, wǒ juéde tāde Zhōngwén zuì hǎo.

"I feel that among these three people, her Chinese is the best."

6.   **YǑU + QUANTITY EXPRESSION + STATIVE VERB TO INDICATE SIZE, DISTANCE, ETC.** In this line, look at the question **Gōngyù yǒu duō dà?** "How big is the apartment?" (lit. "Apartment has how big?") Then, in line 7, look at the sentence **Chàbuduō yǒu sānshiwǔpíng** "It's about 35 ping" (lit. "About has 35 ping"). The verb **yǒu** "have" can be followed by quantity expressions to indicate size, area, years of age, etc. Often the quantity expression is followed by a stative verb. The basic pattern is:

YǑU	QUANTITY EXPRESSION	STATIVE VERB
Yǒu	**sāngōnglǐ**	**cháng.**

"It's three kilometers long." (lit. "It has three kilometers long.")

Some more examples:

Yáo Míng yǒu qīchǐ liùcùn gāo.

"Yao Ming is 7 feet 6 inches tall."

Tīngshuō zhèitiáo lù yǒu yìqiānduō yīnglǐ cháng.

"I heard this road is more than 1,000 miles long."

7. **Píng** is a unit of area equal to 36 square feet or 3.4 square meters that was introduced during the Japanese occupation of Taiwan and is still used there today to indicate the area of apartments and houses. A **píng** is the size of two tatami mats. In Beijing, apartments are usually described as **èrjūshì** or **liǎngjūshì** "two-room apartment" and **sānjūshì** "three-room apartment." Another way to say "two-room apartment" in Beijing would be **liǎng shì yì tīng**, lit. "two bedrooms and one living room."

AV1–9.   **ROOMS AND BUILDINGS.** These words related to rooms and buildings are listed in alphabetical order of the English translations.

Calling About an Advertisement for an Apartment (cont.)

The Taiwanese land-lord answers more of Dunn's questions about the apart-ment and makes an appointment with Dunn for her to view it (continued from the previous lesson).

Basic Conversation 17-4

1. DUNN	**Yǒu méiyou jiājù, diànhuà?**	
	Does it have furniture and a telephone?	
2. TAIWANESE LANDLORD	**Yǒu yìxiē jiǎndānde jiājù xiàng shāfā, cānzhuō, shūzhuō, chuáng, yīguì shem-mede. Méiyou diànhuà.**	
	It has some simple furniture like a sofa, dining table, desk, bed, clothes closet and so on. There's no phone.	
3. DUNN	**Fángzū yíge yuè dàgài shi duōshǎo?**	
	About how much would the rent per month be?	
4. TAIWANESE LANDLORD	**Yíge yuè sānwànkuài, shuǐdiànfèi lìngwài suàn.**	
	30,000 NT per month, with water and electricity not included.	
5. DUNN	**Nà wǒ shémme shíhou lái bǐjiào fāngbian?**	
	So when would it be convenient for me to come?	
6. TAIWANESE LANDLORD	**Nǐ kéyi jīntiān xiàwǔ guòlái, míngtiān shàngwǔ yě kéyi. Zài wǎn jiù pà biérén yǐjīng yào qiānyuē le.**	
	You could come over this afternoon or tomorrow morning. Any later and I'm afraid somebody else might already want to sign a lease.	
7. DUNN	**Wǒ jīntiān xiàwǔ sìdiǎn zuǒyòu dào, fāng bu fāngbian?**	
	If I arrived this afternoon around 4:00, would that be convenient?	
8. TAIWANESE LANDLORD	**Méi wèntí. Guìxìng?**	
	No problem. What's your last name?	
9. DUNN	**Wǒ xìng Dèng, Dèng Lì.**	
	My last name is Deng, Deng Li.	
10. TAIWANESE LANDLORD	**Hǎode, Dèng Xiáojie, sìdiǎn zhōng jiàn.**	
	All right, Ms. Deng, see you at four o'clock.	

11. DUNN   Báibái.
                             Bye.

 **Build Up**

---

1. Dunn
Yǒu méiyou jiājù, diànhuà?   Does it have furniture and a telephone?

---

2. Taiwanese landlord
yìxiē   some [NU+M]
yìxiē jiǎndānde jiājù   some simple furniture
shāfā   sofa [N] (M: **tào**)
cānzhuō   dining table [N] (M: **zhāng**)
xiàng shāfā cānzhuō   like a sofa and a dining table
shūzhuō(r)   desk [N] (M: **zhāng**)
chuáng   bed [N] (M: **zhāng**)
yīguì   clothes closet [N]
Yǒu yìxiē jiǎndānde jiājù xiàng shāfā,   It has some simple furniture like a sofa,
cānzhuō, shūzhuō, chuáng, yīguì   dining table, desk, bed, clothes closet
shemmede. Méiyou diànhuà.   and so on. There's no phone.

---

3. Dunn
fángzū   rent [N]
Fángzū yíge yuè dàgài shi duōshǎo?   About how much would the rent per month be?

---

4. Taiwanese landlord
shuǐfèi   water fee [N]
diàn   electricity [N]
diànfèi   electricity fee [N]
shuǐdiànfèi   water and electricity fee [N]
lìngwài   in addition [MA]
lìngwài suàn   be figured in addition
Yíge yuè sānwànkuài, shuǐdiànfèi   30,000 NT per month, with water and
lìngwài suàn.   electricity not included.

---

5. Dunn
fāngbian   be convenient [SV]
bǐjiào fāngbian   relatively convenient
Nà wǒ shémme shíhou lái bǐjiào   So when would it be convenient
fāngbian?   for me to come?

---

6. Taiwanese landlord
jīntiān xiàwǔ guòlái   come over this afternoon
zài wǎn   further late, any later
biérén   another person, others [PR]
qiānyuē   sign a lease [VO]
biérén yào qiānyuē le   someone else wants to sign a lease
Nǐ kéyi jīntiān xiàwǔ guòlái, míngtiān   You could come over this afternoon or tomorrow
shàngwǔ yě kéyi. Zài wǎn jiù pà biérén   morning. Any later and I'm afraid some-
yǐjīng yào qiānyuē le.   body else might already want to sign a lease.

---

7. Dunn
sìdiǎn zuǒyòu dào   arrive around 4:00
fāng bù fāngbian   convenient or inconvenient

Wǒ jīntiān xiàwǔ sìdiǎn zuǒyòu dào, fāng bù fāngbian?	If I arrived this afternoon around 4:00, would that be convenient?

8.   **Taiwanese landlord**
Méi wèntí. Guìxìng?	No problem. What's your last name?

9.   **Dunn**
Dèng	Deng [SN]
Wǒ xìng Dèng, Dèng Lì.	My last name is Deng, Deng Li.

10. **Taiwanese landlord**
Hǎode, Dèng Xiáojie, sìdiǎn zhōng jiàn.	All right, Ms. Deng, see you at four o'clock.

11. **Dunn**
Báibái.	Bye.

 ## Supplementary Vocabulary

1. **yājīn**	deposit [N]
Yājīn shi liǎngge yuède fángzū.	The deposit is two months' rent.
2. **jiàoshì**	classroom [N] (M: **jiān**)
qiáng	wall [N]
Wǒmen Zhōngwén jiàoshìde qiángshang guàzhe yìzhāng Zhōngguo dìtú.	There's a map of China hanging on the wall of our Chinese language classroom.
3. **yuànzi**	courtyard, yard [N]
zhòng	plant [V]
huā(r)	flower [N] (M: **duǒ** for "a flower")
zài yuànzili zhòng huār	plant flowers in the yard
jiǎn	cut [V]
cǎo	grass [N] (M: **gēn**)
jiǎncǎo	mow the lawn [VO]
Xiānsheng zài jiǎncǎo, tàitai zài yuànzili zhòng huār.	The husband is mowing the lawn, and the wife is planting flowers in the yard.

Grammatical and Cultural Notes

2A.   Note **yìxiē** "some, a little" in **yǒu yìxiē jiǎndānde jiājù** "it has some simple furniture." You've previously seen **zhèixiē** "these" and **nèixiē** "those" (12-2: 8A). Then you learned **xiē** "some" in 15-4, in the phrase **hái yǒu xiē tiáoliào** "there are also some condiments." Actually, **xiē** is an abbreviated form of the full form **yìxiē**, which has the same meaning as **xiē**. **Yìxiē** and **xiē** indicate a small, indefinite number or amount. When they denote an amount of something, they're often interchangeable with **yìdiǎn(r)**. Some more examples with **(yì)xiē**:

Wǒ yǒu (yì)xiē dōngxi yào mài.

"I have some things I want to sell."

Wǒ yǒu (yì)xiē tóngxué xiànzài zài niàn yīxuéyuàn.

"I have some classmates who are now studying in medical school."

Tāde péngyou hěn duō, yǒu xiē shi Zhōngguo rén, yǒu xiē shi wàiguo rén.

"She has lots of friends; some are Chinese, some are foreign."

In 7-2 we learned **yǒude**, which can also mean "some." How are **yìxiē and yǒude** to be distinguished? Both of these can be used as pronoun subjects or to describe a noun subject. However, **yìxiē** can also follow the verb in a sentence, while **yǒude** can never follow the verb. So you can say **Wǒ gěile tā yìxiē shū** "I gave her some books" but you CANNOT say *Wǒ gěile tā yǒude shū.

Yìxiē or **xiē**, in the sense of "a little," can also substitute for **yìdiǎn(r)** in comparative constructions. For example:

> **Nǐ màn xiē zǒu.**   "Walk a little slower."
> **Zhèizhǒng bǐ nèizhǒng hǎo yìxiē.**   "This kind is a little better than that kind."

2B.   **INNOVATIVE PRONUNCIATIONS.** In the speech of some younger Beijing women, the word **yìxiē** is pronounced so that it sounds more like **yìsiē**. In fact, there are a number of new-style pronunciations common among the younger generation in Beijing. These innovative pronunciations include:

a.   Use of **s-** in place of **x-** so that, for example, **hěn xiǎo** "very small" sounds like **hěn siǎo** and **yìxiē** "some" sounds like **yìsiē**.

b.   Use of **z-** in place of **j-** so that, for example, **jiǔ** "nine" sounds like **ziǔ**, **jīntiān** "today" sounds like **zīntiān**, and **jiànshè** "construct" sounds like **ziànshè**.

One of few remaining Japanese-style houses in downtown Taipei

c.   Use of a lightly articulated **v-** in place of **w-** so that, for example, **wèn** "ask" sounds almost like **vèn-** and **wěidà** "great" sounds somewhat like **věidà**. Some speakers may actually articulate a **w-** but spread and press their lips together so that the sound produced sounds like a **v-**.

The innovative pronunciations in (a) and (b) above are most frequently encountered in the speech of younger women from Beijing and environs. Men don't normally use these pronunciations, which are considered feminine. However, the use of **v-** for **w-** appears to be more widespread, being heard even in the speech of television announcers—and in both mainland China and Taiwan. (One common example is **vǎnjiān xīnvén** for **wǎnjiān xīnwén** "evening news.") While you should become familiar with these innovative pronunciations so that you can understand them when heard, it's recommended that in your own speech you use the standard pronunciations you've learned, which are still preferred.

2C.   Notice the use of **xiàng** "like" in **Yǒu yìxiē jiǎndānde jiājù xiàng shāfā, cānzhuō, shūzhuō, chuáng, yīguì shemmede** "It has some simple furniture like a sofa, dining table, desk, bed, clothes closet and so on." You had the verb **xiàng** previously in 13-2 in the sense of "resemble, be like." In Chinese, **xiàng** is frequently used as an introductory verb, much like "like" in English. For example:

> **Xiàng jīntiān tiānqi zhèmme chà, wǒ shízài bú tài xiǎng qù.**
> "Like today, the weather's so bad, I really don't much feel like going."

2D.   **Shāfā**, as you'll probably have guessed, is a phonetic borrowing from English "sofa." Be aware that while **shāfā** usually means "sofa," some Chinese speakers use it for any type of chair or armchair with a soft, resilient cushion, even if it can seat only one person.

4.   Study the structure of **shuǐdiànfèi** "water and electricity fee." This is a combined form of **shuǐfèi** + **diànfèi**. Compare **chēyuèpiào** "individual bus tickets and monthly bus tickets" (from **chēpiào** + **yuèpiào**) that you learned in 9-4.

5A.   **Nà wǒ shémme shíhou lái bǐjiào fāngbian?** "So when would it be convenient for me to come?" This line literally means "In that case, I what time come is comparatively convenient?"

5B.   The common Chinese stative verb **fāngbian** "be convenient" deserves some comment. When refusing a request, rather than saying **Bù xíng** "No," which would be considered too direct, Chinese people often say **Bù fāngbian** "That's not convenient." In fact, **Bù fāngbian** is one of the most common refusals. Of course, you also may turn someone down by saying **Duìbuqǐ, bú tài fāngbian** "I'm sorry, it's not very convenient." In general, **fāngbian** and **bù fāngbian** are used more loosely than in English, as is obvious from the next example:

> **Nǐ bú rènshi Zhōngguo zì, kàn Zhōngwén bàozhǐ bù fāngbian.**
>
> "You can't read Chinese characters, so reading a Chinese newspaper would be inconvenient."

Be sure to distinguish the stative verb **fāngbian** "be convenient" from the adverb **shùnbiàn** "conveniently, in passing, while I'm at it" that you learned in 11-2.

7.   Notice the grammar of **fāng bu fāngbian** "convenient or not convenient." This is a stative verb in an affirmative-negative question and represents an abbreviation of **fāngbian bu fāngbian** (cf. 5-1: 8A on deletion of second syllable of bisyllabic verbs in affirmative part of affirmative-negative questions).

Unit 17: Review and Study Guide

New Vocabulary

ADVERBS
lìkè — immediately
yī — as soon as

ATTRIBUTIVES
guójì — international

EXPRESSIONS
yì-yán-wéi-dìng — be agreed with one word

IDIOMATIC EXPRESSIONS
báibái — "bye-bye"
shìde — "yes"

INTERJECTIONS
hài — (indicates exasperation)

MEASURES
jiān — (for rooms)
píng — (unit of area, 36 sq. ft.)

MOVEABLE ADVERBS
lìngwài — in addition
zuìhǎo — it would be best, had better

NOUNS
qiáng — wall
bào — newspaper
cānzhuō — dining table
cǎo — grass
chuáng — bed

chuānghu — window
chuánzhēn — facsimile, FAX
diàn — electricity
diànfèi — electricity fee
fángzū — rent
fēnjī — extension
gōngyù — apartment
guǎnggào — advertisement
huā(r) — flower
huì — gathering, meeting
jiàoshì — classroom
kòng(r) — free time
kōngtiáo — air conditioning
lǚxíng — trip
shāfā — sofa
shēngyīn — sound; voice
shuǐdiànfèi — water and electricity fee
shuǐfèi — water fee
shūzhuō(r) — desk
xìngqu — interest
yājīn — deposit
yīguì — clothes closet
yīnyuè — music
yīnyuèhuì — concert
yuànzi — courtyard, yard
záyīn — noise, static

NUMERAL + MEASURE
yìxiē — some

PATTERNS
děng... — as soon as..., once...
duì...gǎn xìngqu — be interested in...
duì...yǒu xìngqu — be interested in...
yī...jiù... — as soon as
zhèng zài... — just be in the midst of...

PHRASES
dà shēng — in a loud voice
shìnèi diànhuà — local telephone call
xiǎo shēng — in a low voice, quietly

PLACE WORDS
chúfáng — kitchen
Guójì Jùlèbù — International Club
jùlèbù — club
lǚxíngshè — travel agency
wòshì — bedroom
yùshì — bathroom

PRONOUNS
biérén — another person, others

RESULTATIVE COMPOUNDS
jìxialai — write down, note down

kāiwán	finish holding (a meeting)
mánghuài	extremely busy
náshanglai	take up (to speaker)
náshangqu	take up (away from speaker)
náxiaqu	take down (away from speaker)
shànglai	come up
shàngqu	go up
tīngqīngchu	hear clearly
xiàlai	come down
xiàqu	go down
zūchuqu	rent out

RESULTATIVE ENDINGS

-chūqu	out
-huài	be bad
-qīngchu	clear

-shànglai	up
-shàngqu	up
-xiàlai	down
-xiàqu	down

STATIVE VERBS

ānjìng	be quiet
chǎo	be noisy
fāngbian	be convenient
huài	be bad

SURNAMES

Dèng	Deng
Liú	Liu
Táng	Tang

VERBS

dìng	settle, decide
gǎn	feel
guà	hang, hang up

jì	record
jiǎn	cut
lǚxíng	travel
tí	mention
tíqián	move up (a time or date)
zhòng	plant
zhuǎn	transfer
zū	rent

VERB-OBJECT COMPOUNDS

jiǎncǎo	mow the lawn
kāihuì	hold or attend a meeting
liúhuà(r)	leave a message
qiānyuē	sign a lease
yǒukòng(r)	have free time
zhànxiàn	be busy (of a telephone)

Major New Grammar Patterns

EXTENDED USE OF BǍ: Zhèijǐtiān zhēn bǎ wǒ mánghuàile. "These last few days I've just been incredibly busy." (17-1)

A GĒN B SHUŌ C: Nǐ bié gēn tā shuō wǒ méi qù. "Don't tell her I didn't go." (17-1)

DUÌ...GǍN XÌNGQU/DUÌ...YǑU XÌNGQU: Wǒ duì yīnyuè gǎn xìngqu. "I'm interested in music.",

Nǐ duì shémme yǒu xìngqu? "What are you interested in?" (17-1)

ZHÈNG ZÀI...NE: Wǒ zhèng zài jiǎng diànhuà ne. "I'm speaking on the telephone right now." (17-2)

YĪ...JIÙ...: Tā yí xiàkè jiù huíjiā. "She goes home as soon as class is over." (17-2)

ZUÌHǍO: Nǐ zuìhǎo bié wèn ta. "You'd better not ask him." (17-3)

YǑU + QUANTITY EXPRESSION + STATIVE VERB TO INDICATE SIZE: Yǒu duō dà? "How large is it?", **Tā yǒu qīchǐ gāo.** "She's seven feet tall." (17-3)

YÌXIĒ "some," ZHÈXIĒ "these," NÀXIĒ "those": Yǒu yìxiē jiǎndānde jiājù. "There is some simple furniture." (17-4)

Visiting People (I)

COMMUNICATIVE OBJECTIVES

Once you've mastered this unit, you'll be able to use Chinese to:

1. Make an informal visit to a Chinese friend's home.
2. Pay a formal call on someone at their residence to request a favor.
3. Apologize for being late for an appointment.
4. Engage in appropriate polite talk on arriving at your host's home: greetings, presenting a gift, etc.
5. Politely decline your host's offer of a cigarette.
6. Make a request or respond to a request from someone else, hemming and hawing as appropriate.
7. Accept or decline a dinner invitation.
8. Announce your departure and take leave of your host.
9. Express afterthoughts: "Oh, that's right, I just thought of something…"
10. Engage in appropriate polite talk on departing your host's home.
11. Handle various types of sociolinguistic situations with increased discourse competence and fluency.

Visiting a Friend at Home

John Niu, an American studying Chinese medicine in Beijing, visits the home of his Chinese friend, Li Zhijie. Niu and Li, who are both in their early twenties, know each other well. Li's mother, whom Niu knows from several previous visits, opens the door.

Basic Conversation 18-1

1. NIU **Bómǔ hǎo! Xiǎo Lǐ zài jiā ma?**
Hello, Mrs. Li! Is Little Li home?

2. MRS. LI **Zài, zài. Xiǎo Niúr, nǐ jìnlái zuò ba. Zhìjié mǎshàng jiù lái. Nǐ xiān hē diǎnr chá.**
Yes, he is. Little Niu, come in and sit down. Zhijie will be right here. First have some tea.

3. LI ZHIJIE *(calling from a back room)* **Xiǎo Niúr, duìbuqǐ, wǒ zhèng zài guā húzi ne. Zhè jiù wánle.**
Little Niu, I'm sorry, I'm just in the middle of shaving. I'll be finished in a second.

4. NIU **Xiǎo Lǐ, nǐ máng nǐde, bié jí.**
Little Li, you take your time, don't rush.

5. CHILD *(enters room)* **Wàipó!**
Grandma!

6. MRS. LI **Xiǎo Niúr, nǐ jiànguo wǒde wàisūn Péngpeng ma?**
Little Niu, have you met my grandson Pengpeng before?

7. NIU **Jiànguo, jiànguo.**
Yes, I have.

8. MRS. LI **Péngpeng, nǐ wèn Niú Shūshu hǎo.**
Pengpeng, say hello to Uncle Niu.

9. CHILD **Niú Shūshu hǎo!**
Hello, Uncle Niu!

10. NIU **Péngpeng, nǐ hǎo! Yuè zhǎng yuè gāole.**
Hi, Pengpeng! The more you grow, the taller you get.

11. MRS. LI *(to the child)* **Shì, tǐng gāode la. Péngpeng, qù ba, dào wàimian qù hé xiǎo péngyou wánr qu ba.**
Yes, he is quite tall. Pengpeng, go, go outside and play with your little friends.

(to Niu) **Xiǎoháir zǒngshi zài wūzili dāibuzhù!**
Kids can never stay indoors!

Build Up

---

1. Niu
   bómǔ   aunt (wife of father's older brother) [N]
   Bómǔ hǎo! Xiǎo Lǐ zài jiā ma?   Hello, Mrs. Li! Is Little Li home?

---

2. Mrs. Li
   Niú   Niu (lit. "cow") [SN]
   Zhìjié   Zhijie (given name)
   Zài, zài. Xiǎo Niúr, nǐ jìnlái zuò ba.   Yes, he is. Little Niu, come in and sit down.
   Zhìjié mǎshàng jiù lái. Nǐ xiān hē diǎnr chá.   Zhijie will be right here. First have some tea.

---

3. Li Zhijie
   guā   scrape [V]
   húzi   beard, moustache [N]
   guā húzi   shave [PH]
   wǒ zhèng zài guā húzi ne   I'm just in the middle of shaving
   zhè   right away [A]
   zhè jiù wánle   (I'll) be finished right away
   Xiǎo Niúr, duìbuqǐ, wǒ zhèng   Little Niu, I'm sorry, I'm just in the middle
   zài guā húzi ne. Zhè jiù wánle.   of shaving. I'll be finished in a second.

---

4. Niu
   máng   be busy with (something) [V]
   nǐ máng nǐde   you be busy with your things
   jí   be in a hurry [SV]
   Xiǎo Lǐ, nǐ máng nǐde, bié jí.   Little Li, you take your time, don't rush.

---

5. Child
   wàipó   grandmother (maternal) [N]
   Wàipó!   Grandma!

---

6. Mrs. Li
   wàisūn   grandson (daughter's son) [N]
   Péngpeng   Pengpeng (child's nickname)
   Xiǎo Niú, nǐ jiànguo wǒde wàisūn   Little Niu, have you met my grandson
   Péngpeng ma?   Pengpeng before?

---

7. Niu
   Jiànguo, jiànguo.   Yes, I have.

---

8. Mrs. Li
   wènhǎo   send one's regards to, say hello to [RC]
   wèn Niú Shūshu hǎo   say hello to Uncle Niu
   Péngpeng, nǐ wèn Niú Shūshu hǎo.   Pengpeng, say hello to Uncle Niu.

---

9. Child
   Niú Shūshu hǎo!   Hello, Uncle Niu!

10. Niu

Péngpeng, nǐ hǎo! Yuè zhǎng yuè gāole.	Hi, Pengpeng! The more you grow, the taller you get.

11. Mrs. Li

dào wàimian qù	go outside
xiǎo péngyou	little friend, child [PH]
hé xiǎo péngyou wánr	play with little friends
qù hé xiǎo péngyou wánr qu	go play with your little friends
Shì, tǐng gāode la. Péngpeng, qù ba, dào wàimian qù hé xiǎo péngyou wánr qu ba.	Yes, he is quite tall. Pengpeng, go, go outside and play with your little friends.
zǒngshi	always [A]
wūzi	room [N] (M: **jiān**)
zài wūzili	in a room, indoors
dāi	stay [V]
-zhù	firm [RE]
dāibuzhù	not be able to stay [RC]
Xiǎoháir zǒngshi zài wūzili dāibuzhù!	Kids can never stay indoors!

Supplementary Vocabulary

1. bófù	uncle (father's older brother) [N]
2. wàigōng	grandfather (maternal) [N]
3. wàisūnnǚ(r)	granddaughter (daughter's daughter) [N]
4. liú húzi	grow a beard or moustache [PH]

Grammatical and Cultural Notes

1A.   **VISITING PEOPLE.** Traditionally, you can in China visit relatives and friends most any time without prior arrangement; the idea of telephoning in advance is new, though more and more urban residents are beginning to do this.

In some areas, for example Taiwan, it's customary to remove your shoes on entering someone's home, even if the host says it's not necessary. Always observe carefully what others do; a useful clue is if there are other people's shoes already placed outside or just inside the door. When you remove your shoes, you'll probably be offered slippers. On entering the household, you should greet any elderly people who are present first. It's fine to compliment young children for being cute, good-looking, intelligent, and well-behaved; on the other hand, be careful about commenting on the appearance of members of the opposite sex ("I really love your hair!"); this could be interpreted romantically or as a sexual overture. Compliments about a particular object in the home may make the host feel obligated to give the object to the guest as a gift, so be careful. When visiting someone at home, you should always bring a present (cf. 18-3: 4). If you happen to arrive while people are eating, the host is likely to ask you to join them, even if they're almost done. Similarly, if it's close to meal time when you prepare to leave, you'll usually be invited to stay for a meal. Therefore, if you really don't want to eat or don't want to feel obliged, you shouldn't visit people close to meal times. If Chinese people invite you to eat with them and you're willing to accept their invitation, it's best to decline politely the first time. If they really mean it, they'll almost certainly repeat the invitation. If they don't, it could mean they're worried there isn't enough food. When it comes time to take leave, in America you usually give your own reason for leaving (e.g, "I have to get up early tomorrow morning"); but in China you often give a reason related to the other person (e.g., **Shíjiān bu zǎo le, nǐ lèile ba** "It's getting late, you must be tired"). When the guest leaves, the host must escort him or her a ways; in general, the distance that the host accompanies the

> It's fine to compliment young children for being cute, good-looking, intelligent, and well-behaved; on the other hand, be careful about commenting on the appearance of members of the opposite sex.

guest serves as an indication of the esteem in which the guest is held. If you're the host, always offer to escort your guests when they depart, even if they politely refuse. It's best to escort them to their waiting cars, or to the main gate of your compound. At the very least, you should escort them to the elevator on your level.

1B. The speaker here uses a kinship term, **bómǔ** "auntie," to address the mother of his classmate rather than using **Lǐ Tàitai** "Mrs. Li," as we might in English. It's considered good manners to use **bómǔ** and, for the fathers of classmates, **bófù** "uncle," in this way. To use **xiānsheng** and **tàitai** would be considered too formal and would seem purposely to be creating distance. Kinship terms can be used for many more people than just relatives; for example, au pairs may be called **āyí** "auntie," maids may be called **dàjiě** "big sister," and children whom you don't know may be called **xiǎo dìdi** "little brother" or **xiǎo mèimei** "little sister."

1C. **Zài jiā** means "to be home." **Jiā** "home" functions as a place word, so use of the localizer **-lǐ** with **jiā** is optional. For "He's at home," you can say either **Tā zài jiā** or **Tā zài jiāli**.

2A. Notice here the repetition of **zài**. As we've seen before, it's common to repeat short phrases. While saying **zài** only once would not be incorrect, it would seem rather abrupt.

2B. The addition of the **-r** final to a surname, as here in **Xiǎo Niúr**, is rather unusual.

2C. When a Chinese person invites a guest to come in, he or she will frequently invite the guest to drink "tea" (which sometimes really is tea and sometimes is merely hot water). It's considered good manners for the guest to at least take a sip of what is offered, but it's not necessary to finish it.

3. The adverb **zhè** "right away, right now" is often followed by **jiù** to stress how soon something will happen: **Zhè jiù wánle** "(I'll) be finished right away." Some more examples:

> **Bié zháojí, tā zhè jiù lái.**
> "Don't get excited, she'll be here right away."

> **Nǐ fàngxīn hǎole, wǒ zhè jiù gěi nǐ bàn.**
> "Why don't you just relax; I'll take care of it for you right away."

4A. **Nǐ máng nǐde** literally means "you be busy with your things." In freer English, this could be translated as "you just go ahead and take care of your own business" or, in the context of this conversation, "you just take your time." Cf. **Nǐ mǎi nǐde, wǒ mǎi wǒde** "You buy your things and I'll buy my things" in 13-2. Also common is **Nǐ zǒu nǐde ba** "You go ahead," which can be abbreviated to **Zǒu nǐde ba**. These expressions basically all mean "You take care of your own business and don't concern yourself with me."

4B. **Bié jí** can mean either "don't rush" or "don't get excited." To express "don't rush," some native speakers prefer **bù jí**.

5A. Here the speaker uses a kinship term as a form of greeting: **Wàipó!** "Grandma!" In English, we would probably just say "hello" or "hi," but Chinese people would seldom use **nǐ hǎo** in such a context. Chinese children are taught from early on to call out the titles of their older relatives on entering a room in which they are present. Besides serving as a greeting, this also acknowledges that the child knows his or her relationship to the person being addressed, which is even more important in Chinese society than in Western society (cf. note 8A below).

5B. Instead of **wàipó** "grandmother (mother's mother)," some speakers use the term **lǎolao**.

7. Here, again, a short response is repeated (cf. note 2A above).

8A. **Péngpeng, nǐ wèn Niú Shūshu hǎo** "Pengpeng, say hello to Uncle Niu." As we saw in 6-1, children call a man of their father's generation **shūshu** "uncle" and a woman of their mother's generation **āyí** "auntie." Chinese parents and other caregivers will frequently tell children what to call another person and insist that the child address and greet the person in that way. Either **wènhǎo** "say hello to" or **jiào** "call out" can be used to accomplish this. An example with **jiào**:

Mother:	**Jiào yéye!**	"Say 'Grandfather'"!
Child:	**Yéye!**	"Grandfather!"

In Chinese families, it's considered very important for everyone to know and utter the appropriate kinship term for each other. If children do this appropriately, it confers face on the senior person in the relationship, especially if third parties are present. This proves that the child understands the relationship and, just as importantly, that he or she accepts the hierarchical relationship. In this way, individuals' positions in the Chinese social hierarchy are constantly being reinforced.

8B. If the verb **wènhǎo** "send one's regards to" or "say hello to" has an object, that object is inserted between the **wèn** and the **hǎo** as in **Qǐng nǐ wèn tā hǎo** "please say hello to her." **Wènhǎo** is often used in conjunction with the coverb **tì** "for" or "on behalf of" (16-2: 1A). Example:

> **Qǐng nǐ tì wǒ wèn Wáng Zǒngjīnglǐ hǎo.**
>
> "Please convey my regards to General Manager Wang."

10. Review the use of **yuè...yuè...** "the more...the more..." (15-2: 7).

11A. Notice the repetition of the verb **qù** in **dào wàimian qù hé xiǎo péngyou wánr qu** "go outside and play with (your) little friends." The second **qù**, which is often (as here) in the neutral tone, is completely optional but is very common in Beijing speech.

11B. **Wūzi** "room" is a synonym of **fángjiān** (4-3). **Wūzi** tends to be used more in northern China, while **fángjiān** is used more in southern mainland China and Taiwan. However, for rooms in hotels and other public places, **fángjiān** is used everywhere. Note that **jiān** is the measure for **wūzi**. Also, be aware that the **-wū** in **tóngwū** "roommate" that you learned in 2-2 is the same **-wū** as in **wūzi**. **Tóngwū** literally means "same room."

11C. The verb **dāi** means "stay." It can be used with the postverb **-zài**, for example:

> **Hánjiàde shíhou nǐ dǎsuan dāizai nǎr?**
>
> "Where do you plan to stay during winter vacation?"

11D. The resultative ending **-zhù** indicates that something is fixed in a certain position. In **dāibuzhù** "not be able to stay," the meaning is "they won't stay in one place." Other common examples with this ending are **zhànzhu** "stand still" and **jìzhu** "remember clearly."

Visiting a Friend at Home (cont.)

Li finishes shaving and joins his friend (continued from the previous conversation).

Basic Conversation 18-2

1. LI ZHIJIE **Wǒ láile, wǒ láile! Xiǎo Niúr, duìbuqǐ, ràng nǐ jiǔ děngle.**
I'm coming, I'm coming! Little Niu, sorry to keep you waiting so long.

2. NIU **Méi guānxi, méi guānxi.**
Don't worry about it.

3. MRS. LI **Xiǎo Niúr, zài zhèr chīfàn ba!**
Little Niu, have dinner here!

4. NIU **Bú yòngle. Děng huǐr wǒ gēn Xiǎo Lǐ tánwánle, jiù huíqu.**
That's not necessary. In a little while when I finish talking with Little Li, I'll go home.

5. LI ZHIJIE **Bù, Xiǎo Niúr, nǐ jiù zài zhèr chī ba. Zámmen yìbiānr chī yìbiānr tán.**
No, Little Niu, why don't you just have dinner here. We can talk while we eat.

6. NIU **Nà yě hǎo. Jiǎndān diǎnr, bié tài máfanle!**
Well, all right. But keep it simple, don't go to too much trouble!

7. MRS. LI **Ò, bù máfan, mǎshàng jiù nònghǎo.**
Oh, it's no trouble, it'll be ready in no time.

(after the meal)

8. NIU **Xiǎo Lǐ, shíhou bù zǎole, wǒ gāi zǒule.**
Little Li, it's getting late, I should be going now.

9. LI ZHIJIE **Zài zuò yihuir ba!**
Why don't you sit a while longer?

10. NIU **Bù le, wǒ hái děi shàngjiē mǎi diǎnr dōngxi.**
No, I still have to go out on the street to buy something.

11. LI ZHIJIE **Hǎo ba. Jìrán nǐ hái yǒu shì, wǒ jiù bù wǎnliúle. Yǐhòu yǒukòngr zài lái wánr.**
O.K. Since you still have things to do, I won't make you stay. Come again when you're free.

12. NIU   **Bómǔ, wǒ zǒule. Xiǎo Lǐ, míngtiān xuéxiào jiàn!**
           Mrs. Li, I'll be leaving. Little Li, see you at school tomorrow!

13. LI ZHIJIE **Míngtiān jiàn. Wǒ bú sòngle, màn zǒu!**
               See you tomorrow. I won't see you out, take care!

Build Up

1. Li Zhijie
Wǒ láile, wǒ láile! Xiǎo Niúr, duìbuqǐ,   I'm coming, I'm coming! Little Niu, sorry
ràng nǐ jiǔ děngle.   to keep you waiting so long.

2. Niu
Méi guānxi, méi guānxi.   Don't worry about it.

3. Mrs. Li
Xiǎo Niúr, zài zhèr chīfàn ba!   Little Niu, have dinner here!

4. Niu
děng huǐr	in a little while [PH]
tán	talk [V]
tánwán	finish talking [RC]
wǒ gēn Xiǎo Lǐ tánwánle	I've finished speaking with Li

Bú yòngle. Děng huǐr wǒ gēn Xiǎo   That's not necessary. In a little while when I
Lǐ tánwánle, jiù huíqu.   finish talking with Little Li, I'll go home.

5. Li Zhijie
yìbiān(r)	on the one hand [PW]
yìbiān(r) A yìbiān(r) B	do B while doing A [PT]
yìbiānr chī yìbiānr tán	talk while eating

Bù, Xiǎo Niúr, nǐ jiù zài zhèr chī ba.   No, Little Niu, why don't you just have dinner
Zámmen yìbiānr chī yìbiānr tán.   here. We can talk while we eat.

6. Niu
máfan	be troublesome [SV]
bié tài máfanle	don't go to too much trouble

Nà yě hǎo. Jiǎndān diǎnr,   Well, all right. But keep it simple,
bié tài máfanle!   don't go to too much trouble!

7. Mrs. Li
nòng	do, make [V]
nònghǎo	fix, prepare, finish [RC]

Ò, bù máfan, mǎshàng jiù nònghǎo.   Oh, it's no trouble, it'll be ready in no time.

8. Niu
shíhou bù zǎole	the time is no longer early

Xiǎo Lǐ, shíhou bù zǎole, wǒ gāi zǒule.   Little Li, it's getting late, I should be going now.

9. Li Zhijie
Zài zuò yìhuir ba!   Why don't you sit a while longer?

10. Niu
jiē	street [N] (M: **tiáo**)
shàngjiē	go out on the street [VO]

Bù le, wǒ hái děi shàngjiē mǎi diǎnr dōngxi.	No, I still have to go out on the street to buy something.

11. Li Zhijie

jìrán	since [MA]
jìrán...jiù...	since... [PT]
jìrán nǐ hái yǒu shì	since you still have things to do
wǎnliú	urge someone to stay [V]
wǒ jiù bù wǎnliúle	I then won't urge (you) to stay
Hǎo ba. Jìrán nǐ hái yǒu shì, wǒ jiù bù wǎnliúle. Yǐhòu yǒukòngr zài lái wánr.	O.K. Since you still have things to do, I won't make you stay. Come again when you're free.

12. Niu

Bómǔ, wǒ zǒule. Xiǎo Lǐ, míngtiān xuéxiào jiàn!	Mrs. Li, I'll be leaving. Little Li, see you at school tomorrow!

13. Li Zhijie

sòng	see someone off or out [V]
wǒ bú sòngle	I won't see (you) out
Míngtiān jiàn. Wǒ bú sòngle, màn zǒu!	See you tomorrow. I won't see you out, take care!

Supplementary Vocabulary

1. dàshǐ	ambassador [N]
tánhuà	talk, speak [VO]
Xiǎo Sūn, dàshǐ yào gēn nǐ tánhuà.	Little Sun, the ambassador wants to talk to you.

Grammatical and Cultural Notes

1. In the first line, **Wǒ láile!** means not "I have come!" but rather "I'm coming!" Verbs with the suffix **-le** are often translated into English as present perfect, so **Tāmen láile** would typically mean "They've come." But, depending on the context, **-le** sometimes indicates merely that the action of the verb has begun, not necessarily that the action has already been completed. Therefore, **Tāmen láile** could also mean "They're coming" or "They're on their way."

2. As we've noted before, short phrases like **Méi guānxi** "it doesn't matter" are often said twice for emphasis.

3. **Xiǎo Niúr, zài zhèr chīfàn ba!** "Little Niu, have dinner here!" Around meal times, Chinese people will often invite visitors to stay to eat with them (18-1: 1A). Similarly, if a Chinese guest arrives at your home around meal time or stays until meal time, it would be polite to invite him or her to join you for the meal.

4. **Děng huǐr** "in a little while" is an abbreviation of **děng yìhuǐr**.

4–7. **INVITATIONS.** When invited to something, a guest is expected to decline politely the first time, lest he or she seem too eager to accept, which would be impolite; this is called "ritual refusal." Even if you'd in fact like to accept something, you mustn't seem too eager, since it would then appear you don't care about all the trouble caused for your host. After declining once or twice, you can begin to accept, but it's best to attach polite conditions: yes, you'll take the drink or the food, but only a little; yes, you'll agree to have a meal with the family, but only if it's a very simple meal. In line 6, for example, the speaker accepts but stipulates **Jiǎndān dianr** "Keep it simple," and then adds **Bié tài máfanle** "Don't go to too much trouble." To sum up, we could say that in America, the likelihood of an invitation being accepted decreases each time that it's repeated, while in China the exact opposite is true! Besides the situation in the Basic Conversation, below is another typical situation:

Speaker A: **Nǐ zài wǒmen zhèr chī wǎnfàn ba!** "Why don't you have dinner here with us!"

Speaker B: **Bú yòngle.** "That's not necessary."

Speaker A: **Zhēnde búyào kèqi, nǐ jiù zài zhèr chī ba.** "Really, don't be polite, why don't you just eat here."

Speaker B: **Tài máfanle ba.** "I suppose it would be too much trouble."

Speaker A: **Bù máfan, yìdiǎnr yě bù máfan.** "It's no trouble, no trouble at all."

Speaker B: **Nà...hǎo ba. Jiǎndān yidianr.** "Then...O.K. Keep it simple."

Note how in Speaker B's second-to-the-last comment above she uses **ba** to convey the message "I suppose it would be too much trouble." Then, in her last comment, rather than enthusiastically accepting as we might in English ("Sure!"), she says **Nà...hǎo ba** "Well...O.K., I guess" and then proceeds to stipulate that the meal should be kept simple. How do you know whether an invitation is a ritual invitation or a genuine one? Ritual invitations are often offered toward the end of a visit rather than at the beginning. Also, if you've politely declined once and the host quickly accepts your declining with a comment like **Nà, xiàcì ba** "Well, then next time," you can be sure it was just a ritual invitation. On the other hand, if the host keeps trying over and over again to get you to accept, then it's probably a genuine invitation. If you suspect an invitation is merely a ritual invitation, you can make up most any excuse such as **Xièxie nǐ, kěshi wǒ hái yǒu shì, xiàcì ba** "Thanks, but I have stuff to do, next time." As cultural outsiders, foreigners will usually be forgiven a lot. However, fairly or unfairly, more will often be expected of Chinese-Americans, even if of the second or third generation, simply because they're of Chinese descent and expected to understand the rules of Chinese culture.

Two women having tea in a private home in Taipei

The above comments concern the foreigner as guest. There will, of course, also be times when you're the host. You must then be careful not to accept your guests' ritual refusal of food or drink without coming back once or twice and inviting them again. Indeed, many polite English questions don't translate into Chinese. For example, in English we would ask a guest "Would you like something to drink?" It would seem as though this would translate into **Nǐ yào bu yào hē dianr shémme?** but that would be the wrong question, since a polite Chinese would have to say he or she wants nothing, even if they were very thirsty. A better question would be **Nǐ xiǎng hē dianr shémme?** "What would you like to drink?" Alternatively, many hosts just pour tea or juice without asking. Putting several cans of carbonated drinks on the coffee table and instructing your guests to "help themselves" would not be appropriate in Chinese culture, since they would usually be hesitant to drink without a more specific, repeated invitation.

We've previously mentioned the natural tendency to transfer the grammar and vocabulary of your native language into a foreign language. Be aware that such inappropriate transfer, and the temptation to assume that all in the foreign language is the same as in the native, also applies to culture. So be very careful about making assumptions and always observe those around you carefully! The above discussion of ritual politeness applies to most host-guest situations in China. However, if you're on very familiar terms with someone who is your peer (e.g., two college students who know each other quite well), then matters will be simpler, more direct, and less formal.

5.   **YÌBIĀN(R) A YÌBIĀN(R) B.** The paired adverb pattern **yìbiān(r) A yìbiān(r) B** is used to indicate that one action (action B) occurs while another action (action A) is in progress. It often translates as English "on the

one hand...on the other hand..." or "(do B) while (doing A)." Note that with this pattern, the main or longer action (action A) comes first, with the secondary action (action B) coming last. Oftentimes where in English you'd use an "and," you'd in Chinese use **yìbiān(r) A yìbiān(r) B**. For example, for English "Let's eat and talk," the best equivalent would be **Wǒmen yìbiānr chī yìbiānr tán ba**; in this case, you could NOT say ***Wǒmen chīfàn gēn tánhuà ba**. The basic pattern is:

SUBJECT	YÌBIĀN(R)	VERB PHRASE₁	YÌBIĀN(R)	VERB PHRASE₂
Tā	yìbiānr	chī zǎofàn,	yìbiānr	kàn bào.

"He read the newspaper while he ate breakfast."

Some more examples of the pattern **yìbiān(r)...yìbiān(r)**:

Zhōngguo rén xǐhuan yìbiān hē chá, yìbiān liáotiān.

"Chinese people like to chat while drinking tea."

Zuìhǎo búyào yìbiānr kāichē, yìbiānr kàn dìtú.

"Better not look at maps while you're driving."

Wǒmen xué Zhōngwén, yìbiānr xué shuōhuà, yìbiānr xué xiězì.

"In our study of Chinese, we learn speaking and writing."

The pattern **biān...biān...** is a somewhat more formal equivalent of **yìbiān(r)...yìbiān(r)....** Examples:

Tā biān shuō biān xiào.   "She laughed while she talked."

There is also the pattern **yímiàn...yímiàn...**, which is used in the same way and with the same meaning as **yìbiān(r)...yìbiān(r)....** Example:

Wǒmen yímiàn zǒulù, yímiàn shuōhuà.   "We talked while we walked."

One other related pattern is **yìfāngmiàn..., (lìng) yìfāngmiàn...** "on the one hand..., on the other hand...." Example:

Dàxuésheng yìfāngmiàn yào yònggōng dúshū, (lìng) yìfāngmiàn yě yào huì wánr.

"College students on the one hand should study hard, but on the other they should also know how to have a good time."

6A.   **Nà yě hǎo** literally means "That also is good" and is used to "give in" to a suggestion from someone else which is different from what was originally intended. **Yě hǎo** alone is also quite common as a response to a suggestion or invitation. It's considered less direct than just saying **Hǎo**; the implication is "It doesn't have to be this way, but this way also would be fine."

6B.   Note the **le** in **Bié tài máfanle**. It's common to have a final **le** with negative imperatives.

7.   The verb **nòng** is here a so-called "dummy" verb for **zuò** "make." **Nònghǎo** literally means "do to the extent that something becomes good." **Nòng**, which has the general meaning "do, make, fix, tinker with, get, handle," is a very versatile, all-purpose verb which can substitute for a more specific one that you don't know or can't think of quickly enough. Examples:

Wǒ qù nòng dianr chīde.	"I'll go make something to eat."
Nǐ zài nòng shémme?	"What are you doing?"
Wǒ xiān qù nòng dianr shuǐ lái.	"I'll go get some water first."

> **Zāogāo, wǒ zhǎobudào chēpiào, bù zhīdào nòng nǎr qùle.**
>
> "Rats, I can't find my bus ticket, I wonder where I put it."

Nòng is also frequently used in resultative compounds. For example:

Nǐ bǎ tā nònghuàile!	"You broke it!"
Tā bǎ yīfu nòngzāngle.	"He got his clothes dirty."
Wǒ tàitai bǎ wénzi nòngsǐle.	"My wife killed the mosquito."

> **Wǒ yǐjīng nòngle hǎo jiǔ le, yīzhí nòngbuhǎo, nǐ bāng wǒ nòngnong, hǎo ma?**
>
> "I've been trying to fix it for a long time, and I just can't; you help me fix it, O.K.?"

You've had several other general verbs like **nòng**, including **zuò** "do, make," **gǎo** "do, make," and **gàn** "do." Sometimes these are interchangeable, sometimes not. For example, instead of **Wǒ gǎocuòle** "I got it wrong," you could also say **Wǒ nòngcuòle**. And to say "I got several tickets," you could say either **Wǒ gǎodàole jǐzhāng piào** or **Wǒ nòngdàole jǐzhāng piào**.

8. The common and useful remark **Shíhou bù zǎole** literally means "The time isn't early anymore." You could also say **Shíjiān bù zǎole**. If you wish for whatever reason to leave a function, look at your watch or a clock, act a bit surprised, and say **Ò, shíhou bù zǎole, wǒ gāi zǒule** "Oh, it's getting late, I ought to be leaving now."

9. **Zài zuò yīhuir ba!** "Sit a while longer!" A Chinese host will often invite a guest who has announced his or her intention to depart to stay a while longer. You should try to do the same to your Chinese guests.

10. If a guest truly wishes to depart, all he or she needs to do is give a vague reason and repeat the desire to leave.

11A. Notice the use of **hǎo ba** here as a discourse marker indicating the end of the discussion about whether John Niu should stay longer or not.

11B. **JÌRÁN...JIÙ....** The paired adverb pattern **jìrán...jiù...** means "since" or "given the fact that" (not "since" as in "since a certain time"). **Jìrán** is a moveable adverb and can stand either before or after the subject of the clause it occurs in. However, **jiù** always follows the subject and stands before the verb. Unlike English, where the "since" clause may come first or last (you can say either "Since it's already so late, I don't think I'll go" or "I don't think I'll go, since it's already so late"), in Chinese the clause with **jìrán** normally comes first. The pattern is:

JÌRÁN	PHRASE₁	SUBJECT	JIÙ	PHRASE₂
Jìrán	nǐ hái yǒu shì,	wǒ	jiù	bù wǎnliúle.

"Since you still have things to do, I won't make you stay."

More examples of the pattern **jìrán...jiù...**:

Jìrán nǐ xǐhuan, wǒ jiù sònggei nǐ ba.	"Since you like it, I'll give it to you."
Jìrán nǐ bù zhīdào, wǒ jiù gàosu nǐ ba.	"Since you don't know, I'll tell you."
Jìrán tā jīntiān bù lái, nèmme wǒ yě jiù huíqule.	"Since she's not coming today, I'll head back."
Jìrán nǐ wàngle dàilái, nà jiù suànle ba.	"Since you forgot to bring them, just forget about it."

> **Jìrán nǐ shēntǐ bù shūfu, nǐ jiù huíjiā xiūxi ba.**
>
> "Since you don't feel well, why don't you just return home and rest."

Distinguish carefully between **jìrán...jiù...** and **yīnwei...suǒyi....** With **yīnwei...suǒyi...**, there is a strong flavor of "cause and effect," whereas with **jìrán...jiù...**, the relationship between the first and second clauses is weaker. Also, **jìrán...jiù...** is often used to give suggestions for what to do in the future; it's generally not used to describe past events. For example, take English "Since it rained yesterday, they didn't meet." In Chinese this would be **Yīnwei zuótiān xiàyǔ, suóyi tāmen méiyou kāihuì.** You couldn't say ***Jìrán zuótiān xiàyǔ, tāmen jiù méiyou kāihuì.**

12A. It's considered good manners to announce your departure to all those who greeted you when you arrived.

12B. **Míngtiān xuéxiào jiàn** "See you at school tomorrow" is an abbreviated form of **Wǒmen míngtiān zài xuéxiào jiàn.**

13. As we noted earlier, Chinese hosts are ordinarily expected to escort their guests out of their home to the street, or at least to the door of their building or the elevator on their floor. In informal situations among peers who know each other well, this isn't always necessary, but tradition then calls for an acknowledgement or explanation: **Wǒ bú sòngle** "I won't be escorting you out (even though I know I really should)."

Calling on Someone to Request a Favor

Bill Sanchez, an American graduate student who is conducting research in Taiwan, visits the Taipei home of his friend Cai Yaquan to request a favor. Cai opens the door and lets him in.

Basic Conversation 18-3

1. MR. CAI Sòng Xiānsheng, huānyíng, huānyíng!
Mr. Sanchez, welcome, welcome!

2. SANCHEZ Duìbuqǐ, wǒ yīnwei línshí yǒu diǎn shì, suóyi láiwǎnle.
I'm sorry, I'm late because something came up at the last minute.

3. MR. CAI Méi guānxi.
That's O.K.

(sees Sanchez starting to take off his shoes) Bú yòng tuōxié.
No need to take off your shoes.

4. SANCHEZ Wǒ hái shi tuō hǎole, bǐjiào shūfu. Wǒ yě xǐhuan zhèige xíguàn.
I'll take them off anyway, it's more comfortable. I also like this custom.

(to Mrs. Cai) E, Cài Tàitai, zhè shi yìdiǎn xiǎo yìsi.
Uh, Mrs. Cai, this is a little something for you.

5. MRS. CAI Āiya! Nín tài kèqile. Qǐng zuò, wǒ qù pàochá.
Oh! You're too polite. Please have a seat, I'll go make some tea.

6. MR. CAI *(offers Sanchez a cigarette)* Qǐng chōuyān.
Please have a cigarette.

7. SANCHEZ Ò, wǒ bú huì chōu, xièxie.
Oh, I don't smoke, thanks.

8. MR. CAI Nín zuótiān zài diànhuàli shuō yǒu diǎn shì yào zhǎo wǒ.
You said on the phone yesterday you wanted to see me about some matter.

9. SANCHEZ Éi, bù hǎo yìsi. Yǒu diǎn xiǎo shìqing xiǎng bàituō nín bāng ge máng.
Yes, sorry to bother you with this. There is a little matter I'd like to ask for your help with.

10. MRS. CAI   *(brings a cup of tea)* **Qǐng hē chá.**
                Please have some tea.

11. SANCHEZ   **Xièxie.**
               Thank you.

12. MR. CAI   **Búyào kèqi, qǐng zhí shuō.**
                Don't be polite, please be frank.

13. SANCHEZ   **E, zheige, zheige, e, shìqing shi zhèiyangzide...**
                Uh, well, well, uh, the matter is like this...

Build Up

---

1. Mr. Cai
    Sòng   Song [SN]
    Sòng Xiānsheng, huānyíng, huānyíng!   Mr. Sanchez, welcome, welcome!

---

2. Sanchez
    línshí   at the time when something happens, at the last minute [A]

    línshí yǒu diǎn shì   at the last minute there was a little something
    -wǎn   late [RE]
    láiwǎn   come late [RC]
    Duìbuqǐ, wǒ yīnwei línshí yǒu   I'm sorry, I'm late because something
    diǎn shì, suóyi láiwǎnle.   came up at the last minute.

---

3. Mr. Cai
    Méi guānxi.   That's O.K.

    tuō   take off (shoes, clothes) [V]
    tuōxié   take off one's shoes [VO]
    Bú yòng tuōxié.   No need to take off your shoes.

---

4. Sanchez
    xíguàn   custom, habit [N]
    Wǒ hái shi tuō hǎole, bǐjiào shūfu.   I'll take them off anyway, it's more
    Wǒ yě xǐhuan zhèige xíguàn.   comfortable. I also like this custom.

    Cài   Cai [SN]
    yìsi   intention [N]
    yìdiǎn(r) xiǎo yìsi   "a little something," a gift [IE]
    E, Cài Tàitai, zhè shi yìdiǎn xiǎo yìsi.   Uh, Mrs. Cai, this is a little something for you.

---

5. Mrs. Cai
    pàochá   steep tea, make tea [VO]
    Āiya! Nín tài kèqile. Qǐng zuò,   Oh! You're too polite. Please have a seat,
    wǒ qù pàochá.   I'll go make some tea.

---

6. Mr. Cai
    yān   tobacco, cigarette; smoke [N]
    chōuyān   smoke [VO]
    Qǐng chōuyān.   Please have a cigarette.

---

7. Sanchez
    Ò, wǒ bú huì chōu, xièxie.   Oh, I don't smoke, thanks.

8. Mr. Cai

Nín zuótiān zài diànhuàli shuō yǒu
diǎn shì yào zhǎo wǒ.

You said on the phone yesterday you
wanted to see me about some matter.

9. Sanchez

shìqing	thing, matter [N] (M: **jiàn**)
yǒu diǎn xiǎo shìqing	there is a little matter
bàituō	ask someone to do something [V]
bāngmáng	help [VO]
bàituō nín bāng ge máng	ask you to help

Éi, bù hǎo yìsi. Yǒu diǎn xiǎo shìqing
xiǎng bàituō nín bāng ge máng.

Yes, sorry to bother you with this. There is a
little matter I'd like to ask for your help with.

10. Mrs. Cai

Qǐng hē chá.

Please have some tea.

11. Sanchez

Xièxie.

Thank you.

12. Mr. Cai

zhí	be straightforward, frank [SV]
zhí shuō	speak frankly [PH]

Búyào kèqi, qǐng zhí shuō.

Don't be polite, please be frank.

13. Sanchez

zheige	(pause filler) [I]

E, zheige, zheige, e, shìqing
shi zhèiyangzide...

Uh, well, well, uh, the matter
is like this...

Supplementary Vocabulary

1. chōukòng	find time (to do something) [VO]
kàn	call on, visit [V]

Xièxie nǐ chōukòng lái kàn wǒ.

Thanks for finding time to visit me.

2. guānxi	relationship, connection [N]

Tāmen liǎngge rén shi
shémme guānxi?

What is the relationship between
the two of them?

3. xī	inhale, breathe in [V]
xīyān	smoke [VO]
qū	area, region [N]
xīyān qū	smoking section [PH]
fēixīyān qū	non-smoking section [PH]

Nǐmen fēn bù fēn xīyān qū gēn
fēixīyān qū?

Do you divide it into a smoking section and
a non-smoking section?

Additional Vocabulary: Increasing Your Discourse Competence

1. huàn jù huà shuō	in other words [PH]
2. jǔ ge lìzi ba	let me give an example [PH]
3. zài wǒ kàn	as I see it [PH]
4. tǎnbáide jiǎng	speaking frankly, to be frank [PH]
5. bù mán nín shuō	to tell you the truth [PH]
6. jù wǒ suǒ zhī	so far as I know [PH]

7. zànchéng
   kànfa
Wǒ wánquán zànchéng nínde kànfa.

agree with [V]
way of seeing things, view [N]
I completely agree with you.

8. liánxiǎng
**Nín nèiyàng shuō ràng wǒ liánxiǎngdào
lìngwài yíge wèntí.**

make a mental association with [V]
Your saying that makes me think of another
question.

Grammatical and Cultural Notes

1.   Both speakers in this and the next lesson have rather heavy Taiwanese accents, as recorded on the video and in the conversation for listening. It's good for your listening comprehension to be exposed to such accented Mandarin, but you should mimic and learn for your own use the standard pronunciation of the Build Up sections.

2.   **Duìbuqǐ, wǒ yīnwei línshí yǒu diǎn shì, suóyi láiwǎnle** "I'm sorry, I'm late because something came up at the last minute." This sentence is useful as an apology when you're late for an appointment. You can also simply say **Duìbuqǐ, wǒ láiwǎnle** "Sorry, I'm late."

3.   The verb **tuō** means "take off" and **xié** means "shoes." Contrast the verb-object compound **tuōxié** "take off one's shoes" with the noun **tuōxié** "slippers" (the **tuō** of which is written with a different character that means "drag").

3–4.   When entering someone's home in Taiwan, you usually remove your shoes and change into slippers, both to feel more comfortable and also to keep the inside of the house clean (18-1: 1A). This is the result of Japanese influence during the Japanese occupation of Taiwan from 1895 to 1945 and isn't the custom everywhere in China.

4.   **GIFT GIVING.** When visiting someone's home—especially if you have a favor to ask—you should always bring a gift. There is a Chinese saying that goes **Yǒu qiú yú rén lǐ xiān dào** "When there is a request of someone, a gift arrives first." Appropriate gifts for visiting someone at their home might include fruit, cakes, a basket of imported canned goods, or a bottle of imported spirits. You could also give a hardcover, coffee-table-type book of photographs from your country;* or, if you're still a student, a set of postcards from your native state or perhaps a T-shirt from your home institution. If your hosts have a child, you could give the child a game from your country or a book and CD for learning English. Flowers aren't usually given as a gift, since they're associated with funerals, nor should you give clocks (**sòng zhōng** "give a clock" rhymes with the expression meaning "escort someone to their final resting place"), handkerchiefs (which are used to wipe tears and thus indicate imminent parting), towels (a sign of sadness, since they are handed out at funerals), or any sharp objects like scissors, knives, or letter openers (which symbolize the cutting off of friendships or good luck). The Chinese prefer even numbers to odd ones, so gifts—including bills—are often given in pairs. Don't give anything in fours, whether items or money amounts, since the number **sì** "four" sounds rather like **sǐ** "die." When presenting a gift to someone, use both hands and say **Zhè shi yìdiǎn xiǎo yìsi** "This is a little something." Traditionally, the gift isn't opened in the presence of the giver and may not even be acknowledged, so don't be offended if that should happen to you. Gifts are usually collected quietly and put aside to be opened later in private, so that other guests won't be embarrassed in case they've given lesser gifts, and also so the giver won't have to see the disappointment on the recipient's face if he or she isn't pleased with the gift. Nowadays, among more modern, Western-educated Chinese, sometimes gifts are opened in the giver's presence or the recipient will ask **Kéyi dǎkāi ma?** "Can I open it?" This is especially true if the giver is a foreigner, since some Chinese are aware of the Western custom of opening presents on receipt. Indeed, if a foreigner is present, a

---

* Books generally make good presents but don't give them to business people, as some of these consider them inauspicious since the word for "book" (**shū**) is a homonym with the word for "lose" (also **shū**). Always take into consideration the context: the people involved and the local society. Ask several different people of the appropriate social background if you're uncertain.

situation sometimes exists where the Chinese adjust their behavior to what they think is expected by the foreigner, and the foreigner may do likewise as regards the Chinese—so that the potential for misunderstandings still very much exists! To be sure, the very presence of a non-Chinese skews the situation so that it's no longer completely "normal." However, the likelihood is that the closer your language and behavior adapt to Chinese customs, the more comfortable the Chinese people around you will be, and the more you'll be dealt with as a Chinese person would be.

6–7. **SMOKING ETIQUETTE.** Smoking is still very common in China, mainly among men. This is especially true in business circles, where it's expected that everyone smokes. If you're male, you'll frequently be offered cigarettes (there is definitely a "double standard" here, as elsewhere). At formal banquets, there are often cigarettes and watermelon seeds on the table at the beginning of the event. Frequently, if someone wants to get to know you, say in a train or waiting area, they'll offer you a cigarette to start a conversation: **Xiānsheng chōu gēn yān ma?** "Sir, would you like a cigarette?" You should be careful about how you decline such an invitation, since it could be taken as rejecting the speaker's offer of friendship. If you don't wish to smoke, you could say **Wǒ bú huì chōuyān, xièxie** (cf. line 7 of this Basic Conversation). This literally means "I don't know how to smoke, thanks" but is in fact an equivalent for "I don't smoke." Another way to decline would be to say **Xièxie nǐ, kěshi wǒ shēntǐ bú tài hǎo, dàifu jiào wǒ búyào chōuyān** "Thanks, but I'm not in the best of health, my doctor told me not to smoke."

9A. Learn the noun **shìqing** "thing, matter," which uses the measure **jiàn**. Examples:

zhèijiàn shìqing	"this matter"
hěn duō shìqing	"many things"

Contrast **shìqing** with **dōngxi** "thing" (5-4). The important distinction between these two words is that **dōngxi** refers to concrete, tangible objects while **shìqing**—which can often be replaced by **shì** or **shìr**—refers to abstract things, i.e., "matter" or "affair."

9B. **Bàituō** "ask someone to do something" is a very polite expression, used when you politely request someone to do something. The pattern is **Bàituō nín...**, with the request following. Two more examples:

Bàituō nín sòng wǒ huíjiā.	"Could I ask you please to take me home."
Bàituō nín dào wàimian chōuyān.	"Could I ask you please to go outside to smoke."

9C. **DIFFERENT WAYS TO SAY "HELP."** You've now been introduced to three ways to say "help": **bāng** (13-3), **bāngzhù** (15-1) and, in this lesson, **bāngmáng**.

Bāng is a coverb that takes a following main verb. While it literally means "help," in fact, it often means "do something for someone." Examples:

Wǒ bāng nǐ zhǎo.	"I'll help you look."
Wǒ bāng nǐ dǎ diànhuà.	"I'll make the call for you."
Qǐng nín bāng wǒ xiě, hǎo bu hǎo?	"Could you please write it for me?"
Yào bu yào wǒ bāng nǐ diǎncài?	"Would you like me to order for you?"
Qǐng nǐ bāng wǒ jiějué zhèige wèntí.	"Please help me solve this problem."

If only a noun or pronoun object follows, **bāngzhù** is usually used. Example:

Qǐng nǐ bāngzhù tā.	"Please help her."

However, **bāngzhù** can be abbreviated to **bāng**, so **Qǐng nǐ bāng tā** is also possible.

If you're saying "help" without a following object or verb, then use the verb-object compound **bāngmáng**.

Note that there the word **máng** means "favor" more than it means "be busy." Examples:

Qǐng nǐ bāngmáng.   "Please help." or "Please do me a favor."

Since **bāngmáng** is a verb-object compound, you can insert **(yí)ge**, nouns or pronouns with or without **-de**, or even stative verbs used as adjectives between the **bāng** and the **máng**. Examples:

Qǐng nín bāng ge máng.	"Please help." or "Please do me a favor."
Qǐng nín bāng wǒde máng.	"Please help me." or "Please do me a favor."
Wǒ bāngle tā yíge dà máng.	"I helped him a great deal." or "I did him a big favor."
Lǎo Lǐ bāngle wǒmen hěn duō máng.	"Old Li helped us a lot." or "Old Li did us a lot of favors."
Nǐ fàngxīn, dàjiā dōu huì bāng nǐde máng.	"Relax, everybody will help you."
Tāde máng, nǐ bāngdeliǎo bāngbuliǎo?	"Are you able to help him?"

Xiānsheng, wǒ néng bu néng qǐng nín bāng wǒ yíge máng?

"Sir, could I ask you to help me?" or "Sir, could I ask you for a favor?"

You CANNOT use noun or pronoun objects after **bāngmáng**. In other words, you couldn't say *Wǒ kéyi **bāngmáng nǐ** "I can help you." Instead, you'd have to say **Wǒ kéyi bāng nǐde máng** or **Wǒ kéyi bāng nǐ**. This is because the verb **bāng** already has an object in **máng**, and you can't add a second object. Finally, one other difference between **bāng**, **bāngzhù**, and **bāngmáng** is that while **bāngzhù** and **bāngmáng** can function as nouns meaning "help," **bāng** can only function as a verb.

9D.   **Yǒu diǎn xiǎo shìqing xiǎng bàituō nín bāng ge máng** literally means "There is a little small matter (about which I) want to ask you to help." Note that **bàituō nín bāng ge máng** is a pivot sentence, where **nín** serves as the object in the sentence **(Wǒ) bàituō nín** "I ask you" and simultaneously serves as the subject in the sentence **Nín bāng ge máng** (8-2: 2C). These two sentences are then collapsed into one, with the second **nín** deleted. In other words:

Wǒ bàituō nín.   +   **Nín bāng ge máng.**   →   **Wǒ bàituō nín bāng ge máng.**

9E.   Notice how, in the last part of line 9, the speaker prepares the listener for the request. In this line, and again in line 13, the speaker announces that he will make a request without telling exactly what the request is (and, of course, he had previously given notice on the telephone the day before that he had a request to make). Providing advance hints that a request is about to come and being very careful about the way the request is presented gives the other person a chance to give an excuse or find an "out" if he or she cannot agree to the request, and gives both sides a chance to avoid the loss of face that would occur if a clearly made, full request had to be flatly turned down. Other common formulas for requests include:

Wǒ yǒu yíjiàn shìqing xiǎng gēn nín tántan.

"I have something I'd like to talk to you about."

Bù zhīdào nín néng bu néng bāng wǒ yíge máng?

"I wonder if you could help me with something?"

10.   **Qǐng hē chá** "Please have some tea." Notice that the Chinese host just brings tea without even asking the guest if he wants something to drink. In English we'd ask "Can I get you something to drink?" but in Chinese that would be too direct except for close friends, since Chinese people would feel obligated to answer in the negative. Keep this in mind if you're a host and are entertaining Chinese guests. Many a Chinese guest has spent a visit with an American suffering from thirst simply because he or she ritually refused the first offer of something to drink and there were no further offers (18-2: 4–7).

12.   Notice how Cai says **Qǐng zhí shuō!** "Please speak frankly!" Of course, Sanchez was hoping for exactly this sort of request from Cai, which signals to him that he may proceed with the formal request.

13A.   **PAUSE FILLERS AND HESITATION SOUNDS.** In line 13 of this conversation, there are four pause fillers: two occurrences of **e**, which you've seen before, and two occurrences of **zheige**, which occurs for the first time in this lesson. As a pause filler, **zheige** is frequently, as here, said two or more times: **zheige, zheige**. These pause fillers and hesitation sounds fill in a pause while the speaker thinks of what to say next, and also prevent what is being said next from appearing to be too direct or blunt. Here, the use of **zheige, zheige** to a certain extent even indicates politeness, since it reflects Mr. Sanchez' reluctance to bring up his request and bother Mr. Cai. Other common pause fillers include **a**, **m**, **neige** (often repeated as **neige, neige**), **nà** "in that case," **nèmme** "in that case," **suóyi shuō** "and therefore," **jiùshi shuō** "that is to say," **wǒde yìsi shi shuō** "what I mean is," **Zěmme shuō ne?** "How should I put it?"and **Nǐ zhīdao ma?** "You know?" Pause fillers serve to keep the conversation going and also allow speakers to retain their turn in turn-taking while they search for their next idea or for the "right word." There is considerable variation in the frequency of pause fillers, depending on the individual speaker and the sociolinguistic occasion. Appropriate use of pause fillers and hesitation sounds is useful and important for foreign learners of Chinese (cf. also 7-4: 6C on the related topic of backchannel comments).

13B.   Instead of **zhèiyangzide** "one like this" you could also say **zhèiyangde** or **zhèiyangrde**.

13C.   The utterance **Shìqing shi zhèiyangzide** "The matter is (one) like this" is useful as an introductory phrase when you're bringing up something for explanation or discussion.

SV2.   **GUĀNXI.** You've previously seen the word **guānxi** in the expression **méi guānxi** "it has no relevance (to the matter at hand)" or "never mind." In the present lesson we now learn the word **guānxi** in its basic meaning of "relationship, connection." **Guānxi**, which could be translated as "connections," is a very important concept in Chinese society that is used to get things done both at work and in the social arena. It's all about whom you know and what those people are willing or obligated to do for you—and what you're willing or obligated to do for them. The Chinese are adept at "networking" in order to get things done, save money, gain favors, and generally get ahead in society. They tend to divide the world into two kinds of people: those with whom you have some sort of **guānxi**, on the one hand, and strangers, on the other. For this reason, Chinese people try if possible to identify or create common ground between themselves and their counterparts; for example, any of the interpersonal relationships that start out with the syllable **tóng-** "same" are potentially fertile ground: **tóngxué** "classmate," **tóngshì** "colleague," **tóngzhì** "comrade," **tóngxiāng** "someone from the same home town as oneself," **tóngbāo** "compatriot," etc. Americans like to feel independent and generally dislike the feeling of being beholden to anyone. However, you shouldn't feel guilty at the thought of "using" people, for you'll quickly learn that **guānxi** doesn't operate in one direction only—you'll get asked to help others soon enough. Of course, as a foreigner in Chinese society, you'll be dependent on help by Chinese citizens to a considerable degree. However, you also have much to offer Chinese people through the **guānxi** system: for example, English teaching or practice, access to foreign goods, help with visa applications, helping their children become admitted to U.S. schools, assistance when a Chinese person travels overseas, etc. It can be especially difficult when Chinese people assume that you as an American must have the same kinds of **guānxi** they do, and mistakenly think you can obtain a visa for them because you know someone at the consulate, or that you can get their children into an American college because you know someone there. Try not to see requests made of you by someone you thought of as a friend as a betrayal of that friendship; they're still your friend and you can ask favors of them, too. To a Chinese person, it would seem foolish to have friends and not ask them for help, especially if there is something useful that they can do fairly easily. From the Chinese point of view, this isn't being manipulative but merely being practical and using common sense.

SV3.   **Xīyān qū** literally means "inhale-smoke area" and **fēixīyān qū** literally means "non-inhale-smoke area." The noun **qū** means "area, region, district" and can also be used in other contexts. Examples:

dà Táiběi qū	"the greater Taipei area"
Zhèige qū bú tài hǎo.	"This district isn't very good."

In mainland China there are seldom non-smoking sections in smaller restaurants. Nevertheless, you could explain to the owner that you don't smoke and ask if there is a **fēixīyān qū**. In restaurants or public spaces, Chinese people don't often ask others to refrain from smoking. If you must do this, find an appropriate reason, for example:

Duìbuqǐ, wǒ duì yānde wèidào guòmǐn. Néng bu néng qǐng nín búyào chōuyān? Xièxie!

"Excuse me, I'm allergic to the smell of smoke. Could I ask you not to smoke? Thank you!"

AV1–8.   **INCREASING YOUR DISCOURSE COMPETENCE.** There exist in every language certain common introductory phrases and rhetorical devices used to introduce questions, preface responses, emphasize certain points, make arguments, offer concessions, retake your turn in the conversation, stall for time, or otherwise "manage" speech and influence the outcome of a conversation. Familiarity with some such phrases and devices in Chinese and the ability to use them appropriately can be of great use in attaining your communicative goals, and may give hearers the impression that you're even more fluent and proficient than you really are. Additional Vocabulary 1–8 of this lesson are examples of such introductory phrases; another is line 13 of this Basic Conversation: **Shìqing shi zhèiyangzide...** "The matter is like this...." From here on out, you should keep your own collection of similar phrases that you find useful. To be really effective, these phrases must be rattled off at good speed and with self-confidence, so practice them carefully. The pause fillers described earlier in note 13A of this lesson will also help strengthen your discourse competence.

Calling on Someone to Request a Favor (cont.)

After Sanchez has made his request for a favor, Cai responds (continued from the previous conversation).

 Basic Conversation 18-4

1. MR. CAI		**Sòng Xiānsheng, zhèijiàn shì, wǒ jìnliàng bāng nín dǎtīng dǎtīng. Zuì wǎn lǐbàiwǔ gěi nín dáfù, hǎo ma?** Mr. Sanchez, I'll do my best to help you find out about this matter. At the latest I'll give you an answer by Friday, all right?
2. SANCHEZ		**Zhēn shi tài máfan nín le. Búguò wànyī bù róngyi dǎtīngdào, yě búyào miǎnqiǎng.** I'm really putting you to too much trouble. But if it's not easy to find out, don't try too hard.
3. MR. CAI		**Wǒ zhīdao. Wǒ jìnlì jiù shì.** I know. I'll just do my best.
4. SANCHEZ		**Cài Xiānsheng, wǒ kàn shíhou yě bù zǎole, wǒ jiù bù duō dǎrǎole. Gàocíle.** Mr. Cai, I think it's getting late, so I won't disturb you any more. I'll be on my way.
5. MR. CAI		**Máng shémme? Zài zuò yixia ma.** Why the rush? Sit a bit longer.
6. SANCHEZ		**Bù le, e, gǎi tiān zài lái bàifǎng.** No, uh, I'll come again to visit some other day.
7. MR. CAI		**Ò, duìle, wǒ tūrán xiángqi yíjiàn shì lai. Wǒ zhèige lǐbàiwǔ yào qù Xīnzhú kàn péngyou, bú zài Táiběi. Nín lǐbàiliù dǎ diànhuà gěi wǒ yě kéyi.** Oh, that's right, I just thought of something. This Friday I'm going to go to Xinzhu to see a friend, and I won't be in Taipei. So you could also call me on Saturday.
8. SANCHEZ		**Hǎode.** All right.
9. MR. CAI		**Wǒ sòng nín xiàlóu.** Let me see you downstairs.

10. SANCHEZ   **Bú yòngle, qǐng liúbù.**
                   That's not necessary, please stay inside.

11. MR. CAI   **Nà hǎo.**
                   Well, all right.

                   (they shake hands)

                   Màn zǒu a.
                   Take care.

12. SANCHEZ   **Zàijiàn!**
                   Goodbye!

13. MRS. CAI   **Zàijiàn!**
                   Goodbye!

Build Up

---

1. Mr. Cai
    jìnliàng   to the best of one's ability [A]
    dǎtīng   inquire [V]
    wǒ jìnliàng bāng nín dǎtīng   I do my best to help you inquire
    zuì wǎn lǐbàiwǔ   at the latest on Friday
    dáfù   answer, reply [N]
    gěi nín dáfù   give you an answer
    Sòng Xiānsheng, zhèijiàn shì, wǒ   Mr. Sanchez, I'll do my best to help you find out
    jìnliàng bāng nín dǎtīng dǎtīng. Zuì wǎn   about this matter. At the latest I'll give you
    lǐbàiwǔ gěi nín dáfù, hǎo ma?   an answer by Friday, all right?

---

2. Sanchez
    wànyī   if by chance, in case [MA]
    dǎtīngdào   inquire and find out [RC]
    wànyī bù róngyì dǎtīngdào   if it's not easy to find out about
    miǎnqiǎng   do with great effort, force [V]
    yě búyào miǎnqiǎng   don't try too hard
    Zhēn shi tài máfan nín le. Búguò wànyī   I'm really putting you to too much trouble. But
    bù róngyi dǎtīngdào, yě búyào miǎnqiǎng.   if it's not easy to find out, don't try too hard.

---

3. Mr. Cai
    jìnlì   do one's best [VO]
    ...jiù shì   just, simply [PT]
    Wǒ zhīdao. Wǒ jìnlì jiù shì.   I know. I'll just do my best.

---

4. Sanchez
    dǎrǎo   disturb [V]
    wǒ jiù bù duō dǎrǎole   then I won't disturb anymore
    gàocí   take leave [V]
    Cài Xiānsheng, wǒ kàn shíhou yě bù zǎole,   Mr. Cai, I think it's getting late, so I won't
    wǒ jiù bù duō dǎrǎole. Gàocíle.   disturb you any more. I'll be on my way.

---

5. Mr. Cai
    Máng shémme? Zài zuò yixia ma.   Why the rush? Sit a bit longer.

---

6. Sanchez
    bàifǎng   pay a formal call on someone [V]
    Bù le, e, gǎi tiān zài lái bàifǎng.   No, uh, I'll come again to visit some other day.

7. Mr. Cai

tūrán (B)	suddenly [MA]
xiángqilai	think of [RC]
xiángqi yíjiàn shì lai	think of a matter
zhèige lǐbàiwǔ	this Friday
Xīnzhú	Xinzhu [PW]
qù Xīnzhú kàn péngyou	go to Xinzhu to see a friend
dǎ diànhuà gěi wǒ	call me on the telephone

Ò, duìle, wǒ tūrán xiángqi yíjiàn shì lai.   Oh, that's right, I just thought of something.
Wǒ zhèige lǐbàiwǔ yào qù Xīnzhú kàn péngyou,   This Friday I'm going to go to Xinzhu to see a
bú zài Táiběi. Nín lǐbàiliù dǎ diànhuà gěi   friend, and I won't be in Taipei. So you could
wǒ yě kéyi.   also call me on Saturday.

8. Sanchez
Hǎode.   All right.

9. Mr. Cai

xiàlóu	go downstairs [VO]

Wǒ sòng nín xiàlóu.   Let me see you downstairs.

10. Sanchez

liúbù	"don't bother to see me out" [IE]

Bú yòngle, qǐng liúbù.   That's not necessary, please stay inside.

11. Mr. Cai
Nà hǎo.   Well, all right.

Màn zǒu a.   Take care.

12. Sanchez
Zàijiàn!   Goodbye!

13. Mrs. Cai
Zàijiàn!   Goodbye!

 ## Supplementary Vocabulary

1. **shànglóu**   go upstairs [VO]

Grammatical and Cultural Notes

1A. Notice the preposed topic **zhèijiàn shì** "(regarding) this matter." As we've so often seen before, Chinese speakers frequently mention the topic of the sentence first, after which they proceed with a comment about the topic.

1B. The verb **dǎtīng** "inquire" can also be used as part of an introductory phrase that leads up to a request for information. It smooths the way and makes clear what the speaker intends to do. In this way, it's particularly useful for non-Chinese speakers, since native Chinese when first approached by a foreigner are often so nonplussed that they may miss the first few words of the foreigner's speech. Examples:

Láojià, wǒ dǎtīng yixiar, zhèilù chē dào bu dào Báiduīzi?

"Excuse me, I'd like to ask, does this bus route go to Baiduizi?"

> **Duìbuqǐ, wǒ dǎtīng yixia, nǐmen zhèige bǔxíbān xū bu xūyào Yīngwén lǎoshī?**
>
> "Excuse me, I'd like to inquire, does this cram school need any English teachers?"

1C.   In the sentence **Zuì wǎn lǐbàiwǔ gěi nín dáfù** "At the latest I'll give you an answer by Friday" there is no pronoun **wǒ**. The **wǒ** is understood, since there is a **wǒ** in the first sentence of this utterance. Overuse of pronouns, especially of **wǒ**, is typical of the Chinese spoken by native English speakers. If you use too many **wǒ** in your speech, it makes you sound "un-Chinese" and could possibly even cause you to come across as arrogant.

1D.   If **zuì wǎn** means "at the latest," how do you think you'd say "at the earliest"?*

1E.   **REFUSALS.** In this Basic Conversation, Mr. Cai is being relatively forthcoming and actually invites the other person to call him on Saturday to find out the result of his inquiry, which is a sign that he's probably sincere about offering to help. But what if he had wanted to refuse the request? In that case, he could have said something like this:

> **Shízài bàoqiàn, dànshi zhèijiàn shìqing kǒngpà wǒ zhēnde méiyou bànfǎ bāng nín.**
>
> "I'm truly sorry, but this matter, I'm afraid I really have no way to help you."

However, this would be considered a very strong response and could seriously strain the relationship between the two individuals involved. If Mr. Cai had wanted to appear at least somewhat helpful, he could have added:

> **Búguò wǒ yǒu ge péngyou yěxǔ kéyi bāng nín. Wǒ míngtiān gěi tā dǎ ge diànhuà wènwen kàn.**
>
> "But I have a friend who might be able to help you. I'll call him tomorrow and see."

This could be merely a face-saving excuse, with the other person never hearing about this matter again, or the speaker's connections with his friend might turn out to be the key element in solving the problem at hand. You can never know for sure. (Of course, if it turns out that someone did introduce someone else who was able to solve your problem, then you'll owe two people—the person who solved your problem and the introducer!)

You should know that in polite Chinese society, to refuse a request outright is, in most circumstances, considered somewhat rude and even unacceptable, since it makes the other person lose face. Therefore, what Chinese people say to each other in formal situations can't always be taken at face value. Rather than flatly turn down someone's request, they might give no response at all; or they might say **Hǎo, wǒ bāng nǐ wènwen, guò jǐtiān zài gěi nǐ dǎ diànhuà** "O.K., I'll ask around for you and call you in a couple of days," even if they can't or don't wish to do something; or they might say **Wǒ jìnlì** "I'll try my best" or **Dàgài kéyi ba** "I suppose we could do that" or **Yīnggāi méiyou wèntí** "There should be no problem," and then you might never hear from them again. In Chinese society, this isn't necessarily considered lying; it could be far worse to come out with a brusque **Méiyou bànfǎ** "There's nothing I can do." In general, Chinese are a practical people who believe that telling the truth for its own sake is often not so important as maintaining harmony and preserving face (that of the requester as well as of the person requested). Other fairly polite refusals include **Hǎo, wǒ huì kǎolǜ** "O.K., we'll consider it," **Zhèige děi yánjiū yánjiū** "We'll have to study this," **Zhèige kěnéng bú tài fāngbiàn** "This might not be very convenient" and **Zhèige kěnéng yǒu yidian kùnnan** "There might be some difficulty with this."

2A.   **Wànyī** means "if by chance" or "in case" (lit. "in the one chance in ten thousand that…"). In the video and the conversation for listening, the speaker nasalizes the vowel of the first syllable so that the **-n** almost disappears. Some speakers do this if a syllable ending in **-n** is followed immediately by a syllable beginning with **y-**. Another example of this phenomenon is **yuànyi** "would like," which you learned in 15-4.

---

* Answer: **zuì zǎo**

2B.   Notice that in **bù róngyi dǎtīngdào**, the negative stative verb **bù róngyi** "not be easy" takes the object **dǎtīngdào**, with the resultant meaning "not be easy to find out about."

4A.   The reason for the **yě** in **shíhou yě bù zǎole** is that "the time no longer being early" is only one of several other, unstated reasons why the speaker should be leaving, including the fact that the speaker has already bothered Mr. Cai too long, etc.

4B.   The two phrases **Bù duō dǎrǎole** "I won't disturb (you) anymore" and **Gàocíle** "(I'll) be leaving now" are frequently used when taking leave of someone.

5A.   The **máng** here is the transitive **máng** "be busy with" which can take an object (18-1). **Máng shémme?** means "What's the hurry?" or "Why the rush?" (lit. "What are you busying yourself with?") For example, in chatting with someone about how they pass their day, you could ask **Nǐ měitiān máng shémme?**

5B.   **Zài zuò yixia ma** "Sit a bit longer." As we've seen before, it's very common to invite a guest who has announced her or his decision to depart to sit a while longer.

5C.   The **ma** at the end of **Zài zuò yixia ma** implies that it's obvious that the guest ought to sit a while longer: "Sit for a bit longer—this is obviously something that you ought to do!" Be sure you're clear that this **ma** is not the question **ma** but rather the **ma** that indicates an obvious situation (7-2: 4C).

7A.   As we saw previously in 17-1, the introductory phrase **Ò, duìle** "Oh, yes, that's right" is often used to introduce a change of topic, as when you've just thought of something important that you wish to mention without delay.

7B.   An alternate pronunciation of **tūrán** "suddenly" that you'll hear in Taiwan and occasionally elsewhere is **túrán**. This is how the word is pronounced in the conversation for listening.

7C.   **SPLIT RESULTATIVE COMPOUNDS.** Consider in this line the phrase **Wǒ tūrán xiángqi yíjiàn shì lai** "I suddenly thought of a matter" or "I just remembered something." In the case of resultative compounds ending in the directional endings **-lai** or **-qu**, the object of the verb is either placed in front of the verb as the topic or, as here, is inserted into the verb construction, directly before the **-lai** or **-qu**. In this case, the construction is called a Split Resultative Compound. For example, to express "I just thought of her name," you could say either **Tāde míngzi wǒ xiángqilaile** or **Wǒ xiángqi tāde míngzi laile**. The basic pattern is:

RESULTATIVE VERB	OBJECT OF VERB	DIRECTIONAL ENDING
xiángqi	yíjiàn shì	lai
"think of something"		

Some more examples of split resultative compounds:

Tā náqi bǐ laile.	"He picked up his pen."
Tā pǎohuí jiā qule.	"He ran back home."
Tā zǒujìn wūzili qule.	"She walked into the room."
Tā shuō tā nábuchū qián lai.	"She says she can't get the money out." or "She says she can't come up with the money."
Nǐmen náchū běnzi lái ba!	"You all take out your notebooks!" or "Take it out of your notebooks!"
Wǒ yǐjīng náhuí shūdiàn qule.	"I've already taken it back to the bookstore."
Zhèiběn cídiǎn cháqi zì lai hěn fāngbian.	"This dictionary is convenient for looking up characters."
Tā xiǎngchū yíge hǎo bànfǎ láile.	"She thought of a good way."
Qǐng nǐ bǎ yǐzi bāndào jiàoshìli lai.	"Please move the chair into the classroom."

7D. **Zhèige lǐbàiwǔ** "this Friday." Chinese people are more precise in their use of "this" and "next" than we are in English. In English, "next Friday" is used by some speakers to mean "the next Friday," but by others to mean "Friday of the next week." Chinese **zhèige lǐbàiwǔ** can mean only "Friday of this week," while **xiàge lǐbàiwǔ** can mean only "Friday of next week."

7E. **Xīnzhú** (lit. "new bamboo") is a medium-sized city about 75 kilometers southeast of Taipei. It's known for its excellent **mǐfěn** "rice noodles," for being windy, and for having a majority Hakka population.

7F. Review the two different **kàn** in lines 4 and 7. In line 4, **kàn** means "think" or "consider." In line 7, **kàn** means "visit."

7G. Both **dǎ diànhuà gěi wǒ** and **gěi wǒ dǎ diànhuà** are possible.

7H. The last sentence in this utterance literally means "On Saturday you call me, also is permitted." This is a Topic-Comment sentence, where the topic is **Nín lǐbàiliù dǎ diànhuà gěi wǒ** and the comment is **yě kéyi**. Of course, the word **yě** "too" isn't really logical here, since the speaker has just said that he won't even be in town on Friday! However, using **yě** downplays the speaker's earlier mistake in initially offering to provide an answer by Friday.

10. **Qǐng liúbù** "There's no need to see me out" literally means "Please retain your step." This is commonly said by guests to hosts when the hosts prepare to escort the guests out of their home.

11. Chinese men sometimes shake hands to say goodbye, while other times they just nod and smile. Chinese women shake hands less frequently than men do. In Western-educated circles or when dealing with foreigners, handshaking is more common than when only Chinese are present.

Unit 18: Review and Study Guide

New Vocabulary

ADVERBS

jìnliàng	to the best of one's ability
línshí	at the last minute
zhè	right away
zǒngshì	always

IDIOMATIC EXPRESSIONS

liúbù	"don't bother to see me out"
yìdiǎn(r) xiǎo yìsi	"a little something," a gift

INTERJECTIONS

zheige	(pause filler)

MOVEABLE ADVERBS

jìrán	since
tūrán	suddenly
wànyī	if by chance, in case

NOUNS

bófù	uncle (father's older brother)
bómǔ	aunt (wife of father's older brother)
dáfù	answer, reply
dàshǐ	ambassador
guānxi	relationship, connection
húzi	beard, moustache
jiē	street
qū	area, region
shìqing	thing, matter
wàigōng	grandfather (maternal)
wàipó	grandmother (maternal)
wàisūn	grandson (daughter's son)
wàisūnnǚ(r)	granddaughter (daughter's daughter)
wūzi	room
xíguàn	custom, habit
yān	tobacco, cigarette; smoke
yìsi	intention

PATTERNS

jìrán...jiù...	since...
...jiù shì	just..., simply...
yìbiān(r) A yìbiān(r) B	do B while doing A

PHRASES

děng huǐr	in a little while
fēixīyān qū	non-smoking section
guā húzi	shave
liú húzi	grow a beard or moustache
xiǎo péngyou	child
xīyān qū	smoking section
zhí shuō	speak frankly

PLACE WORDS

Xīnzhú	Xinzhu
yìbiān(r)	on the one hand

RESULTATIVE COMPOUNDS

dāibuzhù	not be able to stay

dǎtīngdào	inquire and find out	**VERBS**		**wǎnliú**	urge someone to stay
láiwǎn	come late	**bàifǎng**	pay a formal call on someone	**xī**	inhale, breathe in
nònghǎo	fix, prepare, finish	**bàituō**	ask someone to do something	**VERB-OBJECT COMPOUNDS**	
tánwán	finish talking	**dāi**	stay	**bāngmáng**	help
wènhǎo	send one's regards to	**dǎrǎo**	disturb	**chōukòng**	find time (to do something)
xiángqilai	think of	**dǎtīng**	inquire	**chōuyān**	smoke
RESULTATIVE ENDINGS		**gàocí**	take leave	**jìnlì**	do one's best
-wǎn	late	**guā**	scrape	**pàochá**	steep tea, make tea
-zhù	firm	**kàn**	call on, visit	**shàngjiē**	go out on the street
STATIVE VERBS		**máng**	be busy with (something)	**shànglóu**	go upstairs
jí	be in a hurry	**miǎnqiǎng**	do with great effort, force	**tánhuà**	talk, speak
máfan	be troublesome	**nòng**	do, make	**tuōxié**	take off one's shoes
zhí	be straightforward	**sòng**	see someone off or out	**xiàlóu**	go downstairs
SURNAMES		**tán**	talk	**xīyān**	smoke
Cài	Cai	**tuō**	take off (shoes, clothes)		
Niú	Niu (lit. "cow")				
Sòng	Song				

Major New Grammar Patterns

YÌBIĀN(R) A YÌBIĀN(R) B: Tā yìbiān chī zǎofàn, yìbiān kàn bào. "She read the newspaper while eating breakfast." (18-2)

JÌRÁN...JIÙ...: Jìrán nǐ hái yǒu shì, wǒ jiù bù wǎnliúle. "Since you still have things to do, I won't keep you." (18-2)

DIFFERENT WAYS TO SAY "HELP": Qǐng nín bāng wǒ xiě, hǎo bu hǎo? "Could you please help me write it?", **Qǐng nǐ bāngzhù tā.** "Please help her.", **Qǐng nǐ bāngmáng.** "Please help.", **Qǐng nín bāng ge máng.** "Please help.", **Nǐ fàngxīn, dàjiā dōu huì bāng nǐde máng.** "Relax, everybody will help you." (18-3)

SPLIT RESULTATIVE COMPOUNDS: Wǒ tūrán xiángqi yíjiàn shì lai. "I suddenly thought of something.", **Tā náqi bǐ láile.** "She picked up her pen.", **Tā pǎohuí jiā qule.** "He ran back home." (18-4)

Visiting People (II)

COMMUNICATIVE OBJECTIVES

Once you've mastered this unit, you'll be able to use Chinese to:

1. Visit a friend or classmate who is ill.
2. Explain why you didn't come to visit your sick friend or classmate earlier.
3. Ask someone how they're feeling and urge them to get enough rest and take good care of themselves.
4. Offer to help someone if they need assistance.
5. Tell someone you'll visit them again soon and invite them to visit you.
6. Pay a formal call on a teacher at her or his home.
7. Thank a teacher for her or his efforts on your behalf.
8. Discuss your progress in learning Chinese pronunciation, grammar, vocabulary, accuracy, and fluency.
9. Ask someone to convey greetings from you to a third party.
10. Take leave of someone politely.
11. Talk about tests: different kinds, your impressions of how you did, whether the results are out yet, etc.
12. Discuss academic life: reports, term papers, theses, courses, grades, credits, and semesters.
13. Talk about mail: buying stamps and sending letters, postcards, and packages.

Visiting a Sick Classmate

Linda Fuentes, a graduate student in art history who is studying Chinese and conducting research in Beijing, visits Hu Xiaoling, a Chinese classmate of hers who is recovering from an illness. Hu's mother opens the door and lets her in.

Basic Conversation 19-1

1. FUENTES **Bómǔ, nín hǎo!**
Hello, Mrs. Hu!

2. MRS. HU **Jìnlái ba. Xiǎolíng zài wòfáng tǎngzhe ne.**
Come in. Xiaoling is lying down in the bedroom.

3. FUENTES **Xiǎolíng, tīngshuō nǐ bìngle. Xiànzài hǎo diǎnr le ma?**
Xiaoling, I heard you were sick. Are you better now?

4. HU XIAOLING **Yǐjīng hǎo duōle. Qíshí yě méi shémme dà bìng. Xièxie nǐ hái pǎolai kàn wǒ.**
I'm already a lot better. Actually, it isn't anything serious. Thanks for coming over to see me.

5. FUENTES **Běnlái zǎo jiù yīnggāi lái kàn nǐ, zhǐ shi zhèjǐtiān mángde hěn, yìzhí méiyou gōngfu, suóyǐ zhí dào jīntiān cái lái. Ò, duìle, gěi nǐ dàile yidianr shuǐguǒ.**
Ordinarily, I should have come to see you a long time ago, it's just that the last few days I was always busy and never had time, that's why I didn't come until today. Oh, that's right, I brought you some fruit.

6. HU XIAOLING **Xièxie nǐ. Nà, nǐ zhèjǐtiān máng shémme ne?**
Thanks. So, what have you been busy with the last few days?

7. FUENTES **Hái bú shi mángzhe qīmò kǎoshì. Tiāntiān dōu kǎo, dōu kuài bǎ wǒ kǎoyūnle!**
I've been busy with final exams, what else? I've been taking tests every day; soon I'm going to get dizzy from all this testing!

Build Up

1. **Fuentes**
Bómǔ, nín hǎo!   Hello, Mrs. Hu!

2.   **Mrs. Hu**

Xiǎolíng	Xiaoling (given name)
wòfáng	bedroom [PW] (M: **jiān**)
tǎng	lie down [V]
zài wòfáng tǎng	lie down in a bedroom
Jìnlái ba. Xiǎolíng zài wòfáng tǎngzhe ne.	Come in. Xiaoling is lying down in the bedroom.

3.   **Fuentes**

bìng	get sick [V]
tīngshuō nǐ bìngle	(I) heard you got sick
Xiǎolíng, tīngshuō nǐ bìngle.	Xiaoling, I heard you were sick.
Xiànzài hǎo diǎnr le ma?	Are you better now?

4.   **Hu Xiaoling**

hǎo duōle	have become much better
bìng	illness, disease [N]
méi shémme dà bìng	don't have any major illness
pǎo	run [V]
pǎolai	run over here, come over [RC]
Yǐjīng hǎo duōle. Qíshí yě méi shémme dà bìng. Xièxie nǐ hái pǎolai kàn wǒ.	I'm already a lot better. Actually, it isn't anything serious. Thanks for coming over to see me.

5.   **Fuentes**

zǎo jiù yīnggāi lái kàn nǐ	should have come to see you long ago
zhǐ shi...	it's only that...
zhèjǐtiān	these last few days
mángde hěn	(I've been) very busy
gōngfu	time [N]
yìzhí méiyou gōngfu	never had time
zhí dào	straight up to, until [PH]
zhí dào jīntiān cái lái	not come until today
Běnlái zǎo jiù yīnggāi lái kàn nǐ, zhǐ shi zhèjǐtiān mángde hěn, yìzhí méiyou gōngfu, suóyǐ zhí dào jīntiān cái lái. Ò, duìle, gěi nǐ dàile yidianr shuǐguǒ.	Ordinarily, I should have come to see you a long time ago, it's just that the last few days I was always busy and never had time, that's why I didn't come until today. Oh, that's right, I brought you some fruit.

6.   **Hu Xiaoling**

Xièxie nǐ. Nà, nǐ zhèjǐtiān máng shémme ne?	Thanks. So, what have you been busy with the last few days?

7.   **Fuentes**

hái bú shi...	if it isn't... [PT]
mángzhe	be busy with
kǎoshì	test [N/VO]
qīmò kǎoshì (B)	final examination [PH]
mángzhe qīmò kǎoshì	be busy with the final exam
kǎo	take a test [V]
tiāntiān dōu kǎo	take a test every day
yūn	be dizzy [SV]
-yūn	dizzy [RE]
kǎoyūn	become dizzy from testing [RC]
bǎ wǒ kǎoyūnle	made me dizzy from testing
Hái bú shi mángzhe qīmò kǎoshì. Tiāntiān dōu kǎo, dōu kuài bǎ wǒ kǎoyūnle!	I've been busy with final exams, what else? I've been taking tests every day; soon I'm going to get dizzy from all this testing!

Supplementary Vocabulary

1. qīzhōng kǎoshì (B)	mid-term examination [PH]
2. pǎoqu	run over there [RC]
pǎolái pǎoqù	run all over the place
Xiǎo háizi zuì xǐhuan pǎolái pǎoqù.	Kids like nothing better than running all over the place.
3. pǎobù	run paces, run [VO]
Wǒ měitiān xiàwǔ pǎobù.	I run every afternoon.
4. zhuàn	earn [V]
zhuànqián	earn money [VO]
mángzhe zhuànqián	be busy earning money
huā	spend (money, time) [V]
huāqián	spend money [VO]
mángzhe huāqián	be busy spending money
Xiānsheng mángzhe zhuànqián,	The husband is busy earning money
tàitai mángzhe huāqián.	while the wife is busy spending it.
5. yǒu yìdiǎn(r)...	be a little... [PT]
yǒu yìdiǎnr yūn	be a little dizzy
Wǒ xiǎng zuò yihuir, wǒ yǒu yidianr yūn.	I'd like to sit down for a while, I'm a little dizzy.

Additional Vocabulary: Testing

1. xiǎokǎo	quiz [N]
2. zhōukǎo	weekly test [N]
3. dàkǎo	final exam [N]
4. kǎojuàn(r)	test paper [N]

Grammatical and Cultural Notes

1. **VISITING THE SICK.** In Chinese society, where even minor illnesses are viewed more seriously than in America, people will go to considerable trouble to visit sick friends or acquaintances in their homes or in the hospital. When they do, they will almost always bring a gift. Suitable gifts for visiting the sick include fruit, cakes, cookies, dry milk powder, tea, homemade foods, and Chinese medicine. Actually, most any food item is fine; even if the sick person can't eat them, family members can. Flowers aren't usually given to the sick, since flowers are used for funerals. Some people believe it's inauspicious to visit sick people at night, as this could be interpreted as meaning that the sick person doesn't have much time left. If you have a friend or acquaintance who is ill, it will be much appreciated if you go visit them. On the other hand, if you're the one who is ill and word gets out, don't be surprised if friends, classmates, teachers, or colleagues come unannounced to your dormitory or home to visit you. Even if their visit is unexpected and inconvenient, you must be careful not to express displeasure, since your visitors' intentions are good.

3–4. **DIFFERENT WAYS TO EXPRESS "SICK."** In line 3, the word **bìng** is a verb meaning "get sick" or "become ill." In line 4, **bìng** is a noun meaning "sickness" or "disease." Study the different uses of **bìng** as exemplified in the Basic Conversation and in the additional examples below:

To say "He/she is sick," say **Tā bìngle** (lit. "He/she has gotten sick"; you CANNOT say *Tā shi bìng or *Tā hěn bìng).

To say "He/she isn't sick," say **Tā méiyou bìng** (lit. "He/she doesn't have an illness"; you CANNOT say *Tā bú bìng).

To say "He/she is very sick," say **Tā bìngde hěn lìhai** (lit. "He/she sicks severely"; you CANNOT say ***Tā hěn bìng**).

4A.   **Xièxie nǐ hái pǎolai kàn wǒ** "Thanks for coming over to see me." The **hái** here means "still" or "even"; the implication is "despite being very busy, you still came over to see me."

4B.   The basic meaning of **pǎo** is "run," but this verb is often used colloquially to mean "go" or "come." Examples of the colloquial use of **pǎo** meaning "go" or "come":

        Tā pǎodao náli qùle?   "Where did he go?"

        Nǐ pǎo zhèr lái gàn shémme? "What did you come here for?"

5A.   **Mángde hěn** means "be very busy." As we explored in 16-3: 3B, the pattern STATIVE VERB + **-de** + **hěn** means "very." Other common examples include **hǎode hěn** "be very good," **duōde hěn** "be very many," and **guìde hěn** "be very expensive."

5B.   **DIFFERENT WORDS FOR "TIME."** Learn the noun **gōngfu** "time" as in **yìzhí méiyou gōngfu** "never have time." The word **gōngfu** is especially colloquial and characteristic of northern Mandarin. You've now had several words that translate as "time": **shíjiān** (3-4), **shíhou(r)** (7-3), **kòng(r)** (17-1), and **gōngfu** (19-1). These are used in somewhat different ways. **Gōngfu** and **kòng(r)** refer to "free time," i.e., time which a person has available for their own use. **Shíhou** is usually used for a point or period in time when something happens. The most general of these terms is **shíjiān**, which can be used almost anywhere. To sum up:

TO EXPRESS FREE TIME, SAY:

        Nǐ yǒu méiyou gōngfu?   "Do you have time?"

        Nǐ yǒu méiyou kòng(r)?   "Do you have time?"

        Nǐ yǒu méiyou shíjiān?   "Do you have time?"

But NOT ***Nǐ yǒu méiyou shíhou?**

TO EXPRESS POINT IN TIME, SAY:

        Nǐ shémme shíhou qù?   "What time will you go?"

        Nǐ shémme shíjiān qù?   "What time will you go?"

But NOT ***Nǐ shémme gōngfu qù?**

And NOT ***Nǐ shémme kòng(r) qù?**

5C.   **Zhí dào jīntiān cái lái** "all the way up until today only then come" or "not come until today." **Zhí** is an abbreviated form of **yìzhí**.

7A.   Look at **Hái bú shi mángzhe qīmò kǎoshì**. This means "If it isn't that I've been busy with final exams" or, in freer English, "I've been busy with final exams, what else?" The **Hái bú shi...** is here a rhetorical device that implies "Of course this is how it is, how could it be otherwise?"

7B.   **Mángzhe qīmò kǎoshì** means "being busy with final exams." **Máng** can be a regular verb meaning "be busy doing something." Other examples:

        Tāmen mángzhe bānjiā.   "They're busy moving."

        Wǒ gēge zài Niǔyuē mángzhe zhuànqián.   "My older brother is busy making money in New York City."

7C.   The word **kǎoshì** can function both as a verb-object compound meaning "to test, to take a test" and as a noun meaning "a test" (in the abstract). On the other hand, if a specific test or exam paper is meant, then the word **kǎojuàn(r)** is used.

7D.   **Qīmò kǎoshì** "final exam" can be abbreviated to **qīmòkǎo**. In Taiwan, these two expressions are pronounced **qímò kǎoshì** and **qímòkǎo** with a Tone Two on the syllable **qí-**.

7E.   **REDUPLICATION OF MEASURES AND NOUNS TO MEAN "EACH" OR "EVERY."** As we saw in 10-3, **tiān** "day" when reduplicated as **tiāntiān** gains the meaning "every day" (the meaning of **tiāntiān** is about the same as **měitiān**). A limited number of measures and monosyllabic nouns can be reduplicated in this manner to add emphasis and mean "each" or "every." These reduplicated forms cannot occur as objects after the verb; to say "I like everyone" you couldn't say ***Wǒ xǐhuan rénrén**; in this case, you would have to prepose the **rénrén** and say **Wǒ rénrén dōu xǐhuan**. These reduplicated forms are often, though not always, followed by the adverb **dōu**. Examples of common reduplicated measures and nouns that mean "each" or "every":

PLAIN FORM		REDUPLICATED FORM	
tiān	"day"	**tiāntiān**	"every day"
nián	"year"	**niánnián**	"every year"
zhāng	"sheet"	**zhāngzhāng**	"every sheet"
běn	"volume"	**běnběn**	"every volume"
rén	"person"	**rénrén**	"everybody"

Here are some more examples of reduplicated measures and nouns within sentences:

Rénrén dōu zhīdao.	"Everyone knows."
Tā tiāntiān dōu lái shàngbānr.	"She comes to work every single day."
Tāmen jiāde rén gègè dōu ài xiào.	"Every single one of the people in their family likes to laugh."
Zhèxiē zhǐ wǒ zhāngzhāng dōu yào.	"I want every sheet of this paper."
Wǒmen zhèr niánnián dōu fāshēng zhèige wèntí.	"This problem occurs here every year."
Lǎoshī jiǎngde huà wǒ jùjù dōu jìde.	"I remember every single sentence of what the teacher said."

It's best to learn these reduplications as you come across them and not to make them up on your own. While **tiāntiān** "every day" and **rénrén** "every person" work fine, ***gǒugǒu** for "every dog" (which the author once, early in his studies of Chinese, mistakenly said) would definitely not!

7F.   Contrast carefully the pronunciation of **tiāntiān** "every day" with that of **qiántiān** "day before yesterday."

7G.   **Kǎoyūn** literally means "take tests to the point where one becomes dizzy."

SV1.   In Taiwan, mainland Chinese **qīzhōng kǎoshì** is pronounced **qízhōng kǎoshì**.

SV5.   **YǑU (YI)DIANR + STATIVE VERB.** Consider in this line **Wǒ yǒu diǎnr yūn** "I'm a little dizzy." **Yǒu (yi)dianr** occurs frequently with stative verbs (sometimes also with certain other verbs) to indicate that something is "a little" something, or that something is "somewhat" something. The literal meaning of this pattern is "have a little...," "be a little...," or "somewhat...." The tones on **yìdiǎnr** are optional, tending to be lost in rapid speech. The basic pattern is:

YǑU	(YI)DIANR	STATIVE VERB
yǒu	yìdiǎnr	wǎn

"be a little late"

More examples of **yǒu (yi)dianr** + VERB:

Wǒ yǒu diǎnr è.	"I'm a bit hungry."
Wǒ yǒu diǎnr bù shūfu.	"I'm a little uncomfortable."
Zhèijiàn shì yǒu diǎn máfan.	"This matter is somewhat troublesome."
Tā zhèijǐtiān yǒu yìdiǎnr máng.	"The last few days she's been a little busy."
Cài hěn hǎochī, kěshi yǒu yìdiǎnr là.	"The food is very good, but it's a little hot."
Lǎobǎn hǎoxiàng yǒu yìdiǎnr bù mǎnyì.	"The boss seems somewhat dissatisfied."
Wǒ yǒu diǎnr bù xǐhuan ta.	"I somewhat dislike him."
Wǒ yǒu diǎnr xǐhuan ta.	"I kind of like him." (e.g., when said by a shy young woman to a confidant about a young man she met recently)

The meaning of the **yǒu (yi)dianr** + VERB pattern is usually negative or infelicitous, indicating less than ideal or less than comfortable conditions, not what you might desire to be the situation or to have happen. (Only the last example above is an exception to this.) For example, you could say **Tāmen màide dōngxi yǒu diǎnr guì** "The things they sell are a little expensive" (i.e., more expensive than you'd have liked); but you could NOT say ***Tāmen màide dōngxi yǒu diǎnr piányi** "The things they sell are a little inexpensive," since "being inexpensive" is normally a desirable quality. Similarly, you could say **Wǒ yǒu yìdiǎn bù gāoxìng** "I'm a little upset" but you could NOT say ***Wǒ yǒu yìdiǎn gāoxìng** "I'm a little happy."

IMPORTANT NOTE: When using this pattern, be careful always to include the **yǒu**. You could NEVER say ***Wǒ yìdiǎnr máng** but should always say **Wǒ yǒu yìdiǎnr máng**. Also, be careful to distinguish the following two patterns:

Zhèitiáo kùzi yǒu yidianr dà.	"This pair of trousers is a little big."
Zhèitiáo kùzi dà yidianr.	"This pair of trousers is bigger (than some other pair)."

In other words, if **yidianr** appears AFTER a stative verb, then comparison with something else is involved; but if **yǒu yidianr** occurs BEFORE a stative verb, then there is no comparison implied and you are merely stating that something "is a little something else."

Visiting a Sick Classmate (cont.)

Fuentes concludes her conversation with Hu and prepares to leave (continued from the previous conversation).

 ## Basic Conversation 19-2

1. HU XIAOLING   **Kǎode zěmmeyàng?**
How did you do on your tests?

2. FUENTES   **Mámahūhū ba. Chéngjī hái méi chūlai ne.**
So-so, I guess. The grades aren't out yet.

(after conversing for a while)

Xiǎolíng, nǐ hǎohāo xiūxi ba. Wǒ bù duō zuòle. Guò jǐtiān zài lái kàn nǐ.
Xiaoling, you rest real well. I'll be going on my way. In a few days, I'll come visit you again.

3. HU XIAOLING   **Chīle fàn zài zǒu ba.**
Why don't you have dinner before you leave?

4. FUENTES   **Bù le, bù le, xièxie nǐ, wǒ děi zǒule. Xiǎolíng, nǐ duō zhùyì shēnti. Bié tài lèile. Yǒu shémme shìde huà, lái ge diànhuà, dàjiā dōu kéyi bāng nǐ.**
No, thanks, I must be going now. Xiaoling, you watch your health. Don't tire yourself out. If there should be anything, give us a call, everybody can help you.

5. HU XIAOLING   **Tài xièxie nǐ le. Yǒu shì wǒ huì shuōde.**
Thanks so much. If there is anything, I'll be sure to let you know.

6. FUENTES   **Bómǔ, wǒ zǒule.**
Mrs. Hu, I'll be going now.

7. MRS. HU   **Xièxie nǐ lái kàn Xiǎolíng. Gǎi tiān zài lái wánr ba.**
Thanks for coming to see Xiaoling. Come again to visit some other day.

8. FUENTES   **Hǎo, yídìng lái. Zàijiàn!**
O.K., I'll definitely come. Bye!

9. MRS. HU   **Zàijiàn!**
Goodbye!

Build Up

1. **Hu Xiaoling**
Kǎode zěmmeyàng?   How did you do on your tests?

2. **Fuentes**
   mámahūhū   so-so, fair; not too bad [IE]
   chéngjī   grade (on test or in course) [N]
Mámahūhū ba. Chéngjī hái méi chūlai ne.   So-so, I guess. The grades aren't out yet.

   hǎohāo(r)   very well
   hǎohāo xiūxi   rest very well
   nǐ hǎohāo xiūxi ba   you rest real well
   wǒ bù duō zuòle   I won't sit anymore
   guò jǐtiān   after a few days
Xiǎolíng, nǐ hǎohāo xiūxl ba. Wǒ bù   Xiaoling, you rest real well. I'll be going on my way.
duō zuòle. Guò jǐtiān zài lái kàn nǐ.   In a few days, I'll come visit you again.

3. **Hu Xiaoling**
   chīle fàn   having eaten
   zài zǒu   then go
Chīle fàn zài zǒu ba.   Why don't you have dinner before you leave?

4. **Fuentes**
   duō zhùyì shēnti   pay more attention to your body
   bié tài lèile   don't get too tired
   yǒu shémme shìde huà   if there is any matter
   lái diànhuà   call on the telephone [PH]
Bù le, bù le, xièxie nǐ, wǒ děi zǒule. Xiǎolíng,   No, thanks, I must be going now. Xiaoling,
nǐ duō zhùyì shēnti. Bié tài lèile.   you watch your health. Don't tire yourself out.
Yǒu shémme shìde huà, lái ge   If there should be anything, give us a
diànhuà, dàjiā dōu kéyi bāng nǐ.   call, everybody can help you.

5. **Hu Xiaoling**
   wǒ huì shuōde   I'll be sure to say
Tài xièxie nǐ le. Yǒu shì wǒ huì shuōde.   Thanks so much. If there is anything, I'll be sure to let
                                                   you know.

6. **Fuentes**
Bómǔ, wǒ zǒule.   Mrs. Hu, I'll be going now.

7. **Mrs. Hu**
   gǎi tiān zài lái wánr   come again to have fun another day
Xièxie nǐ lái kàn Xiǎolíng. Gǎi tiān   Thanks for coming to see Xiaoling. Come again
zài lái wánr ba.   to visit some other day.

8. **Fuentes**
Hǎo, yídìng lái. Zàijiàn!   O.K., I'll definitely come. Bye!

9. **Mrs. Hu**
Zàijiàn!   Goodbye!

Supplementary Vocabulary: Academic Life

1. **xuéqī (B)**	semester, term [N]
shàngge xuéqī	last semester
xiū	study, take (courses, credits) [V]
xuéfēn	credit, credit hour [N]
Wǒ shàngge xuéqī xiūle shíliùge xuéfēn.	Last semester I took sixteen credits.
2. **zhèige xuéqī**	this semester
xuǎn	choose, select [V]
mén	(for courses) [M]
wǔmén kè	five courses
Wǒ zhèige xuéqī xuǎnle wǔmén kè.	This term I chose five courses.
3. **xiàge xuéqī**	next semester
piān	(for theses, reports, essays) [M]
lùnwén	thesis, dissertation [N] (M: **piān**)
bìyè lùnwén	honors thesis [PH] (M: **piān**)
Wǒ xiàge xuéqī yào xiě yìpiān	Next semester I'm going to write an
bìyè lùnwén.	honors thesis.
4. **bàogào**	report [N] (M: **piān**)
xuéqī bàogào (B)	term paper [PH] (M: **piān**)
guānyú	about, concerning [CV]
Nǐde xuéqī bàogào shi guānyú shémmede?	What is your term paper about?

Grammatical and Cultural Notes

2A.   Even if the speaker felt she had done very well on her exams, Chinese politeness and modesty would have prevented her from saying so directly. **Mámahūhū** literally means "horse-horse tiger-tiger" and can be used when you wish to express "O.K.," "so-so," or "neither particularly good nor particularly bad." Here are two more examples:

> Speaker A: **Zuìjìn zěmmeyàng a?**
>
> "How have you been recently?"
>
> Speaker B: **Mámahūhū.**
>
> "So-so."

> Speaker A: **Nǐde Zhōngguo huà jiǎngde zhēn hǎo!**
>
> "You speak Chinese really well!"
>
> Speaker B: **Mámahūhū la.**
>
> "It's only so-so."

2B.   **REDUPLICATED STATIVE VERBS AS ADVERBS.** In this line notice the adverb **hǎohāo** "very well" in the sentence **Xiǎolíng, nǐ hǎohāo xiūxi ba** "Xiaoling, you rest real well." The adverb **hǎohāo** derives, as you may have guessed, from **hǎo** "be good." Actually, the idiomatic expression **mànmān lái** "take your time" (lit. "come slowly") that you learned in 13-2 also involves this type of reduplication. Monosyllabic stative verbs like **hǎo** or **màn** can be reduplicated, that is, doubled to function as adverbs; they then have a stronger, more vivid effect as compared with the basic stative verb. In Beijing speech, the second syllable of such reduplicated monosyllabic stative verbs is typically changed to the first tone, regardless of the tone of the underlying simple stative verb, and the second syllable is often followed by an **-r**. The explicit adverbial marker **-de** can also be added after the **-r**, so that the complete forms would then be **hǎohāorde** "very well" or **mànmānrde** (pronounced as **mànmārde**) "very slowly." To sum up, the basic pattern for reduplicated monosyllabic stative verbs used as adverbs is:

STATIVE VERB	**REDUPLICATED FORM (→ tone 1)**	**-R**	**-DE**
hǎo	hāo	-r	de
"very well"			

More examples of reduplicated stative verbs used as adverbs:

> **Nǐmen yào hǎohāor xuéxí!**
>
> "You all should do a good job studying!"

> **Xiǎomèi, kuàikuāirde pǎo!**
>
> "Little sister, run quickly!" (**kuàikuāirde** is pronounced as **kuàikuārde**)

> **Zhōngguo zì yào mànmānrde xiě cái hǎokàn.**
>
> "Chinese characters should be written slowly; only then do they look good." (**mànmānrde** is pronounced as **mànmārde**)

As we noted, reduplication of monosyllabic stative verbs gives additional emphasis and makes them more vivid. Since reduplication already implies a fairly high degree, the reduplicated stative verbs cannot be further modified by adverbs of degree such as **hěn** or **fēicháng**. So you couldn't say *hěn hǎohāorde or *fēicháng hǎohāorde. The change to Tone One for the second syllable and the addion of **-r** and **-de** are common in Beijing but don't necessarily occur in the Mandarin spoken elsewhere. Therefore, all of the following forms may be encountered, all with the same meaning of "very well":

> hǎohāo
>
> hǎohāor
>
> hǎohāode
>
> hǎohāorde
>
> hǎohǎo
>
> hǎohǎode

Finally, we should mention that not only monosyllabic stative verbs but also bisyllabic stative verbs can be reduplicated to serve as adverbs. Whereas monosyllabic stative verbs reduplicate as A → AA, bisyllabic ones reduplicate as AB → AABB. Moreover, the second of the four syllables is usually neutral tone, while the other three syllables all have their full tones. For example, **gāoxìng** "be happy" becomes **gāogaoxìngxìngde** "very happily." This could occur in a sentence as follows:

> **Gāogaoxìngxìngde shàngbān, píngping'ān'ānde huíjiā.**
>
> "Go to work happily, and come home safely."

Other examples of reduplicated bisyllabic stative verbs are **ānjìng** "be quiet" → **ān'anjìngjìngde** "very quietly" and **qīngsōng** "be relaxed" → **qīngqingsōngsōngde** "very relaxedly." In the case of bisyllabic stative verbs the second syllable of which is neutral tone, the original tone of the second syllable is restored when reduplicated. Example: **qīngchu** "be clear" → **qīngqingchǔchǔde** "very clearly."

2C.   **Wǒ bù duō zuòle** "I won't sit any more," that is, "I'll be leaving now."

3.   Look at the sentence **Chīle fàn zài zǒu ba**. It could be translated as "Having eaten then again go, how about it?" or "Why don't you first eat and then go?" or "Why don't you have dinner with us first, before leaving?" The completed action suffix **-le** attached to the verb **chī** indicates that the action of eating will have been completed prior to the action of departing.

4A.   **Nǐ duō zhùyì shēnti** "Watch your health" (lit. "You more pay attention to body"). This is often said to people who are or have been sick. Other things you can say to sick people include **Xīwàng nǐde bìng kuài yidianr hǎo** "I hope that your illness will become better soon" and **Zhù nǐ zǎo rì kāngfù!** "I wish you that you may recover as soon as possible" (lit. "Wish you early day health restored!").

4B. **Bié tài lèile** literally means "Don't be too tired." In English we might say "Don't do too much" or "Don't overdo it."

5. **Yǒu shì wǒ huì shuōde** means "(If) there is any matter, I'll be sure to say (it)" or "If there is anything, I'll be sure to let you know." Review the **huì...-de** construction that expresses strong likelihood, which we first saw in 13-2: 7C.

7. **Gǎitiān zài lái wánr ba** literally means "Change the day again come play, how about it?", i.e., "On another day come again and have some fun" or "Come visit us again some day soon."

7–8. **POLITE TALK.** Notice that in line 7 as Linda Fuentes prepares to leave, Mrs. Hu invites her to visit their home again in the future and in line 8 Fuentes replies **Hǎo, yídìng lái** "O.K., I'll definitely come." It's important to understand that comments like these are merely **kèqi huà** or "polite talk" and aren't necessarily to be taken literally. Chinese speakers will sometimes say things like **Shémme shíhou dào wǒ jiā lái wánr?** "When will you come to my home to have a good time?" A response such as "O.K., let me check my schedule and see when I have time" would be inappropriate. The best response would probably be something like **Hǎo, wǒ yǒukòngr yídìng lái** "All right, I'll definitely come when I'm free," even if you're not sure whether or not you'll really go. This doesn't mean that Chinese speakers are insincere but rather that Chinese social custom calls for making polite comments like this. (Of course, American society is not so very different; just think of how many Americans will remark "We'll have to get together some time" but then there is never any follow up!) In general, if a comment is repeated many times, then there is a much higher likelihood that it is really meant. In American society, responsibility for successful transmission of a message rests largely with the speaker; if you have something to say, it's your job to say it as clearly and concisely as possible. Communication in Chinese society is much more hearer-based, that is to say, a good deal of the responsibility for ensuring that communication is successful lies with the hearer, who must work diligently through the "small talk" and the "polite talk" to identify and interpret the true intent of a message.

SV2–5. As with the word **xīngqī** "week," use of the measure **ge** is optional before **xuéqī** "semester, term." So you can say either **shàngxuéqī** or **shàngge xuéqī** to mean "last semester," and you can say either **xiàxuéqī** or **xiàge xuéqī** to mean "next semester."

SV2–5. The word for "semester" or "term" is in Taiwan pronounced **xuéqí**.

SV5. **Nǐde xuéqī bàogào shi guānyú shémmede?** "What is your term paper about?" The **shi...-de** in this sentence is the "situational" **shi...-de** that emphasizes a situation or describes how things are (16-3: 3C).

A Farewell Call on a Favorite Teacher

After living in Beijing for a year, American student Randy Lewis is preparing to return to the U.S. The day before he leaves, he visits the home of his favorite Chinese teacher, Professor Ding, to say goodbye. Mrs. Ding opens the door to let him in.

Basic Conversation 19-3

1. LEWIS

Qǐng wèn, zhèr shi Dīng Lǎoshī jiā ma?
Excuse me, is this Professor Ding's home?

2. MRS. DING

Duì, qǐng jìn.
Yes, please come in.

(calls to back room) **Lǎo Dīng, lái kèrén le.**
Old Ding, you have a guest.

3. PROFESSOR DING

(as he enters living room) **Shéi a? Ài, shi nǐ a! Kuài qǐng zuò.**
Who is it? Oh, it's you! Come on, sit down.

4. LEWIS

Lǎoshī, wǒ xiàng nín gàobié laile.
Professor, I've come to bid you farewell.

5. PROFESSOR DING

Nǐ shémme shíhou zǒu a?
When are you leaving?

6. LEWIS

Xiàxīngqīsān.
Next Wednesday.

7. PROFESSOR DING

Āiya, shíjiān guòde zhēn kuài! Zhuǎnyǎn jiù yìnián le. Jìde nǐ gāng láide shíhou, lián yíjù jiǎndānde Zhōngguo huà dōu bú huì shuō. Xiànzài yǐjīng néng duì-dá-rú-liúle.
Gosh, time really passes quickly! In the blink of an eye a year has passed. I remember when you had just come, you couldn't say even a simple phrase in Chinese. And now you can already converse fluently.

8. LEWIS

Duō kuī lǎoshīde bāngmáng. Zhèyìnián wǒ kě zhēn méi shǎo gěi nín tiān máfan.
It's all thanks to your help. This past year I really have put you to too much trouble.

🔘 Build Up

1. Lewis
   Dīng
   Qǐng wèn, zhèr shi Dīng Lǎoshī jiā ma?

   Ding [SN]
   Excuse me, is this Professor Ding's home?

2. Mrs. Ding
   Duì, qǐng jìn.

   Yes, please come in.

   lái kèrén le
   Lǎo Dīng, lái kèrén le.

   a guest has come
   Old Ding, you have a guest.

3. Professor Ding
   Shéi a? Ài, shi nǐ a! Kuài qǐng zuò.

   Who is it? Oh, it's you! Come on, sit down.

4. Lewis
   xiàng
   gàobié
   xiàng nín gàobié
   Lǎoshī, wǒ xiàng nín gàobié laile.

   toward, to [CV]
   bid farewell, take leave [V]
   bid farewell to you
   Professor, I've come to bid you farewell.

5. Professor Ding
   Nǐ shémme shíhou zǒu a?

   When are you leaving?

6. Lewis
   Xiàxīngqīsān.

   Next Wednesday.

7. Professor Ding
   āiya
   shíjiān guòde zhēn kuài
   zhuǎnyǎn
   jìde nǐ gāng láide shíhou
   lián
   lián...dōu...
   lián yíjù jiǎndānde Zhōngguo
   huà dōu bú huì shuō
   duì-dá-rú-liú

   "gosh" [I]
   time passes really quickly
   blink the eyes, glance [VO]
   I remember when you had just come
   even [CV]
   even [PT]
   couldn't say even a simple phrase of Chinese

   reply to questions fluently [EX]

   Āiya, shíjiān guòde zhēn kuài! Zhuǎnyǎn
   jiù yìnián le. Jìde nǐ gāng láide shíhou,
   lián yíjù jiǎndānde Zhōngguo huà
   dōu bú huì shuō. Xiànzài yǐjīng néng
   duì-dá-rú-liúle.

   Gosh, time really passes quickly! In the blink of
   an eye a year has passed. I remember when
   you had just come, you couldn't say even a
   simple phrase in Chinese. And now you can
   already converse fluently.

8. Lewis
   duō kuī
   duō kuī lǎoshīde bāngmáng
   zhèyìnián
   tiān
   máfan
   méi shǎo gěi nín tiān máfan
   Duō kuī lǎoshīde bāngmáng. Zhèyìnián
   wǒ kě zhēn méi shǎo gěi nín tiān máfan.

   be thanks to [PH]
   thanks to the teacher's help
   this year
   add [V]
   trouble [N]
   didn't cause too little trouble for you
   It's all thanks to your help. This past year I
   really have put you to too much trouble.

Supplementary Vocabulary

1. fāyīn	pronunciation [N]
yǔfǎ	grammar [N]
cíhuì	vocabulary [N]
Tāde fāyīn gēn yǔfǎ hái bú cuò,	Her pronunciation and grammar are pretty good,
kěshi cíhuì bú gòu.	but she doesn't have enough vocabulary.
2. biāozhǔn	be standard [SV]
liúlì	be fluent [SV]
Tāde Pǔtōnghuà shuōde yòu biāozhǔn	She speaks Mandarin both correctly and
yòu liúlì.	fluently.
3. shēngchǎn	produce [V]
Nǐmende gōngchǎng shēngchǎn shémme ne?	What does your factory produce?

Grammatical and Cultural Notes

1. Even though there is in Chinese a formal word for professor (**jiàoshòu**) that would be used, for example, as a title on a name card, the term **lǎoshī** is commonly used for professors in direct address or when referring to them in front of others.

2. **INVERTED SUBJECT AND VERB FOR UNSPECIFIED SUBJECTS.** Consider the sentence **Lái kèrén le** "There has come a guest" or "A guest has come" or "Some guests have come." In Chinese, unspecified, indefinite subjects sometimes follow rather than precede the verb. While the sentence **Kèrén láile** would also be correct, the meaning would be a little different; the latter sentence would mean "The guest has come" or "The guests have come," in other words, specific guests that the speaker knows about. The pattern for subject-verb inversion with unspecified subjects is:

VERB	SUBJECT	SENTENCE FINAL PARTICLE
Lái	**kèrén**	**le.**

"A guest has come."

Some more examples of subject-verb inversion with unspecified subjects:

Nàr sǐle bù shǎo rén.	"A lot of people died there."
Láile yíwèi Zhāng Xiānsheng.	"A Mr. Zhang has come."
Nàr xīn kāile yìjiā Rìběn guǎnzi.	"A Japanese restaurant has newly opened there."
Yòu zǒule yíge.	"Another one has departed." (e.g., talking about old friends who have passed on)

4A. Since Professor Ding is the only professor present, it's sufficient (and actually more respectful) to simply say **Lǎoshī** rather than to add the surname and say **Dīng Lǎoshī**. Similarly, to address a university president, you'd normally just say **Xiàozhǎng** without the surname unless, for example, you were at a meeting of university presidents, where you'd then have to distinguish among the different presidents by saying **Zhāng Xiàozhǎng**, **Lǐ Xiàozhǎng** and so on.

4B. The coverb **xiàng**, which means "to" or "toward," is quite common. Besides in the pattern **xiàng...gàobié** "bid farewell to...," **xiàng** can also be used by itself in expressions indicating direction toward, in place of **wàng**. Examples:

xiàng dōng zǒu	"walk toward the east"
xiàng qián kāi	"drive toward the front"

4C. **Lǎoshī, wǒ xiàng nín gàobié laile** "Professor, I've come to bid you farewell." Observe the position of **laile** at the end of this sentence. A more common way of saying this would be **Wǒ lái xiàng nín gàobié**. In Beijing speech, the verbs **lái** and **qù** can sometimes be repeated at the ends of sentences, for example, **Wǒ lái xiàng nín gàobié laile** "I have come to say goodbye to you" or **Tā qù mǎi dōngxi qule** "She went to buy things." In the sentence under consideration here, the first **lái** in **Wǒ lái xiàng nín gàobié laile** has been omitted.

6. Examine **xiàxīngqīsān** "next Wednesday." This could also be said as **xiàge xīngqīsān**; either way is correct. Grammatically, the word **xīngqī** "week" can function either as a noun (in which case it requires the measure **ge** before it) or as a measure (in which case you add a specifier like **xià-** directly). Similarly, you can say either **shàngxīngqī** or **shàngge xīngqī** for "last week." The other word for "week," **lǐbài**, can also function as either noun or measure. More examples:

xiàxīngqī	"next Monday"
xiàge xīngqīwǔ	"next Friday"
xiàlǐbài'èr	"next Tuesday"
xiàge lǐbàiliù	"next Saturday"
shàngxīngqītiān	"last Sunday"
shàngge xīngqīsān	"last Wednesday"
shànglǐbàisì	"last Thursday"
shàngge lǐbàiyī	"last Monday"

Be aware that Chinese **xīngqī** and **lǐbài** are used more strictly than English "week" is. When Chinese people say "next week," they mean "some time during the seven days that begin with the next Monday." So **xiàxīngqīsān** means "Wednesday of the next whole week" (which starts on the following Monday), NOT the next day from now that happens to be a Wednesday. "Wednesday of this week" would be **zhèixīngqīsān** while "Wednesday of last week" would be **shàngxīngqīsān**.

7A. **Zhuǎnyǎn** literally means "turn or revolve the eyes." **Zhuǎnyǎn jiù yìnián le** means "You turn your eyes and it's a year," that is, "In no time at all another year has passed."

7B. **LIÁN...DŌU... AND LIÁN...YĚ....** The paired adverb pattern **lián...dōu...** and its synonym **lián...yě...** both mean "even." The coverb **lián** literally means "link up" or "include." **Lián** is placed before the element to be emphasized (which can be subject, object, or some other element), and **dōu** or **yě** is placed before the verb. The basic pattern is:

LIÁN	(ELEMENT TO BE EMPHASIZED)	DŌU/YĚ	VERB PHRASE
lián	yíjù jiǎndānde Zhōngguo huà	dōu	bú huì shuō

"couldn't speak even a simple phrase of Chinese"

More examples of **lián...dōu...** and **lián...yě...**:

Lián wǒ dōu huì.

"Even I know how."

Xiǎo Wáng fēicháng xǐhuan kàn diànshì, lián chīfànde shíhou dōu kàn.

"Little Wang loves watching TV, he watches even while eating."

Lián nǐ dōu bú qùle, hái yǒu shéi huì qù?

"If not even you are going, who else would there be that would go?"

Lián Wáng Lǎoshī dōu bú rènshi zhèige zì.

"Even Professor Wang doesn't recognize this character."

Zhèige wèntí lián tā dōu jiějuébuliǎo, wǒ dāngrán yě méi bànfǎ.

"Even she can't solve this problem, of course there's nothing I can do."

Tā lián yíkuài qián yě méiyou.

"He doesn't even have one dollar."

Yǐjīng bādiǎn duōle, zěmme lián yíge rén yě méi lái ne?

"It's already past eight, how come not even a single person has come?"

Tā shi Běijīng rén, búguò tā shuō Wànlǐ Chángchéng tā lián yícì yě méi qùguo!

"She's from Beijing, but she said that she hasn't even been to the Great Wall once!"

In **lián...dōu...** and **lián...yě...** sentences, if there is an object and if the sentence is affirmative, then the object cannot be modified by **yī** "one." For example, in English, we could say "You've got everything, even a swimming pool!" But in Chinese this would have to be **Nǐmen shémme dōu yǒu, lián yóuyǒngchí dōu yǒu!** You could NOT say: *****Nǐmen shémme dōu yǒu, lián yíge yóuyǒngchí dōu yǒu!**

8A. Note the phrase **duō kuī** "thanks to" as in **Duō kuī lǎoshīde bāngmáng** "Thanks for your help." Some more examples of **duō kuī**:

Duōkuī tā jiè qián gěi wǒ, wǒ cái néng píng'ānde huíjiā.

"My being able to return home safely is all thanks to her lending me some money."

Duōkuī nǐ tíxǐng wǒ, wǒ cái méi bǎ zhèijiàn shì gěi wàngle.

"My not forgetting about this is all thanks to your reminding me."

Duōkuī nínde bāngzhù, yàoburán zhèipiān bàogào wǒ kě xiěbuchūlai!

"It's all thanks to your help, otherwise I would never have been able to write this report!"

8B. **Wǒ kě zhēn méi shǎo gěi nín tiān máfan** literally means "I indeed really didn't too little for you add trouble," that is, "I really did add a lot of trouble for you" or "I really have put you to too much trouble." This is a good example of the Chinese predilection for indirectness (i.e., if you didn't add too little trouble, then you probably did add a lot of trouble). Two more examples with **méi shǎo**:

Tā yě méi shǎo huā qián.

"He sure did spend quite a lot of money." (lit. "He also didn't spend too little money.")

Wǒ méi shǎo cìhou tā.

"I really did serve him quite a lot." (lit. "I also didn't serve him too little." This was said by an elderly woman recollecting the care she had provided to her husband while he was still alive; **cìhou** means "wait upon" or "serve.")

SV2. In China, where many people speak Mandarin with an accent, it's considered praiseworthy to be able to speak "standard" Mandarin. Therefore, if your pronunciation is reasonably good, you may be told **Nǐde Pǔtōnghuà shuōde hěn biāozhǔn** or **Nǐde Guóyǔ shuōde hěn biāozhǔn**, both of which mean "Your Mandarin is very accurate." Similarly, you could praise your Chinese friends by saying **Nǐde Yīngyǔ shuōde hěn biāozhǔn!**

A Farewell Call on a Favorite Teacher (cont.)

Lewis continues his conversation with Professor Ding and gets ready to leave (continued from the previous conversation).

 Basic Conversation 19-4

1. LEWIS		**Shuō shízàide, yào bú shi nín jiào-xué-yǒu-fāng, wǒ yě bù kěnéng jìnbùde zhèmme kuài.**
		To tell the truth, if it hadn't been for your excellent teaching, I wouldn't have been able to progress so quickly.
2. PROFESSOR DING		**Nǎrde huà. Zhè shi lǎoshī yīng jìnde zérèn ma. Qíshí, zhǔyào hái shi nǐ zìjǐ nǔlìde jiéguǒ.**
		Not at all. This is what a teacher is supposed to do! Actually, this is mostly the result of your own hard work.
		(after conversing for a while)
3. LEWIS		**Lǎoshī, shíjiān bù zǎole, wǒ gāi huíqule.**
		Sir, it's getting late, I should be going back now.
4. PROFESSOR DING		**Zài dāi huǐr ba!**
		Why don't you stay a bit longer?
5. LEWIS		**Bù le, wǒ hái yǒu diǎnr shì.**
		No, I have something else I have to do.
6. PROFESSOR DING		**Hǎo, nà wǒ jiù bù liú nǐ le. Huí Měiguo hòu, dài wǒ xiàng nǐde fùmǔ wènhǎo. Bié wàngle yǒukòng gěi wǒmen láixìn.**
		O.K., then I won't keep you. When you get back to America, give my best to your parents. Don't forget to send us a letter when you have time.
7. LEWIS		**Lǎoshī, zàijiàn!**
		Goodbye, Professor!
		(to Mrs. Ding) **Shīmǔ, zàijiàn!**
		Goodbye, Mrs. Ding!

8. PROFESSOR DING   **Zàijiàn.**
                            Goodbye.

9. MRS. DING   **Zàijiàn.**
                            Goodbye.

 **Build Up**

---

1. Lewis

   shuō shízàide   to tell the truth [PH]
   yào bú shi   if not, if it weren't for [PH]
   jiào-xué-yǒu-fāng   have an especially effective method in one's teaching [EX]
   jìnbù   progress [V/N]
   Shuō shízàide, yào bú shi nín   To tell the truth, if it hadn't been for your
   jiào-xué-yǒu-fāng, wǒ yě bù kěnéng   excellent teaching, I wouldn't have been
   jìnbùde zhèmme kuài.   able to progress so quickly.

---

2. Professor Ding

   nǎrde huà   "not at all" [IE]
   yīng   should [AV]
   jìn   carry out, fulfill [V]
   zérèn   responsibility [N]
   yīng jìnde zérèn   a responsibility one should carry out
   jiéguǒ   result [N]
   nǐ zìjǐ nǔlìde jiéguǒ   the result of your own hard work
   Nǎrde huà. Zhè shi lǎoshī yīng jìnde Not at all. This is what a teacher is supposed to
   zérèn ma. Qíshí, zhǔyào hái shi nǐ zìjǐ do! Actually, this is mostly the result of your own
   nǔlìde jiéguǒ.   hard work.

---

3. Lewis

   wǒ gāi huíqule   I should go back now
   Lǎoshī, shíjiān bù zǎole, wǒ gāi huíqule. Sir, it's getting late, I should be going back now.

---

4. Professor Ding
   Zài dāi huǐr ba!   Why don't you stay a bit longer?

---

5. Lewis
   Bù le, wǒ hái yǒu diǎnr shì.   No, I have something else I have to do.

---

6. Professor Ding

   liú   ask someone to stay [V]
   wǒ jiù bù liú nǐ le   then I won't make you stay
   ...hòu   after... [PT]
   huí Měiguo hòu   after (you) return to America
   dài   for, on behalf of [CV]
   dài A xiàng B wènhǎo   on behalf of A convey regards to B [PT]
   dài wǒ xiàng   on my behalf send regards to
   nǐde fùmǔ wènhǎo   your parents
   xìn   letter [N] (M: **fēng**)
   láixìn   send a letter [VO]
   Hǎo, nà wǒ jiù bù liú nǐ le. Huí Měiguo hòu, O.K., then I won't keep you. When you get back
   dài wǒ xiàng nǐde fùmǔ wènhǎo. Bié wàngle to America, give my best to your parents. Don't
   yǒukòng gěi wǒmen láixìn.   forget to send us a letter when you have time.

7. Lewis
Lǎoshī, zàijiàn!   Goodbye, Professor!

    shīmǔ   wife of one's teacher [N]
Shīmǔ, zàijiàn!   Goodbye, Mrs. Ding!

8. Professor Ding
Zàijiàn.   Goodbye.

9. Mrs. Ding
Zàijiàn.   Goodbye.

 ## Supplementary Vocabulary

1. **jì**   send [V]
    jìgěi   send to [V+PV]
    bāoguǒ   package, parcel [N]
Zhèmme dàde bāoguǒ, nǐ yào jìgěi shéi?   Whom are you going to send such a big parcel?

2. **jì hángkōng**   send by airmail
    míngxìnpiàn   picture postcard [N] (M: **zhāng**)
    tiē   stick [V]
    yóupiào   stamp [N] (M: **zhāng**)
Qǐng wèn, zhèizhāng míngxìnpiàn rúguǒ jì hángkōngde huà, yào tiē duōshǎo qiánde yóupiào?   Excuse me, if I send this postcard by airmail, how much in stamps do I have to stick on it?

Grammatical and Cultural Notes

1A.   **Shuō shízàide** "to tell the truth" is a common introductory phrase. You should try to memorize and often use introductory phrases like this. They will make your speech appear more fluent and give you a bit of extra time to think about what to say next.

1B.   **YÀO BÚ SHI....** The pattern **yào bú shi...** literally means "if is not..." but is usually translated as "if not..." or "if it weren't for...." **Yào bú shi** may precede or follow the subject of the first clause; in the second clause there is almost always an adverb like **jiù** "then," **yě** "also," **hái** "still," or **yídìng**. The pattern is:

YÀO BÚ SHI	CLAUSE₁	CLAUSE₂
Yào bú shi	nín jiào-xué-yǒu-fāng,	wǒ yě bù kěnéng jìnbùde zhèmme kuài.

"If it hadn't been for your excellent teaching, I wouldn't have been able to progress so quickly."

More examples of **yào bú shi...**:

Yào bú shi nǐ gàosu wǒ, wǒ yě bú huì zhīdao.

"If you hadn't told me, I wouldn't know."

Yào bú shi nǐ sòng wǒ qù yīyuàn, wǒde bìng yídìng hǎobuliǎo.

"If you hadn't taken me to the hospital, I'm sure I wouldn't have gotten better."

Zhèxiē zì yào bú shi Wáng Xiáojie xiěde, jiù shi Zhāng Xiānsheng xiěde.

"If these characters weren't written by Ms. Wang, then they were written by Mr. Zhang."

Nèixiē rén yào bú shi Rìběn rén jiù shi Hánguo rén, yídìng bú shi Zhōngguo rén.

"If those people aren't Japanese then they're Korean, they're definitely not Chinese."

The **yào** in **yào bú shi** means "if." Review other meanings of **yào** which you've encountered up to this point in this course: "cost" (3-3); "take time" (3-4); "will" (4-3); "want" (5-1); "request" (8-3); and "should" (14-4).

1C.   The word **jìnbù** "progress" can function both as verb and as noun. In the first example below, **jìnbù** is a verb; in the second example, it's a noun:

Zuìjìn nǐ jìnbùde hěn kuài.

"Recently you've progressed very quickly."

Zuìjìn nǐde jìnbù hěn dà.

"Recently you've made a lot of progress." (lit. "Recently your progress has been great.")

2A.   **Nǎrde huà** literally means "Words from where?", that is, "Why would you say something like that?" In this Basic Conversation, Professor Ding doesn't accept the compliment made him, whereas in America we would often accept and say "Thank you." **Nǎrde huà** has basically the same meaning as **Náli**, which you've seen before as a response for deflecting compliments.

2B.   Note the phrase **yīng jìnde zérèn** "a responsibility that one should carry out." The **yīng** here is semi-literary formal style. More colloquial would be **yīnggāi** or **yīngdāng**.

2C.   The common and important noun **jiéguǒ** means "result." The phrase **nǐ zìjǐ nǔlìde jiéguǒ** literally means "you yourself hard-working's result" or "the result of you yourself being hard-working" or "the result of your own hard work."

3.   **Shíjiān bù zǎole** "The time is no longer early" or "It's getting late" is a useful expression when you wish to leave someone's home. After saying this sentence, you often add something like **Wǒ děi zǒule** or **Wǒ gāi huíqule** and slowly get up to leave.

4.   Even if the host is secretly hoping the guest will leave soon, good etiquette demands that the host indicate his or her wish that the guest stay a little longer. Cf. the note on polite talk in 19-2: 7–8.

5.   If the guest doesn't wish to accept the invitation to stay longer, he or she should say something like **Xièxie nín, kěshi wǒ zhēnde děi zǒule** "Thank you, but I really must go." Indication of the reason for having to leave is common, but a general explanation is usually all that's offered, for example, **Wǒ hái yǒu diǎnr shì** "I still have some things to do."

6A.   **Huí Měiguo hòu...** "After you return to America...." Chinese speakers are in general more sensitive to the literal meaning of **huí** (and **huílai** "come back" and **huíqu** "go back") than are Americans. An American in China who is traveling to America should always say **huí**, since America is where Americans come from. To a Chinese, it would sound strange for an American in China to say ***Xiàlǐbài wǒ dào Měiguo qù**. Instead, you should say **Xiàlǐbài wǒ huí Měiguo qù**.

6B.   **Hòu** is an abbreviated form of **yǐhòu** or **zhīhòu**.

6C.   **DÀI A XIÀNG B WÈNHǍO.** The pattern **dài A xiàng B wènhǎo** literally means "on behalf of A convey regards to B." In freer English, it often translates as "convey someone's regards to someone else." Observe the sentence in the conversation **Dài wǒ xiàng nǐde fùmǔ wènhǎo**, literally "Represent me toward your parents greet," or in more idiomatic English, "Convey greetings to your parents on my behalf." We see here again the use of **xiàng** "to" or "toward" (19-3: 4B). This is rather formal usage. To sum up, the pattern is:

dài   wǒ   xiàng   nǐde fùmǔ   wènhǎo

"send regards on my behalf to your parents"

Another example:

Qǐng nín dài wǒmen xiàng Lín Xiàozhǎng wènhǎo.

"Please convey our regards to President Lin."

Instead of **Dài wǒ xiàng nǐde fùmǔ wènhǎo**, you can also say **Dài wǒ wèn nǐde fùmǔ hǎo**, with the same meaning.

6D.   Be sure to learn the noun **xìn** "letter." The measure for **xìn** is **fēng**, so you say **yìfēng xìn** "a letter." Here is another example with **xìn**:

Tā měicì xiěde xìn dōu hěn cháng.   "Every letter she writes is very long."

7.   **Shīmǔ** is a polite term of address for the wife of one's teacher. So if a Mr. Li were your teacher and he were married, you'd call him **Lǎoshī** and you'd call his wife **Shīmǔ**. This would be considered more proper usage than to call them **Lǐ Xiānsheng** and **Lǐ Tàitai**. The term of address for the husband of one's teacher is **shīzhàng**, so if your teacher were Mrs. Li, then you'd call her **Lǎoshī** and her husband **Shīzhàng**.

SV1.   The verb **jì** means "send (through the mail)." For "send to someone," say **jìgěi**. For "send to some place," say **jìdào**. Examples:

Wǒ yào jìgěi wǒ fùmǔ.   "I want to send it to my parents."

Wǒ yào jìdào Měiguo.   "I want to send it to America."

Wǒ yào bǎ zhèifēng xìn jìdào Měiguo.   "I want to send this letter to America."

Unit 19: Review and Study Guide

New Vocabulary

AUXILIARY VERBS
yīng — should

COVERBS
dài — for, on behalf of
guānyú — about, concerning
lián — even
xiàng — toward, to

EXPRESSIONS
duì-dá-rú-liú — reply to questions fluently
jiào-xué-yǒu-fāng — have an especially effective method in one's teaching

IDIOMATIC EXPRESSIONS
mámahūhū — so-so, fair
nǎrde huà — "not at all"

INTERJECTIONS
āiya — "gosh"

MEASURES
mén — (for courses)
piān — (for theses, reports, essays)

NOUNS
bàogào — report
bāoguǒ — package, parcel
bìng — illness, disease
chéngjī — grade (on test or in course)
cíhuì — vocabulary
fāyīn — pronunciation
gōngfu — time
jiéguǒ — result
jìnbù — progress
kǎoshì — test
lùnwén — thesis, dissertation
máfan — trouble
míngxìnpiàn — picture postcard

shīmǔ — wife of one's teacher
xìn — letter
xuéfēn — credit, credit hour
xuéqī — semester, term
yóupiào — stamp
yǔfǎ — grammar
zérèn — responsibility

PATTERNS
dài A xiàng B wènhǎo — on behalf of A convey regards to B
...hòu — after...
hái bú shi... — if it isn't...
lián...dōu... — even
yǒu yìdiǎn(r)... — be a little...

PHRASES
bìyè lùnwén — honors thesis

duō kuī	be thanks to
lái diànhuà	call on the telephone
qīmò kǎoshì	final examination
qīzhōng kǎoshì	mid-term examination
shuō shízàide	to tell the truth
xuéqī bàogào	term paper
yào bú shi	if not, if it weren't for
zhí dào	straight up to, until

PLACE WORDS

| wòfáng | bedroom |

RESULTATIVE COMPOUNDS

kǎoyūn	become dizzy from testing
pǎolai	run over here, come over
pǎoqu	run over there

RESULTATIVE ENDINGS

| -yūn | dizzy |

STATIVE VERBS

biāozhǔn	be standard
liúlì	be fluent
yūn	be dizzy

SURNAMES

| Dīng | Ding |

VERBS

bìng	get sick
gàobié	bid farewell
huā	spend (money, time)
jì	send
jìn	carry out, fulfill
jìnbù	progress
kǎo	take a test
liú	ask someone to stay
pǎo	run

shēngchǎn	produce
tǎng	lie down
tiān	add
tiē	stick
xiū	study, take (courses, credits)
xuǎn	choose, select
zhuàn	earn

VERB + POSTVERB

| jìgěi | send to |

VERB-OBJECT COMPOUNDS

huāqián	spend money
kǎoshì	test
láixìn	send a letter
pǎobù	run
zhuànqián	earn money
zhuǎnyǎn	blink the eyes, glance

Major New Grammar Patterns

DIFFERENT WAYS TO EXPRESS "SICK": Tā bìngle. "She's sick.", **Tā méiyou bìng.** "She's not sick." (19-1)

DIFFERENT WORDS FOR "TIME": Nǐ yǒu méiyou gōngfu?/Nǐ yǒu méiyou kòng(r)?/Nǐ yǒu méiyou shíjiān? "Do you have free time?", **Nǐ shémme shíhou qù?** "What time will you go?", **Yào duō cháng shíjiān?** "How much time will it take?" (19-1)

REDUPLICATION OF MEASURES AND NOUNS TO MEAN "EACH" OR "EVERY": rénrén "everybody," **tiāntian** "every day," **niánnián** "every year" (19-1)

YǑU (YÌ)DIǍNR + VERB: Wǒ yǒu diǎnr yūn. "I'm a little dizzy.", **Wǒ yǒu diǎnr è.** "I'm a bit hungry.", **Cài yǒu yìdiǎnr là.** "The food is a little spicy hot." (19-1)

REDUPLICATED STATIVE VERBS AS ADVERBS: hǎohāor(de) "well," **mànmānr(de)** "slowly," **kuàikuār(de)** "quickly" (19-2)

INVERTED SUBJECT AND VERB FOR UNSPECIFIED SUBJECTS: Lái kèrén le. "A guest has come.", **Sǐle bù shǎo rén.** "A lot of people died." (19-3)

LIÁN...DŌU... AND LIÁN...YĚ...: Lián wǒ dōu huì. "Even I know.", **Tā lián yíkuài qián yě méiyou.** "He doesn't have even one dollar." (19-3)

YÀO BÚ SHI...: Yào bú shi nín jiào-xué-yǒu-fāng, wǒ yě bù kěnéng jìnbùde zhèmme kuài. "If it weren't for your excellent teaching, I wouldn't have been able to progress so quickly." (19-4)

DÀI A XIÀNG B WÈNHǍO: Dài wǒ xiàng nǐde fùmǔ wènhǎo. "Send my regards to your parents." (19-4)

Leisure Time Activities (I)

COMMUNICATIVE OBJECTIVES

Once you've mastered this unit, you'll be able to use Chinese to:

1. Ask people about their hobbies and discuss your own hobbies when you are asked: music (piano, guitar, violin), singing, watching Peking opera, going to the movies, visiting museums, reading, painting, calligraphy, photography, stamp collecting, chess, checkers, etc.

2. Invite someone to watch a film or attend a Peking opera performance with you, and respond appropriately if someone else invites you to a film or to the opera.

3. Talk about going to the movies: different kinds of films, stars and directors, where in the theater the seats are located, impressions of the movie after seeing it.

4. Discuss your future career plans.

5. Handle computer terminology such as surfing the web, sending e-mails, and sending text messages.

6. Express fractions: "one-third," "three-fourths," etc.

7. Express percent: "10%," "95%," etc.

8. Express decimals: "1.6," "2.85," etc.

P
A
R
T

1

Hobbies

Sally Lee, who is spending her junior year in Beijing, has been invited to the home of a Chinese classmate. After dinner the two young women, who have only recently become acquainted, sit on the sofa and ask about each other's hobbies.

Basic Conversation 20-1

1. CHINESE	**Lǐ Wén, nǐ yǒu shémme shìhào ma?**	
	Sally, do you have any hobbies?	
2. LEE	**Wǒ xǐhuan yīnyuè. Cóng xiǎo zài Měiguo xué gāngqín.**	
	I like music. From the time I was little, I've been studying piano in America.	
3. CHINESE	**Guàibudé cháng kàn nǐ yìbiān zǒu yìbiān hēng diàozi.**	
	No wonder I often see you humming a tune while you walk.	
4. LEE	**Shì ma?**	
	Really?	
5. CHINESE	**Chúle yīnyuè, nǐ hái yǒu qítāde àihào ma?**	
	Besides music, do you have any other hobbies?	
6. LEE	**Hái xǐhuan kàn xiǎoshuōr huòshi cānguān bówùguǎn. Nǐ ne? Nǐde shìhào shi shémme?**	
	I also like to read novels or visit museums. And you? What are your hobbies?	
7. CHINESE	**Huàhuàr, tèbié shi guóhuàr, hái yǒu xiàqí. Wéiqí, Xiàngqí, Tiàoqí, wǒ dōu xià.**	
	Painting, especially Chinese painting, also playing Chinese chess. Go, Chinese chess, Chinese checkers, I play them all.	

Build Up

1. **Chinese**

shìhào   hobby [N]

Lǐ Wén, nǐ yǒu shémme shìhào ma?   Sally, do you have any hobbies?

2. **American**

cóng xiǎo	from the time when I was little
gāngqín	piano [N]
Wǒ xǐhuan yīnyuè. Cóng xiǎo zài Měiguo xué gāngqín.	I like music. From the time I was little, I've been studying piano in America.

3. **Chinese**

guàibudé	no wonder [MA]
hēng	hum [V]
diàozi	tune, melody [N]
hēng diàozi	hum a tune
yìbiān zǒu yìbiān hēng diàozi	hum a tune while one walks
Guàibudé cháng kàn nǐ yìbiān zǒu yìbiān hēng diàozi.	No wonder I often see you humming a tune while you walk.

4. **American**

shì ma	"really?" [IE]
Shì ma?	Really?

5. **Chinese**

chúle yīnyuè	besides music
àihào	interest, hobby [N]
qítāde àihào	other hobbies
Chúle yīnyuè, nǐ hái yǒu qítāde àihào ma?	Besides music, do you have any other hobbies?

6. **American**

xiǎoshuō(r)	novel [N] (M: **běn**)
kàn xiǎoshuōr	read novels
cānguān	visit [V]
bówùguǎn	museum [PW]
huòshi cānguān bówùguǎn	or visit museums
Hái xǐhuan kàn xiǎoshuōr huòshi cānguān bówùguǎn. Nǐ ne? Nǐde shìhào shi shémme?	I also like to read novels or visit museums. And you? What are your hobbies?

7. **Chinese**

huà	paint [V]
huà(r)	painting [N] (M: **zhāng**)
huàhuà(r)	paint paintings [VO]
guóhuà(r)	Chinese painting [N] (M: **fú**)
tèbié shi guóhuàr	it's especially Chinese painting
xià	play (chess or checkers) [V]
xiàqí	play chess [VO]
Wéiqí	Go (a kind of chess) [N]
Xiàngqí	Chinese chess [N]
Tiàoqí	Chinese checkers [N]
Huàhuàr, tèbié shi guóhuàr, hái yǒu xiàqí. Wéiqí, Xiàngqí, Tiàoqí, wǒ dōu xià.	Painting, especially Chinese painting, also playing Chinese chess. Go, Chinese chess, Chinese checkers, I play them all.

 ## Supplementary Vocabulary

1. | | |
|---|---|
| **chàng** | sing [V] |
| **gē(r)** | song [N] (M: **zhī**) |
| **chànggē(r)** | sing a song [VO] |
| **hǎotīng** | be nice-sounding, pretty [SV] |
| **Nǐ chàngde gēr zhēn hǎotīng.** | The songs you sing are really pretty. |

2. **kànshū**   read [VO]
   Wǒ měitiān kàn wǔge xiǎoshíde shū.   I read for five hours every day.

3. **zhào**   take (photographs) [V]
   zhàoxiàng   take photographs [VO]
   bāng wǒ zhào yìzhāng xiàng   take a photo for me
   Qǐng nín bāng wǒ zhào yìzhāng xiàng, hǎo ma?   Please take a picture for me, all right?

Additional Vocabulary: More Hobbies

1. **xià Xīyáng qí**   play Western chess [PH]
2. **jíyóu**   collect stamps [VO]
3. **shūfǎ**   calligraphy [N]
4. **xiě dōngxi**   write things, write [PH]
5. **diàoyú**   fish, go fishing [VO]
6. **dǎliè**   go hunting [VO]
7. **lùyíng**   go camping [VO]
8. **tīng yīnyuè**   listen to music [PH]
9. **tán**   play (a musical instrument) [V]
   tán gāngqín   play piano [PH]
   jíta   guitar [N]
   tán jíta   play guitar [PH]
   lā   pull [V]
   xiǎo tíqín   violin [PH]
   lā xiǎo tíqín   play violin [PH]

Nǐ xǐhuan tán gāngqín, tā xǐhuan tán jíta,   You like to play piano, she likes to play guitar,
wǒ xǐhuan lā xiǎo tíqín.   I like to play violin.

Grammatical and Cultural Notes

1A.   **Lǐ Wén, nǐ yǒu shémme shìhào ma?** "Sally, do you have any hobbies?" Remember that, because this sentence is already a question due to the **ma** at the end, the **shémme** must be interpreted as an indefinite ("some hobbies" or "any hobbies") and couldn't be interpreted as an interrogative ("what hobbies?").

1B.   Contrast **shìhào** "hobby" and **shíhou** "time."

1C.   Some Chinese speakers will cite smoking (**chōuyān**) as one of their "hobbies"! On the other hand, hardly anyone would name bicycle riding as a hobby, as they might in the U.S., since in China it's an important means of transportation.

3A.   **GUÀIBUDÉ.** Guàibudé "no wonder that" is gramatically a negative potential resultative compound composed of the verb **guài** "find strange," **-bù-** "not," and **dé** "can," that is, "cannot find something to be strange." **Guàibudé** expresses a sudden awareness of the reason why something is as it is. **Guàibudé** can function as an independent comment—for example, **Guàibudé!** "No wonder!"—or it can be followed by a sentence, which grammatically functions as the object of **guàibudé**. The meaning and use of **guàibudé** are similar to **nánguài** (7-3: 7A). The basic pattern involving **guàibudé** is:

GUÀIBUDÉ	SENTENCE
Guàibudé	tā hěn shǎo lái.

"No wonder he rarely comes."

More examples of **guàibudé**:

Tā hěn ài chī, guàibudé tā nèmme pàng!

"He loves to eat, no wonder he's so fat!"

> **Tā zhèmme yònggōng, guàibudé zǒng kǎode zhèmme hǎo.**
>
> "She's so diligent, no wonder she always does so well on tests."

> **Nǐ shuō tāmen chūqu lǚxíngle? Guàibudé wǒ zuìjìn méi kànjian tāmen.**
>
> "You say they went traveling? No wonder I haven't seen them recently."

> **Jiāzhōude tiānqi nèmme hǎo, guàibudé Zhōngguo rén dōu xǐhuan bāndao Jiāzhōu qù.**
>
> "The climate in California is so good, no wonder Chinese all like to move to California."

3B. Review **yìbiān(r)...yìbiān(r)...** "on the one hand..., on the other hand..." or "do one thing while you do another" (18-2: 5).

4. The idiomatic expression **Shì ma?** "Is that so?", "Really?", "You don't say?" is extremely common in mainland China but less common in other Chinese speech communities.

5. **Chúle yīnyuè, nǐ hái yǒu qítāde àihào ma?** "Besides music, do you have any other hobbies?" In 15-4: 5B, you were introduced to the patterns **chúle...yǐwài** and **chúle...zhīwài**, both of which mean "besides..." or "except...." In this line of this Basic Conversation, the **yǐwài** or **zhīwài** that usually follows has been omitted. It's not incorrect to omit the **yǐwài** or **zhīwài**, but we recommend you keep it in your own speech.

6. The verb **cānguān** "visit" can take only a place as its object, never a person. To express "visit a person," say **kàn yíge rén**.

7A. **Wéiqí** "Go" (i.e., the Asian board game) is played by two people; the objective is to encircle more territory than the opponent.

7B. In **Xiàngqí** "Chinese chess," which is also for two people, the aim is to take the opponent's general.

7C. **Wéiqí, Xiàngqí, Tiàoqí dōu xià** literally means "Go, Chinese chess, and Chinese checkers, (I) play them all." This is a good example of the Chinese preference to prepose objects, that is, to place objects at the beginning of the sentence, before the verb, rather than in the normal position toward the end of the sentence, after the verb.

SV1. Learn **hǎotīng** "be nice-sounding." As we noted in 6-1: SV3 when you learned **hǎochī** "be good to eat" and **hǎokàn** "be good-looking," **hǎo** can be prefixed to a number of verbs to create stative verbs meaning "be good to...," "be pleasant to...," or "be easy to...." **Hǎotīng** is the word to use for describing songs or music that you like; you couldn't use **piàoliang** "be pretty," which describes only things that are seen.

Students practicing oil painting on campus of National Taiwan Normal University

SV3A. While taking photographs of typical tourist sites is no problem, it's always best to ask for permission before taking photographs of individuals or when near sensitive places such as airports or military installations. The appropriate question is **Kéyi zhàoxiàng ma?** "May one take photographs?"

SV3B. Another common expression that means "take a photograph" is the verb-object construction **pāizhào**.

SV3C. In the U.S., when we're taking a photo and want our subjects to smile, we often say "Say 'cheese'!" In Chinese you try to get people to say the word **qiézi** "eggplant," for which they must open their mouths and spread their lips.

AV3. **Shūfǎ** "calligraphy" literally means "way of writing," since in Classical Chinese **shū** is a verb meaning "to write" and **fǎ** is a noun meaning "way" or "method" (10-3: 3F). In Modern Chinese, **shū** means "that which has been written" or "book."

Hobbies (cont.)

Lee is invited by her classmate to view a performance of the Peking opera The Chronicle of the White Snake (continued from the previous conversation).

 Basic Conversation 20-2

1. CHINESE	**Duìle, nǐ duì Jīngjù gǎn xìngqu ma?**	
	Oh, yes, are you interested in Peking opera?	
2. AMERICAN	**Jīngjù a? Wǒ suīrán bú tài dǒng, dànshi tǐng ài kàn.**	
	Peking opera? Though I don't understand it very well, I do love to watch it.	
3. CHINESE	**Zhèige xīngqīliù wǎnshang wǒ yào gēn fùmǔ yìqǐ qù Rénmín Jùchǎng kàn "Bái Shé Zhuàn." Zhènghǎo duō yìzhāng piào. Nǐ yuànyi gēn wǒ yìqǐ qù ma?**	
	This Saturday evening I'm going to People's Theater with my parents to see Chronicle of the White Snake. I just happen to have an extra ticket. Would you like to go together with me?	
4. AMERICAN	**Tài hǎole! Jǐdiǎn kāishǐ?**	
	Great! What time does it begin?	
5. CHINESE	**Bādiǎn. Wǒ xīngqīliù wǎnshang qīdiǎn yíkè lái zhǎo nǐ.**	
	At 8:00. I'll come looking for you Saturday night at 7:15.	
6. AMERICAN	**Hǎo, zhēn xièxie nǐ!**	
	O.K., thanks so much!	
7. CHINESE	**Zhè hái yòng xiè? Xīngqīliù jiàn!**	
	No need to thank me. See you Saturday!	

 Build Up

1. Chinese

Jīngjù	Peking opera [N]
duì Jīngjù gǎn xìngqu	be interested in Peking opera
Duìle, nǐ duì Jīngjù gǎn xìngqu ma?	Oh, yes, are you interested in Peking opera?

2. **American**
    wǒ suīrán bú tài dǒng   although I don't understand it well
    dànshi tǐng ài kàn   but I very much like to watch
Jīngjù a? Wǒ suīrán bú tài dǒng,   Peking opera? Though I don't understand it very
dànshi tǐng ài kàn.   well, I do love to watch it.

3. **Chinese**

rénmín	people [N]
jùchǎng	theater [PW]
Rénmín Jùchǎng	People's Theater (in Beijing) [PW]
shé	snake [N] (M: **tiáo**)
zhuàn	chronicle, biography [N] (M: **piān**)
"Bái Shé Zhuàn"	"The Chronicle of the White Snake"
zhènghǎo(r)	just, as it happens [MA]
duō yìzhāng piào	there is one ticket too many
zhènghǎo duō yìzhāng piào	there just happens to be an extra ticket

Zhèige xīngqīliù wǎnshang wǒ yào   This Saturday evening I'm going to People's
gēn fùmǔ yìqǐ qù Rénmín Jùchǎng kàn   Theater with my parents to see Chronicle of the
"Bái Shé Zhuàn." Zhènghǎo duō yìzhāng   White Snake. I just happen to have an extra
piào. Nǐ yuànyi gēn wǒ yìqǐ qù ma?   ticket. Would you like to go together with me?

4. **American**
Tài hǎole! Jǐdiǎn kāishǐ?   Great! What time does it begin?

5. **Chinese**
Bādiǎn. Wǒ xīngqīliù wǎnshang   At 8:00. I'll come looking for you Saturday night
qīdiǎn yíkè lái zhǎo nǐ.   at 7:15.

6. **American**
Hǎo, zhēn xièxie nǐ!   O.K., thanks so much!

7. **Chinese**
Zhè hái yòng xiè? Xīngqīliù jiàn!   No need to thank me. See you Saturday!

Supplementary Vocabulary

1. **yánjiū**   study, research [N/V]
    yǒu yánjiū   have expertise
    duì yīnyuè yǒu yánjiū   have expertise in music
Tā duì yīnyuè hěn yǒu yánjiū.   She has great expertise in music.

2. **fēn**   part, fraction [M]
    ...fēnzhī...   (for fractions) [PT]
    sānfēnzhī'èr   two-thirds
Sānfēnzhī'èrde rén méi qù.   Two-thirds of the people didn't go.

3. **bǎifēnzhī...**   ...percent [PT]
    bǎifēnzhīshí   ten percent
Zhǐ yǒu chàbuduō bǎifēnzhīshíde rén qùle.   Only about 10% of the people went.

4. **...diǎn...**   (pattern for decimals) [PT]
    yī diǎn bā   1.8
Lí zhèr yǒu yī diǎn bā gōnglǐ.   It's 1.8 kilometers from here.

5. **yǒuyòng**   be useful [SV]

6. méiyou yòng	not have any use **[PH]**
7. Zhōnghuá	(literary name for "China") **[N]**
gònghéguó	republic **[N]**
Zhōnghuá Rénmín Gònghéguó	People's Republic of China **[PW]**
8. Zhōnghuá Mínguó	Republic of China **[PW]**

Additional Vocabulary: Computer Terminology

1. shàngwǎng	get on the net, surf the net **[VO]**
Wǒ yǒukòngde shíhou, xǐhuan shàngwǎng.	When I have time, I like to surf the net.
2. diànzǐ	electron **[N]**
yóujiàn	piece of mail **[N]**
diànzǐ yóujiàn	electronic mail, e-mail **[PH]**
-men	(plural suffix) **[BF]**
péngyoumen	friends
fā	issue, send out **[V]**
gěi péngyoumen fā diànzǐ yóujiàn	send e-mails to friends
Wǒ cháng yòng wǒde diànnǎo gěi	I often use my computer to send e-mail
péngyoumen fā diànzǐ yóujiàn.	messages to my friends.
3. diànzǐ yóuxiāng	electronic mailbox **[PH]**
Nǐde diànzǐ yóuxiāng shi shémme?	What's your e-mail address?
4. wǎngzhàn	website **[N]**
Zhè shi wǒmen gōngsīde wǎngzhàn.	This is my company's website.
5. duǎnxìn	text message **[N]**
Wǒ gěi nǐ fā duǎnxìn.	I'll text you.

Grammatical and Cultural Notes

1A.   Remember that the expression **duìle** "That's right" often indicates a change of topic, i.e., the speaker has just thought of something new that he or she wishes to introduce into the conversation.

1B.   PEKING OPERA. **Jīngjù** "Peking opera" is also referred to as **Jīngxì**, **Guójù**, or (in Taiwan) **Píngjù**. Combining music, singing, and dance as well as stylized pantomime and strenuous acrobatics, **Jīngjù** is the national drama of China and can be traced back to the Tang Dynasty (618–906). While scenery in **Jīngjù** is minimal, consisting mostly of tables and chairs, costumes and makeup are very bright and colorful, with brilliant, lavishly embroidered costumes and hangings. Language in **Jīngjù** is often in archaic Chinese that is difficult even for native Chinese speakers to understand, hence slides with subtitles in characters are sometimes shown simultaneously. Of course, true Chinese opera lovers would know the story and probably the lyrics before they even go. Striding onto the stage to the sound of strings, woodwinds, drums, and gongs, Peking opera performers somersault across the stage and display their skills in the martial arts. It used to be that only males could perform in Peking opera, but now women perform also. Attending performances of Chinese opera has long been a popular pastime of both ordinary people and the well-to-do. However, the younger generation in China appears to have largely lost interest in Peking opera.

2.   Review the important pattern **suīrán...dànshi...** "although," that was introduced in 16-4: 3B.

3A.   Be careful how you pronounce **jùchǎng** "theater," making sure it doesn't sound like **zhūchǎng** "pig farm"!

3B. **Bái Shé Zhuàn,** one of the most famous and popular Peking operas, is based on a twelfth-century legend which is also recounted in fiction, ballads, and drama. The legend goes as follows: A supernatural white snake, after living an exemplary life on earth for 1,000 years, attains immortality and develops various kinds of magical powers. As it yearns to return to earth, it takes on the shape of a beautiful maiden and meets the young scholar Xu Xian. The maiden and Xu fall in love and marry, and open a medicine shop near West Lake in Hangzhou. The maiden uses her magical powers so that all the medicines they sell become especially potent, with the result that their business prospers. But the Buddhist monk Fa Hai intervenes, telling Xu the true identity of his wife and, with a magic potion, turning the maiden back into a snake. When Xu sees what his wife really looks like, he's so shocked he dies, but his snake-wife brings him back to life with another potion. Then Xu once again comes under the influence of the monk and, to be protected from the snake, allows himself to be locked in a temple. With the assistance of other spirits, the white snake then takes over the temple, so as to liberate her husband. However, Fa Hai is able to mobilize all kinds of spirits and, in the end, is able to keep the snake locked up inside a pagoda.

3C. **Zhènghǎor duō yìzhāng piào** "It just happens that I have an extra ticket" literally means "It just happens that there is one ticket too many." **Duō** is here a verb meaning "be many." Some more examples with **zhènghǎo(r)** "just, be just right, as it happens":

Xiànzài zhènghǎo shí'èrdiǎn.	"It's just 12:00 now."
Zhèishuāng xié zhènghǎo gěi nǐ dìdi chuān.	"This pair of shoes is just perfect for your brother to wear."

7. **Zhè hái yòng xiè?** literally means "This (matter of my inviting you to the Peking opera, you) still need to thank (me for it)?" This is an ironic comment; the implication is "Of course you don't need to thank me for this!" Functional English equivalents of **Zhè hái yòng xiè?** would include "Don't worry about it," "Forget it," and "Never mind."

SV1. Learn the common word **yánjiū,** which can function as both a verb and a noun meaning "research" or "study." Sometimes if you make a request in Chinese society, you'll receive the reply **Wǒmen yánjiū yanjiu** or **Wǒmen yánjiū yixia.** While this literally means "We'll study it," the real meaning may be "No." In other words, this is sometimes nothing more than a face-saving way to decline a request. However, depending on the context, it's of course also possible that this truly means a request or proposal will be "studied."

SV2, SV3, SV4. FRACTIONS, PERCENT, AND DECIMALS. Fractions are created on the following pattern:

DENOMINATOR	FĒN	ZHĪ	NUMERATOR
sān	fēn	zhī	èr

"two-thirds"

The **zhī** in the above pattern is from Classical Chinese and means the same as **-de** in modern Chinese. Thus, **sānfēnzhī'èr** literally means "three parts' two" or "two of three parts." Other common fractions include:

sānfēnzhīyī	"⅓"
sìfēnzhīyī	"¼"
sìfēnzhīsān	"¾"
wǔfēnzhīyī	"⅕"
shífēnzhīyī	"¹⁄₁₀"

More complicated fractions work the same way. For example, ⁵⁄₁₈ would be said as **shíbāfēnzhīwǔ** and ¹²⁄₄₉ would be said as **sìshijiǔfēnzhīshí'èr.**

Percent is expressed, using the same pattern as for fractions, as **bǎifēnzhī...,** literally, "...of a hundred parts."

The pattern is:

BĂI   FĒN   ZHĪ   **NUMBER**

băi   fēn   zhī   èr

"two percent"

More examples with **băifēnzhī...**:

băifēnzhīyī	"1%"
băifēnzhīshí	"10%"
băifēnzhīwŭshí	"50%"
băifēnzhībăi	"100%"

As regards decimals, the word for the decimal point is **diăn**. The number before the decimal point is pronounced like any other number, but the numbers after the decimal point are simply "read off," one digit at a time. The pattern for Chinese decimals is:

NUMBER   **DIĂN**   **INDIVIDUAL DIGIT(S)**

sìshijiŭ   diăn   bā liù

"49.86"

Some more examples of Chinese decimals:

liăngbăi èrshisān diăn liù wŭ	"223.65"
yī diăn èr sì	"1.24"
líng diăn líng wŭ sān qī	"0.0537"

SV7. **Zhōnghuá Rénmín Gònghéguó** "People's Republic of China" has been the official name for mainland China since 1949.

SV8. **Zhōnghuá Mínguó** "Republic of China" was the official name of all China from 1911–1949 and has since 1949 continued to be the official name for Taiwan.

Scene from Beijing Opera about **Sūn Wùkōng** "The Monkey King"

Going to the Movies

In the men's dormitory at Capital Normal University in Beijing, Li Xiaodong asks his American friend John Niu if he would like to watch a movie with him later that afternoon.

Basic Conversation 20-3

1. AMERICAN	**Jìnlái.**	
	Come in.	

2. CHINESE | **Hài!**
Hi!

3. AMERICAN | **Èi, Xiǎodōng!**
Hey, Xiaodong!

4. CHINESE | **Gàn shémme ne?**
What are you up to?

5. AMERICAN | **Xuéxí ne.**
Studying.

6. CHINESE | **Shì ma? E, xiàwǔ nǐ yǒukòng ma? Xiǎng bu xiǎng qù kàn chǎng diànyǐngr?**
Really? Uh, are you free this afternoon? Would you like to go see a movie?

7. AMERICAN | **Kéyi a. Yǒu shémme hǎo piānzi ma?**
Sure. Are there any good films?

8. CHINESE | **Zuìjìn yǒu yíbù xīn piānzi, gāng shàngyǎn, míng jiào "Yuède Zhǔrén." Tīngshuō bú cuò. Jiǎngde shi sānshí niándài Zhōngguo yíge zhùmíng yīnyuèjiāde gùshi.**
Recently there's a new film that just began playing titled "Moon Master." I've heard it's pretty good. It's the story of a famous musician in China in the 1930s.

Build Up

....

1. American
Jìnlái.   Come in.

2. **Chinese**
Hài!   Hi!

3. **American**
   Xiǎodōng   Xiaodong (given name)
Èi, Xiǎodōng!   Hey, Xiaodong!

4. **Chinese**
   gàn   do [V]
Gàn shémme ne?   What are you up to?

5. **American**
Xuéxí ne.   Studying.

6. **Chinese**
   xiǎng bu xiǎng qù kàn   would you like to go to see
   chǎng   (for a showing of a movie) [M]
   diànyǐng(r)   movie [N]
   kàn diànyǐng(r)   see a movie
   kàn chǎng diànyǐngr   see a showing of a movie
Shì ma? E, xiàwǔ nǐ yǒukòng ma?   Really? Uh, are you free this afternoon?
Xiǎng bu xiǎng qù kàn chǎng diànyǐngr?   Would you like to go see a movie?

7. **American**
   piānzi   film, movie [N] (M: **bù**)
Kéyi a. Yǒu shémme hǎo piānzi ma?   Sure. Are there any good films?

8. **Chinese**
   bù   (measure for films) [M]
   yíbù xīn piānzi   a new film
   shàngyǎn   begin to play (of a film at a theater) [V]
   míng jiào   be named [PH]
   yuè   moon [N]
   "Yuède Zhǔrén"   "Moon Master" (film title)
   jiǎng   tell the story of, be about [V]
   jiǎngde shi   what it's about is
   gùshi   story [N]
   jiǎng gùshi   tell a story [PH]
   niándài   decade [N]
   sānshí niándài   the decade of the 1930s
   zhùmíng   be famous, well-known [SV]
   yīnyuèjiā   musician [N]
   yíge zhùmíng yīnyuèjiā   a famous musician
Zuìjìn yǒu yíbù xīn piānzi, gāng shàngyǎn,   Recently there's a new film that just began
míng jiào "Yuède Zhǔrén." Tīngshuō bú cuò.   playing titled "Moon Master." I've heard it's
Jiǎngde shi sānshí niándài Zhōngguo yíge   pretty good. It's the story of a famous musician
zhùmíng yīnyuèjiāde gùshi.   in China in the 1930s.

 Supplementary Vocabulary

A. GENERAL

1. **diànyǐngyuàn**   movie theater [PW] (M: **jiā**)
2. **shuō gùshi**   tell a story [PH]

B. FUTURE CAREERS AND PROFESSIONS

3. **jiānglái**	in the future [TW]
jìhua	plan [N/AV]
Nǐ jiānglái yǒu shémme jìhua?	What are your plans for the future?

4. **dāng**	serve as, work as, act as [V]
yīshēng	medical doctor [N]
Wǒ jiānglái xiǎng dāng yīshēng.	In the future I want to serve as a doctor.

5. **huàjiā**	painter (artist) [N]
6. **gāngqínjiā**	pianist [N]
7. **xiǎoshuōjiā**	novelist [N]
8. **yínhángjiā**	banker [N]

Additional Vocabulary: More Careers and Professions

1. **kuàijìshī**	accountant [N]	7. **lǜshī**	lawyer [N]
2. **jiànzhùshī (B)**	architect [N]	8. **hùshì**	nurse [N]
3. **yáyī**	dentist [N]	9. **xīnlǐxuéjiā**	psychologist [N]
4. **wàijiāoguān**	diplomat [N]	10. **kēxuéjiā**	scientist [N]
5. **gōngchéngshī**	engineer [N]	11. **jūnrén**	soldier [N]
6. **jiātíng zhǔfù**	housewife [PH]		

12. **shēngyì**	business [N]
zuò shēngyì	engage in business [PH]
Zuò shēngyì kéyi zhuàn hěn duō qián.	You can earn a lot of money in business.

13. **zhèngfǔ**	government [N]
wèi zhèngfǔ gōngzuò	work for the government
Wǒ jiānglái yào wèi zhèngfǔ gōngzuò.	In the future I want to work for the government.

Grammatical and Cultural Notes

4A.   The verb **gàn** is an all-purpose general verb meaning "do" or "make," much like **gǎo** (2-4), **nòng** (18-2), or **zuò** (6-2). Be aware that **gàn** is very colloquial and informal, so it would not be used in polite conversation with superiors; for example, you'd NEVER say to your teacher ***Lǎoshī, nín gàn shémme ne?** "Teacher, what are you doing?" However, with peers or within the family, **gàn** is common.

4B.   A fuller form of **Gàn shémme ne?** "What are you doing?" would be **Nǐ zài gàn shémme ne?** or **Nǐ zhèng zài gàn shémme ne?**

4–5.   Notice the sentence final particle **ne** at the end of the Chinese student's question in line 4: **Gàn shémme ne?** "What are you up to?" The same final particle **ne** then reoccurs at the end of the American's response in line 5: **Xuéxí ne** "Studying." As we've seen before, sentence final particle **ne** can indicate present progressive, in other words, that something is currently in progress, which we often indicate in English with the "-ing" form of verbs.

5.   A fuller form of **Xuéxí ne** would be **Wǒ zài xuéxí ne** or **Wǒ zhèng zài xuéxí ne.**

6A.   **Xiǎng bu xiǎng qù kàn chǎng diànyǐngr?** "Would you like to go see a movie?" The measure **chǎng** here is short for **yìchǎng** "one showing of (a movie)." In rapid, colloquial conversation, the number **yī** before a measure is often omitted when it's unstressed and means "a" (but **yī** isn't omitted when it's stressed and means "one").

6B.   Another example of the measure **chǎng** "showing (of a movie)":

Dìyīchǎng shi qīdiǎn, dì'èrchǎng shi jiǔdiǎn bàn.
"The first showing is at 7:00, the second showing is at 9:30."

7A.   The reply **Kéyi a** "O.K." or "Sure" indicates agreement—but a low-key, restrained, understated sort of agreement.

7B.   The nouns **diànyǐng(r)** and **piānzi**, both of which mean "film" or "movie," are often interchangeable. However, the term **diànyǐng(r)** is more general and more common, especially in the phrase **kàn diànyǐng(r)** "see a movie."

7C.   Regarding the pronunciation of **diànyǐngr**, note that if a syllable ending in **-n** is followed immediately by a syllable beginning with **y-, w-, h-**, or a vowel, the **-n** of the first syllable is often not fully pronounced. In this case, the tongue doesn't quite reach the roof of the mouth, and the vowel in the first syllable is nasalized. So **diànyǐngr** is pronounced a little like **diaàyǐngr** (with a nasalized **a**). Other examples of this phenomenon we have encountered previously are **piányi** "cheap" (3-3) and **yuànyi** "would like" (15-4).

8A.   **Míng jiào** is a somewhat more formal variant of the more colloquial **míngzi jiào** "the name is called" or "be named."

8B.   **Jiǎng** here means "tell the story of" or "be about." It may refer to a movie, television show, or book. Learn the phrase **jiǎng gùshi** "tell a story." This can also be said as **shuō gùshi** "tell a story," cf. SV2.

8C.   **Jiǎngde shi...-de gùshi** literally means "What (the new film) tells is the story of...." Everything after the **shi** and before the **...-de gùshi** describes what the story is about.

8D.   Note the noun **niándài** "decade" in **sānshí niándài** "the decade of the 1930s." Some more examples:

liùshí niándài	"the sixties (i.e., the 1960s)"
qīshí niándài	"the seventies"
bāshí niándài	"the eighties"

Some speakers prefer to use **líng** "zero" instead of **shí**, so you'll also sometimes hear **sānlíng niándài** "the 1930s," **wǔlíng niándài** "the 50s," and so forth.

8E.   **-JIĀ AS A SUFFIX INDICATING PROFESSIONS.** Note the suffix **-jiā** in the noun **yīnyuèjiā** "musician." The suffix **-jiā** is attached to nouns (and less frequently to verbs) to form a noun relating to a certain profession. It often corresponds to the English suffixes "-ist" or "-er." Examples:

yīnyuè "music"	+	**jiā**	→	**yīnyuèjiā** "musician"
gāngqín "piano"	+	**jiā**	→	**gāngqínjiā** "pianist" (cf. SV6)
xiǎoshuō "novel"	+	**jiā**	→	**xiǎoshuōjiā** "novelist" (cf. SV7)
yínháng "bank"	+	**jiā**	→	**yínhángjiā** "banker" (cf. SV8)
yǔyánxué "linguistics"	+	**jiā**	→	**yǔyánxuéjiā** "linguist"
huà "painting"	+	**jiā**	→	**huàjiā** "painter" (cf. SV5)

The term **zhuānjiā** "expert, specialist," which was introduced in 8-2, also contains this suffix. Names of professions ending in **-jiā** are normally not used to refer to oneself, as that would be considered immodest. For example, to say "I'm a painter," you might say **Wǒ xǐhuan huàhuàr** "I like to paint." To say "I'm a linguist," you might say **Wǒ shi gǎo yǔyánxuéde** "I do linguistics" or **Wǒ gǎo yǔyánxué gōngzuò** "I do linguistics work." To say "we novelists," you might say **Wǒmen xiě xiǎoshuōde ren** "we people who write novels."

AV1–11.   **CAREERS AND PROFESSIONS.** The names of these careers and professions have been arranged in alphabetical order of the English equivalents.

AV2.   An alternate pronunciation of **jiànzhùshī** "architect" that you'll hear in Taiwan and occasionally elsewhere is **jiànzhúshī**.

Going to the Movies (cont.)

Niu agrees to go to the movie with Li. The two young men go to the box office to purchase tickets, watch the movie, and discuss it as they come out of the movie theater (continued from the previous conversation).

Basic Conversation 20-4

1. AMERICAN		Ò, tài hǎole! Wǒ hái cónglái méi kànguo zhèilèide diànyǐngr ne. Zài shémme dìfang? Jǐdiǎn kāiyǎn?
		Oh, great! I've never before seen this kind of movie. Where is it? What time does it start?
2. CHINESE		Běijīng Túshūguǎn, sāndiǎn bàn. Sāndiǎn wǒ lái zhǎo nǐ, zěmmeyàng?
		At the Beijing Library at 3:30. I'll come looking for you at 3:00, O.K.?
3. AMERICAN		Hǎo a.
		O.K.
4. CHINESE		Hǎo, zàijiàn.
		All right, bye.
5. AMERICAN		Zàijiàn.
		Bye.

(that afternoon, after his Chinese friend has purchased the tickets)

Jǐpáide?
Which row?

6. CHINESE		Wèizi bú cuò. Lóuxià shíwǔpái, shíliù, shíbāhàor. Wǒmen jìnqu ba.
		The seats are pretty good. Downstairs, row 15, numbers 16 and 18. Let's go in.

(when they come out of the theater)

Nǐ juéde zhèige diànyǐngr zěmmeyàng?
What do you think of this movie?

7. AMERICAN		Tài bàngle! Hěn gǎn rén.
		It was fantastic! Very touching.

8. CHINESE   Tāmen shuōde huà, nǐ dōu néng tīngdǒng ma?
                    Could you understand everything they said?

9. AMERICAN   Dà bùfen dōu dǒng. Yǒude dìfang shuōde tài kuài, tīngbutàimíngbai. Búguò
                    diànyǐngde zhǔyào nèiróng wǒ dōu néng lǐjiě.
                    I understood most of it. In some places they spoke too fast and I couldn't understand
                    very well. But I was able to understand the gist of the film.

Build Up

1. **American**
   cónglái   all along, always [A]
   cónglái méi...-guo   have never ever...before [PT]
   cónglái méi kànguo   have never before seen
   lèi   kind, type, category [M]
   zhèilèi   this kind of
   zhèilèide diànyǐngr   this kind of movie
   kāiyǎn   begin to be shown (of a film) [V]
   Ò, tài hǎole! Wǒ hái cónglái méi kànguo Oh, great! I've never before seen
   zhèilèide diànyǐngr ne. Zài shémme dìfang?   this kind of movie. Where is it?
   Jǐdiǎn kāiyǎn?   What time does it start?

2. **Chinese**
   Běijīng Túshūguǎn   Beijing Library [PW]
   Běijīng Túshūguǎn, sāndiǎn bàn.   At the Beijing Library at 3:30.
   Sāndiǎn wǒ lái zhǎo nǐ, zěmmeyàng?   I'll come looking for you at 3:00, O.K.?

3. **American**
   Hǎo a.   O.K.

4. **Chinese**
   Hǎo, zàijiàn.   All right, bye.

5. **American**
   Zàijiàn.   Bye.

   pái   row [M]
   jǐpái   which row
   Jǐpáide?   Which row?

6. **Chinese**
   lóuxià   downstairs [PW]
   lóuxià shíwǔpái   downstairs row 15
   Wèizi bú cuò. Lóuxià shíwǔpái,   The seats are pretty good. Downstairs, row 15,
   shíliù, shíbāhàor. Wǒmen jìnqu ba.   numbers 16 and 18. Let's go in.

   Nǐ juéde zhèige diànyǐngr zěmmeyàng?   What do you think of this movie?

7. **American**
   gǎn   touch, move (emotionally) [V]
   hěn gǎn rén   be very touching for people
   Tài bàngle! Hěn gǎn rén.   It was fantastic! Very touching.

8. **Chinese**
   Tāmen shuōde huà, nǐ dōu néng tīngdǒng ma?   Could you understand everything they said?

9. American

bùfen	part, portion [M]
dà bùfen	greater part, majority, most [PH]
yǒude dìfang	some places, some parts
míngbai	understand [V]
-míngbai	understand [RE]
tīngbutàimíngbai	can't understand very well [RC]
zhǔyào	essential, main [AT]
nèiróng	content [N]
diànyǐngde zhǔyào nèiróng	the main content of the movie
lǐjiě	understand [V]
wǒ dōu néng lǐjiě	I can understand all

Dà bùfen dōu dǒng. Yǒude dìfang
shuōde tài kuài, tīngbutàimíngbai.
Búguò diànyǐngde zhǔyào nèiróng
wǒ dōu néng lǐjiě.

I understood most of it. In some places they
spoke too fast and I couldn't understand very
well. But I was able to understand the gist of the
film.

Supplementary Vocabulary

1. **lóushàng**	upstairs [PW]
2. **yǎnyuán**	actor [N]
3. **dǎoyǎn**	director [N]
4. **diànyǐng míngxīng**	movie star [PH]

Additional Vocabulary: Films and Film Stars

1. **dòngzuòpiàn**	action film [N]
2. **xǐjùpiàn**	comedy film [N]
3. **zhēntànpiàn**	detective film [N]
4. **kǒngbùpiàn**	horror film [N]
5. **àiqíngpiàn**	romantic film [N]
6. **kēhuànpiàn**	science fiction film [N]
7. **zhànzhēngpiàn**	war film [N]
8. **zìmù**	subtitle [N]
9. **nánzhǔjué**	male leading role [N]
10. **nǚzhǔjué**	female leading role [N]

Grammatical and Cultural Notes

1A.   CÓNGLÁI MÉI(YOU)...-GUO. This pattern means "have never ever...before." The **cónglái méi(you)** precedes the verb and the **-guo** is suffixed to the verb. While it's of course possible to use only **méi(you)...-guo**,
the addition of the **cónglái** strengthens the meaning, much like English "never ever...before." The pattern is:

CÓNGLÁI	MÉI(YOU)	VERB	-GUO
cónglái	méi	qù	guo

"have never ever gone"

Some more examples of **cónglái méi(you)...-guo**:

Wǒ cónglái méi jiànguo ta.

"I've never ever seen him before."

Wǒ cónglái méiyou chīguo zhèmme hǎochīde Zhōngguo cài.

"I've never eaten Chinese food as delicious as this before."

> **Wǒ cónglái méi tīngshuōguo nèizhǒng shìqing.**
>
> "I've never ever heard of something like that before."

> **Wǒ cónglái méi shàngguo nèiwèi lǎoshīde kè.**
>
> "I've never ever taken that professor's classes before."

> **Wǒ cónglái méi zhèmme qīngsōngguo.**
>
> "I've never ever felt so relaxed before."

The adverb **cónglái** literally means "always." **Cónglái** is usually followed by a negative, either **méi(you)** or, less commonly, **bù**. **Cónglái bù** does not take a following **-guo** and the meaning is somewhat different. While **cónglái méi(you)...-guo** indicates only that the speaker has never ever done something in the past (but leaves open the possibility that he or she may do so in the future), **cónglái bù** indicates that the speaker has a policy against ever doing something, whether in the past or in the future. Examples with **cónglái bù**:

Wǒ cónglái bù hē jiǔ.	"I don't drink alcohol." (i.e., it's something the speaker just doesn't do)
Wǒ cónglái bù chī zǎofàn.	"I never eat breakfast."
Tā cónglái bù chōuyān.	"She never smokes."

1B. Notice that in this line the speaker happens to say **zhèilèide diànyǐngr** "this kind of movie." After measures like **lèi**, you can often optionally add a **-de**. However, **zhèilèi diànyǐngr** is even more common.

2. Adjacent to **Běijīng Túshūguǎn** "Beijing Library" there is a large movie theater which is referred to by the same name.

5. **Jǐpáide?** literally means "Ones in which row?" This is an abbreviation of the fuller form of this question: **Jǐpáide wèizi?** "Seats in which row?"

7. Instead of **hěn gǎn rén** "be very touching," some speakers prefer **hěn gǎndòng rén**, which has the same meaning.

9A. **Dà bùfen** "the majority" or "most of" is a useful and common term. It's made up of **dà** "big" or "great" plus **bùfen** "part" or "portion." **Dà bùfen** can be used by itself, as in the first example below, or followed by **-de** and a noun, as in the second example. Examples:

Dà bùfen wǒ dōu tīngguole.	"I've listened to most of them." (e.g., a stack of CDs)
Dà bùfende xuésheng xuéde bú cuò.	"The majority of students are learning well."

9B. **Yǒude dìfang shuōde tài kuài** "(In) some places they spoke too fast." **Yǒude dìfang** here means "some places" or "certain parts" of the movie the two young men saw. Such abstract use of **dìfang** is quite common. Another example:

> **Nǐ jiǎngde huà, yǒude dìfang wǒ tóngyì, yǒude dìfang wǒ bù tóngyì.**
>
> "I agree with some aspects (lit. "some places") of what you said, and I disagree with other aspects."

9C. **Tīngbutàimíngbai** is a negative potential resultative compound which literally means "listen and not be able to understand too well," that is, "can't understand very well." Adverbs like **tài** are sometimes inserted into the middle of potential resultative constructions. More examples:

Tā jiǎngde huà, wǒ tīngbutàidǒng.	"I couldn't understand very well what he said."
Zhèiběn shū wǒ kànbutàidǒng.	"I don't understand this book very well."
Wǒ shuìbutàizháo.	"I can't fall asleep very well."

9D. **Míngbai** is a common verb to indicate "understand." A very common question is: **Nǐ míngbai wǒde yìsi ma?** "Do you understand what I mean?" (lit. "You understand my meaning?") Typical answers to that question would be **Míngbai** "I understand" and **Duìbuqǐ, wǒ hái shi bú tài míngbai** "Sorry, I still don't quite understand."

9E. The verbs **dǒng**, **míngbai**, and **lǐjiě**, all three of which occur in this lesson, mean "understand" and are often interchangeable. In 18-2, you were also introduced to **liǎojiě**, which means about the same as **lǐjiě**. One difference among these verbs is that when referring to "understanding a language," only **dǒng** can be used: **Nǐ dǒng Zhōngwén ma?** "Do you understand Chinese?" To say "I don't understand you," don't say *Wǒ bù dǒng nǐ. Instead, say either **Wǒ bù dǒng nǐde yìsi** (in the sense that you can't understand what the other person is saying) or **Wǒ bù liǎojiě nǐ** (in the sense that you find it impossible to figure out what makes the other person tick).

AV1–7. **FILMS.** The names of these types of films are arranged in alphabetical order of the English equivalents. Note carefully that although the word for "film" by itself is **piānzi** (with Tone One on the first syllable), the compound forms for different types of films, such as **kǒngbùpiàn** "horror film," end in **-piàn** (with Tone Four on the final syllable).

AV9–10. **Nánzhǔjué** "male leading role" and **nǚzhǔjué** "female leading role" are also commonly pronounced as **nánzhǔjiǎo** and **nǚzhǔjiǎo**, especially in Taiwan.

Unit 20: Review and Study Guide

New Vocabulary

ADVERBS
cónglái — all along, always

ATTRIBUTIVES
zhǔyào — essential, main

IDIOMATIC EXPRESSIONS
shì ma — "really?"

MEASURES
bù — (measure for films)
bùfen — part, portion
chǎng — (for a showing of a movie)
fēn — part, fraction
lèi — kind, type, category
pái — row

MOVEABLE ADVERBS
guàibudé — no wonder
zhènghǎo(r) — just, as it happens

NOUNS
àihào — interest, hobby
dǎoyǎn — director
diànyǐng(r) — movie
diàozi — tune, melody
gāngqín — piano
gāngqínjiā — pianist
gē(r) — song
gònghéguó — republic

guóhuà(r) — Chinese painting
gùshi — story
huà(r) — painting
huàjiā — painter (artist)
jìhua — plan
Jīngjù — Peking opera
nèiróng — content
niándài — decade
piānzi — film, movie
rénmín — people
shé — snake
shìhào — hobby
Tiàoqí — Chinese checkers
Wéiqí — Go (kind of chess)
Xiàngqí — Chinese chess
xiǎoshuō(r) — novel
xiǎoshuōjiā — novelist
yánjiū — study, research
yǎnyuán — actor
yínhángjiā — banker
yīnyuèjiā — musician
yīshēng — medical doctor
yuè — moon
zhuàn — chronicle, biography

PATTERNS
bǎifēnzhī... — ...percent

cónglái méi...-guo — have never ever... before
...diǎn... — (pattern for decimals)
...fēnzhī... — (for fractions)

PHRASES
dà bùfen — greater part, majority, most
diànyǐng míngxīng — movie star
jiǎng gùshi — tell a story
méiyou yòng — not have any use
míng jiào — be named
shuō gùshi — tell a story

PLACE WORDS
Běijīng Túshūguǎn — Beijing Library
bówùguǎn — museum
diànyǐngyuàn — movie theater
jùchǎng — theater
lóushàng — upstairs
lóuxià — downstairs
Rénmín Jùchǎng — People's Theater (in Beijing)
Zhōnghuá Mínguó — Republic of China

Zhōnghuá Rénmín Gònghéguó
People's Republic of China

RESULTATIVE COMPOUNDS
tīngbutàimíngbai
can't understand very well

RESULTATIVE ENDINGS
-míngbai   understand

STATIVE VERBS
hǎotīng   be nice-sounding, pretty
yǒuyòng   be useful
zhùmíng   be famous, well-known

TIME WORDS
jiānglái   in the future
VERBS
cānguān   visit
chàng   sing
dāng   serve as, work as
gǎn   touch, move (emotionally)
gàn   do
hēng   hum
huà   paint
jiǎng   tell the story of, be about
kāiyǎn   begin to be shown (of a film)

lǐjiě   understand
míngbai   understand
shàngyǎn   begin to play (of a film at a theater)
xià   play (chess or checkers)
zhào   take (photographs)

VERB-OBJECT COMPOUNDS
chànggē(r)   sing a song
huàhuà(r)   paint paintings
kànshū   read
xiàqí   play chess
zhàoxiàng   take photographs

Major New Grammar Patterns

GUÀIBUDÉ: Guàibudé nǐ nèmme pàng! "No wonder you're so fat!" **(20-1)**

FRACTIONS: sānfēnzhī'èr "two-thirds" **(20-2)**

PERCENT: bǎifēnzhīyī "1%" **(20-2)**

DECIMALS: yīdiǎnèrsì "1.24" **(20-2)**

-JIĀ AS NOUN SUFFIX INDICAT-ING PROFESSIONS: yīnyuèjiā

"musician," **xiǎoshuōjiā** "novelist," **yínhángjiā** "banker" **(20-3)**

CÓNGLÁI MÉI(YOU)...-GUO: Wǒ cónglái méi qùguo. "I've never been there before." **(20-4)**

Leisure Time Activities (II)

COMMUNICATIVE OBJECTIVES

Once you've mastered this unit, you'll be able to use Chinese to:

1. Ask people about their favorite sports and leisure time activities and talk about the sports and activities you like: baseball, basketball, soccer, tennis, badminton, Ping-Pong, swimming, jogging, martial arts, kung fu, taiji, dancing, etc.

2. Discuss competitive games that are in progress: Who is playing whom? What is the score? Who is likely to win and lose? etc.

3. Talk about watching television: channels, stations, different kinds of programs, etc.

4. Discuss a visit to the Great Wall: How long is it? When was it built? What is its history? etc.

5. Talk about requesting leave or going on vacation at different times of the year.

Talking About Sports

Tom Ryan, an American who is teaching English in Taiwan for a year, is talking with his Taiwanese friend Huang Jikuan on the campus of National Taiwan Normal University in Taipei. Huang asks Ryan what sports he likes.

 Basic Conversation 21-1

1. HUANG		**Tāngmǔ, nǐ xǐhuan něixiē yùndòng?** Tom, which sports do you like?
2. RYAN		**Wǒ xǐhuan wǎngqiú hàn yóuyǒng. Yǐqián zài Měiguode shíhou yě cháng chénpǎo. Nǐ ne?** I like tennis and swimming. Before, when I was in the States, I also often jogged in the morning. And you?
3. HUANG		**Wǒ xǐhuan dǎ bàngqiú, pīngpāngqiú, ǒu'ěr yě dǎ yǔmáoqiú. Éi, nǐ gèzi zèmme gāo, lánqiú yīnggāi dǎde bú cuò ba?** I like to play baseball and Ping-Pong, and occasionally I also play badminton. Hey, you're so tall, you ought to be pretty good at basketball!
4. RYAN		**Qíshí, wǒ yǐqián zài gāozhōngde shíhou shi lánqiú xiàoduì, búguò xiànzài yǐjīng hěn jiǔ méi dǎle.** Actually, in the past when I was in high school, I was on the school basketball team, but now I haven't played for a long time.
5. HUANG		**Bù jiǎndān! Nà nǐ lái Táiwān zèmme jiǔ, yǒu méiyou xué yìxiē bù yíyàngde yùndòng, bǐrú shuō, Zhōngguo wǔshù, gōngfū shemmede?** Wow! So, having been in Taiwan so long, have you learned some different sports, for example, Chinese martial arts, kung fu, and so forth?
6. RYAN		**Wǒ zìjǐ méiyou, búguò zhù wǒ gébìde shìyǒu dàoshi měige xīngqītiān zǎoshàng dōu huì dào fùjìnde gōngyuán qù xué dǎ tàijíquán.** I myself haven't, but the dormmate who lives next to me, every Sunday morning he'll go to the park nearby to learn how to shadow box.

Build Up

1. Huang

Tāngmǔ	(Chinese for "Tom")
něixiē	which ones, which [QW+M]
yùndòng	sport, athletics, exercise [N]
něixiē yùndòng	which sports
Tāngmǔ, nǐ xǐhuan něixiē yùndòng?	Tom, which sports do you like?

2. Ryan

wǎng	net [N]
qiú	ball [N]
wǎngqiú	tennis [N]
hàn [T]	and [CJ]
yóuyǒng	swimming; swim [N/VO]
wǎngqiú hàn yóuyǒng	tennis and swimming
chénpǎo	jog in the morning [V]
Wǒ xǐhuan wǎngqiú hàn yóuyǒng. Yǐqián zài Měiguode shíhou yě cháng chénpǎo. Nǐ ne?	I like tennis and swimming. Before, when I was in the States, I also often jogged in the morning. And you?

3. Huang

dǎ	play (a sport) [V]
dǎqiú	play a ball game [VO]
bàngqiú	baseball [N]
wǒ xǐhuan dǎ bàngqiú	I like to play baseball
pīngpāngqiú	Ping-Pong [N]
ǒu'ěr	once in a while, occasionally [MA]
máo	feather, hair (on body), fur [N]
yǔmáo	feather, plumage [N]
yǔmáoqiú	badminton, shuttlecock [N]
ǒu'ěr yě dǎ yǔmáoqiú	occasionally also play badminton
gèzi	height, stature, build [N]
nǐ gèzi zèmme gāo	your height is so tall
lánqiú	basketball [N]
lánqiú yīnggāi dǎde bú cuò	basketball you ought to play well
Wǒ xǐhuan dǎ bàngqiú, pīngpāngqiú, ǒu'ěr yě dǎ yǔmáoqiú. Éi, nǐ gèzi zèmme gāo, lánqiú yīnggāi dǎde bú cuò ba?	I like to play baseball and Ping-Pong, and occasionally I also play badminton. Hey, you're so tall, you ought to be pretty good at basketball!

4. Ryan

duì	team [N]
xiàoduì	school team [N]
lánqiú xiàoduì	school basketball team
Qíshí, wǒ yǐqián zài gāozhōngde shíhou shi lánqiú xiàoduì, búguò xiànzài yǐjīng hěn jiǔ méi dǎle.	Actually, in the past when I was in high school, I was on the school basketball team, but now I haven't played for a long time.

5. Huang

bù jiǎndān	not simple, that's quite something
yǒu méiyou xué	have (you) learned
yìxiē bù yíyàngde yùndòng	some different sports
bǐrú	for example [MA]
bǐrú shuō	for example [PH]
wǔshù	martial art [N]

Zhōngguo wǔshù	Chinese martial arts
gōngfū	kung fu [N]
Bù jiǎndān! Nà nǐ lái Táiwān zèmme jiǔ, yǒu méiyou xué yìxiē bù yíyàngde yùndòng, bǐrú shuō, Zhōngguo wǔshù, gōngfū shemmede?	Wow! So, having been in Taiwan so long, have you learned some different sports, for example, Chinese martial arts, kung fu, and so forth?

6. Ryan

wǒ zìjǐ méiyou	I myself haven't
shìyǒu	roommate, dormmate [N]
zhù wǒ gébìde shìyǒu	the roommate who lives next to me
dàoshi	actually, to the contrary [A]
gōngyuán	park (piece of ground) [PW]
dào fùjìnde gōngyuán qù	go to a park in the vicinity
tàijíquán	taiji, shadow boxing [N]
dǎ tàijíquán	practice taiji [PH]
Wǒ zìjǐ méiyou, búguò zhù wǒ gébìde shìyǒu dàoshi měige xīngqītiān zǎoshàng dōu huì dào fùjìnde gōngyuán qù xué dǎ tàijíquán.	I myself haven't, but the dormmate who lives next to me, every Sunday morning he'll go to the park nearby to learn how to shadow box.

Supplementary Vocabulary

1. chénggōng	succeed [V]
Nǐ chénggōngle, zhēn shi tì nǐ gāoxìng!	You have succeeded, I'm really happy for you!
2. bǐfang shuō	for example [PH]
Tāde shìhào hěn duō, bǐfang shuō, kànshū, huàhuàr, dǎ lánqiú shemmede.	She has lots of hobbies, for example, reading, painting, playing basketball and so on.

Additional Vocabulary

1. yùndòngfú	sweat shirt and pants [N] (M: **tào**)
2. yùndòngkù	sweat pants [N] (M: **tiáo**)
3. yùndòngshān	athletic T-shirt [N] (M: **jiàn**)

Grammatical and Cultural Notes

1. Learn **něixiē** "which?" (also pronounced **nǎxiē**). Remember that these forms with **xiē** refer to plural nouns. To review, you've now been introduced to the following:

TERM	ALTERNATE FORM	ENGLISH
zhèixiē	**zhèxiē**	these
nèixiē	**nàxiē**	those
něixiē	**nǎxiē**	which?
yìxiē	**xiē**	some

The above forms with **xiē** can all serve as SPECIFIER + MEASURE phrases that modify a noun, as in **Zhèixiē shū shi wǒde** "These books are mine." Except for **xiē**, they can also all serve as pronouns without a following noun, as in **Zhèxiē shi wǒde** "These are mine." For more information, see 12-2: 8A.

2. Remember that **hàn** "and" is the Taiwan pronunciation of the word which in Beijing is pronounced **hé**. Of course, **gēn** could have been used here just as well.

3A. Learn **dǎqiú** "play a game involving a ball." Since **dǎqiú** is a verb-object compound, to say "What ball games do you like to play?" you should say **Nǐ xǐhuan dǎ shémme qiú?**

3B. The word **máo** is used for feathers on birds, fur on animals, or hair on the body of humans. For hair on the head of humans, use the noun **tóufa**.

4A. Since the speaker on the video and in the basic conversation for listening is from Taiwan, he pronounces **qíshí** "actually" as **qísí**. Remember that the "dropping" of **h** from **sh-** is common in Taiwan and southern China.

4B. **Wǒ yǐqián zài gāozhōngde shíhou shi lánqiú xiàoduì** "I formerly when I was in high school was on the school basketball team." The basic kernel of this topic-comment sentence is **Wǒ shi lánqiú xiàoduì** "I was school basketball team." Obviously, this **shi** doesn't indicate equivalence but rather a loose connection between **wǒ** and **xiàoduì** which the overall context makes clear: "As for me, it was a situation of school basketball team." Some Chinese speakers would prefer **zài** to **shi** and say **Wǒ zài lánqiú xiàoduì**.

4C. **Hěn jiǔ méi dǎle** "haven't played for a long time now." There are two important points concerning this phrase: (1) the **le** at the end indicates time continuing up to the present ("I haven't played for a long time and this situation of not playing continues right up until this very moment"); and (2) the duration of time expression **hěn jiǔ** here precedes the verb because it's a question of negative time spent (cf. 11-2: 2A). Had this involved positive time spent, then **hěn jiǔ** would have followed the verb. Contrast:

Wǒ dǎle hěn jiǔle.	"I've been playing for a long time."
Wǒ hěn jiǔ méi dǎle.	"I haven't played for a long time."

5A. **Bù jiǎndān** literally means "not simple," but here functions as a compliment. The sense is "That's not so easy!" or "That's really quite something!" or "Wow!"

5B. **YǑU MÉIYOU + VERB TO INDICATE QUESTION FORMS OF COMPLETED ACTION VERBS WITH -LE.** First let's review a bit. Take a sentence with a completed action verb with **-le** such as **Tā qùle** "She went." To transform this into a question, we could either add **ma** (**Tā qùle ma?** "Did she go?"), or we could use the affirmative-negative question form, which in standard northern Chinese ends in VERB **-le méiyou** (**Tā qùle méiyou?** "Did she go?"). Here are some more examples of the affirmative-negative question form as used in northern Chinese:

Tā láile méiyou?	"Did he come?"
Tā mǎile méiyou?	"Did she buy it?"
Nǐmen chīfànle méiyou?	"Have you eaten?"

Now, in southern Mandarin (and sometimes even in the Mandarin spoken in the North) you often hear **yǒu méiyou** placed before the verb, rather than having **-le méiyou** follow after the verb. Thus, in Taiwan and most other parts of southern China, in place of the question pattern **Nǐ qùle méiyou?** "Did you go?" you will frequently hear the pattern **Nǐ yǒu méiyou qù?** The basic pattern for this type of question is:

SUBJECT	YǑU MÉIYOU	VERB
Nǐ	yǒu méiyou	qù?

"Did you go?"

Some more examples:

Tā yǒu méiyou lái?	"Has he come?"
Nǐ yǒu méiyou mǎi?	"Did you buy it?"
Nǐmen yǒu méiyou kàndao tā?	"Have you all seen her?"

Either of these alternatives—the pattern with VERB **-le méiyou** or the pattern with **yǒu méiyou** VERB—is fine for you to use, but be aware that the pattern with VERB **-le méiyou** will make you sound more "northern" in your speech, while the pattern with **yǒu méiyou** VERB will make you sound more "southern."

Attention: Though either of these question patterns is fine, do be careful as regards the answers to such questions. The negative answer ("He didn't...") uses **méi** or **méiyou** (e.g., **Tā méi lái** or **Tā méiyou lái** "He didn't come"), but the affirmative answer must use

People playing baseball on campus of National Taiwan Normal University

verb + **-le** (e.g., **Tā láile** "He came"). You CANNOT say ***Tā yǒu lái** for "He came." The latter is a common error in Mandarin as spoken by native speakers of Cantonese and Taiwanese, since those dialects do allow for constructions similar to ***Tā yǒu lái**.

5C.   **KUNG FU.** The type of Chinese martial arts known in the West as kung fu is known in Mandarin as **gōngfū**. Kung fu combines martial arts, techniques and training, and various methods of health maintenance practiced by Chinese people from ancient times up through today. There are many different styles of kung fu. One particularly famous style is the Shaolin style, which was developed at the Shaolin temple at Song Shan near Zhengzhou in Henan Province. The Shaolin style of kungfu includes the dragon, tiger, panther, snake, and crane styles of boxing. Kung fu styles can be roughly divided into the northern and southern styles, as well as the internal and external styles. Nowadays kung fu is a subject of serious academic study and is taught in the physical education departments of many universities in mainland China and Taiwan as well as at private institutes. There are also international organizations dedicated to the promotion of kung fu and the other Chinese martial arts.

6A.   The answer **Wǒ zìjǐ méiyou** "I myself haven't" is short for **Wǒ zìjǐ méiyou xué** "I myself haven't learned (any different sports)."

6B.   The noun **shìyǒu** "roommate" is a synonym of **tóngwū(r)** that you learned in 2-2.

6C.   A fuller form of **zhù wǒ gébìde shìyǒu** "the roommate who lives next to me" would be **zhùzai wǒ gébìde shìyǒu**. The **zài** after **zhù** is often omitted in rapid conversation (cf. **Wǒ zhù sān líng liù** "I'm staying in 306" in 4-3).

6D.   **DÀOSHI.** In line 5, the Taiwanese student asks the American student if he has learned any Chinese martial arts. Notice how the American answers and, in his answer, pay special attention to the adverb **dàoshi**: **Wǒ zìjǐ méiyou, búguò zhù wǒ gébìde shìyǒu dàoshi měige xīngqītiān zǎoshàng dōu huì dào fùjìnde gōngyuán qù xué dǎ tàijíquán.** An expanded translation of this might be: "I myself haven't, but the dormmate who lives next to me, he on the contrary, unlike me, why every Sunday morning he'll go to the park nearby to learn how to shadow box." The adverb **dàoshi** means "contrary to expectations," "on the contrary," "actually," or "but." Also occurring simply as **dào**, this adverb is sometimes best not translated into English but instead expressed by stress or intonation. Here are more examples with **dàoshi** and **dào**:

> **Nǐ jiào biérén qù, nǐ zìjǐ dàoshi bú qù!**
>
> "You told others to go but you yourself, on the contrary, you didn't go!"

> **Qíguài, dàde piányi, xiǎode dào guì.**
>
> "That's strange, the large ones are cheaper, but the small ones on the contrary are more expensive."

> **Shí'èr yuè méi xiàxuě, shíyuè dào xiàle yìchǎng dà xuě.**
>
> "In December it didn't snow, but in October on the contrary there was a big snow."

Dàoshi is sometimes used in the pattern **A dàoshi A, kěshi...**, which means "As for being A, he/she/it on the contrary is A, but...." Example:

> **Tā qióng dàoshi qióng, kěshi rén hěn hǎo.**
>
> "He's poor all right, but he's a good person." (lit. "As for his being poor, he on the contrary is poor, but he's a good person.")

The preceding pattern also occurs with a **bù** "not" in it as **A dàoshi bù A, kěshi....** Example:

> **Jīntiān lěng dàoshi bù lěng, kěshi fēng hěn dà.**
>
> "It isn't cold today, but there is a strong wind."

6E.   **Měige xīngqītiān zǎoshàng dōu huì dào fùjìnde gōngyuán qù xué dǎ tàijíquán** "Every Sunday morning he'll go to the park nearby to learn how to shadow box." Notice **měige xīngqītiān** "every Sunday" and the adverb **dōu** (lit. "in every case") that occurs before the auxiliary **huì**. When you have the specifier **měi-** in a sentence, it's commonly followed by a **dōu** later in the sentence.

6F.   The **huì** in this sentence is the **huì** that means "be likely to" or "will."

6G.   **Tàijíquán** "taiji" or "shadow boxing" is a traditional Chinese sport that is characterized by slow and graceful movements. It's an exercise for the mind as well as the body. Early each morning in parks and some public places in China, you can see people—especially older people—practicing taiji.

SV2. In northern China, the phrase **bǐfang shuō** "for example" is particularly common. In other parts of China, **bǐrú shuō**, which has exactly the same meaning, is often used instead.

Talking About Sports (cont.)

Ryan and Huang continue their conversation and agree to go jogging together the next morning at 6:00 A.M. (continued from the previous lesson).

 Basic Conversation 21-2

1. RYAN

Tā shuō gēn tā yìqǐ xuéde rén chàbuduō dōu shi zhōnglǎonián rén. Nándào niánqīng rén dōu bù xǐhuan dǎ tàijíquán ma?

He says the people learning with him are mostly middle-aged or older people. Don't tell me that young people all dislike practicing shadow boxing?

2. HUANG

Niánqīng rén bǐjiào xǐhuan wǎnshang qù tiàowǔ, huòshi jiàride shíhou dào jiāowài zóuzou. Dǎ tàijíquán děi sìwǔdiǎn zhōng jiù chūmén, duì tāmen lái shuō tài zǎole, qǐbulái.

Young people prefer going dancing in the evening, or during holidays going walking in the countryside. To shadow box you have to go out at 4:00 or 5:00; as far as they're concerned, that's too early, they can't get up.

3. RYAN

Yuánlái shi zhèiyang.

So that's how it is.

4. HUANG

Nǐ gāngcái shuō nǐ yǐqián xǐhuan chénpǎo. Wǒ dàoshi měitiān zǎoshang liùdiǎn dào liù diǎn bàn pǎo bàn'ge zhōngtóu. Zěmmeyàng? Yǒu méiyou xìngqu hé wǒ yìqǐ pǎo?

You just said you used to like jogging. Actually, every morning from 6:00 to 6:30, I run for half an hour. How about it? Would you be interested in running with me?

5. RYAN

Míngtiān wǒmen zài náli pèngmiàn?

Where shall we meet tomorrow?

6. HUANG

Wǒ liùdiǎn zhěng zài tǐyùguǎn qiánmiàn děng nǐ, zěmmeyàng?

At six o'clock sharp I'll wait for you in front of the gym, O.K.?

7. RYAN

Hǎo, yì-yán-wéi-dìng!

O.K., agreed!

🔘 Build Up

1. Ryan

gēn tā yìqǐ xuéde rén	the people learning with him
zhōngnián	middle age [N]
zhōngnián rén	middle-aged people [PH]
lǎonián	old age [N]
lǎonián rén	old people [PH]
zhōnglǎonián rén	middle-aged and older people
nándào...ma	don't tell me that... [PT]
niánqīng rén	young people [PH]

Tā shuō gēn tā yìqǐ xuéde rén chàbuduō
dōu shi zhōnglǎonián rén. Nándào niánqīng
rén dōu bù xǐhuan dǎ tàijíquán ma?

He says the people learning with him are mostly
middle-aged or older people. Don't tell me that
young people all dislike practicing shadow boxing?

2. Huang

tiàowǔ	dance [VO]
wǎnshang qù tiàowǔ	go dancing in the evening
jià	vacation, leave [N]
jiàrì	holiday, day off [N]
jiàrìde shíhou	during holidays
jiāowài	the countryside around a city [PW]
zóuzou	walk around, wander
dào jiāowài zóuzou	go to the countryside to walk
sìwǔdiǎn zhōng	at four or five o'clock
duì...lái shuō	as regards..., for..., to... [PT]
duì tāmen lái shuō	as far as they're concerned, for them
qǐlái	get up [RC]
qǐbulái	not be able to get up

Niánqīng rén bǐjiào xǐhuan wǎnshang
qù tiàowǔ, huòshi jiàrìde shíhou dào
jiāowài zóuzou. Dǎ tàijíquán děi sìwǔdiǎn
zhōng jiù chūmén, duì tāmen lái shuō
tài zǎole, qǐbulái.

Young people prefer going dancing in the
evening, or during holidays going walking in the
countryside. To shadow box you have to go out
at 4:00 or 5:00; as far as they're concerned,
that's too early, they can't get up.

3. Ryan

yuánlái	actually, so [MA]

Yuánlái shi zhèiyang.   So that's how it is.

4. Huang

liùdiǎn dào liùdiǎn bàn	from 6:00 to 6:30
yǒu méiyou xìngqu	are you interested or not
hé wǒ yìqǐ pǎo	run together with me

Nǐ gāngcái shuō nǐ yǐqián xǐhuan chénpǎo.
Wǒ dàoshi měitiān zǎoshang liùdiǎn dào
liù diǎn bàn pǎo bàn'ge zhōngtóu. Zěmmeyàng?
Yǒu méiyou xìngqu hé wǒ yìqǐ pǎo?

You just said you used to like jogging.
Actually, every morning from 6:00 to
6:30, I run for half an hour. How about it?
Would you be interested in running with me?

5. Ryan

pèngmiàn	meet (face-to-face) [VO]
zài náli pèngmiàn	meet where

Hǎo a! Wǒ yě hǎo jiǔ méi pǎole.
Míngtiān wǒmen zài náli pèngmiàn?

Sure! I haven't run for a long time.
Where shall we meet tomorrow?

6. Huang

zhěng	exact, sharp (of clock times) [BF]
liùdiǎn zhěng	six o'clock sharp
tǐyù	physical education [N]
tǐyùguǎn	gymnasium [PW]
zài tǐyùguǎn qiánmiàn	in front of the gym
Wǒ liùdiǎn zhěng zài tǐyùguǎn qiánmiàn děng nǐ, zěmmeyàng?	At six o'clock sharp I'll wait for you in front of the gym, O.K.?

7. Ryan

Hǎo, yì-yán-wéi-dìng!	O.K., agreed!

Supplementary Vocabulary

1. **shèhuì**   society [N]
   tuántǐ   group [N]
   shètuán   organization, club [N]
   jiārù   join [V]
   Tā juédìng jiārù nèige shètuán.   She decided to join that club.

2. **fàngjià**   take a vacation [VO]
   Tāmen fàngle wǔtiān jià.   They took five days of vacation.

3. **qǐngjià**   request leave [VO]
   Lǎoshi, wǒ xiǎng gēn nín qǐng liǎngtiānde jià.   Sir, I'd like to ask you for two days of leave.

4. **chūnjià**   spring vacation, spring break [N]
5. **shǔjià**   summer vacation [N]
6. **hánjià**   winter vacation [N]
7. **jiàoyù**   education [N]

Additional Vocabulary: More Sports

1. **Měishì zúqiú**   American-style football [PH]
2. **páshān**   climb mountains [VO]
3. **duànliàn shēntǐ**   exercise [PH]
4. **jījiàn**   fencing [N]
5. **tiánjìng**   field and track [N]
6. **shǒuqiú**   handball [N]
7. **huábīng**   ice-skate [VO]
8. **táiqiú**   pool, billiards [N]
9. **liūbīng**   ice-skate; roller-skate [VO]
10. **huáchuán**   rowing, crew [VO]
11. **huáxuě**   ski [VO]
12. **lěiqiú**   softball [N]
13. **páiqiú**   volleyball [N]
14. **shuǐqiú**   water-polo [N]
15. **huáshuǐ**   water-ski [VO]
16. **jǔzhòng**   weight-lift [VO]
17. **shuāijiāo**   wrestle [VO]

Grammatical and Cultural Notes

1A. The expression **zhōnglǎonián rén** means **zhōngnián rén gēn lǎonián rén** "middle-aged people and old people." Compare **chēyuèpiào** "individual and monthly tickets" in 9-4.

1B.   **NÁNDÀO...MA.** The pattern **nándào...ma** is very common and indicates surprise or incredulity. It can often be translated as "don't tell me that...," "you don't mean to say that...," "is it possible that...," or "could it be that...." **Nándào** itself is a moveable adverb, so it can occur at the beginning of a sentence or before a verb or adverb. Sometimes the final **ma** is omitted, and sometimes there is a **shuō** right after **nándào**. The basic pattern is:

NÁNDÀO	STATEMENT	MA
Nándào	tā bú shi Zhōngguo rén	ma?

"Don't tell me that she's not Chinese?"

Some more examples of the pattern **nándào...ma**:

Nándào tā lián yíkuài qián dōu méiyou ma?

"Could it be that he doesn't have even a dollar?"

Nǐ nándào shuō bú rènshi wǒ ma?

"You don't mean that you don't recognize me?!"

Zhèmme zhòngyàode shìqing, nándào nǐ hái bù zhīdào ma?

"Such an important matter, don't tell me you don't know yet?"

Nèmme guìde jiāju, nándào yǒu rén yuànyi mǎi ma?

"Such expensive furniture, don't tell me there are people willing to buy it?"

2A.   **Zóuzou** "take a walk" or "wander about a bit" is a reduplicated form of **zǒu** "walk." Compare **kàn** "look" and **kànkan** "take a look." **Zóuzou** has basically the same meaning as **zǒu** but is more colloquial, more understated, and less abrupt.

2B.   **Sìwǔdiǎn zhōng** "four or five o'clock." Review 16-3: 4B on approximate numbers. Cf. also note 1A in this lesson.

2C.   **DUÌ...LÁI SHUŌ.** The pattern **duì...lái shuō** "as regards..." or "for..." is very common and useful. It expresses that, as regards a certain person or persons, a given situation is a certain way. The basic pattern is:

DUÌ	PERSON(S)	LÁI SHUŌ
duì	wǒ	lái shuō

"as far as I'm concerned"

More examples of **duì...lái shuō**:

Duì Zhōngguo rén lái shuō, Chūnjié shi zuì zhòngyàode jiérì.

"For Chinese people, Chinese New Year is the most important festival."

Duì tā lái shuō, xiànzài zuì zhòngyàode shìqing shi zhuànqián.

"As far as she's concerned, the most important thing now is to make money."

Duì niánqīng rén lái shuō, dǎ tàijíquán méiyou tiàowǔ yǒu yìsi.

"For young people, shadow boxing is not as much fun as dancing."

2D.   The resultative compound **qǐlái** basically means "get up." The potential forms would be **qǐdelái** "can get up" and **qǐbulái** "can't get up." You've previously seen **-qilai** as a resultative ending in **kànqilai** "in the looking," **bǐqilai** "in the comparing," etc.

3. **Yuánlái shi zhèiyang** "So that's how it is." You've already been introduced to **yuánlái** in the sense of "originally" or "formerly." In this sentence, you encounter a new use of **yuánlái**, namely, to indicate on the part of the speaker the discovery of new and unexpected information, or of a previously unknown state of affairs. This kind of **yuánlái** can sometimes be translated into English as "so" or "actually." Examples:

> **Yuánlái Lǎo Zhāng shi gǎo jiàndié gōngzuòde ya!**
>
> "So Old Zhang was involved in spy work!"

> **Guàibudé tā yǐjīng zhīdaole, yuánlái shi nǐ gàosu tāde!**
>
> "No wonder she already knows; so you told her!"

> **Wǒ zhǎo yǎnjìngr zhǎole bàntiān le, yuánlái yìzhí zài wǒde bízishang ne!**
>
> "I've been hunting for my glasses for the longest time, and actually the whole time they were on my nose!"

> **Yuánlái nǐ bù xǐhuan chī Sìchuān cài, nánguài nǐ yào shàng Dōngběi guǎnzi!**
>
> "So you don't like Sichuan cuisine; no wonder you wanted to go to a Northeastern-style restaurant!"

4A. Notice how you say "6:00 to 6:30": **liùdiǎn dào liùdiǎn bàn**.

4B. Sports of all kinds are very popular in mainland China and Taiwan. In fact, participating in sports is an excellent way to meet people, make friends, and improve your understanding of Chinese language, society, and culture.

5. **Wǒ yě hǎo jiǔ méi pǎole** "I also for a long time now haven't run" is a good example of negative time spent (11-2: 2A). Here, **hǎo jiǔ** occurs before rather than after the verb because negative time spent is involved. There is a **le** at the end of the sentence because the situation of "not having run for a long time" has continued up to the present.

AV1–17. **SPORTS.** The names of these sports are arranged in alphabetical order of the English equivalents.

AV1. Another word for "American-style football" is **gǎnlǎnqiú**, literally "olive ball."

Watching a Soccer Game on Television

Kevin Johnson is visiting the home of his Beijing University classmate Cao Jianhua. The two young men are sitting in the living room, discussing what television program they should watch.

Basic Conversation 21-3

1. JOHNSON	**Xiànzài yǒu shémme hǎo jiémù?**	
	What good programs are on now?	

2. CAO
Yī píndào yǒu Shìjiè Bēi zúqiúsài, èr píndào yǒu wényì wǎnhuì. Nǐ xiǎng kàn něige?
On channel one there is the World Cup Soccer match, and on channel two there is a variety show. Which one do you want to see?

3. JOHNSON
Hái shi kàn zúqiú ba. Nǎge duì duì nǎge duì?
Let's watch the soccer. Which team is playing against which team?

4. CAO
Yīnggélán duì Bāxī.
England against Brazil.

5. JOHNSON
Nà kuài kāi diànshì ba!
So hurry up and turn on the TV!

(Cao turns on the television set)

Āiya, bǐsài yǐjīng kāishǐle.
Oh, no, the game has already begun.

6. CAO
Hái hǎo, gāng kāishǐ. Yò! Yǐjīng yī bǐ líng la.
At least it only just started. Wow! It's already one to zero.

7. JOHNSON
Ò, hǎo qiú, zhēn bàng! Xiǎo Cáo, nǐ shuō shéi néng yíng?
Oh, good ball, fantastic! Little Cao, who do you think will win?

8. CAO
Nán shuō. Zhèiliǎngge duì dōu shi shìjiè yǒumíngde qiáng duì. Shéi yùnqi hǎo, shéi jiù yíng.
Hard to say. These two teams are both world-famous strong teams. Whoever is lucky will win.

🔘 Build Up

---

1. Johnson

jiémù	program [N]
Xiànzài yǒu shémme hǎo jiémù?	What good programs are on now?

---

2. Cao

píndào	channel [N]
yī píndào	channel one
èr píndào	channel two
shìjiè	world [N]
Shìjiè Bēi	World Cup [PH]
zúqiú	soccer [N]
zúqiúsài	soccer competition [N]
Shìjiè Bēi zúqiúsài	World Cup soccer competition
wényì	literature and art [N]
wǎnhuì	evening party [N]
wényì wǎnhuì	variety show [PH]
Yī píndào yǒu Shìjiè Bēi zúqiúsài, èr píndào yǒu wényì wǎnhuì. Nǐ xiǎng kàn něige?	On channel one there is the World Cup Soccer match, and on channel two there is a variety show. Which one do you want to see?

---

3. Johnson

duì	pair off against; versus [V]
nǎge duì	which team
nǎge duì duì nǎge duì	which team against which team
Hái shi kàn zúqiú ba. Nǎge duì duì nǎge duì?	Let's watch the soccer. Which team is playing against which team?

---

4. Cao

Yīnggélán	England [PW]
Bāxī	Brazil [PW]
Yīnggélán duì Bāxī.	England against Brazil.

---

5. Johnson

kāi	turn on (a machine, light, etc.) [V]
diànshì	television [N]
Nà kuài kāi diànshì ba!	So hurry up and turn on the TV!
bǐsài	competition [N]
Āiya, bǐsài yǐjīng kāishǐle.	Oh, no, the game has already begun.

---

6. Cao

bǐ	compare; to (in comparing scores) [V]
yī bǐ líng	one to zero
Hái hǎo, gāng kāishǐ. Yò! Yǐjīng yī bǐ líng la.	At least it only just started. Wow! It's already one to zero.

---

7. Johnson

Cáo	Cao [SN]
yíng	win [V]
nǐ shuō shéi néng yíng	who would you say can win
Ò, hǎo qiú, zhēn bàng! Xiǎo Cáo, nǐ shuō shéi néng yíng?	Oh, good ball, fantastic! Little Cao, who do you think will win?

8. Cao

nán shuō	hard to say
zhèiliǎngge duì	these two teams
yǒumíng	be famous [SV]
qiáng	be strong [SV]
shìjiè yǒumíngde qiáng duì	world-famous strong team
shéi yùnqi hǎo shéi jiù yíng	whoever's luck is good will win

Nán shuō. Zhèiliǎngge duì dōu shi shìjiè yǒumíngde qiáng duì. Shéi yùnqi hǎo, shéi jiù yíng.

Hard to say. These two teams are both world-famous strong teams. Whoever is lucky will win.

Supplementary Vocabulary

1.	**kàn diànshì**	watch television [PH]
2.	**diànshì jiémù**	television program [PH]
3.	**diànshìtái**	television station [N]
4.	**xīnwén**	news [N]
5.	**xǐjù**	comedy [N]
6.	**liánxùjù**	soap opera, serial [N]
7.	**ruò**	be weak [SV]
8.	**shū**	lose (i.e., not win) [V]
	Nǐ yíngle, wǒ shūle!	You won and I lost!
9.	**píng**	be flat, even; tied (score) [SV]
	Sān píng.	It's tied three to three.

Additional Vocabulary

1. **Yǒuyì dìyī, bǐsài dì'èr.**   "Friendship first, competition second." [EX]

Grammatical and Cultural Notes

2. The noun **shìjiè** can be combined with **hépíng** "peace" (4-2) to create the expression **shìjiè hépíng** "world peace."

3A. **Hái shi**, literally "still," is often used when deciding between alternatives. **Hái shi kàn zúqiú ba** might be translated literally as "(After considering the alternatives,) it might still be better if we watched soccer."

3B. **Nǎge** is an alternate form for **něige** "which." Similarly, you'll sometimes hear **nǎguó** for **něiguó** "(from) which country?" as in **Nǐ shi nǎguó rén?** "From what country are you?"

4. **Yīnggélán** "England" is a formal term for **Yīngguo**.

6A. **Hái hǎo** here means "(On consideration, it's) still good (that the soccer game has only just begun)."

6B. **COMPARING SPORTS SCORES WITH THE VERB BǏ "COMPARE".** Note **yī bǐ líng** "one to zero" (as a score in a sport or other competition). As in English, the higher score is placed first. In the case of a tie score, you give the number of points and add **píng** "tied" (lit. "level"). The corresponding question would be **Jǐ bǐ jǐ?** "How many points to how many points?" or "What was the score?" The basic pattern is:

SCORE OF TEAM 1	BǏ	SCORE OF TEAM 2
yī	bǐ	líng
"one to zero"		

More examples of the use of **bǐ** in comparing scores:

sān bǐ yī	"three to one"
èrshiliù bǐ shíbā	"26 to 18"
bā píng	"eight tied"

7.   **Nǐ shuō shéi néng yíng?** "Who do you think can win?" The **shuō** here means about the same as **xiǎng** "think" or **kàn** "consider."

8A.   **Nán shuō** "(That) is hard to say." Be sure you can use the pattern **nán** + VERB, which basically means "hard to VERB." Before verbs expressing the senses (e.g., taste, sight, hearing, smell), this pattern often best translates as "VERB awful." More examples:

Hěn nán jiǎng.	"It's hard to say."
Nà shízài hěn nán shuō.	"That is really hard to say."
Zhèige cài hǎo nán chī.	"This dish tastes awful."
Zhèige yīnyuè hěn nán tīng!	"This music sounds awful!"

8B.   Notice how **Nán shuō** is used here as a vague response to allow the speaker to avoid committing himself and possibly losing face (and to avoid making the listener feel uncomfortable or lose face in case he should disagree). For all these reasons, vague and noncommital responses like **Nán shuō** and **Nán jiǎng** are very common in Chinese.

8C.   The pattern **A shi shìjiè yǒumíngde B** means "A is a world-famous B." Another example:

Sūn Xiáojie shi shìjiè yǒumíngde gāngqínjiā.

"Ms. Sun is a world-famous pianist."

8D.   **QUESTION WORDS USED IN PAIRS.** Consider the sentence **Shéi yùnqi hǎo, shéi jiù yíng** "Whoever is lucky will win" (lit. "Who is lucky, who then wins"). When question words are used in pairs, they take on an indefinite sense that can be translated into English by the corresponding question word plus "-ever." In the sentence cited, the question word **shéi** "who" takes on the meaning "whoever." The clause in which the second question word occurs often contains a **jiù** "then." Question words in pairs can have various grammatical functions, e.g., as topic or subject, object, place word, or adverb. Examples:

Nǐ chī shémme, wǒ jiù chī shémme.

"I'll eat whatever you eat." (lit. "You eat what, I then eat what.")

Dàrén zuò shémme, xiǎohái jiù zuò shémme.

"Kids will do whatever grownups do."

Nǐ dào nǎr qù, wǒ jiù dào nǎr qù.

"I'll go wherever you go." (lit. "You go where, I then go where.")

Nǐ jǐdiǎn qù, wǒ jiù jǐdiǎn qù.

"Whatever time you go, I'll go." (lit. "You what time go, I then what time go.")

If the subject of the first clause is the same as the subject of the second clause, the subject in the second clause can be deleted. Examples:

Nǐ xiǎng gàn shémme jiù gàn shémme ba.

"Do whatever you like." (lit. "You want do what, then do what.")

Nǐ juéde zěmme zuò hǎo, jiù zěmme zuò ba.

"Do however you feel is best." (lit. "You feel how do good, then how do.")

Sometimes the question word in the second clause has a different function from the question word in the first clause, that is, the two clauses are not parallel. For example:

Shéi yào, wǒ jiù sònggěi shéi.

"Whoever wants it, I'll give it to them." (lit. "Who wants, I then give to who.")

Něizhāng zhuōzi piányi, wǒ jiù mǎi něizhāng zhuōzi.

"I'll buy whichever table is cheaper." (lit. "Which table is cheap, I then buy which table.")

AV1.   A freer rendering of **Yǒuyì dìyī, bǐsài dì'èr** might be "It's not whether you win or lose, but how you play the game." You were introduced to **yǒuyì** "friendship" in 8-2. In Taiwan, instead of **yǒuyì**, people say **yǒuyí**.

Boys from Hong Kong soccer club practicing soccer

An Excursion to the Great Wall

American Professor Peter McCoy's good friend Mei Tingsheng takes him to see the Great Wall of China at Badaling.

 ## Basic Conversation 21-4

1. **MCCOY**
Xiǎo Méi, wǒ zhōngyú dēngshang Cháng Chéng le!
Little Mei, I've finally climbed onto the Great Wall!

2. **MEI**
Shì a. Zhōngguo rén cháng shuō: "Bú dào Cháng Chéng fēi hǎohàn." Xiànzài nǐ yě suàndeshang shi "hǎohàn" le!
Yes. Chinese people often say: "If you don't go to the Great Wall, you're not a brave man." Now you, too, can be regarded as a "brave man"!

3. **MCCOY**
À, zhēn shi míng-bù-xū-chuán. Xiǎo Méi, Cháng Chéng dàodǐ yǒu duō cháng?
Wow, it really lives up to its reputation. Little Mei, how long really is the Great Wall?

4. **MEI**
Hǎoxiàng yǒu liùqiānduōgōnglǐ cháng.
I think it's over 6,000 kilometers long.

5. **MCCOY**
Cháng Chéng shi shémme shíhou jiànde?
When was the Great Wall built?

6. **MEI**
Dàyuē shi zài liǎngqiānduōnián qián, Zhànguó Shídài jiù kāishǐ jiànle. Hòulái lìdài búduànde kuòjiàn. Búguò zhèlide zhèiyíduàn shi Míngcháode shíhou xiūde.
More than 2,000 years ago, during the Warring States Period, they began building it. Later in successive dynasties it kept being expanded. But this section here was built during the Ming.

7. **MCCOY**
Nèige shíhou xiūqilai kě zhēn gòu bu róngyide.
At that time to build it must have really been quite difficult.

8. **MEI**
Kě bu shì! Zhèixiē cáiliàor quán děi kào réngōng bānyùn, sǐle bù zhīdào yǒu duōshǎo rén!
That's for sure! The material all had to be transported by hand. No one knows how many people died!

MAJOR DIVISIONS OF CHINESE HISTORY

PINYIN	ENGLISH	DATES
Xiàcháo	Xia Dynasty	ca. 2100–1600 BCE
Shāngcháo	Shang Dynasty	ca. 1600–1100 BCE
Xīzhōu	Western Zhou Dynasty	ca. 1100–771 BCE
Dōngzhōu	Eastern Zhou Dynasty	770–256 BCE
Chūnqiū Shídài	Spring and Autumn Period	770–476 BCE
Zhànguó Shídài	Warring States Period	475–221 BCE
Qíncháo	Qin Dynasty	221–207 BCE
Xīhàn	Western Han Dynasty	206 BCE–24 CE
Dōnghàn	Eastern Han Dynasty	25–220
Sānguó Shídài	Three Kingdoms Period	220–280
Xījìn	Western Jin	265–316
Dōngjìn	Eastern Jin	317–420
Nánběicháo	Northern and Southern Dynasties	420–581
Suícháo	Sui Dynasty	581–618
Tángcháo	Tang Dynasty	618–907
Wǔdài	Five Dynasties Period	907–960
Běisòng	Northern Song Dynasty	960–1127
Nánsòng	Southern Song Dynasty	1127–1279
Liáocháo	Liao Dynasty	907–1125
Jīncháo	Jin Dynasty	1115–1234
Yuáncháo	Yuan Dynasty	1271–1368
Míngcháo	Ming Dynasty	1368–1644
Qīngcháo	Qing Dynasty	1644–1911
Zhōnghuá Mínguó	Republic of China	1912–
Zhōnghuá Rénmín Gònghéguó	People's Republic of China	1949–

 Build Up

1. McCoy

Méi	Mei [SN]
Xiǎo Méi	Little Mei
zhōngyú	finally, at last [A]
dēng	climb [V]
dēngshang	climb onto [RC]
dēngshang Cháng Chéng	climb onto the Great Wall
Xiǎo Méi, wǒ zhōngyú dēngshang Cháng Chéng le!	Little Mei, I've finally climbed onto the Great Wall!

2. Mei

hǎohàn	brave man [N]
"bú dào Cháng Chéng fēi hǎohàn"	"if you don't get to the Great Wall you're not a brave man" [EX]
suànshang	include, count [RC]
suàndeshang	can count as, can be regarded [RC]
nǐ yě suàndeshang shi hǎohàn	you too can be regarded as a brave man

Shì a. Zhōngguo rén cháng shuō:
"Bú dào Cháng Chéng fēi hǎohàn."
Xiànzài nǐ yě suàndeshang shi "hǎohàn" le!

Yes. Chinese people often say: "If you don't go
to the Great Wall, you're not a brave man."
Now you, too, can be regarded as a "brave man"!

3. McCoy

míng-bù-xū-chuán	have a well deserved reputation [EX]
zhēn shi míng-bù-xū-chuán	it really has a well deserved reputation
dàodǐ(r)	after all, really [MA]
yǒu duō cháng	is how long
Cháng Chéng dàodǐ yǒu duō cháng	the Great Wall really is how long

À, zhēn shi míng-bù-xū-chuán. Xiǎo Méi,
Cháng Chéng dàodǐ yǒu duō cháng?

Wow, it really lives up to its reputation.
Little Mei, how long really is the Great Wall?

4. Mei

gōnglǐ	kilometer [M]
liùqiānduōgōnglǐ	more than 6,000 kilometers
yǒu liùqiānduōgōnglǐ cháng	it's over 6,000 kilometers long

Hǎoxiàng yǒu liùqiānduōgōnglǐ cháng.

I think it's over 6,000 kilometers long.

5. McCoy

jiàn	build [V]

Cháng Chéng shi shémme shíhou jiànde?

When was the Great Wall built?

6. Mei

zài liǎngqiānduōnián qián	over 2,000 years ago
shídài	period [N]
Zhànguó Shídài	Warring States Period [TW]
lìdài	successive dynasties [N]
búduànde	unceasingly, continuously [A]
kuòjiàn	expand [V]
lìdài búduànde kuòjiàn	in successive dynasties it was continuously expanded
zhèlide zhèiyíduàn	this section here
Míngcháo	Ming Dynasty [TW]
xiū	build [V]

Dàyuē shi zài liǎngqiānduōnián qián,
Zhànguó Shídài jiù kāishǐ jiànle. Hòulái
lìdài búduànde kuòjiàn. Búguò zhèlide
zhèiyíduàn shi Míngcháode shíhou xiūde.

More than 2,000 years ago, during the Warring
States Period, they began building it. Later in
successive dynasties it kept being expanded. But
this section here was built during the Ming.

7. McCoy

xiūqilai	in the building [RC]
gòu...-de	quite... , rather... [PT]
zhēn gòu bu róngyide	really quite difficult

Nèige shíhou xiūqilai kě zhēn gòu bu
róngyide.

At that time to build it must have really
been quite difficult.

8. Mei

kě bu shì	"that's for sure" [IE]
cáiliào(r)	material [N]

kào	depend on [V]
réngōng	human labor, manual labor [N]
bānyùn	transport [V]
kào réngōng bānyùn	depend on human labor to transport
sǐle bù zhīdào yǒu duōshǎo rén	there died it's not known how many people there were
Kě bu shì! Zhèixiē cáiliàor quán děi kào réngōng bānyùn, sǐle bù zhīdào yǒu duōshǎo rén!	That's for sure! The material all had to be transported by hand. No one knows how many people died!

Supplementary Vocabulary

1.	**yīnglǐ**	mile [M]
2.	**zhànzhēng**	war [N]
3.	**kuān**	be wide [SV]

Additional Vocabulary

1. **Zài jiā kào fùmǔ, chūmén kào péngyou.** "At home you depend on your parents; when you leave home and go out, you depend on your friends." [EX]

Grammatical and Cultural Notes

1A.   **Zhōngyú** is an adverb that means "finally" or "at last." It's used here in the sense of always having wanted to do something but only now "finally" being able to achieve your goal. **Zuìhòu**, which you learned in 8-4, has the same meaning of "finally" but has a different connotation: **zuìhòu** has a temporal sense, as in "First I did this, then I did that, and then finally (**zuìhòu**) I did something else." Here are two examples that contrast **zhōngyú** and **zuìhòu**:

> **Wǒ yǐqián cháng tīngshuō Běijīng kǎoyā shi Běijīng míngcài, xiànzài zhōngyú chīdàole, zhēn shi míng-bù-xū-chuán.**

> "I've often heard that Peking Duck is a famous Beijing dish, and now I've finally eaten some; it truly has a well deserved reputation."

> **Chī kǎoyāde shíhou, nǐ xiān bǎ tiánmiànjiàng túzai bǐngshang, ránhòu fàngshang cōng, yāròu, zuìhòu zài bǎ bǐng juǎnqilai, jiù kéyi chīle.**

> "When you eat Peking Duck, you first spread the sweet flour sauce onto the pancake, then you put on scallions and the duck meat, and finally you roll up the pancake, and then you can eat it."

1B.   **Wǒ zhōngyú dēngshang Cháng Chéng le!** "I've finally climbed on the Great Wall!" There could have been a completed action **-le** here after **dēngshang** "climbed." In other words, the speaker could have said **Wǒ zhōngyú dēngshang<u>le</u> Cháng Chéng <u>le</u>**. However, with double **le** in sentences with unquantified objects that indicate completed action, the first **-le** is often omitted. Similarly, **Wǒ yǐjīng chī<u>le</u> fàn <u>le</u>** "I've already eaten" often becomes **Wǒ yǐjīng chīfàn le**.

Great Wall near Badaling

1C.   **GREAT WALL OF CHINA.** The full Chinese name for the **Cháng Chéng** "Great Wall" is **Wànlǐ Cháng Chéng** "the 10,000 li long wall." The Great Wall stretches from Shanhaiguan Pass in the east to Jiayuguan Pass in the west, its length totaling over 6,000 kilometers. Construction began in the 7th century BCE, when several of the different states of the time—Qin, Zhao, and Yan—each built walls to protect themselves. During the reign of Qin Shi Huang (221–206 BCE), the so-called "First Emperor" who unified China, these walls were linked into one longer one. In later dynasties, the Great Wall was periodically repaired and reinforced. Most of the present Great Wall was built in the Ming Dynasty. Badaling used to be the main outpost for safeguarding Beijing. The wall at Badaling, one of the most magnificent sections of the wall, is 7.8 meters high and about 5 meters wide, built with rectangular slabs of stones as well as bricks.

2. The meaning of the Classical Chinese morpheme **fēi** is "not be" or "non-." You've encountered it in **fēicháng** "not ordinarily" or "extremely" (15-1) and **fēixīyān qū** "non-smoking section" (18-3).

3A. **Míng-bù-xū-chuán** literally means "(its) fame (is) not emptily spread," that is, "there is a reason for its fame" or "it has a well deserved reputation."

3B. **Cháng Chéng dàodǐ yǒu duō cháng?** "How long really is the Great Wall?" **Dàodǐ** "after all" or "really" is sometimes best translated by stress. Here are some more examples with **dàodǐ**:

> **Nǐmen gōngsī nèmme dà, dàodǐ yǒu duōshǎo rén ne?**
> "Your company is so large, how many people does it really have?"

> **Nǐ shuō yǒu rén zǎoshang liùdiǎn jiù dǎ diànhuà gěi wǒ, dàodǐ shi shéi ne?**
> "You say somebody called me on the phone at 6 a.m.; so who actually was it?"

> **Zhèiběn shū zài zhèr fàngle hǎo duō tiān le, dàodǐ shi shéide ne?**
> "This book has been lying here for quite a few days; whose really is it?"

3C. Notice in this line the question **Cháng Chéng dàodǐ yǒu duō cháng?** "How long really is the Great Wall?" (lit. "Great Wall after all has how long?"). Also note the answer to this question in the next line: **Hǎoxiàng yǒu liùqiānduōgōnglǐ cháng** "It seems to be over 6,000 kilometers in length" (lit. "Seems has more than 6,000 kilometers long"). **Yǒu...cháng** here means "be...in length." Review grammar note 17-3: 6 on **yǒu** + QUANTITY EXPRESSION + STATIVE VERB to indicate size, distance, etc.

4A. **Gōnglǐ** "kilometer" literally means "public mile" and derives from the traditional Chinese unit of length the **lǐ**, which was approximately one-half kilometer. In SV1 you also learn **yīnglǐ** "mile" (lit. "English mile").

4B. Note the **duō** in **liùqiānduōgōnglǐ** "more than six thousand kilometers." Cf. also, in line 6, **liǎngqiānduōnián** "more than two thousand years."

6A. **USE OF ZÀI IN TIME EXPRESSIONS.** Although **zài** "be located at" most commonly describes physical location, it can also describe location in time. Thus, in this line, **zài liǎngqiānduōniánqián** means "more than 2,000 years ago." This **zài** is optional.

6B. Note the **-de** in **búduànde** "unceasingly" or "continuously" and review note 15-1: 1C on the use of **-de** as adverbial modifier to express manner. This **-de** is optional.

7A. The speaker on the video and audio discs says **nàge shíhou** for **nèige shíhou** "(at) that time." Either pronunciation is correct.

7B. **Xiūqilai** means "in the building." Review the pattern VERB + **-qilai** "in the VERB-ing" (6-2: 5A).

7C. **GÒU + STATIVE VERB + -DE.** The word **gòu** followed by a stative verb followed by **-de** means "quite," "pretty," or "rather." This is informal, colloquial usage. The **gòu**, which here functions as an adverb, is the same **gòu** that elsewhere means "be enough" (cf. colloquial English "Today it sure is cold enough," in which "enough" has a meaning similar to **gòu**). In this line, **kě zhēn gòu bu róngyide** means "really not easy at all" or "really quite difficult." **Kě zhēn** "really" is sometimes added for emphasis. The basic pattern is:

GÒU	STATIVE VERB	-DE
gòu	jǐnzhāng	de
"quite intense"		

Some more examples of **gòu** + STATIVE VERB + **-de**:

Zhèjǐtiān kě zhēn gòu lěngde. "These last few days sure have been cold enough."

Nǐ yě gòu mángde. "You're pretty busy yourself."

8A. **Kě bu shì** is an idiomatic expression that means "That's for sure" or "Of course." Sometimes there is also a following **ma**, as in **Kě bu shì ma!** "Of course!"

8B. In 19-3: 2 you were introduced to sentences where subject and verb are reversed, such as **Lái kèrén le** "A guest has come." In this line there is another example of this: **Sǐle bù zhīdào yǒu duōshǎo rén** "There died I don't know how many people." Remember that sentences where the verb comes first always involve an indefinite subject. So while you could say **Sǐle hěn duō rén** "A lot of people died" (since in this sentence "people" is indefinite), you could NOT say *Sǐle Xiǎo Wángde mǔqīn for "Little Wang's mother died" (since Little Wang's mother is a specific individual). Instead, you'd have to say **Xiǎo Wángde mǔqīn sǐle**.

8C. **Sǐle bù zhīdào yǒu duōshǎo rén!** "There died it's not known how many people there were!" or "Nobody knows how many people died!" The subject of the **bù zhīdào** is here unexpressed. A fuller version of this sentence would be **Shéi yě bù zhīdào sǐle duōshǎo rén!** "Nobody knows how many people died!"

Unit 21: Review and Study Guide

New Vocabulary

ADVERBS

búduànde	continuously
dàoshi	actually, to the contrary
zhōngyú	finally

BOUND FORMS

zhěng	exact, sharp (of clock times)

CONJUNCTIONS

hàn	and

EXPRESSIONS

"bú dào Cháng Chéng fēi hǎohàn"	"if you don't go to the Great Wall you're not a brave man"
míng-bù-xū-chuán	have a well-deserved reputation

IDIOMATIC EXPRESSIONS

kě bu shì	"that's for sure"

MEASURES

gōnglǐ	kilometer
yīnglǐ	mile

MOVEABLE ADVERBS

bǐrú	for example
dàodǐ(r)	after all, really
ǒu'ěr	occasionally
yuánlái	actually

NOUNS

bàngqiú	baseball
bǐsài	competition
cáiliào(r)	material
chūnjià	spring vacation
diànshì	television
diànshìtái	television station
duì	team
gèzi	stature, build
gōngfū	kung fu
hánjià	winter vacation
hǎohàn	brave man
jià	vacation, leave
jiàoyù	education

jiàrì	holiday, day off
jiémù	program
lánqiú	basketball
lǎonián	old age
liánxùjù	soap opera, serial
lìdài	successive dynasties
máo	feather, hair (on body), fur
píndào	channel
pīngpāngqiú	Ping-Pong
qiú	ball
réngōng	human labor
shèhuì	society
shètuán	organization
shídài	period
shìjiè	world
shìyǒu	roommate
shǔjià	summer vacation
tàijíquán	taiji
tǐyù	physical education
tuántǐ	group
wǎng	net

wǎngqiú	tennis	**Shìjiè Bēi**	World Cup		
wǎnhuì	evening party	**wényì wǎnhuì**	variety show	**Míngcháo**	Ming Dynasty
wényì	literature and art	**zhōngnián rén**	middle-aged people	**Zhànguó Shídài**	Warring States Period
wǔshù	martial art	**PLACE WORDS**			
xiàoduì	school team	**Bāxī**	Brazil	**VERBS**	
xǐjù	comedy	**gōngyuán**	park (piece of ground)	**bānyùn**	transport
xīnwén	news			**bǐ**	compare; to (in comparing scores)
yóuyǒng	swimming; swim	**jiāowài**	countryside around a city	**chénggōng**	succeed
yǔmáo	feather, plumage			**chénpǎo**	jog in the morning
yǔmáoqiú	badminton, shuttle-cock	**tǐyùguǎn**	gymnasium	**dǎ**	play (a sport)
		Yīnggélán	England	**dēng**	climb
yùndòng	sport, athletics, exercise	**QUESTION WORDS**		**duì**	pair off against; versus
zhànzhēng	war	**nǎxiē**	which ones, which		
zhōngnián	middle age	**RESULTATIVE COMPOUNDS**		**jiàn**	build
zúqiú	soccer	**dēngshang**	climb onto	**jiārù**	join
zúqiúsài	soccer competition	**qǐlái**	get up	**kāi**	turn on (a machine, light)
PATTERNS		**suàndeshang**	can be regarded as		
duì...lái shuō	as regards..., for..., to...	**suànshang**	include, count	**kào**	depend on
		xiūqilai	in the constructing of something	**kuòjiàn**	expand
gòu...-de	quite..., rather...			**shū**	lose (i.e., not win)
nándào...ma	don't tell me that...	**STATIVE VERBS**		**xiū**	build
PHRASES		**kuān**	be wide	**yíng**	win
bǐfang shuō	for example	**píng**	be flat, even; tied (score)	**VERB-OBJECT COMPOUNDS**	
bǐrú shuō	for example			**dǎqiú**	play a ball game
dǎ tàijíquán	practice taiji	**qiáng**	be strong	**fàngjià**	take a vacation
diànshì jiémù	television program	**ruò**	be weak	**pèngmiàn**	meet (face-to-face)
kàn diànshì	watch television	**yǒumíng(r)**	be famous	**qǐngjià**	request leave
lǎonián rén	old people	**SURNAMES**		**tiàowǔ**	dance
niánqīng rén	young people	**Cáo**	Cao		
		Méi	Mei		

Major New Grammar Patterns

YǑU MÉIYOU + VERB TO INDICATE QUESTIONS: Nǐ yǒu méiyou mǎi? "Did you buy it?" (21-1)

NÁNDÀO...MA: Nándào tā lián yíkuài qián dōu méiyou ma? "You mean he doesn't have even a dollar?" (21-2)

DUÌ...LÁI SHUŌ: duì wǒ lái shuō "as far as I'm concerned" (21-2)

COMPARING SPORTS SCORES WITH BǏ: sān bǐ yī "three to one" (21-3)

QUESTION WORDS USED IN PAIRS: Shéi yùnqi hǎo, shéi jiù yíng. "Whoever is lucky will win.", **Nǐ chī shémme, wǒ jiù chī shémme.** "I'll eat whatever you eat.", **Nǐ dào nǎr qù, wǒ jiù dào nǎr qù.** "I'll go wherever you go." (21-3)

GÒU + STATIVE VERB + -DE: Zhèjǐtiān kě zhēn gòu lěngde. "These last few days sure have been pretty cold." (21-4)

Emergencies

COMMUNICATIVE OBJECTIVES

Once you've mastered this unit, you'll be able to use Chinese to:

1. Talk about being sick: going to see the doctor, requesting an English-speaking doctor, staying in the hospital, etc.

2. Discuss specific maladies and illnesses: cold, headache, fever, nausea, pneumonia, pain, etc.

3. Talk about various parts of the body: head, eyes, ears, nose, mouth, arms, shoulders, back, belly, waist, legs, feet, etc.

4. Explain to a passerby or the police if your purse or wallet has been stolen.

5. Describe the physical characteristics of objects.

6. Go to the lost-and-found to retrieve a missing bag.

7. Deal with a vehicular accident: Anyone hurt? Whose fault? Should you call the police or try to negotiate a settlement privately on the spot? etc.

8. Handle other emergency situations: "Help!," "Fire!," etc.

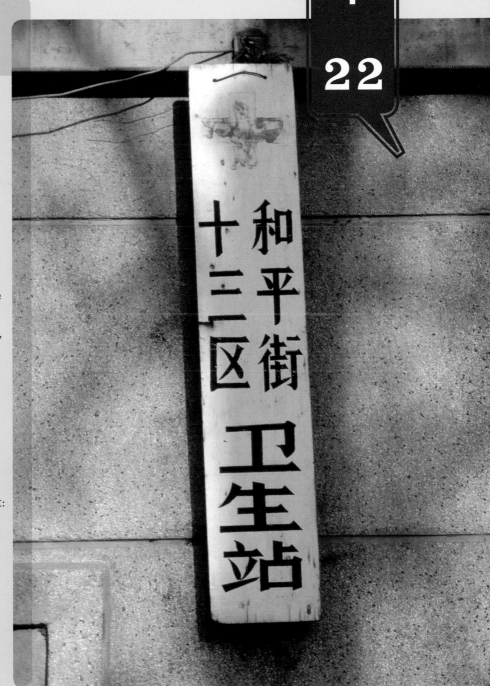

Illness

Ruth Guerriera has been chatting with her friend Ma Cihui in the student coffee shop at Capital University of Economics and Business in Beijing. Guerriera suddenly feels quite ill, so Ma takes her friend to the university hospital.

 ## Basic Conversation 22-1

1. GUERRIERA   **Cíhuī, wǒ juéde hěn bù shūfu.**
Cihui, I don't feel very good.

2. MA   **Shémme dìfang bù shūfu? Nǐ shì bu shi shēngbìng le? Yào bu yao qù yīyuàn kànkan?**
Where does it hurt? Are you sick? Do you want to go to a hospital to see a doctor?

3. GUERRIERA   **Tóu téng, ěxin, xiǎng tù. Húnshēn méi jìnr, hǎoxiàng hái yǒu diǎnr fāshāo. Yěxǔ shi gǎnmàole. Wǒ xiǎng yòngbuzháo qù yīyuàn. Xiūxi liǎngtiān jiù huì hǎode.**
My head hurts, I'm nauseous, and I feel like throwing up. I'm weak all over and I may have a fever. Maybe I caught a cold. I don't think I need to go to a hospital. If I rest for two days then I should be all right.

4. MA   **Xiànzài zǎowǎn qìwēn biànhuà tǐng dàde. Yī bú zhùyì jiù róngyi zháoliáng. Nàobuhǎo hái huì zhuǎnchéng fèiyán. Wǒ xiǎng nǐ zuìhǎo hái shi qù yīyuàn kànkan.**
There's now a huge change in temperature from morning to evening. The minute you're not careful, it's easy to catch cold. If you don't get better, it could even turn into pneumonia. I think you had best go to a hospital to see a doctor.

(to nurse, after they arrive at the hospital)

Tóngzhì, wǒ zhèiwèi péngyou bìngle. Tā bú dà huì shuō Hànyǔ. Néng bu néng gěi tā zhǎo yíwèi dǒng Yīngyǔde dàifu?
Comrade, this friend of mine is ill. She can't speak Chinese very well. Could you find her a doctor who understands English?

5. NURSE   **Nín děng yíxiàr. Nèiwèi dàifu zhèng mángzhe ne.**
Wait just a moment. That doctor is busy right now.

🎧 Build Up

1. Guerriera

Cíhuī	Cihui (given name)
hěn bù shūfu	very uncomfortable
Cíhuī, wǒ juéde hěn bù shūfu.	Cihui, I don't feel very good.

2. Ma

shémme dìfang bù shūfu	what place is uncomfortable
shēngbìng	become sick [VO]
shì bu shi shēngbìngle	is it that you got sick
yīyuàn	hospital [PW]
qù yīyuàn kànkan	go to a hospital to see a doctor
Shémme dìfang bù shūfu? Nǐ shì bu shi shēngbìng le? Yào bu yao qù yīyuàn kànkan?	Where does it hurt? Are you sick? Do you want to go to a hospital to see a doctor?

3. Guerriera

tóu	head [N]
téng	be painful, hurt [SV]
tóu téng	head hurts
ěxin	be nauseous, feel like vomiting [SV]
tù	spit, throw up [V]
ěxin xiǎng tù	be nauseous and want to throw up
húnshēn	entire body [N]
jìn(r)	energy [N]
méi jìnr	have no energy
húnshēn méi jìnr	whole body has no energy
fāshāo	have a fever [VO]
yǒu diǎnr fāshāo	have a little fever
yěxǔ	perhaps, maybe [MA]
gǎnmào	catch cold [V]
yěxǔ shi gǎnmàole	maybe it's that (I) caught a cold
yòngbuzháo	not need to [RC]
yòngbuzháo qù yīyuàn	not need to go to a hospital
xiūxi liǎngtiān	rest for two days
jiù huì hǎode	then it will get better
Tóu téng, ěxin, xiǎng tù. Húnshēn méi jìnr, hǎoxiàng hái yǒu diǎnr fāshāo. Yěxǔ shi gǎnmàole. Wǒ xiǎng yòngbuzháo qù yīyuàn. Xiūxi liǎngtiān jiù huì hǎode.	My head hurts, I'm nauseous, and I feel like throwing up. I'm weak all over and I may have a fever. Maybe I caught a cold. I don't think I need to go to a hospital. If I rest for two days then I should be all right.

4. Ma

zǎowǎn	morning and evening [MA]
qìwēn	temperature [N]
biànhuà	change [N]
qìwēn biànhuà	temperature change
zháoliáng	catch cold [VO]
yī bú zhùyì jiù róngyi zháoliáng	the moment you don't watch out it's easy to catch cold
nào	suffer (from an illness) [V]
nàobuhǎo	suffer from an illness and not get better [RC]
zhuǎnchéng	turn into [V+PV]
fèi	lung [N]
fèiyán	pneumonia [N]
nàobuhǎo hái huì zhuǎnchéng fèiyán	if one doesn't get better it could even turn into pneumonia

Xiànzài zǎowǎn qìwēn biànhuà tǐng dàde.
Yī bú zhùyì jiù róngyi zháoliáng. Nàobuhǎo
hái huì zhuǎnchéng fèiyán. Wǒ xiǎng nǐ
zuìhǎo hái shi qù yīyuàn kànkan.

There's now a huge change in temperature
from morning to evening. The minute you're not
careful, it's easy to catch cold. If you don't get
better, it could even turn into pneumonia. I think you
had best go to a hospital to see a doctor.

bú dà	not very much [PH]
bú dà huì shuō Hànyǔ	can't speak Chinese very well
dàifu	doctor [N]
yíwèi dǒng Yīngyǔde dàifu	a doctor who understands English

Tóngzhì, wǒ zhèiwèi péngyou bìngle. Tā
bú dà huì shuō Hànyǔ. Néng bu néng
gěi tā zhǎo yíwèi dǒng Yīngyǔde dàifu?

Comrade, this friend of mine is ill. She
can't speak Chinese very well. Could you
find her a doctor who understands English?

....

5. Nurse

    zhèng mángzhe ne   is just being busy

Nín děng yíxiàr. Nèiwèi dàifu zhèng mángzhe ne.   Wait just a moment. That doctor is busy right now.

 ## Supplementary Vocabulary

1. kànbìng   see a doctor [VO]

Nǐ yàoshi juéde bù shūfu, zuìhǎo   If you don't feel well, it's best if you
zǎo yidianr qù kànbìng.   go see a doctor as soon as you can.

 ## Additional Vocabulary

A. PARTS OF THE BODY

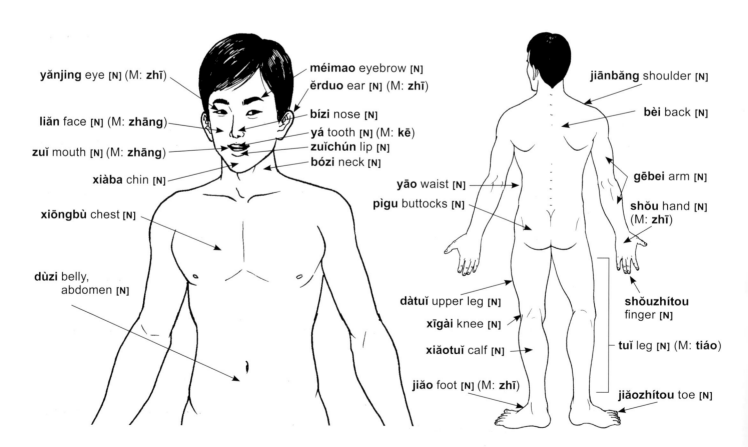

yǎnjing eye [N] (M: zhī)

méimao eyebrow [N]
ěrduo ear [N] (M: zhī)

liǎn face [N] (M: zhāng)

bízi nose [N]
yá tooth [N] (M: kē)

zuǐ mouth [N] (M: zhāng)

zuǐchún lip [N]
bózi neck [N]

xiàba chin [N]

xiōngbù chest [N]

dùzi belly, abdomen [N]

jiānbǎng shoulder [N]

bèi back [N]

gēbei arm [N]

shǒu hand [N] (M: zhī)

yāo waist [N]
pìgu buttocks [N]

dàtuǐ upper leg [N]
xīgài knee [N]
xiǎotuǐ calf [N]
jiǎo foot [N] (M: zhī)

shǒuzhítou finger [N]

tuǐ leg [N] (M: tiáo)

jiǎozhítou toe [N]

B. ILLNESSES AND MEDICAL TERMS

1.	**késou**	cough [V]
2.	**liú bítì**	have a runny nose [PH]
3.	**sǎngzi yǎle**	throat has become hoarse [PH]
4.	**dǎ pēnti**	sneeze [PH]
5.	**lā dùzi**	have diarrhea [PH]
6.	**liúxiě**	bleed [VO]
7.	**fāyán**	be infected, be inflamed [VO]
8.	**guòmǐn**	be allergic [V]
	huāfěn	pollen [N]
	duì huāfěn guòmǐn	be allergic to pollen
9.	**dǎzhēn**	give or get a shot [VO]
10.	**kāidāo**	operate [VO]
11.	**yào**	medicine [N]
	chīyào	take medicine [VO]
12.	**Zhōngyào**	Chinese medicine [N]
13.	**yàofāng**	prescription [N]
	kāi yíge yàofāng	make out a prescription [PH]
14.	**yàofáng**	pharmacy [N]
15.	**zhěnsuǒ**	clinic [PW]
16.	**zhùyuàn**	be hospitalized [VO]
17.	**nèikē**	internal medicine [N]
18.	**wàikē**	surgery [N]
19.	**Xīyī**	Western medicine; doctor of Western medicine [N]
20.	**Zhōngyī**	traditional Chinese medicine; doctor of Chinese medicine [N]
21.	**zhēnjiǔ**	acupuncture and moxibustion [N]

Grammatical and Cultural Notes

2A. **Nǐ shì bu shi shēngbìng le?** "Are you sick?" The **shì bu shi** here literally means "Is it the case that...or not?" This construction is used frequently to create questions and is a little less direct than an affirmative-negative question or **ma** question.

2B. For "I got sick," you can say either **Wǒ bìngle** or **Wǒ shēngbìngle**. **Shēngbìng** "get sick" is a verb-object compound, so its two constituent syllables can be separated. Examples:

Wǒ cónglái méi shēngguo bìng.	"I've never been sick."
Tā shēngle yìchǎng dà bìng.	"He had a serious illness."
Tīngshuō tā shēngle yìzhǒng hěn qíguàide bìng.	"I heard she came down with a strange illness."

Compare **shēngbìng** with the word **bìng**, which can function both as a verb "get sick" and as a noun "illness" (19-1: 3-4).

2C. Distinguish carefully the pronunciation of these two words: **yīyuàn** "hospital" vs. **yīnyuè** "music" (17-1).

2D. As regards the use of the word **yīyuàn** "hospital," in English we say "stay" in a hospital, but in Chinese one says "live" in a hospital, using the verb **zhù**. Example:

Tā zhùle sān'ge xīngqīde yīyuàn. "He stayed in the hospital for three weeks."

2E. **Kànkan** here means "see a doctor." This is a synonym of **kànbìng** "see a doctor" (SV1).

3A. To say "I have a headache," use the double topic-comment construction **Wǒ tóu téng**, lit. "As for me, the head is painful." The same pattern is used for "I have a stomach ache": **Wǒ dùzi téng**. Note that in these expressions, there is no verb **yǒu** "have"; you could NEVER say *__Wǒ yǒu tóu téng__. To say "It really hurts," say **Hǎo téng ó!** In Southern China, instead of **téng**, many speakers use the verb **tòng**, which has the same meaning as **téng**.

3B. **Ěxin** (which can also be pronounced with Tone One on the second syllable as **ěxīn**) means "feel like vomiting, feel nauseated, be nauseous." It can refer both to physical discomfort, as when you're sick, and to mental or emotional discomfort, as when someone makes you feel sick; so it sometimes also has a meaning more like "disgusting." Examples:

> **Wǒ yí kànjian cāngying xīnli jiù juéde ěxin.**
> "As soon as I saw the flies I felt like throwing up."

> **Kàn nèige rénde biǎoqíng, zhēn ràng rén ěxin.**
> "Looking at that person's expression really makes you feel disgusted."

3C. **Húnshēn** means "the entire body," "all over one's body," or "from head to toe," so **Húnshēn méi jìnr** means "My whole body has no energy." Some more examples of **húnshēn**:

> **Tāmen wàngle dài yǔsǎn, húnshēn dōu shīle.**
> "They forgot to take an umbrella, so they're soaked to their skin (lit. "entire body is wet")."

> **Tā pǎole liǎngge xiǎoshí, húnshēn shi hàn.**
> "He ran for two hours; he has sweat over his whole body."

3D. **(Wǒ) yǒu diǎnr fāshāo** "I have a bit of fever." Review the pattern **yǒu (yì)diǎn(r)...** "have a little…," "be a little…," or "somewhat…," which you learned in 19-1: SV5.

3E. The Chinese equivalent of English "I have a cold" is **Wǒ gǎnmàole** and NOT *__Wǒ yǒu gǎnmào__.

3F. **Xiūxi liǎngtiān jiù huì hǎode** here means "If I rest two days, I'll get better." Review the pattern **huì...-de** "be likely to" or "will" that was introduced in 12-2.

4A. **Zǎowǎn** is an abbreviation for **zǎoshang gēn wǎnshang** "morning and evening." Be aware that, in other contexts, **zǎowǎn** can also have the meaning "sooner or later." For example:

> **Wǒ zǎowǎn yídìng huì zhǎo ge jīhui dào Zhōngguo qù lǚxíng.**
> "Sooner or later I'll be sure to find an opportunity to travel to China."

4B. **Xiànzài zǎowǎn qìwēn biànhuà tǐng dàde** "There's now a huge difference in morning and evening temperatures." This is actually a series of four topic-comment constructions, one embedded inside the other. The sentence could be analyzed and translated literally as follows:

TOPIC 1	TOPIC 2	TOPIC 3	TOPIC 4	COMMENT
Xiànzài	**zǎowǎn**	**qìwēn**	**biànhuà**	**tǐng dàde.**

"Now, in the morning and evening, as for the temperature, the change is great."

4C. **Yī bú zhùyì jiù róngyi zháoliáng** "The minute you're not careful, it's easy to catch cold." Note the pattern **yī...jiù...** "as soon as," "the moment," "the minute," or "once" (17-2: 8C).

4D. **Zháoliáng** "catch cold" is a near synonym of **gǎnmào**, which was introduced in line 3. However, besides functioning as a verb, **gǎnmào** can also function as a noun meaning "a cold." Moreover, **gǎnmào** as both verb and noun is used wherever Chinese is spoken, while **zháoliáng** is a colloquial term used mostly in North China.

Jiùhùzhàn

4E. Some stative verbs can be followed directly by verbs (21-3: 8A). **Róngyi** "be easy" is one such stative verb. Notice that the meaning of **róngyi** in the phrase **róngyi zháoliáng** isn't just "easy" but rather "easy to," that is, "easy to catch a cold." Another example of **róngyi** followed directly by a verb in the sense of "easy to":

Zhōngguo huà (bù) róngyi xué.	"Chinese is (not) easy to learn."

4F. **Tā bú dà huì shuō Hànyǔ** "She isn't very well able to speak Chinese" or "She can't speak Chinese very well." **Bú dà** means about the same as **bú tài** "not very much" or "not very well." Examples:

Zhèiyang bú dà hǎo.	"Like this isn't very good."
Tā bú dà cōngming.	"He's not very smart."
Nèiyangr bú dà fāngbian.	"Like that isn't very convenient."
Wǒ bú dà xiǎng qù.	"I don't very much want to go."

4G. **(Nǐ) néng bu néng...?** "Can you/could you...?" is a common and moderately polite way of making a request in Chinese. English works the same way; the expected answer to the English question "Could you close the door?" isn't "Yes, I could" but rather "Sure, I'll be happy to," followed by a response to the request. In neither language is one looking for a true answer to the question asked.

4H. Chinese people often go to the emergency rooms of hospitals even for minor illnesses. Some Chinese people are superstitious about saying the word **zàijiàn** in "unlucky" places like hospitals, funeral homes, jails, or at accident scenes. Remember that the literal translation of **zàijiàn** is "see you again" and implies "see you again in this same place." If you find yourself in a place where you or your interlocutor would rather not appear again, it might be better to use the somewhat formal expression **Bǎozhòng** "Take care of yourself," or you could just say **Wǒ xiān zǒule, wǒmen zài liánxì** "I'll be on my way, we'll be in touch."

SV1. **Kànbìng** "see a doctor (of a patient)" can in some contexts also mean "see a patient (of a doctor)." For example:

Dàifu zhèng zài gěi rén kànbìng.	"The doctor is just seeing a patient."

AV, A. **PARTS OF THE BODY.** Besides the names listed, there are also Chinese names for parts of the body that English lacks or rarely uses, for example, **rénzhōng** (the vertical separation between the skin between your upper lips and your nose), **xiōngkǒu** (the center of the chest right below the breastbone), and **dānyǎnpí** "single eyelid" vs. **shuāngyǎnpí** "double eyelid."

Although the word for "arm" is in dictionaries listed as **gēbei**, in fact many people pronounce this word as **gēbe**. In southern China, many speakers use the word **shǒu**, which in the north means "hand," for both "hand"

and "arm"; these speakers don't use the word **gēbei** at all. For all speakers of Chinese, the meaning of **shǒu** includes part of the arm, unlike English "hand."

The Chinese word **pìgu**, commonly translated as "buttocks," actually includes the buttocks and the hips below the hipbone.

Distinguish **yǎnjing** "eye" from **yǎnjìngr** "eyeglasses."

AV, B.   **ILLNESSES AND MEDICAL TERMS.** These names of illnesses and medical terms have been grouped by semantic category.

AV10.   **Kāidāo** "operate" literally means "open the knife." The direction and meaning of the verb depends on the context. Thus, **Wǒ míngtiān yào kāidāo** can mean either "I'm operating tomorrow" (if you're the doctor) or "I'm having an operation tomorrow" (if you're the patient).

AV11.   In Chinese, to say "take medicine" one says **chīyào**, literally "eat medicine." Many Chinese people, especially older persons, are obsessed with their health and take all kinds of medicines and tonics. When Chinese go to the doctor, they normally expect some kind of treatment, whether an injection, pills, or something else. Penicillin is greatly overprescribed, even for viruses, and IVs are commonly administered even for minor fevers or colds.

AV17–18.   **Nèikē**, usually translated as "internal medicine," basically means that medicine or bandages are in order, while **wàikē** means that surgery is necessary. The location of the malady on the body is irrelevant—a skin allergy would involve **nèikē** even though it's on the surface of the body, while appendicitis (which obviously involves a problem inside the body) would involve **wàikē**.

The Pickpocket

While walking on a street in downtown Taipei, Susan Everett suddenly realizes her purse has been stolen. She calls out and a passerby comes to her assistance. The passerby calls a policeman to the scene.

Basic Conversation 22-2

1. EVERETT

Xiǎotōu! Yǒu rén tōule wǒde píbāo!
Thief! Somebody stole my purse!

2. PASSERBY

Shémme? Zěmme huí shì?
What? What happened?

3. EVERETT

Jiù shi nèige rén! Gǎnkuài zhuāzhù tā, búyào ràng tā pǎodiào. Zhè fùjìn yǒu méiyou jǐngchá?
It's that guy! Hurry up and catch him, don't let him run away. Is there a policeman nearby?

4. PASSERBY

Wǒ qù jiào yíwèi jǐngchá lái.
I'll go call a policeman.

5. EVERETT

(speaking to a policeman who has arrived) **Wǒ shi Měiguo rén, zài Shīdà Guóyǔ Zhōngxīn dúshū. Wǒde píbāo, hùzhào, gèzhǒng zhèngjiàn dōu bèi tōule. Bù zhīdào nèige rén pǎodào nálǐ qùle. Xiànzài zěmme bàn? Wǒ nèixiē dōngxi fēi zhǎohuílai bù kě!**
I'm an American, I'm studying at the NTNU Mandarin Training Center. My purse, passport, and all kinds of IDs were stolen. I don't know where that man ran to. What should I do now? I've got to get those things of mine back!

6. POLICEMAN

Bié jí, bié jí! Wǒmen yídìng jìnlì bāng nǐ zhǎo. Qǐng nǐ xiān gēn wǒ dào jǐngchájú qù yitang.
Don't worry! We'll definitely do our best to help you find them. Please first go to the police station with me.

7. EVERETT

Hǎo ba.
Well, O.K.

Build Up

1. Everett

xiǎotōu	thief [N]
tōu	steal [V]
píbāo	purse [N]
Xiǎotōu! Yǒu rén tōule wǒde píbāo!	Thief! Somebody stole my purse!

2. Passerby

zěmme huí shì(r)	"what's the matter?" [IE]
Shémme? Zěmme huí shì?	What? What happened?

3. Everett

gǎnkuài	quickly [A]
zhuā	catch [V]
zhuāzhù	catch hold of [RC]
gǎnkuài zhuāzhù tā	quickly catch hold of him
diào	fall, drop [V]
-diào	away [RE]
pǎodiào	run away [RC]
búyào ràng tā pǎodiào	don't let him run away
zhè fùjìn	in this vicinity, nearby
Jiù shi nèige rén! Gǎnkuài zhuāzhù tā, búyào ràng tā pǎodiào. Zhè fùjìn yǒu méiyou jǐngchá?	It's that guy! Hurry up and catch him, don't let him run away. Is there a policeman nearby?

4. Passerby

jiào yíwèi jǐngchá lái	call a policeman to come
Wǒ qù jiào yíwèi jǐngchá lái.	I'll go call a policeman.

5. Everett

Shīdà	National Taiwan Normal University (NTNU) [PW]
Guóyǔ Zhōngxīn	Mandarin Center [PW]
Shīdà Guóyǔ Zhōngxīn	NTNU Mandarin Center
hùzhào	passport [N]
zhèngjiàn	identification paper [N]
gèzhǒng zhèngjiàn	every kind of ID
bèi	(indicates passive) [CV]
dōu bèi tōule	were all stolen
pǎodào	run to [V+PV]
pǎodào nǎli qùle	ran to where
xiànzài zěmme bàn	now what should one do
-huílai	come back [RE]
zhǎohuílai	find and get back [RC]
nèixiē	those [SP+M]
nèixiē dōngxi	those things
fēi...bù kě	must [PT]
fēi zhǎohuílai bù kě	must find and get back
Wǒ shi Měiguo rén, zài Shīdà Guóyǔ Zhōngxīn dúshū. Wǒde píbāo, hùzhào, gèzhǒng zhèngjiàn dōu bèi tōule. Bù zhīdào nèige rén pǎodào nǎli qùle. Xiànzài zěmme bàn? Wǒ nèixiē dōngxi fēi zhǎohuílai bù kě!	I'm an American, I'm studying at the NTNU Mandarin Training Center. My purse, passport, and all kinds of IDs were stolen. I don't know where that man ran to. What should I do now? I've got to get those things of mine back!

6. Policeman

jí	be worried, anxious [SV]

bié jí	don't worry
jìnlì bāng nǐ zhǎo	do our best to help you find
jǐngchájú	police station [PW]
dào jǐngchájú qù yitang	make a trip to the police station
Bié jí, bié jí! Wǒmen yídìng jìnlì bāng nǐ zhǎo. Qǐng nǐ xiān gēn wǒ dào jǐngchájú qù yitang.	Don't worry! We'll definitely do our best to help you find them. Please first go to the police station with me.

....

7. Everett

Hǎo ba.	Well, O.K.

Supplementary Vocabulary

1. -huíqu	go back [RE]
pǎohuíqu	run back [RC]
Tā pǎohuíqule.	She ran back.
2. qiánbāo	wallet [N]
Xiǎo Lǐde qiánbāo bèi tōule.	Little Li's wallet was stolen.
3. mà	scold, curse [V]
Tā bèi lǎoshī màle.	She was scolded by the teacher.
4. piàn	trick, deceive [V]
Nǐ bèi tā piànle!	You were tricked by him!

Grammatical and Cultural Notes

1A. **Tōu** means "steal"; this word refers to the taking of something which doesn't belong to one without violence and without the person whose possession is being taken being aware of it. If violence occurs, then the verb to use would be **qiǎng** "rob." **Tōu** and **qiǎng** are distinguished more carefully in Chinese than "steal" and "rob" are in English.

1B. While there is less violent crime in mainland China and Taiwan than in the U.S., there are plenty of pickpockets, so be careful with purses and wallets. Men should never put their wallets in the back pocket of their trousers, and women must be careful with handbags. Pickpockets occasionally work in groups, with one purposely bumping into you to distract you while another steals your purse or billfold, so be careful!

2. A common and useful expression for inquiring about something that has happened or the reason why something has happened is **Zěmme huí shì(r)** "What's the matter?" or "What happened?" This can also be said, with exactly the same meaning, as **Zhè shi zěmme yì huí shì?**

3A. The resultative ending **-zhù** indicates "hold onto something tightly." Contrast: **zhuā** "catch," **zhuāzhù** "catch hold of," **zhuādezhù** "can catch hold of," and **zhuābuzhù** "can't catch hold of." **Dāibuzhù** "can't stay (inside)" (18-1: 11D) was also an example of this resultative ending. Yet other examples are **nábuzhù** "can't hold on to," **zhànbuzhù** "can't stand still," and **jìbuzhù** "can't remember."

3B. Instead of **zhè fùjin** "here in the vicinity," Beijing speakers would say **zhèr fùjin**.

4. **Wǒ qù jiào yíwèi jǐngchá lái** "I'll go call a policeman." This is a so-called pivot sentence (8-2: 2C) and represents the combination of these two sentences: **Wǒ qù jiào yíwèi jǐngchá** "I call a policeman" and **Jǐngchá lái** "The policeman comes." In the first sentence, **jǐngchá** is the object, but in the second sentence, **jǐngchá** serves as the subject. The verb **jiào** commonly serves as a pivot in this way. Sometimes it's best translated as "call," while sometimes it translates better as "tell" or "ask." Another example of **jiào** in a pivot sentence:

Tā jiào wǒ míngtiān zài lái.   "She asked me to come again tomorrow."

5A. **Shīdà** is an abbreviation of **Guólì Táiwān Shīfàn Dàxué** "National Taiwan Normal University," which in English is often abbreviated as NTNU. The Chinese abbreviation, of course, derives from the **Shī** of **Shīfàn** and the **Dà** of **Dàxué** (5-2: 9A).

5B. **EXPRESSING PASSIVE VOICE IN CHINESE.** Examine the following sentence from line 5 of this lesson's Basic Conversation:

Wǒde píbāo, hùzhào, gèzhǒng zhèngjiàn dōu bèi tōule.

"My purse, passport, and all kinds of IDs were stolen."

Now look at these sentences from the Supplementary Vocabulary for this lesson:

Nǐ bèi tā piànle!   "You got tricked by him!"

Tā bèi lǎoshī màle.   "She was scolded by the teacher."

Notice that all of the above sentences contain the coverb **bèi**. The pattern with **bèi** to express passive is:

SUBJECT	BÈI (AGENT)	VERB
Tā	bèi (lǎoshī)	màle.

"She was scolded (by the teacher)."

Note that in the example above, the agent—the part that expresses by whom the action of the verb was performed—is optional. So you could say either **Tā bèi lǎoshī màle** "She was scolded by the teacher" or just **Tā bèi màle** "She was scolded." Here are some more examples of the passive with **bèi**, some of them with and some without an agent:

Tā bèi shāle.	"He was killed."
Tā bèi màle.	"She was scolded."
Yǐzi bèi tā bānzǒule.	"The chair was moved away by him."
Dōngxi dōu bèi nǐ tōule!	"The things were all stolen by you!"
Wǒde xiāngzi bèi názǒule.	"My suitcase was taken away."
Xìn dàgài bèi yóujú nòngdiūle.	"The letter was probably lost by the post office."

Wǒmen shuōde huà hǎoxiàng dōu bèi tāmen tīngjiānle.

"It seems that everything we said was heard by them."

Tāde chēzi bèi zhuànghuàile, hái hǎo tā méi shòushāng.

"Her car was wrecked; at least she wasn't injured."

Note the following concerning the Chinese passive:

(1) In a Chinese passive sentence, the main verb must be transitive, in other words, it must be capable of having an object.

(2) As in the case of **bǎ** (15-3: 1C), the main verb of a **bèi** sentence cannot occur alone but must have a verb suffix such as **-le** or a verb complement attached to it.

(3) As is true of all coverbs, if there is a negative or auxiliary verb, it must precede the **bèi** and cannot precede the main verb. For example, to say "Your things were not taken away" you'd say **Nǐde dōngxi méi bèi názǒu** and NOT *Nǐde dōngxi bèi méi názǒu.

(4) Traditionally, the Chinese passive has been used mostly in adversative or infelicitous senses (i.e., unhappy situations such as "be killed," "be hurt," "be hit," "be stolen," etc.), and such usage is still common. However, due to the influence of Western languages, Chinese grammar has changed, so that now the passive with **bèi** is sometimes used even for happy events. This is especially true of modern written style, as in newspapers and novels.

(5) Not all verbs can occur with **bèi**. For example, most verbs of perception such as **wéndào** "smell" or **gǎnjuédào** "feel" cannot occur with **bèi** (though **kànjian** "see," **kàndào** "see," **tīngjian** "hear," and **tīngdào** "hear" can). Observe carefully how and when your Chinese interlocutors use **bèi**.

(6) In Chinese, sentences with passive constructions are less common than in English. In general, Chinese speakers prefer active voice. Instead of saying "I was told," Chinese speakers would usually say **Yǒu rén gàosu wǒ**, which literally means "There is a person who told me" or "Someone told me."

(7) Besides **bèi**, there are two other coverbs that can be used to express the passive: **ràng** and **jiào**. However, these differ from **bèi** in several ways: (a) they're especially colloquial and seldom written; (b) they're typically "northern" in flavor and seldom used in other parts of China; (c) while **bèi** can be used with or without an agent, **jiào** and **ràng** must have an agent expressed (in lieu of a more specific agent, **rén** "somebody" can be used); and (d) in passive sentences with **ràng** and **jiào**, an optional **gěi** (lit. "give") is often added before the main verb of the sentence. Here are several examples with **ràng** and **jiào**:

Tā jiào wǒ (gěi) dǎle.	"He was hit by me."
Mén jiào fēng (gěi) chuīkāile.	"The door was blown open by the wind."
Táng dōu jiào háizimen (gěi) chīle.	"The candy was all eaten by the children."
Chē jiào Wáng Xiānsheng (gěi) kāizǒule.	"The car was driven away by Mr. Wang."
Tā ràng wǒ (gěi) màle.	"She was scolded by me."
Chá dōu ràng kèrén (gěi) hēwánle.	"The tea has all been drunk up by the guests."
Dàxué ràng dǒngshìhuì (gěi) màile.	"The college was sold by the board of trustees."
Wǒmen shuōde huà ràng tā (gěi) tīngjianle.	"What we said was heard by them."

Having now learned how to create the passive with **bèi**, **ràng**, and **jiào**, you should be careful not to overuse it. As we pointed out earlier, Chinese tends to use active voice much more commonly than passive. Moreover, depending on the context, some verbs may be interpreted in a passive sense without the need for any overt passive marking. That is, the direction of a verb may be outward from the subject as actor, or inward toward the subject as receiver of the action or goal. Study the following examples:

Chēzi yǐjīng màile.	"The car has already been sold."
Tāde fùmǔ gāng líhūnle.	"His parents were just divorced."
Zìdiǎn fàngzai zhuōzishang le.	"The dictionary has been put on a table."
Nèiběn shū qùnián jiù chūbǎnle.	"That book was already published last year."
Tāmen shuō Zhōngguo zǎo jiù jiěfàngle.	"They said that China was liberated long ago."
Tā zài chēhuò zhōng shòule zhòngshāng.	"She was badly hurt in the accident."

5C. Distinguish carefully the pronunciation of these two words, both of which occur in this conversation: **pǎodiào** "run away" (line 3) vs. **pǎodào** "run to" (line 5).

5D. **FĒI...BÙ KĚ.** Consider this sentence from the conversation: **Wǒ nèixiē dōngxi fēi zhǎohuílai bù kě** "Those things of mine must be found." As you already saw in the words **fēicháng** "not ordinarily" or "extremely" (15-1) and **fēixīyān qū** "non-smoking section" (18-3), and in the expression **bú dào Cháng Chéng fēi hǎohàn** "if you don't get to the Great Wall you're not a brave man" (21-4), **fēi** is a Classical Chinese word that means "not".

Bù kě is also Classical Chinese and means "cannot" or "may not"; **bù kě** is the equivalent of modern Chinese **bù kéyi**. The pattern **fēi...bù kě** involves a double negative construction that literally means "cannot not," i.e., "must" or "have to." Sometimes, as in the last example below, the **fēi...bù kě** pattern can also function to indicate strong likelihood. The two parts of the pattern surround the verb phrase of the sentence. The basic pattern is:

SUBJECT	FĒI	VERB PHRASE	BÙ KĚ
Nǐ	fēi	qù	bù kě!

"You've got to go!"

More examples of the pattern **fēi...bù kě**:

Zhèixiē huà nǐ fēi shuō bù kě ma?	"Do you have to say these words?"
Wǒ fēi cānjiā zhèicì huódòng bù kě.	"I must take part in this activity."

Nǐ yàoshi bù duō chuān diǎnr yīfu, fēi gǎnmào bù kě.

"If you don't wear more, you're sure to catch cold."

Wǎnfàn yǐqián, fēi bǎ nǐde fángjiān shōushi gānjìng bù kě!

"You must clean up your room before dinner!"

While we don't recommend you do this, in informal conversation, some speakers drop the **bù kě** at the end of the sentence. Although this would logically seem to give the opposite of the intended meaning, in practice the meaning is actually the same as with the full form; in this case, **fēi** would seem to have changed into an adverb with the meaning "must." Because the **fēi...bù kě** structure is already a double negative, no further negatives can be added, so it can only be used to express positive obligation, not negative obligation. In other words, while you could say **Nǐ fēi qù bù kě** "You must go," you couldn't say *Nǐ fēi bú qù bù kě "You must not go." There are several closely related patterns with the same meaning, including **fēiděi...bù kě** and **fēi...bù xíng**. **Fēiděi** alone is also common and has the same meaning. Here are two examples with **fēiděi...bù kě**:

Yào xiǎng bǎ Zhōngwén xuéhǎo, fēiděi yònggōng bù kě.

"If you want to learn Chinese well, you must study hard."

Duìbuqǐ, wǒ xiànzài fēiděi dào yòu'éryuán qù jiē wǒ háizi bù kě.

"Excuse me, I have to go to the kindergarten to pick up my child now."

6.   **Qǐng nǐ xiān gēn wǒ dào jǐngchájú qù yitang** "Please first go to the police station with me." **Qù yitang** literally means "go a trip," that is, "make a trip" to some place. It would not be wrong to end the sentence with **qù**, but the addition of **yitang** renders the sentence more colloquial and less abrupt.

Lost Bag

Nancy Yates has lost her bag containing her money, student I.D., and library card. She goes to the security guard station at the entrance to National Taiwan Normal University to ask if anyone has found the bag.

 Basic Conversation 22-3

1. YATES		**Xiānsheng, wǒ jīntiān zǎoshang diàole yíge dàizi. Bù zhīdào yǒu méiyou rén jiǎndào?** Sir, I lost a bag this morning. I wonder if anybody picked it up?
2. SECURITY GUARD		**Nǐde dàizi yǒu shémme tèzhēng ma?** Does your bag have any special characteristics?
3. YATES		**Báisè gēn hēisède, dàgài bǐ wǒ zhèige dàizi dà yíbèi. Shàngmian xiězhe "Williams." Lǐmiàn chúle yìqiānduōkuài Táibì yǐwài, hái yǒu wǒde xuéshēngzhèng gēn jièshūzhēng.** It's white and black, probably twice as big as this bag of mine. It has "Williams" written on it. Inside, in addition to over a thousand NT, there are also my student ID and library card.
4. SECURITY GUARD		**Nǐ shi něige guójiāde? Jiào shémme míngzi?** What country are you from? What's your name?
5. YATES		**Wǒ shi Měiguo rén, jiào Yè Nánxǐ.** I'm American, my name is Nancy Yates.
6. SECURITY GUARD		*(checks in back of booth and returns with a bag)* **Nǐ kàn, zhè shì bu shi nǐde dàizi?** Take a look, is this your bag?
7. YATES		**Méi cuò, méi cuò, jiù shi wǒde!** That's right, that's mine!
8. SECURITY GUARD		**Qǐng nǐ jiǎnchá yixia dōngxi shì bu shi dōu zài?** Please examine it to see if everything is there.
9. YATES		*(examines the purse and its contents)* **Wǒ kànkan. Qián, xuéshēngzhèng, jièshūzhèng dōu zài. Zhēn xièxie nǐ!** Let me see. The money, my student ID, library card, they're all there. Thanks so much!

10. SECURITY GUARD   **Méi shémme, yīnggāide. Yǐhòu xiǎoxīn yidian! Máfan nǐ zài zhèli qiān ge míng.**
You're welcome, that's my job. In the future, be more careful! Please sign your name here.

Build Up

---

1. Yates
    diào (T)   lose [V]
    diàole yíge dàizi   lost a bag
    jiǎn   pick up [V]
    jiǎndào   pick up [RC]
    yǒu méiyou rén jiǎndào   is there anyone who picked it up
    Xiānsheng, wǒ jīntiān zǎoshang diàole   Sir, I lost a bag this morning. I wonder if
    yíge dàizi. Bù zhīdào yǒu méiyou rén jiǎndào? anybody picked it up?

---

2. Security Guard
    tèzhēng   special characteristic [N]
    Nǐde dàizi yǒu shémme tèzhēng ma?   Does your bag have any special characteristics?

---

3. Yates
    bèi   time(s) [M]
    dà yíbèi   once again as large
    bǐ wǒ zhèige dàizi dà yíbèi   twice as big as this bag of mine
    shàngmian xiězhe "Williams"   on it there is written "Williams"
    Táibì   NT (Taiwan currency) [N]
    yìqiānduōkuài Táibì yǐwài   in addition to more than 1,000 NT
    xuéshēngzhèng   student I.D. [N]
    jiè   borrow; lend [V]
    jièshūzhēng   library card [N]
    Báisè gēn hēisède, dàgài bǐ wǒ zhèige dàizi   It's white and black, probably twice as big as
    dà yíbèi. Shàngmian xiězhe "Williams." Lǐmiàn this bag of mine. It has "Williams" written on it.
    chúle yìqiānduōkuài Táibì yǐwài, hái yǒu wǒde Inside, in addition to over a thousand NT, there
    xuéshēngzhèng gēn jièshūzhēng.   are also my student ID and library card.

---

4. Security Guard
    guójiā   country [N]
    Nǐ shi něige guójiāde? Jiào shémme míngzi?   What country are you from? What's your name?

---

5. Yates
    Yè   Ye [SN]
    Nánxǐ   (Chinese for "Nancy")
    Wǒ shi Měiguo rén, jiào Yè Nánxǐ.   I'm American, my name is Nancy Yates.

---

6. Security Guard
    Nǐ kàn, zhè shì bu shi nǐde dàizi?   Take a look, is this your bag?

---

7. Yates
    cuò   error, mistake [N]
    méi cuò   "that's right" [IE]
    Méi cuò, méi cuò, jiù shi wǒde!   That's right, that's mine!

---

8. Security Guard
    jiǎnchá   inspect, examine [V]
    jiǎnchá yixia   inspect

Qǐng nǐ jiǎnchá yixia dōngxi shì bu shi dōu zài?	Please examine it to see if everything is there.

9. Yates
Wǒ kànkan. Qián, xuéshēngzhèng, jièshūzhèng dōu zài. Zhēn xièxie nǐ!	Let me see. The money, my student ID, library card, they're all there. Thanks so much!

10. Security Guard
méi shémme	"you're welcome" [IE]
yīnggāide	"something one ought to do" [IE]
qiānmíng	sign one's name [VO]
zài zhèli qiān ge míng	sign (your) name here
Méi shémme, yīnggāide. Yǐhòu xiǎoxīn yidian! Máfan nǐ zài zhèli qiān ge míng.	You're welcome, that's my job. In the future, be more careful! Please sign your name here.

Supplementary Vocabulary

1. **diū**	lose [V]
2. **Rénmínbì**	RMB (PRC currency) [N]
3. **yòngwán**	finish using [RC]
huán	give back [V]
huángěi	give back to [V+PV]
Yòngwánle, qǐng huángěi wǒ.	When you're finished using it, please give it back to me.
4. **jiùmìng**	"help!" [IE]
shīhuǒ	fire breaks out [VO]
Jiùmìng! Shīhuǒ le!	Help! Fire!

Grammatical and Cultural Notes

1. In Taiwan and southern mainland China, **diào** is the verb for "lose." In northern China, **diū** is used instead (SV1).

2. **Nǐde dàizi yǒu shémme tèzhēng ma?** "Does your bag have any special characteristics?" Since there is a **ma** at the end of this sentence, which already makes it a question, the **shémme** here means "any" rather than "what" (12-2: 10).

3A. We can assume that **Báisè gēn hēisède**, literally "White-color and black-colored," derives from a longer sentence like **Wǒde dàizi shi báisè gēn hēisède dàizi** "My bag is a white-colored and black-colored bag."

3B. **BÈI TO EXPRESS "TIMES."** **Bèi** is a measure meaning "times," "once again as," or "-fold" (note that this **bèi** is a completely different word from the **bèi** that indicates passive that you learned in 22-2). Examine this sentence in the Basic Conversation: **(Wǒ diàode dàizi) dàgài bǐ wǒ zhèige dàizi dà yíbèi** "(The bag I lost) is probably once again as big as this bag of mine" or, in smoother English, "(The bag I lost) is probably twice as big as this bag of mine." One very common pattern with **bèi** is as follows:

NOUN₁	BǏ	NOUN₂	STATIVE VERB	NUMBER	BÈI
Wǒ diàode dàizi	**bǐ**	**wǒ zhèige dàizi**	**dà**	**yí**	**bèi.**

"The bag I lost is twice as big as this bag."

More examples of this pattern with **bèi**:

Tāmende fángzi bǐ wǒmende dà yíbèi.   "Their house is twice as big as ours."

Zhōngguo bǐ Rìběn dà hǎojǐbèi.   "China is many times bigger than Japan."

Tā kāichē kāide bǐ wǒ kuài yíbèi.   "He drives twice as fast as I do."

Wǒmen bānde xuésheng bǐ tāmen bānde duō yíbèi.

"Our class has twice as many students as theirs."

There is a second pattern with **bèi** as follows:

NOUN₁	SHI	NOUN₂DE	NUMBER	BÈI
Nǐde gōngzī	shi	wǒde gōngzīde	liǎng	bèi.

"Your pay is twice my pay."

More examples of the second pattern:

Yìbǎi shi shíde shíbèi.   "100 is 10 times 10."

Wǒmen bānde xuésheng shi tāmen bānde liǎngbèi.

"Our class has twice as many students as theirs."

Finally, there is a variant on the second pattern, used only in conversation, that substitutes **yǒu** for **shi**. It is:

NOUN₁	YǑU	NOUN₂DE	NUMBER	BÈI
Tāde niánji	yǒu	wǒde	liǎng	bèi.

"She's twice as old as I am."

Sometimes **bèi** is also used alone. Example:

Zuìjìn shínián nàrde rénkǒu zēngjiāle wǔbèi.

"In the last 10 years the population there has increased by 500%."

For some speakers, the preceding sentence means the population is now six times as large as before, which is strictly speaking the more accurate interpretation; but other speakers interpret the sentence as meaning the population is now five times as much as before.

3C.   The sentence **Shàngmiàn xiězhe** "Williams" means "On it there is written 'Williams.'" As we learned in 9-4: 2A, the suffix **-zhe** can indicate continuous aspect, i.e., that some action or state is continuing over a period of time. Here, the **-zhe** tells us that the name "Williams" continues to be in the state of having been written on the purse; in other words, the action of writing has long since been completed but the results of that action continue. Two more examples of this use of **-zhe**:

Qiángshang guàzhe hěn duō huàr.   "On the walls there are hanging many paintings."

Cānzhuōshang fàngzhe yíge càidān.   "On the dining room table there has been placed a menu."

3D.   **Táibì**, called "New Taiwan Dollar" or NT in English, is the official unit of currency in Taiwan. Common denominations for coins are 1, 5, 10, and 50 dollars. Common denominations for paper currency are 100, 500, and 1000 dollars.

3E.   **JIÈ AS "BORROW" AND "LEND."** **Jièshūzhèng** "library card" literally means "borrow book certificate." The verb **jiè** "borrow, lend" is very common and useful; depending on the context and how it's used, it can mean either "borrow" or "lend." To say "borrow something from someone," the pattern is **gēn...jiè**. The basic pattern can be diagrammed as follows:

BORROWER	GĒN	LENDER	JIÈ	ITEM BORROWED
Wǒ	gēn	tā	jièle	shíkuài qián.

"I borrowed ten dollars from him."

Some more examples of the pattern **gēn...jiè**:

Wǒ kě bu kéyi gēn nǐ jiè yìzhī bǐ?   "Could I borrow a pen from you?"

Bù hǎo yìsi, wǒ zuìjìn shǒutóu bǐjiào jǐn, néng bu néng gēn nǐ jiè yidianr qián?

"I'm embarrassed to ask, but recently I've been kind of short on money; could I borrow some money from you?"

Depending on the context, **jiè** can also mean "lend." For example:

Jīntiān shi xīngqītiān, suóyi túshūguǎn bú jiè shū.

"Today is Sunday, so the library doesn't lend out books."

To say "lend something to someone," the most common pattern is **bǎ** + (ITEM) + **jiègěi** + (PERSON). Examples:

Tā bǎ chēzi jiègěi wǒ le.   "He lent me his car."

Wǒ bǎ yǔsǎn jiègěi tā le.   "I lent her my umbrella."

Qǐng nǐ bié bǎ zhèixiē dōngxi jiègěi biérén!   "Please don't lend these things to others!"

4.   **Nǐ shi něige guójiāde?** "From what country are you?" is quite colloquial and not particularly polite. More polite would be **Nín shi něiguo rén?**, as you learned in 2-1.

10A.   **Méi shémme**, literally "it doesn't have anything" or "there isn't anything," is a common response to expressions of thanks. In function, it's similar to **náli**, **nǎrde huà**, **bú xiè**, and **bú kèqi**, all of which can be translated as "you're welcome" or "don't mention it."

10B.   **Yīnggāide** derives from a longer expression such as **Zhè shi wǒ yīnggāi zuòde shìqing** "This is a thing I'm supposed to do."

SV2.   **Rénmínbì** is the official unit of currency of the PRC, called "yuan" or RMB in English. Common denominations for coins are 10 cents, 50 cents and one dollar. Common denominations for paper currency are 1, 2, 5, 10, 50, and 100 dollars.

The Accident

David Hart, who is employed as interpreter for Delta Airlines in Beijing, collides with a Chinese bicyclist while on his way to work. A passerby joins them in their discussion of how to handle the aftermath of the accident.

 ## Basic Conversation 22-4

1. **HART**

    Zěmmeyàng? Zěmmeyàng? Nín shòushāng le méiyou?

    How are you? Are you O.K.? Did you get hurt?

2. **BICYCLIST**

    Wǒ dào méi shémme dà shì. Búguò, nín qiáo, wǒ zhè kùzi pòle yíge dà kūlong, wǒde zìxíngchē chéngle shémme yàngr le? Yào bú shi wǒ duǒde kuài, hái shuōbudìng yǒu duō wēixiǎn a!

    I'm pretty much all right. But, take a look, a big hole got torn in my pants, and what has become of my bicycle? If I hadn't dodged quickly, who knows how dangerous it could have been!

3. **HART**

    Duìbuqǐ, duìbuqǐ, shízài duìbuqǐ! Shuō shízàide, zhè yě bù quán yuàn wǒ. Wǒ yě shi wèile duǒ yíge guò mǎlùde, jiéguǒ cái bǎ nín zhuàngle.

    Sorry, sorry, I'm really sorry! To tell the truth, this isn't entirely my fault either. I, too, did this to avoid a person who was crossing the street, and it was only thus, as a result, that I hit you.

4. **PASSERBY**

    Zěmme la? Fāshēng shémme shìr le?

    What's going on? What happened?

5. **BICYCLIST**

    Tā bǎ wǒ zhuàngle!

    He hit me!

6. **HART**

    Shì bu shi wǒmen qù zhǎo jiāotōngjǐng?

    Should we go look for a traffic policeman?

7. **PASSERBY**

    Yàoburán zhèiyangr ba. Nǐmen sīliǎo déle. Nín péi tā yìtiáo kùzi, zài péi tā dianr xiūchēfèi. Rúguǒ jiào jǐngcháde huà, nǐ děi dānwu hǎo duō shíjiān, guài bù hé-suànde.

    Or why not handle it like this. Just settle privately. You compensate him for a pair of pants, plus give him a little for repair costs. If you call the police, you'll have to waste a lot of time; it's just not worth it.

8. BICYCLIST   **Kùzi jiù suànle. Nín péi wǒ sānshíkuài qián xiūchē ba.**
Forget about the pants. Just give me 30 RMB in compensation to repair my bike.

9. HART   **Xíng, xíng. Suàn zámliǎ dōu dǎoméi.**
O.K. I guess both of us are out of luck.

 **Build Up**

---

1. Hart

shòushāng	suffer injury, be hurt [VO]
shòushāng le méiyou	did you get hurt or not
Zěmmeyàng? Zěmmeyàng? Nín shòushāng le méiyou?	How are you? Are you O.K.? Did you get hurt?

---

2. Bicyclist

dào	on the contrary, but [A]
wǒ dào méi shémme dà shì	I on the contrary haven't any big matter
qiáo	look [V]
nín qiáo	you take a look
pò	break, tear [V]
kūlong (B)	hole [N]
pòle yíge dà kūlong	there has been torn a big hole
zìxíngchē (B)	bicycle [N] (M: **liàng**)
chéng	become, turn into [V]
yàngr (B)	appearance, shape [N]
chéngle shémme yàngr le	has turned into what shape
duǒ	dodge, avoid [V]
yào bú shi wǒ duǒde kuài	if it were not that I dodged fast
-dìng	fixed, settled [RE]
shuōbudìng	not be able to say for sure [RC]
wēixiǎn (B)	be dangerous; danger [SV/N]
yǒu duō wēixiǎn	how dangerous it is

Wǒ dào méi shémme dà shì. Búguò, nín qiáo, wǒ zhè kùzi pòle yíge dà kūlong, wǒde zìxíngchē chéngle shémme yàngr le? Yào bú shi wǒ duǒde kuài, hái shuōbudìng yǒu duō wēixiǎn a!

I'm pretty much all right. But, take a look, a big hole got torn in my pants, and what has become of my bicycle? If I hadn't dodged quickly, who knows how dangerous it could have been!

---

3. Hart

yuàn	blame [V]
zhè yě bù quán yuàn wǒ	I can't be blamed for all of this
mǎ	horse [N] (M: **pī**)
mǎlù	road [N]
guò mǎlù	cross the road [PH]
duǒ yíge guò mǎlùde	avoid one who is crossing the road
jiéguǒ	as a result [CJ]
zhuàng	bump into, collide with [V]
bǎ nín zhuàngle	collided with you

Duìbuqǐ, duìbuqǐ, shízài duìbuqǐ! Shuō shízàide, zhè yě bù quán yuàn wǒ. Wǒ yě shi wèile duǒ yíge guò mǎlùde, jiéguǒ cái bǎ nín zhuàngle.

Sorry, sorry, I'm really sorry! To tell the truth, this isn't entirely my fault either. I, too, did this to avoid a person who was crossing the street, and it was only thus, as a result, that I hit you.

---

4. Passerby

fāshēng	happen [V]

fāshēng shémme shìr le	there has happened what matter
Zěmme la? Fāshēng shémme shìr le?	What's going on? What happened?

5. Bicyclist

Tā bǎ wǒ zhuàngle!	He hit me!

6. Hart

Shì bu shi wǒmen qù zhǎo jiāotōngjǐng?	Should we go look for a traffic policeman?

7. Passerby

sīliǎo	settle privately [V]
...déle	...and that will do [PT]
nǐmen sīliǎo déle	settle privately and that will do
péi	compensate, pay damages [V]
péi ta yìtiáo kùzi	reimburse her for a pair of pants
xiū	repair [V]
xiūchē	repair a vehicle [VO]
xiūchēfèi	cost of repairing a vehicle [N]
péi tā diǎnr xiūchēfèi	pay her a little for repair costs
dānwu	delay, get held up [V]
dānwu hǎo duō shíjiān	lose a lot of time
hésuàn	be worthwhile [SV]
guài...-de	quite, rather [PT]
guài bù hésuànde	not very worthwhile
Yàoburán zhèiyangr ba. Nǐmen sīliǎo déle. Nín péi tā yìtiáo kùzi, zài péi tā dianr xiūchēfèi. Rúguǒ jiào jǐngcháde huà, nǐ děi dānwu hǎo duō shíjiān, guài bù hésuànde.	Or why not handle it like this. Just settle privately. You compensate him for a pair of pants, plus give him a little for repair costs. If you call the police, you'll have to waste a lot of time; it's just not worth it.

8. Bicyclist

suànle	"forget about it" [IE]
kùzi jiù suànle	never mind about the pants
Kùzi jiù suànle. Nín péi wǒ sānshikuài qián xiūchē ba.	Forget about the pants. Just give me 30 RMB in compensation to repair my bike.

9. Hart

zámliǎ	the two of us [PR]
dǎoméi	be out of luck [SV]
Xíng, xíng. Suàn zámliǎ dōu dǎoméi.	O.K. I guess both of us are out of luck.

Supplementary Vocabulary

1. chēhuò	car accident [N]
2. dòng	hole [N]

Additional Vocabulary

1. jiǎotàchē (T)	bicycle [N] (M: jià)
2. yílù píng'ān	"have a good trip" [EX]
Zhù nǐ yílù píng'ān!	Hope you have a good trip!

Grammatical and Cultural Notes

1A.   This Basic Conversation is in informal, colloquial Beijing dialect.

1B.   **TRAFFIC ACCIDENTS.** Due to the challenging traffic conditions in many parts of China, accidents are unfortunately a frequent occurrence. As a non-native in China, it would be advisable for you to avoid driving a car or motorcycle, unless absolutely necessary. If you do have an accident, stop immediately and render all possible assistance. Be aware that in China, responsibility for traffic accidents is usually shared between both parties rather than ascribed entirely to one party alone, even if the accident is clearly the fault of one side. This is especially the case when a foreigner is involved, since he or she will often be considered wealthier. Minor accidents are often handled via a cash settlement on the spot. Thus, expect to have to part with some money if you're involved in an accident. But most important, show your concern for the other person, especially if injuries are involved, however minor. If more serious injuries occurred, then it would be wise to visit the other person in the hospital or at home to inquire as to how they're doing and wish them well. During such a visit, you should, of course, bring some kind of present or an envelope with cash; a Chinese friend can advise you on the details. To an American lawyer, paying such a visit when one was clearly not at fault might seem to imply guilt. However, not following Chinese custom in such a case is likely to bring about bitter feelings on the part of the Chinese involved, which could create conditions not conducive to a favorable settlement.

1C.   **Nín shòushāng le méiyou?** "Were you injured?" As you learned in 21-1: 5B, the standard northern Mandarin affirmative-negative question form of completed-action sentences ends in VERB + **-le méiyou**, as in **Nín shòushāng le méiyou?** In southern Mandarin, it's common to insert **yǒu méiyou** before the verb rather than ending in **-le méiyou** and instead say **Nín yǒu méiyou shòushāng?** "Were you injured?" Either of these alternatives is fine for you to use, but be careful as regards the affirmative answer to such questions, which must use VERB + **-le** and, in this case, should be **Wǒ shòushāng le** "I was injured." Be aware that you CANNOT say *****Wǒ yǒu shòushāng** for "I was injured." The latter is a common error in the Mandarin spoken by native speakers of Cantonese and Taiwanese, since those dialects do have constructions similar to *****Wǒ yǒu shòushāng**.

2A.   **Qiáo** is a northern Chinese synonym for **kàn**, which could also have been used here. The imperative **Nǐ qiáo** "Look!" is especially common.

2B.   **Wǒ zhè kùzi** "these pants of mine." Normally, this would be **wǒ zhèitiáo kùzi** "this pair of pants of mine" with the measure for pants, **tiáo**. However, in rapid, colloquial speech after the number **yī** or after the specifiers **zhèi-** and **nèi-**, measures are sometimes omitted—but only when the quantity is one (if you were talking about two or more pairs of pants you'd have to use the measure). However, it's never wrong to use the measure and, indeed, we recommend that you always use measures in your own speech.

2C.   **Wǒ zhè kùzi pòle yíge dà kūlong** "In these pants of mine there has been torn a big hole" or "A big hole got torn in my pants" or "There's a big hole in my pants." **Pòle** here means "there has been torn." The verb **pò** "tear" can be interpreted actively or passively depending on the context.

2D.   The noun **zìxíngchē** "bicycle," which literally means "self move vehicle," is used mostly in Beijing and Northern China. In southern mainland China and Taiwan, the most common word for "bicycle" is **jiǎotàchē** (lit. "feet-tread-vehicle," cf. AV1). The measure used for either **zìxíngchē** or **jiǎotàchē** is **liàng**. Remember, as you learned in 11-4, that the verb used for "ride" a bicycle is **qí**, which literally means "straddle" and is used for "riding" bicycles, motorcycles, or horses. Beijing is a great city to explore by bicycle. If you're going to be living in Beijing for more than two or three months, it would be well worth purchasing a bike.

2E.   **Wǒde zìxíngchē chéngle shémme yàngrle?** literally means "My bicycle has become what way?" or "What has happened to my bicycle?"

2F.   Review the use of **yào bú shi** "if not," "if it weren't that," or "if...hadn't" (19-4: 1B). The literal meaning of **Yào bú shi wǒ duǒde kuài, hái shuōbudìng yǒu duō wēixiǎn a!** is "If it weren't that I dodged quickly, still can't say for sure have to what extent danger!" or, in better English, "If I hadn't dodged quickly, who knows how dangerous it might have been!"

2G.   The negative potential resultative compound **shuōbudìng** here retains its basic meaning of "can't say for sure." It derives from the verb **shuō** "say" plus the resultative ending **-dìng** "settle, decide" (cf. the verb **dìng** "settle, decide" that you learned in 17-1). In other contexts, **shuōbudìng** can function as an adverb meaning "perhaps" or "maybe." Examples:

> **Shuōbudìng tāmen yǐjīng zǒule.**
>
> "Maybe they've already left."

> **Nǐ qiáo, tiān tūrán hēile, shuōbudìng yào xiàyǔle.**
>
> "Look, the sky has suddenly darkened, maybe it's going to rain."

> **Shuōbudìng nǐ bìyè yǐhòu yě néng dào Zhōngguo qù gōngzuò.**
>
> "Perhaps you, too, can go to China to work after graduation."

> **Nèige rén zhǎngde zhēn gāo, shuōbudìng tā shi lánqiú yùndòngyuán.**
>
> "That guy is really tall, perhaps he's a basketball player."

2H.   The word **wēixiǎn**, which can function as a stative verb meaning "be dangerous" or as a noun meaning "danger," is in Taiwan pronounced **wéixiǎn**, with Tone Two on the first syllable.

3A.   **Zhè yě bù quán yuàn wǒ** literally means "This also not all blames me" or "This also isn't all my fault."

3B.   **Wǒ yě shi wèile duǒ yíge guò mǎlùde** literally means "I also was a case of in order to dodge someone who was crossing the street."

3C.   **Jiéguǒ** "as a result" is a common and useful conjunction that links sentences expressing cause and result. Note that **jiéguǒ** can be used only with situations that have already occurred, not with future situations. Another example:

> **Lǎoshī gēn tā shuō búyào chídào, jiéguǒ tā hái shi chídàole.**
>
> "The teacher told him not to arrive late, but the result was that he still arrived late."

4.   The verb **fāshēng** "happen" is common and useful. It can sometimes take the postverb **-zài**. Examples:

Nà shi shémme shíhou fāshēngde shìr?	"When did that happen?"
Zěmme huì fāshēng nèiyangde shìqing?	"How could something like that happen?"
Shìqing fāshēngzai 1937 nián 7 yuè 7 hào.	"The event happened on July 7, 1937."

6.   **Shì bu shi wǒmen qù zhǎo jiāotōngjǐng?** "Is it or is it not the case that we go find a traffic policeman?" or "Shall we go look for a traffic policeman?" As is quite common, **shì bu shi** is here used to gently bring up a suggestion. Two more examples of **shì bu shi** used to make suggestions:

> **Xiǎodōng, nǐ shì bu shi wèi wǒmen dú xiàyíduàn?**
>
> "Xiaodong, why don't you read the next paragraph for us?"

> **Wǒmen shì bu shi xiān wènwen Zhāng Xiānshengde yìjian?**
>
> "Shall we first ask Mr. Zhang's opinion?"

7A.   **LAW IN CHINESE SOCIETY.** The concept of law in Chinese society has been quite different from the West. Traditionally, legal institutions in China considered achieving social harmony as their most important task; thus, the harmonious resolution of conflicts (**héjiě**) was the top priority, not determining who was right and who was wrong. In general, Chinese people don't like to have to resort to **fǎ** "the law." To solve a dispute, Chinese will first appeal to **qíng** "affection in human relationships," then to **lǐ** "reason," and only if the preceding don't succeed in solving the problem will they have recourse to **fǎ**. Until recently, there has in China generally been a distrust of the law and a reluctance to turn over accident cases to officials. It's usually considered better to try to resolve such cases directly between the parties involved, especially if they're relatively minor. Often, as happens in this lesson's Basic Conversation, a bystander will try to help mediate between the two sides. This is called **sīliǎo** "handle privately" as opposed to **shàng fǎyuàn** "go to court." In **sīliǎo**, both sides usually have to yield something and compromise. An important factor is whether or not you have a personal relationship (and if so, what kind of relationship) with the other party; to insist on your own point of view or cite official rules and regulations will usually not get you very far. The preceding notwithstanding, we should point out that concepts of law are developing in China and the Chinese government has been making efforts to implement laws and change people's ways of thinking. You, as a non-native, should be very careful about using **sīliǎo** yourselves, since this is complex and, moreover, bystanders will sometimes come and pretend to help you while they actually take advantage of your lack of knowledge of Chinese society. For these reasons, it's in most cases better for you as a foreigner to deal with the foreign affairs police. In fact, in situations like these, even if you speak fluent Chinese, it's sometimes wise to pretend your Chinese is not so good and say something like **Duìbuqǐ, wǒde Zhōngwén bú tài hǎo, wǒ tīngbudǒng nínde huà, wǒmen háishi jiào jǐngchá lái ba** "Sorry, my Chinese is not so good, I don't understand what you're saying, why don't we just call the police."

7B.   **SENTENCE + DÉLE.** **Dé** alone may mean "can," "may," or "will do." A sentence followed by **déle** means "If such-and-such happens, then it will do" or "If such-and-such is done, then it will be O.K." or "All that's needed is such-and-such." This structure, which is especially common in northern Mandarin, is often used to make a suggestion and thereby resolve a problem or conclude a matter. The basic pattern is:

SENTENCE	DÉLE
Nǐ qù	**déle.**

"If you go, then it will be O.K." or "Why don't you just go."

More examples of the pattern SENTENCE + **déle**:

Jiù zhèmme bàn déle.

"Let's just do it like this."

Xiànzài yǐjīng shíyīdiǎn le, wǒmen jiǎndān zài jiāli chī dianr déle, bié chūqu chīle.

"It's already 11:00; why don't we simply eat a little something at home? Let's not go out to eat."

A: Tā shi guójì xuésheng, xiànzài méi dìfang zhù.
B: Nà wǒmen bǎ nèitào gōngyù xiān jiègěi tā zhù déle.

"A: She's an international student and doesn't have a place to stay right now."
"B: Then why don't we just temporarily lend her that apartment for her to stay in."

7C.   A word about the pronunciation of **dānwu** "delay." If a syllable ending in **-n** is followed immediately by a syllable beginning with **w-**, **y-**, **h-**, or a vowel, then the **-n** of the first syllable is often not fully pronounced. In this case, the tongue doesn't quite reach the roof of the mouth, and the vowel in the first syllable is nasalized. So some speakers pronounce **dānwu** as if it were **dāwu** (with a nasalized **ā**). Examples of this phenomenon we had earlier include **piányi** "cheap" (3-3), **zhēn hǎo** "really good" (6-1), **yuànyi** "be willing to" (15-4), **hěn è** "very hungry" (15-4), and **diànyǐngr** "movie" (20-3).

7D.   **GUÀI...-DE.** The **guài...-de** pattern surrounds a positive stative verb expression to mean "quite," "rather," or "very"; and it surrounds a negative stative verb expression to mean "not very." The **guài...-de** pattern is similar in meaning to **hěn** "very" but is more informal, used only in spoken Chinese, and often occurs with negative or adversative ("unhappy") expressions. While a following **-de** is very common, **guài** can also be used alone. The basic pattern is:

GUÀI	STATIVE VERB	-DE
guài	bù hésuàn	de

"not very worthwhile"

Some more examples of **guài...-de**:

Nèige gùshi guài kěpàde.	"That story is quite scary."
Nèige diànyǐngr guài xiàrénde.	"That movie was rather frightening."
Wǒ juéde tā mǎide yīshang guài nánkànde.	"I feel the clothes she bought are quite ugly."

8.   **Suànle**, in the sense "Forget it" or "Forget about it," is also often said by itself.

9.   **Zámliǎ** "the two of us (i.e., you and I)" is an abbreviation of **zámmen liǎngge (rén)**. Remember that **zámmen** is the "inclusive we" that includes the person spoken to (14-1: 1A).

SV1.   In English we say "have" an accident, but in Chinese you can't use *yǒu. Instead, one says **Chū chēhuò le** "An accident has occurred" or **Fāshēng chēhuò le** "An accident has happened."

SV2.   **Kūlong** (cf. line 2 of this Basic Conversation) is the Beijing dialect word for "hole." In most of the rest of China, the word **dòng** is used for "hole."

AV2.   **Yílù píng'ān** literally means "all along the way (may you encounter) peace." This is commonly said to someone who is departing on a long journey to wish them a safe trip, very much as we in English use the French expression "bon voyage." **Zhù nǐ** means "wish you," so the whole sentence literally means "(I) wish you have a good trip!"

Unit 22: Review and Study Guide

New Vocabulary

ADVERBS

dào	on the contrary, but
gǎnkuài	quickly

CONJUNCTIONS

jiéguǒ	as a result

COVERBS

bèi	(indicates passive)

IDIOMATIC EXPRESSIONS

jiùmìng	"help!"
méi cuò	"that's right"
méi shémme	"you're welcome"
suànle	"forget about it"
yīnggāide	"something one ought to do"
zěmme huí shì(r)	"what's the matter?"

MEASURES

bèi	time(s)

MOVEABLE ADVERBS

yěxǔ	perhaps, maybe
zǎowǎn	morning and evening

NOUNS

biànhuà	change
chēhuò	car accident
cuò	error, mistake
dàifu	doctor
dòng	hole
fèi	lung
fèiyán	pneumonia
guójiā	country
húnshēn	entire body
hùzhào	passport
jièshūzhēng	library card
jìn(r)	energy
kūlong	hole
mǎ	horse
mǎlù	road
píbāo	purse
qiánbāo	wallet
qìwēn	temperature
Rénmínbì	RMB (PRC currency)
Táibì	NT (Taiwan currency)
tèzhēng	special characteristic

tóu	head
wēixiǎn	danger
xiǎotōu	thief
xiūchēfèi	cost of repairing a vehicle
xuéshēngzhèng	student I.D.
yàngr	appearance, shape
zhèngjiàn	identification paper
zìxíngchē	bicycle

PATTERNS

...déle	...and that will do
fēi...bù kě	must
guài...-de	quite, rather

PHRASES

bú dà	not very much
guò mǎlù	cross the road

PLACE WORDS

Guóyǔ Zhōngxīn	Mandarin Center
jǐngchájú	police station
Shīdà	National Taiwan Normal University
yīyuàn	hospital

PRONOUNS

zámliǎ	the two of us

RESULTATIVE COMPOUNDS

jiǎndào	pick up
nàobuhǎo	suffer from an illness and not get better
pǎodiào	run away
pǎohuíqu	run back
shuōbudìng	not be able to say for sure

yòngbuzháo	not need to
yòngwán	finish using
zhǎohuílai	find and get back
zhuāzhù	catch hold of

RESULTATIVE ENDINGS

-diào	away
-dìng	fixed, settled
-huílai	come back
-huíqu	go back

SPECIFIERS

nèixiē	those

STATIVE VERBS

dǎoméi	be out of luck
ěxin	be nauseous, feel like vomiting
hésuàn	be worthwhile
jí	be worried, anxious
téng	be painful, hurt
wēixiǎn	be dangerous

SURNAMES

Yè	Ye

VERBS

chéng	become, turn into
dānwu	delay, get held up
diào	fall, drop; lose
diū	lose
duǒ	dodge, avoid
fāshēng	happen
gǎnmào	catch cold
huán	give back
jiǎn	pick up
jiǎnchá	inspect, examine

jiè	borrow; lend
mà	scold, curse
nào	suffer (from an illness)
péi	compensate, pay damages
piàn	trick, deceive
pò	break, tear
qiáo	look
sīliǎo	settle privately
tōu	steal
tù	spit, throw up
xiū	repair
yuàn	blame
zhuā	catch
zhuàng	bump into, collide with

VERB + POSTVERB

huángěi	give back to
pǎodào	run to
zhuǎnchéng	turn into

VERB-OBJECT COMPOUNDS

fāshāo	have a fever
kànbìng	see a doctor
qiānmíng	sign one's name
shēngbìng	become sick
shīhuǒ	fire breaks out
shòushāng	suffer injury, be hurt
zháoliáng	catch cold
xiūchē	repair a vehicle

Major New Grammar Patterns

PASSIVE: Tā bèi lǎoshī màle. "He was scolded by the teacher." **(22-2)**

FĒI...BÙ KĚ: Nǐ fēi qù bù kě. "You must go." **(22-2)**

BÈI TO EXPRESS "TIMES": Tāde fángzi bǐ wǒde dà yíbèi. "Her house is twice as big as mine." **(22-3)**

JIÈ AS "BORROW" AND "LEND": Wǒ néng bu néng gēn nǐ jiè yidianr qián? "Could I borrow some money from you?", **Jīntiān shi xīngqītiān, suóyi túshūguǎn bú jiè shū.** "Today is Sunday, so the library doesn't lend books." **(22-3)**

SENTENCE + DÉLE: Nǐ qù déle. "If you go, then it will be O.K." **(22-4)**

GUÀI...-DE: Nèige gùshi guài kěpàde. "That story is quite scary." **(22-4)**

Hong Kong and Macao

COMMUNICATIVE OBJECTIVES

Once you've mastered this unit, you'll be able to use Chinese to:

1. Discuss aspects of the geography, population, history, politics, economy, society, linguistic situation, language policy, culture, and cuisine of Hong Kong.

2. Discuss aspects of the geography, population, history, politics, society, culture, cuisine, and economy—including the role of gambling and casinos—in Macao.

3. Discuss aspects of the geography, population, history, politics, economy, society, and culture of your own and other countries.

4. Interact appropriately with a host who is showing you around her or his native city.

5. Handle more formal spoken tasks and topics, using some of the higher-level grammatical patterns and vocabulary typical of formal spoken Chinese.

6. Better understand Cantonese-influenced Mandarin.

7. Learn several common expressions in Cantonese.

A Walking Tour of Hong Kong

Tom Brown, a Canadian from Vancouver who majored in Chinese in college, is visiting Hong Kong for the first time. He meets his Hong Kong friend Kenny Lam in a local cafe. The two young men became friends the previous summer in Vancouver, when Kenny was visiting his uncle's family there. Kenny offers to take Tom on a tour of Hong Kong.

 Basic Conversation 23-1

1. LAM   **Jìrán zhè shi nǐ dìyícì lái Xiānggǎng, wǒ yuànyi yìwùde zuò nǐde xiàngdǎo, dài nǐ qù cānguān yixia.**
That's this is your first time in Hong Kong, I'd be happy to volunteer to act as your guide and take you around to see things.

2. BROWN   **Tài hǎole! Zhēn shi tài gǎnxiè nǐ le. Wǒ děng dōu děngbujíle!**
That's awesome! I truly can't thank you enough. I really can't wait!

3. LAM   **Nà wǒmen zǒu ba!**
So off we go!

(on the Star Ferry)

Xiānggǎng shi yóu Xiānggǎng dǎo, Jiǔlóng bàndǎo, Xīnjiè hái yǒu liǎngbǎiduōge dǎoyǔ suǒzǔchéngde. Xiānggǎngde zǒngmiànji shi yìqiān yìbǎiduō píngfāng gōnglǐ, shi Àoménde sānshíbèi, yě shi Xīnjiāpōde liǎngbèi. Xiānggǎngde rénkǒu yǒu qībǎiduōwàn, bāokuò wǔshíduōwàn wàiguo rén, qízhōng Fēilǜbīn rén hé Yìndù rén zuì duō.
Hong Kong is composed of Hong Kong Island, the Kowloon Peninsula, the New Territories, and more than 200 islands. Hong Kong's total area is more than 1,100 square kilometers, which is 30 times that of Macao and twice that of Singapore. The population of Hong Kong is over 7 million, including more than 500,000 foreigners, among which Filipinos and Indians predominate.

4. BROWN   **Nǐ néng bu néng jiǎndānde gěi wǒ jièshao yixia Xiānggǎngde lìshǐ?**
Could you briefly tell me about the history of Hong Kong?

5. LAM   **Dāngrán kéyi. Yīngguo rén zài shíjiǔ shìjì Dìyícì Yāpiàn Zhànzhēng yǐhòu, zhànlǐngle Xiānggǎng, dāngshí zhèli zhǐ yǒu yìxiē xiǎo yúcūn. Hòulái, Zhōngguo hé Yīngguo qiāndìngle Nánjīng Tiáoyuē, Xiānggǎng jiù biànchéngle Yīngguode zhímíndì le. Yìzhí dào yī-jiǔ-jiǔ-qī-nián, Xiānggǎng cái huíguī Zhōngguo, chéng-**

wéi Zhōnghuá Rénmín Gònghéguó Xiānggǎng Tèbié Xíngzhèngqū, bìngqiě shíshī "Yìguó Liǎngzhì," yě jiù shi shuō chúle wàijiāo hé guófáng yǐwài, Xiānggǎng wǔshinián zhīnèi kéyi xiǎngyǒu gāodùde zizhìquán, tāde zīběn zhǔyì jīngjì zhìdù yě bú biàn.

Of course I can. In the 19th century, after the First Opium War, the British occupied Hong Kong; at the time, there were just some small fishing villages here. Later, China and Britain signed the Treaty of Nanking and Hong Kong became a British colony. Not until 1997 did Hong Kong revert to China, becoming the Hong Kong Special Administrative Region of the PRC and implementing "One Country, Two Systems," meaning that except for foreign affairs and national defense, Hong Kong may for 50 years enjoy a high degree of autonomy, without changing its capitalist economic system.

Build Up

---

1. Lam

yìwù	duty, obligation [N]
yìwùde	voluntarily [A]
xiàngdǎo	guide [N]
yìwùde zuò nǐde xiàngdǎo	voluntarily act as your guide

Jìrán zhè shi nǐ dìyícì lái Xiānggǎng, wǒ yuànyi yìwùde zuò nǐde xiàngdǎo, dài nǐ qù cānguān yixia.

Since this is your first time in Hong Kong, I'd be happy to volunteer to act as your guide and take you around to see things.

---

2. Brown

děngbují	can't wait [RC]
wǒ děng dōu děngbujíle	I just can't wait

Tài hǎole! Zhēn shi tài gǎnxiè nǐ le. Wǒ děng dōu děngbujíle!

That's awesome! I truly can't thank you enough. I really can't wait!

---

3. Lam

Nà wǒmen zǒu ba!

So off we go!

dǎo	island [N]
Jiǔlóng	Kowloon [PW]
bàndǎo	peninsula [N]
Jiǔlóng bàndǎo	Kowloon Peninsula [PW]
Xīnjiè	New Territories [PW]
dǎoyǔ	island [N]
zǔchéng	make up, form, compose [V+PV]
A shi yóu B (suǒ)zǔchéngde	A is composed of B [PT]
miànji	area [N]
zǒngmiànji	total area [N]
píngfāng	square [AT]
píngfāng gōnglǐ	square kilometer [PH]
shi Àoménde sānshibèi	it's 30 times that of Macao
shi Xīnjiāpōde liǎngbèi	it's twice that of Singapore
bāokuò	include [V]
qízhōng	among which, within which [PW]
Fēilùbīn	The Philippines [PW]
Fēilùbīn rén	Filipino, Filipina
Yìndù	India [PW]
Yìndù rén	Indian
qízhōng Fēilùbīn rén hé Yìndù rén zuì duō	among which Filipinos and Indians predominate

Xiānggǎng shi yóu Xiānggǎng dǎo, Jiǔlóng bàndǎo, Xīnjiè hái yǒu liǎngbǎiduōge dǎoyǔ

Hong Kong is composed of Hong Kong Island, the Kowloon Peninsula, the New Territories,

suǒzǔchéngde. Xiānggǎngde zǒngmiànji shi yìqiān yībǎiduō píngfāng gōnglǐ, shi Àoménde sānshíbèi, yě shi Xīnjiāpōde liǎngbèi. Xiānggǎngde rénkǒu yǒu qībǎiduōwàn, bāokuò wǔshiduōwàn wàiguo rén, qízhōng Fēilǜbīn rén hé Yìndù rén zuì duō.

and more than 200 islands. Hong Kong's total area is more than 1,100 square kilometers, which is 30 times that of Macao and twice that of Singapore. The population of Hong Kong is over 7 million, including more than 500,000 foreigners, among which Filipinos and Indians predominate.

....

4.   Brown

lìshǐ   history [N]

Nǐ néng bu néng jiǎndānde gěi wǒ jièshao yixia Xiānggǎngde lìshǐ?

Could you briefly tell me about the history of Hong Kong?

....

5.   Lam

shìjì	century [N]
shíjiǔ shìjì	nineteenth century
yāpiàn	opium [N]
Yāpiàn Zhànzhēng	Opium War [PH]
zhànlǐng	occupy, capture [V]
dāngshí	at that time, then [TW]
yúcūn	fishing village [PW]
dāngshí zhèli zhǐ yǒu yìxiē xiǎo yúcūn	at the time there were just some small fishing villages here
qiāndìng	sign [V]
tiáoyuē	treaty, pact [N]
qiāndìng tiáoyuē	sign a treaty
Nánjīng Tiáoyuē	Treaty of Nanking [PH]
biànchéng	become [V+PV]
yìzhí dào yī-jiǔ-jiǔ-qī-nián	right up until 1997
huíguī	revert, return to [V]
huíguī Zhōngguo	be returned to China
chéngwéi	become [V]
xíngzhèngqū	administrative region [N]
tèbié xíngzhèngqū	special administrative region [PH]
Xiānggǎng Tèbié Xíngzhèngqū	Hong Kong Special Administrative Region [PW]
bìngqiě	moreover, furthermore, and [CJ]
shíshī	implement, put into effect [V]
Yìguó Liǎngzhì	One Country Two Systems [PH]
wàijiāo	diplomacy, foreign affairs [N]
guófáng	national defense [N]
wǔshinián zhīnèi	within fifty years
xiǎngyǒu	enjoy (rights, prestige) [V]
gāodù	high degree [AT]
zìzhìquán	autonomy [N]
gāodùde zìzhìquán	high degree (of) autonomy
kéyi xiǎngyǒu gāodùde zìzhìquán	may enjoy a high degree of autonomy
zīběn	capital [N]
zhǔyì	doctrine; -ism [N]
zīběn zhǔyì	capitalism [PH]
jīngjì	economy [N]
zhìdù	system [N]
jīngjì zhìdù	economic system
zīběn zhǔyì jīngjì zhìdù	capitalist economic system

Dāngrán kéyi. Yīngguo rén zài shíjiǔ shìjì Dìyícì Yāpiàn Zhànzhēng yǐhòu, zhànlǐngle Xiānggǎng, dāngshí zhèli zhǐ yǒu yìxiē xiǎo

Of course I can. In the 19th century, after the First Opium War, the British occupied Hong Kong; at the time, there were just some small

yúcūn. Hòulái, Zhōngguo hé Yīngguo qiāndìngle Nánjīng Tiáoyuē, Xiānggǎng jiù biànchéngle Yīngguode zhímíndì le. Yìzhí dào yī-jiǔ-jiǔ-qī-nián, Xiānggǎng cái huíguī Zhōngguo, chéngwéi Zhōnghuá Rénmín Gònghéguó Xiānggǎng Tèbié Xíngzhèngqū, bìngqiě shíshī "Yìguó Liǎngzhì," yě jiù shi shuō chúle wàijiāo hé guófáng yǐwài, Xiānggǎng wǔshinián zhīnèi kéyi xiǎngyǒu gāodùde zìzhìquán, tāde zīběn zhǔyì jīngjì zhìdù yě bú biàn.

fishing villages here. Later, China and Britain signed the Treaty of Nanking and Hong Kong became a British colony. Not until 1997 did Hong Kong revert to China, becoming the Hong Kong Special Administrative Region of the PRC and implementing "One Country, Two Systems," meaning that except for foreign affairs and national defense, Hong Kong may for 50 years enjoy a high degree of autonomy, without changing its capitalist economic system.

Grammatical and Cultural Notes

1A. **HONG KONG.** Hong Kong, known as **Xiānggǎng** in Mandarin, is one of two Special Administrative Regions of China, Macao being the other. Possessing a deep natural harbor and an expansive skyline, Hong Kong is located in the extreme south of China, on the coast next to Guangdong Province. Hong Kong was a British colony from 1841 until 1999, when it reverted to China. Originally a major manufacturing center, Hong Kong has more recently become a service-based economy and leading international financial center, with the banking and insurance industries both of great importance. Hong Kong re-exports to countries around the world many of the products manufactured in mainland China. The native language of most

Star Ferry in Victoria Harbor, Hong Kong

residents of Hong Kong is Cantonese, but more and more people—especially of the younger generation—can understand and speak Mandarin, even though they may have a strong Cantonese accent in their Mandarin. Additional information about Hong Kong is contained in the Basic Conversation for this lesson.

1B. **Yìwùde zuò nǐde xiàngdǎo** means "voluntarily act as your guide" or "volunteer to serve as your guide." Some speakers from Beijing prefer saying this without the **-de** as **yìwù zuò nǐde xiàngdǎo** "voluntarily act as your guide." Here are some more examples with the adverb **yìwù(de)** "voluntarily":

Hěn duō dàzhōngxuéshēng yìwù(de) wèi shèqū fúwù.

"Many college and high school students voluntarily serve the community."

Tāmen dōu shi yìwù lái bāngmángde, bìng méiyou ná qián.

"They all came voluntarily to help, not taking money."

2. The adverb **dōu** in the sentence **Wǒ děng dōu děngbujíle** "I really can't wait any longer" or "I just can't wait any longer" emphasizes and strengthens the meaning of the verb **děngbují**.

3A. **A SHI YÓU B (SUǑ)ZǓCHÉNGDE.** The pattern **A shi yóu B (suǒ)zǔchéngde** means "A is composed of B," "A is formed of B," "A is made up of B," or "A consists of B." In this pattern, **yóu** means "from" and the optional **suǒ** is a nominalizer meaning "one which" or "that which"; if used, **suǒ** makes explicit that **zǔchéngde** is a noun form. A literal meaning of **A shi yóu B (suǒ)zǔchéngde** would be "A is one which is composed from B." The basic pattern is:

A	SHI YÓU	B	(SUŎ)ZŬCHÉNGDE

Xiānggǎng   shi yóu   Xiānggǎng dǎo, Jiǔlóng, hé Xīnjiè   suǒzǔchéngde.

"Hong Kong is composed of Hong Kong Island, Kowloon, and the New Territories."

Two more examples of the pattern **A shi yóu B (suǒ)zǔchéngde**:

Àomén shi yóu Àomén bàndǎo, Dàngzǎi hé Lùhuán liǎngge dǎoyǔ suǒzǔchéngde.

"Macao is composed of the Macao Peninsula and the two islands of Taipa and Coloane."

Zhèige wěiyuánhui shi yóu xiàozhǎng, wǔwèi lǎoshī hé liǎngwèi xuésheng zǔchéngde.

"This committee consists of the principal, five teachers, and two students."

3B. In this line you encounter the word **zǒngmiànji** "total area." The syllable **zǒng** can mean "total," "overall," "general," "main," or "always." Compare the following words you've learned that share the initial syllable **zǒng**:

zǒnggòng	"in all, in total" **(12-4)**
zǒngjīnglǐ	"general manager" **(2-4)**
zǒngmiànji	"total area" **(23-1)**
zǒngshi	"always" **(18-1)**

3C. **Píngfāng** is an attributive that means "square." It can precede various words indicating measurements. Examples:

píngfāng gōnglǐ	"square kilometer"
píngfāng mǐ	"square meter"
píngfāng yīngchǐ	"square foot"
píngfāng yīnglǐ	"square mile"

3D. Examine the two occurrences of **bèi** in the sentence **Xiānggǎngde zǒngmiànji...shi Àoménde sānshíbèi, yě shi Xīnjiāpōde liǎngbèi** "Hong Kong's total area...is thirty times that of Macao and twice that of Singapore." As you learned in 22-3: 3B, **bèi** is a measure that means "times."

3E. **QÍZHONG.** Look at the last sentence of utterance 3, particularly the italicized portion: **Xiānggǎngde rénkǒu yǒu qībǎiduōwàn, bāokuò wǔshiduōwàn wàiguo rén, qízhōng Fēilǜbīn rén hé Yìndù rén zuì duō** "The population of Hong Kong is over 7 million, including more than 500,000 foreigners, among which Filipinos and Indians predominate." The placeword **qízhōng** "among which," "within which," "in which," or "of which," is a common and important word in higher-level, more formal spoken and written Chinese. Here are some more examples of its use:

Kǎoshì zhǐ yǒu wǔge rén jígé, tā shi qízhōng zhīyī.

"Only five people passed the exam, she being one of them."

Táiwān yǒu liǎngqiānsānbǎiduōwàn rén, qízhōng wǔshiduōwàn shi yuánzhùmín.

"Taiwan's population is over 23 million, in which are included over 500,000 aboriginal people."

Měiguo jīngjì mùqián miànduì xǔduō tiǎozhàn, qízhōng zuì dàde shi rúhé jiějué shīyè wèntí.

"The U.S. economy is currently facing lots of challenges, of which the greatest is how to solve the problem of unemployment."

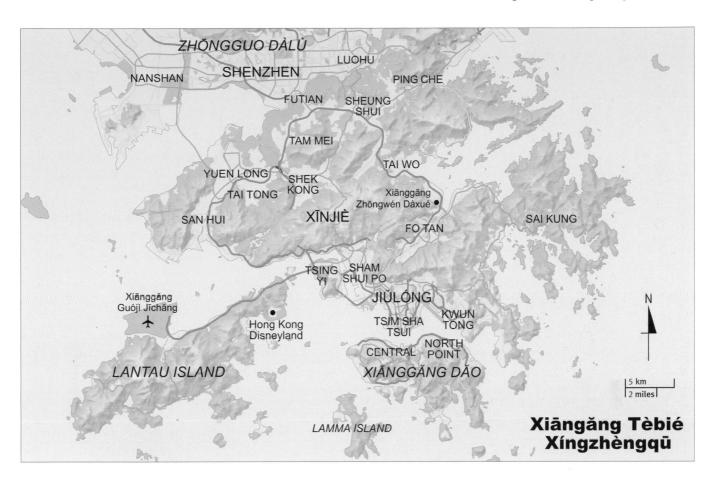

ZHŌNGGUO DÀLÙ

NANSHAN   SHENZHEN   LUOHU   PING CHE

FUTIAN   SHEUNG SHUI

TAM MEI

TAI WO

YUEN LONG   SHEK KONG

TAI TONG   Xiānggǎng Zhōngwén Dàxué ●

SAN HUI   XĪNJIÈ   FO TAN   SAI KUNG

TSING YI   SHAM SHUI PO

JIŬLÓNG

Xiānggǎng Guójì Jīchǎng ✈   KWUN TONG

Hong Kong Disneyland   TSIM SHA TSUI

CENTRAL   NORTH POINT

LANTAU ISLAND   XIĀNGGĂNG DĂO

LAMMA ISLAND

N

5 km
2 miles

Xiānggǎng Tèbié Xíngzhèngqū

5A. **HOW TO EXPRESS "CENTURY."** In this line, note **shíjiǔ shìjì** "nineteen century." In English we use ordinal numbers when describing which century (e.g., "nineteenth century"), but Chinese speakers don't use the specifier **dì-** and instead say the equivalent of "nineteen century." The pattern is:

NUMBER	SHÌJÌ
shíjiǔ	shìjì

"nineteenth century"

Practice the following so they're at the tip of your tongue when you need them:

shíqī shìjì	"seventeenth century"
shíbā shìjì	"eighteenth century"
shíjiǔ shìjì	"nineteenth century"
èrshí shìjì	"twentieth century"
èrshíyī shìjì	"twenty-first century"
èrshi'èr shìjì	"twenty-second century"

The question form is **Něige shìjì?** "Which century?"

5B. **CANTONESE-INFLUENCED MANDARIN.** In this lesson, even though Mr. Lam speaks Mandarin quite fluently, the Mandarin that he speaks has quite naturally been influenced to some extent by his native language, Cantonese. Below are examples of some of the more common pronunciation mistakes made by Cantonese speakers when speaking Mandarin, which you'll hear often if you listen carefully:

zi and **zhi**	→	**ji** (so that **yíge zì** "a character" sounds like ***yíge jī** "a chicken")
ci and **chi**	→	**qi** (so that **chīfàn** "eat" sounds like ***qīfàn**)
si and **shi**	→	**xi** (so that **Tā bú shi wǒde lǎoshī** "She's not my teacher" sounds like ***Tā bú xi wǒde lǎoxī**)
j	→	**g** (so that **jiē** "street" sounds like ***gāai**)
n	→	**l** (so that **nán** "difficult" sounds like **lán** "blue")
hu	→	**w** (so that **Huáng Xiáojie** "Ms. Huang" sounds like **Wáng Xiáojie** "Ms. Wang")

Common grammar mistakes made by Cantonese speakers when speaking Mandarin include:

(1)   **Yǒu** "to have" is often used as an auxiliary before the main verb of a sentence to indicate completed action, replacing standard Mandarin **-le** and **-guo**. Example: ***Nǐ yǒu méiyou qù? –Yǒu, wǒ yǒu qù** "Did you go? –Yes, I did."

(2)   In constructions with **gěi** "to give," the order of direct and indirect object is often reversed. Example: ***Tā kéyi gěi wǒde dìzhǐ nǐ le** "She can give you my address."

(3)   The verb suffix **-guò** "surpass" is often affixed to stative verbs to indicate comparison in place of standard Mandarin comparative constructions with **bǐ**. Example: ***Wǒmende fómiào bù kéyi gāoguò tāmende huíjiào-táng** "Our Buddhist temples are not allowed to be higher than their Islamic ones."

(4)   In Cantonese Mandarin, **-de** is added at the end of many sentences where standard Mandarin would have no **-de**. Example: ***Zhōngguo rén hǎo lǎoshíde** "Chinese people are very honest."

(5)   The adverbs **duō** "more" and **shǎo** "less" may occur after the verb rather than before as in standard Mandarin. Example: **Chī duō yìdiǎn** "Eat a little more."

(6)   The adverb **xiān** "first" often occurs in sentence-final position rather than before the verb as in standard Mandarin. Example: **Nǐmen xiàchē xiān** "You get off the bus first."

Even though the above may sound very complicated and difficult to you, be assured that once you have the opportunity to live in a Cantonese-speaking area (for example, Hong Kong or Guangzhou) and hear Cantonese-influenced Mandarin for a few weeks, your brain will begin making the necessary adjustments, and you'll gradually understand more and more of the Mandarin that you hear spoken around you. Familiarity with the characteristics of Cantonese-influenced Mandarin, as described above, will make your adjustment faster and easier.

A Walking Tour of Hong Kong (cont.)

Tom Brown and Kenny Lam continue their tour of Hong Kong, discussing the Hong Kong economy, local culture, and Cantonese delicacies (continued from the previous conversation).

Basic Conversation 23-2

1. BROWN	*(disembarking from the Star Ferry)* **Tīngshuō Xiānggǎng yíqiè yǐ jīngjì wéi zhǔ.** I've heard that in Hong Kong the economy trumps everything else.
2. LAM	**Duì, kéyi zhèmme shuō. Xiānggǎng shi shìjièshang zhòngyàode jīnróng hé màoyì zhōngxīn zhīyī, yínhángyè tèbié fādá. Xiānggǎng Gǔshì zài shìjièshang páimíng dìwǔ.** Yes, you could say that. Hong Kong is one of the important financial and trade centers in the world, banking being particularly well developed. The Hong Kong Stock Exchange is ranked number five in the world.
3. BROWN	**Nà wénhuà fāngmiàn ne?** And what about in the area of culture?
4. LAM	**Xiānggǎngde yíge tèsè shi tā shi zhēnzhèng Dōngxīfāng jiāohuì rónghéde dìfang. Suīrán yǐqián shi Yīngguode zhímíndì, dàn háishi bǎocúnle hěn duō chuántǒngde Zhōngguo wénhuà, bǐfang shuō, fēngshuǐ duì Xiānggǎng rén jiù shífēn zhòngyào.** One distinctive feature of Hong Kong is that it's a place where the East and West really intersect and merge. Though it used to be a British colony, it has preserved much traditional Chinese culture; for example, feng shui is very important to Hong Kong people.
	(walking on Nathan Road in Kowloon)
5. BROWN	**Wà! Nǐ kàn, zhèmme duō xiàngjī hé diànzǐ chǎnpǐn!** Wow! Look, so many cameras and electronic products!
6. LAM	**Xiānggǎng shi gòuwùzhěde tiāntáng! Shì ge miǎnshuìgǎng, duì yìbānde jìnkǒu shāngpǐn bù zhēng guānshuì.** Hong Kong is a shopper's paradise! It's a free port; it doesn't levy customs duties on ordinary imported goods.

7. BROWN	**Zài zhèli mǎi dōngxi kě bu kéyi jiǎngjià?**
	Can you haggle when you buy stuff here?

8. LAM	**Bǎihuò gōngsī hé bǐjiào dàde shāngdiàn yìbān bù néng jiǎngjià. Xiǎo yìdiǎnde shāngdiàn huò lùtiān shìchǎng kéyi shìshi kàn. Dàn gòuwù qián, zuìhǎo duō qù jǐjiā shāngdiàn bǐjiào yixia jiàqián. Yǒude dìfang mài dàobǎn huò màopáide shāngpǐn, yào xiǎoxīn, miǎnde bèi piàn!**
	At department stores and larger shops generally you can't haggle. At smaller shops or open-air markets you can try. But before you buy, it's best to go to several different stores to compare prices. Some places sell pirated or fake goods; you have to be careful so you don't get cheated!

(in a Cantonese restaurant in Kowloon)

Xiānggǎng rén xǐhuan shàng jiǔlóu yǐnchá.
Hong Kong people like to go to Cantonese-style restaurants to have tea and dim sum.

9. BROWN	**"Yǐnchá" shi shémme?**
	What does yǐnchá mean?

10. LAM	**"Yǐnchá" Guǎngdōng huà jiào "yámchàh," jiù shi hē cháde yìsi.**
	In Cantonese yǐnchá is called yámchàh; it means "drink tea."

11. BROWN	**Nándào wǒmen lái zhèr guāng hē chá ma? Wǒ dùzi hǎo è! Néng bu néng chī yidian dōngxi?**
	You mean we've come here just to drink tea? I'm starving! Could we eat something?

12. LAM	**Nǐ fàngxīn hǎole! Wǒ diǎnle yìxiē Xiānggǎng zuì yǒumíngde diǎnxin: chāshāobāo, xiājiǎo gēn shāomài.**
	Relax! I've ordered some of Hong Kong's most famous dim sum: chāshāobāo, shrimp dumplings, and shāomài.

13. BROWN	**M, hǎochījíle! Xiànzài wǒ zhōngyú míngbai wèishémme dàjiā bǎ Xiānggǎng jiàozuo "měishí tiāntáng" le!**
	Mmm, yummy! Now I finally understand why everybody calls Hong Kong "food heaven"!

 **Build Up**

1. Brown

yíqiè	everything, all [N]
yǐ...wéi zhǔ	take...as the main thing, regard...as the most important component [PT]
yǐ jīngjì wéi zhǔ	regard the economy as the main thing
Tīngshuō Xiānggǎng yíqiè yǐ jīngjì wéi zhǔ.	I've heard that in Hong Kong the economy trumps everything else.

2. Lam

zhòngyào	be important [SV]
jīnróng	finance [N]
...zhīyī	one of... [PT]
yínhángyè	banking industry, banking [N]
fādá	be developed [SV]
yínhángyè tèbié fādá	banking is particularly well developed
gǔshì	stock market, stock exchange [N]
páimíng	be ranked, rank [VO]
páimíng dìwǔ	be ranked number five, be in 5th place
Duì, kéyi zhèmme shuō. Xiānggǎng shi shìjièshang zhòngyàode jīnróng hé màoyì zhōngxīn zhīyī, yínhángyè tèbié fādá. Xiānggǎng Gǔshì	Yes, you could say that. Hong Kong is one of the important financial and trade centers in the world, banking being particularly well developed.

zài shìjièshang páimíng dìwǔ.

The Hong Kong Stock Exchange is ranked number five in the world.

---

3.   Brown

fāngmiàn | aspect, area, side [N]
wénhuà fāngmiàn | in the aspect of culture
Nà wénhuà fāngmiàn ne? | And what about in the area of culture?

---

4.   Lam

tèsè | characteristic, distinguishing feature [N]
zhēnzhèng | real, true, genuine [AT]
Dōngxīfāng | East and West
jiāohuì | connect up, meet, intersect [V]
rónghé | mix together, merge, fuse [V]
zhímíndì | colony [N]
bǎocún | preserve, keep, maintain [V]
chuántǒng | be traditional [SV]
chuántǒngde Zhōngguo wénhuà | traditional Chinese culture
fēngshuǐ | feng shui, geomancy [N]
shífēn | very, extremely [A]
shífēn zhòngyào | very important

Xiānggǎngde yíge tèsè shi tā shi zhēnzhèng Dōngxīfāng jiāohuì rónghéde dìfang. Suīrán yǐqián shi Yīngguode zhímíndì, dàn háishi bǎocúnle hěn duō chuántǒngde Zhōngguo wénhuà, bǐfang shuō, fēngshuǐ duì Xiānggǎng rén jiù shífēn zhòngyào.

One distinctive feature of Hong Kong is that it's a place where the East and West really intersect and merge. Though it used to be a British colony, it has preserved much traditional Chinese culture; for example, feng shui is very important to Hong Kong people.

---

5.   Brown

xiàngjī | camera [N]
chǎnpǐn | product [N]
diànzǐ chǎnpǐn | electronic product, electronics [PH]

Wà! Nǐ kàn, zhèmme duō xiàngjī hé diànzǐ chǎnpǐn!

Wow! Look, so many cameras and electronic products!

---

6.   Lam

gòuwù | buy things, shop [V]
gòuwùzhě | one who buys things, shopper [N]
tiāntáng | paradise, heaven [N]
gòuwùzhěde tiāntáng | a shopper's paradise
miǎnshuì | be exempt from tax or duty [VO]
miǎnshuìgǎng | duty free port [N]
yìbān | general, ordinary [AT]
shāngpǐn | goods, merchandise [N]
yìbānde jìnkǒu shāngpǐn | ordinary imported goods
zhēng | levy, collect (taxes or duty) [V]
guānshuì | customs duty [N]
zhēng guānshuì | levy customs duty

Xiānggǎng shi gòuwùzhěde tiāntáng! Shì ge miǎnshuìgǎng, duì yìbānde jìnkǒu shāngpǐn bù zhēng guānshuì.

Hong Kong is a shopper's paradise! It's a free port; it doesn't levy customs duties on ordinary imported goods.

---

7.   Brown

jiǎngjià | bargain, haggle [VO]
kě bu kéyi jiǎngjià | can you or can't you haggle
Zài zhèlǐ mǎi dōngxi kě bu kéyi jiǎngjià? | Can you haggle when you buy stuff here?

8. Lam

băihuò gōngsī	department store [PH]
shāngdiàn	shop, store [PW]
yìbān	generally, ordinarily [A]
yìbān bù néng jiăngjià	in general you can't haggle
lùtiān shìchăng	open-air market [PH]
shìshi kàn	try and see
gòuwù qián	before purchasing
bĭjiào	compare [V]
duō qù jĭjiā shāngdiàn bĭjiào yixia jiàqián	go to several different stores to compare prices
dàobăn	pirate (a book, film, etc.) [V]
màopái	counterfeit, fake, imitation [AT]
dàobăn huò màopáide shāngpĭn	pirated or fake goods
miănde...	so as to avoid..., lest... [PT]
miănde bèi piàn	to avoid getting cheated

Băihuò gōngsī hé bĭjiào dàde shāngdiàn yìbān bù néng jiăngjià. Xiăo yìdiănde shāngdiàn huò lùtiān shìchăng kéyi shìshi kàn. Dàn gòuwù qián, zuìhăo duō qù jĭjiā shāngdiàn bĭjiào yixia jiàqián. Yŏude dìfang mài dàobăn huò màopáide shāngpĭn, yào xiăoxīn, miănde bèi piàn!

At department stores and larger shops generally you can't haggle. At smaller shops or open-air markets you can try. But before you buy, it's best to go to several different stores to compare prices. Some places sell pirated or fake goods; you have to be careful so you don't get cheated!

jiŭlóu	Cantonese-style restaurant; any large and lavish restaurant [PW]
yĭnchá	drink tea and eat dim sum in a Cantonese-style restaurant [VO]

Xiānggăng rén xĭhuan shàng jiŭlóu yĭnchá.

Hong Kong people like to go to Cantonese-style restaurants to have tea and dim sum.

9. Brown

"Yĭnchá" shi shémme?

What does yĭnchá mean?

10. Lam

"Yĭnchá" Guăngdōng huà jiào "yámchàh," jiù shi hē cháde yìsi.

In Cantonese **yĭnchá** is called **yámchàh**; it means "drink tea."

11. Brown

guāng	only, just [A]
guāng hē chá	only drink tea
dùzi	belly, abdomen, stomach [N]
wŏ dùzi hăo è	my stomach is very hungry

Nándào wŏmen lái zhèr guāng hē chá ma? Wŏ dùzi hăo è! Néng bu néng chī yidian dōngxi?

You mean we've come here just to drink tea? I'm starving! Could we eat something?

12. Lam

diănxin	snack, pastry, dim sum [N]
zuì yŏumíngde diănxin	the most famous snacks
chāshāobāo	steamed white flour bun with barbecued pork filling [N]
xiājiăo	shrimp dumpling [N]
shāomài	small steamed dumpling with pork inside thin wheat flour wrapper [N]

Nĭ fàngxīn hăole! Wŏ diănle yìxiē Xiānggăng zuì yŏumíngde diănxin: chāshāobāo, xiājiăo gēn shāomài.

Relax! I've ordered some of Hong Kong's most famous dim sum: chāshāobāo, shrimp dumplings, and shāomài.

13. Brown

xiànzài wǒ zhōngyú míngbai	now I finally understand
jiàozuo	call; be called, be known as [V]
bǎ A jiàozuo B	call A B [PT]
měishí	fine foods, delicacy [N]
měishí tiāntáng	food heaven [PH]
bǎ Xiānggǎng jiàozuo měishí tiāntáng	call Hong Kong food heaven

M, hǎochījíle! Xiànzài wǒ zhōngyú míngbai wèishémme dàjiā bǎ Xiānggǎng jiàozuo "měishí tiāntáng" le!

Mmm, yummy! Now I finally understand why everybody calls Hong Kong "food heaven"!

Grammatical and Cultural Notes

1A. The Star Ferry, in operation since 1888, runs across Victoria Harbor to connect Tsim Sha Tsui and Hung Hom in Kowloon with Central and Wan Chai on Hong Kong island.

1B. **YǏ...WÉI ZHǓ.** Examine the sentence **Tīngshuō Xiānggǎng yíqiè yǐ jīngjì wéi zhǔ** "I've heard that in Hong Kong everything takes the economy as the most important component." **Yǐ...wéi zhǔ** is an important grammatical pattern typical of higher-level, formal spoken and written Chinese. It literally means "take...to be the main (thing)." Freer translations of this pattern include "regard...as the most important component," "with...being the most important," and "consist mainly of...." The basic pattern is:

YǏ	OBJECT	WÉI ZHǓ
yǐ	jīngjì	wéi zhǔ

"take the economy as the most important thing"

Both noun phrases and verb phrases can occur in the object position. Here are some more examples with the pattern **yǐ...wéi zhǔ**:

Běndìde chūkǒu yǐ diànzǐ chǎnpǐn wéi zhǔ.

"Exports from here consist primarily of electronic products."

Táiwān cài yǐ hǎixiān, jī, gēn nóng tāng wéi zhǔ.

"Taiwanese cuisine consists primarily of seafood, chicken, and thick soups."

Nǐ xiànzài hái shi xuésheng, yīnggāi yǐ xuéxí wéi zhǔ, búyào zhěngtiān xiǎngzhe zuò shēngyi.

"You're still a student, you should consider your studies as the most important thing; don't be thinking about going into business all day long."

2A. **...ZHĪYĪ.** Look at the sentence **Xiānggǎng shi shìjièshang zhòngyàode jīnróng hé màoyì zhōngxīn zhīyī** "Hong Kong is one of the important financial and trade centers in the world." The pattern **...zhīyī** is placed after a noun phrase and means "one of...." The basic pattern is:

NOUN PHRASE	...ZHĪYĪ
shìjièshang zhòngyàode jīnróng zhōngxīn	zhīyī

"one of the important financial centers in the world"

More examples of the pattern **...zhīyī**:

Hāfó Dàxué shi shìjièshang zuì yǒumíngde dàxué zhīyī.

"Harvard University is one of the most famous universities in the world."

Zhèizhī qiúduì shi jīnnián páimíng zuì gāode qiúduì zhīyī.

"This team is one of the highest-ranking teams this year."

Àomén shi shìjièshang píngjūn shòumìng zuì chángde dìqū zhīyī.

"Macao is one of the regions with the longest average life expectancy in the world."

2B.   **PÁIMÍNG.** Examine the use of **páimíng** "be ranked" in the sentence **Xiānggǎng Gǔshì zài shìjièshang páimíng dìwǔ** "The Hong Kong Stock Exchange is ranked number five in the world." The pattern **páimíng dì-**... means "be ranked," "rank," or "be in ___ place." Any number can occur after **páimíng dì-**, for example:

páimíng dìyī	"be ranked number one"
páimíng dì'èr	"be ranked number two"
páimíng dìsān	"be ranked number three"

The question form would be **Páimíng dìjǐ?** "It's ranked number what?" Here are some more examples of the pattern **páimíng dì-**:

Niǔyuē Gǔshì zài shìjièshang páimíng dìyī.

"The New York Stock Exchange ranks number one in the world."

Wǒmen xuéxiào jīnnián páimíng dìbā.

"Our school is ranked number eight this year."

4A.   **Fēngshuǐ** "feng shui" or "geomancy" literally means "wind and water." It refers to the art of selecting favorable locations for houses, businesses, graves, etc. so as to be in harmony with yin and yang, the forces of nature. Business people often consult fengshui masters to determine good locations for stores or offices. If a place is deemed unsatisfactory, then mirrors or other equalizing objects may be added for balance.

4B.   Examine the sentence **Fēngshuǐ duì Xiānggǎng rén shífēn zhòngyào** "Feng shui is very important to Hong Kong people." The pattern **duì...zhòngyào** means "be important to..." or "be important for...." Here is another example of this pattern:

Bǎ Zhōngwén xuéhǎo duì wǒ lái shuō hěn zhòngyào.

"Learning Chinese well is very important to me."

6A.   The verb **gòuwù**, which means "buy things" or "shop," is a more formal equivalent of **mǎi dōngxi**.

6B.   Examine the common noun suffix **-zhě** "one who does something" at the end of the noun **gòuwùzhě** "one who buys things" or "shopper." The noun suffix **-zhě** occurs in many words, for example, **zuòzhě** "author," **dúzhě** "reader," **xiāofèizhě** "consumer," **mùjīzhě** "eyewitness," etc.

6C.   Note the use of **duì** in the pattern **duì...zhēng guānshuì** "levy customs duty on (some product)" as in **Xiānggǎng duì yìbānde jìnkǒu shāngpǐn bù zhēng guānshuì** "Hong Kong doesn't levy customs duties on ordinary imported goods."

7.   The verb-object compound **jiǎngjià** means "haggle" or "bargain" (lit. "discuss price"). Bargaining is traditional in Chinese culture, with most Chinese believing that it's foolish to pay the first price you're quoted. Nowadays, at larger stores and supermarkets in mainland China, Hong Kong, and Taiwan, haggling is no longer commonly practiced, unless one is purchasing in quantity. However, at smaller stores and traditional Chinese markets, it's still quite common to haggle. Even hotel jewelers are usually willing to discount merchandise. It never hurts to ask whether a lower price is possible, but you shouldn't haggle unless you're serious about buying.

8A.   **MIǍNDE...** Toward the end of utterance 8, look at the sentence **Yǒude dìfang mài dàobǎn huò màopáide**

shāngpǐn, yào xiǎoxīn, miǎnde bèi piàn! "Some places sell pirated or fake goods; you have to be careful so you don't get cheated!" The verb construction **miǎnde...** means "save (someone from an undesirable outcome)," "so as to avoid...," "so that...not," or "lest...." The **miǎnde** is usually preceded by a sentence describing the proposed solution to a feared, undesirable outcome; and **miǎnde** is followed by a stative verb, phrase, or sentence that describes the undesirable outcome that is to be avoided. The basic pattern is:

PROPOSED SOLUTION	MIǍNDE	UNDESIRABLE OUTCOME
Yào xiǎoxīn,	**miǎnde**	**bèi piàn!**
"You have to be careful lest you get cheated!"		

Here are some more examples with the pattern **miǎnde...**:

Wǒ xiàwǔ bù lái, miǎnde pèngjian ta.

"I'm not coming in the afternoon, to avoid running into her."

Nǐ zuìhǎo bǎ zhèjǐdiǎn jìxialai, miǎnde yìhuǐr wàngle.

"You better write these several points down, so you don't forget later."

Wǒ zài jiěshì yíbiàn, miǎnde dàjiā nòngbuqīngchu.

"Let me explain one more time, so everyone is clear." (lit. "...lest everyone not be able to be clear about it")

Wǒmen zuìhǎo xiànzài shuōqīngchule, miǎnde jiānglái máfan.

"We better make everything clear now, so we don't have trouble in the future."

Nǐ zuìhǎo zhǔnshí bǎ shū huán'gěi túshūguǎn, miǎnde tāmen fá nǐ qián.

"You better return the book to the library on time, so they don't fine you."

8B. Notice the passive voice with **bèi** in **Yào xiǎoxīn, miǎnde bèi piàn** "You have to be careful, so you don't get cheated." This is the traditional, infelicitous use of **bèi** with verbs indicating unpleasant or undesirable outcomes (cf. 22-2: 5B).

10. The Cantonese word **yámchàh** "drink tea" is written in so-called Yale Cantonese romanization, which is different from Pinyin. There is more information about Cantonese in the next lesson (cf. 23-3: 10).

11. Observe the use of the pattern **nándào...ma** in the question **Nándào wǒmen lái zhèr guāng hē chá ma?** "You mean we've come here just to drink tea?". You first encountered this pattern in 21-2: 1B.

13. **BĂ A JIÀO(ZUO) B.** Look at the following sentence at the end of utterance 13: **Dàjiā bǎ Xiānggǎng jiàozuo "měishí tiāntáng."** The meaning of this sentence is "Everyone calls Hong Kong 'food heaven.'" The pattern **bǎ A jiàozuo B** is a common and useful pattern that means "call A B" (lit. "take A and call it B"). Note that the **-zuo** in **jiàozuo** is optional, so this pattern is sometimes simply said as **bǎ A jiào B**. The basic pattern is:

BĂ	**A**	**JIÀO(ZUO)**	**B**
bǎ	Xiānggǎng	jiàozuo	"měishí tiāntáng"

"call Hong Kong 'food heaven'"

Here are several more examples of the pattern **bǎ A jiào(zuo) B**:

Hěn duō rén bǎ Shànghǎi jiàozuo "xiǎo Bālí."

"Many people call Shanghai 'little Paris.'"

Zhōngguo rén bǎ "brunch" jiàozuo zǎowǔfàn.

"Chinese people call brunch '**zǎowǔfàn**.'"

Dàjiā bǎ Niǔyuē jiàozuo "dà píngguǒ."

"Everyone calls New York the 'Big Apple.'"

Yǒude rén bǎ Qīnghuá Dàxué jiàozuo "Zhōngguode MIT."

"Some people call Tsinghua University 'China's MIT.'"

Wǒmen bǎ nèixiē chéngtiān zhǐ zhīdao niànshūde rén jiàozuo "shūdāizi."

"We call people who only study all day long 'bookworms.'"

Jīlóngde yǔjì hěn cháng, yǔliàng yě duō, suóyi dàjiā bǎ nèige dìfang jiào "yǔgǎng."

"The rainy season in Jilong is long, and the amount of rainfall is great, so everyone calls it 'rain harbor.'"

The Linguistic Situation of Hong Kong

American student John Rogers, who studied Mandarin for three years in college in the U.S., has just arrived in Hong Kong. After his first Chinese class at Yale-China Chinese Language Centre at Chinese University of Hong Kong, he asks his instructor a few questions about the linguistic situation in Hong Kong.

 ### Basic Conversation 23-3

| 1. AMERICAN STUDENT | **Lǎoshī, Xiānggǎngde guānfāng yǔyán shi shémme?** |
| | Professor, what's the official language of Hong Kong? |

| 2. HONG KONG INSTRUCTOR | **Xiānggǎngde guānfāng yǔyán a? Xiānggǎng yǒu liǎngzhǒng guānfāng yǔyán: Zhōngwén hé Yīngwén. Búguò ne, bǎifēnzhījiǔshiwǔ yǐshàngde rén píngcháng shuōde shi Zhōngguode yìzhǒng fāngyán, Guǎngdōng huà.** |
| | The official language of Hong Kong? Hong Kong has two official languages: Chinese and English. However, what over ninety-five percent of the people ordinarily speak is a Chinese dialect, Cantonese. |

| 3. AMERICAN STUDENT | **Wǒ gēn Xiānggǎng rén shuō Pǔtōnghuà, tāmen tīngdedǒng ma?** |
| | If I speak Mandarin with Hong Kong people, will they understand? |

| 4. HONG KONG INSTRUCTOR | **Zhè gēn tāmende jiàoyù shuǐpíng yǒuguān. Rúguǒ shi xuésheng huòzhě shi zuò shēngyìde, yìbān lái shuō dōu néng tīngdedǒng, yě huì shuō, búguò kěnéng huì yǒu yidianr Guǎngdōng qiāng. Kěshi, rúguǒ shi niánji bǐjiào dàde gēn nèixiē jiàoyù shuǐpíng bù gāode, jiù hěn yǒu kěnéng tīngbudǒngle.** |
| | It has to do with their level of education. If it's students or business people, then in general they'll be able to understand and speak it, though it's possible they may have a bit of a Cantonese accent. But if it's older people and the less educated, then it's quite possible they won't understand. |

| 5. AMERICAN STUDENT | **Xiānggǎngde gōnglì xuéxiào jiāo bu jiāo Pǔtōnghuà?** |
| | Do public schools in Hong Kong teach Mandarin? |

| 6. HONG KONG INSTRUCTOR | **Xiānggǎng shíxíng mǔyǔ jiàoyù zhèngcè, yě jiù shi shuō, xiǎoxué hé zhōngxué, jīběnshang dōu shi yòng xuéshengde mǔyǔ, yě jiù shi Guǎngdōng huà, lái shòukè. Dànshi zìcóng yī-jiǔ-jiǔ-qī-nián huíguī Zhōngguo yǐhòu, yìbānde xuéxiào měizhōu dōu yǒu jǐge xiǎoshíde Pǔtōnghuà kè.** |

Hong Kong practices a policy of native language education, that is, in elementary schools and middle schools they basically use the students' native language, Cantonese, for instruction. But since Hong Kong's return to China in 1997, most schools have several hours per week of Mandarin class.

7. AMERICAN STUDENT
Lǎoshī, Xiānggǎng yòng jiǎntǐzì háishi fántǐzì?
Professor, does Hong Kong use simplified or traditional characters?

8. HONG KONG INSTRUCTOR
Xuéxiàoli yìbān dōu yòng fántǐzì lái jiāoxué. Wàibianrde shū a, bàokān a, yìbān yě shi yòng fántǐzì lái yìnshuāde. Búguò ne, zuìjìn jǐnián, kànjian jiǎntǐzìde jīhui bǐ yǐqián duōduōle.
In schools in general they teach traditional characters. Books and periodicals outside are in general also printed in traditional characters. However, in the last few years, you see simplified characters a lot more than before.

9. AMERICAN STUDENT
Lǎoshī, nín kéyi jiāo wǒ jǐjù Guǎngdōng huà ma?
Professor, could you teach me a few phrases in Cantonese?

10. HONG KONG INSTRUCTOR
Kéyi a! Nà, nǐ gēn wǒ shuō: "Yāt, yih, sàam."
Sure! So, repeat after me: "One, two, three."

11. AMERICAN STUDENT
"Yāt, yih, sàam."
"One, two, three."

12. HONG KONG INSTRUCTOR
"Néih hóu!"
"How are you?"

13. AMERICAN STUDENT
"Néih hóu!"
"How are you?"

14. HONG KONG INSTRUCTOR
"Joigin."
"Goodbye."

15. AMERICAN STUDENT
"Joigin." Qǐngwèn, zhè dōu shi shémme yìsi ne?
"Goodbye." Could I ask what it all means?

16. HONG KONG INSTRUCTOR
Ò, "yāt, yih, sàam" jiù shi "yī, èr, sān." "Néih hóu!" jiù shi "Nǐ hǎo!" "Joigin" jiù shi "zàijiàn."
Oh, **yāt, yih, sàam** is "one, two, three." **Néih hóu!** is "How are you?" **Joigin** is "goodbye."

 Build Up

1. American student
guānfāng	official [AT]
guānfāng yǔyán	official language [PH]
Lǎoshī, Xiānggǎngde guānfāng yǔyán shi shémme?	Professor, what's the official language of Hong Kong?

2. Hong Kong instructor
bǎifēnzhījiǔshiwǔ	ninety-five percent
...yǐshàng	more than... [PT]
bǎifēnzhījiǔshiwǔ yǐshàng	more than 95%
bǎifēnzhījiǔshiwǔ yǐshàngde rén	more than 95% of the people
Xiānggǎngde guānfāng yǔyán a? Xiānggǎng yǒu liǎngzhǒng guānfāng yǔyán: Zhōngwén hé Yīngwén. Búguò ne, bǎifēnzhījiǔshiwǔ yǐshàngde rén píngcháng shuōde shi Zhōngguode yìzhǒng fāngyán, Guǎngdōng huà.	The official language of Hong Kong? Hong Kong has two official languages: Chinese and English. However, what over ninety-five percent of the people ordinarily speak is a Chinese dialect, Cantonese.

3.   American student

Wǒ gēn Xiānggǎng rén shuō Pǔtōnghuà,
tāmen tīngdedǒng ma?

If I speak Mandarin with Hong Kong people,
will they understand?

4.   Hong Kong instructor

A gēn B yǒuguān	A is related to B [PT]
shuǐpíng	level, standard [N]
jiàoyù shuǐpíng	educational level [PH]
zuò shēngyì	engage in business, do business [PH]
yìbān lái shuō	generally speaking, in general [PH]
qiāng	accent, intonation [N]
Guǎngdōng qiāng	Cantonese accent
kěnéng	possibility [N]
yǒu kěnéng	there is the possibility, it's possible
hěn yǒu kěnéng tīngbudǒng	it's very possible they won't understand

Zhè gēn tāmende jiàoyù shuǐpíng yǒuguān.
Rúguǒ shì xuésheng huòzhě shì zuò shēngyìde,
yìbān lái shuō dōu néng tīngdedǒng, yě huì
shuō, búguò kěnéng huì yǒu yidiǎnr Guǎngdōng
qiāng. Kěshì, rúguǒ shì niánjì bǐjiào dàde gēn
nèixiē jiàoyù shuǐpíng bù gāode, jiù hěn yǒu
kěnéng tīngbudǒngle.

It has to do with their level of education. If it's
students or business people, then in general
they'll be able to understand and speak it,
though it's possible they may have a bit of a
Cantonese accent. But if it's older people and
the less educated, then it's quite possible they
won't understand.

5.   American student

gōnglì	public [AT]
gōnglì xuéxiào	public school [PH]

Xiānggǎngde gōnglì xuéxiào jiāo bu jiāo
Pǔtōnghuà?

Do public schools in Hong Kong teach Mandarin?

6.   Hong Kong instructor

shíxíng	put into practice, implement [V]
mǔyǔ	native language [N]
mǔyǔ jiàoyù	education in one's native language [PH]
zhèngcè	policy [N]
shíxíng mǔyǔ jiàoyù zhèngcè	practice a policy of native language education
jīběn	basic, fundamental [AT]
jīběnshang	basically [MA]
shòukè	give classes, offer instruction [VO]
yòng xuéshengde mǔyǔ lái shòukè	teach in the students' native language
zìcóng...yǐhòu	since (a certain point in time) [PT]
zhōu	week [M]
měizhōu	every week [SP+M]
jǐge xiǎoshíde Pǔtōnghuà kè	several hours of Mandarin class

Xiānggǎng shíxíng mǔyǔ jiàoyù zhèngcè,
yě jiù shì shuō, xiǎoxué hé zhōngxué,
jīběnshang dōu shì yòng xuéshengde mǔyǔ,
yě jiù shì Guǎngdōng huà, lái shòukè. Dànshì
zìcóng yī-jiǔ-jiǔ-qī-nián huíguī Zhōngguo
yǐhòu, yìbānde xuéxiào měizhōu dōu yǒu jǐge
xiǎoshíde Pǔtōnghuà kè.

Hong Kong practices a policy of native language
education, that is, in elementary schools and
middle schools they basically use the students'
native language, Cantonese, for instruction. But
since Hong Kong's return to China in 1997, most
schools have several hours per week of
Mandarin class.

7.   American student

jiǎntǐzì	simplified Chinese characters [N]
fántǐzì	traditional Chinese characters [N]

Lǎoshī, Xiānggǎng yòng jiǎntǐzì háishi fántǐzì?

Professor, does Hong Kong use simplified or traditional
characters?

8. Hong Kong instructor

jiāoxué	teach [V]
yòng fántǐzì lái jiāoxué	use traditional characters to teach
bàokān	newspapers and periodicals [N]
yìnshuā	print [V]
yòng fántǐzì lái yìnshuā	use traditional characters to print
zuìjìn jǐnián	in the last few years
kànjian jiǎntǐzìde jīhui	opportunity to see simplified characters
bǐ yǐqián duōduōle	much more than before

**Xuéxiàoli yìbān dōu yòng fántǐzì lái jiāoxué.
Wàibianrde shū a, bàokān a, yìbān yě shi yòng
fántǐzì lái yìnshuāde. Búguò ne, zuìjìn jǐnián,
kànjian jiǎntǐzìde jīhui bǐ yǐqián duōduōle.**

In schools in general they teach traditional
characters. Books and periodicals outside are
in general also printed in traditional characters.
However, in the last few years, you see simplified
characters a lot more than before.

9. American student

**Lǎoshī, nín kéyi jiāo wǒ jǐjù Guǎngdōng
huà ma?**

Professor, could you teach me a few phrases in
Cantonese?

10. Hong Kong instructor

Kéyi a! Nà, nǐ gēn wǒ shuō: "Yāt, yih, sàam."

Sure! So, repeat after me: "One, two, three."

11. American student

"Yāt, yih, sàam."

"One, two, three."

12. Hong Kong instructor

"Néih hóu!"

"How are you?"

13. American student

"Néih hóu!"

"How are you?"

14. Hong Kong instructor

"Joigin."

"Goodbye."

15. American student

**"Joigin." Qǐngwèn, zhè dōu shi shémme
yìsi ne?**

"Goodbye." Could I ask what it all means?

16. Hong Kong instructor

**Ò, "yāt, yih, sàam" jiù shi "yī, èr, sān."
"Néih hóu!" jiù shi "Nǐ hǎo!" "Joigin" jiù shi
"zàijiàn."**

Oh, **yāt, yih, sàam** is "one, two, three."
Néih hóu! is "How are you?" **Joigin** is
"goodbye."

Supplementary Vocabulary

1. **...yǐxià**
    lěngdào língdù yǐxià
Běndìde tiānqi chángcháng lěngdào língdù yǐxià.

less than..., below... [PT]
get cold to the point where it's below 0°
The weather here often gets cold to where it's below
zero degrees.

Grammatical and Cultural Notes

2A.   In this line, note **bǎifēnzhījiǔshiwǔ** "ninety-five percent." Review the pattern with **bǎifēnzhī...** to express "percent" that you learned in 20-2: SV2.

2B. **...YĬSHÀNG AND ...YĬXIÀ.** Also in line 2, look at **bǎifēnzhījiǔshiwǔ yǐshàngde rén** "more than 95% of the people." The pattern **...yǐshàng** means "more than...," "over...," or "above." The related pattern **...yǐxià** (cf. SV1) means "less than...," "under...," or "below...." Some speakers use **...yǐshàng** to mean "more than or equal to..." and use **...yǐxià** to mean "less than or equal to...." Both **...yǐshàng** and **...yǐxià** occur most frequently after number expressions, which can involve percentages, numbers of people, temperatures, ages, money amounts, etc. The basic patterns are:

NUMBER EXPRESSION	YĬSHÀNG
bǎifēnzhījiǔshiwǔ	**yǐshàng**
"more than (or equal to) 95%"	

NUMBER EXPRESSION	YĬXIÀ
língdù	**yǐxià**
"below zero (degrees)"	

Here are some more examples:

yībǎikuài yǐshàng	"over a hundred dollars"
yìqiān'ge rén yǐshàng	"more than a thousand people"
shí'èrsuì yǐxiàde háizi	"children ages 12 and below"

4A. **A GĒN B YǑUGUĀN.** At the beginning of utterance 4, look at the sentence **Zhè gēn tāmende jiàoyù shuǐpíng yǒuguān** "This has to do with their educational level." The pattern **A gēn B yǒuguān** means "A is related to B" or "A has to do with B." The basic pattern is:

A	GĒN	B		YǑUGUĀN
Zhè	**gēn**	**tāmende jiàoyù shuǐpíng**	**yǒuguān.**

"This has to do with their educational level."

The negative form of this pattern is **A gēn B wúguān** "A is not related to B" or "A has nothing to do with B." A more colloquial equivalent of this pattern is **A gēn B yǒu guānxi** or, in the negative, **A gēn B méiyou guānxi.** Here are some more examples of these patterns:

Nà gēn zhèngfǔde yǔyán zhèngcè yǒuguān.

"That is related to the government's language policy."

Zhèijiàn shìqing gēn nǐ wúguān!

"This matter has nothing to do with you!"

Nèijiàn shìqing gēn wǒ méiyou guānxi.

"That matter has nothing to do with me."

4B. In this utterance, consider **Hěn yǒu kěnéng tīngbudǒng** "It's very possible that (they) won't understand." In 10-1, you learned **kěnéng** as an auxiliary verb meaning "be possible." Now in this lesson, you learn that **kěnéng** can also function as a noun meaning "possibility." The phrase **yǒu kěnéng** "there is the possibility" or "it's possible" is quite common, as is **hěn yǒu kěnéng** "it's very possible."

6A. **ZÌCÓNG...YǏHÒU.** Examine the phrase **Xiānggǎng zìcóng yī-jiǔ-jiǔ-qī-nián huíguī Zhōngguo yǐhòu** "since Hong Kong's return to China in 1997." In Classical Chinese, **zì** means "from" and in Modern Chinese, as you know, **cóng** also means "from," so not surprisingly, the combination of **zì** and **cóng** into **zìcóng** means "from (a certain point in time)." In smoother English, **zìcóng** is often best translated as "since," but it's important to keep in mind that this is the "since" that means "since a certain point in time" and NOT the "since" that indicates a reason and is a synonym for "because" (the word for the latter kind of "since" is **jìrán**, which you learned in 18-2). **Zìcóng** is typically—though not always—followed at the end of the clause in which it stands by **yǐhòu**, so that the complete pattern then becomes **zìcóng...yǐhòu**. A time expression is inserted between the two parts of the pattern. In the English translation, the clause with "since..." often comes in the second part of the sentence; but in Chinese, the clause with **zìcóng...yǐhòu** ordinarily comes in the first part of the sentence. Also, note that the subject of the two clauses of the sentence may be the same or different (compare the example sentences below). The basic pattern is:

ZÌCÓNG	TIME EXPRESSION	YǏHÒU
zìcóng	huíguī Zhōngguo	yǐhòu

"since reverting to China"

Here are some more examples of the pattern **zìcóng...yǐhòu**:

Zìcóng wǒ débìng yǐhòu, wǒ jiù bù chōuyān le.

"I haven't smoked since I became ill." (subject of first clause same as second clause)

Zìcóng tā nèicì lái yǐhòu, wǒ jiù méi kànjianguo ta.

"I haven't seen her ever since that time she came." (subject of first clause different from second clause)

Zìcóng tā cóng Zhōngguo huílai yǐhòu, dàjiā dōu juéde tā biànle.

"Since she returned from China, everyone feels she changed." (subject of first clause different from second clause)

And here is an example with only **zìcóng**, without a following **yǐhòu**:

zìcóng qùnián chūntiān dào xiànzài   "from the spring of last year until now"

6B.   **ZHŌU "WEEK."** Later in utterance 6, look at **Yìbānde xuéxiào měizhōu dōu yǒu jǐge xiǎoshíde Pǔtōnghuà kè** "Most schools each week have several hours of Mandarin class." The SPECIFIER + MEASURE combination **měizhōu** means "every week" or "per week" (the measure word **zhōu** by itself means "week"). Especially common in written Chinese as a one-character, more formal equivalent of **xīngqī or lǐbài**, **zhōu** can also be used in spoken Chinese. You should become thoroughly familiar with the following expressions:

zhōuyī	"Monday"
zhōu'èr	"Tuesday"
zhōusān	"Wednesday"
zhōusì	"Thursday"
zhōuwǔ	"Friday"
zhōuliù	"Saturday"
zhōurì	"Sunday"
běnzhōu	"this week"
shàngyìzhōu or **shàngzhōu**	"last week"
xiàyìzhōu or **xiàzhōu**	"next week"
měizhōu	"every week"

Note that the word for "Sunday" is **zhōurì** (NEVER *zhōutiān). Be sure to contrast **zhōuyī** "Monday" with **yìzhōu** "one week," **zhōusān** "Wednesday" with **sānzhōu** "three weeks," etc. Study the following example:

Zāogāo, wǒmende jiàqī yǐjīng guòle yìzhōu le!

"Darn, one week of our vacation has already passed."

8. In this line, note **Kànjian jiǎntǐzide jīhui bǐ yǐqián duōduōle** "The opportunity to see simplified characters is much more than before" or, in better English, "There are many more opportunities than before to see simplified characters." The pattern **bǐ** + STATIVE VERB + **duōle** is a variant of the pattern **bǐ** + STATIVE VERB + **-de duō** that you learned in 12-4: 4A. In other words, you could say either **Kànjian jiǎntǐzide jīhui bǐ yǐqián duōduōle** or **Kànjian jiǎntǐzide jīhui bǐ yǐqián duōde duō** with exactly the same meaning.

10. **CANTONESE.** Lines 10–16 contain a number of Cantonese words and expressions. Cantonese is a major regional language of southern China spoken by approximately 70 million ethnic Chinese in Guangdong, Guangxi, Hong Kong, Macao, Viet Nam, Indonesia, Malaysia, Singapore, the U.S., Canada, England, Australia, and New Zealand. Cantonese is one of the world's top 20 languages, having more native speakers than Italian, Polish, or Vietnamese. Due to the pervasive influence of Hong Kong as well as the economic transformation of Guangdong Province, the prestige of Cantonese within China has risen steadily over the past few decades. Cantonese includes many different subdialects including Toishan, the ancestral language of many of the early Chinese-Americans. The Cantonese of Guangzhou is usually considered standard. Hong Kong Cantonese is similar to that of Guangzhou except for some minor pronunciation and vocabulary differences. Cantonese has for centuries had its own written tradition with several hundred so-called "dialect characters" used in informal writing for characters that don't exist in written Mandarin or Literary Chinese. Although Cantonese speakers in both mainland China and Hong Kong nowadays usually read written Mandarin, which they pronounce out loud in Cantonese pronunciation, a few sections of the Hong Kong newspapers, such as cartoons or advertisements, make use of the Cantonese characters. The Cantonese characters can also be found intermixed with letters borrowed from the English alphabet in comic books, popular magazines, informal handwritten notes, and e-mails and text messages such as those students might write to each other. Whereas in the past there had been considerable resistance against Mandarin, knowledge of Mandarin among Hong Kong Chinese people has been noticeably on the increase in recent years due to ever closer links with mainland China. Nevertheless, Cantonese as a dialect is still quite firmly rooted in Hong Kong and Southern China. The Cantonese dialects have preserved many of the features of older forms of the Chinese language. If you read a Tang Dynasty poem out loud in Cantonese pronunciation, many syllables which no longer rhyme in Mandarin will still rhyme in Cantonese. The outstanding linguistic features of the Cantonese dialects include 6–11 tones depending on subdialect (and on how the tones are analyzed); distinction between long and short vowels; a rounded vowel **eu** (somewhat like German "ö" or French "œ"); an initial consonant **ng-**; both **ng** and **m** as independent syllables; final consonants **-m**, **-p**, **-t**, and **-k**; and a rich variety of sentence final particles which, if you're unfamiliar with Cantonese, tend to make the dialect sound especially "sing songy." As for the degree of closeness between Cantonese and Mandarin, a native Mandarin speaker who had never before heard Cantonese would understand only a few isolated words. Cantonese and Mandarin differ most in pronunciation, less in vocabulary, and least in grammar. If you should ever decide to learn Cantonese, you'll find your knowledge of Mandarin to be most helpful. We could say that by learning as much Mandarin as you have by this point, you've already made at least 30% of the necessary "investment" for learning Cantonese!

A Trip to Macao

American Julie Marino, who majored in Chinese and economics at the University of Florida, recently began working at a bank in Hong Kong. One Saturday, she takes a high-speed hydrofoil ferry to Macao, where Vai Pan Lei, a Macanese friend of her father's, meets her at the pier and shows her around town.

 Basic Conversation 23-4

(at the Macao Ferry Terminal)

1. LEI **Qǐngwèn, shi Mǎ Xiáojie, Mǎ Zhūlì Xiáojie ma?**
Excuse me, are you Miss Ma, Miss Ma Zhuli?

2. MARINO **Duì. Nǐ shi Lǐ Xiānsheng ba?**
Yes. And you must be Mr. Lei?

3. LEI **Shìde. Wǒ shi nǐ fùqinde péngyou Lǐ Wěibīn. Huānyíng, huānyíng! Dìyīcì lái Àomén ma?**
Yes. I'm Vai Pan Lei, your father's friend. Welcome! Is this your first time in Macao?

4. MARINO **Shì a. Jiǔwén Àomén lìshǐ yōujiǔ, Pú'ào měishí gèng shi xīyǐn rén. Wǒ zhēn shi děng dōu děngbujíle, lǎo zǎo jiù xiǎng lái cānguān, pǐncháng. Nǐ néng xiān bǎ Àomén dàzhìde jièshao jièshao ma? Bùguǎn shi dìlǐ, lìshǐ háishi wénhuà, wǒ shémme dōu xiǎng zhīdao.**
Yes. I've long heard that Macao has a long history, and what's more that Portuguese-Macanese delicacies are most attractive. I really can hardly wait; I've long wanted to come visit and sample them. Could you first give me a general introduction to Macao? Whether it's geography, history, or culture, I want to know about everything.

5. LEI **Nà yǒu shémme wèntí? Wǒmen yìbiān cānguān, yìbiān shuō. Zǒu ba!**
No problem with that! We'll talk about it while we tour. Let's go!

(walking around the streets of downtown Macao with Marino)

Àomén wèiyú Zhūjiāng kǒu, shi yóu Àomén bàndǎo, Dàngzǎi hé Lùhuán liǎngge lídǎo suǒzǔchéngde. Lí Xiānggǎng chàbuduō liùshíwǔgōnglǐ yuǎn, rénkǒu wǔshíduōwàn, rénkǒu mìdù gāojū shìjiè dìyī.
Macao is located at the mouth of the Pearl River. It's made up of the Macao Peninsula and the two offshore islands of Taipa and Coloane. It's about 65 kilometers from Hong Kong, with a population of over 500,000 and a population density that is the highest in the world.

Shíliù shìjìde shíhou, Pútáoyá rén dìyīcì láidào Àomén, shíjiǔ shìjì hòubànqī, Àomén zhèng-shì chéngwéi Pútáoyáde zhímíndì. Zhè shi Ōuzhōu dìguózhǔyìzhě zài Yàzhōude dìyíge zhímíndì, yě shi zuìhòu yíge. Yī-jiǔ-jiǔ-jiǔ-nián shí'èr yuè èrshí rì, Àomén jì Xiānggǎng zhīhòu huíguī Zhōnghuá Rénmín Gònghéguó, hé Xiānggǎng yíyàng chéngwéi Zhōngguode lìngyíge tèbié xíngzhèngqū.

In the 16th century the Portuguese first came to Macao, and in the latter half of the 19th century Macao formally became a Portuguese colony. This was the first colony of the European colonialists in Asia, and it was also the last one. On Dec. 20, 1999, Macao followed Hong Kong in reverting to the PRC, and like Hong Kong became another Special Administrative Region of China.

Zài "Yìguó Liǎngzhì"-de zhèngcè xià, chúle wàijiāo hé guófáng zhīwài, Àomén yíqiè dōu kéyi wéichí xiànzhuàng, wǔshínián bú biàn. Zǒu, wǒmen qù pángbiān xiǎo xiàngli chángchang Àomén yǒumíngde dàntǎ!

Under the policy of "One Country, Two Systems," except for foreign relations and national defense, everything in Macao can maintain the status quo, not changing for fifty years. Come on, let's go in the little side alley and try Macao's famous egg tarts!

(after eating an egg tart at the egg tart restaurant)

6. MARINO   Àomén hái yǒu nǎxiē míngcài zhíde pǐncháng? Tāmen dōu yǒu xiē shémme tèsè? Wǒmen kéyi diǎn yìxiē ma?
What other famous dishes does Macao have that are worth sampling? What characteristics do they have? Can we order some?

7. LEI   Dāngrán kéyi!
Of course we can!

(eating dinner with Marino in a Macanese restaurant)

Àomén cài shi róuhéle Zhōngguo cài hé wèidao bǐjiào xiánde Pútáoyá cài, zài jiāshang Fēizhōu, Yìndù hé Dōngnányà láide gālí, yēzhī, ròuguì zhèxiē xiāngliào, suǒdúchuàngchūláide. Yǒumíngde cài bāokuò Fēizhōu Jī hé Là Dà Xiā. Àomén cài sè, xiāng, wèi jùquán, chīle jiào rén huí-wèi-wú-qióng.

Macanese food was uniquely created by mixing together Chinese food and Portuguese food, which has a saltier flavor, and then adding spices such as curry, coconut juice, and cinnamon, which come from Africa, India, and Southeast Asia. Famous dishes include African Chicken and Large Chili Shrimp. Macanese food is a perfect combination of color, flavor, and taste. When you eat it, it makes you savor the aftertaste for a long time.

(looking at a casino across the street after dinner)

8. MARINO   Tīngshuō Àomén dǔbóyè shi héfǎde?
I've heard that gambling is legal in Macao?

9. LEI   Méi cuò. Àoménde lǚyóuyè hěn fādá, ér zhèngfǔde jīngjì láiyuán chàbuduō bǎifēnzhīwǔshí shi cóng dǔbóyè láide. Àoménde dǔchǎng shi quán shìjiè zhuànqián zuì duōde.
That's right. Tourism in Macao is very developed, and about 50% of the government's sources of income come from gambling. Macao's casinos are the most profitable in the world.

Búguò yǒu niánlíng xiànzhì, wàiguo rén yào mǎn shíbāsuì, Àomén rén yào èrshiyísuì cái néng rùchǎng. Yǒuqùde shi, Àomén yě shi shìjièshang jūmín píngjūn shòumìng zuì chángde dìqū zhīyī.
But there are age limits; foreigners must be 18 and residents of Macao have to be 21 to be admitted. The funny thing is, Macao is also one of the areas whose residents have the longest average life expectancies in the world.

10. MARINO   Yǒu yìsi! Shì bu shi héfǎde dǔbó ràng tāmen hěn qīngsōng, hěn kuàilè? Ha ha!
That's interesting! I wonder if it's the legal gambling that makes them relaxed and happy? Ha ha!

Build Up

---

1. **Lei**

Qǐngwèn, shi Mǎ Xiáojie, Mǎ Zhūlì Xiáojie ma?   Excuse me, are you Miss Ma, Miss Ma Zhuli?

---

2. **Marino**

Duì. Nǐ shi Lǐ Xiānsheng ba?   Yes. And you must be Mr. Lei?

---

3. **Lei**

Shìde. Wǒ shi nǐ fùqinde péngyou Lǐ Wěibīn.   Yes. I'm Vai Pan Lei, your father's friend.
Huānyíng, huānyíng! Dìyīcì lái Àomén ma?   Welcome! Is this your first time in Macao?

---

4. **Marino**

jiǔwén	have heard of for a long time [IE]
yōujiǔ	be very old, be age-old [SV]
lìshǐ yōujiǔ	have a long history
Jiǔwén Àomén lìshǐ yōujiǔ	have long heard Macao has a long history
Pú'ào	Portuguese-Macanese [AT]
Pú'ào měishí	Portuguese-Macanese delicacies
xīyǐn	attract [V]
xīyǐn rén	attract people
Pú'ào měishí gèng shi xīyǐn rén	furthermore Portuguese-Macanese delicacies attract people
lǎo zǎo	very early, for a long time now [PH]
lǎo zǎo jiù xiǎng lái cānguān	have been wanting to come visit for a long time now
pǐncháng	taste, sample [V]
dàzhì	generally, roughly, for the most part [A]
dàzhìde jièshao	introduce in a general sort of way
bǎ Àomén dàzhìde jièshao jièshao	introduce Macao in a general way
bùguǎn...	no matter..., regardless... [PT]
dìlǐ	geography [N]
bùguǎn shi dìlǐ, lìshǐ háishi wénhuà	no matter whether it's geography, history, or culture
wǒ shémme dōu xiǎng zhīdao	I want to know everything

Shì a. Jiǔwén Àomén lìshǐ yōujiǔ, Pú'ào měishí gèng shi xīyǐn rén. Wǒ zhēn shi děng dōu děngbujíle, lǎo zǎo jiù xiǎng lái cānguān, pǐncháng. Nǐ néng xiān bǎ Àomén dàzhìde jièshao jièshao ma? Bùguǎn shi dìlǐ, lìshǐ háishi wénhuà, wǒ shémme dōu xiǎng zhīdao.

Yes. I've long heard that Macao has a long history, and what's more that Portuguese-Macanese delicacies are most attractive. I really can hardly wait; I've long wanted to come visit and sample them. Could you first give me a general introduction to Macao? Whether it's geography, history, or culture, I want to know about everything.

---

5. **Lei**

wǒmen yìbiān cānguān yìbiān shuō	we'll talk while we tour

Nà yǒu shémme wèntí? Wǒmen yìbiān cānguān, yìbiān shuō. Zǒu ba!   No problem with that! We'll talk about it while we tour. Let's go!

wèiyú	be located at, be situated at [V+PV]
Zhūjiāng	Pearl River [PW]
kǒu	mouth; opening [N]
Zhūjiāng kǒu	mouth of the Pearl River
Àomén wèiyú Zhūjiāng kǒu	Macao is located at the mouth of the Pearl River
Dàngzǎi	Taipa (name of island in Macao) [PW]
Lùhuán	Coloane (name of island in Macao) [PW]
lídǎo	offshore island [N]
mìdù	density [N]

rénkǒu mìdù	population density [PH]
gāojū	be high (in rank), occupy (a high position) [V]
rénkǒu mìdù gāojū shìjiè dìyī	population density is the highest in the world
Pútáoyá	Portugal [PW]
hòubànqī	latter half [TW]
shíjiǔ shìjì hòubànqī	latter half of the 19th century
zhèngshì	formally, officially [A]
zhèngshì chéngwéi Pútáoyáde zhímíndì	formally became a Portuguese colony
dìguózhǔyìzhě	imperialist [N]
rì	day of the month (formal style) [M]
shí'èr yuè èrshí rì	December 20
jì...zhīhòu	follow... [PT]
jì Xiānggǎng zhīhòu	follow after Hong Kong
lìng-	another [SP]
lìngyíge tèbié xíngzhèngqū	another Special Administrative Region
zài...zhèngcè xià	under the policy of... [PT]
zài "Yìguó Liǎngzhì"de zhèngcè xià	under the policy of "One Country, Two Systems"
wéichí	maintain [V]
xiànzhuàng	present conditions, status quo [N]
wéichí xiànzhuàng	maintain the status quo
wǒmen qù pángbiān xiǎo xiàngli	let's go in the little alley off to the side
dàntǎ	egg tart [N]
chángchang Àomén yǒumíngde dàntǎ	taste Macao's famous egg tarts

Àomén wèiyú Zhūjiāng kǒu, shi yóu Àomén bàndǎo, Dàngzǎi hé Lùhuán liǎngge lídǎo suǒzǔchéngde. Lí Xiānggǎng chàbuduō liùshiwǔgōnglǐ yuǎn, rénkǒu wǔshíduōwàn, rénkǒu mìdù gāojū shìjiè dìyī. Shíliù shìjide shíhou, Pútáoyá rén dìyīcì láidào Àomén, shíjiǔ shìjì hòubànqī, Àomén zhèngshì chéngwéi Pútáoyáde zhímíndì. Zhè shi Ōuzhōu dìguózhǔyìzhě zài Yàzhōude dìyíge zhímíndì, yě shi zuìhòu yíge. Yī-jiǔ-jiǔ-jiǔ-nián shí'èr yuè èrshí rì, Àomén jì Xiānggǎng zhīhòu huíguī Zhōnghuá Rénmín Gònghéguó, hé Xiānggǎng yíyàng chéngwéi Zhōngguode lìngyíge tèbié xíngzhèngqū. Zài "Yìguó Liǎngzhì"de zhèngcè xià, chúle wàijiāo hé guófáng zhīwài, Àomén yíqiè dōu kéyi wéichí xiànzhuàng, wǔshínián bú biàn. Zǒu, wǒmen qù pángbiān xiǎo xiàngli chángchang Àomén yǒumíngde dàntǎ!

Macao is located at the mouth of the Pearl River. It's made up of the Macao Peninsula and the two offshore islands of Taipa and Coloane. It's about 65 kilometers from Hong Kong, with a population of over 500,000 and a population density that is the highest in the world. In the 16th century the Portuguese first came to Macao, and in the latter half of the 19th century Macao formally became a Portuguese colony. This was the first colony of the European colonialists in Asia, and it was also the last one. On Dec. 20, 1999, Macao followed Hong Kong in reverting to the PRC, and like Hong Kong became another Special Administrative Region of China. Under the policy of "One Country, Two Systems," except for foreign relations and national defense, everything in Macao can maintain the status quo, not changing for fifty years. Come on, let's go in the little side alley and try Macao's famous egg tarts!

---

6. Marino

míngcài	famous dish, famous food [N]
zhíde	be worth, deserve [AV]
nǎxiē míngcài zhíde pǐncháng	which famous dishes are worth sampling

Àomén hái yǒu nǎxiē míngcài zhíde pǐncháng? Tāmen dōu yǒu xiē shémme tèsè? Wǒmen kéyi diǎn yìxiē ma?

What other famous dishes does Macao have that are worth sampling? What characteristics do they have? Can we order some?

---

7. Lei

Dāngrán kéyi!

Of course we can!

róuhé	mix together [V]
róuhéle Zhōngguo cài hé Pútáoyá cài	has mixed together Chinese food and Portuguese food
wèidao bǐjiào xián	the flavor is relatively salty

wèidao bǐjiào xiánde Pútáoyá cài	Portuguese food, which has a relatively salty flavor
Fēizhōu	Africa [PW]
Dōngnányà	Southeast Asia [PW]
Fēizhōu, Yìndù hé Dōngnányà láide	came from Africa, India, and S.E. Asia
gālí	curry [N]
yēzhī	coconut juice [N]
ròuguì	cinnamon [N]
zài jiāshang gālí, yēzhī, ròuguì	then again add curry, coconut juice, and cinnamon
xiāngliào	spice [N]
dúchuàng	create as something unique
suǒdúchuàngchūláide	something that was uniquely created
jiào	make, cause [V]
huí-wèi-wú-qióng	"savor the aftertaste a long time" [EX]
jiào rén huí-wèi-wú-qióng	make people savor the aftertaste for a long time

Àomén cài shi róuhéle Zhōngguo cài hé wèidao bǐjiào xiánde Pútáoyá cài, zài jiāshang Fēizhōu, Yìndù hé Dōngnányà láide gālí, yēzhī, ròuguì zhèxiē xiāngliào, suǒdúchuàngchūláide. Yǒumíngde cài bāokuò Fēizhōu Jī hé Là Dà Xiā. Àomén cài sè, xiāng, wèi jùquán, chīle jiào rén huí-wèi-wú-qióng.

Macanese food was uniquely created by mixing together Chinese food and Portuguese food, which has a saltier flavor, and then adding spices such as curry, coconut juice, and cinnamon, which come from Africa, India, and Southeast Asia. Famous dishes include African Chicken and Large Chili Shrimp. Macanese food is a perfect combination of color, flavor, and taste. When you eat it, it makes you savor the aftertaste for a long time.

---

8. Marino

dǔbó	gamble [V]
dǔbóyè	the gambling industry [N]
héfǎ	be legal [SV]

Tīngshuō Àomén dǔbóyè shi héfǎde?   I've heard that gambling is legal in Macao?

---

9. Lei

lǚyóu	tour [V]
lǚyóuyè	the tourism industry [N]
lǚyóuyè hěn fādá	tourism is very developed
ér	and, moreover [CJ]
zhèngfǔ	government [N]
láiyuán	source, origin [N]
zhèngfǔde jīngjì láiyuán	the government's source of income
dǔchǎng	casino [PW]
quán shìjiè zhuànqián zuì duō	earn the most money in the whole world
niánlíng	age [N]
xiànzhì	limit, restriction [N]
niánlíng xiànzhì	age limit [PH]
wàiguo rén yào mǎn shíbāsuì	foreigners must be 18 years old
rùchǎng	enter; be admitted [VO]
yǒuqù	be interesting, funny, amusing [SV]
yǒuqùde shi...	the interesting thing is that...
jūmín	resident, inhabitant [N]
píngjūn	average, mean [AT]
shòumìng	life span, life [N]
píngjūn shòumìng	average life expectancy [PH]

Méi cuò. Àoménde lǚyóuyè hěn fādá, ér zhèngfǔde jīngjì láiyuán chàbuduō bǎifēnzhī-wǔshí shi cóng dǔbóyè láide. Àoménde dǔchǎng shi quán shìjiè zhuànqián zuì duōde. Búguò yǒu niánlíng xiànzhì, wàiguo rén yào mǎn shíbāsuì, Àomén rén yào èrshiyīsuì cái néng

That's right. Tourism in Macao is very developed, and about 50% of the government's sources of income come from gambling. Macao's casinos are the most profitable in the world. But there are age limits; foreigners must be 18 and residents of Macao have to be 21 to be admitted.

rùchǎng. Yǒuqùde shi, Àomén yě shi shìjièshang jūmín píngjūn shòumìng zuì chángde dìqū zhīyī.

The funny thing is, Macao is also one of the areas whose residents have the longest average life expectancies in the world.

....

10. Marino
   qīngsōng
   ràng tāmen hěn qīngsōng, hěn kuàilè
   ha ha
   Yǒu yìsi! Shì bu shi héfǎde dǔbó ràng tāmen hěn qīngsōng, hěn kuàilè? Ha ha!

   be relaxed, easy [SV]
   makes them relaxed and happy
   (sound of laughter) [I]
   That's interesting! I wonder if it's the legal gambling that makes them relaxed and happy? Ha ha!

Grammatical and Cultural Notes

1.   **MACAO.** Macao, also spelled Macau, is known as **Àomén** in Mandarin. It's one of China's two Special Administrative Regions, Hong Kong being the other. Macao is situated about 50 miles west of Hong Kong on the western side of the Pearl River delta bordering Guangdong Province to the North and the South China Sea to the south. Consisting of the Macao Peninsula and the islands of Taipa and Coloane, Macao was both the first and the last European colony in Asia, having been under Portuguese control from 1557 until 1999, when it reverted to China. The residents of Macao, called Macanese, number well over 500,000 and live on only a little over 11 square miles of land area, with the result that Macao is one of the most densely populated regions in the world. Tourism, gambling, and garment manufacturing are the three most important sectors of Macao's economy. Even though Cantonese is the native language of almost all Macanese, knowledge of Mandarin has increased greatly among the local population in the last two decades and is considerably higher than in Hong Kong,

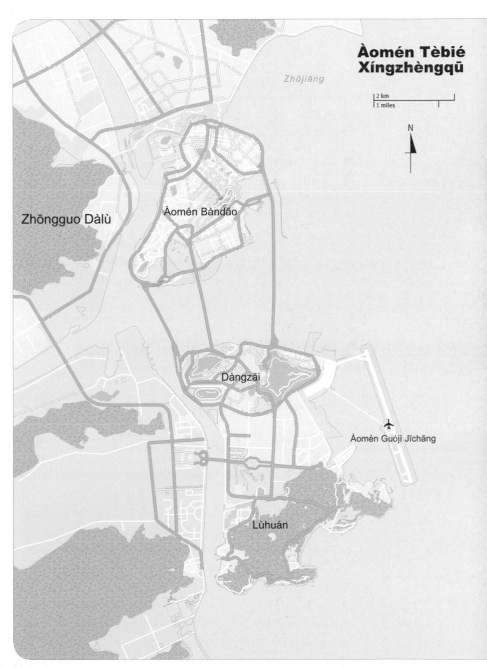

in part due to the large number of mainland tourists, especially gamblers. Additional information about Macao is contained in the Basic Conversation for this lesson.

Rua de São Paulo in Macao with ruins of St. Paul's in background

4A. FORMAL-STYLE SPOKEN CHINESE. All languages have different styles or "registers," that is, different varieties of language used for particular purposes in particular settings, that may range from very informal to very formal, depending on the occasion and the participants. The register used will, among other things, influence the choice of vocabulary and grammar. In Chinese, in part because of the legacy and influence of Classical Chinese, the differences between colloquial and formal registers are even larger than in many other languages. Several expressions in this Basic Conversation are in relatively formal style. In utterance 4, **jiǔwén** "have heard of (something) for a long time" is a set expression from Classical Chinese that is used in spoken Mandarin only in fairly formal contexts. In more colloquial spoken style, this would be said as **zǎo jiù tīngshuōguo**. In utterance 5, there are several more examples of formal-style spoken Chinese:

wèiyú	"be located at"
gāojū	"be high (in rank)"
rì	"day of the month" (equivalent to spoken-style **hào**)
jì...zhīhòu	"follow..."
zài...zhèngcè xià	"under the policy of..."

Having nearly completed this course in spoken Chinese, you're now approaching the intermediate level. From now on, as you consolidate your proficiency in Chinese at the intermediate level and move on to the advanced level, it will become increasingly important for you to start gaining a "feel" for what is colloquial-style Chinese and what is formal-style Chinese and, to the best of your ability, to use the vocabulary and grammar associated with these different styles on the appropriate occasions. Your eventual goal should be to attain the communicative ability of a college-educated native speaker and always adjust your language appropriately to the occasion. For example, if you're in a tea house or bar speaking with Chinese people of your age and position whom you know well, you would use colloquial style; and if you're giving a talk, attending a business meeting, or attending a formal banquet, you would use formal style. Even though as non-natives you'll be "forgiven" for many kinds of mistakes, be aware that sounding too formal in informal contexts can create distance; and sounding too informal in formal contexts can detract from the message you wish to communicate and cause people not to take you seriously. Of course, gaining a fluent command of both informal and formal styles in Chinese isn't so easy and will take time; but be assured that this is doable, as no small number of non-natives have accomplished this successfully. As always, the first step is listening closely to, and observing carefully the behavior of native Chinese speakers in society. As you gain experience, you can gradually begin mimicking them and then build on what you've heard and observed from others for your own creative language use.

4B. As you learned in 16-4, **lǎo** can mean "very," so **lǎo zǎo** means "very early" or "for a long time now." The phrase **lǎo zǎo jiù xiǎng lái cānguān** means "(I've) been wanting to come visit for a long time now."

4C. Be sure you understand the phrase **Wǒ shémme dōu xiǎng zhīdao** "I want to know everything." This is another example of the pattern QUESTION WORD + **dōu** + VERB to indicate indefinites such as "everything" or "anything" or "nothing" that you learned in 14-1: 2.

4D. **BÙGUǍN...** In this utterance, we take up the important pattern **bùguǎn...** "no matter if...," "no matter whether...," "regardless...," or "it doesn't matter whether...." In this pattern, **bùguǎn...** is usually followed by a **dōu** later in the sentence. The basic pattern is:

BÙGUǍN...	CLAUSE₁	CLAUSE₂
Bùguǎn	shi dìlǐ, lìshǐ háishi wénhuà,	wǒ shémme dōu xiǎng zhīdao.

"No matter whether it's geography, history, or culture, I want to know everything."

More examples of **bùguǎn...dōu**:

Bùguǎn shéi qù dōu xíng.

"It doesn't matter who goes." (lit, "No matter who goes, it's all fine.")

Bùguǎn tā gàosu nǐ shémme, nǐ dōu búyào xiāngxìn!

"No matter what he tells you, don't believe it!"

Bùguǎn zhèijiàn shì chéng bu chéng, wǒ dōu hěn gǎnjī nǐde bāngzhù!

"Regardless of whether or not I'm successful in this matter, I'm very grateful for your help!"

Huáng Tàitai bùguǎn mǎi shémme dōngxi, dōu yào mǎi zuì hǎo, zuì guìde.

"No matter what Mrs. Huang buys, she always wants to buy the best and most expensive."

Tā hěn yǒu yǔyán tiāncái, suóyǐ bùguǎn xué shémme yǔyán, tā dōu xuéde yòu kuài, yòu hǎo.

"She has real language talent, so no matter what language she learns, she learns it both fast and well."

There are two near synonyms of **bùguǎn...**, namely, **búlùn...** and **wúlùn....** The meanings and usage of these are the same as for **bùguǎn...**, except that **búlùn...** and **wúlùn...** are slightly more formal. Here is one example of each:

Búlùn duō lèi, Lǎo Táng dōu yào bǎ dāngtiān gāi zuòde shì zuòwán cái xiūxi.

"No matter how tired he might be, Old Tang doesn't rest until he has finished doing the things he was supposed to do that day."

Wúlùn Xiǎo Shī zěmme nǔlì, tā kǎoshì dōu zǒngshi kǎobuhǎo.

"No matter how hard Little Shi tries, he always does badly on tests."

5A. In the second sentence of this utterance, note the sentence **Wǒmen yìbiān cānguān, yìbiān shuō** "We'll talk about it while we tour." Do you remember the pattern **yìbiān(r) A yìbiān(r) B** "(do B) while (doing A)"? If not, refer back to 18-2: 5, where it was first introduced.

5B. Did you notice the noun suffix **-zhě** at the end of the word **dìguó-**

Macao street scene with one of the many casinos visible in background

zhǔyìzhě "imperialist"? As we learned in 23-2: 6B, the suffix **-zhě** means "one who does something," in this case, "one who engages in imperialism" (since **dìguózhǔyì** means "imperialism").

5C.   The specifier **lìng-** means "another," so **Zhōngguode lìngyíge tèbié xíngzhèngqū** means "another special administrative region of China." Note that **lìng-** can occur only before the number **yī** "a, an, one." Here are some more examples with **lìng**:

> **Míngtiān lìngyíge rén yào lái.**
> "Tomorrow another person will come."

> **Nà shi lìngyìhuí shì, gēn zhèijiàn shì wúguān.**
> "That's another matter, which is unrelated to this matter."

> **Nǐ wèishemme zǒngshi cóng yíge jíduān tiàodao lìngyíge jíduān?**
> "Why are you always jumping from one extreme to the other?"

5D.   The noun **dàntǎ** "egg tart" has an alternate pronunciation **dàntà**.

6.   In line 6, the auxiliary verb **zhíde** "be worth, deserve" is well worth learning. Some speakers pronounce this word with a Tone Two on the second syllable as **zhídé**. More examples:

> **Zhèiběn shū hěn zhíde kàn.**
> "This book is well worth reading."

> **Wǒ juéde nèige dìfang zhíde qù kànkan.**
> "That place is worth going to take a look at."

> **Yídùn fàn yībǎiduōkuài, yǒu yìdiǎn bù zhíde.**
> "Over a hundred bucks for a meal, it's not really worth it."

7A.   The long sentence in this utterance that begins with **Àomén cài shi...** is grammatically quite complex. When faced with a complex sentence like this, the first thing to do is to figure out the "skeleton" or basic structure of the sentence, temporarily setting aside the descriptive parts. What is the subject or topic? What is the verb or predicate? If there is an object, what is it? If there is a phrase ending in **-de**, focus on the noun that occurs after the **-de** and for the time being set aside the descriptive parts before the **-de**. The following breakdown of the sentence at hand will serve as an example:

> (a) **Àomén cài shi...dúchuàng-chūláide.** "Macanese food was uniquely created."

Senado Square in the historic center of Macao

(b) **Àomén cài shi róuhéle Zhōngguo cài hé...Pútáoyá cài...suǒdúchuàngchūláide.**
"Macanese food was uniquely created by mixing together Chinese food and Portuguese food."

(c) **...wèidao bǐjiào xiánde Pútáoyá cài...**
"Portuguese food, which has a saltier flavor"

(d) **...zài jiāshang Fēizhōu, Yìndù hé Dōngnányà láide gālí, yēzhī, ròuguì zhèxiē xiāngliào...**
"then add spices such as curry, coconut juice, and cinnamon, which come from Africa, India, and Southeast Asia"

(e) **Àomén cài shi róuhéle Zhōngguo cài hé wèidao bǐjiào xiánde Pútáoyá cài, zài jiāshang Fēizhōu, Yìndù hé Dōngnányà láide gālí, yēzhī, ròuguì zhèxiē xiāngliào, suǒdúchuàngchūláide.**
"Macanese food was uniquely created by mixing together Chinese food and Portuguese food, which has a saltier flavor, and then adding spices such as curry, coconut juice, and cinnamon, which come from Africa, India, and Southeast Asia."

7B.   **THE CAUSATIVE VERB JIÀO.** At the end of utterance 7, we come across the sentence **Àomén cài...chīle jiào rén huí-wèi-wú-qióng** "Macanese food...(when you've) eaten (it), (it) makes a person savor the aftertaste for a long time." **Jiào** "tell (someone to do something)," "cause (someone to do something)," or "make (someone do something)" is a so-called causative verb. After the **jiào**, there is always a human object, which in turn serves as the subject of a following sentence that has been embedded within the main sentence. The basic pattern is:

SUBJECT OF SENTENCE₁	JIÀO	OBJECT OF JIÀO AND SUBJECT OF SENTENCE₂	PREDICATE OF SENTENCE₂
Tā	jiào	wǒ	zài zhèr děng tā.

"She asked me to wait for her here."

Here are some more examples of the causative verb **jiào**:

Nǐ jiào tā zǎo yidianr huílai!	"Tell him not to come back too late!"
Nǐ jiào tā qù mǎi yìpíng jiàngyóu.	"Tell her to go and buy a bottle of soy sauce."
Bié jiào wǒ zuò nèiyangde shìqing!	"Don't make me do something like that!"
Yīshēng jiào tā xiūxi liǎngge lǐbài.	"The doctor told him to rest for two weeks."

Měicì wǒmen zuò fēijī dōu jiào wǒ māma hěn zháojí.

"Every time we take a plane it makes my mother very worried."

Zhèiliàng qìchē lǎo pāomáo, jiào wǒ hěn shēngqì.

"This car keeps breaking down, which makes me very angry."

8A.   Examine the question **Tīngshuō Àomén dǔbóyè shi héfǎde?** "I've heard that gambling is legal in Macao?" First, this is an intonation question, which is the reason there is no affirmative-negative verb construction or final **ma**. Second, note that **Àomén dǔbóyè shi héfǎde** consists of a topic (**Àomén**) and a comment on that topic (**dǔbóyè shi héfǎde**); and then that comment in turn consists of a secondary topic (**dǔbóyè**) and a comment on that topic (**shi héfǎde**). A literal translation of the whole question might be: "I have heard that, if you're talking about Macao, gambling is legal?"

8B.   **Héfǎ** is a stative verb that means "be legal"; the literal translation of **héfǎ** is "be in accordance with the law." The reason that the **shi...-de** pattern has been used in the embedded sentence **Dǔbóyè shi héfǎde** "Gambling is legal" is to emphasize a situation or stress that "that's how it is" (cf. 16-3: 3C). Here is another example sentence with **héfǎ**:

Nǐ yīnggāi yòng héfǎde bànfa lái jiějué wèntí.

"You should solve the problem using legal means."

9.   In sentence 9, the conjunction **ér** means "and" or "moreover." The speaker has made one point (that tourism in Macao is very developed) and now uses **ér** to make clear that he is going to present an additional point (that 50% of the government's revenues come from gambling). The conjunction **ér** is common in ordering the various linguistic components in formal Chinese discourse.

Unit 23: Review and Study Guide

New Vocabulary

ADVERBS

dàzhì	generally, roughly, for the most part
guāng	only, just
shífēn	very, extremely
yìbān	generally, ordinarily
yìwùde	voluntarily
zhèngshì	formally, officially

ATTRIBUTIVES

gāodù	high degree
gōnglì	public
guānfāng	official
jīběn	basic, fundamental
màopái	counterfeit, fake, imitation
píngfāng	square
píngjūn	average, mean
Pú'ào	Portuguese-Macanese
yìbān	general, ordinary
zhēnzhèng	real, true, genuine

AUXILIARY VERBS

zhíde	be worth, deserve

CONJUNCTIONS

bìngqiě	moreover, and
ér	and, yet, but

EXPRESSIONS

huí-wèi-wú-qióng	"savor the after-taste a long time"

IDIOMATIC EXPRESSIONS

jiǔwén	have heard of for a long time

INTERJECTIONS

ha ha	(sound of laughter)

MEASURES

rì	day of the month (formal style)
zhōu	week

MOVEABLE ADVERBS

jīběnshang	basically

NOUNS

bàndǎo	peninsula
bàokān	newspapers and periodicals
chǎnpǐn	product
chāshāobāo	steamed white flour bun
dàntǎ	egg tart
dǎo	island
dǎoyǔ	island
diǎnxin	snack, pastry, dim sum
dìguózhǔyìzhě	imperialist
dìlǐ	geography
dǔbóyè	the gambling industry
dùzi	belly, abdomen, stomach
fāngmiàn	aspect, area, side
fántǐzì	traditional Chinese characters
fēngshuǐ	feng shui, geomancy
gālí	curry
gòuwùzhě	one who buys things, shopper
guófáng	national defense
gǔshì	stock market, stock exchange
jiǎntǐzì	simplified Chinese characters
jīngjì	economy
jīnróng	finance
jūmín	resident, inhabitant
kěnéng	possibility
kǒu	mouth; opening
láiyuán	source, origin
lídǎo	offshore island
lìshǐ	history

lǚyóuyè	the tourism industry
měishí	fine foods, delicacy
miànjī	area
miǎnshuìgǎng	duty free port
mìdù	density
míngcài	famous dish, famous food
mǔyǔ	native language
niánlíng	age
qiāng	accent, intonation
ròuguì	cinnamon
shāngpǐn	goods, merchandise
shāomài	small steamed dumpling
shìjì	century
shòumìng	life span, life
shuǐpíng	level, standard
tèsè	characteristic
tiāntáng	paradise, heaven
tiáoyuē	treaty, pact
wàijiāo	diplomacy, foreign affairs
xiājiǎo	shrimp dumpling
xiànzhì	limit, restriction
xiànzhuàng	present conditions, status quo
xiāngliào	spice
xiàngdǎo	guide
xiàngjī	camera
xíngzhèngqū	administrative region
yāpiàn	opium
yēzhī	coconut juice
yínhángyè	banking industry, banking
yíqiè	everything, all
yìwù	duty, obligation
zhèngcè	policy
zhèngfǔ	government

zhìdù	system
zhímíndì	colony
zhǔyì	doctrine; -ism
zīběn	capital
zìzhìquán	autonomy
zǒngmiànji	total area

PATTERNS

...yǐshàng	more than...
...yǐxià	less than..., below...
...zhīyī	one of...
A gēn B yǒuguān	
	A is related to B
A shi yóu B (suǒ)zǔchéngde	
	A is composed of B
bǎ A jiào(zuo) B	call A B
bùguǎn...	no matter..., regardless...
jì...zhīhòu	follow...
miǎnde...	so as to avoid..., lest...
yǐ...wéi zhǔ	take...as the main thing
zài...zhèngcè xià	under the policy of...
zìcóng...yǐhòu	since (a certain point in time)

PHRASES

bǎihuò gōngsī	department store
diànzǐ chǎnpǐn	electronic product, electronics
gōnglì xuéxiào	public school
guānfāng yǔyán	official language
jiàoyù shuǐpíng	educational level
lǎo zǎo	very early, for a long time now
lùtiān shìchǎng	open-air market
měishí tiāntáng	food heaven
mǔyǔ jiàoyù	education in one's native language
Nánjīng Tiáoyuē	Treaty of Nanking
niánlíng xiànzhì	age limit
píngfāng gōnglǐ	square kilometer
píngjūn shòumìng	
	average life expectancy
rénkǒu mìdù	population density
tèbié xíngzhèngqū	
	special administrative region
Yāpiàn Zhànzhēng	
	Opium War
yìbān lái shuō	generally speaking, in general

Yìguó Liǎngzhì	One Country Two Systems
zīběn zhǔyì	capitalism
zuò shēngyi	engage in business, do business

PLACE WORDS

Dàngzǎi	Taipa (name of island in Macao)
Dōngnányà	Southeast Asia
dǔchǎng	casino
Fēilǜbīn	The Philippines
Fēizhōu	Africa
Jiǔlóng bàndǎo	Kowloon Peninsula
Jiǔlóng	Kowloon
jiǔlóu	restaurant
Lùhuán	Coloane (name of island in Macao)
Pútáoyá	Portugal
qízhōng	among which, within which
shāngdiàn	shop, store
Xiānggǎng Tèbié Xíngzhèngqū	
	Hong Kong Special Administrative Region
Xīnjiè	New Territories
Yìndù	India
yúcūn	fishing village
Zhūjiāng	Pearl River

RESULTATIVE COMPOUNDS

děngbují	can't wait

SPECIFIERS

lìng	another

STATIVE VERBS

chuántǒng	be traditional
fādá	be developed
héfǎ	be legal
qīngsōng	be relaxed, easy
yōujiǔ	be very old, be age-old
yǒuqù	be interesting, funny, amusing
zhòngyào	be important

TIME WORDS

dāngshí	at that time, then
hòubànqī	latter half

VERBS

bǎocún	preserve, keep, maintain
bāokuò	include
bǐjiào	compare
chéngwéi	become

dàobǎn	pirate (a book, film, etc.)
dǔbó	gamble
dúchuàng	create as something unique
gāojū	be high (in rank), occupy (a high position)
gòuwù	buy things, shop
guānshuì	customs duty
huíguī	revert, return to
jiào	make, cause
jiāohuì	connect up, meet, intersect
jiāoxué	teach
jiàozuo	call; be called, be known as
lǚyóu	tour
pǐncháng	taste, sample
qiāndìng	sign
rónghé	mix together, merge, fuse
róuhé	mix together
shíshī	implement, put into effect
shíxíng	put into practice, implement
wéichí	maintain
xiǎngyǒu	enjoy (rights, prestige)
xīyǐn	attract
yìnshuā	print
zhànlǐng	occupy, capture
zhēng	levy, collect (taxes or duty)

VERB-OBJECT COMPOUNDS

jiǎngjià	bargain, haggle
miǎnshuì	be exempt from tax or duty
páimíng	be ranked, rank
rùchǎng	enter; be admitted
shòukè	give classes, offer instruction
yǐnchá	drink tea and eat dim sum

VERB + POSTVERB

biànchéng	become
wèiyú	be located at, be situated at
zǔchéng	make up, form, compose

Major New Grammar Patterns

A SHI YÓU B (SUǑ)ZǓCHÉNGDE: **Xiānggǎng shi yóu Xiānggǎng dǎo, Jiǔlóng, hé Xīnjiè suǒzǔchéngde.** "Hong Kong is composed of Hong Kong Island, Kowloon, and the New Territories." (23-1)

QÍZHONG: **wǔshiduōwàn wàiguo rén, qízhōng Fēilǜbīn rén hé Yìndù rén zuì duō** "more than 500,000 foreigners, among which Filipinos and Indians predominate" (23-1)

SHÌJÌ: **shíjiǔ shìjì** "nineteenth century" (23-1)

YǏ...WÉI ZHǓ: **Tīngshuō Xiānggǎng yíqiè yǐ jīngjì wéi zhǔ.** "I've heard that in Hong Kong everything takes the economy as the most important component." (23-2)

...ZHĪYĪ: **Xiānggǎng shi shìjièshang zhòngyàode jīnróng hé màoyì zhōngxīn zhīyī.** "Hong Kong is one of the important financial and trade centers in the world." (23-2)

PÁIMÍNG: **Xiānggǎng Gǔshì zài shìjièshang páimíng dìwǔ.** "The Hong Kong Stock Exchange is ranked number five in the world." (23-2)

MIǍNDE...: **Yào xiǎoxīn miǎnde bèi piàn!** "You have to be careful lest you get cheated!" (23-2)

BǍ A JIÀO(ZUO) B: **Dàjiā bǎ Xiānggǎng jiàozuo "měishí tiāntáng."** "Everybody calls Hong Kong 'food heaven.'" (23-2)

...YǏSHÀNG AND ...YǏXIÀ: **bǎifēnzhījiǔshiwǔ yǐshàngde rén** "more than 95% of the people"; **língdù yǐxià** "below zero (degrees)" (23-3)

A GĒN B YǑUGUĀN: **Zhè gēn tāmende jiàoyù shuǐpíng yǒuguān.** "This has to do with their educational level." (23-3)

ZÌCÓNG...YǏHÒU: **Xiānggǎng zìcóng 1997 nián huíguī Zhōngguo yǐhòu** "since Hong Kong's return to China in 1997" (23-3)

ZHŌU: **zhōuyī** "Monday," **zhōu'èr** "Tuesday," **zhōusān** "Wednesday," **zhōusì** "Thursday," **zhōuwǔ** "Friday," **zhōuliù** "Saturday," **zhōurì** "Sunday," **běnzhōu** "this week," **shàngyìzhōu** "last week," **xiàyìzhōu** "next week," **měizhōu** "every week" (23-3)

BÙGUǍN...: **Bùguǎn shi dìlǐ, lìshǐ háishi wénhuà, wǒ shémme dōu xiǎng zhīdao.** "Whether it's geography, history, or culture, I want to know everything." (23-4)

CAUSATIVE VERB JIÀO: **jiào rén huí-wèi-wú-qióng** "make people savor the aftertaste for a long time" (23-4)

Singapore and Malaysia

COMMUNICATIVE OBJECTIVES

Once you've mastered this unit, you'll be able to use Chinese to:

1. Discuss aspects of the geography, population, history, politics, economy, society, linguistic situation, and culture of Singapore.
2. Discuss aspects of the geography, population, history, politics, economy, society, linguistic situation, and culture of Penang, Malaysia.
3. Discuss aspects of the geography, population, history, politics, economy, society, linguistic situation, and culture of your own and other countries.
4. Talk about the natural world, its flora and fauna: names of various flowers, trees, and animals.
5. Discuss environmental concerns: destruction of the natural environment, animals facing extinction, etc.
6. Discuss the different names for "Mandarin" in mainland China, Taiwan, Singapore, and Malaysia, and the similarities and differences among these different varieties of Mandarin.
7. Talk about schools and school systems: private, public, and independent schools; Chinese community schools; coeducation, etc.
8. Discuss the purchase of a laptop computer: models, functions, features, multimedia, Wi-Fi, software, operating systems, applications, place of manufacture, warranty, etc.
9. Handle more formal spoken tasks and topics, including some of the higher-level grammatical patterns and vocabulary typical of formal spoken Chinese.
10. Better understand Hokkien-influenced Mandarin.

Conversation at Singapore Botanic Gardens

Matt Wilkinson is an American student who is in Singapore for the summer to continue his study of Mandarin at National University of Singapore's Centre for Language Studies. He recently met Mae Tan, a Mandarin-speaking Singaporean who is the daughter of a business associate of Matt's father. Today being Saturday, Mae has offered to take Matt to Singapore Botanic Gardens on an outing.

 Basic Conversation 24-1

1. AMERICAN

Mae, zhèxiē rèdàide huā gēn shù shízài tài piàoliangle! Nǐ néng bu néng gěi wǒ jiǎndānde jièshao yixia Xīnjiāpō Zhíwùyuán?
Mae, these tropical flowers and trees are really very pretty! Could you tell me a little about Singapore Botanic Gardens?

2. SINGAPOREAN

Dāngrán kéyi. Jù wǒ suǒzhī, zhèige zhíwùyuán yǐjīng yǒu jiāngjìn liǎngbǎiniánde lìshǐ le, shi yóu Yīngguo rén Sir Stamford Raffles zài yī-bā-èr-èr-nián chuànglìde. Zhèige zhíwùyuán duì Xīnjiāpōde gòngxiàn hěn dà. Bǐfang shuō, duì Dōngnányà jīngjì shífēn zhòngyàode xiàngjiāo shù jiù shi zài zhèli péizhíde.
Of course I can. So far as I know, this botanic garden already has a history of nearly 200 years. It was founded by the Englishman Sir Stamford Raffles in 1822. This botanic garden has made a big contribution to Singapore. For example, the rubber tree, which is extremely important to the Southeast Asian economy, was cultivated here.

3. AMERICAN

Wǒ hái yǒu yíge wèntí. Xīnjiāpō dà bùfende rén dōu shi Huárén ma?
I have another question. Are most people in Singapore Chinese?

4. SINGAPOREAN

Dàyuē bǎifēnzhīqīshí shi Huárén, qíyúde zhǔyào shi Mǎlái rén hé Yìndù rén, zài jiāshang yìxiē cóng quánqiú qítā guójiā láide rén.
About 70% are Chinese; the remainder are mainly Malays and Indians, plus some people from other countries all over the globe.

5. AMERICAN

Xīnjiāpō rén shǐyòng shémme yǔyán?
What languages do Singaporeans use?

6. SINGAPOREAN

Xīnjiāpō yǒu sìzhǒng guānfāng yǔyán: Huáyǔ, Mǎláiyǔ, Tǎnmǐ'ěryǔ gēn Yīngyǔ. Dà bùfende rén kéyi shǐyòng zhìshǎo liǎngzhǒng yǔyán, yǒude rén huì shuō sān-sìzhǒng yǔyán. Dànshi suóyǒude rén dōu yǐ Yīngyǔ wéi zhèngshìde gōngzuò yǔyán.
Singapore has four official languages: Chinese, Malay, Tamil, and English. Most

people can use at least two languages, and some people can speak three or four languages. But all people use English as their formal working language.

7. AMERICAN   **Nǐmende Huáyǔ gēn Zhōngguode Pǔtōnghuà hé Táiwānde Guóyǔ yǒu shémme bù yíyàng?**

What is the difference between your "Huayu" and China's "Putonghua" and Taiwan's "Guoyu"?

8. SINGAPOREAN   **Xīnjiāpōde Huáyǔ kěnéng dàiyǒu cǐdì fāngyánde yīndiào, yǒu yíbùfen cíhuì shòudàole běndì qítā sānzhǒng yǔyánde yǐngxiǎng. Búguò, Xīnjiāpōde Huáyǔ gēn Pǔtōnghuà hé Guóyǔ jīběnshàng kéyi shuō shi dà-tóng-xiǎo-yì.**

Singapore's "Huayu" may carry the intonation of local dialects, and there's a part of the vocabulary that has been influenced by the other three local languages. But Singapore's "Huayu" can basically be said to be largely the same as "Putonghua" and "Guoyu."

 Build Up

1. American
    rèdài   the tropics [N]
    rèdàide huā gēn shù   tropical flowers and trees
    zhíwù   plants, vegetation [N]
    zhíwùyuán   botanic garden [PW]
    Xīnjiāpō Zhíwùyuán   Singapore Botanic Gardens [PW]
    **Mae, zhèxiē rèdàide huā gēn shù shízài tài   Mae, these tropical flowers and trees are really
    piàoliangle! Nǐ néng bu néng gěi wǒ   very pretty! Could you tell me a little about
    jiǎndānde jièshao yixia Xīnjiāpō Zhíwùyuán?**   Singapore Botanic Gardens?

2. Singaporean
    jù wǒ suǒzhī   according to what I know [PH]
    jiāngjìn   be close to, nearly be, almost be [V]
    jiāngjìn liǎngbǎinián   nearly 200 years
    yǒu jiāngjìn liǎngbǎiniánde lìshǐ   has a history of almost 200 years
    chuànglì   found, create, establish [V]
    shi yóu Sir Stamford Raffles chuànglìde   it was founded by Sir Stamford Raffles
    gòngxiàn   contribution [N]
    duì Xīnjiāpōde gòngxiàn hěn dà   its contribution to Singapore is great
    duì Dōngnányà jīngjì shífēn zhòngyào   be extremely important to the Southeast Asian economy
    xiàngjiāo   rubber [N]
    xiàngjiāo shù   rubber tree [PH] (M: **kē**)
    péizhí   cultivate (plants or human talent) [V]
    jiù shi zài zhèli péizhíde   it was cultivated here
    **Dāngrán kéyi. Jù wǒ suǒzhī, zhèige zhíwùyuán   Of course I can. So far as I know, this botanic
    yǐjīng yǒu jiāngjìn liǎngbǎiniánde lìshǐ le, shi yóu   garden already has a history of nearly 200 years.
    Yīngguo rén Sir Stamford Raffles zài yī-bā-èr-èr-   It was founded by the Englishman Sir Stamford
    nián chuànglìde. Zhèige zhíwùyuán duì Xīnjiāpō-   Raffles in 1822. This botanic garden has made a
    de gòngxiàn hěn dà. Bǐfang shuō, duì Dōngnányà   big contribution to Singapore. For example, the
    jīngjì shífēn zhòngyàode xiàngjiāo shù jiù shi zài   rubber tree, which is extremely important to the
    zhèli péizhíde.**   Southeast Asian economy, was cultivated here.

3. American
    dà bùfende rén   the majority of people
    Huárén   Chinese person, Chinese [N]
    **Wǒ hái yǒu yíge wèntí. Xīnjiāpō dà bùfende   I have another question. Are most people in
    rén dōu shi Huárén ma?**   Singapore Chinese?

4. Singaporean

dàyuē bǎifēnzhīqīshí shi Huárén	about 70% are Chinese
qíyú	other, the remaining, the rest [AT]
qíyúde	the others, the remainder
Mǎlái rén	Malay (person)
Yìndù rén	Indian (person)
qíyúde zhǔyào shi Mǎlái rén hé Yìndù rén	the others are mainly Malays and Indians
zài jiāshang	and in addition add to that, plus
quánqiú	the whole world, the entire globe [N]
quánqiú qítā guójiā	other countries all over the globe
cóng quánqiú qítā guójiā láide rén	people who've come from other countries all over the globe

Dàyuē bǎifēnzhīqīshí shi Huárén, qíyúde zhǔyào shi Mǎlái rén hé Yìndù rén, zài jiāshang yìxiē cóng quánqiú qítā guójiā láide rén.

About 70% are Chinese; the remainder are mainly Malays and Indians, plus some people from other countries all over the globe.

5. American

Xīnjiāpō rén shǐyòng shémme yǔyán?   What languages do Singaporeans use?

6. Singaporean

Huáyǔ	Chinese (language) [N]
Mǎláiyǔ	Malay (language) [N]
Tǎnmǐ'ěryǔ	Tamil (language) [N]
zhìshǎo	at least [A]
zhìshǎo liǎngzhǒng yǔyán	at least two languages
suǒyǒu	all, every [AT]
suǒyǒude rén	all people
zhèngshì	be formal [SV]
gōngzuò yǔyán	working language [PH]
zhèngshìde gōngzuò yǔyán	formal working language
yǐ Yīngyǔ wéi zhèngshìde gōngzuò yǔyán	take English to be the formal working language

Xīnjiāpō yǒu sìzhǒng guānfāng yǔyán: Huáyǔ, Mǎláiyǔ, Tǎnmǐ'ěryǔ gēn Yīngyǔ. Dà bùfende rén kéyi shǐyòng zhìshǎo liǎngzhǒng yǔyán, yǒude rén huì shuō sānsìzhǒng yǔyán. Dànshi suǒyǒude rén dōu yǐ Yīngyǔ wéi zhèngshìde gōngzuò yǔyán.

Singapore has four official languages: Chinese, Malay, Tamil, and English. Most people can use at least two languages, and some people can speak three or four languages. But all people use English as their formal working language.

7. American

Nǐmende Huáyǔ gēn Zhōngguode Pǔtōnghuà hé Táiwānde Guóyǔ yǒu shémme bù yíyàng?

What is the difference between your "Huayu" and China's "Putonghua" and Taiwan's "Guoyu"?

8. Singaporean

dàiyǒu	carry, bear [V]
cǐdì	this place, here [PW]
fāngyán	dialect [N]
yīndiào	accent, intonation, tone [N]
dàiyǒu cǐdì fāngyánde yīndiào	carry the intonation of local dialects
yǒu yíbùfen cíhuì	there is a part of the vocabulary
shòudào	receive [RC]
yǐngxiǎng	influence [N]
shòudào...yǐngxiǎng	be influenced by... [PT]
shòudàole sānzhǒng yǔyánde yǐngxiǎng	be influenced by three languages
dà-tóng-xiǎo-yì	be mostly the same except for minor differences, be largely the same [EX]

Xīnjiāpōde Huáyǔ kěnéng dàiyǒu cǐdì fāng-yánde yīndiào, yǒu yíbùfen cíhuì shòudàole

Singapore's "Huayu" may carry the intonation of local dialects, and there's a part of the vocabulary

běndì qítā sānzhǒng yǔyánde yǐngxiǎng. Búguò, Xīnjiāpōde Huáyǔ gēn Pǔtōnghuà hé Guóyǔ jīběnshàng kéyi shuō shì dà-tóng-xiǎo-yì.

that has been influenced by the other three local languages. But Singapore's "Huayu" can basically be said to be largely the same as "Putonghua" and "Guoyu."

Additional Vocabulary: Flowers and Trees

(A) FLOWERS

1. jiǔchónggé	Bougainvillea [N] (M: **duǒ**)
2. kāngnǎixin	carnation [N] (M: **duǒ**)
3. júhuā	chrysanthemum [N] (M: **duǒ**)
4. shuǐxiān	daffodil [N] (M: **duǒ**)
5. mòlìhuā	jasmine [N] (M: **duǒ**)
6. zǐdīngxiāng	lilac [N] (M: **duǒ**)
7. bǎihé huā	lily [N] (M· **duǒ**)
8. liánhuā	lotus [N] (M: **duǒ**)
9. héhuā	lotus, water lily [N] (M: **duǒ**)
10. lánhuā	orchid [N] (M: **duǒ**)
11. mǔdān	peony [N] (M: **duǒ**)
12. méihuā	plum blossom [N] (M: **duǒ**)
13. méigui huā	rose [N] (M: **duǒ**)
14. xiàngrìkuí	sunflower [N] (M: **duǒ**)
15. yùjīnxiāng	tulip [N] (M: **duǒ**)

(B) TREES

16. zhúzi	bamboo [N] (M: **kē**)
17. yēzi shù	coconut tree [N] (M: **kē**)
18. bǎishù	cypress tree [N] (M: **kē**)
19. fēngshù	maple tree; Chinese sweet gum [N] (M: **kē**)
20. xiàngmù	oak tree [N] (M: **kē**)
21. gǎnlǎn shù	olive tree [N] (M: **kē**)
22. sōngshù	pine tree [N] (M: **kē**)
23. báihuà	white birch [N] (M: **kē**)

Grammatical and Cultural Notes

1.   **SINGAPORE.** Singapore or **Xīnjiāpō** is an independent city-state located in Southeast Asia, just off the southern tip of the Malay peninsula. It was founded as an English colony by Sir Stamford Raffles in 1819 and continued as a British colony until 1963, when it merged with Malaysia. Two years later Singapore became fully independent. The population of Singapore is over 5 million, of which about 70% are of Chinese ethnic origin, with the remainder being of Malay or Indian origin. Singapore is a major manufacturing center and also a major financial hub. Oil refining is a major industry, and its port is one of the largest in the world. The location for this Basic Conversation, Singapore Botanic Gardens or **Xīnjiāpō Zhíwùyuán**, is a lush sanctuary situated just a few minutes from the heart of Singapore. Founded by Sir Stamford Raffles in 1822, in its early years it played an important role in fostering agricultural development in Singapore and throughout Southeast Asia through the collecting, growing, and distribution of potentially useful plants. One of its greatest successes was the introduction and promotion of the rubber tree or **xiàngjiāo shù**, which became a major crop that brought prosperity to much of Southeast Asia. Additional information about Singapore is contained in the Basic Conversation for this lesson.

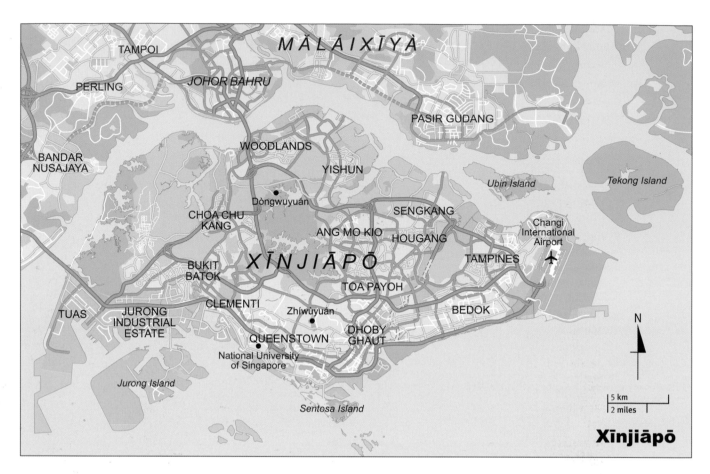

2A. The phrase **jù wǒ suǒ zhī** "according to what I know," "based on what I know," or "so far as I know" is common and useful. Frequent use of introductory phrases like **jù wǒ suǒ zhī**, when appropriate, will make you sound more fluent and natural, and will give you a bit of extra time to mentally prepare the rest of what you wish to say.

2B. **Jiāngjìn** is a verb that means "be close to," "nearly be," "almost be," or "approach." However, it's a somewhat unusual verb, as it doesn't take suffixes like **-le**, **-guo**, or **-zhe**. Here are some more examples with **jiāngjìn**:

> **Yǒu jiāngjìn yìbǎige rén cānjiāle zuótiānde huódòng.**
>
> "There were almost 100 people who took part in yesterday's activity."

> **Zuótiān wǎnshang Xiǎo Táng huílaide shíhou, yǐjīng jiāngjìn bànyè.**
>
> "When Little Tang returned last night, it was nearly midnight."

> **Gùgōng yǒu jiāngjìn qībǎiniánde lìshǐ le.**
>
> "The Imperial Palace in Beijing has nearly 700 years of history."

> **Zhèizuò lóu yǐjīng jiāngjìn wángōng.**
>
> "This building is already nearly completed."

2C. In 14-4: 1D, you learned that the coverb **yóu** can mean "by" and indicate the person who performs the action of the verb. Keep this in mind as you study the sentence **Zhèige zhíwùyuán...shi yóu Yīngguo rén Sir Stamford Raffles zài yī-bā-èr-èr-nián chuànglide** "This botanic garden...was founded by the Englishman Sir Stamford Raffles in 1822."

2D. When faced with a long and complex sentence containing a clause with a **-de** followed by a noun, a good strategy is to temporarily ignore the **-de** and what comes before it, and instead focus on the noun that comes after the **-de**. Once you have figured out the "skeleton" or basic structure of the sentence, you can place the descriptive **-de** phrase back in the sentence. For example, take the sentence **Duì Dōngnányà jīngjì shífēn zhòngyàode xiàngjiāo shù jiù shi zài zhèli péizhíde**. If that sentence seems difficult, then temporarily delete everything through the **-de** phrase, so you have: **Xiàngjiāo shù jiù shi zài zhèli péizhíde** "The rubber tree was cultivated here." Once you're clear about the meaning of this part, you can put the **-de** phrase back in and find out the details of the description of the rubber tree that the speaker gave: **Duì Dōngnányà jīngjì shífēn zhòngyàode...** "...which is extremely important for the Southeast Asian Economy."

2F.   Contrast **xiàngjiāo** "rubber" with **xiāngjiāo** "banana," that you learned in 12-4. We could even add **shù** "tree" to both of these and then contrast **xiàngjiāo shù** "rubber tree" with **xiāngjiāo shù** "banana tree."

4.   **Qíyúde** "the others" is a synonym of **qítāde** that you learned in 7-2.

6.   The attributive expression **suǒyǒude** "all" (lit. "that which there is") precedes the noun that it describes. More examples:

> **Suǒyǒude xuéshēng dōu qù kāihuì le.**   "All the students went to a meeting."
>
> **Wǒ bǎ wǒ suǒyǒude qián dōu jiègěi tā le.**   "I lent all my money to her."

8A.   **SINGAPORE MANDARIN.** About 75% of the population in Singapore is of Chinese ethnic origin, mostly of Hokkien, Cantonese, Hakka, Teochew, or Hainanese background. Many older people can still speak their native dialects as well as some Mandarin, but younger people are usually more fluent in English and Mandarin, though the Mandarin they speak has been influenced by various Southern Chinese dialects. Even though the official standard is as in Beijing, the pronunciation of Singapore Mandarin as spoken by most people is rather like in Taiwan and Southern China, with **-h-** being dropped in the initials **zh-**, **ch-**, and **sh-**; finals **-ing** and **-eng** merging with **-in** and **-en**; and almost total lack of the **-r** suffix. There are in Singapore Mandarin many loanwords from Hokkien, Cantonese, Malay, and English. Some of the grammar of Singapore Mandarin has also been influenced by Hokkien or Cantonese. Much of what is true of Singapore Mandarin is also true of Mandarin as spoken in Malaysia and Indonesia.

A traditional Chinese medicine shop in Singapore

8B.   **SHÒU(DÀO)...YǏNGXIǍNG.** Be sure to learn the pattern **shòudào...yǐngxiǎng** "be influenced by..." (lit. "receive...influence"), as it's common and important. This pattern sometimes also occurs without the **-dào** as **shòu...yǐngxiǎng**. An attributive phrase ending in **-de** typically occurs between the **shòu(dào)** and **yǐngxiǎng**. The basic pattern is:

SUBJECT	SHÒU(DÀO)	ATTRIBUTIVE PHRASE WITH -DE	YǏNGXIǍNG
Yǒu yíbùfen cíhuì	shòudàole	běndì qítā sānzhǒng yǔyánde	yǐngxiǎng.

"There's a part of the vocabulary that has been influenced by the other three local languages."

More examples of the pattern **shòu(dào)...yǐngxiǎng**:

Xīnjiāpō rén jiǎngde Huáyǔ shòudàole běndì qítā yǔyánde yǐngxiǎng.

"The Chinese that Singaporeans speak has been influenced by the other local languages."

Nǐ kéyi kànchulai, tā huàde huàr shi shòule Fǎguo yìnxiàngpài huàjiāde yǐngxiǎng.

"You can tell that her paintings have been influenced by the French impressionist painters."

Wǒ shi shòudàole wǒ tóngwūde yǐngxiǎng zhīhòu, cái kāishǐ duì Zhōngguode yǔyán hé wénhuà fāshēng xìngqude.

"Only after being influenced by my roommate did I start becoming interested in Chinese language and culture."

8C.   The expression **dà-tóng-xiǎo-yì** "be mostly the same except for minor differences" is useful when making comparisons in somewhat formal conversation. The literal meaning of this expression, which derives from Classical Chinese, is "big same small different," meaning that in major aspects there is similarity but in smaller, more minor areas there are differences. The basic pattern into which this expression fits is **A gēn B dà-tóng-xiǎo-yì**.

AV1–15.   **NAMES OF FLOWERS.** These names for various flowers are listed in alphabetical order of the English translations. Note that **duǒ** is the measure used for single flowers, **shù** is the measure for a bouquet of flowers, and **kē** is the measure for the plant.

AV16–23.   **NAMES OF TREES.** These names for various trees are listed in alphabetical order of the English translations. Those tree names that occur in the Basic Conversation for this or previous lessons have not been repeated here. Note that **kē** is the measure used for all trees.

For the remaining pages of **Unit 24**, **Part 2** through **Unit 24**, **Part 4**, plus the Review & Study Guide, "What Next? Notes to Learner" and many other useful resources, please refer to the disc.

Chinese-English Glossary

This glossary contains all the Chinese vocabulary introduced in the Basic Conversation and Supplementary Vocabulary sections of *Intermediate Spoken Chinese*. The following information is included for each entry: the Chinese word, spelled in Pinyin, printed in **bold**; one or more English equivalents; the word class of the Chinese word [in brackets]; and the numbers of the unit and part where the Chinese word was introduced (in parentheses). For example:

Chinese	English	Word Class	Unit & Part
jìnlì	do one's best	[VO]	(18-4)

The entries are arranged in alphabetical order of the Pinyin spellings, spelled one syllable at a time, with the vowel **u** preceding **ü**. Syllables are listed in order of tone, i.e., in the order Tone One, Tone Two, Tone Three, Tone Four, followed by Neutral Tone. For entries consisting of more than one syllable, we go through the first syllable tone by tone before considering the second syllable. For example:

bā	bān
bá	bānjiā
báyuè	bàn(r)
bǎ	bàngōngshì
bà	bāng
ba	bāngmáng
-bǎi	

Capitalization, hyphens (-), apostrophes ('), periods (...), and the optional (**r**) suffix are disregarded for purposes of alphabetization. In the case of two entries with identical spelling, order is determined based on order of introduction in the textbook.

The purpose of this glossary is to refresh your memory of words that have previously been introduced but which you may have forgotten. Since each entry includes the number of the unit and part in the textbook where the item first occurred, you are encouraged to refer back to that part for more detailed information. Do not attempt to learn new words from this glossary; keep in mind that a Chinese word means something only in a certain grammatical and semantic context and that English translations can be misleading.

A
a (pause filler) [P] (11-3)
āiya "gosh" [I] (19-3)
ài (indicates strong sentiment) [I] (16-1)
àihào interest, hobby [N] (20-1)
ānjìng be quiet [SV] (17-3)
ānzhuāng install [V] (24-4)

B
Bāxī Brazil [PW] (21-3)
bǎ (moves object before verb) [CV] (15-3)
bǎ A jiào(zuo) B call A B [PT] (23-2)
báibái "bye-bye" [IE] (17-1)
báicài cabbage [N] (12-3)
bǎifēnzhī... percent [PT] (20-2)
bǎihuò gōngsī department store [PH] (23-2)

bàifǎng pay a formal call on someone [V] (18-4)
bàituō ask someone to do something [V] (18-3)
bānguolai move over [RC] (13-4)
bānyùn transport [V] (21-4)
bàndǎo peninsula [N] (23-1)
bāng help [V] (13-3)
bāngmáng help [VO] (18-3)
bāngzhù help [N/V] (15-1)
bàngqiú baseball [N] (21-1)
bāo wrap [V] (12-4)
bāoguǒ package, parcel [N] (19-4)
bāokuò include [V] (23-1)
bāoqilai wrap up [RC] (12-4)
báo be thin (in dimensions) [SV] (15-3)
báobǐng pancake [N] (15-3)
bǎo be full, satiated [SV] (16-4)

-bǎo full, satiated [RE] (16-4)
bǎocún preserve, keep, maintain [V] (23-2)
bǎohù protect [V] (24-2)
bǎoxiūqī warranty period [N] (24-4)
bǎozhèng guarantee [V] (12-3)
bào newspaper [N] (17-3)
bàogào report [N] (19-2)
bàokān newspapers and periodicals [N] (23-3)
bàotíng newspaper kiosk [PW] (12-2)
bàozhǐ newspaper [N] (12-2)
bēi glass, cup (for beverages) [M] (15-1)
Běijīng Túshūguǎn Beijing Library [PW] (20-4)
bèi (indicates passive); by [CV] (22-2)
bèi time(s) [M] (22-3)

běn(r) (for books, dictionaries) [M] (12-2)

běnlái originally [MA] (13-4)

běnzi notebook [N] (12-2)

bíqilai compare [RC] (13-2)

bǐ compare; to (in contrasting scores) [V] (21-3)

bǐ writing instrument [N] (12-2)

bǐbushàng not be able to compare [RC] (16-4)

bǐfang shuō for example [PH] (21-1)

bǐjìběn diànnǎo notebook computer [PH] (24-4)

bǐjiào compare [V] (23-2)

bǐrú for example [MA] (21-1)

bǐrú shuō for example [PH] (21-1)

bǐsài competition [N] (21-3)

bìyè lùnwén honors thesis [PH] (19-2)

biānhào serial number [N] (11-4)

biànchéng become [V+PV] (23-1)

biàndāng box lunch [N] (16-3)

biànfàn simple meal [N] (16-1)

biànhuà change [N] (22-1)

biāozhǔn level [N] (14-3); be standard [SV] (19-3)

biǎo watch (for telling time) [N] (13-4)

bié kèqi "don't be polite" [IE] (15-4)

biérén another person, others [PR] (17-4)

bīng ice [N] (12-1)

Bīngchéng Penang [PW] (24-3)

bīnggùn(r) ice pop [N] (12-1)

bǐng pancake, biscuit [N] (15-3)

bìng illness, disease [N] (19-1); get sick [V] (19-1)

bìngqiě moreover, furthermore, and [CJ] (23-1)

bófù uncle (father's older brother) [N] (18-1)

bómǔ aunt (wife of father's older brother) [N] (18-1)

bówùguǎn museum [PW] (20-1)

bú dà not very much [PH] (22-1)

bú dào Cháng Chéng fēi hǎohàn "if you don't go to the Great Wall you're not a brave man" [EX] (21-4)

bú shì ma "isn't it?", "isn't that so?" [IE] (24-2)

bú yàojǐn be unimportant; "never mind" [IE] (11-1)

búduànde unceasingly, continuously [A] (21-4)

búyào kèqi "don't be polite" [IE] (16-3)

bǔkè make up a class [VO] (16-1)

bǔxíbān cram school [N] (16-1)

bù step, pace [M] (16-3)

bù (measure for films) [M] (20-3)

bù gǎn dāng "do not dare accept" [IE] (16-2)

bù hǎo yìsi be embarrassing, be embarrassed [PH] (11-2)

bù rú... not be as good as [PT] (16-2)

bù zhīdào (I) wonder [A+V] (13-3)

bùfen part, portion [M] (20-4)

bùguǎn... no matter, regardless [PT] (23-4)

c

cái not until, just [A] (12-3)

cáiliào(r) material [N] (21-4)

cài vegetable [N] (12-3); dish of food [N] (14-1)

Cài Cai [SN] (18-3)

càichǎng market [N] (12-3)

càidān(r) menu [N] (14-1)

cānguān visit [V] (20-1)

cānjiā take part in [V] (14-3)

cāntīng dining room; dining hall, restaurant [PW] (16-4)

cānzhuō dining table [N] (17-4)

cánrěn be cruel [SV] (24-2)

cāozuò operate, manipulate [V] (24-4)

cāozuò xìtǒng operating system [PH] (24-4)

Cáo Cao [SN] (21-3)

cǎo grass [N] (17-4)

chāshāobāo steamed bun [N] (23-2)

chāzi fork [N] (14-1)

chá tea [N] (16-4)

chàbuduō about the same [PH] (13-1)

chǎnpǐn product [N] (23-2)

cháng taste [V] (15-2)

chángjiàn be commonly seen, common [SV] (24-2)

chángkù long pants [N] (13-4)

chǎng showing (measure for movies) [M] (20-3)

chàng sing [V] (20-1)

chànggē(r) sing a song [VO] (20-1)

chāoshì supermarket [N] (13-2)

chǎo be noisy [SV] (17-3)

chǎofàn fried rice [N] (14-4)

chǎomiàn fried noodles [N] (14-4)

chēhuò car accident [N] (22-4)

chénpǎo jog in the morning [V] (21-1)

chènshān shirt [N] (13-4)

chēng weigh, weigh out [V] (13-1)

-chēng fill to the point of bursting [RE] (16-4)

chéng become, turn into [V] (22-4)

chénggōng succeed [V] (21-1)

chéngjī grade (on test or in course) [N] (19-2)

chéngwéi become [V] (23-1)

chībǎo eat one's fill [RC] (16-4)

chībuxià can't eat [RC] (15-3)

chīchēng eat until one bursts [RC] (16-4)

chīdào succeed in eating [RC] (16-3)

chīdelái can or like to eat something [RC] (15-2)

chīguàn be used to eating something [RC] (15-2)

chīsù eat vegetarian food [VO] (13-1)

Chóngqìng Chongqing (city in Sichuan) [PW] (11-1)

Chóngqìng Nán Lù Chongqing South Road [PW] (11-1)

chōukòng find time (to do something) [VO] (18-3)

chōuyān smoke [VO] (18-3)

chūkǒu export [V/N] (12-3); exit [PW] (13-2)

-chūqu out [RE] (17-3)

chúfáng kitchen [PW] (17-3)

chúle...yǐwài besides, except for [PT] (15-4)

chúle...zhīwài besides, except for [PT] (15-4)

chúzhípiào stored-value ticket [N] (11-2)

chuān put on, wear (shoes, socks, clothes) [V] (13-3)

chuántǒng be traditional [SV] (23-2)

chuánzhēn facsimile, FAX [N] (17-2)

chuānghu window [N] (17-3)

chuáng bed [N] (17-4)

chuànglì found, create, establish [V] (24-1)

chūnjià spring vacation [N] (21-2)

cíhuì vocabulary [N] (19-3)

cǐdì this place, here [PW] (24-1)

cì fish bone [N] (16-1)

cōng scallion [N] (15-3)

cóng...qǐ starting from..., beginning from... [PT] (11-4)

cónglái all along, always [A] (20-4)

cónglái méi...-guo have never ever... before [PT] (20-4)

cuì be crisp [SV] (12-3)

cuò error, mistake [N] (22-3)

cuòguo miss [RC] (11-3)

D

dáfù answer, reply [N] (18-4)

dǎ play (a sport) [V] (21-1)

dǎ duìzhé give a 50% discount [PH] (13-4)

dǎ tàijíquán practice taiji [PH] (21-1)

dǎqiú play a ball game [VO] (21-1)

dǎrǎo disturb [V] (18-4)

dǎsuan plan [AV/V] (14-3)

dǎtīng inquire [V] (18-4)

dǎtīngdào inquire and find out [RC] (18-4)

dǎzhé give a discount [VO] (13-4)

dà bùfen greater part, majority, most [PH] (20-4)

dà duōshù great majority [PH] (24-3)

dà shēng in a loud voice [PH] (17-3)

dà xióngmāo giant panda [PH] (24-2)

dàhòunián year after next [TW] (24-2)

dàjiā everybody, everyone [PR] (15-1)

dàlù mainland [PW] (11-1)

dà-pái-cháng-lóng form a long line [EX] (11-4)

dàsǎo wife of oldest brother [N] (16-3)

dàshǐ ambassador [N] (18-2)

dà-tóng-xiǎo-yì be largely the same [EX] (24-1)

dàxiǎo size [N] (13-3)

dàzhì generally, for the most part [A] (23-4)

dàzìrán nature [N] (24-2)

dāi stay [V] (18-1)

dāibuzhù not be able to stay [RC] (18-1)

dài put on, wear (watch, hat, jewelry) [V] (13-4)

dài take the place of [V] (16-4); for [CV] (19-4)

dài A xiàng B wènhǎo on behalf of A convey regards to B [PT] (19-4)

dàifu doctor [N] (22-1)

dàikè teach in place of someone [VO] (16-4)

dàiyǒu carry, bear [V] (24-1)

dānwu delay, get held up [V] (22-4)

dàn egg [N] (14-1)

dàn but [CJ] (15-2)

dàntǎ egg tart [N] (23-4)

dāng serve as, work as, act as [V] (20-3)

dāngshí at that time, then [TW] (23-1)

Dàngzǎi Taipa (island in Macao) [PW] (23-4)

dāozi knife [N] (14-1)

dǎo island [N] (23-1)

dǎoméi be out of luck [SV] (22-4)

dǎoyǎn director [N] (20-4)

dǎoyǔ island [N] (23-1)

dào (for courses of food) [M] (14-4)

dào on the contrary, but [A] (22-4)

dàobǎn pirate (a book, film, etc.) [V] (23-2)

dàodǐ(r) after all, really [MA] (21-4)

dàole...dìbù reach the point where [PT] (24-2)

dàoshi actually, contrariwise [A] (21-1)

...déle and that will do [PT] (22-4)

-de (adverbial marker) [P] (15-1)

dēng climb [V] (21-4)

dēngshang climb onto [RC] (21-4)

děng and so on, et cetera [BF] (24-3)

děng... as soon as, once [PT] (17-2)

děng huǐr in a little while [PH] (18-2)

děngbují can't wait [RC] (23-1)

Dèng Deng [SN] (17-4)

dìbù point, situation, condition [N] (24-2)

dìguózhǔyìzhě imperialist [N] (23-4)

dìlǐ geography [N] (23-4)

dìtiě subway [N] (11-2)

dìtú map [N] (12-2)

diǎn count, check [V] (12-4); order, choose [V] (14-1)

...diǎn... (for decimals) [PT] (20-2)

diǎncài order dishes of food [VO] (14-1)

diǎnxin snack, pastry, dim sum [N] (23-2)

diàn shop, store [N] (11-3)

diàn electricity [N] (17-4)

diànfèi electricity fee [N] (17-4)

diànshì television [N] (21-3)

diànshì jiémù television program [PH] (21-3)

diànshìtái television station [N] (21-3)

diànyǐng(r) movie [N] (20-3)

diànyǐng míngxīng movie star [PH] (20-4)

diànyǐngyuàn movie theater [PW] (20-3)

diànzǐ chǎnpǐn electronic product, electronics [PH] (23-2)

diào fall, drop [V] (22-2); lose [V] (22-3)

-diào away [RE] (22-2)

diàozi tune, melody [N] (20-1)

Dīng Ding [SN] (19-3)

dìng reserve, book [V] (14-3); settle, decide on [V] (17-1)

-dìng fixed, settled [RE] (22-4)

dìnggòu order [V] (24-4)

diū lose [V] (22-3)

Dōngběi the Northeast, Manchuria [PW] (14-4)

Dōngnányà Southeast Asia [PW] (23-4)

dòng (for buildings) [M] (11-3)

dòng hole [N] (22-4)

dòufu tofu [N] (14-1)

dú study; read aloud [V] (12-1)

dúchuàng create as something unique [V] (23-4)

dúlì be independent [SV] (24-3)

dúshū study [VO] (12-1)

dǔbó gamble [V] (23-4)

dǔbóyè gambling industry [N] (23-4)

dǔchǎng casino [PW] (23-4)

dùzi belly, abdomen, stomach [N] (23-2)

duǎn be short (not long) [SV] (13-4)

duǎnkù short pants [N] (13-4)

duànnǎi wean [VO] (24-2)

duì to, toward [CV] (14-4); pair off against [V] (21-3)

duì team [N] (21-1)

duì (for pairs) [M] (24-2)

duì-dá-rú-liú reply to questions fluently [EX] (19-3)

duì...gǎn xìngqu be interested in... [PT] (17-1)

duì...lái shuō as regards [PT] (21-2)

duì...shúxi be familiar with... [PT] (14-4)

duì...yǒu xìngqu be interested in... [PT] (17-1)

duìmiàn across [PW] (11-2)

duìzhé 50% discount [N] (13-4)

dùn (for meals) [M] (16-1)

duō kuī be thanks to [PH] (19-3)

duō xiè "many thanks" [IE] (12-3)

duōméitǐ multimedia [N] (24-4)

duōmínzú multi-ethnic [AT] (24-3)

duōshù majority [N] (24-3)

duōyuán diverse [AT] (24-3)

duǒ dodge, avoid [V] (22-4)

E

ěxin be nauseous, feel like vomiting [SV] (22-1)

è be hungry [SV] (15-4)

èi "yeah" [I] (11-4)

ér and, moreover [CJ] (23-4)

F

fādá be developed [SV] (23-2)

fāpiào itemized bill; receipt [N] (13-4)

fāshāo have a fever [VO] (22-1)

fāshēng happen [V] (22-4)

fāyīn pronunciation [N] (19-3)

fānqié tomato [N] (12-3)

fántǐzì traditional characters [N] (23-3)

fànguǎn(r) restaurant [PW] (14-1)

fànwǎn rice bowl [N] (14-1)

fāngbian be convenient [SV] (17-4)

fāngmiàn aspect, area, side [N] (23-2)

fāngyán dialect [N] (24-1)

fángzi house [N] (11-3)

fángzū rent [N] (17-4)

fàng put, place [V] (14-2)

fàngjià take a vacation [VO] (21-2)

fàngshang put on [RC] (15-3)

fàngxīn be at ease, relax [VO] (11-1)

fàngzai put in, put on [V+PV] (15-3)

fēi...bù kě must [PT] (22-2)

fēicháng extremely [A] (15-1)

Fēilǜbīn The Philippines [PW] (23-1)

fēixīyān qū non-smoking section [PH] (18-3)

Fēizhōu Africa [PW] (23-4)

féi be fatty (of food) [SV] (13-1)

fèi lung [N] (22-1)

fèiyán pneumonia [N] (22-1)

fēn divide, separate [V] (14-3); part, fraction [M] (20-2)

fēnchéng divide into [V+PV] (14-3)

fēnjī extension [N] (17-2)

fēnqī fùkuǎn pay by installments [PH] (24-4)

...fēnzhī... (for fractions) [PT] (20-2)

fèn(r) (for newspapers, magazines) [M] (12-2)

fēngfù be abundant [SV] (15-3)

fēngshèng be sumptuous [SV] (16-4)

fēngshuǐ feng shui, geomancy [N] (23-2)

fēngwèi(r) special local flavor [N] (14-4)

fūren madam, lady [N] (15-1)

fúwùyuán attendant, waiter, waitress [N] (16-1)

fù pay [V] (16-1)

fùjìn in the vicinity, nearby [PW] (13-1)

fùkuǎn pay a sum of money, pay [VO] (24-4)

fùqián pay money [VO] (16-1)

G

gālí curry [N] (23-4)

gǎi change [V] (16-1)

gǎitiān on some other day [TW] (16-1)

gānbēi drink a toast [VO] (15-2); "Cheers!", "Bottoms up" [IE] (15-2)

gǎn dare to [AV] (16-2)

gǎn feel [V] (17-1); touch, move (emotionally) [V] (20-4)

gǎnkuài quickly [A] (22-2)

gǎnmào catch cold [V] (22-1)

gǎnxiè thank [V] (15-1)

gàn do [V] (20-3)

gāngcái just now, just [TW] (16-1)

gānghǎo just, as it happens [MA] (13-4)

gāngqín piano [N] (20-1)

gāngqínjiā pianist [N] (20-3)

gāodù high degree [AT] (23-1)

gāogēn(r)xié high-heeled shoes [N] (13-3)

gāojí be high-class [SV] (14-3)

gāojū be high (in rank) [V] (23-4)

gàobié bid farewell, take leave [V] (19-3)

gàocí take leave [V] (18-4)

gàosu tell [V] (11-3)

gē(r) song [N] (20-1)

gébì next door [PW] (12-2)

gè- each, every [SP] (15-2)

gèzi height, stature, build [N] (21-1)

...gēn...bǐqǐlái comparing A and B [PT] (13-2)

...gēn...yíyàng A is the same as B [PT] (13-3)

gēn...jiǎng tell (someone something) [PT] (11-3)

gēn...shuō tell (someone something) [PT] (11-3)

gēn...yǒuguān be related to [PT] (23-3)

gēn(r) (for long and thin things) [M] (12-1)

gōngchē public bus [N] (11-2)

gōngchǐ meter [M] (11-3)

gōngfū kung fu [N] (21-1)

gōngfu time [N] (19-1)

gōngjìng bù rú cóng mìng "to show respect is not as good as following orders" [EX] (16-2)

gōnglǐ kilometer [M] (21-4)

gōnglì public [AT] (23-3)

gōnglì xuéxiào public school [PH] (23-3)

gōngnéng function, feature [N] (24-4)

gōngshēng liter [M] (11-4)

gōngyòng public [AT] (11-3)

gōngyòng cèsuǒ public toilet [PH] (11-3)

gōngyòng diànhuà public telephone [PH] (11-3)

gōngyuán park (piece of ground) [PW] (21-1)

gōngyù apartment [N] (17-3)

gōngzuò yǔyán working language [PH] (24-1)

gònghéguó republic [N] (20-2)

gòngxiàn contribution [N] (24-1)

gòu be enough [SV/A] (14-1); reach [V] (16-3)

gòu...-de quite... , rather... [PT] (21-4)

gòubuzháo be unable to reach [RC] (16-3)

gòudezháo be able to reach [RC] (16-3)

gòuwù buy things, shop [V] (23-2)

gòuwùzhě one who buys things, shopper [N] (23-2)

gūjì reckon, estimate [V] (14-3)

gǔshì stock market, stock exchange [N] (23-2)

gùshi story [N] (20-3)

guā scrape [V] (18-1)

guā húzi shave [PH] (18-1)

guà hang, hang up [V] (17-2)

guài...-de quite, rather [PT] (22-4)

guàibudé no wonder [MA] (20-1)

guānfāng official [AT] (23-3)

guānfāng yǔyán official language [PH] (23-3)

guānshuì customs duty [N] (23-2)

guānxi relationship, connection [N] (18-3)

guānyú about, concerning [CV] (19-2)

guǎnlǐ manage, administer, control [V] (24-2)

guǎnzi restaurant [PW] (16-4)

-guàn be used to [RE] (15-2)

guāng only, just [A] (23-2)

guǎnggào advertisement [N] (17-3)

guìtái counter [N] (13-2)

guófáng national defense [N] (23-1)

guóhuà(r) Chinese painting [N] (20-1)

guójì international [AT] (17-1)

Guójì Jùlèbù International Club [PW] (17-1)

guójiā country [N] (22-3)

Guóyǔ Mandarin (language) [N] (11-1)

Guóyǔ Zhōngxīn Mandarin Center [PW] (22-2)

guǒzhī juice [N] (16-4)

-guò (indicates motion past or by) [RE] (11-3)

guò mǎlù cross the road [PH] (22-4)

guòlai come over [RC] (13-4)

-guòlai (movement from there to here) [RE] (13-4)

guòqu go over, pass by [RC] (13-4)

-guòqu (movement from here to there) [RE] (13-4)

-guo (expresses completed action) [P] (16-1)

H

ha ha (sound of laughter) [I] (23-4)

hái bú shi... if it isn't... [PT] (19-1)

háishi or [CJ] (12-1)

hǎi ocean, sea [N] (16-2)

hǎiliàng great capacity for drinking alcohol [IE] (16-2)

hài "hi" [I] (16-1); (indicates exasperation) [I] (17-1)

hánjià winter vacation [N] (21-2)

hàn with [CV] (13-2); and [CJ] (21-1)

Hàn-Yīng Chinese-English [AT] (12-2)

hǎo very [A] (11-2)

hǎo lei "all right," "O.K." [IE] (14-2)

-hǎo so that something is good [RE] (12-1)

hǎohàn brave man [N] (21-4)

hǎole "all right," "O.K." [IE] (11-4)

hǎotīng be nice-sounding, pretty [SV] (20-1)

hàomǎ(r) number [N] (13-3)

hē drink [V] (14-2)

hēzuì get drunk [RC] (15-2)

hé river [N] (16-2)

héfǎ be legal [SV] (23-4)

héshì be the right size, fit [SV] (13-4)

hésuàn be worthwhile [SV] (22-4)

hēng hum [V] (20-1)

hóng xīngxing orangutan [PH] (24-2)

hóuzi monkey [N] (24-2)

hòu be thick [SV] (15-3)

...hòu after [PT] (19-4)

hòubànqī latter half [TW] (23-4)

hú lake [N] (16-2)

húzi beard, moustache [N] (18-1)

hútòng(r) alley [N] (13-1)

hùzhào passport [N] (22-2)

huā spend (money, time) [V] (19-1)

huā(r) flower [N] (17-4)

huāqián spend money [VO] (19-1)

Huárén Chinese person, Chinese [N] (24-1)

Huáshè Chinese community [N] (24-3)

Huáwén Chinese language [N] (24-3)

Huáyǔ Chinese language [N] (24-1)

huà paint [V] (20-1)

huà(r) painting [N] (20-1)

huàhuà(r) paint paintings [VO] (20-1)

huàjiā painter (artist) [N] (20-3)

huài be bad [SV] (17-1)

-huài be bad [RE] (17-1)

huānyíng guānglín "welcome" [IE] (11-4)

huán give back [V] (22-3)

huángěi give back to [V+PV] (22-3)

huánjìng environment, surroundings [N] (24-2)

huídào come back to [V+PV] (16-2)

huíguī revert, return to [V] (23-1)

huílai come back [RC] (16-2)

-huílai come back [RE] (22-2)

huíqu go back [RC] (16-2)

-huíqu go back [RE] (22-2)

huí-wèi-wú-qióng "savor the aftertaste a long time" [EX] (23-4)

huì gathering, meeting [N] (17-1)

huì...-de be likely to, would, will [PT] (13-2)

húnshēn entire body [N] (22-1)

huò or [CJ] (11-2)

huòshi or [CJ] (11-2)

J

jī chicken [N] (13-1)

jīběn basic, fundamental [AT] (23-3)

jīběnshang basically [MA] (23-3)

jīdàn chicken egg [N] (14-1)

jīdàn tāng egg soup [PH] (14-1)

jīròu chicken meat [N] (13-1)

jí be in a hurry [SV] (18-1); be worried, anxious [SV] (22-2)

-jíle extremely [PT] (13-1)

jíshì(r) urgent matter [N] (14-2)

jì record [V] (17-2)

jì send [V] (19-4)

jì...zhīhòu follow [PT] (23-4)

jìchéngchē taxi [N] (11-1)

jìgěi send to [V+PV] (19-4)

jìhua plan [N/AV] (20-3)

jìlǜ discipline [N] (24-3)

jìrán since [MA] (18-2)

jìrán...jiù... since... [PT] (18-2)

jìxialai write down, note down [RC] (17-2)

jiā pick up (with chopsticks) [V] (15-3)

jiācài pick up food (with chopsticks) [VO] (15-3)

jiācháng cài home-style cooking [PH] (16-4)

jiājù furniture [N] (11-3)

jiājù diàn furniture store [PH] (11-3)

jiāmǎn fill up [RC] (11-4)

jiārù join [V] (21-2)

jiāyóu add gasoline, buy gas [VO] (11-4)

jiāyóuzhàn gasoline station [PW] (11-4)

jiǎrú if [MA] (13-4)

jiǎrú...-de huà if... [PT] (13-4)

jià vacation, leave [N] (21-2)

jiàqián price [N] (11-4)

jiàrì holiday, day off [N] (21-2)

jiān (for rooms) [M] (17-3)

jiǎn cut [V] (17-4)

jiǎn pick up [V] (22-3)

jiǎncǎo mow the lawn [VO] (17-4)

jiǎnchá inspect, examine [V] (22-3)

jiǎndān be simple [SV] (15-1)

jiǎndào pick up [RC] (22-3)

jiǎntǐzì simplified characters [N] (23-3)

jiàn see [V] (11-2)

-jiàn see, perceive [RE] (12-4)

jiàn build [V] (21-4)

jiànkāng health [N] (15-2)

jiāng ginger [N] (15-4)

jiāng will, would (formal style) [AV] (24-2)

jiāngjìn be close to, nearly be, almost be [V] (24-1)

jiānglái in the future [TW] (20-3)

jiǎng tell the story of, be about [V] (20-3)

jiǎng gùshi tell a story [PH] (20-3)

jiǎngjià bargain, haggle [VO] (23-2)

jiàng thick sauce [N] (15-3)

jiàngyóu soy sauce [N] (15-4)

jiāohuì connect up, meet, intersect [V] (23-2)

jiāowài countryside around a city [PW] (21-2)

jiāoxué teach [V] (23-3)

jiǎozi dumpling [N] (15-4)

jiào make, cause [V] (23-4)

jiàoshì classroom [N] (17-4)

jiào-xué-yǒu-fāng have an effective method in teaching [EX] (19-4)

jiàoyù education [N] (21-2)

jiàoyù shuǐpíng educational level [PH] (23-3)

jiàozuo call; be called, be known as [V] (23-2)

jiē street [N] (18-2)

jiēfēng give a welcome dinner [VO] (16-2)

jiéguǒ result [N] (19-4); as a result [CJ] (22-4)

jiémù program [N] (21-3)

jiéshěng save [V] (13-2); be frugal [SV] (13-2)

jiéyùn mass rapid transit, MRT [N] (11-2)

jiějué solve [V] (11-1)

jiè borrow; lend [V] (22-3)

jièshūzhèng library card [N] (22-3)

jīn catty (unit of weight) [M] (12-3)

jīnróng finance [N] (23-2)

jǐn only [A] (15-3)

jìn carry out, fulfill [V] (19-4)

jìn(r) energy [N] (22-1)

jìnbù progress [V/N] (19-4)

jìnkǒu import [V/N] (12-3)

jìnlì do one's best [VO] (18-4)

jìnliàng to the best of one's ability [A] (18-4)

jīngjì economy [N] (23-1)

Jīngjù Peking opera [N] (20-2)

jǐngchájú police station [PW] (22-2)

jìng toast, drink to [V] (15-1)

jiǔ liquor [N] (14-2)

Jiǔlóng Kowloon [PW] (23-1)

Jiǔlóng bàndǎo Kowloon Peninsula [PW] (23-1)

jiǔlóu Cantonese-style restaurant [PW] (23-2)

jiǔwén have heard of for a long time [IE] (23-4)

jiǔxí banquet [N] (14-3)

...jiù shì just, simply [PT] (18-4)

jiùmìng "help!" [IE] (22-3)

jūmín resident, inhabitant [N] (23-4)

júzi orange [N] (12-4)

jù sentence, phrase [M] (15-1)

jù wǒ suǒzhī "according to what I know" [PH] (24-1)

jùcān get together for a meal [VO] (15-1)

jùchǎng theater [PW] (20-2)

jùlèbù club [PW] (17-1)

jùzi sentence [N] (15-1)

juánqilai roll up [RC] (15-3)

juǎn roll up [V] (15-3)

juézhǒng become extinct, die out [V] (24-2)

K

kāfēi coffee [N] (13-2)

kāi turn on (a machine, light) [V] (21-3)

kāihuì hold or attend a meeting [VO] (17-2)

kāiwán finish holding (a meeting) [RC] (17-2)

kāiyǎn begin to be shown (of a film) [V] (20-4)

kàn consider, think [V] (11-4); call on, visit [V] (18-3)

kàn diànshì watch television [PH] (21-3)

kànbìng see a doctor [VO] (22-1)

kàndào see [RC] (11-3)

kànjian see [RC] (12-4)

kànshū read [VO] (20-1)

kǎo bake, roast [V] (15-2)

kǎo take a test [V] (19-1)

kǎoshì test [N/VO] (19-1)

kǎoyā roast duck [N] (15-2)

kǎoyūn become dizzy from testing [RC] (19-1)

kào depend on [V] (21-4)

kē school subject, branch of study [N] (24-3)

kě be thirsty [SV] (15-4)

kě bu shì "that's for sure" [IE] (21-4)

kělè cola [N] (16-4)

kěnéng possibility [N] (23-3)

kěxī be a shame, be a pity, regrettable [SV] (24-2)

kèqi be polite [SV] (15-4)

kèrén guest [N] (15-2)

kètīng living room [PW] (16-4)

kōngtiáo air conditioning [N] (17-3)

kòng(r) free time [N] (17-1)

kǒu mouth; opening [N] (23-4)

kūlong hole [N] (22-4)

kūzào be dull, dry, uninteresting [SV] (24-3)

kǔ be bitter [SV] (14-2)

kùzi pants [N] (13-4)

kuàilè be happy [SV] (15-1)

kuàizi chopsticks [N] (14-1)

kuān be wide [SV] (21-4)

kuòjiàn expand [V] (21-4)

L

là be peppery hot [SV] (14-2)

làjiāo hot pepper [N] (14-2)

la (combined form of **le** and **a**) [P] (11-1)

lái bring, give [V] (12-4); (indicates one is about to do something) [AV] (15-1); (verb substitute) [V] (15-2)

-lái (indicates motion toward the speaker) [RE] (11-3)

-lái...-qù VERB all over the place [PT] (11-3)

lái diànhuà call on the telephone [PH] (19-2)

láiwǎn come late [RC] (18-3)

láixìn send a letter [VO] (19-4)

láiyuán source, origin [N] (23-4)

lánqiú basketball [N] (21-1)

lǎo be tough (of food) [SV] (16-1); very [A] (16-4)

lǎo zǎo very early, for a long time now [PH] (23-4)

lǎohǔ tiger [N] (24-2)

lǎonián old age [N] (21-2)

lǎonián rén old people [PH] (21-2)

le (indicates action continuing up to the present) [P] (11-1)

lèi kind, type, category [M] (20-4)

lei (sentence final particle) [P] (14-2)

lěngpán(r) cold dish [N] (14-4)

lí(r) pear [N] (12-3)

Lí Shān "Pear Mountain," Li Shan [PW] (12-3)

lídǎo offshore island [N] (23-4)

lǐjiě understand [V] (20-4)

lìdài successive dynasties [N] (21-4)

lìkè immediately [A] (17-3)

lìshǐ history [N] (23-1)

lián even [CV] (19-3)

lián...dōu... even [PT] (19-3)

liánxì contact [V] (14-4)

liánxùjù soap opera, serial [N] (21-3)

liǎng ounce (50 grams) [M] (14-2)

liàng qiǎn little capacity for drinking alcohol [IE] (16-2)

-liǎo be able to [RE] (14-2)

Línjí Ringgit (Malaysian currency) [M] (24-4)

línshí at the time when something happens [A] (18-3)

lìng- another [SP] (23-4)

lìngwài in addition [MA] (17-4)

liú ask someone to stay [V] (19-4)

Liú Liu [SN] (17-1)

liú húzi grow a beard or moustache [PH] (18-1)

liúbù "don't bother to see me out" [IE] (18-4)

liúhuà(r) leave a message [VO] (17-2)

liúlì be fluent [SV] (19-3)

liúxià leave behind [RC] (14-4)

lóngzi cage [N] (24-2)

lóushàng upstairs [PW] (20-4)

lóuxià downstairs [PW] (20-4)

Lùhuán Coloane (island in Macao) [PW] (23-4)

lùtiān shìchǎng open-air market [PH] (23-2)

lǚxíng travel [V] (17-2); trip [N] (17-2)

lǚxíngshè travel agency [PW] (17-2)

lǚyóu tour [V] (23-4)

lǚyóuyè tourism industry [N] (23-4)

lùnwén thesis, dissertation [N] (19-2)

M

máfan be troublesome [SV] (18-2); trouble [N] (19-3)

Málà Zábànr Sesame Hot Spicy Medley [PH] (16-3)

mámahūhū so-so, fair [IE] (19-2)

Mápó Dòufu Pockmarked Old Woman's Tofu [PH] (14-1)

mǎ horse [N] (22-4)

Mǎlái Malay [AT] (24-3)

Mǎláiyǔ Malay language [N] (24-1)

mǎlù road [N] (22-4)

mǎyǐ ant [N] (14-1)

Mǎyǐ Shàng Shù Ants Climbing a Tree [PH] (14-1)

mà scold, curse [V] (22-2)

mǎidān pay the check, figure up the bill [IE] (16-1)

màiwán finish selling, be sold out [RC] (11-2)

mán...-de quite [PT] (16-1)

mántou steamed bun [N] (14-2)

mǎn be full [SV] (11-4); reach age or time limit [V] (14-2)

-mǎn full [RE] (11-4)

màn be slow [SV] (11-1)

màn yòng "take your time eating" [IE] (16-3)

mànmān lái "take one's time" [IE] (13-2)

máng be busy with (something) [V] (18-1)

mánghuài extremely busy [RC] (17-1)

máo feather, hair (on body), fur [N] (21-1)

màopái counterfeit, fake, imitation [AT] (23-2)

Méi Mei [SN] (21-4)

méi cuò "that's right" [IE] (22-3)

méi shémme "you're welcome" [IE] (22-3)

méi wèntí "no problem" [IE] (11-1)

méijièyǔ language or medium of instruction [N] (24-3)

méiyou yòng not have any use [PH] (20-2)

měishí fine foods, delicacy [N] (23-2)

měishí tiāntáng food heaven [PH] (23-2)

mén (for courses) [M] (19-2)

ménqiánqīng drink up alcohol before leaving [EX] (16-4)

mèng dream [N] (11-2)

mǐ rice (uncooked) [N] (14-2)

mǐfàn rice (cooked) [N] (14-2)

mìdù density [N] (23-4)

miǎnde... so as to avoid, lest [PT] (23-2)

miǎnqiǎng do with great effort, force [V] (18-4)

miǎnshuì be exempt from tax or duty [VO] (23-2)

miǎnshuìgǎng duty free port [N] (23-2)

miàn flour; pasta, noodles [N] (15-3)

miànbāo bread [N] (13-1)

miànbāo diàn bakery [PH] (13-1)

miànji area [N] (23-1)

miànlín face, be faced with [V] (24-2)

miào temple, shrine [N] (11-3)

míng jiào be named [PH] (20-3)

míngbai understand [V] (20-4)

-míngbai understand [RE] (20-4)

míng-bù-xū-chuán have a well deserved reputation [EX] (21-4)

míngcài famous dish, famous food [N] (23-4)

Míngcháo Ming Dynasty [TW] (21-4)

míngxìnpiàn picture postcard [N] (19-4)

mótuōchē motorcycle [N] (11-4)

Mò Mo [SN] (15-1)

mǔyǔ native language [N] (23-3)

mǔyǔ jiàoyù education in one's native language [PH] (23-3)

mùqián at present, currently [TW] (24-2)

Mùzhà Muzha (suburb of Taipei) [PW] (11-2)

N

ná hold, take [V] (12-1)

náguoqu take over [RC] (13-4)

náhǎo hold well, hold firmly [RC] (12-1)

nálai bring here [RC] (13-4)

náqu take away [RC] (13-4)

náshanglai take up (to speaker) [RC] (17-2)

náshangqu take up (away from speaker) [RC] (17-2)

náxiaqu take down (away from speaker) [RC] (17-2)

nǎxiē which ones, which [QW+M] (21-1)

nǎiyóu cream [N] (12-1)

nándào... don't tell me that [PT] (21-2)

Nánjīng Tiáoyuē Treaty of Nanking [PH] (23-1)

nánnǚ tóngxiào coeducation [PH] (24-3)

nào suffer (from an illness) [V] (22-1)

nàobuhǎo suffer from illness and not get better [RC] (22-1)

nǎrde huà "not at all" [IE] (19-4)

nèirén one's wife (polite) [N] (16-3)

nèiróng content [N] (20-4)

nèixiē those [SP+M] (22-2)

nèn be tender [SV] (16-1)

niándài decade [N] (20-3)

niánlíng age [N] (23-4)

niánlíng xiànzhì age limit [PH] (23-4)

niánqīng rén young people [PH] (21-2)

niànshū study [VO] (12-1)

nìngyuàn would rather, prefer to [AV] (24-4)

niú cow, ox [N] (13-1)

Niú Niu (lit. "cow") [SN] (18-1)

niúròu beef [N] (13-1)

nòng do, make [V] (18-2)

nònghǎo fix, prepare, finish [RC] (18-2)

nǚxiào girls' school [N] (24-3)

O

ó (indicates interest or excitement) [P] (11-1)

ǒu'ěr once in a while, occasionally [MA] (21-1)

P

pà fear [V] (14-2)

pái row [M] (20-4)

páimíng be ranked, rank [VO] (23-2)

pánzi dish, plate [N] (14-4)

pǎo run [V] (19-1)

pǎobù run paces, run [VO] (19-1)

pǎodào run to [V+PV] (22-2)

pǎodiào run away [RC] (22-2)

pǎohuíqu run back [RC] (22-2)

pǎolái run over here, come over [RC] (19-1)

pǎoqù run over there [RC] (19-1)

pàochá steep tea, make tea [VO] (18-3)

péi compensate, pay damages [V] (22-4)

péizhí cultivate (plants or human talent) [V] (24-1)

pèi coordinate, arrange [V] (14-4)

pèngmiàn meet (face-to-face) [VO] (21-2)

píbāo purse [N] (22-2)

píjiǔ beer [N] (14-2)

piān (for theses, reports, essays) [M] (19-2)

piānzi film, movie [N] (20-3)

piàn trick, deceive [V] (22-2)

piàoliang be pretty, look nice [SV] (12-3)

píndào channel [N] (21-3)

pǐncháng taste, sample [V] (23-4)

pīngpāngqiú Ping-Pong [N] (21-1)

píng(r) bottle [M] (14-2)

píng (unit of area, 36 sq. ft.) [M] (17-3)

píng be flat, even; tied (of scores) [SV] (21-3)

píngfāng square [AT] (23-1)

píngfāng gōnglǐ square kilometer [PH] (23-1)

píngguǒ apple [N] (12-4)

píngjūn average, mean [AT] (23-4)

píngjūn shòumìng average life expectancy [PH] (23-4)

píngzi bottle [N] (14-2)

pò break, tear [V] (22-4)

pòfèi go to great expense [V] (16-1)

pòhuài destroy, damage [V] (24-2)

Pú'ào Portuguese-Macanese [AT] (23-4)

Pútáoyá Portugal [PW] (23-4)

pútao grape [N] (12-4)

pǔbiàn be widespread, common [SV] (13-2)

Q

qīmò kǎoshì final examination [PH] (19-1)

qīzhōng kǎoshì mid-term examination [PH] (19-1)

qí ride, straddle (bicycle, motorcycle, horse, etc.) [V] (11-4)

qíguài be strange [SV] (11-2)

qíyú other, the remaining, the rest [AT] (24-1)

qízhōng among which, within which [PW] (23-1)

qǐdào...zuòyong have a...function or effect [PT] (24-2)

qǐlái get up [RC] (21-2)

-qǐlái (general resultative ending) (12-4)

qìshuǐ(r) soda [N] (16-4)

qìwēn temperature [N] (22-1)

qìyóu gasoline [N] (11-4)

qiān sign [V] (24-2)

qiānbǐ pencil [N] (12-2)

qiāndìng sign [V] (23-1)

qiānmíng sign one's name [VO] (22-3)

qiānyuē sign a lease [VO] (17-4)

qiánbāo wallet [N] (22-2)

qiǎn be shallow [SV] (16-2)

qiāng accent, intonation [N] (23-3)

qiáng wall [N] (17-4)

qiáng be strong [SV] (21-3)

qiángdà be powerful [SV] (24-4)

qiáo look [V] (22-4)

qiē cut, slice [V] (13-1)

qíncài Chinese celery [N] (12-3)

qīngcài green vegetable [N] (12-3)

-qīngchu clear [RE] (17-3)

qīngsōng be relaxed, easy [SV] (23-4)

qǐng shāo hòu "please wait briefly" [IE] (13-4)

qǐngjià request leave [VO] (21-2)

qǐngkè treat (someone to something) [VO] (16-1)

qióng be poor [SV] (12-4)

qiú ball [N] (21-1)

qū area, region [N] (18-3)

quánqiú the whole world, the entire globe [N] (24-1)

quēshǎo lack, be short of [V] (24-3)

qúnzi skirt [N] (13-4)

R

rèdài the tropics [N] (24-1)

réngōng human labor, manual labor [N] (21-4)

rénkǒu mìdù population density [PH] (23-4)

rénmín people [N] (20-2)

Rénmín Jùchǎng People's Theater [PW] (20-2)

Rénmínbì RMB (PRC currency) [N] (22-3)

rì day of the month (formal style) [M] (23-4)

rónghé mix together, merge, fuse [V] (23-2)

róuhé mix together [V] (23-4)

ròu meat [N] (13-1)

ròuguì cinnamon [N] (23-4)

ròusī(r) meat shred [N] (14-1)

rùchǎng enter; be admitted [VO] (23-4)

rùkǒu(r) entrance [PW] (13-2)

ruǎnjiàn software [N] (24-4)

ruò be weak [SV] (21-3)

S

sè xiāng wèir jùquán "color, aroma, and taste are all complete" [EX] (16-4)

shāfā sofa [N] (17-4)

shālā salad [N] (12-3)

shālācài lettuce [N] (12-3)

shāngdiàn shop, store [PW] (23-2)

shāngpǐn goods, merchandise [N] (23-2)

shàngcài bring food to a table [VO] (14-2)

shàngjiē go out on the street [VO] (18-2)

shànglai come up [RC] (17-2)

-shànglai up [RE] (17-2)

shànglóu go upstairs [VO] (18-4)

shàngqu go up [RC] (17-2)

-shàngqu up [RE] (17-2)

shàngshì come on the market [VO] (13-3)

shàngwǎng go online, get on the Internet [VO] (24-4)

shàngyǎn begin to play (of a film at a theater) [V] (20-3)

shāomài steamed dumpling [N] (23-2)

shāowēi somewhat, slightly [A] (11-3)

sháozi spoon [N] (14-1)

shé snake [N] (20-2)

shèhuì society [N] (21-2)

shètuán organization, club [N] (21-2)

...shemmede and so on [PT] (13-2)

shēn be deep [SV] (16-2)

shēngbìng become sick [VO] (22-1)

shēngchǎn produce [V] (19-3)

shēnghuó life [N] (15-1)

shēngyīn sound; voice [N] (17-3)

shèngxia be left over [RC] (11-2)

Shīdà National Taiwan Normal University [PW] (22-2)

shīhuǒ fire breaks out [VO] (22-3)

shīmǔ wife of one's teacher [N] (19-4)

shīpéi "sorry to have to leave" [IE] (16-3)

shīzi lion [N] (24-2)

Shí Shi [SN] (16-2)

shídài period [N] (21-4)

shífēn very, extremely [A] (23-2)

shípǐn food product; groceries [N] (13-1)

shípǐn diàn grocery store [PH] (13-1)

shíshī implement, put into effect [V] (23-1)

shítou stone [N] (16-2)

shíxíng put into practice, implement [V] (23-3)

shì city, municipality [N] (12-2)

shì try [V] (12-2)

shì ma "really?" [IE] (20-1)

shìde "yes" [IE] (17-3)

shìhào hobby [N] (20-1)

shìjì century [N] (23-1)

shìjiè world [N] (21-3)

Shìjiè Bēi World Cup [PH] (21-3)

shìnèi diànhuà local telephone call [PH] (17-1)

shìqing thing, matter [N] (18-3)

shìyǒu roommate, dormmate [N] (21-1)

...shi yóu...(suǒ)zǔchéngde be composed of [PT] (23-1)

shōu accept [V] (13-4)

shǒu hand [N] (11-3)

shǒubiǎo wristwatch [N] (13-4)

shòu endure, suffer [V] (14-2)

shòubuliǎo not to be able to endure [RC] (14-2)

shòudào receive [RC] (24-1)

shòudào...yǐngxiǎng be influenced by [PT] (24-1)

shòukè give classes, offer instruction [VO] (23-3)

shòumìng life span, life [N] (23-4)

shòushāng suffer injury, be hurt [VO] (22-4)

shū book [N] (12-2)

shū lose (i.e., not win) [V] (21-3)

shūcài vegetable [N] (12-3)

shūdiàn book store [PW] (12-2)

shūzhuō(r) desk [N] (17-4)

shúxi be familiar [SV] (14-4)

shǔjià summer vacation [N] (21-2)

shù tree [N] (14-1)

shùxué mathematics [N] (24-3)

shuākǎ imprint a credit card [VO] (13-4)

shuāng pair [M] (13-3)

shuǐ water [N] (16-4)

shuǐdiànfèi water and electricity fee [N] (17-4)

shuǐfèi water fee [N] (17-4)

shuǐguǒ fruit [N] (12-4)

shuǐpíng level, standard [N] (23-3)

shùnbiàn conveniently, in passing [A] (11-2)

shùnlì be smooth [SV] (15-1)

shuō gùshi tell a story [PH] (20-3)

shuō shízàide to tell the truth [PH] (19-4)

shuōbudìng not be able to say for sure [RC] (22-4)

sīliǎo settle privately [V] (22-4)

-sǐ to the point of death [RE] (11-1)

sòng see someone off or out [V] (18-2)

Sòng Song [SN] (18-3)

suān be sour [SV] (14-2)

suàn figure, calculate [V] (13-3); consider as [V] (16-4)

suàndeshang can count as, can be regarded [RC] (21-4)

suànle "forget about it" [IE] (22-4)

suànshang include, count [RC] (21-4)

suīrán... although... [PT] (16-4)

suíbiàn "as you wish" [IE] (14-1)

suíyì "as you like" [IE] (16-2)

suǒ (for schools, hospitals, houses) [M] (24-3)

suǒyǒu all, every [AT] (24-1)

T

Táibì NT (Taiwan currency) [N] (22-3)

Táiwān Yínháng Bank of Taiwan [PW] (11-1)

tàijíquán taiji, shadow boxing [N] (21-1)

tán talk [V] (18-2)

tánhuà talk, speak [VO] (18-2)

tánwán finish talking [RC] (18-2)

Tǎnmǐ'ěryǔ Tamil language [N] (24-1)

tāng soup [N] (14-1)

táng (for classes) [M] (16-1)

Táng Tang [SN] (17-1)

Tángcù Lǐjī Sweet and Sour Pork [PH] (16-3)

tǎng lie down [V] (19-1)

táozi peach [N] (12-4)

tè especially [A] (11-4)

tèbié especially [A] (11-4)

tèbié xíngzhèngqū special administrative region [PH] (23-1)

tèdì especially [A] (16-3)

tèsè characteristic, distinguishing feature [N] (23-2)

tèzhēng special characteristic [N] (22-3)

téng be painful, hurt [SV] (22-1)

tí mention [V] (17-1)

tíqián move up (a time or date) [V] (17-1)

tíyì propose [V] (15-2)

tǐyù physical education [N] (21-2)

tǐyùguǎn gymnasium [PW] (21-2)

tì for [CV] (16-2)

tiān add [V] (19-3)

tiāntáng paradise, heaven [N] (23-2)

tián be sweet [SV] (14-2)

tiánmiànjiàng sweet flour sauce [N] (15-3)

tiánshí dessert [N] (14-4)

tiāo pick out, select [V] (12-4)

tiáoliào condiment, seasoning [N] (15-4)

tiáoyuē treaty, pact [N] (23-1)

tiáozhěng adjust [V] (11-4)

Tiàoqí Chinese checkers [N] (20-1)

tiàowǔ dance [VO] (21-2)

tiē stick [V] (19-4)

tīngbutàimíngbai can't understand very well [RC] (20-4)

tīngdào hear [RC] (12-4)

tīngjian hear [RC] (12-4)

tīngqīngchu hear clearly [RC] (17-3)

tíngchē park a car, park [VO] (11-4)

tíngchēchǎng parking lot [PW] (11-4)

tóng with [CV] (14-4)

tóng...liánxì contact (someone) [PT] (14-4)

tóngshí at the same time [MA] (15-1)

Tǒngyī 7-Eleven® (store) [PW] (11-2)

tǒngyī unite, unify [V] (11-4)

tōu steal [V] (22-2)

tóu head [N] (22-1)

tūrán suddenly [MA] (18-4)

tú smear, daub [V] (15-3)

túzai smear on [V+PV] (15-3)

tǔsī white bread [N] (13-2)

tù spit, throw up [V] (22-1)

tuántǐ group [N] (21-2)

tuō take off (shoes, clothes) [V] (18-3)

tuōxié take off one's shoes [VO] (18-3)

W

wà "wow" [I] (15-4)

wàzi sock [N] (13-3)

wàigōng grandfather (maternal) [N] (18-1)

wàijiāo diplomacy, foreign affairs [N] (23-1)

wàipó grandmother (maternal) [N] (18-1)

wàisūn grandson (daughter's son) [N] (18-1)

wàisūnnǚ(r) granddaughter (daughter's daughter) [N] (18-1)

wán finish [V] (11-2)

-wán finish [RE] (11-2)

wánquán completely [A] (13-3)

wǎn bowl [M] (14-1)

-wǎn late [RE] (18-3)

wǎnhuì evening party [N] (21-3)

wǎnliú urge someone to stay [V] (18-2)

wànyī if by chance, in case [MA] (18-4)

wǎng net [N] (21-1)

wǎngqiú tennis [N] (21-1)

wēixiǎn be dangerous; danger [SV/N] (22-4)

wéichí maintain [V] (23-4)

Wéiqí Go (kind of chess) [N] (20-1)

Wèi Wei [SN] (16-2)

wèi for [CV] (16-3)

wèir smell, aroma [N] (16-3)

wèidao taste [N] (15-2)

wèile... in order to, for [PT] (13-2)

wèiyú be located at, be situated at [V+PV] (23-4)

wén smell something [V] (15-4)

wényì literature and art [N] (21-3)

wényì wǎnhuì variety show [PH] (21-3)

wènhǎo send one's regards to [RC] (18-1)

wèntí problem [N] (11-1); question [N] (11-1)

wòfáng bedroom [PW] (19-1)

wòshì bedroom [PW] (17-3)

wūzi room [N] (18-1)

wúqù be uninteresting, dull [SV] (24-3)

wúxiàn wireless, Wi-Fi [AT] (24-4)

wǔshù martial art [N] (21-1)

X

xī inhale, breathe in [V] (18-3)

Xīcān Western-style food [N] (14-3)

xīyān smoke [VO] (18-3)

xīyān qū smoking section [PH] (18-3)

xīyǐn attract [V] (23-4)

xíguàn custom, habit [N] (18-3)

xǐ wash [V] (14-1)

xǐjù comedy [N] (21-3)

xǐshǒujiān bathroom [PW] (14-1)

xì department [N] (12-1)

xìtǒng system [N] (24-4)

xiā shrimp [N] (13-1)

xiājiǎo shrimp dumpling [N] (23-2)

xià play (chess or checkers) [V] (20-1)

xià frighten [V] (11-1)

-xià down [RE] (14-4)

xiàlai come down [RC] (17-2)

-xiàlai down [RE] (17-2)

xiàlóu go downstairs [VO] (18-4)

xiàqí play chess [VO] (20-1)

xiàqu go down [RC] (17-2)

-xiàqu down [RE] (17-2)

xiàsǐ frighten to death [RC] (11-1)

xiān...zài... first...then... [PT] (15-3)

xiān zǒu yíbù "take one step first" [IE] (16-3)

xiān-gān-wéi-jìng drink bottoms up before someone else to show one's respect [EX] (16-2)

xián be salty [SV] (14-2)

xiàn(r) filling [N] (15-4)

xiànjīn cash [N] (13-4)

xiànzhì limit, restriction [N] (23-4)

xiànzhuàng present conditions, status quo [N] (23-4)

xiāngdāng quite, rather, pretty [A] (24-2)

Xiānggǎng Tèbié Xíngzhèngqū Hong Kong Special Administrative Region [PW] (23-1)

xiāngjiāo banana [N] (12-4)

xiāngliào spice [N] (23-4)

xiāngyóu sesame oil [N] (15-4)

xiángqilai think of [RC] (18-4)

xiǎngyǒu enjoy (rights, prestige) [V] (23-1)

xiàng resemble, be like [V] (13-2)

xiàng toward, to [CV] (19-3)

xiàng (for documents, clauses, items) [M] (24-2)

xiàngdǎo guide [N] (23-1)

xiàngjī camera [N] (23-2)

xiàngjiāo rubber [N] (24-1)

xiàngjiāo shù rubber tree [PH] (24-1)

Xiàngqí Chinese chess [N] (20-1)

xiàngzhēng symbol, emblem [N] (24-2)

xiàngzi lane [N] (11-3)

xiǎo háizi small child [PH] (15-1)

xiǎo nánshēng little boy [PH] (13-4)

xiǎo nǔshēng little girl [PH] (13-4)

xiǎo péngyou little friend, child [PH] (18-1)

xiǎo shēng in a low voice, quietly [PH] (17-3)

xiǎochī snack [N] (16-3)

xiǎode know [V] (11-2)

xiǎodòu red bean [N] (12-1)

xiǎoshuō(r) novel [N] (20-1)

xiǎoshuōjiā novelist [N] (20-3)

xiǎotōu thief [N] (22-2)

xiàoduì school team [N] (21-1)

xiē some [M] (12-2)

xiédìng agreement [N] (24-2)

Xīnjiāpō Zhíwùyuán Singapore Botanic Gardens [PW] (24-1)

Xīnjiè New Territories [PW] (23-1)

xīnkǔ endure hardship [SV] (16-4)

xīnwén news [N] (21-3)

xīnxiān be fresh [SV] (12-3)

xīnxíng new type of, new model of [AT] (24-4)

Xīnzhú Xinzhu (city in northern Taiwan) [PW] (18-4)

xìn letter [N] (19-4)

xìnyòngkǎ credit card [N] (13-4)

xínghào model, model number [N] (24-4)

xíngzhèngqū administrative region [N] (23-1)

xìngqu interest [N] (17-1)

xiū study, take (courses, credits) [V] (19-2); build [V] (21-4); repair [V] (22-4)

xiūchē repair a vehicle [VO] (22-4)

xiūchēfèi cost of repairing a vehicle [N] (22-4)

xiūqilai in the building [RC] (21-4)

xūyào need [N] (13-3)

xuǎn choose, select [V] (19-2)

xuéfēn credit, credit hour [N] (19-2)

xuéqī semester, term [N] (19-2)

xuéqī bàogào term paper [PH] (19-2)

xuéshēngzhèng student ID [N] (22-3)

Y

yā zhēn'gān(r) duck gizzard and liver [PH] (15-2)

yājīn deposit [N] (17-4)

Yālí(r) Ya pear [N] (12-4)

yāpiàn opium [N] (23-1)

Yāpiàn Zhànzhēng Opium War [PH] (23-1)

yāròu duck meat [N] (13-1)

yāzī duck [N] (13-1)

yān tobacco, cigarette; smoke [N] (18-3)

yán salt [N] (15-4)

yánjiū study, research [N/V] (20-2)

yǎnyuán actor [N] (20-4)

yáng sheep [N] (13-1)

yángròu mutton [N] (13-1)

yàng(r) kind, variety [M] (12-1)

yàngr appearance, shape [N] (22-4)

yāo weigh out [V] (12-4)

yào bú shi if not, if it weren't for [PH] (19-4)

yàoburán otherwise, or [MA] (11-2)

yàojǐn be important [SV] (11-1)

yēzhī coconut juice [N] (23-4)

yěxǔ perhaps, maybe [MA] (22-1)

Yè Ye [SN] (22-3)

yī...jiù... as soon as [PT] (17-2)

yīfu clothes [N] (13-4)

yīguì clothes closet [N] (17-4)

yīshēng medical doctor [N] (20-3)

yīyuàn hospital [PW] (22-1)

yíkuài(r) together [A/PW] (16-1)

yímín immigrant, migrant [N] (24-3)

yíqiè everything, all [N] (23-2)

yíyàng one kind; the same [NU+M] (13-3)

yǐ take [CV] (16-4)

yǐ A dài B take A to substitute for B [PT] (16-4)

yǐ...wéi zhǔ regard...as most important [PT] (23-2)

yǐbiàn... so that, in order that [PT] (14-4)

yǐjí and [CJ] (15-3)

...yǐnèi within [PT] (13-4)

...yǐshàng more than [PT] (23-3)

...yǐxià less than, below [PT] (23-3)

yìbān general [AT] (23-2); generally [A] (23-2)

yìbān lái shuō generally speaking [PH] (23-3)

yìbiān(r) on the one hand [PW] (18-2)

yìbiān(r) A yìbiān(r) B do B while doing A [PT] (18-2)

yìdiǎn(r) xiǎo yìsi "a little something," a gift [IE] (18-3)

yìdiǎn(r) yě bù... not at all, not the least bit [PT] (13-1)

Yìguó Liǎngzhì One Country Two Systems [PH] (23-1)

yìhuǐr jiàn "see you in a little while" [IE] (11-3)

yìsi intention [N] (18-3)

yìwù duty, obligation [N] (23-1)

yìwùde voluntarily [A] (23-1)

yìxiē some [NU+M] (17-4)

yì-yán-wéi-dìng be agreed with one word [EX] (17-1)

yìzhí always, all along [A] (15-2)

yīndiào accent, intonation, tone [N] (24-1)

yīnyuè music [N] (17-1)

yīnyuèhuì concert [N] (17-1)

yīnyuèjiā musician [N] (20-3)

yínháng bank [PW] (11-1)

yínhángjiā banker [N] (20-3)

yínhángyè banking industry, banking [N] (23-2)

yǐnchá drink tea and eat dim sum [VO] (23-2)

Yìndù India [PW] (23-1)

Yìnní Indonesia [PW] (24-2)

yìnshuā print [V] (23-3)

yīng should [AV] (19-4)

yīnggāide "something one ought to do" [IE] (22-3)

Yīnggélán England [PW] (21-3)

yīnglǐ mile [M] (21-4)

yíng win [V] (21-3)

yǐngxiǎng influence [N] (24-1)

yìngyòng apply [V] (24-4)

yìngyòng ruǎnjiàn software application [PH] (24-4)

yòng use [V] (14-1); using, with [CV] (14-1)

yòngbuzháo not need to [RC] (22-1)

yòngwán finish using [RC] (22-3)

yōujiǔ be very old [SV] (23-4)

yóu oil [N] (11-4)

yóu by [CV] (14-4)

yóujià price of gasoline [N] (11-4)

yóujú post office [PW] (11-3)

yóupiào stamp [N] (19-4)

yóuyǒng swimming; swim [N/VO] (21-1)

yóuyú... because of, due to [PT] (24-2)

yǒu yìdiǎn(r)... be a little [PT] (19-1)

yǒukòng(r) have free time [VO] (17-1)

yǒumíng be famous [SV] (21-3)

yǒuqián be rich [SV] (12-4)

yǒuqù be interesting, funny, amusing [SV] (23-4)

yǒuyòng be useful [SV] (20-2)

yòushǒu right hand [PW] (11-3)

yòushǒubiān right-hand side [PW] (11-3)

yúcūn fishing village [PW] (23-1)

yúkuài be happy [SV] (15-1)

yúlè entertainment, recreation [N] (24-4)

Yúxiāng Ròusī Fish Fragrant Meat Shreds [PH] (14-1)

yǔfǎ grammar [N] (19-3)

yǔliàng rainfall [N] (16-2)

yǔmáo feather, plumage [N] (21-1)

yǔmáoqiú badminton, shuttlecock [N] (21-1)

yǔwén language and literature [N] (24-3)

yùbei prepare [V] (16-3)

yùshì bathroom [PW] (17-3)

yuán dollar (monetary unit) [M] (11-4)

yuánlái actually, so [MA] (21-2)

yuánzhūbǐ ball-point pen [N] (12-2)

yuánzhùmín native people [N] (24-3)

yuàn blame [V] (22-4)

yuànyi like to, be willing to [AV] (15-4)

yuànzi courtyard, yard [N] (17-4)

yuè moon [N] (20-3)

yuè...yuè... the more...the more... [PT] (15-2)

yūn be dizzy [SV] (19-1)

-yūn dizzy [RE] (19-1)

yùndòng sport, athletics, exercise [N] (21-1)

Z

záyīn noise, static [N] (17-3)

zázhì magazine [N] (12-2)

zài...zhèngcè xià under the policy of... [PT] (23-4)

zàizuò be present (at a banquet or meeting) [V] (15-2)

zámliǎ the two of us [PR] (22-4)

zámmen we (you and I) [PR] (14-1)

zànshí temporarily, for the time being [A] (24-4)

zànzhù support, sponsor [V] (24-3)

zǎo jiù long ago, long since [PH] (15-2)

zǎowǎn morning and evening [MA] (22-1)

zérèn responsibility [N] (19-4)

zěmme huí shì(r) "what's the matter?" [IE] (22-2)

zěmme zhèmme... how come so [PT] (12-3)

zèngsòng present as a gift [V] (24-2)

Zhànguó Shídài Warring States Period [TW] (21-4)

zhànlǐng occupy, capture [V] (23-1)

zhànxiàn be busy (of a telephone) [VO] (17-2)

zhànzhēng war [N] (21-4)

zhǎng rise, go up [V] (11-4)

zháoliáng catch cold [VO] (22-1)

zhǎohuílai find and get back [RC] (22-2)

zhào take (photographs) [V] (20-1)

zhàogu care [N] (15-1); take care of [V] (15-1)

zhàoxiàng take photographs [VO] (20-1)

zhè right away [A] (18-1)

zhèixiē these [SP+M] (12-2)

zheige (hesitation sound) [I] (18-3)

zhēnzhèng real, true, genuine [AT] (23-2)

zhēng levy, collect (taxes or duty) [V] (23-2)

zhěng exact, sharp (of clock times) [BF] (21-2)

zhèng zài... just be in the midst of [PT] (17-2)

zhèngcè policy [N] (23-3)

zhèngfǔ government [N] (23-4)

zhènghǎo(r) just, as it happens [MA] (20-2)

zhèngjiàn identification paper [N] (22-2)

zhèngshì formally [A] (23-4); be formal [SV] (24-1)

zhī (for pens, pencils) [M] (12-2)

...zhīnèi within [PT] (13-4)

...zhīyī one of [PT] (23-2)

zhí be straightforward, frank [SV] (18-3)

zhí dào straight up to, until [PH] (19-1)

zhí shuō speak frankly [PH] (18-3)

zhíde be worth, deserve [AV] (23-4)

zhímíndì colony [N] (23-1)

zhíwù plant, vegetation [N] (24-1)

zhíwùyuán botanic garden [PW] (24-1)

zhǐ paper [N] (12-2)

zhìdù system [N] (23-1)

zhìshāng intelligence, IQ [N] (24-2)

zhìshǎo at least [A] (24-1)

zhìzào manufacture [V] (24-4)

Zhōngcān Chinese-style food [N] (14-3)

Zhōnghuá (literary name for "China") [N] (20-2)

Zhōnghuá Mínguó Republic of China [PW] (20-2)

Zhōnghuá Rénmín Gònghéguó People's Republic of China [PW] (20-2)

zhōngjiān in the middle [PW] (15-3)

zhōngnián middle age [N] (21-2)

zhōngnián rén middle-aged people [PH] (21-2)

zhōngyú finally, at last [A] (21-4)

zhǒng kind [M] (12-2)

zhòng plant [V] (17-4)

zhòngyào be important [SV] (23-2)

zhōu week [M] (23-3)

Zhōu Zhou [SN] (11-3)

zhōumò weekend [N] (15-4)

zhū pig [N] (13-1)

Zhūjiāng Pearl River [PW] (23-4)

zhūròu pork [N] (13-1)

zhǔ boil [V] (15-4)

zhǔrén host [N] (15-2)

zhǔshí staple food, main food [N] (14-2)

zhǔxiū major in; major [V/N] (12-1)

zhǔxí chairman [N] (14-3)

zhǔyào mainly [A] (15-4); essential, main [AT] (20-4)

zhǔyì idea, plan [N] (13-2)

zhǔyì doctrine; -ism [N] (23-1)

zhù wish [V] (15-1)

-zhù firm [RE] (18-1)

zhùmíng be famous, well-known [SV] (20-3)

zhùyì pay attention to [V/VO] (11-3)

zhuā catch [V] (22-2)

zhuāzhù catch hold of [RC] (22-2)

zhuānyè major, specialization [N] (12-1)

zhuǎn transfer [V] (17-2)

zhuǎnchéng turn into [V+PV] (22-1)

zhuǎnjìnlái turn in [RC] (11-3)

zhuǎnyǎn blink the eyes, glance [VO] (19-3)

zhuàn turn, go around [V] (11-3)

zhuàn earn [V] (19-1)

zhuàn chronicle, biography [N] (20-2)

zhuànqián earn money [VO] (19-1)

zhuāng install [V] (24-4)

zhuàng bump into, collide with [V] (22-4)

zhuō (for banquets) [M] (14-3)

zīběn capital [N] (23-1)

zīběn zhǔyì capitalism [PH] (23-1)

zìcóng...yǐhòu since [PT] (23-3)

zìdiǎn dictionary [N] (12-2)

zìjǐ oneself [PR] (14-4)

zìrán be natural [SV] (24-2)

zìrán huánjìng natural environment [PH] (24-2)

zìxíngchē bicycle [N] (22-4)

zìzhìquán autonomy [N] (23-1)

zǒnggòng in all [A] (12-4)

zǒngmiànji total area [N] (23-1)

zǒngshi always [A] (18-1)

zū rent [V] (17-3)

zūchuqu rent out [RC] (17-3)

zúqiú soccer [N] (21-3)

zúqiúsài soccer competition [N] (21-3)

zǔchéng make up, form, compose [V+PV] (23-1)

zuì become drunk [V] (15-2)

-zuì drunk [RE] (15-2)

zuìhǎo it would be best, had better [MA] (17-3)

zuǒshǒu left hand [PW] (11-3)

zuǒshǒubiān left-hand side [PW] (11-3)

zuò by (car, boat, train, airplane) [CV] (11-1)

zuò shēngyì engage in business [PH] (23-3)

zuòdōng serve as host [VO] (16-1)

zuòfàn cook [VO] (14-3)

zuòmèng have a dream [VO] (11-2)

zuòyong function, effect [N] (24-2)

Index of Grammatical and Cultural Topics

This index is intended to assist you in locating information on the major topics presented in the Grammatical and Cultural Notes that accompany each lesson of *Intermediate Spoken Chinese*. The numbers and letters after each topic refer to the unit, part, and number of the relevant note. For example, 14-2: 6C would indicate that information about that entry can be found in Unit 14, Part 2, note 6C.

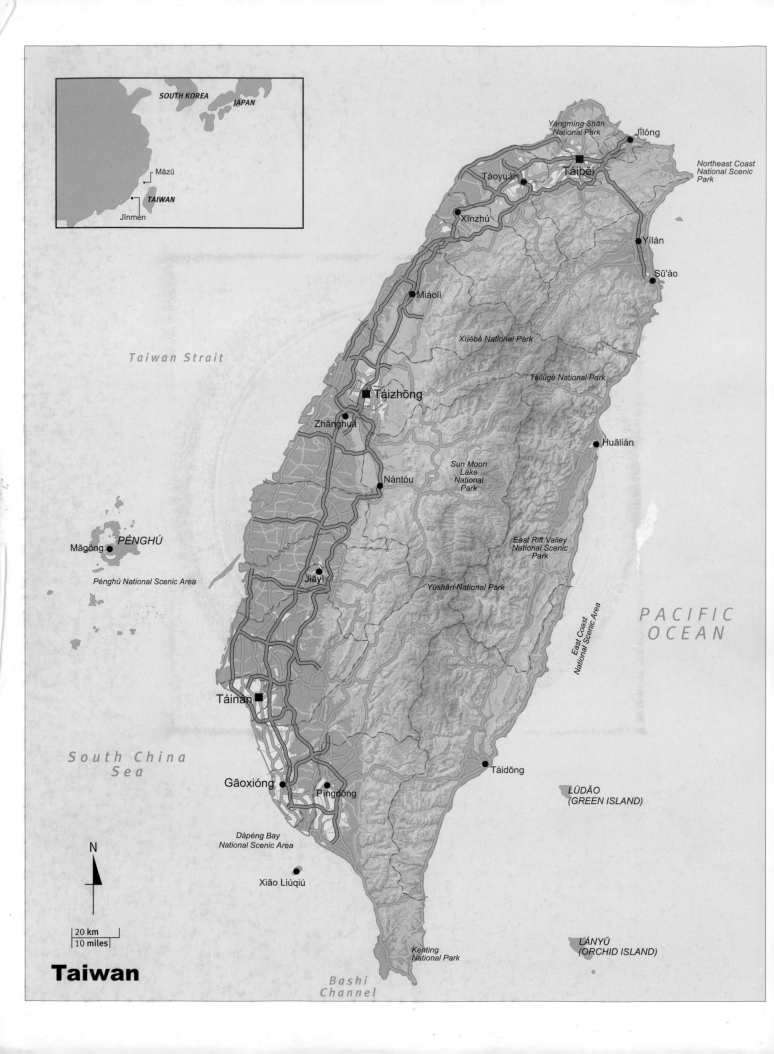

SOUTH KOREA

JAPAN

Măzŭ

TAIWAN

Jīnmén

Yángmíng Shān
National Park

Jīlóng

Northeast Coast
National Scenic
Park

Táoyuán

Táiběi

Xīnzhú

Yílán

Sū'ào

Miáolì

Xuěbà National Park

Táilŭgé National Park

Taiwan Strait

Táizhōng

Zhānghuà

Huālián

Nántóu

Sun Moon
Lake
National
Park

PÉNGHÚ

Măgōng

East Rift Valley
National Scenic
Park

Pénghú National Scenic Area

Jiāyì

Yùshān National Park

PACIFIC
OCEAN

East Coast National Scenic Area

Táinán

South China
Sea

Táidōng

Gāoxióng

Píngdōng

LÙDǍO
(GREEN ISLAND)

Dàpéng Bay
National Scenic Area

N

Xiăo Liúqiú

20 km
10 miles

LÁNYǓ
(ORCHID ISLAND)

Kenting
National Park

Bashi
Channel

Taiwan